THE RED MILLIONAIRE

THE RED MILLIONAIRE

A POLITICAL BIOGRAPHY OF
WILLI MÜNZENBERG,
MOSCOW'S SECRET PROPAGANDA

TSAR IN THE WEST

SEAN McMEEKIN

Yale University Press   New Haven & London

Copyright © 2003 by Sean McMeekin.
All rights reserved.
This book may not be reproduced, in whole or in part, including illustrations, in any form (beyond that copying permitted by Sections 107 and 108 of the U.S. Copyright Law and except by reviewers for the public press), without written permission from the publishers.

Designed by James J. Johnson and set in Monotype Walbaum by Duke & Company.
Printed in the United States of America.

Library of Congress Cataloging-in-Publication Data

McMeekin, Sean, 1974–
  The red millionaire : a political biography of Willi Münzenberg, Moscow's secret propaganda tsar in the West / Sean McMeekin.
    p.   cm.
Includes bibliographical references and index.
  ISBN 0-300-09847-2 (alk. paper)

  1. Münzenberg, Willi. 2. Communists—Germany—Biography. 3. Propaganda, Communist—History. 4. Communism—Germany—History—20th century. 5. Communism—Soviet Union—History—20th century. I. Title.
  HX273.M376 2003
  327.1247′0092—dc21   2003011828

A catalogue record for this book is available from the British Library.

The paper in this book meets the guidelines for permanence and durability of the Committee on Production Guidelines for Book Longevity of the Council on Library Resources.

10 9 8 7 6 5 4 3 2 1

CONTENTS

Note on Transliteration and Translations — vii

List of Initials of Organizations and Publications — viii

Introduction: Who in the World Is Willi Münzenberg? — 1

PART 1. *A Call to Arms*

    1. Erfurt — 7
    2. Zurich — 18
    3. Stuttgart — 74
    4. Berlin — 86
    5. Moscow — 91

PART 2. *The Red Millionaire*

    6. Selling the Famine — 103
    7. Building Socialism — 123
    8. Germany Red or Black — 144
    9. Follow the Money — 163
    10. Hollywood East — 174
    11. Preempting the Peace — 193
    12. The Red Millionaire — 204
    13. Tango with the Devil — 222

PART 3. *Flight*

  14. The Fire This Time   255
  15. Reckoning   270
  16. A Paris Exile   295

Notes   309

Select Bibliography   371

Acknowledgments   381

Index   385

NOTE ON TRANSLITERATION AND TRANSLATIONS

For Russian-language words, I have used the Library of Congress transliteration system throughout, with the exception of commonly used spellings of famous names (Trotsky, Zinoviev, Gorky, and so on).

I have left well-known foreign-language periodicals, especially newspapers, in their original languages *(Pravda, L'Humanité, Rote Fahne, Welt am Abend, Berlin am Morgen)*. I have rendered lesser-known titles of Münzenberg-controlled publications into English when doing so helps illuminate their meaning *(Soviet Russia in Pictures, Hammer and Sickle, Propaganda as a Weapon)*. For ease of reference for those wishing to pursue future research, I cite these periodicals by their original titles in the endnotes.

Unless otherwise indicated, translations are my own.

INITIALS OF ORGANIZATIONS AND PUBLICATIONS

AIZ	*Arbeiter Illustrierte Zeitung*
ARA	American Relief Administration
Cheka	All-Russian Extraordinary Commission for Combating Counter-Revolution and Sabotage
ECCI	Executive Committee of the Communist International (Comintern)
FSR	Friends of Soviet Russia
IAH	Internationale Arbeiterhilfe (International Worker Relief)
KPD	Kommunistische Partei Deutschlands (German Communist Party)
MOPR	Mezhdunarodnaia Organizatsia Pomoshchi Revolutsioneram (International Red Aid)
M-Russ	Mezhrabpom-Russ (Mezhdunarodnaia rabochaia pomoshch'—International Worker Relief)
NDV	Neue Deutsche Verlag
NEP	New Economic Policy
NKVD	People's Commissariat of International Affairs
NSDAP	Nationalsozialistische Deutsche Arbeiterpartei (National Socialist German Workers' Party)
PCF	Parti Communiste Français (French Communist Party)
Pomgol	All-Russian Public Committee to Aid the Hungry
SA	Sturmabteilung (Storm Troop Section)
SOPADE	Sozialdemokratische Partei Deutschlands (German Social Democratic Party—acronym used by the party in exile after 1933)
SPD	Sozialdemokratische Partei Deutschlands (German Social Democratic Party)
SPS	Sozialistische Partei der Schweiz (Swiss Socialist Party)
USPD	Unabhängige Sozialdemokratische Partei Deutschlands (Independent Social Democratic Party of Germany)
WEB	Western European Bureau (of the Comintern)

THE RED MILLIONAIRE

INTRODUCTION *Who in the World Is Willi Münzenberg?*

W illi Münzenberg is little remembered today, but there was a time, not so long ago, when the utterance of his name aroused fear, loathing, and admiration among the world's political classes. In the ideological warfare that convulsed Europe after the First World War, Münzenberg demonstrated formidable talents in the black arts of propaganda. At the height of his influence, Münzenberg controlled from his Berlin headquarters a seemingly invincible network of Communist front organizations—charities, publishers, newspapers, magazines, theaters, film studios, and cinema houses —which stretched, on paper at least, from Buenos Aires to Tokyo. Many of the interwar period's most famous intellectuals—Upton Sinclair, Henri Barbusse, Albert Einstein, Bertolt Brecht, and John Dos Passos—came under his ever-expanding organizational spell. The Nazi journalist Joseph Goebbels, who also operated out of Berlin, admired and feared his Communist rival's propaganda machine, and when Hitler came to power in 1933, Münzenberg's media empire was immediately slated for destruction. It is a measure of Münzenberg's still formidable reputation that even after he was expelled from the Central Committee of the German Communist Party in 1938, his movements in Paris were closely shadowed by agents of both Hitler's Gestapo and Stalin's NKVD. In Münzenberg's mind lodged many potentially explosive secrets about the finances and personnel of the Communist International, secrets that, but for a tantalizingly incomplete paper trail of documents, many of which are only now becoming available, followed him to his grave.[1]

To his legion admirers, Willi Münzenberg was a singular beacon of hope for war-ravaged Europe, a hero whose fund-raising campaigns built bridges between the ever-fragile Soviet experiment in "proletarian" government and Western socialists. To his critics, Münzenberg was a dangerous media demagogue who preyed on naïve fellow-traveling sympathizers to reap a personal fortune—a "Communist Hugenberg" or a "Red Millionaire."[2]

There is an element of truth in both of these caricatures, first drawn by Münzenberg's contemporaries, and then endorsed uncritically by historians alternately sympathetic or hostile to communism.[3]

To emphasize Münzenberg's bland progressive virtues, however, or to ascribe cynicism to this consummate political operator, is to miss the point of his spectacular career in communism. Willi Münzenberg was not unique in his admiration of the Soviet Union, nor in his espousal of pacifism, anti-imperialism, antifascism, and all the other great progressive causes of his time. If Münzenberg had merely been a sympathizer, as opposed to a hard-core Communist devoted to the principles of violent revolution, he never would have remained a trusted confidant in Moscow's ruling circles for two decades. There was nothing cynical about his revolutionary rhetoric, or his often ferocious speeches devoted to accelerating class warfare. He believed sincerely in the Revolution.

Nor did Münzenberg draw his power from a widely reputed entrepreneurial prowess.[4] Although unrivaled in the scale of the investments he made with Moscow's money, Münzenberg was a stranger to corporate profits. Every business he touched—reaching across sectors as diverse as mechanized agriculture, caviar, oil, cars, cigarettes, publishing, along with film production and distribution—hemorrhaged red ink. Had Münzenberg truly been more businessman than Bolshevik, his political fortunes would never have risen as meteorically as they did, nor fallen so precipitously and irreversibly once Stalin finally turned against him in 1937.

Yet another historical myth that has obscured understanding of Münzenberg's career is the Kremlin's alleged use of his media "trust" to lubricate the foreign operations of the NKVD.[5] Münzenberg displayed, to be sure, an impressive capacity for distributing Moscow gold through the dozens of corporate fronts he invented. Unlike the business trust of the American magnate Armand Hammer, however—whose principal raison d'être was to launder espionage funds for Moscow—Münzenberg's fronts were far too cash-thirsty themselves to subsidize spying to any significant degree.[6] So reckless was Münzenberg in launching new firms, often leveraged to the hilt through private German bank loans, that the Kremlin could barely keep up with servicing his debts. Neither profit-maker nor money launderer, Münzenberg was, rather, the Comintern's junk bond king. Knowing that the Bolsheviks placed politics well before profits, Münzenberg believed to the end that the Kremlin would bail out every last one of his expensive media adventures.

And why not? Because he had joined Lenin's tiny cadre of friends and confidants in Zurich, during World War I, when the Communist movement still languished in obscurity, Münzenberg could overawe even the most persistent creditors with his senior status. The Bolsheviks trusted few non-Russians in the Communist movement, especially those who had not struggled with them in the Revolution. Münzenberg, as the only member of Lenin's inner circle from Zurich who did not accompany the future dictator on his fateful train ride to Petrograd, became by default the highest-ranking Bolshevik "outsider" in Europe, answerable only to the Kremlin. As such, Münzenberg became a real thorn in the flesh of socialists who resented Moscow's manipulation of European politics, not to mention a major irritant to colleagues in his own German Communist Party, who did not appreciate having an unaccountable Bolshevik commissar in their midst. Nowhere did the Bolshevik invasion of the European Left have more serious consequences than in Germany, and nowhere was this invasion more blatantly on display than in the Münzenberg media "trust," whose mysterious finances inspired endless speculation by critics on both sides of the political spectrum.

Certainly Münzenberg did not doubt the impregnability of his position in Communism. Although he believed wholeheartedly in the cause, Münzenberg had no qualms about employing ideologically dubious means to further Communist ends. In his exuberant, reckless lying, Münzenberg often out-"Bolsheviked" the Bolsheviks, riding the Russian Revolutionary show pony so ruthlessly that the poor animal had to stop and catch its breath. And so when this fickle, violent, and ultimately ungrateful animal, whose virtues Münzenberg was still tirelessly proclaiming to the world, at last snorted and heaved and bucked its most ferocious foreign partisan off for good, the ride was over. For Münzenberg, revolutionary Marxist-Leninism had long since been the only show in town.

But what a tremendous ride it was while it lasted! Few of history's great salesmen have been carried to such dizzying heights by their star attraction, which never failed to attract gasps of admiration as it was peddled to the far corners of the globe. True, the glamour of utopia-in-power was shadowed by rumors of uncivilized brutality as it passed from War Communism into catastrophic famine in 1921, sponsored political terrorism abroad throughout the 1920s, and forced the collectivization of Ukrainian agriculture over millions of peasant corpses in the early 1930s. But these rumors were easily chalked up to anticommunist propaganda, or the events themselves to direct sabotage by foreign enemies of the utopia. Those Western sympathizers who churned through Münzenberg's propaganda thresher, meanwhile, often saw their careers mysteriously promoted or their lives suddenly ruined as they acquired notoriety and the enmity of their governments.

But risks to livelihood and limb did not lead all prospective Communists to shy away. The risks, Münzenberg rapidly learned, were part of the attraction. In fact, bloody rehearsals in class warfare proved effective political advertising, nowhere more so than in Münzenberg's native Germany. And if Communist calls for an invasion of central Europe by the Red Army, to be accompanied by the forcible expropriation of private property and the elimination of millions of class enemies, helped to rally mass support for right-wing extremist parties who vowed to exterminate Communists before they could exterminate everyone else, then all the better. The rise of openly fascist parties throughout Europe would merely unmask the latent "social fascism" of the mainstream Socialist parties, alerting workers not yet conscious of their historical mission that the moment of apocalyptic reckoning, the true world Communist Revolution, was at hand. Spurred on by such inescapable conclusions of dialectical reasoning, from his seat in the cockpit of a global propaganda empire, Willi Münzenberg planned to lead Germany, and with her all of Europe, into the cataclysmic class war that would destroy capitalism forever.

PART 1

A Call to Arms

We shall go forth to all nations, to all brothers and sisters, and fire them with enthusiasm for Socialism.

—Willi Münzenberg, 1914

CHAPTER 1 *Erfurt*

Willi Münzenberg was born on 14 August 1889—the same year as Hitler—in Erfurt, a charming old southeast Prussian town located in what is now Thuringia. He lived there until he was four years old, when his mother Mina's death left Willi at the mercy of his itinerant father, who after a lackluster military career bounced from one mediocre job to another in civilian life. Willi remembered attending eight different elementary schools in various obscure villages near Erfurt, Gotha, and Weimar, none of which made much of an impression on him. He made few friends, and didn't keep those he made for long. He had two older brothers, but they had both started military service by the time Willi was in school and rarely came back to visit. Willi's sister, also much older, passed in and out of his life more frequently than his brothers, but he would eventually lose contact with her, too. His father's second wife, a farmer's daughter from the village of Friemar, did her best with Willi, but he did not take kindly to his stepmother. The principal, and almost unrivaled, influence on Willi's early development was therefore his father.

This was unfortunate, for the man responsible for bringing Willi Münzenberg into the world was not much of a role model. Himself the bastard son of a hot-tempered and hard-drinking Prussian Junker, Baron von Seckendorf, who in a moment of lust took advantage of his chambermaid, Karl Münzenberg seems to have inherited the baron's recklessness, without, however, the latter's wealth and social standing. As a warrant officer during the Franco-Prussian War of 1870–71, Karl acquired a taste for French wine and for violence. Discharged in 1873, he entered civilian life having internalized all the arrogance of the Prussian officer corps but none of its self-discipline. He worked variously as a gamekeeper, barber, and innkeeper, but his real passion was always for hunting. Powerfully built and easily angered, Karl Münzenberg slept with loaded guns hanging over his bed, and he was known to retrieve them from the bedroom for emphasis if disputes arose with friends during a card game. He was also not above using them to threaten his wife and children. When he flew into a rage, though, any object at hand might be used to administer a beating—sticks, chains, whips, pots and pans. Stories of his erratic and dangerous behavior were legends in the Münzenberg household, and when young Willi went to bed at night, he would sometimes include in his nightly prayers the request that "my father not shoot me dead."[1]

Of course, what we know about Willi's father comes to us only from Münzenberg's autobiographical writings, all tailored in some way to further the socialist cause, so these horror stories of bourgeois patriarchal decadence must be taken with a grain of salt. Violent and irascible Karl Münzenberg may have been, but his son in all likelihood did not cower in bed every night afraid of being murdered in his sleep.

Still, there were undoubtedly grounds for serious conflict between father and son. Unlike his healthy, industrious older brothers, who both uncomplainingly fulfilled their father's command to serve in the army as soon as they met the age requirements, Willi was a nervous, sensitive, physically frail child who showed more interest in reading than in war games. To please his father, Willi would sometimes put on the comically oversized soldier's uniforms his brothers would send home for him, but he never dreamed of entering the army as they had. On his father's command, Willi did take up the piano but ultimately balked at the discipline required. It became clear very quickly that he had neither the talent nor the desire to become a musician, and he remembered the lessons as "torture."

The climactic episode in Willi's short-lived musical career painfully underscored his troubled relationship with his father. While Willi was struggling through "Guter Mond du gehst so stille" one day in preparation for his next lesson, his father asked what song he was playing. Thinking his father was too drunk to tell the difference, Willi offered that he was trying to master "Torgauer Marsch," the old man's favorite tune. For this lie the young smart aleck received a beating he would not soon forget. Swinging wildly at his son with a chain, old Karl Münzenberg missed and smashed an oil lamp instead, shattering it into pieces. Blaming Willi for the broken lamp, he grabbed a rope hanging nearby and threw it at his terrified son, ordering him to hang himself in punishment. In tears, Willi fled into the attic, where his stepmother found him hours later, asleep with the rope still in his hands. There would be no more piano lessons for young Willi.[2]

Ultimately, though, Willi's father may have affected his son's development more through his lengthy absences than by his periodic use of the lash to instill discipline. When the old man wasn't manning the desk at the hostel in a small village near Weimar in which he lived for the longest period, he was usually out drinking or chasing after game in the forest—in truth, he had little time for his son. Left alone for most of his childhood, Willi developed a precocious dramatic imagination. At age four, he staged weddings with young companions from his neighborhood. Without fail, Willi would insist on playing the preacher. When he was a bit older, Willi acted out cowboys-and-Indians and cops-and-robbers scenarios, inspired by the popular Wild West stories of Karl May, and began to conceive of elaborate theatrical scenes involving large numbers of people. At age twelve, he organized a miniature folk festival involving costumes and games in his father's village, and (if we can believe his later boast) induced all the children in town, and nearly half the adults, to take part.

At the inn, meanwhile, young Willi often ran the show when his father was off on the hunt and his stepmother socialized with neighbors. He served the customers, played cards with them, read them stories from the village newspaper, and tried to follow their political discussions.[3] When the Boer War broke out in 1899, Willi immediately absorbed the fanatical anti-British sentiments of most older Germans, read everything he could about the conflict, and one day set off from home on a fanciful quest to join his beloved Boers. When the Prussian police, several days later, returned the young dreamer to his father's inn, old Karl Münzenberg was not amused. Of course, the restless wanderlust of this onetime soldier may have itself inspired his son's fancy; but he had wanted Willi to become a real soldier, not wander off in a childish dream state.[4]

After he had completed his primary schooling at age fifteen, Willi was apprenticed in a barbershop. The barber was a prickly old disciplinarian, a veteran like Willi's father, and his relationship with his young charge ran into predictable difficulties. Willi resented the long hours and subservient attitude required of a barber's apprentice, and his work ethic was not impressive. When a new apprentice arrived, ignorant and servile and yet stronger and more industrious than Willi, the two fought constantly. One day during an argument, the new arrival availed himself of a loose brick and bopped poor Willi on the head. Münzenberg, briefly hospitalized after the incident, had no desire to return to the scene of his humiliation. Doubtless his father would have forced Willi to press on in learning the barber's trade; but while his son was recuperating, the old man, thrashing about in a drunken stupor, accidentally shot himself in the head while cleaning his pistols. From then on, young Willi Münzenberg, for better or for worse, would have to fend for himself.

Following in the footsteps of his older sister, who had come to visit him in the hospital, Willi returned in 1905 to Erfurt, where the economy was now booming, and quickly found unskilled work sorting scrap leather in the Lingel shoe factory. The job wasn't difficult, and the hours were more reasonable than in the barbershop, but the tedium of factory life was hardly suited to a restless, imaginative boy like Willi. Whenever he could, he visited the city's lending library, and for a while spent many of his precious spare hours reading. Mostly he devoured the same old Karl May stories he had always enjoyed, whose promise of adventure and excitement contrasted depressingly with his own dead-end job.

The job did give Willi something he had never had before: a constant supply of companions. In a large manufacturing operation employing some fifteen hundred workers, Willi shared the lowly duties of leather waste sorting with a small contingent of unskilled workers who, for the most part, were just as young and inexperienced as he was. Soon Willi spent all his meal breaks with his fellow scrap sorters, and he even improved on his modest weekly salary of four and a half gold marks by charging a commission for the food he purchased for his companions' daily meals. Willi's evenings, too, were increasingly devoted to social carousing, as his companions played pranks on older townsfolk, spied on and frightened young couples, and read trashy dime novels aloud to each other, taking particular enjoyment in tales of the dark exploits of freemason societies. Inspired by the freemasons, Willi's as yet free-floating group of companions dreamed of instituting their own secret society, and according to Münzenberg would have drunk each other's blood to pledge brotherhood, if they had been able to afford the wine considered necessary to seal such an oath. Short of entwining their collective fate in blood, Willi's factory compatriots did at least decide to found a social club, with Münzenberg as president, that for a time remained dedicated to soccer and card playing.

It was not long before Münzenberg's group of youthful dreamers discovered politics. An older worker in the shoe factory, with whom Willi was sometimes paired up, informed Münzenberg one day about a debating club called Workers Educational Association Propaganda, which met weekly in a pub on Erfurt's Grafengasse. Neither Münzenberg nor his young cohorts knew what the word "propaganda" meant, but it conjured up sufficiently dark images of underground activities and secret handshakes that four or five of them resolved to visit the pub together. The first time around, Münzenberg and his cohorts hesitated downstairs, afraid to ascend to the second floor where the intense group of debaters, mostly unionized metal and shoe factory workers in their twenties, convened. Willi, however, returned the next week with the one other companion whose curiosity outweighed his fear, and they sat through the whole meeting. Neither understood a word of the discussion, but Münzenberg was impressed with the elaborate organizational protocol and the solemn tone of the main speakers. He returned alone two or three more times before he, too, tired of the incomprehensible speeches and decided he would rather spend the time with his friends.[5]

Although he had been too shy to speak up at the first meetings he attended, Münzenberg's evident curiosity and serious bearing had made an impression on Propaganda's chairman, Georg Schumann. Schumann, a radical, was dissatisfied with the moderate political practice of the German Social Democratic Party (SPD). Party Secretary August Bebel, a roughshod former carpenter popular with the SPD's rank-and-file workers, consistently upheld the banner of revolutionary Marxism in his often electrifying speeches— but his rhetoric was rarely backed up by action. Even as the SPD, Europe's largest socialist party, forced through resolutions condemning deviations from Marxist orthodoxy at the congresses of the Second International,[6] its leaders were hamstrung inside Germany by reform-minded union chiefs, whose huge membership rolls and deep pockets gave them effective veto power over the SPD on strike coordination and other social protest actions.[7] Frustrated by his party's reluctance to live up to its revolutionary ideals, Schumann was on the lookout for impressionable young men whose energy could be harnessed against the older, increasingly timid functionaries who staffed the SPD bureaucracy.[8]

When he learned through contacts in Münzenberg's shoe factory that the silent young man who had showed up at several Propaganda meetings had taken ill, Schumann took to visiting Willi regularly, bringing him books, newspapers, and other reading materials to keep him occupied and, not incidentally, to introduce him to Marxist doctrine. Although he was an indifferent student in primary school, Willi had always loved reading, and he devoured the texts Schumann provided him. Away from the factory for four weeks in all, Willi received during his convalescence a haphazard crash course in the classics of German socialism, from the liberal antinationalistic poetry of Heinrich Heine and Ferdinand Freiligath to the abstruse Marxist tomes of Friedrich Engels and Karl Kautsky, along with contemporary polemics and pamphlets. He certainly didn't understand all the theories, but he picked up enough socialist catch phrases to begin proselytizing his pals as soon as he returned to the factory.[9]

After Münzenberg started dragging his unskilled factory comrades down to the pub on Grafengasse, the demographics of Schumann's debating society altered dramatically. By the following summer, the Workers Association—now christened the Erfurt Freie Jugend, or "Free Youth"—counted more than thirty members, twice as many as when Willi had joined. More than half were now under twenty. Willi's teenage friends, although coarser in speech and far less knowledgeable about socialism than the older workers, dominated the debating sessions by sheer force of numbers. While certain older members of the group resented the changes wrought by Münzenberg's aggressive recruiting, Schumann couldn't have been more pleased with the influx of young blood. When Schumann was offered the chairmanship of the Socialist Youth Organization of the whole state of Thuringia early in 1907, he gladly accepted the position and turned the reins of the Erfurt Free Youth over to his successful young protégé.

Why did Willi prove such an effective recruiter? Clearly he had abundant intellectual curiosity and a strong enough personality to dominate his young male colleagues in the factory. But arranging the procurement of lunch supplies and scheduling social functions was one thing; getting hormone-crazed teenagers to devote their free time to intellectually demanding, rigorously organized social activism was something else entirely. The Lingel shoe factory employed both men and women, and if we can believe Willi's later descriptions, life on and near the factory floor presented both sexes with considerable erotic opportunities. In fact, in Willi's own observation, older female workers frequently eyed the youngest boys in the factory, and were not above taking advantage of their inexperience. That Willi himself took no part in such sexual shenanigans is abundantly clear, and it is quite possible that his modesty gave him a moralistic aura that was appealing to other young men offended by the bawdy realities of factory life. For both moral and physical reasons, Willi did not smoke or drink, and his teetotaling can only have accentuated the pristine eccentricity that set him apart.[10]

Willi's intellectual curiosity and eccentricity, however, may have been less important than a certain fanaticism, a moral intensity in his eyes, which was impossible to ignore. In the earliest known photograph of Münzenberg, a Free Youth group snapshot taken at Jena in 1907, Willi is positively dwarfed by the older, taller, stouter Young Socialist leaders of Imperial Germany, but one can see in his eyes a fiery confidence, an unmistakable belief in himself that transforms the apparent absurdity of a diminutive teenager-visionary into the visage of a serious young man with dignity and bearing (figure 1). When he first began to recruit colleagues from the factory to join the Free Youth, Willi later recalled, "it was as if I was overcome with propaganda fever and I wouldn't let up until almost the last young worker in my workspace joined the association and came to the meetings." Georg Schumann could not have chosen a better acolyte.[11]

It is important to emphasize the role of this mentor in unleashing the ideological fury of Willi Münzenberg, for their relationship was representative of a major historical development. The rapid evolution of Schumann's Workers Educational Association occasioned by Willi's aggressive recruiting grew alongside a seemingly irresistible wave of youthful energy transforming European politics, as hundreds of athletic, religious, and worker-related youth leagues mushroomed across the Old Continent in the last decade before the First World War. Many of the most popular groups were explicitly patriotic. Socialist youth organizations throughout Europe aimed to counter this nationalist surge with attacks on the iniquities of the compulsory draft, appealing to shy, sickly, or otherwise nonconformist young men who dreaded the prospect of entering the army. The young leaders of these groups were usually recruited by ambitious older radicals like Schumann, who recognized in poor, independent, and largely ignorant teenagers such as Willi Münzenberg potentially powerful allies in efforts to disturb a social order in which they felt themselves to have little or no stake.[12]

In the ranks of German Socialism, the "youth" cause was first officially launched by Eduard Bernstein, a Revisionist SPD journalist who founded a Young Apprentices League in Berlin in 1904 in reaction to a scandalous series of suicides by maltreated apprentices. Yet Bernstein's gradualist approach to social reform ultimately proved less appealing to impressionable young men of Münzenberg's ilk than the no-holds-barred rhetoric of Karl Liebknecht and Rosa Luxemburg, who wrote for Franz Mehring's radical *Leipziger Zeitung*.[13] Bebel and other party spokesmen were always careful to assure Germany's conservative ruling establishment that the SPD supported military service and would even endorse just wars fought in Germany's national interest—especially against Russia, perceived to be the most reactionary and labor-unfriendly country in Europe. Because of the especially harsh discipline of the Prussian army, Bebel was vulnerable with the young on the military issue, and Luxemburg and Liebknecht exploited this vulnerability skillfully with antimilitarist propaganda aimed at men approaching draft age. The nationwide work stoppage in Russia that nearly brought down the tsar during the Revolution of 1905 introduced a new radical tactic for them to promote in the youth groups—the romantic sounding "general strike."[14]

By 1906, when Schumann took Willi under his wing, the key concepts

FIGURE 1. Young Socialist conference, Jena, 1907. Münzenberg is the diminutive boy in the middle of the front row, flanked by two taller men on either side of him. Source: Münzenberg, *Die Dritte Front*.

of Socialist radicalism were well established. Opportunistic "bourgeois" elements had invaded the SPD and the unions carrying the disease of Revisionism, distracting the masses from the ultimate goal of seizing the means of production; military service was the principal means by which Europe's young men were corrupted by the bourgeois social order; and the "general strike" was the only weapon capable of destroying militarism and bringing about the overthrow of bourgeois society. Young Willi Münzenberg couldn't possibly have understood all of the ideological disputes giving rise to the radical Young Socialist catechism, but he grasped the basic concepts instinctively, especially the antimilitary stance, which seemed to vindicate his own refusal to volunteer for the army like his brothers. His friends might not have understood the ideology either, but they were happy to join in the Free Youth's rhetorical jam sessions.[15]

By promoting youth radicalism, Schumann and others like him were playing with fire, and they knew it. Nothing could have frightened German conservatives more than the prospect of teenagers, indoctrinated in socialist theory, refusing to perform their military service. This was well understood by such realistic German labor leaders as Robert Schmidt, SPD Reichstag deputy and chairman of the national Trade Union Council, who warned in a keynote speech at the 1908 Trade Union Congress of the dangers of young men "ramming their heads into the steel wall of [German] militarism."[16]

Emboldened by the SPD's first real electoral setback in 1907, after years of dramatic gains, Germany's chancellor Prince Bernhard von Bülow pushed through a Law on Associations in May 1908 that, though expanding rights of association by adults, deemed organized political activity by juveniles a punishable offense. In order to avoid legal difficulties under the new Association Law, Bebel resolved to smother the Socialist youth organizations in a web of paternalism, denying their autonomy and absorbing them all into a new Central Authority for Germany's Working Youth.

The damage, though, had already been done. Under the new Law of Associations, Liebknecht himself was sentenced to eighteen months in prison for the "treasonous" intent to abolish the German army reflected in his pamphlet *Militarism and Antimilitarism*, and many of his young followers would soon be arrested as well. The prerogatives of legality and political legitimacy, which the SPD had worked so hard to achieve since the days of Bismarck's ban on the party from 1878 to 1890, had been effectively nullified.

Then again, being thrown in jail was not always the end of the world, and in fact it offered radicals the undeniable political benefits of publicity and notoriety. Münzenberg discovered this when he was arrested while agitating for Youth Apprentices in spring 1907. Informed in his cell that his arrest had merited an article in the *Erfurter Allgemeine Anzeiger*, Willi felt "proud" of what he had done. Local fame meant that his agitation came increasingly under surveillance, and run-ins with the Erfurt police became common.

During one such episode later in 1907, Willi displayed remarkable self-assurance. He had been distributing a Socialist pamphlet titled "Upward into the Light" when he was called down to police headquarters for questioning. When the officer on duty held the rag up in front of Münzenberg's face and demanded, "What is hidden behind [this pamphlet]," Willi answered with a naïve look of incomprehension, "You are, Herr Inspektor." Not certain whether the teenage activist was hopelessly dense or was merely being cheeky, the inspector considered the matter at length before angrily letting Willi go.

The periodic arrests of Münzenberg's legions of Free Youth teenagers in 1907 and 1908 infuriated the local Erfurt SPD leaders, who had to pay the fines. On their salaries of four and a half marks a week, Willi and his unskilled worker-comrades could hardly afford the twenty marks usually levied for the offense of political agitation. Nor could the Free Youth organization itself afford such a sum—twenty marks constituted, according to the membership figures Willi later remembered, almost two whole years' worth of Free Youth revenue in Erfurt. When Willi was sent to Berlin in October 1908 as Erfurt's delegate to a Youth Socialist Congress, he traveled fourth class and stayed with local delegates, as he couldn't afford a hostel room on the meager allowance the Free Youth provided him for the trip. (He was so tired, in fact, from the uncomfortable journey and accommodations, that he slept through most of the first day's sessions.) Financially speaking, Erfurt Free Youth was small potatoes without the support of the SPD, so it proved an easy task to absorb it into the local party apparatus in accordance with Bebel's directive.[17]

Willi and his friends put up a token struggle, protesting verbally when the SPD formally dissolved the Free Youth and all other such groups on 31 January 1909, but they knew the game was up. It was made clear that fines occasioned by youth activities not sanctioned by the party would no longer be paid. The only meetings permitted the former Free Youth members, meanwhile, were now chaired by local SPD leaders, who frequently brought in outside speakers in the hope that the restless young radicals might listen up and learn something. Whether or not they listened, they certainly stopped speaking out regularly at the formal sessions, and it was not long before Willi's friends started meeting on their own time, unofficially, to talk politics and stage mock debates and Reichstag sessions. Although Willi and his cohorts enthusiastically joined SPD demonstrations against the three-class state voting system held throughout Prussia in 1909, the party's absorption of the Free Youth effectively frustrated their capacity for independent activism, and the police troubles quieted down. The effort by Bebel and the unions to cut off dangerous radicalism in the youth movement was, in Erfurt at least, a success.[18]

Of course, it was not only policemen and SPD bureaucrats who had looked askance at Willi's increasingly belligerent proselytizing after he took over the Free Youth. In the Lingel shoe factory, Münzenberg's first imprisonment for political radicalism in 1907 led to a warning that he would be fired if arrested again. This did not stop him from continuing quietly to recruit in the factory for Erfurt Free Youth, nor from fraudently obtaining two days' leave to attend the Berlin Socialist Youth Congress in September 1908 (killing off a "nonexistent aunt" for this purpose, as he later recalled with glee).[19]

When the local SPD clipped his wings by asserting control over the Free Youth later that autumn, Willi's political activities were curtailed, and he avoided further brushes with the police that might have cost him his job. Still, he was not muzzled entirely. When Münzenberg, in August 1909, circulated a petition through the shoe factory asking fellow workers to endorse a general strike in Sweden, he was finally given his walking papers. He tried, for a time, to scare up work in Erfurt's many other thriving factories, but although jobs were certainly available he found that his radical reputation had destroyed his prospects with nearly every employer in town.

Unemployed, with the local job market closed off to him, Willi set off on the road from Erfurt with a friend several weeks after his twentieth birthday to "tramp the country," planning a course to the southwest, through Hessen and the lower Rhine Valley, toward Alsace-Lorraine and into France. There, his somewhat fanciful mind presumed, he would find better work and a new life without further hassles with the Prussian police and the paternalistic despots of the German SPD. Apart from his short trip to Berlin for the Youth Conference of 1908, Willi had never set foot outside of Thuringia. He had only three marks in his pocket. Still, his experience as the chairman of the Erfurt Free Youth had furnished him with political experience, political contacts, and a fervent belief in the righteousness of his radical, if still rather vague, political philosophy. It was the height of Indian summer, and the world seemed ripe with possibility.

CHAPTER 2 *Zurich*

Willi's first attempt to leave the struggles of Erfurt behind was short-lived. His money was rapidly depleted by the costs of food and lodging as he and his friend made their way southwest through the forests of Thuringia. In Hessen, Willi and his companion stopped in Offenbach-am-Main to look for work. The two were nearly broke when they met up with members of Offenbach's Youth Socialist group, who arranged a modest disbursement of unemployment relief from the local union for the two wanderers. Willi's friend, homesick, used the money to return to Erfurt; but Willi was determined to press on. He passed briefly through Frankfurt, Mainz, and Mannheim before lodging in Pirmasens, which the Youth Socialists of Offenbach had informed him boasted many shoe factories. Pirmasens is located right on the border of Lorraine (which although largely French-speaking was then a German province, annexed along with Alsace after the Franco-Prussian war of 1870–71), so it also seemed like a perfect stepping stone on the way to Willi's ultimate destination. With his experience in the shoe business, Willi expected to find work easily there. And he might have done just that, but for a mishap that cut short his entire journey. Charmed by a scruffy-looking young comrade he met while checking into a local youth hostel, Münzenberg chose to share a room with his new "friend," who claimed to have local union contacts. Unfortunately, the deceitful comrade awoke early the next morning to steal Willi's work clothes, which were cleaner and newer than his own. The innkeeper, who felt bad about the theft, furnished Willi with a pair of trousers and boots that were, unfortunately, much too big for him.

Embarrassed and defeated, Willi turned around and headed back for Erfurt. His money from the Offenbach union relief fund ran out quickly, and he had to subsist on wild fruits and berries and some bread he had packed for the trip. Exhausted and malnourished, Willi had fallen ill by the time he reached Heidelberg, and spent a very unpleasant night there coughing up blood in the police station. Somehow he recovered enough strength to forge on the next day through the west Thuringian forest, living off the land and reaching the outskirts of Erfurt a week later.

Willi did not stay for long, however. The return journey from Pirmasens had weakened him, and he had to swallow his pride and move in with his older sister while he recovered. When he was well enough to move about again, he found a poorly paid job hawking wares in a booth in the town market, before his Free Youth buddies found him an unskilled job like his previous one, this time in the Hesse shoe factory. The political obstacles Willi had encountered on the job market before he left had evidently been smoothed over now that the Free Youth, to Willi's dismay, was defunct after his long absence, and posed no apparent threat to the employers of Erfurt. But labor peace was hardly what Willi wanted.

Hoping to reinvigorate his sense of political purpose, Willi sent a letter to Friedrich Ebert, the future president of Weimar Germany who was then chairman of the SPD's Central Youth Committee, asking for permission to revive the Erfurt Free Youth. Ebert's reply was not encouraging. Willi was referred to local SPD headquarters, whose leaders, he knew, had no intention of allowing the Free Youth to flourish again. Münzenberg probably expected such a reply and could hardly have been surprised at the rejection of his request. But Ebert's predictable response entrenched still further Willi's already bitter resentment of the SPD establishment, which had neutralized the one institution—Erfurt's autonomous Free Youth—that had given meaning and direction to his life.

By early July 1910, Willi had saved up enough money to survive another several weeks on the road, and he set off again in search of employment, this time in a more southerly direction. His objective, once again, was France, although he wanted to try a different path so as not to repeat the earlier debacles. His route this time passed through the Black Forest, zigzagging through Bavaria, past Lindau on the Bodensee, and finally over Schaffhausen into Switzerland, where his first stop was Zurich.

Based on his positive experience in Offenbach, Willi searched for and quickly found the Youth Bureau of the Swiss Social Democratic Party (SPS). He was warmly welcomed there by SPS Youth chairman Max Bock, who, upon hearing of Willi's leadership experience in Erfurt, immediately offered to find work and lodgings for the weary traveler. Still clinging to his goal of reaching France, however, Willi pressed on to the west, through Luzern, Meiringen, Interlaken, and Thun, stopping over at last in Bern, where Bock had given him the address of another youth group.

With his money running low, Willi accepted a job the Bern Young Socialists found for him at the Hotel Stern, where he was responsible for unloading and tapping barrels of wine. The hours were long, usually from dawn until closing, and Willi didn't much like the work. But his boss loved having this young teetotaler—here was the first wine boy he had ever employed who didn't drink away the profits!—and was sorry to see Willi go, when Bock sent notice in August that an especially promising job had opened up back in Zurich for a pharmacist's assistant. Having worked only a few weeks at the hotel, Willi didn't even have enough money saved for a train ticket to Zurich, but his Young Socialist friends came to his aid again and sent him on his way.[1]

Aussersihl

Münzenberg's new job in Zurich was perfectly suited to the life of an ambitious young radical. The pharmacist who hired him was a Socialist sympathizer, who didn't care that Willi knew nothing about pharmaceuticals (nor did Münzenberg have fluent Latin, as Bock had hinted to secure the job for him), so long as his politics were admirable. Willi's weekly salary, although not huge, represented more than he had ever gotten before, and he even received an advance of ten Swiss francs upon taking the job to help him settle in Zurich. More important, his new boss gave Willi as much time off as he desired, and this allowed him to plunge immediately into political activism.[2]

When Willi entered the radical scene in Zurich, the largest and most exciting youth group around was the Aussersihl district *Jungburschenverein* (Youth Socialist Union), which met in Zurich's Volkshaus, just down Stauffacher Strasse from Münzenberg's apartment on Werdplatz near the River Sihl. This group, although nominally affiliated with the SPS and other Socialist youth groups throughout Switzerland, was older and more radical than its brethren. It had been founded by an enigmatic pastor named Paul Pflüger in 1901 under the auspices of Zurich's Johanneskirche.[3]

Pflüger, a jolly, hard-drinking socialist, optimistically subtitled his church association a "union of like-minded young laborers for the goal of instruction and friendship," but under his haphazard leadership the group proved susceptible to destructive alien influences. While Pflüger dithered and drank through the group's first decade, the Aussersihl Youth Socialist Union was invaded by bearded old anarchist exiles from France, Russia, and Austria, whose heady message of virtuous violence, expressed in a provocative rag they called the *Scorpion,* was taken well to heart by their young charges. At one point, the *Scorpion* issued an unequivocal defense of the Russian Social Revolutionary Tatiana Leontiev, who had mistakenly murdered a Swiss man in Interlaken, believing him to be a Russian government official on vacation. "We believe," intoned the *Scorpion*, "that a good deed or the intention of doing one—whatever the result of such—is unimpeachable. We believe furthermore that it is irrelevant whether or not, when the dice are thrown, an innocent bystander is struck down by accident."[4]

While the old men celebrated randomly directed assassinations, their young charges frolicked about unsupervised in a two-story house in the meadow of Aussersihl Park near the Johanneskirche, which had been turned over to the group by the City of Zurich on the assumption that Pflüger was going to use it for educational purposes. Here the young "socialists" conducted wild séances involving skulls and thighbones, planned pranks at the expense of other church youth groups, and generally brawled with each other or anyone else who happened to be nearby. When the Aussersihl hooligans went on "nature" outings, they did not merely go hiking in the mountains as did most Swiss youth groups. Rather, a special "action committee" would schedule elaborate war games, violent athletic competitions, and "other merrymaking," as one group circular promised its members.[5]

This wild atmosphere clearly struck a chord with Willi, who seemed to have found the kind of no-holds-barred secret society he and his factory pals had dreamed of creating in Erfurt. Willi took part happily in the pranks and stunts, and was exposed for the first time to anarchist literature, from heretical works of the renegade German socialist Johann Most,[6] to Max Stirner's dense philosophical classic *The Ego and His Own*, to German translations of Bakunin. His favorite author, though, was the exiled Russian prince, geographer, and political crackpot Peter Kropotkin, who had oddly transmuted Darwin's concept of the "struggle for existence" into the idea that the youth associations mushrooming in Europe proved that people, like animals, flock naturally together to protect themselves against threats to their species—such as government oppression, international capitalism, and the urban disease of individualism, which by contrast drove people apart.[7]

The anti-authoritarian rhetoric in such works appealed greatly to Münzenberg after his sour experiences with the tightly organized German SPD. When this logic led Willi's Aussersihl cohorts to abolish the offices of director and session chairman, the group's freewheeling contrast with the hierarchies of the SPD was happily borne out. With his modest salary, Willi certainly didn't mind when his comrades voted further to stop paying dues in accordance with their anti-organizational philosophy. The aged Socialist theorists who sometimes addressed the Aussersihl youth in the Zurich Volkshaus seemed stiff and outmoded, and it was fun to watch unruly young anarchists heckle the old men down to size, humiliating such SPS establishment figures as Heinrich Brandler and Otto Lang.

Such radical acts, although innately satisfying to young men experimenting with anarchist beliefs, were inevitably self-defeating. When the foolish young radicals in the Aussersihl Youth Socialist Union stopped paying their dues, the group's revenues unsurprisingly dwindled rapidly until they were almost wholly dependent on what subsidies their Socialist elders in Zurich might offer—and the SPS was becoming more and more outraged at the disrespectful behavior of the Aussersihl hooligans. Although Willi had never personally objected to the rude outbursts made during the addresses by SPS leaders, he and several like-minded young members gradually grew frustrated with the anarchists' antics and resolved to expel the ringleaders from the group. Willi was dispatched as messenger one night in the winter of 1910–11, and when he found the young firebrands in question hanging about in Zurich's Langasse—a bar district notorious for brawling—he received a "sound thrashing" after he delivered the bad news. Although Münzenberg was bruised and the group had been drained of both money and members, his brave intervention gave the Aussersihl comrades a chance for a fresh start.[8]

Under Willi's leadership, the group began to accept some discipline in 1911. In place of the long-standing regime of carousing, brawling, and heckling, Münzenberg's charges gradually accustomed themselves to serious debate. Weekly discussion sessions were held on a wide-ranging variety of topics, such as the poetry of Heine and Freiligrath, the history of socialism in Switzerland, class struggle in the Middle Ages, the fight against tuberculosis, the causes of inflation, the roots of the current Italian-Turkish war, the novels of Tolstoy, and the duties and rights of Youth Socialist Union members. Certain of the topics (such as Heine and Freiligrath) reflected Willi's own interests, but most were the brainchild of Fritz Brupbacher, an eccentric Zurich physician, notorious for his support for birth control, who had become friendly with Münzenberg during his visits to Youth Socialist meetings in the Volkshaus public meeting hall.

Brupbacher, an idealistic SPS member with anarchist sympathies, had always taken an interest in the Aussersihl group, and when Willi assumed control of the group in 1911, he became its unofficial guru. Brupbacher had been holding a weekly socialist salon at his house for years, where aspiring young intellectuals presented book reports on literary classics that they often spent weeks preparing. Both Münzenberg and his Aussersihl comrade Heinrich Frisch began attending regularly in 1911. Willi's own project that year was on Dostoevsky's *Crime and Punishment*, a work he found very difficult —although his report was given a passing mark by Brupbacher, who considered himself an expert on Russian literature. Besides Dostoevsky, his salon also discussed the works of Gogol, Turgenev, the socialist Alexander Herzen, and Tolstoy. Willi certainly didn't have time to plow through all the books assigned, but he acquired more than a passing interest in the harsh conditions of the poor in Tsarist Russia, accentuated in no small part by the stories told by the young Russian émigré Maler Margolis who frequented the salon. Münzenberg also took part in the vigorous discussion of Henrik Ibsen's *A Doll's House* that occupied the group in mid-August 1912, which was probably his first exposure to feminist ideas.[9]

Fritz Brupbacher, then, did much to encourage Münzenberg's intellectual pretensions, and Willi, in turn, encouraged those of his young followers. In the spirit of proletarian self-improvement, Willi asked his young comrades to make regular contributions to a writing journal, dangling before them the carrot of literary recognition: the best pieces would appear in the periodical *Freie Jugend* (Free Youth), edited by Max Bock of the SPS's Youth Bureau, or even sent off to the party or union press. To give them a taste of the glories that might await them, Münzenberg paraded before them his new friend Max Barthel, a former factory worker from Dresden whose "worker poetry" had so impressed a rich socialist sympathizer that he now traveled through Europe as a kind of professional proletarian bard. Together, Münzenberg and Barthel published some rough poems by aspiring Aussersihl writers in a collection called *Weihnachtsglocken* (Christmas Bells) that was supposed to be the initial volume in a lengthy series devoted to "proletarian literature." But most such efforts ended up on the cutting room floor. Perhaps giving up on the limited literary potential of his comrades, Münzenberg filled the next installment in the series, didactically styled "A Collection of Serious and Cheerful Poems to Recite at Worker Festivals," mainly with his and Barthel's own poems, along with some by Freiligrath, Heine, Schiller, Turgenev, and others.[10]

Münzenberg also wrote a series of overtly political plays, most of which, drawing on his own household experience that he was now mythologizing into dogma, centered on conflicts between young workers and tyrannical father figures. Years later, Willi would cringe upon remembering the didactic drivel he spent so much time writing and promoting. (When Brupbacher asked Willi on one such occasion if he was still writing poetry, Münzenberg threatened to stop speaking to him if he brought up the subject again.) But at the time, Willi and his comrades were intoxicated by the thrill of self-expression, and their poems and plays reflected a sincere belief in the importance of proletarian literary self-improvement for the future of socialism.[11]

Willi's enthusiastic embrace of Brupbacher's pet intellectual obsessions gave the Aussersihl Youth Socialists something to talk about when they met every week, but there was still the problem of recruiting new members to replace the anarchist contingent that had been expelled. To this end Münzenberg advertised screenings of short nature films and cultural documentaries at which his assistants would probe the audience for young men of radical sympathies. Willi also organized contacts with nonproletarian, mostly Catholic youth associations, which allowed him to greatly increase the Youth Socialists' unofficial ranks of sympathizers, but did little to increase the number of dues-paying members.[12]

Münzenberg's most ingenious recruiting ploy was to reach out to women by distributing leaflets advertising a discussion on the theme "Whom should the young working girl marry?" Perhaps thinking that some mysterious bachelor was going to present himself for marriage, fifty girls showed up, of whom well over half left immediately after Willi's rambling fifteen-minute introductory speech. Although no transcript of this speech exists, a glance at the separate home education–type sessions later scheduled for Zurich's girl Socialists hints that it was no feminist manifesto. Still, of those that stayed through Willi's speech, no less than six enlisted in the movement, including a shy, dark-haired beauty named Adele Kluser, who soon became Willi's steady girlfriend and eager office helper. Münzenberg, now twenty-two years old, was still slightly built, but his handsome features, intense eyes, and growing confidence as a leader certainly worked in his favor with the new female recruits.[13]

Such coups helped increase Münzenberg's prestige in Aussersihl, but they cannot be said to have greatly expanded the youth group's clout in Zurich politics. When negotiations between employers and striking painters and metalworkers reached an impasse in summer 1912 and a general strike was proclaimed in the city, Willi's charges joined enthusiastically in downtown demonstrations, but played no role in either the proclamation of the strike or the settlement that ended it. Münzenberg later recalled heroically pedaling his bike frantically all over town, trying to rally Zurich's young behind the strikers, but in truth there was little he and his youth comrades could offer other than moral support. By contrast, Max Bock, the SPS youth chairman, as a leading union representative in Zurich, helped organize the strike directly, for better or worse.

Although Willi had evidently not yet managed to expand the Aussersihl Youth Socialist Union into a serious political force by 1912, the general strike in Zurich did provide impetus in his own political career. The municipal council, which included four SPS representatives, did not look kindly on Max Bock's role in the strike, which had quickly degenerated into violent clashes between demonstrators and city police before it was settled. Bock was arrested and soon thereafter expelled from the party, leaving vacant both his seat as chairman of the SPS's Youth Bureau, and his job as editor of *Free Youth*. As the leader of Zurich's main Youth Socialist organization, the largest in all of Switzerland, Münzenberg was chosen to replace Bock in both positions, and set to work with his customary intensity to make them his own.[14]

Although nominally Willi's authority in the Swiss Youth Socialist movement was now greatly expanded, his power was still quite limited. *Free Youth* was distributed nationally, but had a circulation of only about two thousand.[15] Its operating budget was underwritten almost entirely by subsidies from the SPS, and even so it was running chronic deficits. Moreover, Willi's personal authority in Aussersihl had been almost unquestioned, whereas now he was directly under the thumb of the Swiss Socialist Party bureaucracy. He was forced to stand by helplessly as his friend and mentor, Brupbacher, was expelled from the party after publishing an obnoxious diatribe in *Free Youth*. (Brupbacher, viewing the polite reception Socialists had offered Kaiser Wilhelm II during an official state visit to Switzerland as appeasement of Europe's "bourgeois" ruling establishment, wrote angrily that he would never pay "five cents for Swiss democracy.")[16] And when Münzenberg, seeking to take advantage of the Second International's November 1912 meeting in nearby Basel, hired the biggest hall in Zurich and invited visiting SPD luminaries Liebknecht and Luxemburg to address his Youth Socialist comrades, the SPS forbade the Germans to attend, thus delaying once again the realization of the young man's political ambitions. This was not merely a matter of prestige; a Liebknecht or Luxemburg speech would have drawn huge crowds and been a major fund-raising coup for the Youth Bureau: Münzenberg was charging admission.[17]

Eager to distance himself from SPS leaders who, in his mind, increasingly resembled the SPD functionaries who had cut him down to size in Erfurt, Münzenberg campaigned throughout 1913 for the political "independence" of the Socialist youth organizations—which meant in practice that he would need to raise his own funds. He was helped in this aim by several enthusiastic editorial assistants from *Free Youth*, who were all unattached bachelors with plenty of time on their hands. Willi Trostel, for example, was forty-seven years old, and yet still lived at home with his parents. So did Willi's Italian co-worker, Guilio Mimiola. Longtime Youth Socialist organizer Edi Meyer, meanwhile, roomed with Münzenberg, and so was at his constant disposal. Aided by these eager workaholics, Willi began frantic preparations for financial independence in November and December and set 1 January 1914 as the target date for launching the new secretariat. Münzenberg discovered to his horror in December that *Free Youth* was in debt to its printer for more than fifteen hundred francs. Were four hundred francs of the principal not paid by 2 January, printing would be halted. At the time, there were only thirty francs in the Youth Bureau treasury, which were covering ordinary expenses.

Somewhat romantically, Münzenberg, Meyer, Trostel, and Mimiola agreed together to hock their personal belongings to make up the deficit; and one girl from the editorial office even offered to sell her hair. Before such drastic steps were taken, the men rounded up their youth cohorts and barnstormed New Year's parties given by Zurich's various socialist sympathizers, scaring up piecemeal donations from partygoers that, remarkably, added up to 430 francs by morning. With the printer's debt paid off, the Youth Secretariat was open for business as planned on 1 January, and Willi was unanimously proclaimed the national secretary of the autonomous Youth Socialist movement of Switzerland.[18]

Münzenberg's earlier promotion from the leader of the Aussersihl Youth Socialist Union into chairman of the SPS's Youth Bureau had entailed an impressive-sounding promotion without much increase in political authority. But his new designation as autonomous Swiss Socialist Youth "secretary" represented a major step in Münzenberg's career. He was now on salary, paid one hundred francs a month by the new Youth Secretariat, plus expenses. Consequently, he quit his job in the pharmacy where he had worked, albeit on flexible hours, since 1910. Münzenberg was now free to spend all of his time organizing, beseeching, dictating, writing, recruiting, and delegating. He had become a professional politician.[19]

Münzenberg and his roommate, Meyer, transformed their modestly sized apartment on Zurich's Werdplatz into a veritable post office, as they dispatched recruitment letters, fund-raising plans, and executive circulars to youth groups all over Switzerland. When Willi wasn't answering mail or drafting propaganda, he traveled across the country, proselytizing young men in every town and hamlet he passed through on the virtues of socialism. Within months, new Youth Socialist branches, directly answerable to Münzenberg, were established in the towns of Dietikon, Flumental, Interlaken, Langnau, Roschach, Thalwil, Uster, Siggertal, and many others. In the first year of the Youth Secretariat, Münzenberg organized 336 meetings in Switzerland, and attended almost as many in person. In all, Willi's recruiting more than doubled the active membership in Socialist Youth organizations in Switzerland in the first year of his secretaryship, from 944 members in mid-January 1914 to 2,074 in January 1915.[20]

With Secretariat funds, no fewer than fifty-four delegates were dispatched to an international Youth Socialist congress held in Stuttgart in late spring 1914, and it seemed the energetic Swiss group was in the vanguard of Europe's Youth Socialist movement. The text of Münzenberg's address to the Stuttgart Congress, held just weeks before the outbreak of the First World War, gives some idea of the heady utopian spirit then animating the Swiss Youth Secretariat, and of Willi's own growing confidence and stature:

> Legend has it that two thousand years ago, the Holy Spirit filled Jesus' disciples, so that they went forth and taught all the world's peoples. A legend perhaps, but I know that this spirit of Pentecost must fill us today. We shall go forth to all nations, to all brothers and sisters and fire them with enthusiasm for Socialism.[21]

Rhetoric aside, Willi's clout even in the world of Swiss Socialism was still fairly small. His secretariat commanded, in spring 1914, little more than a thousand dues-paying Youth Socialist members in all of Switzerland, along with about thirteen hundred "passive" members in some way affiliated with the local youth branches. This was a power base sufficient to support an all but financially autonomous Youth Secretariat, which could put out *Free Youth* once a month, send delegates to international conferences, and not incidentally, pay Münzenberg's monthly salary and travel budget. Willi had come far from his humble beginnings in Erfurt, but he still chafed at his junior status in Socialist politics. All this changed, however, with Europe's plunge into war in 1914.

Bern

Even to socialists who had long suspected the worst of "capitalist" governments, the Great War came as a shock. Many moderate socialists shared the optimistic belief of liberal economists that the interlocking "commercial interdependence" of the great powers would deter the outbreak of a major war. Those less sanguine had banked their hopes not on the self-interest of international capital, but on their own capacity for preventive action—had not, after all, the Second International socialist congresses convened at Stuttgart (1907), Copenhagen (1910), and Basel (1912), all issued antiwar resolutions that obliged the member parties of all belligerent powers to sabotage imperialist aggression? As late as 29 July, socialists, after an emergency meeting of the International in Brussels, locked arms in the streets, singing the *Internationale* and shouting "War on war!"

Behind them, the socialist press all over Europe thundered with denunciations of militarism. But Europe's socialists did not prevent the war. In those countries where they had a parliamentary voice, most importantly in France and Germany, socialists voted unanimously for war credits less than a week after the pacifist rhetoric of Brussels. Worse still, apart from a few voices of dissent, leading socialists in the belligerent countries genuinely rallied behind their nation's war efforts, particularly in Germany. Leading the charge were the supposedly antiwar Youth Socialist groups, many of which happily dissolved themselves in a frenzy of patriotism. In a spasm of martial madness, the internationalist pretensions of European socialism vanished into thin air.[22]

If the war's outbreak helped to resolve political dilemmas for socialists in the belligerent countries, however, it brought paralysis to their counterparts in Europe's neutral nations. What was a good internationalist socialist to do, as he saw his putative ideological brothers take up arms in the service of national "bourgeois" armies? In Switzerland, this was not an abstract question. In front of their eyes, Swiss socialists watched helplessly as many resident citizens of France, Germany, and Austria, both volunteers and draftees, swarmed the train stations of Zurich, Geneva, and other large cities. Should they protest? Argue with the crowds? Make public proclamations of international solidarity, to remind departing belligerents with socialist leanings of their more idealistic prewar selves?

There was probably little that socialists like Münzenberg could do in Switzerland to sabotage belligerents' army enlistments, but this did not stop some of them from trying. Zurich's always rambunctious unions convened an antiwar rally early in August at the Velodrome. The first speaker, a moderate SPS functionary named Johann Sigg, disappointingly offered the crowd little but the hope that international solidarity could be rebuilt after the war, counseling against efforts to sabotage belligerents' war efforts. Enraged by this display of passivity, Münzenberg rushed the podium before poor Sigg had even finished and launched into a feverish attack on socialists who had betrayed internationalism in supporting the war, exhorting his young comrades never to march off and die for "capitalism." Willi's speech, too, was forcibly interrupted, by SPS chairman Hermann Greulich, a timorous man who assured the socialists in attendance that he would "pour a good amount of water into this tempestuous young man's wine." Sensing he had gone too far, Willi backed down and remained silent for the rest of the rally. But he found another outlet for his outrage soon thereafter, when he led a contingent from the Youth Secretariat on a march to Zurich's Hauptbahnhof, where they sought to drown out the chorus of departing Austrian patriots singing "Gott beschütze Franz den Kaiser" with their own breathless chanting of the *Internationale*.[23]

Because he was safe in neutral Switzerland Münzenberg could, of course, afford the luxury of unequivocal pacifist idealism in a way that his Youth Socialist counterparts in belligerent countries could not. But there should be no doubting his sincerity. He laid out his views very clearly in the first wartime issue of *Free Youth*, proclaiming on the cover a "war on war," and declaring that the war's objectives for all the belligerents were the same: "territorial gains, new colonies, and along with them new profit-enhancing markets." He stopped short of proposing measures of sabotage, but made it clear that he viewed the socialist establishment as complicit in the war and saw the only hope for the future in the ranks of "proletarian youth."[24]

Münzenberg's antiwar views seem unremarkable next to the widespread revulsion that years of brutal trench warfare would ultimately inspire, but in autumn 1914, his passion was not shared by everyone. Morale in all the belligerent armies was high, even after the initial German offensives of August and September had run aground. There was, on the various home fronts, as yet little serious opposition to the war. By the sheer abdication of their claim to speak for the international "proletariat," war-accepting and war-neutral socialists had all but ceded the political arena to fresh voices like Münzenberg's. Robert Danneberg, the Austrian chairman of the Second International's Youth Bureau, was no partisan of the Habsburg war effort, but he refused to organize opposition. Danneberg shut down his Vienna office entirely, hanging a note on the door explaining that "during the war the [International Youth bureau] will be temporarily closed."[25]

Danneberg's passivity was a godsend to the indefatigable Münzenberg, who set about on his own organizing an international antiwar conference. Throughout the first autumn and winter of the war, Willi's assistants in the Swiss Youth Secretariat took advantage of Münzenberg's networking at the Stuttgart conference of spring 1914 to gain pledges from Youth Socialist leaders from neutral Scandinavia, Denmark, and Italy to attend the antiwar congress. Ultimately, invitations were extended to Stuttgart colleagues from the belligerent countries as well, with less successful results. Although expressing support in principle for Münzenberg's conference, Youth Socialist leaders in France, Germany, and Austria were loath to defy their parent parties and declined to attend.[26]

Danneberg had himself been responsible for setting up the Stuttgart gathering at which Willi had made his fruitful international contacts, but he refused to take seriously Münzenberg's plans to convene a similar, though far more dramatic, conference, in the neutral Swiss capital of Bern for Easter Week, 1915. His only reply to Münzenberg's numerous queries was a short note in mid-November informing his rival-in-waiting that he was unable to "comment on your proposal at this time." Although Münzenberg continued to report to Vienna right up to the Easter conference, Danneberg's inability to recognize the Bern initiative as a threat to his authority ensured his own political eclipse.[27]

Münzenberg was not alone in exploiting the suddenly dormant institutional structures of the International to launch an antiwar crusade over the heads of the socialist establishment. On the suggestion of Inessa Armand, the radical Bolshevik editor of *Rabotnitsa* (Working Woman), Clara Zetkin published an appeal "To the Socialist Women of All Nations" in the *Berner Tagwacht* on 10 December 1914 on behalf of the Second International Women's Bureau, which she headed. Zetkin's article sparked preparations for a conference that ultimately met, although without much publicity, from 26 to 29 March 1915, in Bern. Moderate pacifist women delegates from Britain, France, the Netherlands, Switzerland, and Italy dominated the sessions, allowing little to be resolved beyond vague collective statements on the importance of ending the war. But Armand—a Russian who in fact was acting on behalf of her lover, Vladimir Ilyich Lenin, then quietly assembling a circle of dissident socialist radicals in Bern—provided the real drama, arguing provocatively against including useless "pacifist phrases about peace" in the conference resolutions, before proposing unsuccessfully that the women should instead agree on the need for "insurrectionary activity" to bring down belligerent governments.[28]

Just a week after the women's gathering, Münzenberg's antiwar Youth Socialist conference convened in the very same building, and followed an uncannily similar political dynamic. Everyone but the Russians agreed on a relatively moderate resolution, written jointly by the senior Swiss delegate, Robert Grimm, and a transplanted polyglot Russian representing neutral Italy, Angelica Balabanoff, which condemned the war without committing socialists to any particular action.[29] In fact, the Russian delegates were not even in the hall when the Grimm-Balabanoff resolution was passed. Led, once again, by Armand, they had staged a theatrical walkout, ostensibly to protest the assignment of one vote per country resolved on at the beginning of the conference. (They wanted two per national delegation, with Russian Poland counted separately from Russia.) Armand's ploy attracted the attention she desired: the voting allotment was changed in accordance with Russian wishes, and the other delegates agreed to hear her minority proposal. Like her resolutions at the women's conference, Armand's admonition to use the war as a springboard to insurrection was written by Lenin, and was voted down soundly by thirteen to three, even with the new voting rules.[30]

The crucial difference between the two conferences, however, was that Zetkin's pacifist moderates had merely spoken on behalf of socialist "women" in the abstract, while the delegates from neutral Denmark, Scandinavia, Holland, Bulgaria, and Italy who had come together at Münzenberg's urging represented thousands of dues-paying Youth Socialist members. In light of the history of voting allotments in the Second International, the Russians' pretension to greater representation was, in fact, absurd. Traditionally one vote was given to a socialist delegation for every thousand active members at its disposal in its host country. The Russian and Polish delegates at Bern were exiles from tsarism, and had, in 1915, only a sketchy underground following behind them in the countries they putatively represented. This is why Münzenberg, although feeling a certain rhetorical kinship with the Bolsheviks' radical intransigence, made no overtures to them and allowed Grimm and Balabanoff to carry the hall with a moderate resolution that offended none of the neutral delegations. Norway, Sweden, and Denmark alone counted some 31,000 active Youth Socialists, more than ten times as many as the other Bern delegations combined.[31]

The assembled Youth Socialist delegates at Bern, recognizing the impotence of Danneberg's old Youth Bureau, voted unanimously to create an autonomous International Youth Secretariat, with Münzenberg as secretary. The expansion of Willi's authority in the socialist world was pronounced. His new bureau commanded the loyalty of more than thirty thousand young men and women, some fifteen times the size of his Swiss power base.[32]

The break with the Second International occasioned by Münzenberg's Bern conference, then, was not merely symbolic. The youth delegates there transferred their allegiance from Vienna to Zurich, and their money would follow. For each thousand members, Youth Socialist member organizations would contribute twenty-five Swiss francs in annual dues, retroactive to 1 January 1915, which gave Münzenberg's office a budget of over six thousand francs. Although not an enormous sum—Münzenberg's Swiss Youth Secretariat turned over more—this revenue was enough to underwrite the publication of a new quarterly journal, *Youth International*, with a circulation in the tens of thousands; a team of couriers that smuggled prohibited antiwar propaganda into France, Germany, and Italy, ultimately reaching both the Eastern and Western fronts; and the creation of a special "Karl Liebknecht fund" to underwrite legal or medical costs for arrested or injured antiwar activists. Perhaps the most ambitious political creation of Münzenberg's Bern conference was an antiwar "International Youth Day," which was meant to replace the May Day tradition bequeathed to the world by the Second International.[33]

Whereas Danneberg's Youth Bureau had been merely an afterthought of the Second International, Münzenberg's International Youth Secretariat constituted an independent political force. Recognizing this, Liebknecht, Trotsky, and other emerging figures in the socialist antiwar opposition from belligerent countries contributed articles to Münzenberg's *Youth International*. Lenin and other exiles in Switzerland began using Münzenberg's courier service for their own correspondence with colleagues in their home countries, and a crucial communications link was established between the International Youth Secretariat and the underground Socialist opposition movement in Berlin, soon to christen itself the "Spartacist League."[34]

The German opposition Socialist Edwin Hörnle titled his contribution to the inaugural issue of *Youth International* on 1 September 1915 "The International is Dead! Long Live the International!" A new International had of course not yet been truly launched, but Münzenberg's Bern triumph helped clear the deck of pretenders and placed Youth Socialism clearly in the vanguard. It would not be long, however, before older, more experienced radicals would get into the act.

Zimmerwald

Nineteen-fifteen was a depressing year for pacifists. The brief winter calm that descended on Europe after the great battles of summer and early autumn 1914 was deceptive. Already in January, the war spread to the Middle East as an Ottoman army, aided and abetted by the Germans, marched across the Sinai desert in an attempt to take the Suez Canal from the British. This unsuccessful offensive, coupled with the Turks' ill-judged effort to ignite a Muslim "holy war" against the Russians in the Caucasus, inspired the Western Allies to relieve Russia by forcing open the Dardanelles, which blockaded Russia's only warm-water ports in the Black Sea. This waterway, though, was narrow and heavily mined, and protected by heavy artillery fire from the shore. It proved impassable, which led British, French, and Australian troops into the epic, but ultimately futile struggle to storm the elevated Turkish positions at Gallipoli.

On the Western Front—which both sides had heavily fortified after the German offensive had bogged down into a strategic stalemate—spring 1915 saw the first installments of futile trench warfare, as French and British offensives against nearly impregnable German positions collapsed in a sea of blood and tangled barbed wire. On 22 April, the war in the West took an especially sinister turn, as the Germans launched the first effective poison gas attack. Release of this airborne killing agent would soon accompany offensives by either side when the wind was right.

In the East, the stalemate was temporarily broken by a German-Austrian offensive at Gorlice-Tarnow in early May that opened the route to Warsaw and Brest-Litovsk, bringing about the encirclement of over three hundred thousand Russian soldiers. But this defeat only stiffened Russian resolve, and did nothing to dent Russia's nearly endless manpower reserves or its munitions production, which was just beginning to crank up in summer 1915, achieving virtual parity with German capacity by September. Russia's Western allies, meanwhile, although defeated in 1915 everywhere but at sea and in minor colonial skirmishes in Africa, showed no signs of weakening morale. In short, the prospect for breakthrough victories or voluntary peace initiatives on the part of belligerent countries were everywhere put to rest in 1915, and the war's end was nowhere in sight.

Against this backdrop of carnage, thirty-eight socialist leaders representing the antiwar opposition in eleven different countries, belligerents and neutrals alike, gathered in Bern's Eigerplatz on 5 September 1915, crowded into a tiny convoy of horse-drawn carriages, and slowly made their way up into the Alps. Lev Trotsky later famously remarked that "half a century" after the birth of Marx's First Workingman's International in 1864, "it was still possible to fit all the internationalists in Europe into four coaches."[35]

Certainly little attention was paid to the political convoy. There were no spies or reporters along (aside from the delegates themselves, many of whom were journalists). The destination chosen by Robert Grimm, the moderate Swiss Socialist who had organized the affair, all but guaranteed isolation. He had reserved a run of rooms for an innocuous-sounding "ornithological society" meeting in a country inn known as the *Beau Séjour* in the pristine

Alpine village of Zimmerwald, a quaint valley settlement surrounded by white-capped peaks about six miles south of Bern. Only fifty miles to the northwest, the French and German armies faced each other near the village of Bonfol, at the far eastern edge of the Western Front, observed warily by the Swiss militia army just across the border. But the war could not have seemed further away for the socialist delegates who came together in hushed secrecy amidst the splendid isolation of Zimmerwald to hammer out an antiwar statement that might give hope to the peace lovers of the world.

The setting of the Zimmerwald conference was undoubtedly tranquil, and peace was the theme of the day. But the relations between the delegates who met there were hardly peaceful. Mindful of the disruption caused by Lenin's protégés at the Bern conferences in spring, Grimm had hesitated almost to the last minute before inviting the Bolshevik leader. Since the publication of Lenin's classic Marxist treatise on political tactics, *What Is to Be Done?* in 1902, in which he had scorned socialists' naïve expectations of a "spontaneous" mass proletarian uprising and proposed instead the formation of an elite "vanguard" party made up of a hard core of professional revolutionaries, the Russian had been the enfant terrible of European socialism, a man whose dictatorial philosophy, he himself often conceded, could be suited only to Russia's vast empire of illiterate peasants under the absolutist rule of the tsar. Lenin's views remained offensive to socialists from democratic countries, and few of them enjoyed listening to this "little man with the narrow eyes, rusty beard, and monotone voice," as one International colleague described him. At the preliminary planning meeting for Zimmerwald, held in Bern in July 1915, Lenin's deputy, Grigori Zinoviev, proposed that only unequivocally antiwar socialist delegations be allowed to attend; his desired list excluded delegates from the belligerent countries. Grimm and the other moderates shot Zinoviev down easily, and they went out of their way to recruit socialist delegates from the French, Austrian, and German opposition that summer. Grimm's efforts ensured that Lenin would be greatly outnumbered at the conference. But he would not be able to bottle the Russian up entirely.[36]

At Zimmerwald, Lenin was relatively silent, or so it seemed. He made few speeches and acquiesced quietly after his favored resolution, drafted by the exiled left-wing SPD journalist Karl Radek, was rejected in favor of a statement, penned by Trotsky, which condemned the war and urged international socialist efforts to "summon the working class" to "begin the struggle for peace," without making any explicit instructions as to how this might be done. Lenin even voted in favor of Trotsky's text, making sure, however, to submit a brief statement establishing his reservations: the majority resolution provided no tactical guidelines and did not break clearly enough with the "opportunism" of the socialists who had supported the war. The conference did establish a new International Socialist Executive Committee, dominated by Grimm and Balabanoff, but refrained from declaring this move a repudiation of the Second International, as Lenin would have preferred. On almost every issue, Lenin and his small core of supporters were soundly defeated, to no one's surprise. There would be no new Socialist International; no expulsions of the socialist "traitors" who had voted for war credits; no plans for internationally coordinated insurrectionary activity. Because the vote on the majority resolution was unanimous, the Zimmerwald delegates were able to publicize it as a principled statement of international socialist unity. But they all knew that proclamations of unity were a sham.[37]

Such disagreement over doctrine and "tactics" may appear, at first glance, relatively arcane. After all, every last socialist at Zimmerwald opposed the war; all mourned the tragic "impotence" of the Second International, which had been unable to prevent its outbreak; and all of them wanted desperately to convert the majority socialists and unions of France, Germany, Austria, and England to the antiwar cause. Further, every single one of the delegates shared an affinity for the basic principles of Marxism, believing wholeheartedly in the existence of a universal "proletarian" class that merely needed to be awakened from its wartime hibernation, as workers at last were torn loose from the mirage of "social patriotism" and realized their true international brotherhood.

Despite these apparent grounds for agreement, however, a political wedge of historic significance was forged at Zimmerwald. Lenin did not carry the floor at the conference, but he succeeded in cementing a core group of followers, including Zinoviev, Radek, and the radical Swiss union leader Fritz Platten. He also succeeded in circulating at the conference a polemic he had recently drafted, *Socialism and War*, which would soon be making the rounds of the socialist underground, most importantly in Germany. The principal inspiration for Lenin's pamphlet was Clausewitz's classic treatise *On War*, which Lenin had read the preceding spring. Warfare was, according to Clausewitz, "the continuation of politics by other, namely violent, means." The goal of socialists, Lenin believed, should thus be to use the European war for their own political ends, uniting behind the slogan, "transformation of the imperialist war into a civil war."[38] "Peace," by contrast, "was a slogan of philistines and priests."[39] Grimm and the moderates had recoiled from Lenin's proposals for good reason: most socialists really did abhor the violence of the war, and the Leninists were demanding more violence, not less.

In effect, Lenin had called the bluff of international Socialism at Zimmerwald. What *Socialism and War* demanded—the promotion of mutinies that would topple the belligerent governments, leading to civil wars certain to be won by the "proletarians" who had foolishly been armed by "capitalists" to fight an "imperialist" war—was in fact very close to what Marx himself had envisioned, and even explicitly endorsed, in the form of the Paris Commune born of the Franco-Prussian War in 1871, whose advent was as near an approximation of his historical theories as would appear in his lifetime.[40] Lenin's "civil war" slogan, although deemed "extremist" and "sectarian" by his Zimmerwald critics, was entirely in the spirit of the socialist *Internationale:*

> The kings intoxicate us with gunsmoke,
> Peace between ourselves, war on the tyrants.
> Let us bring the strike to the armies,
> Fire into the air and break ranks!
> If they insist, these cannibals,
> On making us into heroes,
> They'll know soon enough that our bullets
> Are for our own generals![41]

Lenin, by 1915, had already taken the Marxist theory of class struggle to its inevitably violent conclusion. The Leninist chorus still lacked vocal support; but the tune, once hummed by a few, would prove increasingly hard to resist.

Red Sunday

The day after the Zimmerwald conference adjourned, Lenin's small group of supporters met to affirm their allegiance to Radek's defeated draft resolution as a theoretical basis for action and declared themselves, somewhat grandly, the "Zimmerwald Left." In the beginning, there were all of eight of them, and they had no political headquarters, no base of supporters, and no money. Not even Lenin's fellow Russian socialists adhered as a group to the Zimmerwald Left. Trotsky and the Mensheviks were resolutely opposed, denouncing Lenin's group in *Nashe Slovo* as "extremists and sectarians." In Berlin, Liebknecht and Luxemburg, who had been in prison during the September 1915 conference, although sharing Lenin's contempt for the weak majority resolution passed there, preferred to establish their own faction, independent of Lenin's. They declared themselves the "Spartacist League" on 1 January 1916. Even Radek, who was Lenin's closest ally at Zimmerwald, wavered when the Zimmerwald Left tried to establish a new theoretical journal in the winter of 1915–16: he wanted to collaborate openly with the Dutch Opposition Socialists whose funds were to underwrite the enterprise, while Lenin insisted on absolute editorial control. The impasse killed the journal, *Vorbote,* before the first issue even appeared. Lenin's insistence on rigid doctrinal adherence made it difficult to recruit allies, but then this rigidity was both the strength and the weakness of a "vanguard" party. The very isolation of the Zimmerwald Left would, in time, make it increasingly attractive to socialists who longed for a clean break from tradition. One of Lenin's first, and most important, converts was Willi Münzenberg.[42]

It is easy to see why the violent eschatology promoted by the Zimmerwald Left appealed to Münzenberg. Lenin's contempt for empty pacifist rhetoric, his conspiratorial insistence on the need for concerted action, the romantic-sounding adventure he foretold of wholesale mutinies and civil war—such heady notions were tailor-made for the energetic Young Socialist organizer. Münzenberg's reputation as an uncontrollable firebrand, in fact, had ensured that Grimm did not invite him to Zimmerwald, a conference convened without the blessing of the SPS, whose position on the war was even more conservative than Grimm's moderate pacifism. (The party supported full mobilization of the Swiss militia to defend the country against possible attacks by belligerent armies.) Grimm feared igniting a wholesale split in the SPS, and was wary of allowing Münzenberg to join forces with his fellow Zurich radical, Fritz Platten, at Zimmerwald. Grimm's suspicions were well founded. When Lenin's Zimmerwald Left began meeting weekly in Zurich in autumn 1915, Münzenberg accompanied Platten out of curiosity and soon became a regular at the fashionable cafés—the Stüssihof, the Schwarzer Adler, and the Weisser Schwänli—where the group held their political discussions.

Münzenberg had first met Lenin during the Bern conference of April 1915. Lenin, it is true, had nearly made a mockery of the proceedings by stage-managing Armand's divisive walkout. But in doing so, he had indirectly flattered Münzenberg, by deeming his Young Socialist conference worthy of such manipulation.

Münzenberg repaid the compliment by listening attentively at the Zimmerwald Left café discussions. Before long, Lenin reciprocated by attending Youth Socialist meetings, where he often challenged Münzenberg's charges in debate. The intense Russian gave no quarter when he argued with Youth Socialists, showing them the same intellectual respect he accorded

Münzenberg. "At last," wrote Münzenberg's friend Ferdinand Böhny of Lenin's courting of the youth group, "we had met a grown-up, clever man who argued seriously with us."[43] To better exploit his new political base, Lenin moved permanently from Bern to Zurich in February 1916. Over the next year, Münzenberg was a frequent guest at the single-room apartment Lenin and Krupskaya shared in the Spiegelgasse, and Lenin often visited Münzenberg's residence as well, below the river on Werdplatz.

The grounds for Münzenberg's ideological conversion were fairly simple. Before the Bern conference, he had concentrated on the problem of ending the war, by demanding that socialists in belligerent countries vote down war credits, and by suggesting (although he was careful not to demand directly) that recruits refuse to perform military service. The unspoken assumption behind Münzenberg's position, according to Lenin, was that war, under the existing "capitalist" world order, could be brought to an end, whereas in true Marxist ideology, capitalist war was inevitable and endemic. The goal of socialists, then, should not be *Entwaffnung*, or general disarmament, but rather *Bewaffnung*, the arming of the proletariat, accompanied by selective *Entwaffnung* of the "bourgeois" population.

The key, then, was not to deprive the belligerent armies (or Switzerland's militia) of soldiers, but to infiltrate them with ideological allies and turn the armies "Red." As Lenin instructed proletarians in the unsuccessful minority resolution for the Kienthal Conference of April 1916 (which was largely a replay of Zimmerwald), "*Lay down your weapons. Turn them against the common foe!*—the capitalist governments." Lenin's military stance wasn't really new—Karl Liebknecht had famously invoked the goal of "legal" penetration of the army at his 1907 trial for lèse-majesté. But if Lenin wasn't original, he was refreshingly honest, proclaiming his revolutionary intentions far more explicitly than had the slippery Liebknecht. In any case, the radical line played better in Zurich's Volkshaus than in the courts of Wilhelmine Germany. Willi's Young Socialists were progressively worn down by Lenin's disarming bluntness, to the point where, in Münzenberg's recollection, "we would have walked through fire for him."[44]

Lenin's program also helped Münzenberg solve a political dilemma regarding the Swiss militia draft. Switzerland may not have been a belligerent, but the Western Front ran dangerously right up to her borders and her militia army was fully mobilized for war. The Swiss authorities did not look kindly on efforts to undermine the militia's effectiveness, and were on ready alert for agitators promoting draft resistance. Münzenberg, although passionate in his contempt for Europe's "capitalist" warmongers, generally kept his pacifist rhetoric vague in the first year of the war, calling for disarmament and denouncing "militarism," while being careful not to endorse treasonous behavior. For example, in a 1915 circular instructing local Young Socialist leaders on speech topics for section meetings, Münzenberg emphasizes the iniquities of military justice, the "abuses" of "military dictatorship," and the Swiss government's use of the school system to indoctrinate chauvinistic values of "militarism"—but despite his obvious intention of promoting resistance to military service he makes no mention of the draft, and it is clear he wants his charges to follow the same discretion.[45]

By contrast, a similar circular from summer 1916, by which time Münzenberg had fallen under Lenin's spell, outlines the military question in more aggressive terms and yet it is clear the Young Socialist leader does not, strictly speaking, advocate refusal of military service. The proposed themes of discussion begin with overarching Marxist theory ("aims of militarism"; "forms of militarism"; "militia vs. people's army"; "aggressive and defensive wars") and conclude with revolutionary practice: "the placement of revolutionary soldiers" and "practical measures taken as a consequence."[46] Although Lenin's influence had "revolutionized" his goals, Münzenberg was now also theoretically within the bounds of legality on the military issue (at least on the narrow issue of draft resistance).

Such ideological distinctions had, of course, not impressed Liebknecht's judges in 1907, and they were likewise lost on the Swiss police, who were fond of Münzenberg's antimilitary rhetoric neither before nor after his conversion to Leninism. The boisterous pacifist rhetoric of *Free Youth* in the first winter of the war, Münzenberg's Bern Youth Conference of April 1915, his International Secretariat's distribution of antiwar literature across the border, and even his sale of antiwar stamps to raise funds, had all attracted the attention of the Swiss government. The meetings Münzenberg held in the Zurich Volkshaus, meanwhile, were generally open to the public by design—and frequently attended by law enforcement officials. Although Münzenberg was keen to avoid the legal pitfall of explicitly demanding resistance to military service, he was not above provoking a government he knew was beginning to watch him closely. And Zurich's cantonal authorities took the bait on Tuesday 1 August, when a group of about five hundred rowdy antiwar demonstrators, led by Münzenberg's assistant Willi Trostel, ran into a police cordon on Bahnhofstrasse, Zurich's ritzy shopping thoroughfare. The young militants refused to disperse, and the police opened fire. Several marchers were struck, although no one was killed, and a number of bystanders were injured in the resulting stampede.[47]

The exact circumstances of the Bahnhofstrasse incident remain murky. Münzenberg himself, for example, wasn't there, although he almost certainly organized the demonstration that ultimately provoked the bloodshed. No record of the Volkshaus meeting directly preceding the fateful antiwar demonstration exists, but it is likely the demonstration plans were announced there—in the presence of the usual contingent of police observers, who apparently used this intelligence to stake out Bahnhofstrasse.[48]

Whether intentionally provoked or not, the Tuesday "massacre" (as it was instantly styled by Münzenberg and his staff) was a godsend for Münzenberg, igniting a firestorm of publicity that buoyed recruiting efforts. He had already drawn a fairly steady stream of recruits during the war, tripling Youth Socialist membership rolls from 944 to 3,500. But the new wave of enlistments was without precedent. As messages of condolence poured in from all over Switzerland for victims of the "massacre," Willi's missionaries barnstormed the country and established no less than thirty-seven new local branches counting one thousand dues-paying members. "Sympathy" demonstrations were organized in over a hundred towns, drawing an average of four hundred participants apiece, who were hustled for donations and sold subscriptions to *Free Youth* and the *Youth International*. Over a thousand Swiss francs were collected for the "Karl Liebknecht Fund," and so many new subscribers were signed on that *Free Youth* moved from a monthly to a biweekly format. Demand was so robust that the subscription price was soon doubled to three Swiss francs a year.[49]

The sudden swelling of Münzenberg's militant youth movement in the wake of a violent confrontation with the government was not looked upon kindly by the SPS. The radicalism of the youth groups had long been a thorn in the side of the parent party, which, like its counterparts in the belligerent countries, had put social peace above ideological principle in supporting mobilization during the war. Aggressive street protests had always been seen as dangerous and counterproductive by the SPS brass. Max Bock had been expelled from the party for his role in the Zurich general strike of 1912, and Münzenberg might have met a similar fate in 1916, had not his growing fame meant that his expulsion could have sparked loud protests. Provoked by the aggressive posturing of Münzenberg's minions in August, the Zurich cantonal police turned to the national militia for help in preserving public order, and the army began regular surveillance of youth gatherings. Münzenberg and Switzerland's law enforcement officials were eye to eye, and both were itching for a fight. Desperate to prevent another incident that would blacken Swiss socialism, the SPS summoned an emergency conference and banned party members from participating in Münzenberg's planned nationwide demonstrations marking International Socialist Youth Day on "Red Sunday," 3 September.[50]

The SPS ban was prudent and, in the event, probably saved Münzenberg's career in Switzerland. Red Sunday had been widely advertised all spring and summer. After the embarrassment of the Tuesday "massacre," the government had no intention of allowing Münzenberg's angry young men to disturb public order again. On 2 September, the executive government in Bern issued a sweeping resolution banning any and all "demonstrations and processions on public streets or squares that are deemed to endanger public peace, order, and security, or the national defense."[51] The decree did not mention Münzenberg's Young Socialists by name, but it was understood by all concerned as aimed directly at the International Youth Day on the morrow. The army was put on full alert, and garrisons in every large city were ordered to be "ready to move" at 2 A.M.[52] Had Münzenberg ordered his followers to take the streets, it is likely there would have been enormous bloodshed, far surpassing the modest casualty figures of the Tuesday "massacre." Moreover, there would have been no doubting Willi's personal responsibility this time, so widespread had been the publicity for Red Sunday. Münzenberg, if he himself were not injured, would certainly have been arrested and deported from Switzerland immediately, with blood on his hands. But without the party behind him, he decided not to chance it, and called off the demonstrations at the last minute.[53]

At least, this is the explanation he gave to his Young Socialist branch leaders. In his "cease and desist" order to the youth sections, Münzenberg took pains to avoid the appearance of surrendering to superior force. "It is entirely possible for us to rise in the streets against a world of bourgeois enemies," he counseled them, "but it is impossible to take the streets against our own party." So Red Sunday was off, but Münzenberg counseled that Youth Socialist leaders should take advantage of their free time that day to go "house to house" informing citizens of the government's latest "shameful action" against its workers, using the demonstration ban as a spur to recruitment. Undoubtedly this message was disappointing for young militants who had been gearing up for International Youth Day for months, but it was better than walking into a "bloodbath."[54]

However he tried to spin it, the government's successful suppression of Münzenberg's Red Sunday plans was a humiliating defeat. Youth Socialists held a number of small protest meetings in September, but they generally confined themselves to indoor settings that would not violate the government ban. Münzenberg himself had to cancel one speaking engagement in Wartburg, near Davos, after the local population raised an outcry against the notorious foreign antimilitary agitator daring to proselytize their sons.[55]

Emboldened by their success in quieting Young Socialist agitation, Zurich's cantonal authorities now called Münzenberg and his assistants down to police headquarters to justify their antimilitary propaganda. Pressed to the wall, Münzenberg put forward a torturous legalistic defense, claiming that Youth Socialists had formally taken "no position on the questions of antimilitarism," and that anyway the individual sections affiliated with his Youth Secretariat were "accountable for their own goals and actions." Both of these statements were misleading, if not downright falsehoods: Münzenberg had long instructed his sections quite specifically on military questions, both on how to talk and how to act. To his credit, though, he was more honest in defending his "personal position." "I am a Marxist," he declared, "and [the goal of] disarmament is incompatible with this [ideology] at the current moment. I am thus against the refusal of military service." The Zurich police may not have been unduly impressed by this claim for the legality of Leninism, but they recognized the difficulty of prosecuting it, and let Willi go.[56]

Münzenberg had suffered a serious defeat, but it was not without its silver lining. Media attention surrounding Red Sunday was even more extensive than it had been following the Tuesday "massacre," and much of the coverage this time was concerned with Münzenberg himself. In fact, the Public Prosecutor's office in Bern considered deporting him in early September, but declined to do so on the grounds that his expulsion could spark "new unrest" in the streets. After Red Sunday, Willi Münzenberg's notoriety passed a certain point of no return in Switzerland, and consideration of any further measures to be taken against him, by either the SPS or the Swiss government, would be informed by fears of a public scandal.[57]

Münzenberg's Red Sunday defeat also emboldened his rhetoric. In one angry executive circular, he questioned the parent party's prerogative to order the Young Socialists around, based as it was on a meager annual subsidy of one thousand francs. (Paltrier still was union support—they had forked over all of two hundred francs in the last three years.) Displaying rhetorical firepower he had evidently honed during several years of antiwar speeches, Münzenberg now all but incited his Youth Socialist charges to class war. "They say were are too radical," Münzenberg declaimed, "but in these times one cannot be radical enough." After all, on Red Sunday, "our enemies ... proceed[ed] against us with cannons and machine guns." Against such violently disposed class enemies, it was clear that "we cannot answer with peace resolutions." Socialist agitation, Münzenberg concluded, "will remain meaningless so long as we don't succeed in advocating workers' interests radically enough . . . against the arrogant contempt of the rich."[58] Faced with a hostile alliance between the SPS and the Swiss government, Münzenberg's legions had accepted a cease-fire in the streets on Red Sunday. But this was an uneasy truce, which Münzenberg was clearly prepared to break when doing so would be to his advantage.

Stockholm

Münzenberg's struggles with the Swiss authorities in 1916 reflected the unprecedented political opportunities opened up by the world war, but also the ultimate impotence of revolutionaries faced down by armies loyal to their governments. In the months before the failure of Red Sunday, Münzenberg's followers had probably succeeded in infiltrating the Swiss militia with dozens, perhaps even hundreds of "revolutionaries" who would refuse to fire on comrades demonstrating in the streets. But the vast bulk of the army, as Münzenberg well knew, was fervently loyal to the Swiss Republic, and in its wartime state of full mobilization was a formidable enemy. This was the essential problem faced by every leader in the European socialist opposition: disciplined national armies ruled the continent from the English Channel to the Urals, armies hostile not only to public antiwar demonstrations but also to any substantial movement of people and materials not essential to the war effort. Years of attrition at the front had radicalized the war's opponents and made them ripe for socialist propaganda; but the armies were still there, and socialists had little prospect of seizing power without their support.[59]

By 1917, however, the first significant cracks began to appear in Europe's military edifice. The death of Emperor Franz Josef in November 1916, who had ruled over his multiethnic subjects since 1848, greatly loosened the always tenuous bonds holding together the many nationalities of Austria-Hungary and made them ripe for Entente propaganda that sought to divide the empire. On the Western Front, casualty rates had been so astounding in the battles of 1916 that the disastrous French offensive at Chemin des Dames that opened 1917 led to a wave of so-called "mutinies," as soldiers refused to continue flinging themselves against the enemy trenches. In all the belligerent armies, conscripts complained of bad food, of futile offensive battles that had gained little, of "shirkers" on the home front who avoided the risks of life at the front and earned good wages, of the ever detestable industrial "profiteers" who were gaining materially from the war.[60]

Nowhere were these complaints more rampant than in Russia, where conscripts were neither well armed, well paid, nor particularly patriotic—certainly not in comparison with British or French soldiers, many of whom were volunteers. Russia's overheated war economy, run on loose credit, had fueled a wild inflation devastating the agricultural sector, with landlords unable to afford wages. This in turn had sparked a massive peasant migration into the booming war factories of Petrograd. And when food and fuel supplies to the northern capital plummeted in winter 1916–17, sending prices skyrocketing, thousands of workers took to the streets during a break in the cold weather in early March, looking for food. They were soon smashing up food shops and fighting the police, the Cossacks, and those few army units who dared oppose them. Within days, the bulk of the Petrograd army garrison had mutinied; workers' and soldiers' committees (Soviets) were sprouting up all over the capital; the heretofore impotent national parliament (Duma) established a Provisional Committee to work on forming a new government; and the tsar, at his country palace outside the city, abdicated his throne.

The momentous events of the February Revolution in Petrograd struck Europe like a thunderclap. Well-informed observers had long known that morale in the Russian army was fragile, and damaging strikes had frequently rocked the empire's urban production centers in 1915 and 1916, but no one expected the government to disintegrate so totally, in a matter of days, due to unrest in the capital. It was not clear at first what the tsar's fall meant for the military balance of power, but it was obvious that the fluid situation in Petrograd offered a ripe opportunity for political subversion. Since the earliest days of the war, the Central Powers had been financing various political schemes to sabotage the Russian war effort, from Vienna's "Union for the Liberation of the Ukraine" (which also subsidized Lenin after he endorsed the Ukrainian national cause) to Berlin's organization of strikes in Russian munitions factories in January 1916. The German Foreign Office had been granting covert subsidies to various Russian exile groups in Switzerland since 1915, and was even underwriting Trotsky's *Nashe Slovo*, published in Paris. When the Petrograd Soviets, in their "Appeal to the Peoples of the World" issued in late March 1917, made clear their intention to continue the war against the Central Powers, Berlin resolved to make use of its Russian allies-in-exile to undermine them.[61]

There is a considerable residue of legend surrounding the circumstances of Lenin's famous journey through Germany in a "sealed train car" in April 1917 on his way to Petrograd. Münzenberg himself dramatized the events in his memoir *Die Dritte Front*, recalling a high-level meeting he attended with Lenin, Radek, and Fritz Platten in a back room of the Zurich restaurant "Eintracht" on 19 March, where the impatient Russian paced furiously around the room before finally resolving to negotiate passage with the German ambassador in Bern. So desperate was Lenin to reach Petrograd and the Revolution that he would go, even if his route "went through hell itself" (that is, Germany). Münzenberg elsewhere wrote of the Bolsheviks' departure, "I no longer remember if it was Lenin or Radek who said to me in departing, 'Either we'll be swinging from the gallows in three months or we shall be in power.'" In *To the Finland Station*, Edmund Wilson highlights the drama of the Eintracht "meeting of the exiles," after which "it was arranged with the German ambassador in Switzerland that a party was to be sent through Germany." Famously, Lenin was harassed by a group of fellow Russian socialists at the Zurich Hauptbahnhof on 8 April, who were adamant that his acceptance of a German transport permit would compromise his political position in Russia. But he brushed them off without a word, so certain of the importance of his mission that no protests could budge him.[62]

Lenin certainly had contempt for the Germans who "permitted" his voyage, but to fashion a melodrama out of his efforts to make the trip at any cost is historically misleading. It was in fact the German Foreign Office, and not Lenin, which took the initiative and organized Lenin's journey. Specifically, it was the shadowy figure of Alexander Israel Helphand, known to socialists and intelligence services alike by his pen name "Parvus," who arranged Lenin's trip, just as he had overseen the distribution of German subsidies to Russian revolutionary groups since 1915. Parvus, a Jew educated in Odessa, was a truly enigmatic character, a passionate yet pragmatic, multilingual socialist who had played a major role in Petrograd during the Russian Revolution of 1905, and who was also a controversial propagandist in the prewar SPD. Parvus was larger than life, both in his appetite (Rosa Luxemburg referred to him, half-affectionately, as "the fat one") and his sexual passions (he bore children by three of his many wives and was reputed to hold orgies in his various mansions in Zurich, Berlin, and Copenhagen). His hatred of the tsarist regime, which had banished him to Siberia after the 1905 Revolution, was intense, and he decided soon after the war broke out in 1914 that a German victory was the best means to bring about a socialist revolution in Russia. When he offered his services to the Foreign Office in

January 1915, he bluntly declared that "the interests of the German government are identical with those of the Russian revolutionaries." Soon after the February Revolution of 1917, Parvus advised the Germans that the "extreme revolutionary movement will have to be supported, in order to intensify anarchy"—and this meant Lenin, who, he believed, "was much more raving mad" than all the other exiles. On 3 April 1917, the Foreign Office approved five million gold marks for Parvus's plans to "anarchize" Russia, and five days later, Lenin was sent on his way.[63]

Lenin knew Parvus was in charge of his journey, and that the Germans were offering much more than safe passage across the Reich. Although disliking each other personally, Lenin and Parvus had been in contact since 1915 through their mutual friend Jakob Fürstenberg (known to socialists as "Kuba"), who would later become the first director of the Soviet Central Bank. Kuba managed a firm owned by Parvus, which had special import and export licenses from the German Foreign Office. The two men oversaw a huge portion of the illicit trade being carried out during the war between Germany and Russia through the northern neutral capitals, mainly Copenhagen and Stockholm, and used their employees to contact strike committees and other revolutionary cells within the Russian empire. They also helped the German military distribute defeatist propaganda on the Russian side of the Eastern Front. After the Foreign Office provided its large subsidy, the scope of this propaganda expanded dramatically and it began to promote Lenin and the Bolshevik antiwar position explicitly. When Lenin's train, carrying forty other Russian exiles along with his key non-Russian lieutenants, Platten and Radek, reached Stockholm, Parvus was waiting with both money and instructions. Lenin, not wanting to compromise himself politically, refused to meet the man responsible for his journey, but Radek negotiated with Parvus on his behalf, and apparently secured German financing of the Bolshevik Party inside of Russia on the understanding that it would proselytize for a defeatist peace (which Lenin was planning to do anyway). Soon after Lenin's arrival in Petrograd the Bolsheviks, who had been struggling to put out *Pravda* on a regular basis, were able to finance three major daily newspapers aimed at members of the armed services alone, including *Soldatskaia Pravda* (for domestic garrisons), *Okopnaia Pravda* (for troops at the front), and *Golos Pravdy* (for sailors).[64]

Karl Radek, a sophisticated, somewhat cynical Austro-Hungarian polyglot of Jewish descent, was much better disposed toward the controversial Parvus than the other Bolsheviks, and the two established an important political nexus in Stockholm. Radek was granted nearly unlimited funds for setting up a "Bolshevik Foreign Mission" in the Swedish capital, which was to keep Lenin's colleagues and allies abroad in contact with the Bolsheviks once they were firmly reestablished in Russia. The Foreign Mission, at Lenin's insistence, was dominated by a triumvirate of anti-German Poles —Radek, Kuba, and a Bolshevik engineer who had worked for Siemens's Moscow branch during the war, V. V. Vorovski (known as Orlovsky). This was doubtless because the Bolshevik propaganda organs Radek established, notably *Korrespondenz Prawda*, were published in German, still the official language of international socialism, and Lenin wanted to avoid any appearance of being "pro-German" as he propagated his antiwar message. But Lenin's efforts to wash his hands of the Germans were problematic: the Stockholm Foreign Mission used the German diplomatic communications network to relay Bolshevik messages back and forth from Petrograd (and passed on what they learned to the German Foreign Office), and they almost certainly distributed German money to Lenin. Rumors to this effect were exploited by Kerensky on the occasion of a failed Bolshevik uprising in Petrograd against the Provisional Government on 16–17 July, when he had telegrams published that seemed to incriminate the Bolsheviks of treasonous collaboration with the Germans. The case, however, was soon dropped for political reasons, and Radek's Foreign Mission remained intact.[65]

Although Münzenberg accompanied his friends Lenin, Radek, and Platten at the Zurich train station, he was unable to join them on their historic trip, because, unlike them, he was still a German citizen. This was more than an accident of birth. Of the four Zimmerwald Left allies, only Münzenberg was actively engaged in sabotaging the war effort in his native Germany through his Youth Socialist underground network. Moreover, his military status in Germany was unclear. Although he was often referred to in hostile Swiss papers as a "refractory" or draft shirker, in truth Münzenberg had presented himself to the German consulate in Zurich in October 1916, submitted to a medical exam, and been placed on the deferred list as "employable." Had he accompanied Lenin on the trip across Germany, it is quite possible he would have been forcibly conscripted into military service or worse, arrested for his antimilitary propaganda.[66]

Still, Münzenberg was favorably impressed when Lenin, Platten, and Radek succeeded in crossing Germany without incident. And the youth secretary had a further interest in joining Radek in Stockholm. The Executive Bureau of Münzenberg's International Socialist Youth Secretariat, which had last met in Zurich in February 1916, was scheduled to convene in May 1917 in the Swedish capital. Most of the other members of the executive were from the northern neutrals, and it made sense to meet in Stockholm, where preparations were already under way between the various Scandinavian parties to host an ambitious socialist conference meant to take advantage of the Petrograd revolution and end the war through a display of international solidarity.

By late April 1917, when Münzenberg applied to the German ambassador in Bern for a transit visa, Stockholm was already a hothouse of international political intrigue. Parvus was holding meetings not only with Radek and the Bolsheviks, but also with the SPD leaders Philipp Scheidemann and Friedrich Ebert on the pretense that they were to coordinate German Socialist policy with the Petrograd Soviets to bring about a mutual peace without annexations (except in the Balkans). Parvus was playing a complicated double game, trying to secure good relations with the SPD leadership in case that party came to power through a German socialist revolution, with his whole scheme depending, however, upon the Bolsheviks' seizure of power in Petrograd, to be followed by their acquiescence in a German military victory. As part of this double game, Parvus convinced the Foreign Office to approve Münzenberg's safe passage to Stockholm on 25 April 1917, on the putative grounds that the Youth Socialist secretary would "work for peace."[67] Two days later, Berlin agreed that Münzenberg could accompany a second trainload of Russian exiles (mostly Mensheviks) on the way to Stockholm, on condition that a German army liaison officer escort him.[68] The German Foreign Office's insistence on a military escort may have been made in light of Münzenberg's ambiguous draft status, or possibly to prevent him from agitating for peace inside of Germany (to do so in Stockholm, presumably in the direction of Petrograd, was a different matter).

Münzenberg certainly took a significant risk when he crossed over the Swiss border into Germany on 28 April 1917, and it is unlikely that meeting his northern comrades in the secretariat was the only purpose of the trip. According to a 29 March 1917 letter later confiscated by the Swiss government, Münzenberg had in fact been invited to Stockholm in May 1917 under the auspices of a highly secret plan concocted by the British Foreign Office to coordinate strikes and antiwar propaganda on the fronts in Germany with envoys from the Russian Provisional Government—thus he may have himself scheduled the youth conference there as a cover. The other principals mentioned in this letter are Radek, who, as we know, soon thereafter arrived in Stockholm on Lenin's train; and the left-wing SPD lawyer Paul Levi, an orthodox German Marxist who had gained notoriety during the war by staging a series of successful hunger strikes to resist the draft, and who was to act as liaison for the German revolutionaries in London. The British, it seems, were offering unlimited funding for defeatist propaganda, and planned to use two hundred planes to drop some five million peace pamphlets across German lines in order to stimulate mutinies during the planned British-French offensives later that spring.[69]

In the event, the British scheme probably came to nothing. By the time Münzenberg was in Stockholm in early May, the Allied offensives had already collapsed and the Germans were attacking, their morale undamaged; and Radek was busy cranking out antiwar propaganda aimed at the Russian front. No record of Münzenberg's activities in Stockholm during the first three weeks of May 1917 exists, outside his own report on the executive meeting of 19–20 May. At the least, Münzenberg probably visited Radek at the Foreign Mission to establish lines of communication with the Bolsheviks that he could exploit for the Youth International. This may have been all he was hoping to accomplish, and in any case he was back in Switzerland by 24 May.[70]

We may never know why Münzenberg really went to Sweden in May 1917—he took pains to conceal the intent of the trip in his memoir *Die Dritte Front*, even moving the dates of the Youth Bureau meeting forward from May to August—or why, exactly, the German Foreign Office, at Parvus's urging, approved the ambiguous voyage.[71] The trip's results, however, were disastrous for Münzenberg's position in Switzerland. Already a favorite punching bag of the conservative Swiss press after the scandal of Red Sunday, Münzenberg was now further tarred, due to Berlin's arrangement of his voyage to Stockholm, as a possible German agent. Because of his known association with Lenin, who would soon be sending shock waves through the political world with a series of attempted coups d'état against the Russian Provisional Government, Münzenberg had a lot to answer for. His already tenuous relations with the Swiss government were now balanced precariously on the edge of a political explosion.

Solothurn

Although Münzenberg had ultimately gained little from his trip to Stockholm, he returned to Switzerland full of confidence in himself and his movement. The Swiss Young Socialists had stayed largely out of public view since Red Sunday, but Münzenberg had used the months of relative quiet to expand the ranks of his followers, exploiting various "cultural" and "educational" fronts for recruiting and fund-raising that were designed to frustrate police surveillance. The new cultural initiative was also more sophisticated, and effective, than Münzenberg's pretentious efforts to promote "proletarian literature" before the war. There were, for example, his widely publicized "culture nights" held in the Zurich Volkshaus, at which local singers, musicians, and poets of note would give recitals bearing absolutely no relation to socialism—although the gate revenues, at half a franc a person, went into Youth Socialist coffers. Münzenberg also bought literary classics that were not exclusively socialist and resold them to all comers out of his apartment headquarters, including the collected works of Schiller, Freiligrath, Heine, and Goethe, and even a German translation of Charles Dickens's *Oliver Twist*. He made sure, moreover, that Swiss socialists realized it was "a crime" to buy books "anywhere else than from the 'Freie Jugend' bookstore in Zurich at 40 Werdstrasse." Then there was the audacious campaign to lure children into the movement through a network of forty "Socialist Sunday Schools" founded and entirely funded by Münzenberg's secretariat.[72]

Some of these overtures to party outsiders were politically risky, but the gains seemed to outweigh the disadvantages. "Bourgeois" sympathizers who dropped by an event or two may not have made ideologically reliable activists, but they had more disposable income than young factory workers and could afford one-time donations as high as five francs, for which they were given a "passive membership" badge. Münzenberg also shrewdly exploited one of his pet issues, the fight against alcoholism, to lure in bourgeois sympathizers. His eye-catching pamphlets, fronted with moralistic slogans such as "Avoid alcohol! Avoid trash literature!" helped secure a substantial donation in 1916 from a large Swiss foundation that specialized in children's health problems. Münzenberg also used this angle in defending the Youth Secretariat after his arrest in September 1916, claiming that no less than half of his five thousand members were teetotalers. Zurich's police inspectors may not have been fooled by Münzenberg's efforts to portray himself as a friend of law and order, but hundreds of middle-class sympathizers were, and it must have been richly satisfying to raid their pockets for support.[73]

Ever mindful of the humiliating police crackdown on street demonstrations after Red Sunday, Münzenberg raised his political dissembling to an art form in 1917, creating a sort of firewall between his communication with loyal followers and his public persona. Münzenberg had long taken care to tailor speeches to different audiences, making sure his rural recruiters, for example, refrained from attacking organized religion. At a conference in Solothurn in April 1917, shortly before his trip to Stockholm, Münzenberg disappointed the more militant members of the secretariat by ruling out the possibility of a general strike, a strategy that after Russia's February Revolution had gained renewed currency as the best means of bringing down belligerent governments. He took this position, in part, because he knew full well the SPS bitterly opposed the general strike, and he was then negotiating an agreement that would have formally recognized the supremacy of the parent party in exchange for an allotment of youth votes at party congresses.[74]

Münzenberg was also aware, however, that the Swiss police were eavesdropping on the conference. On the last day of the Solothurn gathering, Sunday 8 April, at around 3 P.M., Münzenberg smirked at his adversaries by ordering everyone who could not produce evidence of active membership in the Youth Socialist organization to clear out of the conference room, as he was now going to discuss the "military question." This could not have pleased the police observer who had just sat through three days of interminable political speeches on orders from the Public Prosecutor's Office in Bern precisely in order to gather evidence of Münzenberg's propagation of "antimilitary propaganda."[75]

All of this dissembling, of course, would be fruitless if other Young Socialist leaders were to let fly with improperly radical statements in public, so one of Münzenberg's main priorities in 1917 was to discipline his lieutenants. His attack on the general strike at Solothurn was principally aimed at three members of the Swiss Youth Secretariat Executive Committee who, he knew, favored the idea. Two of these, Alfred Bucher and Ernst Marti, both wide-eyed idealists barely twenty years old, swiftly fell into line after Solothurn. The third radical, Jakob Herzog, an older, wizened man, proved a tougher nut to crack (figure 2). Frustrated in the secretariat, Herzog joined forces with a notorious anarchist, Toni Waibel (a "psychopath," in Münzenberg's estimation), and the two ran, successfully, for the Executive Committee of Zurich's Youth Socialist local, while Münzenberg was in Sweden. This was a deliberate provocation, staged in Münzenberg's old district of Aussersihl. It was also later ruled illegal. Herzog continued, however, to stir up opposition to Münzenberg, and won over Youth Socialist groups in Davos, Aarau, Rheinach, and Hard. Münzenberg's hold over these and several other districts was loosened, but at the national level he had no trouble putting down the rebellion, securing a unanimous vote to eject Herzog from the Youth Secretariat.[76]

Herzog's ultimate expulsion for "anarchism" was emblematic of a very old socialist tradition dating from Marx's feud with Bakunin, which had ultimately doomed the First International in the 1870s. Anarchists had been

FIGURE 2. Members of the new international Youth Secretariat, Zurich, 1915. Münzenberg is in the bottom left corner. Directly behind him is his faithful Italian assistant, Guilio Mimiola. Jakob Herzog, Münzenberg's future rival, is seated on the table, third from the right. Source: Münzenberg, *Die Dritte Front*.

expelled from the Second International as well, and no socialist party worth its salt could afford to tolerate loose cannons like Herzog whose insubordination had the potential to set off a vicious cycle of dissident rebellions. Of course, Bakunin had not gone quietly—he took more than half of the First International's followers with him—and Herzog wouldn't, either.

The source of Herzog's antipathy to Münzenberg was, ultimately, quite personal. Whereas Münzenberg, a German citizen, had fled the martial pressures of his native land to take advantage of the political freedoms of Switzerland, Herzog was a Swiss who had done the opposite, crossing the border in 1914 to work with the socialist underground in Berlin toward sabotaging the German war effort. He was arrested there and spent several months in prison before being expelled to Switzerland, where he joined Münzenberg's secretariat in Zurich. Münzenberg's all-expenses-paid trip to Stockholm in May 1917, under German military escort, did not impress him. In Germany hundreds of antiwar activists, many of them working on behalf of Münzenberg's Youth International, had been imprisoned since 1914—and here was their putative leader, consorting with the enemy! In his pamphlet polemic against Münzenberg, Herzog stopped just short of accusing his adversary of being a German agent, but did say may have been even harsher: Münzenberg was a "Judas" who had "betrayed" the socialist movement with his "cowardice."

This was a low blow and certainly unfair to Münzenberg, but it was meant as a challenge. The issue in Herzog's formulation was, "who is really the revolutionary?"—Herzog, always in the front lines, risking his skin for the cause; or Münzenberg, who had proceeded, according to Herzog, through a series of Machiavellian calculations in his long progression from "anarchist" into "anarchist-killer" during his rise to prominence in the Swiss movement, always ready to retreat or cut deals with the government or the parent party if it served his purposes. Herzog credited Münzenberg with omnipotent powers of persuasion that allowed him "brutally to crush underfoot every opinion that's not his own." Herzog conceded that his adversary commanded the loyalty of the Youth Secretariat—and all its cash resources—while he was forced to defend himself with only his own "meager resources." Clearly Münzenberg no longer did his own dirty work—both the grounds for Herzog's expulsion and the official denunciation of Herzog's heresy were written up by his underlings. Münzenberg's charm, his brazen self-confidence, and the aura of prestige he had gained through his association with leading figures of the Zimmerwald Left—all these factors seem to have made his position in the Youth Secretariat impregnable.

Although Herzog had besmirched his honor, Münzenberg was content to let his opponent stew in his own juices, refusing to dignify Herzog's attacks by responding to them personally.[77]

There was one other expulsion for reasons of executive discipline that occupied Münzenberg in summer 1917, one aimed not at the anarchist "Left" but at weak-kneed tendencies on the "Right" stemming from the recruitment of nonproletarian intellectuals into the movement. The victim was a man named Heinzmann, about whom little is known either before or after his brief stint as a member of the Youth Secretariat. He seems, however, to have made a very strong impression on Münzenberg, who took the time to write a long letter to him in early July 1917 justifying his expulsion with real, heartfelt reluctance. The cause of the break was somewhat arcane, relating to Heinzmann's persistent efforts to distribute a utopian novel by the American socialist Edward Bellamy to Young Socialists over the objections of the secretariat. Whatever the exact reasons for the expulsion, Münzenberg's letter is a remarkable document that offers us a precious glimpse of his evolving political philosophy after his encounters with Lenin, free of the pressing tactical concerns that often obscured his real views. It was also Münzenberg's first, and in all probability last, effort to come to personal terms with a comrade he had individually betrayed on behalf of the collective movement he saw as a higher cause.[78]

"I was once in the same situation as you," Münzenberg began, recalling his years in Erfurt, when his mind was alight with the poetry of Heine and Freiligrath and he dreamed of finding "a place, where before long . . . the well-being of mankind should bloom." But he soon found that even in the socialist movement, men were beset with the "same failings and frailties as in all other groups." This was at first depressing, but Münzenberg did not hang his head for long, as his nature was better suited to relentless work than to passivity. Long experience in the Swiss Youth Socialist movement eventually taught Münzenberg that "the task of a revolutionary cannot be to seek out a world that corresponds to his ethical taste, but rather [he must] help change the present, existing world in such a way as suits his views of right and justice." The dialectical dilemma was this: faced with an "unbridgeable swamp," with the imagined revolutionary future on the other side, one could either sit around, "writing poems about the promised land, heaving forth sigh after sigh" (this was presumably what Heinzmann was doing in promoting Bellamy's sentimental utopian novel), or one could "rouse oneself and adapt to the unalterable, persevering with bold resolution through the remaining obstacles to reach the sunny shore."

In the current conditions of human society, Münzenberg explained, "no better humans will be able to develop." Revolutionaries were forced to work with the "weak powers" at their disposal, which could only be strengthened by "organizing" people against their own passive inclinations. In this way, the "dialectical process" churned onward, preparing the way for the eventual revolution that would create a new, better social man.[79]

In his rush to reach the other shore, Herzog had forgotten the necessity of relentless organization. Heinzmann's problem was that he was so wrapped up in visions of the world to come that he never ventured into the revolutionary waters in the first place.

Helvetiaplatz

By disciplining his followers, Münzenberg was able to avoid useless confrontations with the Swiss authorities during the summer of 1917 and well on into the autumn. But even the most careful tactician, with the most sensitive grasp of the dialectical twists and turns of the political arena, cannot always stay ahead of onrushing events. Münzenberg's erstwhile mentor Lenin, for example, had almost destroyed himself in a series of three unsuccessful Bolshevik putsches in Petrograd in April, June, and July, and might have been ruined in summer 1917, if Kerensky's Provisional Government had decided to stage a show trial highlighting Lenin's treasonous contacts with the German enemy. But Kerensky feared alienating the Workers' Soviets, the Mensheviks, and other socialist intellectuals who all sympathized with Lenin (even if they disapproved of his violent tactics), and so no such trial was ever held. Only a handful of Bolsheviks were arrested, none of their followers' weapons were confiscated, and Lenin carried on his open conspiracy to seize power from the safety of Finland.

When the German army counterattacked after the disastrous "Kerensky offensive" of July, reaching Riga on the Baltic late in August, reports of another imminent Bolshevik putsch set off a panic in the Provisional Government. A fateful misunderstanding ensued between Kerensky and the headstrong general he had appointed commander of the Petrograd military district, Lavr Georgievich Kornilov, whom he suspected of preparing a military coup. Fatally, Kerensky sacked his commander, and the resulting confusion in the military command left Petrograd all but defenseless. When a renewed German offensive pitched loyal Russian forces into retreat within three hundred miles of the capital in mid-October, sparking controversial preparations for the evacuation of the Provisional Government from Petrograd, the Central All-Russian Soviet, controlled by Mensheviks and other moderate workers' parties, turned against Kerensky, and the disunited capital was ripe for the taking. On 6 November 1917 the Bolsheviks ordered their armed supporters, mainly sailors from Kronstadt, to seize Petrograd's rail stations, post offices, telephone and telegraph centers, banks, bridges, and military command posts (all guarded lightly or not at all by this time). The operation succeeded within hours. The Bolsheviks balked before storming the better-guarded Winter Palace, where ministers from the Provisional Government held out until their cadets abandoned them the following evening. The palace was finally taken with only five casualties, and the ministers (excluding Kerensky, who had escaped) were arrested at 2:10 A.M. on 8 November in the tsar's old dining room, as the clock reads to this day. Lenin, after throwing his forceful will into a vacuum of power and governmental incompetence, was in power.[80]

News of Lenin's historic coup reached Zurich on 9 November 1917. Reports describing the October Revolution (as it was dated using the Julian calendar) were at first somewhat sketchy, as many journalists found it difficult to disentangle just what had happened in Petrograd. The Swiss Socialist Party, like most of its Western counterparts, reacted coolly, not certain just what to make of the Bolsheviks' stage-managed "Revolution" achieved on behalf of, if not exactly with the help of, the Russian proletariat (who of course only represented a small fraction of the population in what was in any case in an overwhelmingly peasant country). To orthodox socialists, questions concerning the details of the event were crucial. Did the new government have the endorsement of the Soviets? Would elections to the Assembly still be held? Who exactly was represented on the new "Council of People's Commissars" which now replaced Kerensky's Cabinet? And did they have the workers' support? As fighting still raged for weeks in Moscow, where the Bolsheviks' support was even scantier than in Petrograd, these were all very open questions.

Swiss pacifists showed no such reticence, however. To many sympathizers on the left, the Bolshevik victory meant, regardless of its implications for European Socialism, that the war could at last be brought to a close. Lenin had after all been proselytizing for peace (albeit on his own self-serving terms) since 1914, and his victory in Petrograd unleashed a wave of euphoria among those committed to ending the war by any means. Two of the leading spokesmen of the pacifist cause from the Socialist opposition were Max Rotter, an Austrian draft deserter, and Max Dättwyler, an excitable Swiss peace activist with anarchist leanings who had once spent time in an insane asylum. Both of these men had been pushing for a general strike ever since the February Revolution in Petrograd, and they had taken clear stands in favor of draft resistance. Neither was nearly as famous as Münzenberg, and for this reason they seem to have escaped police harassment before the Bolshevik triumph in Petrograd spurred them to tip their hand in a mad rush to end the European war all by themselves, in Zurich.

The pacifists' plan was simple. There were about three thousand workers employed in weapons factories in downtown Zurich, and if they could be persuaded not to work in light of the Bolshevik victory, then a wave of imitation munitions strikes would overtake Europe, no more shells would reach the front, and the war would be over. This, at any rate, was the plan Dättwyler described to a gathering of several dozen pacifists in the Helvetiaplatz, in front of the Zurich Volkshaus, at 8 P.M. on Thursday evening, 15 November. Inspired by Dättwyler's passionate speech, the demonstrators marched to a nearby weapons plant owned by Scholer & Cie on Zentralstrasse and harassed the managers sufficiently that the night shift was interrupted and the workers sent home. The marchers tried to repeat the feat at another factory nearby, but were cut off by a police cordon hastily formed in the wake of the first incident. The demonstrators agreed to disperse if the night shift was called off, and the plant's owners, with police encouragement, agreed. Dättwyler and Rotter, on their way back to the Helvetiaplatz, beguiled friendly reporters from the Socialist paper *Volksrecht* with stories of their brave triumph over the forces of militarism. This interview was conducted under a street lantern on the steps of Münzenberg's apartment at Werdplatz, and the youth secretary, observing from his window, invited the two pacifists in to talk over their actions.[81]

Münzenberg was not greatly impressed by Dättwyler's dubious triumph. The two had clashed once before, at a meeting in the Restaurant "Eintracht" Münzenberg had called in mid-September 1917 to debate the pacifism question. Münzenberg gave Dättwyler a chance to make his case, but spoke out strongly himself against open draft resistance and the closing of munitions factories, both of which he viewed as premature, as the Swiss army was still strongly loyal to the government. The two men did not meet again until 15 November, when Münzenberg, although cordially welcoming Dättwyler, again refused to directly endorse the munitions strike plan. He may, of course, have seen Dättwyler as a potential rival. In any case, Dättwyler had already gotten *Volksrecht* to bite on the story, and it seemed likely that with a little publicity, the pacifists might develop a large following in Zurich. Unwilling entirely to concede the field of maneuver to Dättwyler, Münzenberg agreed to print up flyers for the pacifists advertising a follow-up meeting the next night, but let it be known he would not himself attend. Dättwyler's bragging, along with Münzenberg's placards, ensured that the Zurich police would be ready when the pacifists gathered again on the Helvetiaplatz the next evening.[82]

Münzenberg himself retained a careful distance from Dättwyler's second Helvetiaplatz demonstration, but many Youth Socialists did not. Herzog's followers were there in force, and Herzog himself joined Dättwyler on the podium. When a riot police battalion at last moved in to suppress the demonstration, dozens were injured in the resulting mêlée, although no shots were fired. Herzog himself was beaten, and both he and Dättwyler were arrested. It was the fortune, or misfortune, of the demonstrators that the district police headquarters were less than a half a block away on Ankerstrasse. The recently dispersed crowd was soon besieging the station, demanding the release of their comrades. The pacifists were not strong enough to break through the police cordon, but a number of hotheads succeeded in bombarding the police with stones, which sparked a new round of beatings and prompted the local units (all city officers) to call in reinforcements from the canton level, who were better armed. By about midnight, the skirmishing at the cordon line finally died down and the demonstrators went home.[83]

Münzenberg was nowhere near the violence of 16 November, but this did not prevent him, of course, from capitalizing on its implications. To join Dättwyler on Friday evening would have meant endorsing strikes aimed at sabotaging the Swiss army, a stance that would have immediately ruined Münzenberg's precarious standing with the Swiss government. Once Dättwyler's demonstrators had been ruthlessly suppressed, however, the political issue was now police brutality—and this was fair game. Besides, once word got around about the "casualties" of 16 November, the provocation was sure to be immense and Münzenberg would be a fool not to play it for all it was worth. He decided, therefore, to take part in the protest against "the police attacks" his own flyers announced the next day, and authorized protest speeches by several other members of the Youth Secretariat, including the radicals Bucher and Marti, who he had earlier disciplined for their stance on the general strike, along with his friend and political collaborator, Willi Trostel.

The Saturday demonstration began at around 8 P.M., once again on Helvetiaplatz, where Bucher, Marti, and Trostel, among others, addressed the crowd and demanded Dättwyler's release from jail. Münzenberg did not speak at Helvetiaplatz, but he did lead a delegation of marchers to the north, across the River Sihl and over Paradeplatz to Bahnhofstrasse, where they stopped in front of the offices of the *Neue Zürcher Zeitung*, the leading conservative daily in town, which had been vociferous in denouncing Dättwyler and the rioting of the previous two nights. Tipped off to the marchers' objective by observers at Helvetiaplatz, a cordon of city police, with bayonets fixed, blocked the marchers from storming the offices. This was good political theater, and Münzenberg took advantage of the situation to incite the crowd with a speech denouncing police brutality.

Not all the protesters, however, were there to hear it. Some had gone instead to the Aussersihl police headquarters, protesting the violence of the night before by hurling stones at station windows, shattering glass in all directions. The police stormed the crowd, and many tried to escape to the north, up Ankerstrasse in the direction of Bahnhofstrasse and the *Neue Zürcher Zeitung*, but the heavily armed cantonal police cut them off at Zweierplatz near the St. Jakobskirche. Several officers fired, and at least one protester was killed. In panic, demonstrators threw up a makeshift barricade made out of nearby construction materials and tried to hold the square. Fortunately, the battle for Zweierplatz ended relatively quickly and bloodlessly. Soldiers from the *Landsturm*, a special reserve unit of the Swiss militia army made up of older men, most in their fifties, who were traditionally used as mediators in domestic conflicts, were called in. True to form, they refrained from firing across the barricade, and gradually the resisters came out to capitulate. Regular infantry, who set up machine gun batteries and fired them over the Volkshaus to disperse the crowds, also secured Helvetiaplatz. At the police station on Ankerstrasse, though, angry demonstrators continued to throw stones at the police, who fired repeatedly and felled several more victims. In all, nearly thirty protesters were injured, two of them seriously, and three were dead, along with one police officer.[84]

The scale of the 17 November rioting was a shock to Swiss political sensibilities. This was Zurich, after all, the cosmopolitan center of German Swiss culture, a city so easygoing and tolerant it had become the exile capital of Europe. And the country, whatever demonstrators shouted about militarism, was not at war! Barricades in peaceful Zurich? The provocation started by Dättwyler seemed, to moderates and conservatives, to have no political rationale whatsoever. There was little, if any, resistance to the militia draft in Switzerland, and the workers in the munitions factories had not been complaining about anything at all. The SPS had not played any role in the demonstrations (although after the scattered violence of 16 November, the party had called a solidarity march for the nineteenth), and its leaders had little sympathy for Dättwyler's extreme pacifist views, or with the October

Revolution in Petrograd that provided the occasion for his initiative. The only explanation for the whole disaster, it seemed, was "Bolshevism," which somehow had already infected Switzerland in the wake of Lenin's triumph.

Although neither Münzenberg nor his Youth Socialists had instigated the November demonstrations, it was inevitable that the wrath of the conservative press, and the government, would fall upon them. They were, after all, known associates of Lenin and the Bolsheviks; they were notorious opponents of "militarism," whatever their putative position on the draft and the general strike; and the whole sequence of bloody events had unfolded in Aussersihl, in their backyard, literally in Münzenberg's neighborhood. Münzenberg may not have endorsed Dättwyler's views, but he had received the ringleader in his apartment and done nothing publicly to renounce or distance himself from the pacifists' munitions plant initiative (it was soon discovered that Münzenberg had even offered financial support to Dättwyler that night). Jakob Herzog may have been expelled from Münzenberg's secretariat, but he was still recognized by the police as a leading Youth Socialist, and he played a central role in inciting the crowd into a violent mood on Friday evening. Most importantly, Münzenberg himself was right in the thick of the protests that had led to the greatest casualties. On Sunday, his secretariat collaborators Trostel and Marti, who had both spoken the previous night at Helvetiaplatz, were arrested. Münzenberg was picked up on Monday, and his apartment was immediately raided for incriminating propaganda material on the military question. The national government in Bern, however, did not even wait for this evidence to arrive before decreeing Münzenberg's expulsion from Switzerland on 19 November 1917.

The national government's swift response to the troubles in Zurich reflected a visceral fear of violent insurrection that was not wholly without justification. The arrests of Dättwyler, Herzog, and several others had not prevented the bloody clashes on the evening of the same day; nor had the resulting incarceration of twenty-four stone-throwing rioters prevented the renewal of street violence during the following night's protests. Only the army's intervention had stopped the escalating violence between the police and demonstrators on 17 November, and the full military occupation of Zurich that followed, coupled with the arrests of Münzenberg and his men, at last restored peace, order, and quiet to the city. When two terrorist bombs, both powered by highly refined (and expensive) explosive material, were found in Zurich on the day following Münzenberg's arrest, rumors of foreign financing of the weekend riots gathered steam. In addition, the undeniably foreign support base of Münzenberg's International Youth Secretariat lent credence to Bern's suspicions that the German exile was working for distant paymasters (although the Swiss government soon admitted it had no proof of any such connections). At the very least, it was clear to the Swiss authorities that Münzenberg's youth sections had become a virulent breeding ground of "revolutionary and anti-military tendencies," and it was thus in the interest of national security to corral them as quickly as possible.[85]

It was not only the pressing interest of public safety, however, which lay behind Münzenberg's own arrest. Government lawyers in Bern had apparently been among the most avid readers of *Free Youth* and *Youth International*, and they now had little trouble pointing to instances in reprints of Münzenberg's public speeches of propaganda aimed at "revolutionizing" the army—including, significantly, the address in Stockholm in May 1917 in which he celebrated the February Revolution as a triumph over "social patriotism." Münzenberg's frequent contacts with the Bolsheviks in Zurich were duly noted. Münzenberg had even published his own refusal of military service, in a defiant open letter to the German military registration office, in *Volksrecht* on 28 September 1917. Whatever the exact nature of Münzenberg's participation in the Zurich riots, the grounds for prosecuting his "anti-military propaganda" endangering the effectiveness of the army were many. Legally, his expulsion seemed an open-and-shut case.[86]

Münzenberg's supporters did not see it that way, of course. The inevitable outcry over the youth secretary's arrest was, at first, slow in coming, but this was merely because Bucher, Marti, and Trostel, three of Münzenberg's most competent collaborators, were arrested along with him. The authors of the first Münzenberg-less executive circular signed anonymously, as if to emphasize their helplessness, as "the rest of the Central Committee." Within a week, however, Münzenberg's old friend Fritz Platten (who after being refused entry at the Russian border while on Lenin's train in April had returned to Switzerland) had taken over the Youth Secretariat. Platten quickly set about turning the November arrests into an international cause célèbre. Trostel, released from prison early in 1918, faithfully assembled six years worth of Münzenberg's scribblings into a flattering volume titled *What Did Münzenberg Want?* which made it seem as if the youth secretary had been occupied exclusively with cultural and educational policy during the explosive war years. The new Bolshevik government in Russia dispatched an official protest to Bern (although this undoubtedly did not help Münzenberg's legal case!) and before long the Zurich police barracks housing Münzenberg was flooded with hundreds of angry letters from Young Socialists all over Europe demanding his release.[87]

The point was further emphasized in large protest demonstrations held in the winter of 1917–18 in Zurich, Luzern, Basel, and Bern, along with smaller "sympathy marches" in Rome, Berlin, and Stockholm. Years of relentless networking had evidently paid serious dividends. Münzenberg had so impressed one radical socialist during his visit to Sweden that this fan translated into Swedish an autobiographical play called "Jungvolk" Münzenberg had written years earlier, offering the royalties from its sale for his hero's legal defense. The editors of the Münzenberg-less *Free Youth*, reinforced by Platten and Willi Trostel, recovered their rhetorical powers sufficiently to launch a blistering attack on the Swiss government. Münzenberg, they declaimed, had been the principal victim of a great "reactionary flood" which had "shed proletarian blood on the streets of Zurich on 17 November 1917." "Let us free him," the editors proclaimed to socialists of the world, "from the claws of the reactionary beast!"[88]

Rhetorically speaking, the case for Münzenberg's release was an easy sell, but legally it was much tougher going. Münzenberg would not have been able to make a case at all if he had been immediately deported, as the government had ordered. But the genuine pride most Swiss government officials took in their country's liberal asylum policies worked to Münzenberg's advantage, and Bern refused to deport the German draft dodger across the border to certain military detention. "I cannot return to Germany," Münzenberg himself declared in a statement not notable for its courage, and his prosecutors agreed.[89]

There was still the possibility of sending Münzenberg to France or Italy. But this was rejected by Münzenberg's lawyer, Albert Keller, on the grounds that the youth secretary was "known to the Entente powers as a trusted colleague of Lenin and Trotsky"—who were regarded by the Allies as paid German agents. Keller wanted to buy time by claiming the impossibility of deportation, but to do so he was forced to emphasize embarrassing political facts. Münzenberg was not only an avowed, and adamant, draft resister, he was also an ally of revolutionaries who had toppled the Provisional Government in Russia while reputedly in the pay of a foreign power. This was not much of a legal case for acquittal, and in recognition of its weakness, Keller reverted to a veiled threat: Münzenberg's deportation would give "inducement to undesirable new unrest."[90]

Aside from raising the specter of a renewal of street violence, Keller was grasping at straws, but it must be said that he did so with flair. His client, he confidently wrote Bern, "was not only in no way dangerous to the public, but rather is a young man animated by high ideals." Münzenberg's revolutionary socialist beliefs, Keller assured the Swiss government, were also shared by "many highly regarded thinkers and politicians." Surely it was unreasonable to deport Münzenberg simply for being a revolutionary![91]

Where Keller was sincerely obtuse, Münzenberg was bold but slippery. In a remarkably brazen letter to the Swiss government, penned from prison in Zurich on 27 December 1917, Münzenberg outlined the dialectical underpinnings of his stance on military service. "Antimilitarism," he wrote, represented in his view "all movements, ideas, and . . . general spiritual life which align themselves against . . . the solution of national and social problems [on the battlefield]." This was an internationalist worldview that had nothing to do, Münzenberg explained, with the "vulgar conception [of pacifism] reflected in the expression of individual resistance to the draft." True, this was a revolutionary philosophy that ultimately envisioned "great upheavals" necessary to usher in "the final goals of [Socialism]"; but Switzerland's particular liberal traditions meant that it would be "one of the last countries to experience this revolution."[92]

Münzenberg had thus opposed Dättwyler's demonstrations, he claimed, because they promoted "violent revolution in Switzerland today," whereas Münzenberg knew that the achievement of socialism in the peaceful republic would require years of relentless education and propaganda. In this connection, he outlined the four principal goals of his wartime work as Swiss youth secretary: proletarian pedagogy; exposing workers to art and literature; battling the evils of drinking and smoking, which distracted workers from their political work; and mobilizing apprentices into Youth Socialism. Such lawful priorities, Münzenberg informed the Swiss government, he had fought to uphold against impatient hotheads such as Herzog, who, if Münzenberg were deported, would radicalize Youth Socialists behind a program of incessant street violence.[93]

All this was more or less true, so far as it went—but of course Münzenberg's differences with Dättwyler and Herzog were merely tactical, and it is astounding that he admitted this in a legal "defense" that openly confessed his strategic aim of ultimately overthrowing the Swiss government in a socialist revolution.

Bravado had served Münzenberg well before in escaping legal entrapment, but this time he had met his match. The Public Prosecutor's Office in Bern promptly issued a stinging twenty-five-page rebuttal that set out to prove that the "legality" defense of Münzenberg's antimilitary activities was merely "shadow-boxing *(Spiegelfechterei)*." Münzenberg's wartime editorials were flush with radical exhortations to "go on the offensive," "sharpen the class war," to conduct "systematic revolutionary propaganda in the army." The youth secretary may not have endorsed every disruptive strike or protest, depending on tactical considerations, but Münzenberg nevertheless had written in 1916 that "the only political school of the proletariat is through battle." Only "active participation in demonstrations, in [strike] actions, in revolutionary struggles," Münzenberg evidently believed, "builds [true] proletarian activists."[94]

The best gauge of Münzenberg's views on the supposedly "vulgar" issue of individual resistance to the draft, meanwhile, was his own public explanation of his own refusal to serve in the German army. "I would like especially to emphasize," he had written in his open letter to the German military registration board, "that I am not refusing to serve on ethical or strict pacifist grounds." In fact, if Münzenberg had harbored a realistic hope of "making propaganda in the army," he would gladly have served, but it was clear that the German military was loyal to its bourgeois masters and "a revolutionary socialist can only be in a state of pitiless struggle against the current German ruling classes." Münzenberg's proud abdication of military service, the poor militia record of his Youth Socialists (several of whom had claimed under questioning to be shirking on his orders), his association with the Bolsheviks, both his and his staff's participation in the violent 17 November demonstrations—all the evidence pointed to the necessity of deporting "a dangerous revolutionary agitator, who is systematically preparing the [Swiss] Young Socialists for active participation in a social revolution and for igniting a civil war among us."[95]

Dangerous or not, Münzenberg was still in Switzerland, and he would remain there until a friendly country was found that would receive him. While the Zurich cantonal police were waiting for Bern to deport Münzenberg, the Youth Socialists harassed them with letters demanding his release, visited him in prison, and staged protest demonstrations. A key protest theme was Münzenberg's traditionally poor health, which did not augur well for a long jail term. In his first two months in the Zurich police barracks, Münzenberg weakened significantly and this was apparent to his jailers. Potentially, Münzenberg's failing health could fan the flames of socialist protest even more widely, as Keller hinted none too subtly in a letter to Bundesrat president Müller in late January, and it was perhaps for this reason that Münzenberg was released on bail of five thousand francs, paid by a rich friend from nearby Pfäffikon named Gustav Nüssli. Münzenberg himself had smoothed the political waters for his release by shrewdly informing his lawyer, in a letter clearly intended for the eyes of his captors, that he saw "it as self-evident that in the time until the execution of my sentence of expulsion I will refrain from any political activity."[96]

This promise was, as we might expect, somewhat disingenuous. Münzenberg's imprisonment had not merely affected his health; it had deprived him of the stimulation of constant political activity, which had seeped into his blood and become second nature. Münzenberg recalled of his first days in the municipal barracks in Zurich being "numbed by the void" of inactivity. Above all, he missed the ritual of the postman's arrival at his apartment headquarters on Werdplatz, which had for so long given him a reason to get out of bed in the morning. Münzenberg did receive letters in prison, from as far away as Stockholm and Moscow, but it simply wasn't the same. Small wonder, then, that as soon as he was let go in late January Münzenberg set furiously to work catching up on old correspondence, putting together new propaganda pamphlets and posters, and sketching out a brochure called *The Struggle and Triumph of the Bolsheviks* based the second-hand impressions he had of the October Revolution in Petrograd. For several weeks, Münzenberg refrained from public speaking, thus theoretically adhering to the bail conditions he had agreed to (even if he was certainly carrying on "political activity" in private). And he kept the authorities informed of his changes of address within Zurich. But cease-fires are made to be broken, and the nationwide army surveillance of Münzenberg's movements was bound to turn up something sooner or later. His struggle with the Swiss authorities was only beginning.[97]

Witzwil

In the event, it was a relatively minor breach, a speech given to a small Youth Socialist gathering in Birsfelden near Basel, which put Münzenberg in the doghouse again. Although this was a clear violation of the terms of his parole, and Münzenberg was brought back to Zurich for further questioning, he was not thrown back into the police barracks where he had suffered the past winter. His bail situation was, in fact, somewhat paradoxical —there was not much risk of flight, as Münzenberg himself was the one who refused to go to Germany, while the French and Italian governments had made it clear they would not receive him. The problem was not that Münzenberg was trying to leave Switzerland, but rather the exact opposite: the Swiss government desperately wanted him to leave, but there was nowhere to send him. Thus he was allowed to remain at large in Zurich, although under close surveillance.[98]

Bern was truly in a pickle. The mainstream press was outraged that Münzenberg was still in Switzerland, and a number of leading industrialists were beginning to petition the government for an immediate deportation. Swiss Opposition Socialists, meanwhile, had gone into paroxysms over Münzenberg's arrest and didn't want him deported at all. Further imprisonment might imperil Münzenberg's health, enraging Youth Socialists; an expulsion to Germany, where harsh punishment would await the draft deserter, would almost certainly be met with rioting by even moderate socialists; and to do nothing was an outrage to almost everyone else. Trying to capitalize on the government's predicament, in late April, Münzenberg's longtime ally Fritz Platten proposed a resolution in the Swiss parliament overturning the deportation decree. This was a rash move. Platten's proposal was defeated soundly, receiving support only from the small Socialist parliamentary minority, and a counterresolution was overwhelmingly passed the next day demanding that Münzenberg be deported without delay.[99]

But this was hoping for too much. While the issue of Münzenberg's deportation seemed simple in the statehouse in Bern, it was not so easy in Zurich, where he still enjoyed widespread popular support and where the memory of the November riots was raw. On the advice of the State Prosecutor, the Justice Department of the Canton of Zurich wired Bern in mid-May that an involuntary deportation to Germany, the only country that wanted to take Münzenberg, would be disastrous for public order. This view was seconded by the Public Prosecutor's Office in Bern, which advised against such a step in a report to the government on 25 May 1918, although not without a significant note of rancor. While unwilling to violate "our traditions" by extraditing the draft resister to face military incarceration in Germany, the Public Prosecutor's office declared that "Münzenberg is politically dead and will take part in no more public agitation." The Bundesrat agreed in its executive session on 31 May, and Münzenberg was imprisoned once again, this time far enough away from Zurich so as to satisfy widespread concerns about the continued threat he posed to public security.[100]

The Swiss authorities were now getting serious with Münzenberg. They exiled him to Witzwil, a rural penitentiary in the Bernese Oberland where his companions would no longer be fellow political prisoners from cosmopolitan Zurich, but real criminals. Even so, there was an element of the ridiculous to the whole affair—Münzenberg was seen off at Zurich's Hauptbahnhof by political well-wishers who besieged him with flowers, and his police escorts lugged a whole trunk of books onto the train at his request. In an incongruously polite letter to the Swiss government, penned just before he was packed off to prison on 6 June, Münzenberg thanked his adversaries for their consideration, offered to pay the costs of his internment (the request was politely denied), and assured them he would use the time in isolation from Zurich to study French.[101]

Münzenberg may very well have intended to learn some French while serving time at Witzwil, but he was certainly not going to acquiesce quietly, as he hinted, in his removal from active political life. Just two days after his arrival, Münzenberg wrote to his lawyer with "burning impatience," demanding Keller look into the possibility of deportation to a neutral country such as Holland. Münzenberg himself had already launched queries at the American consulate in Zurich. (U.S. military intelligence, unfortunately for Münzenberg, had been following the case closely, and wired Bern in June that the German agitator must "not come to the United States under any circumstances.") Münzenberg also gave Keller more material to work with by complaining about the size of his cell and of persistent migraines. He went to work on the Witzwil prison director, too, securing for himself a larger bed, an extra milk ration, special work clothes, a pleasant job doing light garden work, and full freedom of movement inside the penitentiary, as well as liberal visiting hours for his political friends and unhindered correspondence with the outside world. Although he was evidently receiving the royal treatment, Münzenberg filed a complaint with the Bundesrat, claiming that he was being treated, in violation of international legal standards, in the same manner as common criminals (a claim the prison director promptly refuted with overwhelming evidence to the contrary—Münzenberg in fact gained over ten pounds in his first month at Witzwil).[102]

Münzenberg's real objection to his situation at Witzwil was to his frustrating political isolation at a time of great upheaval. "I am literally becoming a vegetable," Münzenberg wrote to Platten on 4 August. The "useless, almost laughable [nature] of my current existence," he explained, "is bringing me to the brink of despair." In late July, the other members of the International Youth Secretariat had met without him in Copenhagen to discuss the war situation, with Balabanoff in charge. The thought of such important matters proceeding in his absence was "burning every hour in [his] soul."[103]

Münzenberg was following military developments in the newspapers, with a close eye on how they affected his possibilities for getting out of Switzerland. The Entente Powers, reinforced by the arrival of thousands of American doughboys in the spring, were poised for a major breakthrough on the Western Front. In the East, the Bolsheviks had gladly surrendered to Germany at Brest-Litovsk in early March 1918 to escape the "imperialist war" and concentrate on crushing domestic opposition, but they quickly regretted this decision when the Germans moved swiftly to occupy White Russia, the Ukraine, and the Crimea. Concerned about the possibility of renewed German aggression, Trotsky, now war commissar, invited French and British troops to land at the northern Russian port of Murmansk. But this military collaboration of convenience between the Communists and the Western Powers rapidly descended into outright hostility due to a bizarre saga on the Trans-Siberian Railway involving liberated Czech and Hungarian prisoners-of-war who had taken opposite sides in the rush to reinforce the Western Front.[104]

With the Entente now in a virtual state of war with his Bolshevik friends, Münzenberg all but gave up on the West and turned his attention to Russia. If Platten could arrange for German draft deserters currently exiled in Switzerland to be sent East, with German permission, to "place themselves at the disposal of the Bolshevik regime," Münzenberg thought it would be a great "moral coup" for Socialism, which would not incidentally allow him again to "make [his] life useful for the movement." If this did not work, he informed Platten, he was going to look into the possibility of escaping from prison, sneaking across the border into France, and then illegally crossing into Germany.[105]

Judging from this last confidence, Münzenberg may not have been too far off the mark in complaining that his mind was turning to mush from lack of activity. Certainly his normally acute political sense was dulled, perhaps due to the cozy treatment he was receiving at Witzwil—otherwise he would not have spoken so openly of his desire to serve the Bolshevik regime or mentioned his dreams of escape. His letter to Platten was intercepted by the Swiss authorities, who decided to move Münzenberg to another prison where his activities could be more closely watched. On 28 August, he was transferred to Meilen, a cantonal facility on Lake Zurich, under strict terms: all further correspondence with Münzenberg and visits to his prison suite would have to be approved by the State Prosecutor. Bern had clearly had enough of Münzenberg's political intrigues.[106]

Meilen

Münzenberg was treated just as well at Meilen as he had been in Witzwil. He was even placed in the prison's so-called "best room," a suite with a view of Lake Zurich used for prominent political prisoners (such as his friend Platten, a frequent guest). Of course, physical comfort did not do much to soothe his political restlessness. Münzenberg was permitted a limited number of political visitors, and his girlfriend Adele Kluser, to whom he was now engaged, made a number of preconjugal visits (in fact Münzenberg later bragged that he was allowed to bring Adele into the director's suite, and that he used the same chambers when his illicit lover, Fanny Awensparger, came into town).[107] Judging from the sparse police files from the Meilen period, Münzenberg gave up for a while on political correspondence. Bottled up at last after years of relentless organizing and propagandizing, he turned inward and began writing an autobiography.[108]

Münzenberg's "Lebenslauf" or uncompleted autobiography, preserved in the Swiss police archives, provides much of the piecemeal information we have about his early years, but is far more revealing in what it tells us about his political development at the close of the First World War. It is a bracingly ideological document, in which Münzenberg refracts an entire universe of childhood experience through the distorting lens of socialism. He does so, however, with care, showing an intellectual sophistication entirely lacking in his earlier forays into didactic theater and pedagogy. Münzenberg catalogues his father's sins of alcoholism and domestic violence, for example, less to explain his own political promotion of teetotaling and clean living (although the connection is made obvious) than to heap moral outrage on the "bourgeois" institution of the family. "How was it possible," he asks after reciting a litany of his father's abuses of both wife and children, "that such a man could torment a family for forty years ... without neighbors or the authorities intervening?"[109]

This was not meant as a rhetorical question. The evil was allowed to continue, in Münzenberg's interpretation, by the complicity of his mother in her own oppression. Although he had scarcely known her—she died just before his fourth birthday—Münzenberg now judged his mother harshly. The daughter of a poor but proud Thuringian farmer, Mina Münzenberg was, in her son's reconstruction, "like all German workers and peasants, boundlessly satisfied and servile." She had fallen for Karl Münzenberg's impressive uniform and remained stupefyingly loyal to him, even after he began to drink away the money she herself earned. She was, in short, Mother Courage, a tool of the system who foolishly propped up the very bourgeois institution—socially respectable marriage—responsible for her suffering. "O Mother," Münzenberg now cried in strained compassion to a woman he barely knew, "oh lachrymose and deeply afflicted martyr of your sex! In your suffering, o Mother, in your pain you are unequaled in greatness, now and for always." Doubtless Münzenberg felt real regret that he had not gotten to know his mother better. But she was now, for him, primarily a symbol, who should warn others by her example of the uselessness of collaborating with one's oppressors.[110]

Although veering periodically into such melodrama, Münzenberg's first stab at autobiography is on the whole an effective and moving piece of work, making its ideological points by subtle demonstration rather than by openly arguing them. We sympathize with the nervous young man left to his own devices by parental neglect, we root for him in his intermittent struggles with his father, we are pleased when he finally overcomes his loneliness in the camaraderie of factory life. It is at first somewhat jarring when, toward the end of the tale, we are treated to a brief tirade against Revisionism and the "bourgeois elements" who had invaded the prewar SPD, but even this polemic wins us over: how could a young idealist possibly be on the side of crotchety old men who dismissed dreams of "proletarian revolution" as "mere romantic fantasies"? Swept up in the excitement of socialist politics after years of aimless lethargy, Münzenberg was understandably seized with "propaganda fever," and so might we have been, too.[111]

Münzenberg's autobiography could have itself been a real propaganda success, but due to onrushing historical circumstances he was never able to complete it. With the Entente armies, buttressed by American troops, advancing on all fronts, the German government began putting out feelers for an armistice in early autumn, and morale in the kaiser's army finally began to collapse. On 29 October, sailors in Germany's High Seas Fleet refused orders to steam out and attack the vastly superior British fleet, a suicide mission conceived by the Admiralty as a way to redeem the navy's honor and avoid an ignominious surrender. Soldiers' councils, spontaneously formed in a manner reminiscent of the February Revolution in Petrograd, were soon in charge of the main port city of Kiel, and their emissaries rapidly spread the mutiny to army garrisons throughout northern Germany. When rebellion in the north was followed by secession in the south, where the radical socialist Kurt Eisner proclaimed an independent Bavarian Republic on 7 November, the tottering imperial government in Berlin under Chancellor Max von Baden saw itself threatened with an imminent dissolution of Bismarck's Reich. On the ninth, Baden resigned and announced the kaiser's abdication, a new government was formed under moderate Majority Socialist leader Friedrich Ebert, and the German Republic was proclaimed. With the war over, and a general amnesty proclaimed throughout the land, it was now possible for Münzenberg to be expelled to Germany without being sent to military prison. On 9 November 1918, the day of the kaiser's fall, Münzenberg wired the Swiss government that he was ready to be deported to Germany, and Bern agreed (although denying Münzenberg's request for five days of free movement in Zurich to arrange his affairs).[112]

On 12 November 1918, Münzenberg was expelled from Switzerland, accompanied by his fiancée Adele Kluser. Characteristically, he was unable to reach the border without providing yet more evidence of his inexhaustible capacity for political intrigue. Fritz Platten joined the Münzenberg party in Pfäffikon, on the outskirts of Zurich, and tried to convince the police to let him, an upstanding member of parliament, drive the German himself to the border (the two planned to give a joint speech in Schaffhausen, where Platten's car was waiting). The ruse was short-lived. Platten was taken into custody in Schaffhausen and sent back to Zurich, unable to watch his friend cross the border at Stein-am-Rhein, near Singen. Willi Münzenberg was now Germany's problem.[113]

An Exile No More

In all, Münzenberg had spent more than eight years in Switzerland, during which time he acquired invaluable political experience at both the local and international level. He had entered Zurich an anonymous, penniless orphan, and now left it behind as possibly the most notorious political agitator in recent Swiss history, at a time when the neutral Alpine republic did not lack for charismatic revolutionaries. Münzenberg had mastered sophisticated techniques of indirect revolutionary propaganda and fund-raising; learned how to exploit "bourgeois" fellow travelers for both money and political cover; become adept at political dissembling, which preserved his freedom of action for future "revolutionary" offensives; and ruthlessly established dominance over his staff by purging undisciplined troublemakers. He was the trusted associate of many of the leading figures in international Socialism, including Lenin, Zinoviev, and Radek—who in war-torn Russia had achieved the unprecedented feat of actually attaining political power. And all this by the age of twenty-nine, when Münzenberg's exact contemporary Hitler, though now (unlike Münzenberg) a seasoned war veteran, was still a year away from joining his first political party.

On a more personal level, Münzenberg had used his charisma to lure legions of young men and women into the socialist movement. Among them was his politically adept mistress, Fanny, who proved an effective Young Socialist organizer in her hometown of Winterthur (which was close enough to Zurich to allow for frequent romantic liaisons). Then there was Münzenberg's

FIGURE 3. Münzenberg's Youth International comrades on the eve of his arrest in fall 1917, Zurich. Münzenberg is sixth from the left, flanked by his longtime loyalist Willi Trostel (fifth from the left, with mustache), with Ernst Marti and Fritz Platten immediately to the right of Münzenberg. Emil Arnold is on the far right. Source: Münzenberg, *Die Dritte Front*.

ever loyal girlfriend Adele Kluser, who endured his dalliances and often reckless political behavior, seemingly without complaint.

But it was not merely lovers that became enamored of Willi. Stalwart members of the Swiss Youth Secretariat such as Bucher, Martin, and Trostel came to feel an intense attachment to Münzenberg, which was manifest in the loyalty they demonstrated during the expulsions of 1917. A group of five lower-ranking activists all made special note of Münzenberg's personal magnetism when interviewed sixty years later.[114]

In a photograph taken late in 1917, Münzenberg exudes a jaunty confidence as he is flanked by his trusted lieutenants (figure 3). The years in Zurich have clearly been good to him. His stylishly coiffed hair flatters his always-handsome face, punctuated by a slight mischievous glow in his eyes that contrasts sharply with the earnest visages of his followers. Münzenberg's overwhelming confidence in himself could not be more obvious; it is as if he is privy to a powerful secret that he is not about to share with his colleagues.

By inhaling the intoxicating political freedoms of neutral Switzerland during the war, Münzenberg had shifted his already precocious socialist career into overdrive, but this momentum would not be easy to sustain. Unlike Radek, Münzenberg had not gone to work for Lenin in the new Soviet government, so he had no position of power to fall back on once he had left Switzerland. More importantly, Münzenberg himself had no real political base in Germany. Eight years of self-imposed exile had alienated Erfurt's radical son from his native land, allowing him to ascend the ranks of international politics without risk of arrest in Germany. Münzenberg's political talent was undeniable, but so, too, was his estrangement from German socialism, and both his strengths and this apparent weakness would be put to the test in the revolutionary maelstrom of postwar Germany.

CHAPTER 3 *Stuttgart*

Münzenberg's first experiences in postwar Germany were not auspicious. The border crossing at Singen was not well lit, and soon after Münzenberg crossed it on the evening of 12 November, he lost his footing and fell into a muddy ditch. The hands that helped him to his feet belonged to a German soldier, who promptly turned him over to the military police for questioning. The next morning, Münzenberg was marched to departmental headquarters in Singen's Hauptbahnhof, and was dismayed by the peace and quiet in the town. "I was shocked," he later recalled, "to see nothing of the Revolution; I had imagined that all the houses would be flying the Red Flag and that happy crowds would fill the streets." Although an amnesty for deserters and shirkers had been proclaimed in the state of Württemberg, the army in Singen was still following the procedural letter of military administration, and Münzenberg's registration status had to be cleared up before he would be let go. To his great good fortune, he was recognized by one of the officers at headquarters, who had served as a military attaché in Bern; the man took a great interest in politics, had avidly followed Münzenberg's case in the papers, and was excited to meet him. After Münzenberg disingenuously promised this friendly officer to "put in a good word for him in the SPD" (a party Münzenberg had been estranged from for ten years!), the young agitator was released and hopped on the first northbound train.[1]

The reception in Stuttgart was altogether more pleasant. Münzenberg had used a few spare moments in the Singen train station to dispatch telegrams to colleagues from the Spartacist movement, and at the Stuttgart Hauptbahnhof, his friends Edwin Hörnle and Max Barthel were waiting for him on the platform. Barthel, while retaining intermittent contact with his prewar co-conspirator in the publication of hack proletarian literature, had, unlike Münzenberg, spent the war in Germany, and even served a tour of duty on the Western Front. After finishing his service in October 1918, Barthel joined the editorial board of the Stuttgart *Rote Fahne* (Red Flag), the paper of the left-wing Spartacist viewpoint in the Independent Social Democratic Party (USPD), the faction of the prewar SPD that had broken off to oppose the war in 1917. After Barthel took him in, Münzenberg promptly published a recruiting appeal to the "young workers of Württemberg" in *Rote Fahne*. He devoted most of his editorial energy, however, to reviving the old *Youth International*, which at last reappeared on 30 November. The local USPD leadership certainly did not mind that Münzenberg was sticking to youth affairs, and two days after his arrival in Stuttgart he was given an office in the state parliament house for his International Youth Secretariat.[2]

Although Münzenberg was certainly excited to be back on the German political scene, it is hard to escape the conclusion that his heart was still in Switzerland. Frustrated by the lack of political excitement in Stuttgart, Münzenberg memorably remarked to Barthel that "revolutions are the locomotives of world history, but in Swabia they still travel by puff-puff."[3] Just three days after his arrival in Stuttgart, Münzenberg sent his Swiss fiancée Adele Kluser, who had dutifully accompanied him across the border into Germany, back to Switzerland on a reconnaissance mission. She was to retrieve his belongings in Zurich, settle a few debts, and arrange publication of a book her beloved Willi had earlier assembled on the wartime activities of the Youth International.

In the meantime, Münzenberg reestablished contact with his collaborators in the Swiss movement. He wired Platten on 14 November, asking for copies of Bolshevik propaganda from Russia and anything else that might be of use for the International Youth Secretariat. Further telegrams were dispatched the next day to Trostel in Zurich and to Isaak Schweide, an Italian citizen of Argentinian origin who represented Italian-speaking Switzerland in the Swiss Youth Secretariat, in Ascona, inviting both to a Youth Secretariat meeting optimistically scheduled for 7 December 1919 in Stuttgart. Münzenberg's early December executive meeting was not to be, in part because of the unmistakable imprint of his own hand in organizing it: his telegrams were intercepted by Swiss army intelligence, on the lookout for any material on which his name appeared, and Schweide and Trostel were both immediately arrested. Trostel's apartment was also searched, but nothing indicating further illegal traffic with Münzenberg was found, and Trostel was released. Schweide was not so lucky: a political exile in wartime Switzerland, he had assured the Swiss authorities earlier in 1918, after numerous run-ins, that he was retiring from politics for "health reasons." Münzenberg's ill-fated telegram exposed Schweide's lie, and the Argentine-Italian agitator was summarily deported.[4]

Münzenberg may not have known initially that his various instructions were being intercepted in Bern, but the lack of immediate response made it obvious by early December that they were not reaching their destinations. He therefore dispatched Barthel to Zurich to check up on political matters south of the border. The fact that he ordered Barthel to do this is significant in itself: Münzenberg's old friend now occupied an important place on the left wing of German socialism as the Stuttgart editor of *Rote Fahne*, and was in this sense Münzenberg's political superior in Germany. That Barthel consented to leave his editorial office in Stuttgart right in the midst of the German Revolution on a highly risky mission to Zurich—from which he himself could expect little possible benefit—was powerful testament to the force of Münzenberg's personality.

Unfortunately, Barthel made the same mistake as Münzenberg in wiring to Zurich by open telegram soon after he had crossed the Swiss border near Romanshorn. When Ernst Marti met Barthel on the platform at Zurich's Hauptbahnhof, the police were waiting and both were summarily thrown in jail. Barthel, although not yet as experienced in the kind of political dissembling Münzenberg had developed into an art form during the war, held up well under questioning. He even produced a few impressive whoppers, such as that he had merely been dispatched by Münzenberg to Zurich to clear up "technical matters" regarding an upcoming Youth Secretariat conference (such as passing out invitations in person). Marti, meanwhile, played dumb in truly inspired fashion. When asked why Münzenberg had sent Barthel to Zurich, Marti replied that he was uncertain, "because Barthel was arrested as soon as I met him and I didn't get to speak with him."[5]

Marti and Barthel were being questioned plainly on the pretext their activities were intertwined with the recent expellee Münzenberg, and the youth secretary's notorious name now enveloped the entire Swiss movement in a cloud of suspicion. In recognition of this growing danger, Münzenberg's old roommate Edi Meyer saw fit to send a letter to Bern of his own volition, acquitting himself of crimes of which he had not yet been accused. Not all were as shrewd in maneuvers of self-defense as Marti and Meyer, however. A Polish philosophy student, Leonie Kascher, implicated no one but herself in a gushy personal letter sent to Münzenberg late in November, in which she foolishly asked him to forward propaganda materials from Germany, including copies of *Rote Fahne*. Before long Emil Arnold, Münzenberg's successor as Swiss Youth Secretary, was imprisoned as well, apparently because Marti mentioned his name under questioning.[6]

All of these arrests reflected Bern's visceral fear of communist infiltration (they were classified in police records as "relating to Bolshevik operations"), a fear already more acute in Switzerland than nearly anywhere else because of a wave of bank transfers following Lenin's seizure of power: Zurich's famous banks were now flush with the looted wealth of Imperial Russia. Münzenberg, to Bern, was Bolshevik enemy number one, and political association with him was now the kiss of death.[7]

This unpleasant truth was experienced by no one so painfully as by Münzenberg's patient fiancée, Adele Kluser. To be sure, Kluser had her own reasons for returning to Zurich, where her parents lived, and where she retained her own apartment and a job as forwarding agent for the printer Conzett & Cie. But Münzenberg had specifically ordered Kluser, among other politically hazardous errands, to expedite publication of his little book about the Youth International. Münzenberg's selfish attempt to publish this vanity volume was at the heart of the whole disastrous saga of arrests. The union press in Bern he had enlisted, apparently unimpressed with the market prospects of a book glorifying a defunct organization, informed Kluser that they would not print unless twelve hundred francs were forthcoming—money neither she nor Münzenberg had. When Kluser mentioned Münzenberg's cash shortfall under police questioning on 7 December, it was obvious that she was in over her head. Asked to justify her acquaintance with various Socialist figures known to be associates of the Bolsheviks, poor Kluser simply exclaimed, "I got to know all of these people through Münzenberg!" Because Münzenberg involved her in his machinations, this modest Catholic girl, from a very proper Swiss family, would now be spending her Christmas holiday in the Zurich police barracks.[8]

Despite having reentered Germany at a time of unprecedented political opportunity, then, Münzenberg was still reliving the former glories of the wartime Youth International. And yet his plans were rapidly coming unraveled. To avoid embarrassment, he postponed the Youth Secretariat meeting planned for 7 December in Stuttgart by ten days. He also moved the setting to Berlin, where most youth delegates would be convening anyway for the first national Congress of Soldiers' and Workers' Councils on the banks of the River Spree, near the stock exchange. Unaware his messages were being intercepted, Münzenberg persistently wired to Zurich, hoping to meet up in Berlin with Barthel, Kluser, and his former Swiss colleagues, after which time he planned to travel to Norway in January to renew links with the Youth Socialists of Scandinavia.[9]

But the Swiss police investigations ensured that there would be no holiday reunion of Münzenberg's Zurich friends. The Youth Conference in Berlin was a flop, attended by only a handful of delegates, including, significantly, Francesco Misiano from Italy, whose loyalty at this time of the Youth International's lowest political ebb Münzenberg would not soon forget. Yet the trip to Berlin was not a total failure—Münzenberg at last met his heroes Luxemburg and Liebknecht, and seemed to strike it off well with Liebknecht in particular, who agreed to speak alongside Münzenberg at a gathering of Youth Socialists in Neukölln. Münzenberg also had a long talk with Leo Jogisches, Luxemburg's longtime lover and chairman of the Spartacist League. Münzenberg also attended the Congress of Workers' and Soldiers' Councils where, to his chagrin, the Spartacists were overwhelmingly defeated by the hated Majority Socialists, who convinced the councils to abdicate political power to a National Assembly to be elected in January. But for all the excitement, Münzenberg's attempt to revive the Youth International was a failure, and so he gave up on the idea of going to Norway and returned to Stuttgart instead.[10]

On the return trip to Württemberg, Münzenberg came down with pneumonia, and this was why, he later claimed, he dropped out of political sight for several weeks—at a critical time when the Spartacists convened in Berlin and voted to form the German Communist Party (KPD) in formal affiliation with Moscow. From what we know of Münzenberg's persistent health problems, it is certainly possible that he spent nearly three weeks recovering indoors, missing the historic Spartacist conference merely by accident. Still, there were other preoccupations that must have weighed heavily on Münzenberg's mind. His beloved Youth International was floundering and his most trusted political lieutenants were out of reach in Switzerland. Münzenberg's fiancée Adele, with whom he had planned to spend the holiday season, was in jail in Zurich, and it was entirely, inescapably his fault that she was there, suffering due to his own vanity and ambition. No correspondence survives from this bleak period in Münzenberg's life, but it is clear that he took a serious interest in Kluser's fate, hiring his own expensive lawyer Keller for her, a step he took for none of the others who had been imprisoned on his account.[11]

Whether by accident or design, then, Münzenberg was aloof from German politics when the KPD was founded, and this was not necessarily a bad thing. The birth of German Communism was a messy affair, leaving political scars on those who survived the delivery that would not soon disappear. The basic motivation for allying with Moscow at this point in time was that the Spartacists, after their resounding defeat at the conference of Workers' and Soldiers' Councils on 19 December, were isolated and had little to recommend themselves to potential recruits besides their political intransigence. There were potential allies on the left wing of the USPD, and it was largely the prospect of winning these politicians over that prompted Spartacus to align with Moscow in its historic New Year's conference, held from 30 December 1918 to 1 January 1919 in the Banquet Hall of the Prussian Chamber of Deputies. Unfortunately for the Spartacists' political cohesion, however, this recruiting call for disaffected USPD converts attracted many other radicals as well, and the KPD's founding congress was invaded by a potent brew of angry anarchists and army deserters then stampeding around Berlin, who all wished to join the most extreme political faction imaginable. Most Spartacist leaders believed that the German working masses were not yet radicalized enough to take over the means of production, and wanted time to build their political base before attempting to seize power. But despite the passionate exhortations of Rosa Luxemburg and Paul Levi, the leading advocates of electoral participation, a vote of sixty-two to twenty-three at the KPD's founding congress ruled in favor of a boycott of the upcoming elections for the National Assembly, a vote that so disturbed Luxemburg, in particular, that she immediately considered disbanding the party she had played so large a role in creating.[12]

Luxemburg's disillusionment with the uncomfortably radical resolutions of the KPD's founding congress may seem counterintuitive in light of her reputation as an uncompromising idealist of the Socialist cause. But in fact, her reaction to the electoral boycott was wholly in character and provides a vivid illustration of the imaginative limitations of orthodox German Socialism. Luxemburg was certainly a radical, a famously bitter opponent of Friedrich Ebert and the practical bureaucratic mentality he embodied in the SPD, but she opposed men such as Ebert less out of antipathy to their moderate political temperament than out of outrage at their betrayal of the Marxist tradition. Luxemburg, a diminutive Polish Jew with a limp and a deformed shoulder—traits sharply offset, however, by a powerful speaking voice— was the queen of orthodoxy in the Second International, sparing no one in her denunciations of deviations from the party line. It was Luxemburg who had led the attacks on Bernstein's Revisionism; she who had denounced the great French pacifist Jean Jaurès, for the sin of desiring to cooperate with "bourgeois" political parties, as "the great corrupter"; and she who had issued the most celebrated defense of the principles of socialist "democracy" as against Lenin's proposal for the dictatorship of an elitist "vanguard party."[13]

After the kaiser's fall in November 1918, Luxemburg awkwardly applied her understanding of Marxist theory to the fluid political situation. She celebrated the workers' councils that ostensibly had arisen to represent the German proletariat, even while she lamented their failure to stage a real social revolution. The Spartacus program, drafted by Luxemburg and first published in *Rote Fahne* on 14 December 1918, called for the immediate dissolution of the army, the police, the state parliaments, and the municipal governments, with the soldiers' and workers' councils taking over the entire administration of the country. Barring such fantastic developments, though, Spartacus would itself assume no role in any German government. If the working masses were not ready for revolution—as their 19 December vote in favor of abdicating power to an elected National Assembly implied— then Spartacus shouldn't be, either. To Luxemburg, the electoral boycott passed at the KPD's founding congress was an inexplicable spasm of political ignorance, which would spoil the Spartacists' chances to win new supporters. The hotheads who demanded action now, regardless of where the workers stood, were insulting the Marxist tradition, and this is why Luxemburg could not stomach them.[14]

Just as the Spartacists had feared, an uprising led by uncontrollable radical elements shook Berlin less than a week after the KPD was founded, and Luxemburg's efforts to contain political reality inside of her theories were dealt a serious blow. When Emil Eichhorn, a popular USPD deputy appointed Berlin Police President after the kaiser's fall, was sacked by the Prussian government on 4 January for suspected "revolutionary" sympathies, hundreds of workers took to the streets in protest. A joint proclamation published the next morning by the left-leaning Berlin USPD leaders in *Freiheit* and by the Communists in *Rote Fahne* led even greater numbers to demonstrate for Eichhorn on Alexanderplatz that afternoon, where Liebknecht, among others, addressed the crowds from the balcony of police headquarters. Inspired by the impressive turnout, Liebknecht and Wilhelm Pieck of the KPD's Central Committee (Zentrale) met later that evening with representatives of the USPD and the Revolutionary Shop Stewards, a shadowy group with ties to radical unions elsewhere in Germany.[15] The conspirators declared themselves a "Revolutionary Committee" and resolved to overthrow Ebert's government. Luxemburg and Levi both protested this decision on Monday, but failed to win over the KPD Zentrale, which endorsed the Revolutionary Committee and called for a general strike. This was not the revolution Luxemburg had wanted, but it was the revolution she got.

Luxemburg's problem was analogous to the one Münzenberg had faced when Dättwyler's "peace" riots broke out right under his nose in Zurich in November 1917; but in Berlin the stakes were much higher. The KPD's leaders did not merely take part in the rioting that soon engulfed all of Berlin. On 6 January 1919 they publicly proclaimed their desire to overthrow the government, and showed how serious their intentions were when their followers seized key positions in the city, including Eichhorn's police headquarters, the Government Printing Office, the Main Railroad Office, and the Wolff Telegraph Bureau. For several days chaotic violence reigned in the city, as workers and soldiers supporting the Revolutionary Committee clashed in the streets with those loyal to Ebert's government. The *Vorwärts* building on Lindenstrasse, which served as SPD party headquarters, actually changed hands several times.

The Provisional Government's counteroffensive began in earnest on Wednesday 8 January, with Ebert's declaration of war on "Spartacus," whose members he blamed exclusively for the uprising. Using reliable troops from the army's Berlin garrison, the SPD's own paramilitary units, and for the final blow, the notorious Freikorps units recently cobbled together from the mass of disbanded former soldiers as a bulwark against Bolshevism, Ebert succeeded in suppressing the rebellion by force. By 11 January, most of the city was firmly in government control, and four days later, Luxemburg, Liebknecht, and Pieck were captured by a neighborhood militia in the Wilmersdorf apartment where they had gone into hiding with affluent socialist friends. Turned over to the army's Guard Cavalry Rifle Division for questioning, Luxemburg and Liebknecht were murdered while in custody later that day, although Pieck escaped unharmed (possibly by convincing the soldiers he was someone else).[16]

Because Liebknecht had been one of the principal instigators of the uprising, we might say that he died a martyr's death for communism. But in Luxemburg's case the sense of tragic, futile irony is inescapable. She died a scapegoat for an aborted revolution she had not wanted and at first tried to prevent, a victim of just the kind of "spontaneous," undirected revolutionary violence she had always advocated in theory, but which in practice proved both ineffectual and fatal.

In Stuttgart, meanwhile, news of the Ebert government's crackdown on Spartacus in Berlin sparked a large protest demonstration on 9 January 1919, called by local representatives of the KPD and USPD, the Red Soldiers'

League, and the Stuttgart Youth Socialists. It is unclear whether Münzenberg played a role in organizing the event, but his health had evidently recovered sufficiently for him to join Zetkin, Hörnle, and several others in haranguing the crowds in front of the Schlosshof, the Labor Ministry, and in the market square. In the square he called for the dismissal of the local SPD government and the assumption of administrative power by the workers' and soldiers' councils.[17]

As in Berlin, the radicalism of the ringleaders proved extremely divisive. By the afternoon progovernment workers and soldiers were fighting Spartacists in the streets, and the tide of the battle swung back and forth on into the evening. At some point late in the afternoon, a group of armed pro-Spartacist workers seized control of the *Stuttgarter Tageblatt* building, and Münzenberg and Hörnle set immediately to work pumping out a propaganda rag they styled "The Red Flood" *(Die rote Flut)* which was meant to put a definitive stamp on the day's events. But this was still a very provisional sort of putsch, and Münzenberg and Hörnle stopped work on the evolving copy no less than three times to check on the situation on the street. Twice, they descended all the way to the entrance steps to argue with progovernment soldiers, apparently tiring the poor enlistees out enough with their rhetoric that the two were left alone to write.

By midnight, progovernment forces had surrounded the building in sufficient numbers that its storming seemed imminent, and it was at about this time that Münzenberg later claimed to have collapsed from exhaustion. Physically this was not an unlikely possibility, but Münzenberg's "collapse," suspiciously, offered those inside a last-ditch chance to camouflage a retreat: Hörnle and several friends now carried their fallen comrade out the front door of the building on the pretext of taking him home to recuperate. Although the would-be escapees' path was blocked by the progovernment forces, a young soldier friendly to the Spartacists intervened, pretending to arrest the Münzenberg party. He took them into custody, only to let them slip away on a side street. Still, two days later Münzenberg and his friend Barthel (who had returned after being expelled from Switzerland in early January) were arrested in their apartment, later to be charged with high treason. Once more, the flame of Spartacus, lit in a manner not of its leaders' choosing, fluttered briefly behind a wave of Red Flags, and quickly died out.[18]

The ease with which Münzenberg backed down in January suggests that he had a better sense of the Spartacists' real chances of attaining power in Stuttgart than did Liebknecht and Pieck in Berlin. A less charitable interpretation would be that Münzenberg lacked the guts to risk his skin when the chips were down, but this is merely another way of saying that his political survival instincts were acute. In fact, Münzenberg's strategic calculations were fairly shrewd. He rode the wave of unrest as far as it would take him, using the drama of the moment to give a bold speech and launch a new propaganda organ, but he slipped quietly out of sight before being caught in any uncontestable acts of treason. He was able to claim, to other Spartacists, that he had been in the thick of the action, while maintaining in court that he had displayed no intention of overthrowing the government. And both claims were, more or less, convincing, judging by Münzenberg's acquittal from treason charges in June 1919 by a friendly jury, as well as the general rejoicing by radical unionists and Spartacists in Stuttgart that followed his release. Clearly, the lessons in political dissembling Münzenberg learned in Zurich had paid off.[19]

There is a stubborn tendency among historians—and the general voting public in democracies—to admire steadfastness and consistency in political figures. But the talent for indirection, the ability to wait before committing to certain positions (or not to commit at all), the capacity to step down and distance oneself from one's own actions as Münzenberg did in Stuttgart—such subtle, unheroic virtues should never be discounted in assessing a political career. Liebknecht and Luxemburg won lasting fame and the admiration of generations of historians by risking their necks in a reckless bid for power in January 1919, but it is difficult to say exactly what was gained, and for whom, by their martyrdom. Spartacus did not ignite the rioting in January, but the Berlin Spartacists' unambiguous attempt to exploit the situation ultimately placed the onus for the January debacle on their own shoulders. The Berlin USPD leaders, by contrast, disavowed the putsch as soon as it spun out of control, and so were able to retain some political respectability. All Spartacus gained from the tragedy in Berlin was a reputation for irresponsible political troublemaking that would prove impossible for the KPD to shake.[20]

While in prison in spring 1919, Münzenberg penned a sarcastic account of the events, *Down with Spartacus!* which offers up a series of transparently obtuse objections to the Spartacus program from the mind of an intellectually challenged Majority Socialist. "The Spartacists want the dictatorship of a minority and terror," we read, only to learn rapidly that such a view is blatant slander, and in fact the KPD actually favors a "dictatorship of the majority in the interest of the whole." Against the most devastating anti-Spartacist argument—the claim that Spartacus is treasonously working for Bolshevik Russia, Germany's former enemy—Münzenberg turns the tables, accusing

Ebert's "bourgeois" government of collaboration with the victorious Entente Powers, whereas a Spartacist government in Germany would have annulled all unjust "capitalist" war reparations. Because Allied soldiers were now at war with the Bolshevik regime, the Spartacists' friendly relations with Moscow would mean "peace in the East" if they achieved power, with the Entente Powers' capitalist tyranny beaten back by a "Socialist Empire" stretching "from the Rhine to the Urals." Those who cried "Down with Spartacus" were actually working for Germany's enemies, while the Communists were, by contrast, the Entente's worst nightmare.[21]

What is clever about this pamphlet is that, despite his sarcastic rhetoric and aggressive posturing, Münzenberg takes no real position on the January uprising beyond vaguely endorsing the political goals all Spartacists agreed on. The uncompromising line taken by the KPD's new chairman Paul Levi after the failed Spartacist putsch offers an instructive contrast to Münzenberg's sharp but noncommittal tone.

To prevent a replay of the January disaster, Levi understandably moved to purge the party of its more uncontrollable elements, disbanding the Red Soldiers' League in summer 1919 and swinging regional sections in line with a series of dictatorial resolutions passed at the KPD Congress at Heidelberg in October. But the zealous manner in which he did all this helped pigeonhole Levi as a tiresome opponent of any and all spontaneous social protests, an effete intellectual with no stomach for bold revolutionary action. His increasingly shrill denunciations of the various communist putsches of 1919, from the Spartacist uprising of January to Bela Kun's March Revolution in Hungary to the short-lived "Bavarian Soviet Republic" of April, did not endear him to activists who had risked their lives in the streets, and there was scarcely a whimper from rank-and-file KPD members when Levi was finally sacked in 1921.[22]

Münzenberg, on the other hand, burned no bridges to fellow Communists even though he disowned "putschist" tactics in *Down with Spartacus!* No one endorses putsch tactics after they fail—but as Münzenberg realized, there is a way to criticize them without insulting those who were swept up in the promise of action.

By maneuvering carefully through the ideological minefield of the "putsch" debate, Münzenberg was able to emerge from prison in a strong political position. In his testimony at his June trial for treason, Münzenberg remained free of acrimonious hand-wringing over an uprising gone wrong: he concentrated instead on what the Spartacists would have done to help the working man if the putsch had gone right. Before a friendly jury and a friendly judge who allowed him to expostulate at length, Münzenberg scarcely bothered to deny his treasonous intention of overthrowing the inept bourgeois regime. "Jawohl!" he gleefully proclaimed, the Spartacists would have nationalized the banks—and instead of bankrupting poor Germany by paying the Entente's reparations and allowing the capital flight sure to follow economic collapse, they would have distributed the country's remaining wealth to the veteran invalids, widows, and ordinary working-class soldiers who had been victimized by the war. In this way Münzenberg played to the gallery in similar fashion to the way Hitler would at his own trial for treason after the Nazis' Beer Hall Putsch. The unrepentant Spartacist made such a strong impression on the party faithful that he was elected chairman of the Württemberg State KPD that summer.[23]

Still, the central problem facing Münzenberg when he had been imprisoned following the Spartacist uprising—the Youth International's decline into irrelevance—had not gone away. The situation in Zurich was bleak. Although Kluser, Trostel, and Arnold had all been released from prison by early spring 1919, there was no money left in the old Youth International Treasury.[24] Almost certainly the cash flow problem could have been cleared up in March 1919, had Münzenberg been able to secure official patronage at the First Congress of the new Communist International in Moscow, but although he was invited, he was then still in prison and could not attend. An attempt to revive the wartime Youth International in Vienna in late summer 1919 fizzled quickly when Münzenberg himself was expelled from Austria for carrying an improper passport. In late October, while returning from the annual KPD Congress in Heidelberg, Münzenberg was informed that a new warrant had been issued for his arrest in the state of Württemberg. He learned of this in time to switch trains several stations before Stuttgart. After instructing friends to collect his papers there, Münzenberg set off for Berlin, where he was to host the next Youth International congress, rescheduled after the Vienna fiasco, in November. Aside from the brief excitement of January, Stuttgart had not offered Münzenberg much in the way of political stimulation. Now he would try his luck in the German capital.

CHAPTER 4 *Berlin*

Berlin was an obvious destination for Münzenberg once he became a fugitive in Württemberg, and not merely because it was Germany's political epicenter and home to the headquarters of the KPD Zentrale (though after the crackdown on the Spartacists the party had gone underground). In the disillusioned aftermath of Germany's defeat in 1918, the Prussian capital teemed with disbanded soldiers, political refugees (many of them Russians fleeing the Bolsheviks, like Vladimir Nabokov), and currency speculators from all over the world, offering in its human chaos a possibility for anonymity unmatched elsewhere in Germany. Everyone, it seemed, was seeking his or her fortune on the banks of the River Spree, from the thousands of beggars and war cripples panhandling for scraps from the rich, to soldiers setting up gun stalls to cash in on the most ubiquitous asset left over from the trenches, to foreign businessmen cynically snapping up properties at cut rates due to the wild inflation set off by a war financed almost entirely on credit. Already the inflation had begun to erode moral restraints, making a mockery of thrift and modesty and putting a premium on conspicuous consumption. Berlin was rapidly becoming Europe's postwar Babylon, with all-night dance cabarets, exuberant pornography, and plenty of women renting their bodies to any men who could afford them. Count Harry Kessler, a charismatic Prussian aristocrat nicknamed "the Red Count" for his socialist sympathies, described living in postwar Berlin as "dancing on a volcano."[1]

Berlin was not quite so much fun, of course, for those who couldn't afford the good life, but the city still offered plenty of political excitement for struggling exiles and conspirators seeking refuge in its vastness. Münzenberg arrived in the Prussian capital without papers in late October 1919, and immediately rented rooms in different parts of the city to keep the Prussian police guessing as much as possible as to his whereabouts. The most important property was a carpenter's shop in Schöneberg, where he set up a secret printing press. In October, thousands of invitations and propaganda leaflets were pumped out there and delivered via couriers to Youth Socialist groups all over Europe. These documents provided detailed instructions on alternative meeting places and times for the upcoming youth conference in Berlin, in the strictest confidentiality, so as not to tip off anyone who might inform the Prussian police.

By leaving Stuttgart Münzenberg had forfeited his position as chairman of the Württemberg KPD, but this apparent demotion may have come as a relief. He now lovingly devoted his time to putting together the logistics of an underground Youth International, with friendly contacts on Germany's borders with Switzerland, Austria, and Lithuania who could help delegates get across national frontiers safely. These meticulous preparations proved successful in getting bodies to Berlin, in happy contrast to the weakly attended event the previous year. On 20 November 1919, youth delegates from all over Europe, including a large Russian delegation, met in the back room of a pub in the working-class district of Neukölln. Further meetings were held later that week in other bars in nearby Lichtenberg, as well as in the carpenter's shop in Schöneberg; but it was the Neukölln Berliner Bürgerbrau that Münzenberg would later strain to immortalize as the birthplace of the Communist Youth International.

Although Münzenberg's first successful postwar youth conference was most strongly attended by those same northern moderates whose regular contributions had financed the Zurich secretariat during the war, Scandinavian patronage was about to be jettisoned in a historic changing of the guard. It seems clear that Münzenberg made contact sometime in early November 1919 with Bolshevik emissaries to scare up money for the Youth Secretariat, including Karl Moor, a wealthy Swiss patron of the socialist cause who had been friendly with Lenin and Radek since 1904 and who now quietly distributed both Moscow's and his own money to favored revolutionaries in Europe. Another important contact was James Reich, alias Thomas, the liaison man for the Comintern's Western European Bureau (WEB), who had set up a Bolshevik front in a Charlottenburg bookshop on Leibnizstrasse, which he used to distribute cash and advice to the KPD brass.[2]

We may certainly conclude that Münzenberg did Moscow's bidding at the Berlin conference, where the main priority was to win the delegates over to a policy of "centralization" of authority under the auspices of the Communist International. As a sop to skeptical Scandinavians wary of losing the political voice that seemed warranted by their large domestic member bases and the financial support this had always guaranteed, Münzenberg included a phrase about the need for the youth organizations' "independence" in the final conference resolutions. But this independence was conditioned by the contradictory demand that each national Youth organization establish its political priorities "on the basis of the program of that [adult] political party in their country that belongs to the Third [Communist] International." Whereas at Bern in 1915, Münzenberg had played to the northern moderates because they held the purse strings, he was now playing to Moscow's tune. Not even the thirty-thousand-member strong Swedish Youth could come close to the Soviet government in financial clout. Nor could Scandinavian Youth Socialists, however well organized, possibly compete with the prestige of Russian revolutionaries such as Lenin and Zinoviev, who were also Münzenberg's friends.[3]

Münzenberg would later make a lot of noise about his efforts to preserve the "independence" of the youth organizations, but this was disingenuous. Naturally he wanted to maintain the same personal independence he had enjoyed as youth secretary in Zurich. As far as the other delegates were concerned, though, the central priority lay in firmly establishing their loyalty to Moscow. Münzenberg's specific political goal at the Berlin conference was to purge the wartime Youth International of unreliable sections who were thinking of joining the revived Second International, convened in Bern at the urging of British socialists early in 1919. Münzenberg laced his speeches in Berlin with oblique attacks on deviant tendencies in the movement, excoriating the "petty bourgeois" ideas of "pacifist and intellectual youth circles." Properly trained, Youth Communists would become "the vanguard of the Red Army" and later, "confidence men" in their national Communist parties. Far from fighting heroically for the autonomy of the youth groups, Münzenberg in fact wanted his charges to resign themselves to a complementary role in international Communism, to realize that they must "march side by side with their adult revolutionary comrades."[4]

Although the Berlin conference was generally a success, the terms of entry into the new Youth International were not to everyone's liking. Münzenberg's first significant action after the delegates disbanded was a trip to Copenhagen, where he hoped to ward off a defection in the Danish youth section to the Majority Socialists. Delegates from the other Scandinavian countries had called the Copenhagen meeting, and Münzenberg was afraid they were all considering abandoning the Communist International. Clearly the stakes in Copenhagen were high, for otherwise there would have been little reason for Münzenberg to risk a clandestine voyage to Denmark in the bitter cold of December, under a false passport, with a live warrant for his arrest in Germany.

Whatever the true stakes of the trip for Münzenberg, it certainly provided him with a good story to tell. He crossed into Denmark in the middle of a thunderstorm, stowed away in a hired fishing vessel, where he feared for his life as it crashed about helplessly on the waves. Although he survived the frigid night at sea, before he could reap any political fruits from the voyage, he was recognized in Copenhagen and arrested. (He tried to deny being Münzenberg, but his picture was on file with the police, having appeared in publications of the Danish Youth Socialist organization.) After spending the holidays in prison, Münzenberg was expelled in early January. Upon approaching the German border by train, he hid in a cattle car and slipped out undetected, losing himself quickly in a crowd of drunken sailors. Münzenberg made it back to Berlin without further incident, relieved to have his freedom, but having gained nothing from the adventure.[5]

The Prussian police had not yet found any of Münzenberg's various flats in Berlin, but he still had to be careful when moving about the city. Little correspondence or other material survives from this period, but we may surmise that Münzenberg was reasonably successful in staying underground, for there were no run-ins with the police in spring 1920. Münzenberg's youth followers seem to have been relatively quiet during the so-called Kapp Putsch of 13–17 March, when the "National Association," an antirepublican umbrella organization composed of disgruntled army leaders such as Generals Erich Ludendorff and Walther Freiherr von Lüttwitz, marched troops on Berlin. Although General Hans von Seeckt refused to defend the capital with the regular army, and Ebert and his government fled to Dresden, the putsch fizzled quickly in the face of a general strike staged in Ebert's defense by the (mostly noncommunist) Berlin unions, who were aided in turn by a cut-off of coal supplies to the capital on the part of the national miners' union. Communists in western Germany used the general strike as an excuse to march armed guerrilla bands of supporters across the Ruhr industrial belt, temporarily capturing a number of city centers. In Berlin, however, the KPD notoriously played no role in the strike, with the Central Committee even issuing an ugly resolution proclaiming that "the revolutionary proletariat ... will not lift a finger for the democratic republic." Münzenberg may not have agreed with this sentiment, but there is no evidence that he played any role whatsoever in thwarting the short-lived Kapp regime.[6]

Münzenberg kept a low profile in spring 1920, and in fact became so invisible that he himself complained in June that neither Thomas, nor anyone else at WEB, was returning his mail. Münzenberg disliked Thomas, a short, somewhat awkward man most Communists knew as "Fatty," and the sentiment seems to have been mutual. Münzenberg didn't enjoy being dependent on Thomas for official Comintern funds (although he frequently circumvented WEB by getting casual handouts from Karl Moor), and Thomas, in turn, wasn't excited about extending this largesse to Münzenberg.[7]

The only way to resolve such an impasse was, of course, to go to Moscow. Luckily for Münzenberg, the Second Congress of the Comintern was scheduled to meet in July 1920. Invited once more to represent the Youth International in Moscow, as he had been while detained in prison the previous year, Münzenberg was certain that he could secure a direct patronage link by hitting up his old Bolshevik friends.

But he almost didn't make it. On the night before he was scheduled to leave Berlin, Münzenberg was arrested while sitting in a café and taken to police headquarters, where he was presented with the Stuttgart warrant from 1919, along with one relating to his draft evasion in 1917. When he was arraigned the following morning, Münzenberg found himself hauled into court with "about forty petty thieves and pimps" arrested the previous evening. In his pristine manner he stood out from the others so clearly that the judge, a "jovial old man," demanded to know why he was there. Thinking quickly, Münzenberg replied that he had, to his utter surprise, been picked up on a warrant for avoiding military service back in 1917. When the judge, who fortunately did not recognize Münzenberg from the newspapers, found the suspect's file, the 1917 warrant was in fact sitting on top of the more recent documentation, and so the little ruse fooled the old man. "Those fellows . . . must have been drunk again," the bamboozled magistrate assured Münzenberg, and released him immediately. The mistake was soon discovered, but by the time the police resumed searching for the Young Communist organizer, he was already crossing the Baltic Sea, disguised as a Russian war prisoner being repatriated to the Soviet Union.[8]

CHAPTER 5 *Moscow*

After the Bolsheviks evacuated European Petrograd for the ancient Russian capital of Muscovy in March 1918, the Moscow Kremlin rapidly assumed an almost mystical status for socialists all over the world. Inside the stone walls of this great fortress, constructed by Italian architects in the fifteenth century, Lenin's embattled communist regime holed up as if in hiding from its many domestic and foreign enemies. Outside the gates of the Kremlin, the war raged on, even after the Bolsheviks surrendered to Germany at Brest-Litovsk in March 1918. There was the first armed White resistance to Red rule, launched by the generals Alekseev and Kornilov in the Don Cossack region in winter 1917–18; the revolt of the Czechoslovak Legion along the trans-Siberian railway in summer 1918; the establishment of two anti-Bolshevik armies in the east, headquartered at Samara and Omsk, in Siberia; and the Polish invasion of White Russia in the west, launched in April 1920. Until March 1920 the various White forces were also supported by the Western Allies, chiefly Great Britain, who supplied the anti-Bolshevik armies in the north through Murmansk, and in the south by way of Novorossiisk on the Black Sea.

This war of self-preservation started off poorly for the Bolsheviks, who had foolishly dissolved the imperial army after assuming power in November 1917. But their new Red Army, formed under War Commissar Trotsky in 1918, ultimately took advantage of the superior manpower reserves, munitions factories, and rail network of central Great Russia, and was able to turn the tide against the Whites, Czechs, partisans, and Poles, who were all on the retreat when the Second Comintern Congress met in July 1920.

The First Congress, which met in March 1919 while Münzenberg was in jail, had been intended as a coming-out party for the world's first communist regime, but due to the logistical complications of wartime was so poorly attended as to be something of a farce. Of the fifty-four delegates there theoretically representing the global proletariat, only five actually arrived in Moscow from abroad—and only one of these actually carried a mandate from a national political party. A motley assortment of released political prisoners and military attachés visiting Moscow from the West were invited at the last minute to give the congress an international flavor, but it was unquestionably a Russian show from start to finish, dominated by the five official delegates of the Russian Communist Party: Lenin, Trotsky, Zinoviev, Nikolai Bukharin, and Georgii Chicherin.[1]

By contrast, the Second Comintern Congress a year later was attended by over a hundred legitimate foreign delegates, some of whom actually represented organized Communist parties—although these were mostly still embryonic offshoots of larger, long-established Socialist parties. Along with Münzenberg, many emerging stars of international communism made their first appearance in Moscow in summer 1920. From Paris, there was Marcel Cachin, a onetime philosophy professor who would remain a Kremlin favorite in the French Communist Party well into the 1930s and 1940s; from Italy, Giacinto Menotti Serrati, one of the most popular socialist orators of prewar Europe; from Switzerland, the prolific Geneva-based journalist Jules Humbert-Droz; and from Germany, Clara Zetkin, the grand dame of the Second International, who would reprise her role as the unofficial, silver-haired socialist queen mother in Lenin's Third International.

The vastly improved attendance of the Second Comintern Congress reflected a dramatically improved military situation. In 1919, the Red Army had been pressed by White and Allied resistance for most of the year on three separate fronts, to the north, south, and east. By spring 1920, the Allies had dropped out of the conflict entirely and, despite continued partisan resistance in the Ukraine, the war was essentially reduced to one major theater, against Poland in the west. After some early setbacks in April and May, the Bolsheviks were largely on the offensive. By midsummer, the Red Army was on the gates of Warsaw, and the Bolsheviks were swept up in "revolutionary delirium," in the words of Richard Pipes: Lenin was planning the immediate "sovietization" of Hungary, Czechoslovakia, and Rumania, as he cabled to his trusted Red Army field commander, Joseph Stalin, in Kharkov on 23 July.[2] Although such grand visions proved unrealistic, the Bolsheviks' sweeping military successes in 1920 made possible, at the least, the successful voyage of European Comintern delegates through northern ports on the Baltic Sea, now that military lines no longer had to be crossed to reach Moscow.

The Red Army's success also altered the political equation significantly. The waxing of revolutionary confidence in Soviet Russia over the past year had been accompanied by its waning in the West. From the crushing of a great wave of postwar strikes in France to the bloody obliteration of short-lived "Soviet" regimes in Bavaria and Hungary, 1919 had been a humiliating year for European revolutionaries. The prestige of European radicals was sinking just as the Bolsheviks' was ascending into the stratosphere. This imbalance was reflected in the condescending tone of the pamphlet Lenin prepared for the Second Congress, *"Left Wing" Communism, an Infantile Disorder*, which counseled foreign comrades to exhibit greater patience and discipline, ruling out aggressive putsches on the grounds that European Communists were too weak to prevail over their enemies.[3]

Foreign delegates and their Russian counterparts, then, would clearly not be meeting on equal terms in summer 1920. Still, the risk of Bolshevik domination hardly dampened the enthusiastic mood of most of the Comintern's first pilgrims. For socialists who had been fed only second-hand stories about the Bolsheviks' exciting experiment in proletarian dictatorship, merely crossing the Russian border was enough to ignite the imagination. As Münzenberg and his Spartacist companions rode a wood-fired locomotive east after disembarking at the Estonian port of Narva, they were simply "thrilled," he later wrote, "after all the dangers and difficulties to stand at last on the soil of the Soviet Union."[4]

It must have been a great relief, too, for Münzenberg to set foot at last on political ground where he was welcome. After several years' worth of on-and-off imprisonment in Switzerland, detention in Stuttgart, and tiring efforts to evade the Prussian police in Berlin, Red Russia promised respite from the hazardous life of a revolutionary. Not that Münzenberg would get much rest—in fact, he stayed up all night after arriving in Petrograd in mid-July, reminiscing with his old comrade Zinoviev about the heady days of the Zimmerwald Left. It was then White Nights in Petrograd, the time of year so beloved of hooligans, lovers, conversationalists, and other voluntary insomniacs.

Next day the endless meetings and tours began, as Münzenberg was feted by an assortment of unions, Young Communist Leagues, "proletarian children's' homes," and other Bolshevik organizations. He was particularly impressed by the transformation of the tsar's summer palace (Tsarskoe selo), the imperial retreat beyond Petrograd's western suburbs where the last Romanov, Nicholas II, had preferred to live. Tsarskoe selo had been turned into a school for workers' and soldiers' children offering a "collectivist" education. The children there, Münzenberg later recalled, "stormed us like wild animals," proudly showing off their artwork, compositions displayed on bulletin boards, and other sketchings. No less proudly, the children being indoctrinated in the former palace of the tsars belted out the *Internationale* later that afternoon, to Münzenberg's delight.[5]

The pageantry prepared in Petrograd for the incoming Comintern delegates was no less exuberant than the children of Tsarskoe selo. The first spectacle awaiting them was a memorial service at Mars Field, used in the tsarist era as a military parade ground, where the Bolsheviks commemorated the fallen heroes of the October Revolution.

In case foreign visitors were not yet impressed with the legend of Red October, the Bolsheviks staged a lurid reenactment of *The Storming of the Winter Palace* on the steps of the now-silent Petrograd Stock Exchange, where some twenty thousand technicians, actors, and extras acted out a didactic melodrama, scripted by Maxim Gorky. Witnesses estimated the size of the crowd of spectators to be one hundred thousand.[6] There could not have been a much more majestic backdrop for the Gorky extravaganza. Red Flags blustered in the wind atop the nearby Winter Palace, warships on the Neva lit up the Soviet star with searchlights, and Nevsky Prospekt was overflowing with thousands of Russians and honored foreign guests, taking in the spectacle. "It was like a dream," Münzenberg later wrote of this outsized miracle of political agitprop. For him, it was a dream come true.

If Petrograd was the city of spectacle, however, Moscow was the seat of power, and it was there that the Communist International was truly born. The Second Congress met for only several largely ceremonial days in the former imperial capital in mid-July, before relocating to the throne room of the Kremlin in Moscow, where it met for two whole weeks. Here, delegates from all over the world watched in awe as Lenin mounted the rostrum beneath the Red Flag of the Revolution, with three gold-embroidered imperial thrones at his back, to deliver the gala address. Lenin's triumphant speech, Münzenberg recalled, was greeted by a deafening standing ovation.[7] The Bolsheviks were now literally enthroned as masters of the international Communist movement.

If the sessions in the Kremlin throne room symbolized the Comintern's formal power relationships, however, much of its real business was conducted informally, in face-to-face encounters between leading Communists who enjoyed the Bolsheviks' confidence. Münzenberg keenly understood this. Immediately upon his arrival in Moscow, he paid a visit to his old friend Radek in the luxurious new headquarters of the Comintern Executive, installed in the palatial former residence of a German sugar magnate, which had housed the German embassy up to 1918. Radek had recently replaced

Angelica Balabanoff as the Comintern's executive secretary. Despite her friendship with Lenin, Balabanoff had proved insufficiently "Bolshevik" for the position, having placed philanthropic activity above propaganda in her spending priorities.[8] Radek, by contrast, had no difficulty with the concept of unlimited spending for agitprop, and we may surmise that he took care to assure Münzenberg of this when the two were reunited in Moscow.

After reminiscing with Radek, Münzenberg quickly shored up old Zürich friendships with German-speaking Russian comrades such as Georgii Chicherin, who was now the head of the Soviet Commissariat for Foreign Affairs; Anatolii Lunacharskii, the First Soviet Commissar for Popular Enlightenment; and of course, Lenin. The Bolshevik dictator had not forgotten the youth secretary who had provided him with a political base during the difficult wartime years. Reminding Münzenberg of a running argument the two had carried on in Zürich about the possibility of seizing power in Russia by force, Lenin chided his old charge boastfully, "and who, then, was right?" Through such informal banter with his Zimmerwald comrades, Münzenberg helped reinforce his status as one of the "Old Bolsheviks" who enjoyed the confidence of the Kremlin.[9]

Although most foreign delegates who made the trip to Moscow approached the Second Congress as a forum for genuine debate, all the important questions on the agenda had actually been decided long beforehand, in the Kremlin. Unless they accepted every one of the soon to be infamous Twenty-One Conditions drafted for membership in the Communist International, national political parties could neither call themselves "Communist" nor count on any patronage from Moscow. The conditions demanded absolute subordination, based on a military model of the chain of command: national Communist parties were merely "sections" of the International, taking unbreachable marching orders from the Moscow-based Executive Committee of the Communist International (ECCI), which was to function as a "General Staff." The disciplining of the foreign Communist delegates was the main event; the much-vaunted Second Congress debates on such matters as electoral and colonial policy were merely sideshows.[10]

To a certain extent, the inevitable capitulation of most of the small national parties to Moscow's will was itself a sideshow, with real attention focused only on delegates from large countries with strong socialist traditions: France, Italy, and above all Germany. Germany was not merely the largest country in Europe and its geopolitical fulcrum; it was also the birthplace of Marx and the country, apart from Russia, which most excited Lenin's own imagination. German was chosen as the official language of the Comintern, the language of its debates and its written protocols, and securing the loyalty of the German party was, procedurally speaking, the central order of business at the Second Congress. In fact, the Twenty-One Conditions had originally been merely Eighteen—the last three were tacked on during the debates in order to drive a final wedge between the "Left" German USPD delegates (Arthur Crispien and Wilhelm Dittmann) and their "Right" counterparts (Ernst Däumig and Walter Stoecker). The four USPD men had taken a vow before arriving in Moscow to remain united through the congress, but this pledge fell victim to the Twenty-One Conditions, which by the end of the congress had split the Independent German Socialists down the middle, with Crispien and Dittmann assenting and Däumig and Stoecker balking, just as the Bolsheviks had planned.[11]

There were, to be sure, dissident voices raised at the pivotal Second Congress, a phenomenon that would not often recur at future Moscow gatherings. Münzenberg himself joined a chorus of protest against the directive that communists must participate in elections, ironically finding himself aligned on this question with two former enemies from Zürich days, the onetime anarchists Jacob Herzog and Toni Waibel (who were representing Switzerland). And there were other, more subtle expressions of dissent. Dittmann and Crispien, according to Münzenberg, were willing to swallow the Twenty-One Conditions but not the yellowish water in their hotel rooms, about which they spent much of the Congress complaining.[12]

But such grousing could not taint the overwhelming nature of the Bolsheviks' triumph at the Second Congress. All of the power and prestige was now theirs, and they were not about to let go anytime soon. Of course, the prestige of the powerful rests ultimately on the admiration of the less powerful, and the Bolsheviks recognized the need to cultivate and exploit this admiration. One way in which they did this at the Second Congress was by organizing a special VIP propaganda voyage through recently reconquered territories in the Ukraine, which in one stroke was to drive home the immensity of the task the Bolsheviks were assuming in "sovietizing" an entire continent, even while advertising to Ukrainian dissidents that Moscow was awash in foreign friends.

Touring the Ukraine on a specially outfitted military train, Münzenberg and forty other prominent foreign Comintern delegates, including Angelica Balabanoff and his old friend Max Barthel, witnessed the war's devastation, and also the harsh facts of Bolshevik military government. Streets were now patrolled by Red Army soldiers who stopped nearly everyone they encountered for document checks, as they tried to root out resistance to Red rule. Smaller train stations, Münzenberg remembered, were often overflowing with wounded soldiers sent back from the front, who were waiting, usually in vain, for ever-elusive medical supplies and medical personnel. According to Barthel, the group visited a "concentration camp" set up for speculators, military turncoats, and other enemies of the people. One such turncoat, however, remained dangerously at large: the legendary Ukrainian partisan Nestor Makhno, an anti-authority peasant anarchist commanding a force of thousands of fiercely loyal men. Makhno, whom Orlando Figes has described as the "Pancho Villa of the Russian Revolution," had fought both for and against the Reds. He was apparently in one of his anti-Bolshevik moods when he tried, no less than three times, to assassinate the visiting delegation of foreign Communists.[13]

Although this obscure episode has received, to my knowledge, no treatment by historians of the Russian Revolution and Civil War, it must surely be considered one of the most significant "what-ifs" in the history of the Communist International. If Balabanoff, Münzenberg, and the rest of the foreign notables had been murdered by partisans while under Soviet military escort, the Bolsheviks' prestige in Europe would almost certainly have sunk precipitously, with potentially fateful consequences for the future autonomy of the German, French, and Italian Communist parties, among others. Luckily for Moscow, Makhno failed resoundingly, and this problem was never confronted.

In spite of such dangers and intermittent unpleasantnesses, the trip was eye-opening for everyone, and Münzenberg greatly enjoyed himself. Most of the locals, he remembered, greeted the foreign Comintern delegates with real enthusiasm, although this enthusiasm probably did not reflect ideological commitment. The bitterly poor Ukrainians, after years of war, were suffering from near starvation, and the VIP train of foreign Bolshevik sympathizers was amply equipped not only with weapons but with foodstuffs (the restaurant car, according to Barthel, was so lavishly outfitted that its curtains had to be drawn when the delegation stopped in the smaller stations, lest the locals lose themselves in jealous agony and storm the train). Perhaps the enthusiastic reception was tied to expectations of better times: the arrival of foreigners granting benediction to the Bolsheviks might have seemed a divine signal that the fate of long-suffering Russia was about to turn around. "If even the popes from abroad are in favor," Barthel recalled one peasant remarking, "then the Bolsheviks, these scoundrels, must be in the right and will win."[14]

By the time the delegation reached Odessa, nearly everyone was in high spirits. Münzenberg and Barthel spent one raucous evening in a villa overlooking the Black Sea sampling some French cognac provided by a local party operative. Münzenberg, for so long a teetotaler, got drunk after only a few sips, so drunk that he started belting out old Thuringian folk songs. Münzenberg couldn't sing to save his life, according to Barthel, but the Russians were glad to indulge their new German comrade, and before long everyone was singing along as if in international brotherhood.[15]

After returning to Moscow in mid-August, Münzenberg was furnished with some truly essential materials for his Youth Secretariat in Berlin: a horde of diamonds, which he stitched into the cuffs of his jacket.[16] The Kremlin was not merely the new seat of power and prestige in the socialist world, but of unheard-of-wealth: sacks and sacks of jewels confiscated from the Romanovs, who in 1917 had been by far the world's richest royal family with an estimated net worth of over $9 billion, the equivalent of over a hundred billion dollars today. The Bolsheviks' seizure of these treasures meant they could now offer potentially unlimited patronage to leaders of foreign Communist parties.

It also put such foreigners squarely in their place: Moscow was now the master of international Communism, and they its loyal servants. Because youth issues had been relatively ignored at the Second Congress, Münzenberg himself did enjoy some breathing space in the coming months, when the established Socialist parties of Europe were invaded, one-by-one, by Comintern emissaries trying to split their ranks. Münzenberg's recruitment efforts, in fact, now brought the Communist Youth International to its organizational peak, with forty-nine national organizations counting eight hundred thousand members.[17]

But Münzenberg's time would come too. Although he was undoubtedly loyal to the Kremlin—he even published articles in favor of the Twenty-One Conditions—Münzenberg planned to keep his Youth Secretariat headquarters in Berlin. Such geographical distance from Moscow could lead to just the kind of de facto independence from ECCI that the Twenty-One Conditions were designed to squash. Zinoviev therefore politely demanded that Münzenberg change the location of the next Youth International meeting from Berlin to Moscow. Although wary of alienating his Bolshevik friends, Münzenberg was not ready to give up control of the Youth Bureau. Privately, he protested Zinoviev's instructions in a personal letter. "The ECCI," he wrote, "has neither the right nor cause to move our Youth Bureau congress to Moscow."[18]

Needless to say, ECCI did not agree. Münzenberg did put in a token protest against Moscow's decision in *Youth International*, but he surely must have known the game was up.[19] Moscow was evidently determined to undermine his personal control over the Communist Youth International, just as the SPD had clipped his wings in the prewar days. Once again, the deciding issue was money. As Münzenberg had tacitly admitted in 1909 when he left Erfurt, the Socialist Free Youth had been unable to survive without SPD subsidies. And in 1921 he recognized perfectly well that, without ECCI's endorsement, any organization he ran would be now cut off from the Kremlin's generous coffers.

The radical youth movement had dominated Münzenberg's life for nearly fifteen years, and the loss of the Youth Bureau was deeply upsetting to him. Still, it was not enough to turn him against Moscow. He knew that he enjoyed the confidence of Zinoviev, Radek, and Lenin, and this was far more important in the Communist world than any single mandate. A man of Münzenberg's experience, talent, and inexhaustible political energy was invaluable to the Kremlin, and the Bolsheviks refrained from attacking him directly at the Third World Congress in July 1921, even as they stripped him of his youth portfolio. Although forced to leave the youth movement behind, Münzenberg was still a loyal servant at Moscow's disposal, and it was not long before Lenin found use for him.

PART 2

The Red Millionaire

"I want you to spend millions, many many millions."

—Lenin, 1920

CHAPTER 6 *Selling the Famine*

In May and June 1921, a ghastly drought descended upon European Russia. The Volga flowed at its lowest level in years, its waters only weakly replenished by the spring thaw. Wells ran dry and "grain was burned as it came up from the ground." Hungry peasants ate this burnt wheat, along with grass, weeds, and bark, to keep from starving. The few existing grain reserves were quickly exhausted, and many famished peasants fled their villages, rampaging through the countryside looking for food. Typhus, cholera, typhoid fever, and smallpox raged through the affected area, rumors of cannibalism were rampant, and famine walked the land. By early summer, nearly a quarter of the landmass of European Russia, bounded by Viatka in the north, Astrakhan in the south, Penza in the west, and Ufa at the foot of the Ural mountains in the east, had become almost inhabitable. The lands of the famine region were ordinarily among the most fertile in all of Russia, and there was no surplus elsewhere to be had. Even the great breadbasket of the Ukraine, traditionally a source of outsize agricultural reserves and grain exports, was suffering severe drought and was itself on the verge of famine. On 26 June 1921, the official Soviet organ *Pravda* finally admitted that Russia was facing a humanitarian catastrophe the likes of which the world may never have witnessed: a population of "about twenty-five million" was on the brink of starvation, with no relief in sight.[1]

The raging battles of the Civil War of 1918–20 had certainly disrupted agricultural production on vast swathes of productive land, but in truth the Bolsheviks' own economic policies had contributed most to the crushing scale of the famine. It was hardly a secret that the Soviet government had since its inception been waging a violent struggle with its peasant subjects over the ever-dwindling food supply, in which urban workmen, armed by the Kremlin, descended upon the countryside to purge village soviets of non-Bolsheviks and murder farmers who refused to supply their surplus to the cities. This "food army" met furious resistance nearly everywhere it went, to the point where most peasants reduced their cultivation to a subsistence level, or failed to grow anything at all. The Bolshevik policy of forced requisitions led to a disastrous decline in agricultural production by spring 1920, when the harvest dropped to less than half of prewar levels.[2]

After serious drought struck in the summer of 1920, the Soviet government—far from easing up on requisitions as one might have expected with the Civil War at last all but won—stepped them up to the highest levels yet, with food detachments confiscating supplies from travelers on the rivers and roadways as well as from peasants in the villages. German communes along the drought-plagued lower Volga were invaded by an armed government gang, which the terrified peasants began referring to as the "Iron Broom." "Like roaring lions," one villager later recalled, "they came to the settlements, . . . all houses, barns, stables, cellars, lofts were searched and literally swept of everything they contained down to the last dried apple and the last egg . . . and woe to the farmer, in whose house flour, or any other produce was found; he was tortured and whipped to the blood."[3]

Elsewhere in the German Volga colonies, food army detachments mutinied and gave grain back to the people, only to provoke even more brutal revenge measures against the population once Communist reinforcements had arrived. Over eight thousand Bolshevik food requisitioners were murdered by angry peasants in 1920 alone,[4] but the number of peasant victims was undoubtedly far higher. Throughout the drought region in South Russia, the meager reserves produced during the fall harvest of 1920 were confiscated by Bolshevik food battalions that winter, leaving the entire region utterly defenseless when an even worse drought appeared in spring 1921.[5]

Remarkably, the Soviet government reacted to indications that a colossal famine was developing in its most productive agricultural region by intensifying the policies that had contributed so much to the famine in the first place. As late as the end of July 1921, at a time when millions of refugees were already besieging Russia's train stations and staggering into towns and cities, scrambling to get out of the famine regions by any means necessary, Lenin was ordering his armies of food requisitioners to step up their war against the peasantry. In a 30 July 1921 telegram to provincial Communist functionaries, Lenin demanded that local party leaders create "rural Communist cells" to assist village soviets in "tax" (i.e., food) collections, and "provide the food agencies with the necessary party authority and the total power of the state apparatus of coercion."[6] By this point, such obtuse policy decrees were largely moot, as there was little government left in the famine area to carry them out. But we should take note of the contempt Lenin displayed here for millions of starving subjects. Far from confronting his own grave responsibility for the famine, the Bolshevik dictator continued to blame the peasants for their stubborn resistance to his requisitions, long after there was no food left to requisition.

Only such contempt can explain Lenin's failure even to mention the famine in public, a task he delegated to a commission of Russian notables convened specially for the purpose. It would be hard to exaggerate the cynicism involved in the Bolsheviks' creation of an "All-Russian Public Committee to Aid the Hungry" (Pomgol), a government-controlled group fronted by prominent non-Communists such as the liberals Ekaterina Kuskova and S. N. Prokopovich, along with regime-friendly writers like Maxim Gorky, whose aid plea "To All Honest People" was released to the international press corps on 23 July 1921. As soon as Gorky's "nonpartisan" appeal had served its purpose, publicizing the famine in the West in a manner sufficiently respectable to secure an agreement with Herbert Hoover's American Relief Administration (ARA) to dispense massive humanitarian aid to the Volga area, Pomgol's non-Communist members (except Gorky) were arrested.[7]

Lenin's contempt for the peasants starving to death in the Volga region was matched only by his hatred of the people he had called in to feed them. Hoover's aid workers were in Lenin's opinion "mercenaries," who embodied all the "baseness" of American materialism—a view shared by Lenin's many left-wing admirers in America, who regarded the ARA's distribution of needed foodstuffs in Belgium and other beleaguered regions of Europe after World War I, with some justification, as an anti-Bolshevik crusade. When the ARA relieved Budapest in spring and summer 1919, helping take the edge off the desperate economic situation that had given Bela Kun a pretext for his short-lived communist coup, the *New Republic* accused Hoover of displaying "an implacable hostility to Bolshevism." This charge was rekindled in the U.S. media as soon as the ARA began negotiating with the Soviet government two years later, with the *Nation* speculating that Hoover might "use his food to overturn the Soviet government."[8]

Hoover himself never made any secret of his hostility to Bolshevism, and when his ARA negotiators met with their Bolshevik counterparts at Riga in August 1921, they insisted on absolute independence from Soviet government interference in their operations, as well as on the release of U.S. nationals from Soviet prisons.[9] Lenin's negotiators agreed to the ARA's terms at Riga—on paper—but Lenin was so infuriated by Hoover's demands that he immediately ordered his secret police (the Cheka) to infiltrate the arriving battalions of American aid workers. "The main thing," Lenin wrote his colleague Molotov three days after hiring Hoover, "is to identify and mobilize the maximum number of Communists who know English, [and] to introduce them into the Hoover commission."[10] "One must punish Hoover," he explained further in a memo to the Politburo, "one must *publicly slap his face*, so that the whole world sees."[11]

Naturally it was humbling for Lenin to turn to "bourgeois" leaders like Hoover to bail him out of a self-inflicted human catastrophe, but he was hardly going to do this without taking steps to whitewash the embarrassing situation. Beyond ordering the Cheka to infiltrate the ARA, Lenin launched a preemptive political strike against Hoover's men, declaring on 2 August 1921 in a public decree to the "workers of the world" that "the capitalists of all countries . . . seek to revenge themselves on the Soviet Republic. They are preparing new plans for intervention and counterrevolutionary conspiracies." Before they had even gone to work alleviating the Volga famine, Hoover's aid workers were to be placed under suspicion of "counterrevolutionary" activities.[12]

Lenin handpicked the propagandists in charge of this smear campaign from his old Zimmerwald Left circle. As a sort of foreign corollary to the "nonpartisan" Russian Pomgol, he named his Polish lieutenant Karl Radek and his German friend Willi Münzenberg to front a new "Foreign Committee for the Organization of Worker Relief for the Hungry in Soviet Russia," with the ever-useful figurehead Clara Zetkin added to the mix as "honorary chairwoman." Nominally the new committee was split in two, with Radek in charge in Moscow and Münzenberg to take the reins for the European branch in Berlin; but since the objective was to disguise the Kremlin's hand in the campaign, it is likely that Lenin meant for Münzenberg's Berlin office to run the show. Münzenberg's mission was to distract attention from Hoover's "bourgeois" aid efforts by directing a widely publicized campaign to collect relief funds from "workers," even while subtly selling the famine itself as evidence of the diabolical designs of western "capitalist" governments to sabotage the Soviet regime by starving its citizens.[13]

The new assignment provided badly needed balm to Münzenberg's sagging ego during a difficult summer in which he had lost control over the Communist Youth International. Lenin's young protégé set out immediately to make the famine whitewash campaign his own. Shortly after he returned to Berlin from the Third Comintern Congress in early August, Münzenberg advertised an exploratory conference of European left notables in the Hotel Baltie, to which representatives of "proletarian" (but not necessarily Communist) organizations, such as independent unions, were ostentatiously invited.

Münzenberg's public appeal on 12 August 1921 to "join the aid campaign," though, was a bit presumptuous, as many non-Communist European union leaders had already been organizing relief drives without Communist help. If anyone should have been giving orders that month, it was by all rights Edo Fimmen, secretary of the Amsterdam-based International Federation of Trade Unions, who had a successful track record of relieving food shortages in central Europe dating back to winter 1918. At the time of Münzenberg's appeal, in fact, Fimmen was already negotiating details with the Russian embassy in Berlin regarding a shipment of food aid he had already put together through his unions. Fimmen, an imposing former Dutch oil executive, towered physically over the diminutive Münzenberg, as the latter learned to his chagrin when they met on 13 August to discuss the new "aid" venture: Fimmen slapped Münzenberg "cheerfully" on the back and suggested he leave famine relief to the trade unionists.[14]

With typical bravado, the young German organizer made no effort to defer to his more experienced rival in the Hotel Baltie. Little matter that Fimmen already had funds, foodstuffs, and thousands of loyal activists at his disposal; Münzenberg had a mandate from the Moscow Kremlin, which authorized him to assemble "all worker organizations, unions, and comrades" on earth into "a unified aid campaign," and he was going to do this with or without Fimmen's help. Münzenberg therefore insisted on absolute loyalty to his new committee, which was to funnel all cash contributions collected internationally through Germany, where foodstuffs and medicines would be purchased before being transported to the Volga region. To counter Fimmen's inevitable suspicions that he was fronting some new Muscovite scheme to infiltrate Europe's independent labor unions, Münzenberg disingenuously assured him that "no political motivation on the part of the Comintern whatsoever" lay behind the new initiative, but merely "the truly terrible emergency" facing twenty million Russian famine sufferers.[15]

Fimmen had heard such fine phrases before, and he was not about to declare loyalty to Münzenberg's committee without getting some guarantees. No matter what his unions did, Fimmen complained, they were denounced by Communists everywhere as "social patriots" and "social traitors," and he was wary of working with the "same people" who had "up to the present time always slandered and attacked us." Just recently, Fimmen had written to ECCI in Moscow and to the Russian unions directly to inquire about contributing to the Volga relief effort. These polite entreaties had been "met with slanders." Perhaps, Fimmen's assistant Oudegeest playfully suggested, Münzenberg had "heard nothing" of these insults, being too young to know about such things. But how, Fimmen feared, were outsiders to know that agreements they reached with Zetkin and Münzenberg in Berlin would be honored by "Zinoviev, Chicherin" and their ilk in Moscow?[16]

Tellingly, Münzenberg danced around these insinuations without ever directly responding to them. "It would be very difficult for you," he admonished his skeptical Dutch rivals to the laughter of the Communists present at the table, "to bring forward real proof that lies or slanders against the Trade Union International were propagated officially by the Comintern or the Russian government." This cynical "denial" Oudegeest viewed as too "ridiculous" to be worthy of retort; and so Münzenberg was allowed to continue pouring on the humbug. The only way to bring the various factions of the Left together in the aid campaign, he claimed, was to schedule yet another international conference—at which Fimmen's Trade Union International would be joined by Europe's Socialist parties, who would then all agree to send all the money they collected to Berlin.[17]

But why should non-Communist organizations accustomed to bitter Communist invective against their "opportunism" give their money to Münzenberg? If centralization of the international Volga aid efforts was truly imperative, Fimmen reasonably suggested, why not insist that funds be channeled through his own secretariat in Amsterdam, whose track record was proven? (In fact something like this transpired less than a week later, when Ramsay MacDonald, secretary of the so-called "Two and a Half" or "Vienna" Socialist International, responded to Münzenberg's invitation to join forces with the Berlin committee by vowing to send all of his funds instead through Fimmen in Amsterdam.) Fimmen's refusal to pledge loyalty to Münzenberg occasioned an icy accusation from Münzenberg's KPD colleague Wilhelm Koenen, who told the Dutch trade union secretary, "you have taken a very grave responsibility on yourself" for perpetuating the divisions still hampering the famine relief efforts. Fine, Fimmen understandably retorted, and "we will assign this responsibility to you." With this exchange of mutually irrefutable accusations, the meeting in the Hotel Baltie sputtered finally to a close.[18]

It is characteristic of the personality of Willi Münzenberg that, despite the total lack of common ground he had reached with Edo Fimmen on issues of substance, the two became fast friends and would continue corresponding for years after this seemingly hostile encounter. Somehow Münzenberg knew how to express contempt with a smile, to brush off fundamental dis-

Selling the Famine

agreements as trivial, to win over rivals personally even as he ignored their complaints and repeatedly demanded the impossible of them without ever coming close to gaining their true consent. In part this was a simple matter of chutzpah—during his long war of words with the Swiss prosecutor's office in 1918, Münzenberg had won the grudging respect of his interlocutors even as he exasperated them with his brazen demands and frequent lies. At the Hotel Baltie, what seems to have won Fimmen over is Münzenberg's cheerful open-door policy toward even noncommittal allies. The two men had agreed on nothing concrete, and yet Fimmen did not rule out holding further meetings with the "Münzenberg committee," as he revealingly called it at one point (only to be corrected by the other delegates, who reminded him that Münzenberg represented a "Foreign Committee" of the Russian government). Dealing with the Russians was, for Fimmen at least, a less appealing prospect than dealing with Willi Münzenberg.[19]

Still, it was hardly encouraging that Münzenberg's new "fundraising" committee was racked by infighting over control of its cash flow—before the cash even started flowing. Clearly little, if any, funding would be forthcoming from party outsiders; but Münzenberg had not won over Communist Party insiders yet, either. Ostensibly his new committee could claim any monies raised by national Communist parties based on its Kremlin mandate to unite international fund-raising efforts, but Fimmen's refusal to cooperate could easily imperil Münzenberg's credibility. Münzenberg took this possibility seriously, and in fact blamed Fimmen in his first circular to the Communist parties of Europe, dispatched on 18 August 1921, for the delay in getting his committee off the ground. Formally at least, the KPD endorsed Münzenberg's new venture at a party congress in late August, but it would be stretching the truth to say the party brass were impressed with what his committee offered. Not until Münzenberg met with members of the KPD Zentrale personally on 1 September did they finally agree to publicize the hunger relief drive in the party press. It is reasonable to assume, meanwhile, that they did so reluctantly. *Rote Fahne* ran only one brief notice advertising Münzenberg's committee on 2 September 1921, then dropped the issue. Before long, Münzenberg was blaming the KPD as fervently as Fimmen for hampering his propaganda efforts.[20]

From Münzenberg's dispatches to his bosses in Moscow in the early days of the Volga campaign, one gets the impression that the Berlin office spent more time searching for scapegoats for its own ineptitude than raising funds for the famine sufferers. Aside from Fimmen and the KPD, there was ECCI itself, which, Münzenberg complained early in September, had come through with "neither directives, nor instructions, nor [agitprop] material, nor articles, nor [even] the brochures Radek promised [us]; in short, [we have received] nothing."[21] With materials expected from Moscow missing and party publicity lacking, Münzenberg was forced to do his own agitprop, which created the unfortunate impression that his committee was raising funds merely in order to advertise itself. "The broad working masses," he wrote to Zinoviev on 21 September 1921, "would not understand ... if we were collecting [their] pfennigs on the one hand, and on the other spending great sums for posters and other printed materials." Non-Communist workers, it seems, were already suspicious of the ostensibly "nonpartisan" nature of Münzenberg's front committee, declining to collaborate in the fund-raising campaign due to the feeling that, by doing so, they would "be strengthening the Communist Party."[22] Paradoxically, more overt KPD involvement was needed in Münzenberg's propaganda efforts, so as to keep the hands of his own committee members clean. Already the Communists were irrevocably associated in German workers' minds with Soviet Russia, and, Münzenberg observed in frustration in early October, there was "a strong anti-Russian voice" influencing the masses of SPD and USPD workers. This, too, helped explain his committee's inability to stimulate much interest in the Volga famine in Germany.[23]

Things weren't much better elsewhere in Europe. In a circular addressed to national Communist Party leaders on 9 September 1921, Münzenberg wrote angrily that, with the partial exception of France, "little has been done [anywhere]."[24] Frustrated by the lack of response to his appeals, Münzenberg's rhetoric grew more shrill, pitching his relief campaign as nothing less than a preemptive strike against Franco-Polish preparations for "military intervention against Soviet Russia" which depended on Russia's continued weakness.[25] Still the parties failed to respond, and without their help, collections by "Münzenberg" committees for the Volga famine barely inched along. In nearby Czechoslovakia, for example, a positively anemic total of about ten thousand crowns, or about eight dollars at the going rate of exchange, had been collected by October.[26]

More substantial sums were being raised by Communists in the wealthier countries of western Europe, but they were hesitating before turning it over to Münzenberg. The French party, which had collected a million francs by late October, or nearly $150,000, preferred to buy supplies themselves rather than send them to Berlin.[27] To rally flagging spirits, Münzenberg convened a kind of emergency meeting, at which he ordered emissaries to visit Scandinavia, the Balkans, and Italy, where the campaign had never really begun.[28] Fund-raising in Germany, at least, did pick up somewhat, when a special "collections week" (which the KPD refused to publicize, to Münzenberg's great embarrassment) kick-started at least some token Communist interest in the Volga famine.[29]

By 20 October 1921, Münzenberg was able to report to Moscow that nearly two and a half million deutschmarks, or about twelve thousand dollars, had been turned over to his committee for the purchase of food and medicine.[30] On this date the first ship with 350 tons of aid supplies purchased by Münzenberg's committee finally set sail from Hamburg—slightly more than two months after his relief campaign was launched.[31] By contrast, the first ARA ship, laden with over 700 tons of food rations ready for immediate distribution, had been sent off as soon as Hoover had reached his agreement with the Soviet authorities in late August and arrived in Petrograd on 1 September—and this ship was the first of hundreds more ARA vessels to arrive that autumn.[32]

Boris Souvarine, the tart-tongued French Communist Party secretary whose propensity for making independent, honest judgments would soon get him sacked by Moscow, painted a devastating picture of the impotence of Münzenberg's committee in a letter he sent to Zinoviev from Berlin in October. Souvarine's suspicions had already been raised in France, the one country in Europe in which Communists had actually raised serious money for the Volga famine. In Paris, Münzenberg's October "action week" initiative had struck everyone as superfluous in light of the preparations under way for a major fund-raising event timed to coincide with the anniversary of the Russian Revolution in early November. With so many "special events" on the docket, Souvarine complained, "[our] speechmakers are out of breath, [our] newspapers don't know what to say anymore, and the public grows tired of meetings where no one learns anything new." Meanwhile contrary instructions about relief operations were arriving from ECCI in Moscow, which had told the national parties that grain was supposed to be purchased directly, and Münzenberg's group in Berlin, which insisted on straight cash donations, used to purchase grocery items (flour, sugar, meat, fat, milk, beans, cocoa, etc.) in Germany.

As confused as things were in Paris, though, Souvarine was simply shocked to witness the incompetence on display in Berlin. In typical Münzenberg style, the Berlin committee had begun publishing a "news" bulletin before it had actually done anything. By mid-October 1921, it was publishing no less than three bulletins a week. "No one," Souvarine observed, read this bulletin, and there was in his view little point in publishing it, especially in light of the fund-raising record of the Germans, which was the poorest in all of Europe. Offended by Souvarine's lack of tact, the Germans on Münzenberg's committee refused to abandon the famine bulletin (although they grudgingly agreed to scale production back to one issue a week). Overall, Souvarine found Münzenberg's committee emblematic of all that was wrong in international Communism generally: there were "too many commissions and committees working on the same projects, all ignoring one another and what the others are doing."[33]

One has to admire Münzenberg's audacity, though. Each week in the fall of 1921 he sent more bad news to Moscow, more evidence of his committee's utter futility, and yet this did not prevent him from asking ECCI for more money. In a particularly downbeat October letter to Zinoviev and Radek, Münzenberg complained about his meager office budget, which prevented him from hiring enough help to take the administrative load off his own shoulders or to free him for needed foreign travel.[34] Aside from the remarkable admission here that his fund-raising committee needed outside funding to function normally, this letter reveals volumes about Münzenberg's spending priorities: executive staff support and international travel came first. Next, we may assume based on his insistence on publishing a bulletin no one was reading, came propaganda. Certainly famine relief came last. Not only had the meager funds raised by Münzenberg's committee failed to underwrite any actual aid shipments during its first two months, but Münzenberg confessed before the first ship sailed on 20 October that he had all but exhausted the fund-raising possibilities in central Europe. In Berlin itself barely four hundred thousand marks, or about two thousand dollars, had been collected, and yet in attaining even this modest sum, Münzenberg claimed, he had "nearly reached the boundaries of the possible."[35]

Münzenberg's approach to a special famine fund-raising day, scheduled to coincide with the Russian Revolution anniversary on 7 November, splendidly illustrated both his shamelessness and his utter failure to galvanize the working masses his committee supposedly represented. With the parties dragging their feet and Fimmen (as always) refusing to play along with his plans, Münzenberg sought to win attention by boldly inverting the usual logic of radical labor agitation. Instead of asking workers to take to the streets to celebrate the advent of the world's first "proletarian dictatorship," he demanded they remain on the job on 7 November—and give their earnings from that day to him. This was a nifty idea, and it had Moscow's approval. But the parties weren't biting, least of all the KPD, which was still smarting from a failed uprising in March 1921 that had cost the party millions of dues-paying members, and was hoping itself to ride the Russian Revolution anniversary celebrations back to financial solvency through "a whole series of other fund-raising [events]."[36]

At the very least, Münzenberg hoped the KPD would help advertise an array of plays, concerts, and other artistic events he had planned for Sunday 6 November, the day before the Revolution anniversary. But Münzenberg's daily communiqués to the party brass in late October were roundly ignored, and no help came. On Friday 28 October, Münzenberg at last succeeded in getting a verbal promise from the editors of *Rote Fahne*, on the phone, to publicize the planned famine relief events in that weekend's issue, but even this promise was broken. In the event, Münzenberg's grand schemes for the anniversary came to naught. Even the scheduled send-off of his committee's second aid shipment was postponed, due (he claimed) to last-minute delays in receiving promised supplies from Switzerland and the Netherlands—and ultimately no recourse was left to Münzenberg but to blame others for his failure. The KPD, he at last found himself "forced" to report to ECCI, had not devoted its formidable party apparatus "for even one day" to his famine relief campaign.[37]

In Münzenberg's defense, it must be conceded that he faced significant competition getting attention in the European political climate of fall 1921. The situation in Germany, with inflation raging and the Communist party reeling from a series of botched putsches going back to the Spartacist uprising of 1919, was only an extreme example of the economic and political devastation still gripping the Continent after the ravages of World War I. It was hard for European workers, themselves struggling just to put food on the table, to get too excited by tales of starvation in the Volga region thousands of miles away—and those who did exhibit interest in the Russian famine were for the most part already giving whatever money they could to Fimmen's Trade Union International or its affiliates. Münzenberg's orbit, no matter what he pretended to the contrary, was still confined to Communist voters and sympathizers, and even these were distracted by issues closer to home. European Communists were, for the most part, too preoccupied with their own fund-raising problems to care much about Münzenberg's.

The exception that best proved this rule was the United States, where Communist sympathizers, with no domestic political possibilities of note, flooded the New York City–based "Münzenberg" committee with mountains of cash, to Münzenberg's own great surprise. The fund-raising well in Europe may already have been running dry, but across the Atlantic it was positively overflowing. The Münzenberg-affiliated "Friends of Soviet Russia" committee (FSR), founded in early August 1921, literally raised more money in its first two months than it knew what to do with. As of 15 October 1921, more than $125,000 had been collected, of which about $65,000 had already been used to purchase famine relief supplies, with roughly $8,000 sunk on top of this into agitprop and administrative expenses—leaving an astounding total of $50,000 just sitting idly in the bank, at a time when Münzenberg had yet to raise $10,000 in all of Europe.[38] More astonishingly, this cash was arriving in the form of thousands of spontaneous individual and small-group donations—some for as little as fifty cents—whereas the far less impressive sums Münzenberg was collecting in Europe came principally from large, established union organizations. Despite little help from organized labor, FSR committees spread across America in 1921, with local branch offices opening up in Boston, Philadelphia, Baltimore, Chicago, Cleveland, Kansas City, Seattle, and even smaller cities like Rochester, Erie, and Salt Lake City. With the tiny American Communist Party still only an irrelevance in American politics, the Volga famine cause struck a powerful chord with charitable Americans sympathetic to the Russian Revolution.[39]

It is impossible to know exactly what motivated all of these Americans to donate money to FSR during a period when the United States, coming down hard from a wartime production boom, was suffering through a serious economic downturn. Some of these donors at least, we may surmise, combined a humanitarian interest in the starving peasants of Soviet Russia with a strong hostility toward Hoover's ARA and the other "bourgeois" charities (such as the Quakers, the Federated Council of the Churches of Christ, and the American Red Cross) who were also raising funds for Volga famine relief. FSR's slogan, as prescribed by Münzenberg's Berlin Secretariat in line with Lenin's own preemptive decree impugning the ARA on 2 August 1921, was "Famine Relief Without Counter-Revolutionary Conditions." "Give," explained the letterhead on which FSR appeals were printed, "not only to feed the starving, but to save the Russian Workers Revolution. Give without imposing imperialistic and reactionary conditions as do Hoover and others."[40]

FSR thus followed the line of the *New Republic* and the *Nation* (in whose pages it frequently advertised) in assailing the ARA for extinguishing the flames of Bolshevism in postwar Europe. This argument was dramatically visualized in a none too subtle FSR cartoon titled "The Hoover Plan!" which featured a brawny, overweight Hoover-ogre, sporting a grotesquely unfashionable "Uncle Sam" top hat, as he offers a tiny food package to an impoverished worker with "Soviet Russia" printed on his overalls, while concealing a bloody dagger behind his back. In the bottom right corner we see where the blood issued from: the mangled corpse of a young proletarian representing "Soviet Hungary." Such aggressively anticapitalist cartoons may have appealed to the various immigrant left groups—Finnish Socialist Clubs, Progressive Societies of Lithuanians, Estonian Workers' Alliances, etc.—which proved the most reliable contributors to the FSR.[41]

Not all of the FSR's supporters, though, were radical East European exiles, and it would be unfair to the many generous donors moved by humanitarian sentiment to imply that Münzenberg's cynical anti-Hoover smear campaign lay behind FSR's striking fund-raising success. Perhaps in response to donors' complaints, FSR toned down the nasty rhetoric late in 1921, dropping the negative slogans about "counterrevolution" and instead focusing in its agitprop literature on its own positive endorsement from the Soviet regime.[42] To some of the Bolsheviks' American sympathizers, this government endorsement, reinforced by the attractive moniker "Friends of Soviet Russia," may have been seen as a stamp of authenticity Hoover and his American Relief Administration simply couldn't match. How else are we to explain spontaneous gifts such as the following, which was reported to Moscow by a stunned FSR representative early in 1922: "An individual came to the office today, took $1,000 in cash out of his pocket, said 'anonymous' and walked out. Several days ago a farmer-preacher came in, gave us his wife's $500 pltinum [sic] diamond watch. All over the country such incidents occur."[43]

At the root of the FSR's success in the United States was a methodical work ethic that Münzenberg would have loved to duplicate if he could. Nearly everything the FSR did issued right from the Münzenberg playbook, with the difference that in New York, there were a lot more money and voluntary man-hours to be had than in destitute postwar Berlin. The Friends of Soviet Russia merged Münzenberg's key organizational principles—regular newsletters distributed to committee members, reams of redundant-sounding "special" collection events, and above all the centralization of the cash flow—with American pluck and can-do cheer, which meant that impossible-sounding directions from FSR headquarters were actually followed. The men composing the national FSR leadership were Communist sympathizers, but they were also respectable professionals, for the most part doctors and lawyers, who kept scrupulous accounts and earned the confidence of FSR's activists and donors. FSR circulars softened blatant demands for cash with a reassuringly bland, all-American tone of organizational professionalism:

> Money is the thing to go after just now. Push the contributions lists.... Having collected the funds, send them in promptly. Immediate wholesale shipments are needed or millions will die. Urge quick action all round. All contributions

will be receipted for at once and published acknowledgements will be made. A monthly statement will be issued and attested to by a Certified Public Accountant.... all checks and money orders to be made payable to Dr. Jacob W. Hartmann, Treasurer.

The swift pace of collections in the United States testifies to the effectiveness of such appeals, which commanded an obedience Münzenberg could only have dreamed of in Berlin.

FSR leaders also came up with a few original collection schemes, wholly in the spirit of the kinds of agitprop Münzenberg had mastered in wartime Switzerland, but with an American twist. Thus the dual fund-raising/propaganda whammy of wearable "FRIENDS OF SOVIET RUSSIA" buttons, which FSR sold for ten cents apiece at charity events ("Not only do they bring in funds, they also advertise your relief campaign"). Local FSR branches receiving perishable food surpluses from America's overproducing farms were encouraged to resell them for cash.[44] One American propaganda innovation that particularly impressed Münzenberg was the sale of "theme" stamps to the famine relief campaign. As soon as he learned of this, he wrote to Bela Kun at Comintern headquarters, asking that Moscow furnish him with old stocks of both tsarist and Soviet Russian stamps that he might sell to stimulate interest in the Volga famine.[45]

Such innovations were badly needed in Europe, where the fund-raising by Münzenberg committees remained anemic. At an international conference Münzenberg convened in Berlin early in December, the Austrian delegate, Paul Friedländer, spoke for many when he suggested the whole campaign should be "liquidated" rather than risk further political embarrassment. And yet, as Münzenberg's "honorary chairwoman," Clara Zetkin, pointed out to Friedländer in a rare moment of candor, the Volga campaign was not about "philanthropy" at all, but was rather "a question of revolutionary solidarity, of politics." Leaders of Münzenberg committees who fretted about low fund-raising totals were missing the point: their job was not to collect cash, but to publicize the famine and all it portended for the future of Soviet Russia, and by extension, the global proletariat.[46]

To this end, at the Berlin conference Münzenberg proposed a broad array of gung-ho, American-style propaganda initiatives to liven up the boring fund drives that had so conspicuously failed to inspire Old World "proletarians." All across Europe, he ordered, Communists should organize Christmas collection weeks, hitting up party members for holiday gifts to their starving Russian comrades; they should pin up relief posters, designed by the German artist and Communist sympathizer Käthe Kollwitz, on the win-

Selling the Famine

dows of bookstores and smoke shops where prosperous, fashionable Europeans often did their Christmas shopping; and they should stake out grocery stores, where patrons would be asked to contribute canned goods and other nonperishable items. Once the Comintern came through on its long-ago promise to send Münzenberg a huge cache of pictures taken in the famine region, then photographic exhibits should be organized to publicize the relief campaign. Some of these photos could also be used to spruce up an illustrated monthly magazine Münzenberg had launched in Berlin late in November called *Sowjet-Russland im Bild* (Soviet Russia in Pictures), which he promised later to reproduce in different languages when sufficient funding and materials were available. Russian stamps, ordered from Comintern headquarters, could be sold to raise cash and visibility. The Soviet government had also promised to supply film footage from the famine areas, which Münzenberg hoped to show at festivals for a profit.[47]

The trouble with such optimistic plans was that they assumed the existence of a pool of competent, enthusiastic collaborators that still wasn't there. Uncut Volga famine film footage arrived as requested in mid-December, but it was not to Münzenberg's liking and the money he needed to rent time in the well-equipped but expensive editing studios in Berlin-Babelsberg was not forthcoming from Moscow.[48] The starving-Russians aesthetic was going over well in neither bourgeois nor proletarian neighborhoods during the holiday season. In most districts, Münzenberg reported to Radek three days before Christmas, "people want to know absolutely nothing about this [famine] crap."[49] The Russian stamps, at least, arrived early in January, but the promised photographs from Moscow got lost in the mail, leaving Münzenberg with little new material to fill his illustrated monthly.[50] And relations between Münzenberg's committee and the KPD leadership deteriorated even further in winter 1921–22, with *Rote Fahne* continually refusing to publicize the famine relief drive, to the point where Münzenberg complained that the newspaper was deliberately "sabotag[ing]" his campaign.[51]

It was not in Münzenberg's nature, however, to admit defeat. Both the FSR and his most successful European fund-raising affiliates—the French, Dutch, and Italians—insisted on buying their own supplies and sending them directly to Russia, instead of sending cash to Berlin. This didn't stop Münzenberg, though, from taking credit for such shipments in his agitprop literature. In fact Münzenberg went so far as to count sums collected by Communist party organizations acting independently of his committee, along with monies raised by Fimmen's Trade Union International, which actively refused to associate with Berlin, in the greatly inflated fund-raising totals he published in his committee bulletin. Through a relentless correspondence with Communist colleagues, Münzenberg was able to get recalcitrant national parties to begin sending some money to Berlin in early 1922, but the sums they coughed up were minuscule. Communists in Amsterdam, for example, sent Münzenberg 4,850 Dutch guilders, or around $2,000, a sum comparable to the total amount raised in Berlin in autumn 1921 but which represented less than 2 percent of the amount the Dutch party had collected. The French and Italians were not quite as stingy, but they, too, turned over less than a tenth of their Volga aid revenue.[52]

Whichever way you looked at it, the money arriving at Münzenberg's Berlin office represented the merest trickle of the global fund-raising efforts for the Volga famine, but in his propaganda literature he somehow made it sound like a mighty stream. "500 Million—½ Billion Marks raised through the Foreign Committee to Aid the Starving in Russia" blared the cover headline of Münzenberg's international bulletin in German, French, and English in late April 1922—a total that shrank precipitously if you read through the fine print. In fact barely thirty million marks of this had ever made its way to Berlin, and even this total was misleading due to the runaway German inflation. In hard currency terms Münzenberg's take was a not very impressive-sounding $100,000 U.S., or roughly one six-hundredth the amount raised by Hoover's ARA, the organization Münzenberg had been hired to upstage and malign.[53]

But who read the fine print? Certainly not Münzenberg's overseers in Moscow, who were anyway less concerned with the cash flow in Berlin than in how the campaign was being publicized. And Münzenberg's publicity output wasn't bad. His American affiliates weren't sending much money directly to Berlin, but their fund-raising cornucopia was all over the Communist press and even the mainstream newswires, especially after Hoover began attacking the FSR for using the famine to spread Soviet propaganda, thereby sparking a war of words that splashed onto the front page of the *New York Times* in February.[54] Münzenberg's illustrated monthly *Soviet Russia in Pictures,* meanwhile, followed the hunger bulletin in attaining trilingual publication in June 1922, in an issue which also saw the first actual photos of aid facilities funded by Münzenberg's committee in the Volga region, some ten months after the campaign began. Considering the fact that *Soviet Russia in Pictures* still had no paying advertisers and thus was probably not being read by anyone other than Münzenberg's friends and collaborators, trilingual publication was a dubious achievement, but it was something. Illustrated famine pictorials, American media scandals, phantom fund-raising figures in the billions—Münzenberg's numbers may not have checked out, but his committee was certainly gaining in visibility.[55]

The shrewdest move Münzenberg made in promoting his committee was doubtless his diversion of aid revenues to support a team of loyalists who looked after his interests in Moscow. Things were, at first, slow getting off the ground back in Russia, since relief supplies from Berlin were so long in coming. Once the first official Foreign Committee shipment arrived in Petrograd in November 1921, the Russian government placed buildings at Münzenberg's disposal in Petrograd and Moscow for processing the aid. Franz Jung, a German writer who had moved to Russia to work in the Comintern's press department, assembled a makeshift staff befitting the title of Münzenberg's Foreign Committee from the ranks of former German and Austrian prisoners of war who had won their freedom by vowing fidelity to the Bolsheviks in 1918. Jung had good contacts, both in the Cheka (though Alexander Eiduk, a Latvian intelligence officer recently appointed to the impressive-sounding position of "Representative Plenipotentiary of the Russian Socialist Federated Soviet Republic to All Foreign Relief Organizations") and in Red Army intelligence (the GRU), which had taken Jung on a special guided tour of the famine regions before he set up shop in Moscow. Münzenberg began sending cash to Moscow in December 1921 to grease the wheels of Jung's growing operation, and expressed full confidence in Jung in his communiqués to ECCI.[56]

Jung had little in the way of administrative experience, but his political instincts were acute, and the operation he masterminded in Russia was nothing if not political. With Eiduk's help, Jung secured transport lines going directly to the most visible urban areas in the famine zone, which were not incidentally home to the kinds of "proletarians" so beloved of Communists. Hoover could go ahead and feed millions of Volga peasants; Münzenberg's committee would take care of the much smaller number of skilled workers. Jung therefore routed food and medical supplies from Petrograd to industrial cities such as Kazan, where packing materials, sledge runners, carriage wheels, hatchets, and locks were traditionally produced; Orenburg, home to leather and metal factories; Saratov, a mecca of textile manufacturing; and the coal-mining towns of Chelyabinsk and Samara. The idea was to feed and clothe targeted groups of unemployed laborers, who could then be put back to work when their health improved, and to put their offspring in special showcase children's homes to be used in promoting the image of Münzenberg's committee abroad.

Such a program offered the advantage of being very limited in scope.

This was especially important in light of the modest distribution capacity of Jung's men, who proved incapable even of handling the tiny amounts of supplies Münzenberg sent to Petrograd. Of the 230 freight cars of aid materials sent to Russia through Münzenberg committees by 1 January 1922, Jung turned over nearly half to the Russian Red Cross, whose transport and distribution capacity was far greater. He divided the remainder between Kazan, Orenburg, Saratov, Samara, Chelyabinsk, and several smaller industrial cities.[57]

And yet even this smaller amount proved difficult for Jung's people to handle. En route to Orenburg, for example, one entire train car filled with sugar got wet, and when the sugar was later dried out, it turned "hard as stone" and was thus inedible. Other cars laden with wheat flour and corn arrived rotten and had to be thrown out. The little produce that made it to Orenburg in edible shape had to be turned over to the local authorities for further distribution, as only one Jung employee had accompanied the transport train, and he was unable to follow up on the entire shipment. Still, enough aid somehow got through to open up two high-profile children's homes, named according to Münzenberg's instructions after Karl Liebknecht and Rosa Luxemburg, which were soon housing, feeding, and schooling about two hundred young Russians from working-class families. Jung also sent cash to subsidize new jobs for the children's parents in Orenburg's leather factories, and by summer 1922, eighteen color photographs of the operation had been sent back to Berlin.[58]

In every substantial way, the Münzenberg-Jung relief operation paled in comparison to Hoover's, but then, Münzenberg's goals in the famine relief campaign were not about substance. Where ARA worked in terms of speed and volume, bringing grain and seed in bulk to relieve as many starving Russians as possible as quickly as possible, Münzenberg wanted his people to include among their much less voluminous supplies perishables (meat and milk) and luxuries such as sugar, which raised the spirits of the few Russians lucky enough to receive them but did nothing for the millions who didn't.

The objective, of course, was to create attractive scenes of happy well-fed workers and "worker children" which could be photographed and disseminated in Münzenberg's media organs in the West. Münzenberg took this goal one step further in spring 1922, promoting the sale of special aid packets, each equipped with ten kilograms of fleshy food items fit for proletarians (flour, sausage, bacon, meat conserves, dried milk, sugar, tea), which could be purchased by Communist sympathizers for individual famine sufferers.

This idea proved modestly popular, especially in France, Germany, and Argentina, where most of the nearly ten thousand dollars worth of aid packets sold over the next year were purchased. Aid packets certainly made for good publicity, regardless of the fact that Münzenberg was never able to produce receipts proving that any of them had reached their intended beneficiaries, as the French, among others, later complained.[59]

Ultimately Münzenberg resolved to limit the scope of Jung's aid operation to a segment of politically marketable proletarian children small enough (twenty thousand) to be adopted permanently by the Berlin relief committee.[60] This population was only the tiniest fraction of the eleven million people Hoover's ARA was feeding daily by spring 1922, but then Hoover's goal was to beat the famine—a feat successfully achieved that summer, when reports of starvation in the Volga region virtually ceased—while Münzenberg's was to milk it politically for as long as possible. With Jung's foreign aid workers looking after their nourishment, housing, and schooling in Marxist doctrine, these young proletarians became poster children of international Communism, their faces plastered across the pages of Münzenberg's illustrated "workers' pictorial" as symbols of the new Russia.[61]

The children's parents, too, were fed by Jung's operation, but in their case the key propaganda objective lay not in the feeding itself, but in putting them back to work. To this end Münzenberg began diverting cash from the general collection fund in winter 1921–22 to purchase needed machine tools, spare parts, agricultural equipment, and the like which could be sent to Russia, and picked up the travel costs of Western specialists who would accompany the factory equipment east. It is unclear whether he had formal authorization from Moscow to do this. There is evidence, in fact, that the scheme was cooked up by Münzenberg and Jung together, without Comintern approval.[62]

In any case, Jung undoubtedly showed impressive initiative in helping to reopen defunct factories and mechanize dilapidated farms in the famine zone, whoever was authorizing him to do so. In most cases this meant using famine aid as a quid pro quo for a share of future factory output, on the principle that Jung's employees, by "providing raw material and food which enables the work to be done," were entitled to "part of the production." Thus Jung laid claim to 50 percent of the leather produced in Orenburg's three tanneries; an undisclosed "premium" on the coal mined in Samara; a weight percentage of the heavy construction and transport equipment produced in Kazan; 60 percent of the catch at the fisheries in the Tsaritsyn region and the Donets basin; and one-third of the agricultural land and its produce in one of the German Volga communes (although the Germans stubbornly refused to turn the land over).

What Jung planned to do with these materials was not yet clear, as he freely admitted that his organization had no means of bringing them to market. Food transport to the famine regions had been provided free of charge by the Soviet authorities, but bringing finished goods back out again was another question. Perhaps the Comintern, Jung demanded, could secure "transport, taxation, and customs priveleges [sic]" that would extend the relief committee's extraterritorial status into industrial production and transport. Then Münzenberg could contract abroad with established capitalist firms to distribute Russian goods from the famine region, firms that could inject yet more capital into the Volga regions' outdated factories and thereby secure Münzenberg's position there.[63]

In many ways Jung was beginning to slip out of Berlin's control in his dealings in the Volga area. Although Münzenberg had clearly given Jung the go-ahead in the evolution of the food aid operation toward *Wirtschaftshilfe* ("industrial assistance"), he may have intended for this shift to be a limited propaganda gesture, in which efforts to bring targeted Russian factories back to life could be photographed for his workers' pictorial. In a series of carefully written letters to Zinoviev and other allies at Comintern headquarters the following July, Münzenberg began distancing himself from Jung even as he was clearly benefiting from the industrial takeovers Jung was forging in his name.[64]

It is hard to believe, though, that Münzenberg had absolutely no idea what was going on in the economically devastated Volga region, where hundreds of run-down factories were languishing idly, just waiting for someone to lay claim to them. His own protestations and those of his bosses in Moscow aside, the transformation of Münzenberg's totally unsuccessful famine relief operation into a playground for foreign aid profiteers was well under way by summer 1922, and he was doing nothing to stop it. Münzenberg may not have succeeded in sending much food aid to the Volga region, nor in blaming the famine on the West in the ranks of global public opinion. But the foreign Communists he had hired to look after his interests in Moscow had already sunk their tentacles into the chaotic Russian economy in the name of the global proletariat his committee claimed to represent, and they were not about to let go. Flush with cash skimmed off the American aid bounty and with Kremlin subsidies so secret that they remain unknown to this day, Münzenberg's men in Russia were in a prime position to stake their claim in the wild free-for-all of the early Soviet economy.

CHAPTER 7 *Building Socialism*

The Volga famine was only the most dramatic example of the social apocalypse in Soviet Russia resulting from Bolshevik policies. Much as agricultural production sank to near zero when the Kremlin stepped up its war on the peasantry after defeating the White armies in the Civil War, so too did the output of industrial and consumer goods in Russia drop precipitously in response to Moscow's efforts to ban market activity by force. Between 1918 and 1920, a series of Soviet decrees outlawed private trade and retail, while nationalizing (at least in theory) not only agriculture but also industry, mining, banking, and joint-stock companies that held concessions for foreign distribution and sales. Even money was formally abolished, and the private possession of hard currency, jewels, and other valuables was outlawed. The result of all this was economic catastrophe. Handicapped in part by a wave of strikes staged in opposition to the new regime's high-handed management methods, which crippled over three-quarters of Russia's state factories in the first six months of 1920, industrial production sank to less than 20 percent of its prewar level, and the supply of consumer goods fell even further.

Statistics, though, tell only part of the story. As the economy collapsed, civilized life virtually ceased, with the cities literally emptied of people. Half of Moscow's two million people died or disappeared, many returning to the country like Doctor Zhivago, to escape Bolshevik harassment and get closer to the food supply. Petrograd's population dropped from almost two and a half million at the time of the February Revolution to under 750,000 by autumn 1920. Those who remained had to wait in often interminable lines for food, clothing, and other essentials, which were strictly, although not always logically, rationed. Once vibrant urban streets were soon overrun with weeds, as there was no one with the energy or motivation to maintain them. State theaters all but ceased to function as their actors, artists, and musicians were sent on permanent rural tours so they could eat.[1]

Things were not much better in the countryside, where it was sometimes difficult to tell the difference between the government's own ragtag food army and the armed bands of private marauders who held up trains and pillaged towns. The Red Army demobilizations at war's end in 1920 merely compounded the chaos, with seemingly the whole country erupting in rebellion. According to the conservative estimates of the Soviet government's own intelligence apparatus, the Cheka, over one hundred separate peasant uprisings occurred in February 1921 alone, many of them eclipsing in scale the great Pugachev "bunt" rebellion of the eighteenth century. This was also the month of the naval mutiny at Kronstadt near Petrograd, which Trotsky brutally suppressed with over fifty thousand Red Army troops. In Tambov province, about two hundred miles southeast of Moscow, an anti-Bolshevik jacquerie erupted over the winter of 1920–21 which the whole population supported. Minsk and Smolensk in White Russia likewise fell to anti-Bolshevik partisans. Further east, rebel armies in the Caucasus counted thirty thousand men under arms, with an unknown number of nomadic warriors wreaking havoc along the nearby steppes between Ufa and the Caspian. Armed peasant partisans in western Siberia, near the Ural mountains, numbered over sixty thousand, and by 1921 they controlled the regions surrounding Omsk, Chelyabinsk, Tomsk, Yekaterinburg, and the Tiumen'. Everywhere the Red Army was overstretched just to hold on to its gains in the Civil War, and in many cases regular units were simply withdrawn, to be replaced gradually by Chekists who deployed a strategy of mass arrests and random executions to terrify the populace.[2]

Even the most hard-hearted Bolshevik had to concede by 1921 that, whatever the true cause of the Volga famine, the Bolsheviks' forcible economic policies had been a social disaster. On practical grounds alone, it was clear that resistance to the government's armed requisitions detachments was beginning to threaten the survival of the Communist regime. Implicitly Lenin himself admitted this when, at the Tenth Communist Party Congress in March 1921, he suggested a new course in dealing with the agricultural sector in which peasants were to fulfill their obligation to the state by paying a tax in kind, or *prodnalog*, instead of forfeiting the bulk of their output to meet requisition quotas (the *prodrazverstka*). The new course was described by Lenin's Politburo ally Lev Kamenev, in a masterfully revealing euphemism, as "introducing political tranquility to the peasantry."[3] Although armed requisitions continued that spring, Lenin's new policy allowed peasants, theoretically, to sell their own surpluses and thus cleared the ideological path for the revival of private trade and by extension, private manufactures.

Over the next year, as the Volga famine deepened, liberalization decrees started coming fast and furious from Moscow. After 19 July 1921, licenses to sell agricultural and manufactured goods could be obtained legally. In August, the market in nonmunicipal buildings was reopened, and in December private publishing houses were legalized. In April 1922 Russians were at last allowed once again to own foreign currency and precious metals including gold, and silver. The following July, all Soviet citizens over the age of eighteen were given the right to set up "small-scale manufacturing enterprises," and could contract with the free market both to buy raw materials and sell finished goods.[4] In this way the Communists came nearly full circle, legalizing virtually all private economic activities they had once banned (although the Kremlin retained control over banking, energy, and large-scale industry, which Lenin famously called the "commanding heights" of the economy). In retrospect the Bolsheviks' aggressive bans on private economic activity and their forced monopolizations during the three-year period from 1918 to 1921 acquired the aggressive-sounding label of "War Communism," while the reforms that dismantled this system came collectively to be known as the "New Economic Policy" or NEP.

Historians can argue until they are blue in the face about the true ideological meaning of NEP. One thing, however, is abundantly clear: the economic reforms of 1921–22 represented an ideological retreat no less embarrassing for the Bolsheviks than their controversial hiring of Herbert Hoover to feed the starving Volga peasants. Just to preserve his hold on power, Lenin was forced to abandon key Communist principles, granting peasants and tradesmen enough freedom to revive the free market he had tried to destroy. To kill paper inflation and restore the money economy, Lenin even had to mimic hated bourgeois values by introducing a gold-based ruble called the *chervonets*, which was backed by bullion and foreign reserves (although he promised that, once Communism had overtaken the world, gold would then be employed only for building toilets).[5] Although initially intended to be used only for debt settlements between large state concerns, the *chervontsi* were soon in regular circulation, a visible rebuke to the now abandoned Bolshevik dreams of a world free of gold and money.

Worse still, Lenin was forced to grovel before Western creditors whose help, like Hoover's, he needed in spite of himself. Everywhere the Russian economy was paralyzed by shortages of necessary materials, from food and fuel to iron and copper reserves, and these had to be purchased abroad if industrial production was ever to get off the ground. The transport sector, likewise, was in pitiful shape, and capital was desperately needed just to get the trains running reliably enough to distribute raw materials where they were required. And yet the unsavory reputation of the Bolshevik government, still viewed as an outlaw regime by the Western Allies who had until recently been trying to overthrow it, presented a serious obstacle to any kind of serious foreign investment. In part NEP was designed precisely to encourage the influx of foreign capital; yet this could hardly be openly proclaimed by a Communist regime that rejected the principles of capitalism.

So it was hardly surprising that Lenin resolved upon a policy of stealth, courting potential investors through a kind of secret economic diplomacy. The idea was to offer state "concessions" to a select group of private Western capitalists, who would then promote investment in the Russian economy by word of mouth, while also petitioning their governments to lift the trade embargoes still being enforced against the Soviet Union. As Lenin explained this policy to his aides, such concessions were the "bait" which would ensnare needed capital.

The first Westerner to fall for the bait was Armand Hammer, the son of an imprisoned American Communist, who arrived in Russia in fall 1921 carrying a letter of introduction from his father's New York–based pharmaceutical business, Allied Drug & Chemical. After accepting a concession to operate an abandoned asbestos mine in the Ural Mountains (which was in fact all but worthless), Hammer returned to the United States to spread the message to impressionable American businessmen that NEP heralded the beginning of the end of communism. What he didn't tell them was the price of his concession: the Cheka had infiltrated his business to the core.[6]

That winter, while Lenin was still waiting for publicity surrounding the ideologically suspect Hammer "concession" to work its magic in the West, his search for capital inspired even more desperate measures. A 26 February 1922 Politburo decree ordered local Soviet leaders to confiscate icons, jewelry, and other valuables from churches in their districts. While there was a flimsy pretense about helping the famine victims ("Turn Gold into Bread!" went the slogan), in reality this brutal campaign of armed robbery was designed to shore up hard currency reserves for the upcoming diplomatic conference at Genoa in April, where Lenin hoped to negotiate trade accords from a position of strength. As he explained in a top secret Politburo directive on 19 March 1922,

> We must . . . carry out the confiscation of church valuables in the most decisive and rapid manner, so as to secure for ourselves a fund of several hundred million gold rubles (one must recall the gigantic wealth of some of the monas-

teries and abbeys). Without this fund, no government work in general, no economic construction in particular, and no defense of our position in Genoa especially is even conceivable.[7]

With currency reserves finally rising due to the church confiscations and the glow of the Hammer concession beginning to attract attention in New York, the Bolsheviks felt confident enough at Genoa to spurn the Western Allies and cut a secret deal with the Germans, at nearby Rapallo, in which Berlin and Moscow renounced mutual claims arising from the war and agreed to cooperate covertly in weapons development. The German government further promised to "support and facilitate" the work of private firms that signed contracts with the Soviet government.

Rapallo may have been good nuts-and-bolts diplomacy, but it was bad politics. Internationally, Rapallo was no less embarrassing to the Kremlin than the Volga famine—a number of German Communists, for example, criticized the treaty in the Reichstag before receiving contrary instructions from Moscow—and Lenin was no more going to give German industrialists carte blanche in the Russian economy than he was going to let Hoover's aid workers or Hammer's American capitalist colleagues into his country without heavy surveillance. Just as a duplicate "proletarian" aid organization had been needed to hide the embarrassment of Hoover's role in alleviating the Volga famine, so now was an international communist front needed to camouflage the role of German and American capitalists in rebuilding the shattered Soviet economy.[8]

The obvious candidate was Münzenberg's Foreign Workers' Aid Committee, which had already begun shedding its (anyhow unsuccessful) famine relief functions in favor of Hammer-style industrial concessions. There was a kind of crude political synergy in Jung's modus operandi of shares for aid, which provided a justification for taking over potentially valuable properties from local authorities who might otherwise have resisted. Ironically, it was the ethnic Germans living on fertile land in the Volga communes who most fervently resisted the takeovers forged by Jung's German-dominated committee; local leaders of native Russian descent acquiesced much more easily to the foreign aid invaders. Jung's operation was legitimately "international" on its face: of the 180 foreign managers he hired in 1922, roughly 30 percent were German, 25 percent Hungarian, 15 percent Rumanian, 10 percent French, and 8 percent Polish, with the remainder split up among American, Norwegian, Finnish, and Swiss nationals. He could therefore stake a plausible claim to be representing the global proletariat, plausible enough at least to intimidate most skeptical natives. And the equipment Jung was able to import really did come from foreign Communists (if not literally from "proletarians")—both from Münzenberg's Berlin office and from FSR in New York, which began sending American-made Fordson tractors, bought with monies diverted from the famine relief collection windfall, to the Volga region in spring 1922.[9]

Lenin and his allies in the Politburo gave their official blessing to the rapidly evolving Münzenberg-Jung "industrial assistance" program in early April 1922, in the form of a secret start-up infusion of ten billion Soviet paper rubles *(sovznaki)*, issued directly from the Soviet Central Bank. In theory, this was only a "credit," a sort of expense account guaranteed by the Soviet government, to which title of the properties involved would also legally revert once the Münzenberg-Jung committee, usually known as "Internationale Arbeiterhilfe" or "International Worker Relief" (IAH), was dissolved.[10] In effect, the Kremlin was extending this credit to itself. The Politburo expected to retain strict control over Jung's "foreign" industrial takeovers, which were anyway devoted to Soviet propaganda. Thus it sent 240 reliable Russian Communist Party comrades to assist him in overseeing the various concerns in the Volga region, enough to outnumber the 180 foreign managers under Jung's control. The Politburo also formally subordinated the whole operation to the trusted Chekist Alexander Eiduk, who until spring 1922 had been in charge of liaison with (i.e., spying on) Hoover's ARA.[11]

Whoever had final authority to dispose of it, the sum is significant if we consider the desperate poverty of the time. Although massively distorted by the wild inflation of 1922—in the absence of any reliable tax revenue to buttress their theft of Church wealth, the Bolsheviks were printing paper rubles en masse to cover government operating expenses—the amount "lent" to Jung's operation was still comparable to the total amount the Soviet government had spent on famine relief.[12] The fact that the Bolsheviks extended it to Jung's operation, meanwhile, tells us a great deal about the bizarre logic of NEP. Rather than simply occupying more productive land and factories with the army and nationalizing them by fiat—this had been the failed strategy of War Communism—the Kremlin would subsidize a "foreign relief committee" based in Berlin to help it take control of a wide range of properties in the name of the global proletariat, while retaining ultimate title itself. In effect, the Russian Communist Politburo was trying to disguise its own dictatorship by pretending to turn nationalized property over to foreigners. And, since these foreigners answered to Lenin's loyal Zimmerwald comrade Willi Münzenberg, they could be described in Communist media organs not as foreign capitalists employing Russian workers—although this is how they were undoubtedly seen by their employees—but rather as model proletarians, helping build socialism in Soviet Russia.

Certainly these concessions were not granted on the basis of managerial competence. Neither Münzenberg, a lifelong politician, nor Jung, a writer, had any experience running businesses before 1922, and their inexperience showed. Jung began complaining of inadequate staff support as early as January 1922, when he asked Münzenberg to send more German-speaking secretaries, stenographers, and typewriters to Moscow—a request it would take Münzenberg more than four months to fulfill.[13] The IAH shipments of machine tools, tractors, and spare parts were endlessly delayed in spring 1922, in part because of strikes by German dock loaders at the Baltic port of Stettin—laborers who apparently weren't keen enough to service the needs of Münzenberg's "worker relief" committee. Ironically, labor unrest was a recurrent leitmotif in the early days of the industrial assistance campaign—both in Germany, where Münzenberg found himself stranded at one point in late winter due to a rail strike, unable to get to Moscow to lobby for the new campaign, and in Petrograd, where the boisterous dockworkers' unions demanded summer salary premiums for social insurance and compensation for the inevitable winter downtime, when the northern ports closed. "It is impossible," complained a disgruntled administrator from the IAH Petrograd branch office in summer 1922, "to work under these conditions." Such, though, were the realities of the business world, and the IAH had to face them along with everyone else.[14]

After April 1922, Münzenberg and Jung did have the advantage of bank credits backed by the full authority of the Kremlin, but this was a mixed blessing. In Communist circles, word traveled quickly that Jung's organization had cash to blow, and would-be profiteers were soon homing in on IAH concessions like bees to honey. In mid-May, Jung dispatched a certain comrade Januschek from Moscow to Nizhny-Novgorod with a shipment of milk and gift parcels, which were to be used to open up an IAH home for the children of workers in a toy factory. In early June, several truckloads of flour were sent on top of this, and a bank credit of some 180 million *sovznaki* was extended, which Januschek, along with a Hungarian comrade named Natonek, used to purchase toys and ship to America for profit. Jung had definitely not authorized this, although he thought Münzenberg might have. In any case, both men agreed by mid-June that the questionable operation best be "liquidated," and they were able to hush the matter up before it broke in the Communist press.[15]

Even bolder than Januschek was Hal Ware, an American Communist who won a concession to mechanize agriculture in the village of Toikino, near Perm at the foot of the Ural mountains. The purpose of this "Kuzbus" concession, as it was called by the American comrades who accompanied Ware to Russia, was political. The Bolsheviks wanted to create a model collective farm in the former famine region—moreover in an area that had recently been plagued by partisan anti-Communist uprisings—to symbolize the renaissance of the regime. Toikino was only one of thousands of villages that might have fit the bill, with its labor force reduced dramatically during the Civil War and famine, and so many horses killed off as well that the few citizens left had little means of plowing the fields.[16] An unspoken consideration that singled Toikino out was the locals' mildly, but not incorrigibly, negative attitude toward the Bolsheviks ("workers dissatisfied, peasants hostile," one observer noted), which made them prime material for a propaganda offensive. The Kremlin would thus send Ware and his men to Perm, along with the American tractors, at state expense, and Jung was to provide them further with food, fuel, supplies, and spare parts. Everything was set for a model propaganda operation, with donated American technology, German logistical support, and Russian peasant labor photogenically harnessed together under the auspices of the "International Worker Relief."[17]

As soon as the American tractors reached Perm, the troubles began. The low-lying land between the train station in Perm and Toikino was wet and pockmarked with streams and other obstacles. Revolution, civil war, and famine had decimated the regional infrastructure, to the point where thirty bridges were impassable. En route to Toikino, Ware and his men "mobilized" about two hundred farmers to fix the roads and bridges, offering IAH food supplies in return for the labor. On top of this unexpected expense, they had to purchase huge amounts of scarce fuel back in Perm, plus building materials to put up garages to house the tractors, along with barns, silos, and tents for the crews to live in. Everyone had to eat, too, of course, and when one factored in the fifty tons of groceries bought in nearby Kieselkop, some thirty-nine million Soviet paper rubles had been thrown into the operation before it even began. After all this, it turned out that not enough seed had been procured to start planting in summer 1922, and Ware had to turn to nearby localities for help, granting them shares in the venture in exchange for the seeds he needed to get going.[18]

If we read the one surviving letter Ware sent to Jung in Moscow from the field, meanwhile, it is not hard to guess what Ware's own objective in the operation was: to milk the IAH for everything it was worth. Despite having already spent huge amounts of IAH-fronted cash on seed, fuel, and supplies, Ware claimed in early August that more of each of them was "urgently needed," along with more tents and other household goods. Overall, he complained, "camp equipment" was "not sufficient to house a full double crew." And yet, despite facing such supply shortages and "unusually trying conditions," Ware claimed the plowing was already proceeding swimmingly, so much so that village councils from miles around were submitting requests for him to plow their land as well. If Jung would furnish the necessaries, he suggested, he could mechanize the whole region, proving to the Bolsheviks in the process that "industrial combines who control land become almost entirely independent of the peasantry."[19]

Grand collectivization schemes aside, Ware was himself clearly operating independently of the needs of the peasants. According to the report of an American Communist who worked under him, Ware treated the locals "like dogs," denying them adequate rations while his American cronies "had enough food to last them a year and more" and were "gorging themselves, overeating" on pork, bacon, and milk. Ware's buddies monopolized all the good tents, and slept on "fine beds" with "good sheets," while the Russian hands, despite a surplus of fifteen American-made mattresses that remained unused, slept on the bare ground or, at best, on "some hay" in small leaky tents. Apart from three American consultants who worked hard in the fields and were kind to the peasants, teaching them the ins and outs of mechanized farming, none of Ware's men did any work beyond bossing the Russians around with a "dictatorial and superior attitude."

Despite having contributed no capital themselves, Ware and his wife, Jessica Smith, consistently refused to acknowledge the role of either the FSR or Jung's Russian IAH in financing the operation, but rather "made it appear it was all their personal favor to the Russian people." Ware corrected one Communist who invited the peasants to eat breakfast with the Americans for failing to make clear that it was "Comrade Ware" who was issuing the invitation. Smith was even more obnoxious, insisting in early autumn that a small contingent of Russians, who had already mastered operating the tractors, be fired for "having been too proud to be her valets and for being too dignified." Ware granted her wish. Russians from nearby villages who came to see the Toikino operation out of curiosity received even worse treatment. Smith, on one such occasion, "personally chased away an inoffensive peasant with a baseball club," and followed this up by threatening to shoot "anybody, Communist or non-Communist, who came around [her] kitchen."

So overbearing was the Ware couple that rumors coursed through the surrounding area that the "American government and capitalists... had come to take our land away."[20]

Ware and his cronies were only individual bad apples, but their profiteering boded poorly for the IAH's ambitious tractor operation, which was meant to showcase Russia's industrial reconstruction for the world. To give the organization credibility in the Ural region, where most of the tractors were to be sent, the IAH children's homes were heavily concentrated there, in the urban centers of Yekaterinburg, Chelyabinsk, and in a number of smaller cities near Perm. Jung's men set up dozens of these homes, named after foreign ideological heroes such as Liebknecht, Luxemburg, Radek, and Karl Marx himself, with an eye to promoting the IAH among the local populations. With the Kremlin's subsidies, they were able to hire a sizable contingent of schoolteachers in 1922, whose job was to indoctrinate the organization's young charges in the virtues of Communism. In one showcase home named after Lenin in the town of Zlatousk, no less than fifteen instructors monitored the ideological progress of workers' children (of whom 24 percent were still "counterrevolutionary" when the IAH arrived, perfect material for a political turnaround).

No matter how many loyal ideological foot soldiers the IAH hired, though, there were always rotten low-lifes who squandered good will with their rank actions. The children's home in Yekaterinburg was an exercise in wastefulness, with uneaten rice and bread regularly thrown out without care and filthy clothes and linens left to mildew for days on end. When Edwin Hörnle, Münzenberg's old friend from Stuttgart, visited it early in 1923, he was shocked at the indifference of the IAH staff to the unsanitary conditions, under which the children had themselves grown despondent and unwilling to learn, work, or do just about anything. Many were suffering from head lice. Conditions were more pleasant at the IAH facility in Chelyabinsk, which was spread out over fifteen picturesque vacation villas—pleasant enough to attract the attention of several foreign aid ruffians. One of them, Comrade Winninger, made off with IAH cash intended for purchasing children's clothes, although not before he shocked the female IAH attendants by seducing an eighteen-year-old girl in their charge. Winninger's criminal counterpart, who may or may not have been working with him, sank even lower, raping a forty-five-year-old Russian IAH employee, a deaf and dumb mother of two children.[21]

Overall, Hörnle reported that the children's homes in the Urals were characterized by poor food rations, dirty or nonexistent clothes and bed sheets, and "embittered and worn out" employees who had no idea what they were doing. A typical, and revealing, complaint Hörnle encountered while visiting the homes was that "we are receiving no instructions, nor answers [from Moscow] to our questions." It seemingly never occurred to these Communist officials to exercise initiative in improving living conditions for the children in their care. The one relative bright spot was classroom instruction (i.e., indoctrination), which Communists clearly preferred to household management. But even in the schools, Hörnle complained, more staffers were urgently needed.

But these were mere details. A much more serious problem, in Hörnle's view, was that the IAH was not winning recognition with the Russian population. After traveling throughout the showcase IAH facilities in the Ural region on behalf of the Berlin office, Hörnle concluded that "the IAH's propaganda all over Russia has totally failed." The industrial and agricultural takeovers were premised upon the organization's ability to feed workers, but very few locals, after the whole period of the Volga famine of 1921 and the spread of permanent children's relief homes after famine's end in 1922, had even heard of the IAH. Most Russians, Hörnle observed, "know the ARA and the Red Cross." ARA posters were everywhere, and were impossible to ignore. Peasants especially were grateful to Hoover's aid organization, and whenever they came into town they went straight to the local ARA building to line up for food. But if you asked just about anyone about the IAH, "they were simply astonished [to hear that such a thing as] International Worker Relief exists." Only much more vigorous IAH agitprop, Hörnle suggested in a revealing turn of phrase, "would ... show the indifferent masses of Russia what international solidarity is."[22]

If the food-for-shares rationale for the IAH's industrial takeovers in the Ural region was increasingly questionable in light of the organization's inability to deliver the aid it promised, the concessions Jung won in Moscow and Petrograd seemed to follow no other logic than imperial whim. One gets the impression, in fact, that NEP in its early stages was in large part a simple divestiture of responsibility: the Bolsheviks, having failed in their efforts to control the entire Russian economy, were now turning over troublesome enterprises to anyone willing to take them. If this was the plan, then Jung undoubtedly showed himself a willing accomplice, taking over title to a mechanical workshop and a soap factory in Petrograd, along with an astonishing array of prime real estate in the capital.

Significantly, most of the Moscow properties were concentrated in several prestigious neighborhoods, where IAH employees would be living and working. Thus Jung's central headquarters, housed in a large prerevolutionary mansion on Tverskaia-Iamskaia, was just down the street from a restaurant, a hair salon, a food and clothing cooperative, and a woodworking shop that were all turned over to the IAH in summer 1922. On nearby Malaia Dimitrovka, the organization acquired a residential building, a car garage, a laundry facility, and an outpatient clinic for IAH employees. Choice apartments were also distributed to IAH staffers in the prestigious neighborhoods of Bol'shaia Bronnaia near the Patriarch Ponds and on Ostozhenka, along with a number of dachas in Sokolniki Park. The IAH obtained these facilities, Jung blandly explained at a staff meeting in August 1922, because of "the need for our Moscow office to expand."[23]

And expand it did. While Münzenberg's Berlin committee was still caught up sending directives to Russia concerning famine aid packages and children's homes, Jung's Moscow office was rapidly abandoning any pretense of being in the aid business, diving headlong instead into the chaos of NEP. Literally the Russian IAH headquarters began feeding on itself. In order to pay salaries for the ever-expanding executive staff (by June 1922, at two hundred and growing), several of Jung's assistants began reselling sugar and cocoa destined for the famine zone. The start-up credit of ten billion Soviet paper rubles was apparently not enough for Jung, who complained in late June 1922 that he was soon going to need that much each month, just for his own office.[24] By the end of the summer, salary expenses for the Moscow staff had shot up another 50 percent, totaling about a fourth of administrative costs for the whole Russian IAH empire, which was burning *sovznaki* at an astonishing rate of sixty billion a month. Nearly all of this cash came from the dumping of aid supplies on the black market, especially cocoa, which was fetching close to eighty million Soviet paper rubles per pood (about thirty-three pounds).[25]

When Münzenberg visited Moscow in June 1922 to check out the sprawling IAH empire, he claimed to be doing so in order to clean up Jung's administrative mess. Certainly this was part of his intention. But if we pay attention to what Münzenberg actually did (as opposed to what he said), it seems more accurate to say that he wanted to get in on the action. According to Münzenberg's own admission, no one bothered to respond to the complaints about Jung's profiteering he sent to Comintern headquarters in June and July, nor did Zinoviev or Radek give the slightest feedback on how the IAH's evolution toward "industrial assistance" was proceeding.[26] This did not stop Münzenberg, however, from acting on his own initiative. While in Moscow in June, he ordered Franz Schäfer, a German Communist, and Tangelevich, a Russian friend, to keep an eye on Jung, mandating that any official Russian IAH directives must be accompanied by the signatures of at least two of these men.[27] When he left Moscow in July, Münzenberg invited several FSR representatives to Berlin to incorporate a joint American-German firm that would take legal title to all the Russian concessions Jung had acquired to date—and any his office would acquire in the future. The parent company, christened "Industrie- und Handels-Aktiengesellschaft: Internationale Arbeiterhilfe für Sowjet-Russland" (though this moniker was soon mercifully shortened in office shorthand to "Aufbau") would be based in Berlin, but the financing would come from New York, where Juliet Stuart Poyntz, the American Communist leader who would later recruit dozens of Soviet spies on U.S. soil, was to play the role of FSR rainmaker. The aid money was in America, the fire sale of industrial, agricultural, and real estate concessions in Russia—and Münzenberg wanted a permanent piece of both.[28]

The corruption involved in the creation of "Aufbau" was staggering. First of all, the corporation was initially capitalized with the revealingly meager sum of one million deutschmarks, or about two thousand dollars at summer 1922 exchange rates, which was itself skimmed off Berlin's proceeds from the FSR fund-raising bounty. FSR and other IAH affiliates were expected to expand this modest pool of capital by floating a so-called "workers' loan"—a cash grab to be backed not by the IAH but by the Soviet government.[29] With the monies thus raised, along with the still buoyant famine aid revenues coming in from FSR, IAH would purchase "groceries, tools, machines, [and] raw materials" that might "support Russian labor relations and the condition of workers in Soviet Russia"—little matter that Münzenberg was already planning to liquidate the ineffectual aid campaign on which his whole scheme was premised.[30] In exchange for this dubious service, Münzenberg and four trusted IAH friends, including the American Juliet Poyntz, the Dutchmen John William Kruyt and Johannes Brommert, and the Italian Francesco Misiano, laid claim to any revenues produced by Jung's industrial empire, plus those that might accrue from future concessions in film, forestry, or precious minerals such as manganese.[31]

For better and for worse, Münzenberg was now knee-deep in the aid profiteering racket, and there was no going back. While he could still blame subordinates for incompetence or malfeasance, he could no longer pretend to ignorance of the IAH's sometimes ideologically questionable activities in Soviet Russia. According to Eiduk and Schäfer, Münzenberg personally sanctioned the dumping of children's clothes donated by IAH committees on the black market, which began in September 1922.[32] The reason he did so was undoubtedly to juice up the cash flow of the Russian IAH operation, which was still living way beyond its means. At an executive IAH meeting in late September 1922, in fact, Münzenberg resolved to petition the Soviet state bank for another credit, this time of one hundred billion Soviet paper rubles.[33] The idealistic workers' loan clearly offered more in the way of ideological satisfaction than ready cash—and Münzenberg needed the latter above all, to stake his claim in the Russian economy while the getting was good.

Keying in on the acquisitions game in NEP-era Russia is crucial to understanding the conflicted nature of the IAH, which in its actions was never anything remotely close to what it claimed to be in its propaganda. Tacitly Münzenberg and his collaborators revealed an awareness of the problem soon after the shift to "industrial assistance" began, when Franz Schäfer tried to establish separate "commercial" and "transport" branches inside the Russian IAH organization over the course of the summer of 1922 in order to isolate these accounts from the aid program.[34] The idea was to set up a kind of political firewall, to cut off the IAH's (potentially) profitable private ventures from its public charity mandate. In much the same way, Münzenberg had incorporated "Aufbau" to insulate the IAH from any suspicion of having a "capitalist" profit motive. But this incorporation, like Schäfer's efforts to paper over the various improprieties of Russian IAH, was mere administrative sleight of hand. In reality, all of the accounts were mixed together, and neither Münzenberg, Jung, Schäfer, nor anyone else with access to IAH revenues hesitated to spend this money entirely as they saw fit.

Even if most IAH leaders were ideologically inconsistent in practice, though, there was a certain logic to keeping up appearances. A visitor who strolled into Münzenberg's Berlin headquarters, which from summer 1922 on were housed inside the Soviet embassy on the Unter den Linden just several blocks from the Brandenburg Gate, would have had no idea that the IAH was mixed up in private commerce. Most of the staff members were idealistic volunteers, or drew a modest pay of about two or three dollars per week. Many were women, attracted to the IAH's charitable mandate. In one room, a girl from Leipzig kept files on the Russian children's homes; down the hall, another young German woman catalogued and captioned pictures from the famine zone for *Soviet Russia in Pictures*. "The place," Münzenberg's wife Babette Gross later recalled, "was a beehive. A constant stream of foreign visitors passed through the offices." To the uninformed observer —as well as to its own employees—IAH headquarters would have seemed the embodiment of everything the organization had always claimed to be, an international aid clearinghouse for famine victims in Soviet Russia.[35]

If you looked more closely, however, as early as 1922 the IAH's own propaganda indicated that a subtle transformation was under way. Even before Münzenberg began talking about "liquidating" the hunger campaign in late summer, the editors of *Soviet Russia in Pictures* were quietly abandoning famine photos of starving children, instead displaying pictures of showcase IAH industrial properties such as the Moscow boot factory and the tractors of Toikino. *The New Russia*, the book version of the illustrated monthly, interspersed photos from IAH operations together with scenes from the Revolution and Civil War in such a way as to make setbacks the Bolsheviks had faced, from the Kronstadt rebellion to the famine to the concessions of NEP, look like political triumphs. Thus the Bolsheviks' victory over the Kronstadt rebels was celebrated in two flattering Red Army action shots, serenaded by a cynical Lenin quote explaining that "oppressed classes" who failed to master the use of weapons were fated to remain "slaves." A picture of Petrograd *subbotniki*, or forced Sunday labor conscripts, was misleadingly captioned, "voluntary labor of female Communists." The Volga famine was depicted through photographs of happy worker children receiving instruction in IAH homes. NEP was represented by attractive images of IAH fisheries, farms, and tractors.[36]

In this way a durable IAH aesthetic, largely independent of the fleeting famine campaign, crystallized around the idea of Russia's industrial "reconstruction." It was a muscular aesthetic, embodied in the new title of Münzenberg's illustrated workers' monthly, which after October 1922 was known as *Hammer and Sickle*. The new Münzenberg aesthetic was trumpeted in the Soviet media in summer 1923, when a series of IAH press releases were sent around to Bolshevik organs such as *Izvestia, Pravda, Trud, Rabochaia Gazeta*, and *Economicheskaia Zhizn'* promoting the new line. To back up the promised agitprop campaign, the Russian IAH office began assembling statistics and visual evidence of current Soviet exports and imports, agricultural output, university enrollment, union activity, and the like, which could be reproduced in Münzenberg's publications in the West.[37] From now on, images of strength, growth, and vigor would dominate IAH descriptions of life in Soviet Russia. NEP, instead of an ideological retreat, would be promoted as a visionary effort to industrialize a battered, backward, yet right-thinking nation. And the IAH's own industrial assistance program symbolized not the sordid reality of private acquisition of former state properties by insider deals, but rather the collective efforts of the proletarians of the world to "build socialism."

Increasingly the IAH was a house of illusions, where up was down and vice versa. The "industrial assistance" program, much more so than the famine relief mandate, was riddled with logical contradictions. Ostensibly the new mandate allowed the IAH to import laborers from anywhere in the world to assist in rebuilding the Russian economy; but the vast majority of foreign IAH employees in Russia were not workers but managers—political commissars, basically, assigned to manage properties based on Bolshevik whim. In theory, capital was to be raised in the West by way of an authentically proletarian "workers' loan." In reality, most of the IAH's funding came directly from the Kremlin—which, in turn, had stolen much of its capital from Russia's rich and the Church—or from Communist sympathizers in the "capitalist" United States, whose generous donations in kind were often cynically dumped on the black market. Even some of the American tractors sent to the Ural region were later resold to ambitious private farmers for cash.[38] Finally, industrial assistance was meant somehow to lead to international labor solidarity and the dissolving of class tensions—and yet foreign IAH managers often mistreated their Russian workers, leading instead to greater mistrust and xenophobia.

Only a total lack of transparency in its operations prevented the IAH's mistreatment of hired hands from escalating into a full-blown scandal in the Communist world. Information about Hal Ware's misdeeds in Toikino, for example, was so thoroughly hidden from public view that Lenin himself gullibly wrote to Ware, praising his noble efforts on behalf of the Russian people.[39] Ware's reputation certainly did not suffer in American Communist circles, where he later organized famously effective espionage cells, recruiting Whittaker Chambers and Alger Hiss, among others.[40] Likewise, the poor conditions in IAH children's homes in the Ural region, along with the robbery and rape scandal, remained internal secrets. Rumors about the "terrorization" of the workers at the IAH fishery in Astrakhan were not quite so successfully hushed up, but they were anyway drowned out by the seemingly more pertinent scandal of the loss of over three-quarters of the year's catch there in 1923 due to the ignorance of the IAH managers, who had allowed the fish to spoil before it was properly salted and preserved.[41]

Many of the other problems IAH managers ran into with their workers reflected a typical pattern of the time. There was simply too many desperate Russian workers to be had, and not enough real work to give them to do, nor enough room to house them. The "terrorization" of the hired hands at the Astrakhan fishery was doubtless due at least in part to the difficulty of controlling a fluctuating staff of over three hundred workers (which topped out at one point near six hundred) while housing them in barracks built for eighty to a hundred.[42]

Back in Moscow, IAH headquarters had expanded so ludicrously in 1922 that a bloodletting in 1923 was all but inevitable. Several employees—including, significantly, the chief accountant and cashier—were fired in spring 1923 for malfeasance. Most of the hundreds of Russian IAH Moscow employees axed that year, though, were let go merely for being redundant. Under Jung, the staff had peaked at over two hundred. When prodded, his immediate successors found they could make do with less than half this number (although no one wanted to get rid of the seven chauffeurs who served the top functionaries).[43] When prodded further, they learned it was possible to live with one-third as many executive manservants as had Jung, about seventy-five fewer, in fact—although a Comintern commission established to audit the IAH in May 1923 thought this was still forty too many.[44]

All in all, concluded Wilhelm Kress, a German Communist hired member of the commission, in every corner of Münzenberg's Russian business empire there were simply "too many employees."[45] There were too many hangers-on, too, according to the commission, which somewhat callously recommended that all non-IAH employees be evicted from the mansion on Tverskaia-Iamskaia that served as both headquarters and residence for the organization's top brass (except for Münzenberg and other Berlin executives, who stayed at the Hotel Lux on Tverskaia when they were in town).[46]

Such ruthlessness might have been justified if the IAH was bringing discipline and productivity to the enterprises it took over, but the evidence of that was scant. None of the IAH concessions in the Russian economy came close to breaking even in their first year, and there was little sign any of them ever would, either. The Moscow boot factory, an ideal IAH concession in that it benefited from the importation of German equipment, bled red from day one. The equivalent of twelve thousand dollars was spent renovating the facility in summer 1922, but this did not seem to improve productivity, as the production of felt boots that autumn ran at a net loss of over 100 percent.[47] More renovations were ordered the following spring, but not all the capital improvement in the world could compensate for the IAH's managerial incompetence. By summer 1923, the boot factory was no longer producing or selling much of anything. From September to December 1923, revenues dropped to zero, although the facility was still burning over four thousand dollars a month.[48] Little wonder Münzenberg planned to unload the operation on the Soviet government at the end of the 1923 fiscal year.

Other IAH facilities lost money for the mundane reason that most of their customers were nonpaying IAH employees. This was the case with the outpatient clinic and the car garage, neither of which produced any revenue at all. The hair salon had at least some paying customers, but its losses still ran over 800 percent.[49]

Managerial incompetence and employee favoritism accounted for much of the IAH's track record of business failure, but a more fundamental problem was the total lack of financial accountability within the organization. With a steady supply of aid revenues still coming into Berlin (especially from the FSR in America), and the famine relief operation essentially over by early autumn 1922, Münzenberg could afford to branch out and throw money wherever he wanted. Thus, he sank nearly fifty thousand dollars into several Soviet film studios, without much chance of recouping it in the near future. Another thirty thousand dollars went to buy German cars, which Münzenberg hoped to resell in the Soviet Union for profit. Huge sums were devoted to machines and spare parts sent to Russia, over a hundred thousand dollars for the tractor operation alone. By way of preliminary accounting, Münzenberg himself estimated that he had earmarked about four hundred thousand dollars toward IAH "industrial assistance" by June 1923, an investment that had to date yielded only about seventy thousand dollars in revenue.[50]

The one exception that proved the rule of IAH waste and mismanagement was the "workers restaurant" on Tverskaia-Iamskaia, which ironically began turning a profit in 1923—as soon as it no longer catered to the working class. At the insistence of the rich young NEP speculators or "nepmen" who began frequenting the place, the photographs of stolid, happy productive proletarian labor brigades that had graced the walls when the IAH restaurant opened in 1922 were progressively abandoned over the next year for racier images of decadent partygoers. Even the multilingual banner that had greeted patrons with Karl Marx's immortal exhortation, "Proletarians of the world, unite!" was replaced with "agreeably sensual decorations." The IAH workers' restaurant was transformed, in short, into an upper-class cabaret. Because authentic proletarians could no longer afford to eat there, Russian IAH administrator Otto Roth complained to Münzenberg in June 1923, the restaurant no longer held "any propaganda value for the IAH." A commission appointed to audit the IAH agreed, recommending the restaurant be sold for political reasons (though Münzenberg, significantly, balked at the suggestion).[51]

If the problem with the restaurant's managers was that they were following market forces instead of ideology, the problem everywhere else in the IAH empire was just the opposite. As Münzenberg himself put the matter in June 1923, IAH personnel on the whole were "good Communists, but poor businessmen."[52] A good example of this was a Swiss agronomist, Comrade Schaffner, who was hired by the IAH to take over an enormous farm collective known as the "Pinaevo" property south of Chelyabinsk near the border with Turkestan (now Kazakhstan). Schaffner published an elaborate scheme for modernizing the farm in the pages of Münzenberg's new theoretical journal, *Rote Aufbau*. But Schaffner's plans were "careless," according to Jakob Fausch, the IAH auditing commission member who went to check up on Pinaevo in May 1923. First of all, the farm had required a major infusion of livestock—but Schaffner had not constructed shelter for the hundreds of Swiss cattle he brought in, putting the whole population at risk whenever the first winter storm hit. Schaffner also failed to pay his staff for several months, poisoning relations with his employees and alienating local union authorities. The Pinaevo land remained fertile, but in Fausch's view, the IAH would be unable to profit from it so long as it was managed by a man who understood so "little about operating a business."[53]

IAH administrators were no more effective in bringing goods to market. In one particularly egregious instance, a shipment of sixty tons of fish from the IAH facility at Tsaritsyn arrived in Saratov, where the local IAH commissar, Rosenberg, left the fish to rot for nearly a month in the local train station. Somehow Rosenberg eventually found a buyer willing to part with five hundred gold rubles for the fish without having seen the product—but he promptly forfeited all of his questionable profits and more when the local police, tipped off by the buyer about the defective merchandise, forced him to dump the rotten fish in the Volga and pay for the clean-up of the station storage facilities he had used. Having literally caused a stink in Saratov, the IAH was left with little choice, according to auditing commission member Wilhelm Kress, but to liquidate its operations there, firing Rosenberg and recalling his sister, too (who had been in charge of the local IAH children's homes).[54]

Undoubtedly the greatest IAH fiasco was the mechanized farming mecca Jung tried to create in the Ural Mountains. The Toikino operation Hal Ware was botching was only the beginning. Jung envisioned a huge agricultural collective, powered by four hundred American tractors, which would surround a modern city of concrete. By 1923, only twenty-two tractors had arrived in the Urals, but Jung had already diverted the equivalent of 300,000 gold-backed rubles ($150,000), some of which came from a questionable dollar loan he secured from a friend who controlled the largest American tailor's union, into a firm he himself created, Ural A-G.[55] Other gullible foreign investors ponied up another $100,000.[56] Jung used this cash to stock massive quantities of seed, fuel, and supplies. His plans were all over the Russian press, with the Bolsheviks' full endorsement. The whole scheme was constructed on an enormous mountain of debt.

Unfortunately for Jung and all of his investors, the fifteen thousand desiatins (forty thousand acres) of land set aside by the Soviet government turned out to be uneven, rock-strewn and all but impervious to the methods of mechanized agriculture. Inevitably, many of the tractors broke down after being used by inexperienced operators on totally unsuitable land. It was only then that Jung's commissars, true idiots savants, learned that there was no one in Russia qualified to fix most of the machines, which required unobtainable American specialists for servicing. A year went by, and despite all the sound and fury absolutely nothing had been cultivated. Good press turned to bad, and there was nothing left for Münzenberg to do but to turn tail, disown Jung, and count his losses. Ultimately an in-house legend about the origins of the Ural A-G debacle was born, in which an out-of-control Jung at one point "stuck a gun under Münzenberg's nose to prevent him from examining the accounts," but this was hooey. As Otto Roth admitted at the Berlin IAH Congress in June 1923, Jung's widely admired plan had failed for the mundane reason that no one in either the Russian IAH organization or the Soviet government knew enough about mechanized agriculture to scout out land suitable for the operation.[57]

Every member of the IAH auditing commission dispatched by the Comintern to audit the organization's sprawling properties in spring 1923 reached the same conclusion: from now on, production needed to be managed by experienced Western experts, and goods must be sold "according to commercial principles."[58] As for administration and accounting, they had to follow Western models too. Specifically, the mess at Moscow headquarters could only be cleaned up if the IAH adopted "American or German double-entry bookkeeping methods." To survive, the IAH had to become, well, more capitalist.[59]

Although their report ultimately had little concrete effect, the auditors who tried to make sense of the IAH's Russian operations in spring 1923 had hit upon a fundamental paradox at the heart of communism that could not be explained away. No matter what they claimed to be doing, IAH and other Communist functionaries who took over Russian properties during NEP were acting no less as capitalists than the private nepmen who rose up to compete with them, with the caveat that the latter were doing so with competence. However odious their "speculation" appeared to Russians struggling in poverty, nepmen grew wealthy by responding to market forces, something most Communists were temperamentally incapable of doing. Among IAH properties only the "workers' restaurant" on Tverskaia-Iamskaia had found a real niche in the Russian economy—yet by transforming the place into a cabaret catering to nepmen who could actually pay, the IAH managers there had violated the ideological rules their concession was based on in the first place. If the other bloated dinosaurs of the IAH empire followed suit and began turning profits after bringing in capitalist managers who knew how to run a business, they would have violated charter IAH principles no less than had the restaurant. Economic viability for Communists, no less than for capitalists, ran squarely through the profit ledger—but to admit this truth was to call the whole Communist ideal into question.

It is not surprising, then, that Münzenberg's response to the scathing IAH audit was to deny everything—without denying anything. The auditing commission report, he wrote to the Comintern Secretariat on 27 June 1923, "is not only superficial but is absolutely incoherent." Because the commissioners commented only on myriad particular occurrences, they "concealed" any possible view of the whole, coming inevitably to "erroneous conclusions." Without responding to any of the individual allegations of graft, incompetence, or malfeasance (doing so, we presume, might have concealed the larger truths at hand), Münzenberg declared his "sharpest protest" against the auditing commission, and vowed to come to Moscow personally to uphold the honor of the IAH.[60]

Münzenberg would never succeed in refuting the auditing commission's allegations, but he was never forced to implement their recommendations, either. The auditors' report was embarrassing enough—it almost ruined the June 1923 IAH Congress, which was attended by several SPD spies who later washed Münzenberg's dirty laundry in public, causing a major scandal on the German left—but in Moscow it had a very short shelf life.[61] At Comintern headquarters, there were much bigger things afoot in summer 1923, and to Münzenberg's pleasant surprise, the low-grade industrial disasters of the IAH's Russian operations had dropped off the radar screen almost entirely by August. For neither the first nor the last time, Münzenberg was able to postpone a reckoning with the consequences of his actions simply by tumbling headlong into other adventures.

CHAPTER 8 *Germany Red or Black*

Since his arrest in Stuttgart during the Spartacist uprising of January 1919, Münzenberg had remained largely aloof from German political affairs. Like most Communists in Berlin, he had been caught unawares by the right-wing Kapp Putsch in March 1920 and played no role in the general strike that overthrew the short-lived regime. The following year, Münzenberg was busy preparing his last stand for keeping the Youth International in Berlin when the ill-starred Communist-led uprising known as the "March action" struck Germany like a thunderclap. Wrapped up in youth affairs, Münzenberg did not participate in the acrimonious debate over tactics that engulfed the KPD after the unsuccessful March action— in which hundreds of activists perished, and thousands more were arrested and convicted of various treasonable offenses.[1] After 1921, Münzenberg was far too wrapped up in the Russian operations of the IAH to pay close attention to political developments in Germany.

All this changed, however, with the French occupation of the Ruhr ordered by conservative premier Raymond Poincaré on 11 January 1923. Only the day before, the KPD had proposed a nationwide general strike in an open letter to the SPD and the unions, aiming to bring down the government of Chancellor Wilhelm Cuno, a nationalist businessman. But this invitation, like most of the KPD's calls for united action that periodically interrupted the usual vitriol against the "reformist" German labor establishment, was ignored, and Poincaré's Ruhr move instead breathed sudden life into Cuno's government, as the nation rallied in opposition to the French occupation.[2]

Revealingly, the initial responses of Münzenberg and other KPD leaders to the Ruhr crisis paralleled those of the most extreme right-wing party, Adolf Hitler's National Socialist German Workers' Party (NSDAP). Alone on the right, Hitler refused to exploit the Ruhr crisis and even withdrew his party from a coalition of nationalist parties that supported Cuno's policy of passive resistance. Recruiting Ruhr resisters might temporarily swell the ranks of the NSDAP, but Hitler's long-term political strategy dictated that he avoid submerging his extremist movement in a general patriotic upwelling that would blunt its sharp identity. Hitler thus mocked Cuno's policy of passive resistance as a futile effort to "kill the French by loafing," blaming the occupation instead on the impotence of a Weimar republican establishment that had invited the contempt of the French.[3]

Münzenberg's first published commentary on the Ruhr occupation vividly illustrates the convergence between Communist and Nazi responses to the crisis. In the pages of *Hammer and Sickle* in February 1923, Münzenberg wrote that the tasks of French and German Communists were complementary: the French must do battle with Poincaré's "military junta," while their German comrades struggled against the nationalist "rabble-rousers" of Weimar Germany. Far from inciting German workers to resist the French imperialist invaders, Münzenberg in fact wanted them to focus their attention on the Weimar regime, heeding the words of the revolutionary martyr Karl Liebknecht: "the enemy resides in our own land."[4] He might well have been quoting Hitler, who wrote at about the same time that "the real enemy of the German people lurks within its gates."[5]

Taking a position on the Ruhr occupation so emphatically at odds with prevailing national sentiment was risky for a nationalist extremist like Hitler—whose rapidly expanding NSDAP now had to fend off rumors of French financing—and it was no less problematic for the Communists. The awkwardness of the KPD's stance was highlighted for all to see in February, when the French banned publication of all newspapers in the occupied zone except Communist ones, the occupiers' idea being to split German opposition forces by painting the KPD as pro-French. This state of affairs was so embarrassing that the KPD's main regional organ, the *Ruhr Echo*, resorted to printing deliberate insults to the French in order to be included in the press ban with the others.[6]

Tactical confusion aside, Münzenberg and other German Communists were not, of course, genuinely pro-French any more than Hitler was. But the KPD, unlike the NSDAP, did have one permanent foreign commitment that complicated the party's position during the Ruhr crisis: its dependence on Soviet Russia. At first, the party's special relationship with the Bolshevik regime seemed to offer political advantages. The German government had, in fact, been quietly cozying up to Moscow for several years. The Rapallo Treaty of April 1922 had provided for military collaboration between the two countries as well as mutual debt write-offs and trade accords. The Rapallo accords were, of course, deeply distasteful to the Western Allies, and anything the KPD might do to strengthen the Moscow-Berlin détente might be a real thorn in the side of the French Ruhr operation.

In the spirit of Rapallo, Karl Radek announced in *Rote Fahne* on 8 March 1923 that the Russian government was shipping twenty million pounds of Ukrainian wheat flour to the Ruhr, to be distributed free of charge.[7] Cuno's government had not asked Moscow for food aid, but it was undeniable that many Germans had sunk into poverty because of passive resistance. Russia, meanwhile, had just enjoyed several good harvests in a row—thanks in large part to the seeds provided by Hoover's ARA during the Volga campaign.

This was an intriguing reversal of the famine aid program whose loose ends Münzenberg was still tying up in Berlin: now the grain would be coming west, marking the Bolsheviks' recovery from the depths of civil war and famine, just as central Europe was sinking into economic chaos. Moscow's decision to ship grain to the Ruhr, in fact, seems to have caught Münzenberg by surprise, so caught up was he in cleaning up the lingering messes of the Russian food aid program.[8] Although himself still quite busy with the old accounts, Münzenberg gladly dispatched his IAH colleague Max Wagner to Hamburg to meet the first shipment of Ukrainian wheat, which arrived on 29 March 1923.[9] Here, it seemed, was a golden opportunity to exploit the Ruhr situation politically in a way that could embarrass both the French, whose brutal occupation policy had evidently created a human crisis, and the German regime, which, in light of the Russian aid deployment, appeared incapable of providing for all of its citizens. "Russian bread," Radek declared, "is a weapon against both Poincaré and Cuno."[10]

The involvement of the Russians in the Ruhr crisis, however, opened up a Pandora's box of problems for the Communists. The grain shipment was accompanied by a number of Russian trade representatives who made propaganda speeches, and this provoked a wave of suspicion in Berlin. The Russians might even have been detained by the Prussian police, in fact, but for the intervention of the German Foreign Office, which was keen to preserve the spirit of Rapallo.[11] Further complications ensued in May, when a sudden inflationary spike sparked a wave of violent wildcat strikes and labor riots in the Ruhr. Recalling the recent Russian food aid tour of the Ruhr, the German Foreign Office suspected foul play by Soviet agents, and rumors of Bolshevik subversion in the Ruhr enveloped Berlin. The allegations were serious enough that Radek himself went to the German Foreign Office in person to demand proof of the charges. Although Soviet agents had, in fact, been advising the KPD's underground military apparatus (M-group) and clandestine intelligence network (N-group) in the Ruhr since early February 1923, the Prussian police could turn up no evidence of Russian involvement in the May riots, and a full-scale diplomatic scandal was averted, for the time being.[12]

Historians have speculated for years about the Bolsheviks' intentions during the Ruhr crisis, with some even suggesting they were toying with the possibility of a fascist overthrow of the Weimar government.[13] The most intriguing evidence centers around Radek's notorious speech in Moscow on 20 June 1923, in which he lavished praise on a right-wing German paramilitary thug named Albert Leo Schlageter who was regarded as a martyr, having been executed by the French occupation forces in late May. Clearly Radek's speech, and the wide publicity it received in the Communist press, were designed to appeal to disgruntled "petty bourgeois" Germans who had been flocking into the arms of Hitler's NSDAP. More socially respectable German race-nationalists of the *völkisch* movement's salon set, such as the elegant Nazi sympathizer Count Ernst zu Reventlow and his allies at the right-wing magazine *Gewissen*, had been stretching out olive branches to KPD leaders since the start of the Ruhr crisis, praising the Communists' "active forces" and welcoming any overtures in the direction of "national-Bolshevi[sm]."[14] Radek, according to former Soviet spy Walter Krivitsky, entered into serious negotiations with Count Reventlow, who was friendly with both Hitler and the enigmatic general cum revanchist politician Erich Ludendorff, about the terms of a possible political alliance.[15] Yet by mid August, Radek was carefully distancing himself from Reventlow, claiming that the *völkisch* movement's anti-Weimar fervor was misguided because it focused its hatred on foreigners and Jews, while sparing German capitalists like steel magnate Hugo Stinnes.[16]

Radek was far from the only one in the Communist camp flirting with fascism in 1923. Hitler himself might have approved one *Rote Fahne* headline from late May for the Nazis' own *Völkische Beobachter:* "Down with the government of national shame and betrayal of the people!"[17] KPD recruiters used similar phrases when they ventured into political territory traditionally hostile to Communism, such as the universities.[18] Notoriously, Ruth Fischer, a "left" oppositionist elected to the KPD Zentrale for the first time in late January, exhorted Communists at one point during this campaign to "trample the Jewish capitalists down, hang them from the lampposts."[19] Only slightly less odious was the *Rote Fahne* piece attacking German People's Party leader Gustav Stresemann's "Jewish Chamber of Commerce," which ran in early August.[20] Longtime KPD Zentrale member Hermann Remmele went so far as to meet with Nazis in Stuttgart, admonishing them to go ahead and "fight Jewish finance capital," so long as they fought (not exclusively Jewish) "industrial capital" as well.[21]

There was certainly common ideological ground here to be exploited. Still, we should be careful about reading too much into the Communists' flirtation with fascism in summer 1923. Especially with Lenin himself now all but incapacitated by a series of strokes, the Bolsheviks' German policy was far from coherent during the Ruhr crisis. Whether by accident or intentionally confusing design, the Kremlin was toying with a number of political possibilities, recruiting anti-Weimar malcontents from other radical movements while continuing quietly to assure the German Foreign Office that Communists supported the passive resistance in the Ruhr, all the while keeping the world guessing about Russian intentions. Was Moscow pragmatically courting a military alliance with Cuno's suddenly bellicose outlaw regime? Or flirting with the fascists who wanted to supplant that very regime, possibly to join forces in an extremist alliance of "national Bolshevism" that would turn the guns of Rapallo on Paris? Or doing both at once?

To complicate matters further, Zinoviev and his assistants at ECCI spent much of spring and summer 1923 assembling an "antifascist" front organization that aimed to ensnare pacifists, moderate socialists, and liberal intellectuals into the Communist camp. Significantly, the first "pacifist" noises coming from Moscow were linked to concerns about aggressive Polish designs on White Russia. ECCI invited European labor representatives to meet in Cologne on 18 March 1923 "to unite against the imperialist war that is being prepared through mobilization in Poland."[22] Perhaps wary of submitting themselves to the imperatives of Soviet foreign policy, neither the Second International nor the Amsterdam Trade Union International sent delegates to this conference, but this snub did not stop Moscow from presumptuously announcing the formation of a "Provisional International Committee for the Struggle against Fascism," with Clara Zetkin as honorary chairwoman.[23] Zetkin herself delivered the keynote antifascist address at the enlarged ECCI meeting in Moscow on 20 June 1923—which, as if to highlight Moscow's ideological double-dealing, was immediately followed by Radek's Schlageter speech.[24] Between Radek's fascist bridge building, the KPD Zentrale's Jew-baiting, and Zetkin's pacifistic antifascism, Kremlin watchers must have been spinning in circles.

Or was it possible to reconcile neofascism with antifascism, to unite bellicose threats against "capitalist" governments with appeals to antiwar idealists—to build, in short, a counterintuitive coalition of angry would-be warriors and radical pacifists? If such a task of ideological conjuring was possible, then surely it must fall to no less a propaganda mastermind than Münzenberg, whose utterly inconsequential campaign to alleviate the Communists' self-inflicted Volga famine had somehow sold itself to thousands of sympathizers as the sole savior of Soviet Russia. Out of boredom with his IAH duties, in fact, Münzenberg himself had asked Zinoviev for the new antifascist portfolio while in Moscow in late April. After two years of uninspiring fundraising and capital-squandering logistics, he explained to his old Zurich comrade, "I want to do more political work." At Zinoviev's behest, Münzenberg was named secretary of the new "Action Committee in the Struggle Against Fascism and War" by ECCI on 18 May 1923.[25]

Much as the long-suffering IAH secretary ached for a new cause at which to throw his frustrated energies, however, the antifascist initiative remained, for a considerable time, stuck. Münzenberg's own people in Berlin, for a start, refused to let him leave his post, at least not until after the upcoming IAH World Congress in June.[26] Münzenberg was certainly not going to miss the June meeting, which he had been promoting far and wide for months. Still, to indicate that he was serious about leaving, he proposed to Moscow that his old friend from the Youth International, the Italian Francesco Misiano, succeed him as IAH secretary.[27] Münzenberg's choice was not approved by ECCI, whose members, at Zinoviev's urging, insisted that only a Russian replace their trustworthy comrade from the Zimmerwald Left.[28] And before Münzenberg could find a successor to Moscow's liking, he changed his own mind about quitting the IAH, once the results of the long-awaited audit of its Russian commercial enterprises were relayed to Berlin during the June Congress. So embarrassing was the verdict pronounced by the auditing committee that Münzenberg decided to handle the damage control himself.[29] In July, he traveled to Moscow to lobby Radek and Zinoviev on behalf of the IAH's continued economic relevance for Soviet Russia, all but forgetting about the ongoing Ruhr crisis.[30] Only in August was Münzenberg able to take up the new antifascist initiative full-time, once he had cleared away the stench from the IAH's disastrous spring audit.

In the meantime, Münzenberg's men in Berlin had begun to carve out an antifascist political line that played on pacifists' fears of renascent militarism and exploited the anti-Entente sentiments of the German population, even while serving the needs of Soviet foreign policy. The key to this ideological confection was the resurgence of Soviet Russia, whose prestige was on the rise again, now that the famine of War Communism had given way to the recovery of NEP. A new, deceptively simple slogan—"Hands off Soviet Russia!"—distilled the complex into the essence.[31] Your average sympathizer might have had no idea that Communists really believed the French Ruhr occupation was linked with a recent threat by the English to abandon the Anglo-Russian Trade Agreement of 1921 in a nefarious plan by Entente capitalists to march their armies into Russia over the corpses of the German labor movement. But a slogan expressing the idea that the workers' paradise in the East, merely by its conspicuous, shining existence, inspired plans by the evil capitalists of the world to sabotage it—that could attract attention viscerally.[32]

Such a slogan carried even more appeal, of course, if a gallery of famous intellectuals conspicuously endorsed it. Thus the "Hands off Soviet Russia" campaign was adorned by the signatures of Albert Einstein, the French novelist Henri Barbusse, the fashionable Bolshevik scribe Maxim Gorky, and the muckraking American novelist Upton Sinclair (whose known Communist sympathies Münzenberg often cynically exploited, forging Sinclair's signature whenever it seemed appropriate).[33] Along with Münzenberg's notable Berlin friends such as the artist Käthe Kollwitz, the music historian Adolf Weismann, and the banker Hugo Simon, these celebrities were listed as charter members of the "Society of the Friends of the New Russia" founded in June 1923.[34]

So it was that the fuzzy-sounding "Friends of Soviet Russia" idea, so successful for the IAH in America during the Volga famine, migrated across the Atlantic at the height of the Ruhr crisis, by which time Russia, delivered from its own hunger by Hoover, was helping to feed Germany. The German economy was imploding, the ravages of hyperinflation were decimating the life savings of millions of Germans—and yet the cause that lit up the IAH's star house intellectuals during the fateful summer of 1923 was a largely nonexistent military threat to the existence of Soviet Russia. Ironically, the antifascist cause Münzenberg had seized on as a ticket out of the IAH began to breathe a semblance of life into that long-floundering organization, and particularly into its German branch, whose prospects he had so long discounted. The Berlin intelligentsia had not been conspicuously generous during the Volga aid campaign, nor were they as yet much exercised about poverty in their own country. But when the IAH merged the fear of fascism with admiration of Soviet Russia, the combination was irresistible.[35]

Thus Münzenberg, as it turned out, did not need to choose between the traditional Soviet propaganda of the IAH and the struggle against fascism. Ideologically, the two campaigns turned out to be natural brethren: the bellicose Bolshevik boasting of the IAH's flagship *Hammer and Sickle* could be complemented by an antifascist aesthetic that was simply its mirror image. After spending August studying the fascist press on orders from ECCI, Münzenberg accomplished the trick in grand style with an antifascist parody he provocatively styled *The Swastika*.[36] The inaugural cover of *Swastika* depicts a terrified bourgeois citizen clinging desperately to the flimsy branches of "democracy," about to fall into a pit of "fascist" knives that will bludgeon him. In the opposite cover graphic, a crisply dressed Red Army officer has planted the flag of the USSR on top of an immovable granite embankment that rises above a black sea of "counterrevolution." The only way to escape the fascist threat, then, was obviously to pitch camp with Soviet Russia. A cartoon parodying the Nazis rounded out the inaugural issue: a bearded Viking manchild chugs beer out of a ram's horn, while holding up a giant swastika-bearing shield: here was "the moral regeneration of the German people."[37]

Hitler's paramilitary thugs clearly offered ripe terrain for political satire, but Münzenberg's antifascist vision extended well beyond the Nazis. Perhaps a bit too emboldened by the generally positive response to the debut issue, Münzenberg dared in the second *Swastika* to depict President Fritz Ebert —his long-ago enemy from the prewar Youth Socialist days—striding imperially in front of the Weimar statehouse over a pile of "worker" corpses, his clothes splattered with blood. As if to ensure his new publication would never again see the light of day, Münzenberg included in the same issue unflattering caricatures of SPD finance minister Rudolf Hilferding, former warlord Ludendorff, and perhaps most foolishly, of General Hans von Seeckt, who as commander of the regular army (Reichswehr) was probably the most powerful man in Germany. None of the four were amused, and the Prussian police acted quickly to suppress Münzenberg's obnoxious propaganda creation.[38] The antifascist aesthetic, however, was born, and with his somewhat toned-down follow-up to *Swastika*, the *Chronicle of Fascism*, Münzenberg would continue to entertain the Berlin IAH intelligentsia until well into 1924.

The threat posed by fascism was, of course, not merely an aesthetic issue, and the Communist promotion of antifascism was helped along immeasurably by the fact that a whole array of German nationalist parties, armed to the teeth, really were conspiring to seize power in 1923. In a manner eerily reminiscent of the collusion between key members of the Italian political establishment and Mussolini's Blackshirts that had facilitated the fascists' successful March on Rome in 1922, shadowy figures both inside and outside the German government had seized on the Ruhr crisis as a pretext for mobilizing underground armies to be placed at the disposal of anyone bold enough to set the nation on a new course. In fact, one of Germany's leading political intriguers, industrial tycoon Hugo Stinnes, met with Italian envoys sent by Mussolini himself in September 1923, to discuss ways of ending the Ruhr crisis. General Seeckt, supreme commander of the Reichswehr, was approached by a number of leading conservatives during the summer months, including Bavarian State Commissioner Gustav von Kahr. They wanted the famously noncommittal general—after he refused to take sides during the Kapp Putsch of 1920, he was sometimes referred to as the "Sphinx with the Monocle"—to throw in his lot at long last with the antirepublican forces.[39]

And then there was Bavaria. Since the Reichswehr had crushed Munich's ill-fated "Soviet Republic" in 1919, Germany's southern capital of touchy particularism had become a safe haven for right-wing paramilitary groups, many of which had been banned elsewhere in Germany. Hitler's NSDAP and its armed wing of "storm troopers" (*Sturmabteilung*, or SA) were only the most notorious members of the "Kampfbund," a sort of right-wing army assembled in 1923 out of the many groups making up the Bavarian *völkisch* movement, which was allowed to stage provocative maneuvers with relative abandon. While the Kampfbund's numbers were insignificant compared to those of the regular Reichswehr, its fanatics were well financed and heavily armed, fortified by an underground network of munitions depots in Munich's hinterland.[40]

The specter of the "Black Hundreds" evoked by Communist propaganda, then, was no phantom. And the antifascist line, aside from appealing to intellectuals, carried tremendous political potential in the German labor movement. The right-wing parties were not merely armed; they were also winning huge numbers of new members in 1923, mainly from more moderate conservative parties such as the German National People's Party. A similar trend toward extremism was clearly in the offing on the left, as the SPD's moderate stock slid downward with each uptick in the inflationary spiral of the economy. Millions of workers, disappointed by the declining leverage of the unions during the Ruhr occupation—which saw recently won gains, such as the eight-hour day, fall victim to the economic crisis—were abandoning moderation in search of new political solutions.[41] Even worse than losing the eight-hour day was losing one's job, and by the end of 1923, less than 30 percent of the German labor force was fully employed. A significant percentage of the white-collar unemployed were turning to the Nazis in 1923, but most blue-collar laborers remained squarely hostile to the Right.

All of these factors might have led millions of struggling workers permanently into the Communist tent in 1923 at the expense of the SPD—

whose centrists would then have correspondingly lost ground to the party's left wing. Cooperation between the Communists and the left-leaning SPD governments of Thuringia and Saxony was, in fact, already paying serious dividends, especially in Saxony, where the KPD's own paramilitary forces were allowed to stage exercises without molestation, much as Hitler's SA enjoyed freedom of movement in Bavaria. The Saxon "Red Hundreds," although covertly advised by Soviet agents, included both SPD and KPD men, and if their operational base had been extended significantly beyond Saxony, they might have posed a real threat to the right-wing "black" paramilitaries conspiring against the republic.[42]

But the men behind the Red Hundreds, however authentically antifascist, were in truth no more prorepublican than Hitler's "blackest" storm troopers. As the wicked caricatures of Münzenberg's *Swastika* suggest, the Comintern's definition of the fascist enemy drew little distinction among those it viewed as enemies of communism, lumping bloodthirsty extremists like the Nazis together with Reichswehr generals and moderate SPD Cabinet members, not to mention President Ebert himself, a living symbol of the Weimar Republic if there ever was one. Hitler may have been correctly perceived by Zetkin and other pacifist types as an enemy of the "proletariat," but then so, according to the party press, was nearly everyone else to the right of the KPD Zentrale.

The Communists, moreover, were just as complicit in conspiratorial antirepublican plotting as the Right. Although the party's M- and N-groups had been relatively quiet in the Ruhr for most of the year, preparations for insurrectionary activity began in earnest in late summer, just as the Nazis were sharpening their sabers in Munich. The crucial decision to pursue a "revolutionary" course in autumn 1923 was made in the Kremlin, possibly at a Politburo meeting on 23 August 1923, and was communicated to KPD Chairman Heinrich Brandler in Moscow early in September. Brandler himself at first had reservations about switching the KPD's tactical course so suddenly, but was progressively won over by Trotsky and Zinoviev, among others, to an aggressive policy that envisioned arming fifty to sixty thousand workers in Saxony with the collusion of the SPD government there (into which the Communists would enter). Once the Saxon Red Hundreds were strong enough to resist an invasion by the Reichswehr, the proletarian masses of Germany would then presumably gain the courage to join the insurrection, and it would be only a matter of time before the government fell and the German Soviet Republic was proclaimed.[43]

Back in western Germany, meanwhile, the Ruhr crisis was heating up to fever pitch. French-supported demonstrations by Rhenish separatists in Cologne and nearby cities in the Rhineland on 23 and 24 September sparked violent counterdemonstrations by both the Left and Right. In Düsseldorf, armed Communists actually joined forces with right-wing paramilitaries and even local police officers in street fighting against separatist agitators, many of whom were violent criminals set loose by the French to wreak havoc with passive resistance.[44] The clashes on the Rhine, however, much like the on-again, off-again resistance in the Ruhr, were understood by the Communists as merely a rehearsal for the real action to come in Saxony. In late September, the remaining Soviet advisers in the Ruhr began moving their secret military formations east to reinforce the Saxon Red Hundreds. Ominously, the KPD's underground apparatus of M- and N-groups was now buttressed by terrorist cells ("T-groups") whose aim was to "demoralize [the country] by assassinations"; and "Z-groups" designed to infiltrate the Reichswehr and police.[45]

Armed terrorists on both sides of the political spectrum, then, were ready for action, just itching for a fight against the republican regime they hated so much. As the strange events in Düsseldorf suggest, however, the policy of passive resistance provided a powerful outlet for political energy against the French. So long as fascists and antifascists could fight side by side against a foreign enemy, the government's flank was somewhat protected against would-be putschists. Passive resistance had wreaked havoc with Germany's economy—the Ruhr region was the source of four-fifths of Germany's coal deposits, and a huge share of the nation's heavy industrial capacity—and ruined the public finances, as the printing presses had gone wild to subsidize the idle German population in the occupied area, fueling a devastating hyperinflation. By September the mark had fallen to about one hundred million to the dollar; by October the figure was in the billions, by November in the trillions.[46] But abandoning passive resistance would have incited the wrath of German patriots, and such a courageous move was well beyond the capacity of Cuno, a novice chancellor who enjoyed only very shaky support in the Reichstag until the SPD abandoned him for good on 12 August 1923.

Cuno's successor, Gustav Stresemann, was made of sterner stuff, and as a former monarchist and outspoken wartime "annexationist," he had patriotic credentials to cushion the political blow of bowing to the French. Still, even Stresemann found it difficult to abandon Cuno's popular policy. Only after the British government, long cold toward the Ruhr occupation, finally endorsed the French policy on 19 September, did he reconcile himself to the inevitable. On 26 September 1923, Stresemann, with deep reluctance, announced the end of passive resistance. That same fateful day, President Ebert declared a state of emergency in Germany, transferring formal executive authority to Defense Minister Otto Gessler (although the real power was now in General Seeckt's hands). With the crutch of passive resistance abandoned and the Reichswehr in charge the battle lines were drawn: it was now life or death for the Weimar Republic and its enemies.

"The decisive moment will arrive no later than in four-five-six weeks," Zinoviev wired Berlin from the Kremlin on 1 October 1923, and immediately Communists in both Russia and Germany plunged into a frenzy of revolutionary activity. All through October, one leading Russian Bolshevik recalled, "Moscow was in the throes of violent excitement."[47] The Russian capital was bedecked with banners and posters proclaiming the glory of the German revolution. Government decrees placarded throughout central Moscow advised Russian children to learn German, because "the German October stood at the gates."[48] At the Soviet war college, Radek regaled packed auditoriums with tales of the upcoming German revolution, before departing for Germany himself. On 8 October, KPD deputy Hermann Remmele mounted the rostrum of the Reichstag and promised to destroy Germany's "White dictatorship" by erecting a "Red dictatorship." "Hand guns and machine guns," he declared, "are better weapons than all the speeches made in parliament." As if to emphasize Remmele's point, a division of the Red Hundreds clashed openly with Nazi storm troopers near the Thuringian-Bavarian border the following evening. Next day, on 10 October, *Rote Fahne* printed a letter from the most powerful man in the Politburo, Joseph Stalin, which erased any doubts that the revolutionary hour was at hand. Congratulating the KPD in advance for events that had yet to transpire, Stalin proclaimed that the "approaching revolution in Germany" would be the "most important world event of our time." Not merely would Berlin be made Red, but the Prussian metropolis would soon take Moscow's place as the "center of world revolution." If they weren't ready long before, Stalin's euphoric letter made certain the German authorities would be on full alert when the world revolution finally landed in the heart of Prussia.[49]

Concrete preparations for the German revolution were no less euphoric. In Russia, a strategic reserve of grain was transported to Petrograd, to be placed at the disposal of a victorious Communist regime in Germany.[50] The Red Army's mobile cavalry divisions began staging threatening maneuvers near the Polish border, and thousands of reliable Russian Communist functionaries were put on alert, to be dispatched to Berlin on short notice.

In all, more than $1 million in hard currency from the Kremlin's coffers was thrown at the operation, and by mid-October Berlin was swarming with Soviet spies, middlemen, and dollar-carrying arms procurement agents. Most of the cash and personnel came in through the Soviet Embassy on the Unter den Linden just a quarter-mile or so down from the Brandenburg Gate. Jacob Mirov-Abromov, the German liaison for the Comintern's Department for International Liaison, ran a virtual bank from his Embassy offices, located just upstairs from Münzenberg's lair at IAH.[51]

Revolutions, as the Bolsheviks knew, are won by superior force on the ground, and in the absence of a Russian invasion of Prussia—before which Poland would have had to be crushed—this meant that a Red Army would have to be raised in Germany. Pëtr Aleksandrovich Skoblevsky, a victorious Bolshevik general from the Russian Civil War, was dispatched to Germany in September. Under Skoblevsky's Supreme Command, the KPD began fashioning an underground army out of the preexisting M-groups, divided up into six German military districts approximating those of the Reichswehr (although excluding Bavaria, which was conceded to the "blacks"): West, Northwest, Central, Berlin, Southwest, and East Prussia. The Red Hundreds stepped up their periodic training exercises in politically friendly regions such as Saxony, although many soldiers still lacked guns. A few firearms were stolen from private citizens, and makeshift bombs were manufactured at home out of fuses and dynamite pilfered from construction sites. Address lists of fuel, food, weapons, and clothing stores were optimistically sent in to Berlin by local party committees, in the hope that the Communists could supplement their ever-deficient supplies of necessary wartime materiel with raids on existing depots once the fighting broke out. The signal to rise would be a call for a general strike or some impressive-sounding labor conference; then partisan warfare would be unleashed in the countryside, from the (presumably secure) "proletarian" base in Saxony. The Reichswehr would everywhere encounter superior force and surrender its weapons, and the revolution would spread until the Hammer and Sickle at last flew over Red Berlin, capital of the future Communist world-system.[52]

All this might have happened, had the German Communists really mobilized millions of followers behind the revolutionary policy, provided them with arms, and somehow kept such preparations from arousing the attention of the Reichswehr and the government. Yet by October 1923, none of these crucial conditions were met. The party's confusing ideological experiments had hampered its recruitment possibilities severely. Although the membership rolls gradually increased during the Ruhr crisis, there were still fewer than three hundred thousand registered Communists in Germany by autumn. Of these, no more than perhaps fifty thousand had been supplied with arms by October.[53] The Communists were wearing insurrection on their sleeves, and after the publication of Stalin's letter in *Rote Fahne,* any chances of revolutionary success in Germany were blown out of the water.

The decision for insurrection, however, had already been made, and so the Communists sleepwalked right into an ambush. Just several days after three members of the KPD Zentrale entered the Saxon state government of SPD Minister President Erich Zeigner on 10 October 1923, the local army commander, General Alfred Müller, announced a ban on the proletarian Red Hundreds and "similar" military organizations. The Communists refused to dissolve their army, ordered their men to take up arms, and on the fourteenth dispatched two deputies to join the neighboring state government of Thuringia. General Müller, unfazed, placed the Saxon police under the authority of the Reichswehr on the 16th, thereby rendering Zeigner and the Communists in his Cabinet effectively powerless.[54]

There was still, however, one last desperate card for the Communists to play. Because the army commanders of East Prussia and Silesia were forbidding transport of foodstuffs (mostly potatoes) grown in eastern Germany, a severe food shortage had descended upon the heavily populated areas of central Germany—and the Bolsheviks had grain to burn in Petrograd. Münzenberg and his IAH lieutenants had, until mid-October, played little part in the KPD's preparations for a German revolution, but the burgeoning hunger crisis in central Germany, coupled with the KPD's entry into the governments of Saxony and Thuringia, provided an opportunity. Münzenberg had learned of the Bolsheviks' strategic grain reserve after arriving in Moscow in late September, and at his insistence, the grain was earmarked for IAH distribution in Germany. After returning to Germany in mid-October, Münzenberg announced a gift of nearly eight hundred tons of Russian grain for the new "workers' government" of Thuringia with great fanfare, and soon thereafter placed an additional two thousand tons at the disposal of the Saxon government on the twentieth. Once the Russians got their act together, he further promised, another twenty thousand tons would be on the way. It was not much, but at this point the beleaguered left coalition governments of Thuringia and Saxony would take what they could get.[55]

The day after Münzenberg's food gift to the Saxon government was announced in *Rote Fahne,* Reichswehr battalions descended from Prussia into Saxony, and the Communist insurrection was over before it started. The joint SPD/KPD government would not be officially deposed for over a week, but once the army had surrounded Dresden, the issue was decided. Recognizing the futility of further resistance, Münzenberg and the other KPD leaders returned to Berlin on the night of 22–23 October 1923 to lick their wounds. A brief flash of revolutionary excitement was provided by KPD hotheads in Hamburg, who, oblivious to the meaning of the events in Saxony, rashly attacked local police stations on the twenty-third, providing the "German October" with its only Red martyrs.[56] But, aside from several dozen Communist corpses (and about a dozen police victims), the Russians had ultimately bought very little with their money. The failure of Hitler's putsch in Munich on 8–9 November, and the ban on the NSDAP announced by General Seeckt on 23 November, might have cheered up German Communists—except that the restoration of order in Bavaria, coupled with the introduction of a new *Rentenmark* pegged against the dollar (soon further dissolved into a *Reichsmark* [RM] backed by gold), signaled the end of the Ruhr crisis and all the explosive possibilities its chaos had offered to revolutionaries. Even the usually excitable Ruth Fischer refused Radek's order to stage demonstrations in Berlin protesting the deposition of the Saxon government.[57] On the same day the Nazi party was banned, the KPD was itself declared illegal. The Red Flag would not fly over Berlin—not for a long while, anyway.

Aftermath: From Red Army to Red Soup Kitchens

Resounding political defeats in the history of Communism have nearly always been followed by lengthy bouts of recriminations and opportunistic maneuvering for position, and the bungled October action of 1923 was no different. In official party lore, Heinrich Brandler was the principal scapegoat. Brandler was deemed guilty of backing down too easily when the Reichswehr called the Communists' bluff, instead of staging a fighting retreat. Because Radek had been the Bolsheviks' principal man on the ground in Germany, he too received a lion's share of blame for October. Trotsky, too, merely by his friendly association with Radek and Brandler, lost further ground against the ascending triumvirate of Bolsheviks who were now set to replace the ailing Lenin—Stalin, Zinoviev, and Kamenev. In Germany, the principal beneficiary of Brandler's fall was Ruth Fischer, who, by throwing in her lot with Zinoviev against Brandler and Radek, would now be given the reins of the KPD Zentrale, along with her young allies from the so-called "Berlin left opposition," Arkadi Maslov and Ernst Thälmann.[58]

The scapegoating of Brandler, Radek, and Trotsky was, of course, nonsensical. The policy pursued in Dresden had been made in Moscow, with total disregard for the balance of armed force on the ground in Germany. This policy had been supported by just about everyone in the KPD Zentrale, and by all the leading Bolsheviks in Moscow, Stalin and Zinoviev prominent among them. Just the same, prudence dictated that Communists distance themselves from the failures of 1923 as quickly and thoroughly as possible: the earlier one had (retroactively) realized the bankruptcy of the revolutionary policy, the better.

No one was better at this game than Münzenberg. Just hours after the failure of the Beer Hall Putsch in Munich on 9 November 1923, Münzenberg wrote Zinoviev that the Nazis' defeat proved that a period of political moderation was opening up in Germany (yet again revealing how much Nazis and Communists had in common). "Brandler and certain other comrades," he wrote, had wanted to "rise up to no purpose." By contrast, Münzenberg had long ago realized that the "question of a German revolution is a much more protracted one."[59] This was certainly the correct line to take in the aftermath of October, whether or not Münzenberg had really taken it actually in October as he claimed (and I have found no evidence that he did). In the ascendant Zinoviev (as opposed to Willi's other Zurich comrade Karl Radek, whose star was now in decline), he had furthermore chosen the right man to whom to make the pitch.

Münzenberg also had a staff of loyalists in Moscow to look after his interests, and he set them to work immediately after the disaster in Dresden. Because the granting of Russian food aid was one of the few propagandistic bright spots of the recent events, Münzenberg hit on the idea of a German "famine relief campaign" as balm for the wounded egos of October. At the urging of Münzenberg's longtime loyalist Max Barthel, who had recently been assigned to the Russian IAH office, on 25 October 1923 the Comintern's "Orgburo" granted the IAH a three-month Communist fund-raising monopoly for an "aid action for Germany."[60] On 1 November, Barthel sent a circular from Moscow to all of the IAH's local branches in Russia, demanding they scale back "commercial" activities and focus immediate attention on fund-raising and publicity for the German relief effort.[61] The same day, Barthel sent a deliberately flattering memo to Zinoviev asking the old Bolshevik for a "sound bite" that could be used to drum up interest in the German hunger situation—in his own handwriting if possible.[62] Zinoviev's casually penned words of wisdom were promptly dispatched to Berlin, to be splashed across the front page of Münzenberg's new IAH bulletin on the *Famine in Germany*.[63] The official blessing on the IAH's newfound mission of directing German famine relief for the Comintern, was granted by ECCI on 10 November 1923, in a resolution that simultaneously, officially—and belatedly—liquidated the IAH's scandal-plagued Russian relief campaign.[64]

Münzenberg had meanwhile plunged into the so-called German aid campaign with his usual abandon. As always, agitprop came first. The new *Famine in Germany* bulletin was appearing in German, French, and English editions by early November.[65] Without waiting for authorization from Moscow, Münzenberg appropriated a thousand dollars from the IAH's hard currency reserve for setting up soup kitchens in Berlin.[66]

With this furious rush of activity, Münzenberg hoped to forge a fait accompli that Moscow couldn't disavow. Thus in a "personal" 28 October 1923 letter to the Comintern's Orgburo budget chief Iosif Piatnitskii, he described his accomplishments to date on the German hunger campaign with typical exaggeration ("committees are springing up in every country!"), before warning that he couldn't keep borrowing money from other IAH campaigns much longer. If full Comintern financing did not come through by November 1, Münzenberg warned, he would have to suspend the campaign indefinitely.[67] This was a bluff—Münzenberg had never been loath to divert funds into exciting new projects, with or without Kremlin authorization— but it may have helped accelerate the ponderous Comintern bureaucracy. In addition to endorsing Münzenberg's campaign with formal executive resolutions, Piatnitskii appointed a special Kremlin liaison to the IAH's German hunger campaign on 6 November 1923, and on Münzenberg's request, the ECCI agreed to order all national Communist sections to cooperate fully with the new IAH campaign.[68]

The IAH's own national branches had been putting word out as well, but their appeals were mostly ignored. Few Communist parties in Europe wanted to waste more of their scarce fund-raising energy on the IAH's pet propaganda projects. The French Communist editors of *L'Humanité*, for example, were so enraged about the IAH's failure to explain what had happened to the "aid packets" from the Russian relief that they refused even to publicize the new campaign.[69]

French skepticism about the new campaign was actually quite warranted, although not for the reasons first given in Paris. Regardless of the IAH's poor track record, the new "famine" relief campaign was a dubious cause on its merits, as Münzenberg knew better than anyone, because Germany was not in fact experiencing a famine in 1923. True, the Ruhr crisis had caused widespread distress and disrupted the flow of agricultural goods to the market, as farmers remained reluctant to sell their output for near-worthless paper money. The state of near-wartime mobilization of early autumn had wreaked further havoc with supply routes—this was why the Russian strategic grain reserve had been placed at the IAH's disposal for use in Saxony and Thuringia.

But Germany in fact experienced a bumper harvest in summer 1923, and the Prussian minister of agriculture announced this fact on 12 October.[70] The IAH's new German campaign was not, in fact, about famine relief at all. Although Russian food aid was the ostensible inspiration for the new initiative, Münzenberg revealingly spent little time in late autumn 1923 organizing grain shipments. Barthel's first request to ECCI asked not for more grain but for money.[71] To lend credibility to Barthel's request, his signature was authorized for the IAH accounts at Prombank, and this authorization was forwarded to ECCI as a hint to deposit cash there for the new German campaign.[72] During a closed, Communists-only session of the IAH World Congress in December 1923, Münzenberg all but admitted he was out to raid his supporters' pocketbooks, recommending national IAH delegates not send foodstuffs to Germany, because cash was "more useful."[73] As always in IAH fund-raising campaigns, monies raised were to be dispatched forthwith to Berlin, instead of being used to buy grain on the international market or in other rashly independent actions.[74]

What Münzenberg meant to do with this money, meanwhile, was politically inspired. Famine or no famine, there were certainly a lot of malcontents in Germany who had been economically ruined in 1923, not least in Berlin. Several hundred thousand were unemployed there by year's end, and a not insignificant number had died of hunger or by taking their own lives during the late stages of the inflation.[75] "Red" soup kitchens, Münzenberg pointed out at the IAH World Congress in December, could easily feed "three to ten thousand people daily," and if the ostensibly nonpolitical directors of these facilities would receive the proper instruction, they could spread Communist doctrine subtly and indirectly, without fear of arrest—at a time when the party was banned and under strict surveillance. In the open public sessions of this congress, Münzenberg understandably stressed the humanitarian aspects of the soup kitchen idea, rallying the IAH's house intellectuals and various hangers-on behind the arresting slogan that "Germans are going hungry in front of overflowing granaries." Yet behind closed doors, he assured the IAH's Communist functionaries that the purpose of the kitchens was to continue preparations for "the Revolution" while the political striking power of the party was "crippled."[76] Thus the official ideological line of the campaign forbade politically unreliable persons from handing out food in IAH soup kitchens—while simultaneously demanding that such reliably revolutionary personalities maintain a cooperative relationship with local municipal authorities so as not to attract suspicion.[77]

The sums of money turned over in the early days of the IAH's German hunger campaign were not huge, but it still must be counted among Münzenberg's agitprop successes. By February 1924, more than fifty-eight soup kitchens had been established in Berlin alone, blanketing the working-class districts of Wedding, Prenzlauer Berg, Friedrichshain, and Lichtenberg.[78] Outside the capital, IAH soup kitchens were fewer and farther between, but wherever one had sprung up, a local IAH fund-raising committee had soon followed. Halle, Hamburg, Frankfurt, and Breslau had been relative backwaters during the Volga famine drives of 1921–22. Inspired by the soup kitchen campaign (and the prospect of circumventing the KPD ban), Communists in each city now contributed their fair share of functionaries to the IAH's international orbit of committees.[79]

Inevitably, the mushrooming of Red soup kitchens attracted the unfavorable attention of the police in at least some towns. But such attention must have seemed a compliment to Münzenberg. With the KPD silenced by the November ban, the IAH was no longer merely an afterthought, but a real troublemaker on the German political scene. Münzenberg forwarded the most "scathing" government report handed down on the IAH to Moscow as a badge of honor. How could the IAH secretary not have been proud of the "proof" offered by the police inspectorate of Gelsenkirchen, near Essen, that the IAH was surreptitiously building "a mass organization for the KPD": no less than ten thousand membership cards had already been printed in this small town, with the cost of joining the IAH running at half a gold mark apiece.[80]

The Red soup kitchens gave the IAH a relevance it had never before had in Germany, and this raised Münzenberg's status in the German Communist world significantly. Once again, the Comintern's most shameless guru of agitprop had fashioned a winning cause out of the trash heap of failed Communist polices, defying inertia, economics, logic, and political gravity. Furthermore, the German relief campaign must have come as particularly welcome distraction for Münzenberg from the ongoing scandals in Soviet Russia. In the nick of time, a new cause célèbre had appeared on the horizon, offering in its wake a wonderful catharsis of nonstop activity, fresh propaganda material, and old friendships renewed. But if the messes of the past could sometimes be pushed cavalierly aside to make way for new excitements, they could not be avoided forever.

CHAPTER 9 *Follow the Money*

While the antifascist initiative and the new German "famine relief" drive did much to improve Münzenberg's political standing in the KPD, neither promised to ease ongoing tensions between the International Worker Relief and other national Communist parties. The pointblank refusal by the French to join the German hunger campaign escalated still further a war Münzenberg was already waging with his enemies over control of Comintern cash flow, which was beginning to dry up now that the Bolsheviks had blown so much of the looted wealth of Imperial Russia on the botched German adventures of 1919, 1921, and 1923. So desperate for funds were the leaders of the American Communist Party by late 1923, according to Münzenberg, that they deputized a party member who also worked for the FSR to lift twenty-five thousand dollars directly from the safe in the FSR's office, located in the Flatiron Building on Broadway not far from Union Square.[1]

Dramatic as this single theft may have been, it appears to have scarcely made anyone bat an eye at ECCI, so common was this kind of embezzlement becoming. Although Zinoviev and Piatnitskii expressed sympathy with Münzenberg's case, they finally punted the matter on in late December 1923, asking the IAH secretary to content himself with a Comintern circular ordering member parties in the future not to "divert collections to purposes other [than that for which they were collected]."[2] Münzenberg himself was, of course, as guilty as anyone of "diverting" funds to other purposes, as the entire Volga campaign had made painfully clear. In this sense, there was a sort of poetic justice in ECCI's nonbinding resolution on the matter, as if the Kremlin had decided to let embezzlers be embezzlers, so long as they weren't caught red-handed.

In the absence of Kremlin intervention in his financial disputes with the Communist member parties, the finances of Münzenberg's strange corporate empire continued to flounder. IAH debts were piling up in Russia at Kremlin-controlled banks such as Gosbank—none more important than the obligations for the "workers' loan" the bank had assumed in spring, debts that were already running in the tens of thousands of dollars. The same was happening at Prombank, to the extent that it seemed foolish to continue to pretend that the IAH "owned" its far-flung commercial concerns, since it couldn't even pay for their ordinary operating expenses.[3] By October, for example, the house of horrors known as the IAH fishery on the Volga near Astrakhan had run through the entire fifteen thousand dollars Münzenberg had sunk into the operation in January 1923 out of proceeds from the workers' loan—and this was without paying seven thousand dollars in rent and permit fees owed to the Soviet Central Board of Fisheries.[4] The Moscow boot factory was still draining over four thousand dollars a month, and producing nothing, although some of its earlier output was still being sold out of an IAH warehouse store in Moscow.[5]

And those were the businesses that actually sold things. Most of the other outposts in Münzenberg's commercial empire in the USSR, such as the Moscow apartments and dachas, the outpatient clinic, garage, and hair salon, along with his 25 percent share in Hotel Lux, served mainly as perks to keep IAH employees happy.[6]

By the end of 1923, the Russian IAH office had no reliable source of income other than Soviet bank credits.[7] Certainly the one remaining "aid" operation—the children's homes in the Urals and their accompanying propaganda schools—was not helping, as it was running losses more than ten times revenues, even with the ever robust donations from the FSR still arriving in Moscow via Berlin. A minor exception to the general rule of red ink was embodied in the Volga famine "care packages" still being sold to gullible donors in the United States. Such sales netted over a thousand dollars in "profit" from September to December 1923, because there were, in fact, no famine victims left to buy food packets for.[8] But such blatant fraud was hardly worthy of celebration.

All this, however, represented mere pennies compared to Jung's tractor boondoggle in the Urals, which had produced such an impressive mountain of debt as to be, in a backhanded way, a financial asset. It is hard to imagine the director of the Finance Department of the Russian IAH office keeping a straight face as he signed off on a balance sheet for Ural-AG in December 1923 listing no less than 317,268.98 gold rubles in debits as against one hundred thirty *chervontsi* of credits, leaving net obligations of 317,138.98 gold rubles, or nearly $160,000.[9] Clearly little of this money, which had been fronted mainly by gullible foreign investors and the members of an American tailors' union defrauded by Jung, was ever going to be returned in the way of profits. And yet Münzenberg continued to list the Ural-AG property as collateral for the workers' loan, the obligations for which the Russian IAH office was beginning to pay out incrementally (although the Kremlin was actually footing the bill, through Gosbank).[10] As if this was not enough, Münzenberg went so far in autumn 1923 as to suggest rolling over the debts piling up at the Pinaevo property in southern Russia, near the border of what is now Kazakhstan, into the Ural-AG accounts, on the specious logic that both concerns were agricultural.

The Münzenberg method of financial house cleaning was, in short, to throw bad money after bad wherever possible (as with Pinaevo's debts being subsumed into those of Ural-AG), and liquidate lower-profile financial messes (such as the fishery, the boot factory, the outpatient clinic, and the children's homes) by "generously" offering to turn their debt-ridden operations over to the Soviet government. This was what Münzenberg did in late October 1923, at the same time he was petitioning ECCI for the new "German hunger" mandate. By giving up on these concerns—except for the profitable, though controversially un-"proletarian" restaurant, which Münzenberg, significantly, refused to let go of—he was tacitly admitting that his "industrial assistance" campaign, by means of which the Soviet government had theoretically enlisted the expertise of the global proletariat through the IAH to modernize a range of Russian industries and make them more efficient, was an abysmal failure. All the Kremlin had received from Münzenberg for these concessions was fraud, mismanagement, and debt. The German hunger campaign, then, was clearly aimed at reasserting the IAH's sullied reputation as an "aid" organization in Moscow, just as its commercial empire was crashing into ruins.[11]

On the aid front, meanwhile, Münzenberg had his sights on the accounts of another cash-rich Communist organization whose fund-raising clout dwarfed his own. Whereas the IAH had progressively tied itself up in dozens of nearly incoherent missions, the International Red Aid (MOPR) had since its inception in 1921 carried out a simple, and eminently useful, task: paying the legal bills of Communist Party activists jailed for political offenses. Nearly all of the Comintern's member parties gave high fund-raising priority to MOPR causes, and the organization was guaranteed a share of funds raised through the Kremlin-controlled unions belonging to the "Red Labor

International," or Profintern, as well. The Soviet Union's government-controlled domestic unions, in particular, consistently coughed up thousands of rubles to MOPR in the name of "labor solidarity."

Throughout the winter of 1923–24, Münzenberg and MOPR carried on a fund-raising turf war over the German hunger campaign, with MOPR dominating the field inside Russia, and cutting the IAH off from the German-speaking regions of Czechoslovakia and Switzerland as well. Münzenberg did have the better of the draw in Germany itself, where new IAH locals formed due to the soup kitchen initiative were generously beginning to underwrite some of MOPR's activities, supporting families of arrested party activists in Berlin, Hamburg, and elsewhere.[12] But Münzenberg overplayed this hand, exaggerating his German expansion in dispatches to Moscow to the point where MOPR leaders had credible grounds for complaint. In some cases, Münzenberg bragged, the IAH had even paid for the defense of MOPR personnel themselves, who due to the organization's traditionally high profile in Germany had been heavily targeted by the police during the winter crackdown on the KPD.[13]

Such boasting played right into the hands of MOPR's lobbyists in Moscow, who won both of the Kremlin's early decisions on the fund-raising fight in winter 1924. If Münzenberg was doing so well with the German campaign, Piatnitskii and Zinoviev seem to have decided, then surely he could share some of its bounty with MOPR—specifically, 10 percent of monies raised outside of Russia, and no less than 25 percent in countries where MOPR was still weak, such as Canada and South Africa. Adding insult to injury, Moscow refused to order reciprocal revenue sharing inside the Soviet Union, where MOPR, according to Misiano, had as of April 1924 still not turned over a kopek to the IAH.[14]

This was all very bad news, but it was not the worst. Even while Münzenberg was being ordered to turn over a percentage of his meager international fund-raising proceeds to the very rival doing most to undercut them, the most reliable source of cash flow in his entire organizational empire—the FSR—was being invaded by the enemy. Israel Amter, international secretary of MOPR, had seized on the favorable Kremlin decisions as grounds to move in for the kill. In a telegram from Moscow to American Communist Party headquarters in New York City, Amter cited a string of Comintern resolutions in order to create the misleading impression that the IAH itself was going to be liquidated in three months.[15] Amter's telegram further weakened Münzenberg's position in New York, where, as we have seen, Communist Party leaders had seldom shown compunction about laying claim to FSR funds. If the Kremlin failed to stop Amter's intrigues, Münzenberg wrote in a desperate direct plea to Zinoviev in late April, the consequences for the German relief drive—and the IAH more generally—could be "catastrophic."[16]

For once, Münzenberg's melodramatic tone may have been justified. The IAH's public reputation as a "fund-raising" organization had never really gotten off the ground in western Europe, nor in Russia, where the manifest failures of the industrial assistance program were there for all to see. But on the other side of the Atlantic Ocean, there were still thousands of believers. FSR care packages for Volga victims were being sold to gullible donors in the United States until late in 1923, and the German hunger campaign struck a powerful chord, especially among the large German population in the Midwest. In early 1924, FSR headquarters were moved to Chicago, presumably to accommodate the shift in the organization's fund-raising locus.[17] Nearly fifty thousand dollars had been raised for Münzenberg's new hunger campaign by April, with cash coming in at a pace not seen since 1921.[18] Because of the FSR's move to Chicago, jealous Communist rivals in New York had yet been able to get their hands in this trough. But if the rumors spread by Amter about the IAH's imminent demise gained a foothold in Chicago, there was no telling how long Münzenberg could stave off a hostile takeover of his greatest fund-raising asset.

The risk posed by Amter's attack on FSR was a real one, but in truth Münzenberg had never really had exclusive control of the organization's funds in the first place. Of the more than one million dollars donated to the FSR by unions and individuals in the organization's first three years, little more than a tenth had been sent directly to Berlin. Aside from domestic agitprop and film distribution expenses, FSR leaders had always shown strong initiative in purchasing foodstuffs, clothes, machine tools, parts, tractors, and the like, and sending them directly to Russia. The percentage of FSR aid revenues turned over to Berlin increased, logically, with the onset of the German hunger campaign in November 1923, but only from 10 percent to about 25 percent. Although less than Münzenberg wanted, this amount still represented, by far, the most significant source of IAH revenue.[19]

Besides, FSR was much more than a cash cow. Only in America did the IAH really do what Münzenberg tirelessly claimed it was doing—carry the Communist flag outside the boundaries reached by the parent party, win over sympathizers, and not least, collect money from them. The IAH children's homes and commercial properties in the Soviet Union may have been run into the ground, but no one knew this in the United States, where the FSR's prestige in left-wing circles remained unblemished. Its supporters included such intellectual luminaries as the journalist Max Eastman, the muckraking novelist Upton Sinclair, the poet Mary Heaton Vorse, and even Helen Keller.[20] Perhaps more significantly, thousands of ordinary Americans continued to flood FSR with letters requesting photographs of children receiving "care packages" or information about Russian relatives who had disappeared in the days of the Red Terror. The Chicago office, run by an energetic young Communist named Rose Karsner, was both a real and a symbolic asset, and Münzenberg was desperate to hold onto it.[21]

Once more, though, all he got from the Kremlin was a punt. A Comintern executive resolution handed down in May 1924 nominally disowned Amter's claim that the IAH was being dissolved, but offered no concrete guidelines to help Münzenberg recover any revenues that might have been lost due to the confusion.[22] Without Moscow's active backing, Münzenberg was, ultimately, powerless in American Communist circles. The FSR's new Chicago office stopped sending cash to Berlin sometime in August, and Amter's agents had seized control of the FSR accounts there by December.[23] Although Rose Karsner and one old FSR comrade, Jay Lovestone, remained loyal to Münzenberg, they were now outnumbered by MOPR loyalists in the Chicago office, who insisted there was "no room in America for two [Communist aid] organizations."[24]

The only good news for Münzenberg came in Germany, where the KPD had been relegalized in time to participate in the May 1924 Reichstag elections. In his correspondence with Zinoviev after the failed German October, Münzenberg had consistently sung the praises of Ruth Fischer and her so-called Berlin Left allies who had taken over the reins of the party.[25] In exchange for this support, Fischer put forward Münzenberg's name for a Reichstag slot in the May 1924 elections, from Electoral District 19 (Hesse-Nassau, near Frankfurt-am-Main). Münzenberg had no particular connection to this district, but this was hardly out of the ordinary in the parliamentary system of the Weimar Republic, where the major parties consistently ran favored figures in whichever district offered the best chance to win seats. And win Münzenberg did, along with sixty-two other German Communists, who surprised nearly everyone by actually increasing their share of the vote despite Germany's recent economic stabilization. From May 1924 until the last days of the Weimar Republic, Münzenberg, as a Reichstag deputy, would enjoy immunity from prosecution, mail franking privileges, a rail ticket, and untold other perks unavailable to IAH functionaries who would continue to toil at great risk on his behalf.

His Reichstag triumph notwithstanding, Münzenberg's clout in the

Kremlin had, in truth, fallen to its lowest ebb since he had lost control of the Youth International in 1921. Fed up with years of corruption in the Russian IAH commercial labyrinth—the latest complaints related to the diversion of "German hunger" donations into the Astrakhan fishery—the Comintern executive finally began reining in the IAH by absorbing its Russian office into the organizational structure of the Russian Communist Party, which had, of course, always financed its operations anyway.[26]

The administrative shake-up in Moscow alarmed Münzenberg enough that he sent a long letter to Moscow in late December 1924 reasserting his legal claim to all of the IAH's far-flung concessions and properties through the joint American-German firm Aufbau he had incorporated in Berlin. In a legal sense, he declared, every single IAH venture in publishing, manufacturing, or film, anywhere in the world, belonged ultimately to Aufbau and its board of directors (which he incidentally headed).[27]

But this declaration, like the original claim to these properties found in Aufbau's incorporation documents from summer 1922, was unilateral and had little force behind it without the backing of the Kremlin. Münzenberg's concerns in the Soviet Union, just like his punchless efforts to raise funds for German "famine" victims there, had always depended ultimately on the Soviet government (which is to say, the Russian Communist Party), and there was nothing different now, except that the Kremlin was being more assertive than previously in pointing out this fact. From Piatnitskii and Zinoviev at ECCI to Stalin and Kamenev in the Russian Politburo, Münzenberg answered to many bosses, and at the moment, none of them were delivering what he wanted for the IAH. Small wonder, then, that in December 1924 Münzenberg tried yet again, as he had in June 1923 at the time of the embarrassing auditing commission report, to quit the struggling organization, sounding out Bela Kun in the Comintern's agitprop department in December about the possibility of replacing Hugo Eberlein as KPD propaganda tsar.[28]

But there was no way the Kremlin was going to let Münzenberg off the hook that easily. With the MOPR controversy still swirling and the IAH's commercial empire in Russia stumbling along on the brink of bankruptcy, it was not a good time to bring in a replacement. Münzenberg still enjoyed the personal confidence of Zinoviev, whether or not Kremlin gold was currently available for his pet propaganda projects. In any case, it is unlikely Münzenberg really wanted to leave the IAH—he was certainly not about to forfeit his claim to Aufbau's far-flung properties. What Münzenberg truly wanted to disown in December 1924 was the messy "aid" business, where MOPR was beating him handily.

He should, however, have been careful what he wished for. Although no one in the Kremlin called his bluff to quit the IAH, Münzenberg's few remaining streams of aid revenue were running dry by the end of 1924. He secured no Kremlin subsidies at all for Berlin IAH headquarters for the rest of the winter. With both of his principal lifelines in the aid game—aid donations in America and Kremlin subsidies—severed for the foreseeable future, there was little for Münzenberg to do but cut back on expenses in Berlin, abandon his plans for agitprop expansion, and slash his bloated executive staff just to stay afloat. The bloodletting of winter 1925 was long overdue, and for that reason turned out to be exceptionally brutal. The Berlin IAH staff had peaked at close to seven hundred back in fall 1923; Münzenberg would now slash the payroll close to zero. All nonessential support staff were given notice on 1 February. Seven more upper-level bureaucrats, including several of the highest-ranking women in the organization, were fired later that week. Subsidies from Berlin headquarters for the rapidly expanding German domestic branch of the IAH were suspended in March, and the paid staffers at the Neue Deutsche Verlag (NDV), the publishing house Münzenberg had recently incorporated to circumvent *Rote Fahne* after it refused to continue publishing IAH inserts, would all be replaced by Münzenberg's wife Babette Gross, who would subsist on his coin.

In this way Münzenberg freed up enough money to send several of his most important assistants abroad on recruiting trips. The Dutch Communist Wilhelm Kruyt was dispatched to Amsterdam; the secretary of the domestic German IAH committee, Paul Scholze, to Vienna; and the Frenchman F. Levassor to Paris. But these men would have to earn this perquisite: with minimal staff, each would now be responsible for administering close to a dozen divisions of the IAH's international empire.[29]

Most of these responsibilities were fantasies, of course. If there really were fully operative national committees raising funds for IAH causes in the dozens of countries listed in the new mandates for Levassor, Kruyt, and Scholze, Münzenberg would hardly have needed to slash their staff budgets and beg for more Moscow gold. The way to loosen the Kremlin's purse strings, he had acutely recognized during the Volga aid campaign of 1921, was to cultivate an impression of ubiquitous activity, while conspicuously making "economies" to create the appearance of fiscal responsibility. Münzenberg, after outlining the new staff duties, now wrote up a streamlined prospective monthly budget for spring 1925, with a checklist of reasonable-sounding monthly subsidies for both national branches and Berlin office expenses (e.g., $200 for "the Balkans," $250 for the NDV, and $300 for office rent).

The budget deviously hid the organization's indulgent spending habits in nebulous categories such as "salaries" and "communications" ($2500), "unforeseen expenses" ($1000) and Aufbau ($4000). Significantly, Münzenberg asked for $500 per month to kick-start a new IAH office in America, where FSR had once been entirely self-supporting. In all, Münzenberg suggested, Moscow should pony up $10,000 a month to lubricate his operations—and this was just for the "normal" budget, which did not include perks like travel and vacation pay.[30]

These budget figures were only optimistic projections, an ideal scenario for the IAH if ECCI decided not to eliminate his organization entirely. But Münzenberg's financial blueprint of April 1925 is revealing: it represents the first time he abandoned the pretense that the IAH was self-supporting. To justify his new demands, Münzenberg again promised the Kremlin that he would liquidate the IAH's failing commercial concerns.[31] To cover his political flank, Münzenberg dashed off an obsequious letter to his old friend Zinoviev in early May—signing off in the latest servant-master idiom of Bolshevism, "I place myself as always entirely at your disposal"—in which he promised to use his propaganda organs to counter a supposed wave of anti-Bolshevik reaction sweeping over Europe.[32] Münzenberg repeated this pledge in an even more obsequious letter to Stalin, in which he humbly asked the master of the Russian Politburo for a flattering recent picture of him to be put on the cover of the next issue of the IAH's illustrated monthly (formerly *Hammer and Sickle,* now restyled *Arbeiter Illustrierte Zeitung* or *AIZ*).[33]

Summer came and went, however, and still no Kremlin gold arrived in Berlin. So tight were finances that Münzenberg was forced to suspend publication of a special AIZ photomontage series on the "Terror in the Balkans" which had followed the Bulgarian Communists' audacious terrorist bombing of Sveta Nedelya Cathedral in Sofia on 16 April 1925, during a service at which the entire government and military leadership was in attendance. Amazingly, every one of the targeted officials survived, although 120 bystanders did not.[34]

Not until late autumn, when the hated auditing commission conducted a new audit for ECCI, was the fate of the IAH really put on the table in the Moscow Kremlin. And the verdict was not good. There would be no intervention by Moscow to return the FSR's accounts to Münzenberg. Worse, due to his ineptitude in the commercial arena, his principal creditor, Prombank —owed over seven hundred thousand gold rubles—was allowed to foreclose on most of the IAH's remaining Russian properties. In recognition of its de facto bankruptcy, Münzenberg's industrial empire would go into a kind of receivership, with managerial control to be gradually handed over to Prombank-appointed directors, and the whole process overseen by the Kremlin.[35]

In all likelihood, Münzenberg welcomed the inevitable liquidation of his failing industrial concerns. He had himself "threatened" many times to liquidate them, although of course he had wanted cash in exchange for doing this. For him, the foreclosure was an excuse to retool the IAH as an exclusively media-oriented organization devoted purely to Soviet propaganda.

Such, at any rate, was the mission Münzenberg outlined in yet another prospective monthly IAH budget in December 1925, which had the undeniable merit from Moscow's perspective of being half the size of the one he had written up earlier that spring. The new budget was also more realistic, abandoning the now nonexistent American section, and demanding appropriately modest outlays for other countries where MOPR had taken over Münzenberg's turf, such as Switzerland (thirty dollars a month) and Czechoslovakia (fifty dollars a month). The only expense that Münzenberg wanted to increase significantly was for the China office in Peking, through which, for five hundred dollars a month, he promised to spearhead Moscow's new "anti-imperialism" offensive in Asia. In all, Münzenberg was asking for "merely" five thousand dollars a month for the IAH, of which a hefty 30 percent would go for his own headquarters in Berlin. This amount, he lied, was roughly what the IAH used to draw from its Russian commercial operations, which were now being turned over to Prombank.[36]

The December budget represented a genuine retrenchment of IAH activities, and it is not surprising that ECCI, in the main, approved it.[37] On nearly every front, Münzenberg had lost ground in the Moscow budget wars. He had been all but wiped off the map in the United States, and rebuffed by the Russian unions. Most embarrassingly, the IAH debt pyramid scheme once known as "industrial assistance" had finally collapsed under its own weight. As Misiano dryly explained in a postmortem on the *Wirtschaftshilfe* campaign delivered to ECCI in late May 1926, the "most important reasons" for the IAH's commercial collapse were "too many ventures, no [financial] means, [too] many debts."[38]

But there were still enough Communist sympathizers in Europe to warrant a nebulously defined front organization such as the IAH, which could envelop left-wing circles in a mist of pro-Soviet propaganda that was at least moderately more credible than that promoted directly by parent parties. This new, seemingly limited mandate in fact offered Münzenberg exactly what he wanted. With the days of unexciting aid shipments and industrial capital-squandering logistics behind him, Münzenberg could now shift his full attention to the field of agitprop, which had always excited him the most. Nothing, he was convinced, offered better potential for pro-Soviet publicity than the movies.

CHAPTER 10 *Hollywood East*

If there was a silver lining buried somewhere inside the scandal-ridden depths of Münzenberg's commercial empire, we might best look for it in the record of the IAH's well-publicized foray into the international film business. European cinema was just coming into its own in the 1920s, the golden age of silent film, and fortunately for Münzenberg, the most vibrant production centers in postwar Europe were almost without question his own dual haunts, Berlin and Moscow. Probing for inspiration amidst the cultural ruins of Europe's two postwar pariah states, German and Russian directors in their turn introduced to the world such avant-garde classics as R. Wiene's *Cabinet of Dr. Caligari* (1919), Fritz Lang's *Doctor Mabuse* (1922), and Sergei Eisenstein's *Battleship Potemkin* (1925). Münzenberg's acquisition of the German distribution rights for *Potemkin* was merely the most prominent coup for the IAH, which also brought German films to Russia and produced its own movies through its Soviet subsidiary, the celebrated film collective Mezhrabpom-Russ (M-Russ), which featured the talents of both renowned director Yakov Protazanov and Russia's most popular stage actor, Ivan Moskvin.[1]

Whereas Münzenberg's murky involvement in Russian agriculture, real estate, and heavy industry has excited little interest among historians of the NEP, his entry into the more glamorous motion picture industry has elicited favorable scholarly attention. Through efficient management of M-Russ, Vance Kepley claims, Münzenberg's men were able to draw profits that were then "reinvested in the company's expanded production schedule." Because of the IAH's ostensible independence from the Soviet authorities, Kepley explains, M-Russ was unafraid to pour money into ideologically risky films such as Protazanov's ambitious sci-fi extravaganza *Aelita* (1924). Such political risk-taking meant that M-Russ "consistently outperform[ed] other Russian companies at the box office."[2]

Such putative successes in Moscow, to be sure, would mainly have been due to the work of the Berlin IAH secretary's far-flung staff appointees, but Münzenberg himself is often given personal credit for the IAH's distribution coups on the international market. "Without Münzenberg's internationalist vision and entrepreneurial skills," Ian Christie argues, "it seems doubtful, to say the least, that Soviet cinema would have achieved its fame and outreach in the 1920s, faced with obstacles both commercial and political on all sides."[3] Kepley goes even further in his praise, crediting "the communist-entrepreneur Willi Münzenberg" with the establishment of the only "worldwide socialist film organization" ever to rival the monolithic domination of "world-capitalist cinema."[4]

Upon closer view, however, Münzenberg's "entrepreneurial skills" turn out to have been no less conspicuously absent from his entry into the film industry than they were from all his other commercial concessions in the USSR. Those who claim otherwise have based their interpretations on a naïve and uncritical reading of the IAH's own propaganda, which for obvious reasons flatters both Münzenberg and the early Soviet film industry in equal measure. The data out of which such sympathetic film scholars fashion what appears to have been a commercially viable industry are shaky and consistently unreliable.[5]

In fact, Münzenberg's Russian and German subsidiaries, like Soviet film producers more generally, were awash in Bolshevik subsidies without which they would not have stayed afloat. The money "invested" in M-Russ productions came not from commercial profits (which never materialized) but from the Kremlin. Any capital contributed by Berlin was either embezzled from other IAH ventures or from Comintern accounts (all directly subsidized by Moscow), staked rashly on credit, or backed by gullible foreign "capitalist" investors, who were fleeced in the process. It is unlikely, moreover, that penetration of Soviet films into the Western market would have been significantly less broad without Münzenberg's "internationalist vision." The IAH was not the only channel of distribution chosen by Russian filmmakers, nor was it, by a long shot, the most efficient. Even the *Potemkin* coup in Germany, for which Münzenberg may legitimately take some credit, was in financial terms a failure at best, a fact that has understandably been obscured by the movie's near-universal acclaim by film critics.

If Münzenberg was a poor excuse for an entrepreneur, however—in this as in every other business he touched—then it must also be said he was certainly one of the most successful salesmen in film history, with the caveat that the product he was actually selling, aside from the usual pro-Soviet publicity, was himself. Merely by showing Soviet-produced films somewhere, anywhere, Münzenberg could claim to be indispensably furthering the communist cause, and he did so with all his characteristic boldness. In the heady, experimental early years of the Soviet film industry, with its funhouse economics and makeshift production standards, Münzenberg was right in his element. Up was down, down was up, and when it came to budgeting—in an ironic parallel to the notorious excesses of capitalist Hollywood—the sky was the limit.

Münzenberg's involvement in film distribution grew directly out of his original IAH mandate from September 1921, which envisioned film festivals featuring Russian-made famine outtakes that would complement the various print bulletins and action committees.[6] One might think such propagandistic shorts, known as *agitki*, would be an easy sell, and maybe even a lucrative source of fund-raising income, once they had been produced. Certainly this was the Comintern's intention in sending two uncut *agitki* to Münzenberg's international hunger committee in Berlin in December 1921, on the understanding that any revenues accrued from ticket sales be used exclusively for the Volga relief effort.[7]

But then, nothing turned out to be so easy in the IAH's famine relief campaign. Once the footage had been thoroughly examined, most of it turned out to be choppy and "uninteresting," in Münzenberg's not so humble opinion.[8] Merely to make the footage presentable, he decided, would require weeks of editing, and the Berlin office would have to rent time in the expensive studios of Berlin-Babelsberg to do this. When copying costs, censor fees, and so on were factored in, Münzenberg figured it would take about four hundred thousand marks (about two thousand dollars at the current rates) just to get things moving.[9] Provisionally, Münzenberg set aside four thousand marks from the IAH's cash reserves for film processing in mid-December, while dispatching an urgent request for the "required" four hundred thousand marks to Moscow on the sixteenth. Mindful of the reputation for shady finance the Berlin Hunger Committee had already acquired in Moscow, Münzenberg promised to pay this sum back within six months, with interest, out of the revenues he expected the films to generate. To his chagrin, Münzenberg's funding request, which he reiterated repeatedly over the coming weeks in growing desperation, was ignored, in part because ECCI was having trouble keeping up with the furious pace of correspondence from Berlin.[10]

Doubtless Münzenberg intended to honor such a significant debt incurred to the Kremlin, but merely the fact that he asked for this loan reveals volumes about the shaky financial terms on which he entered the film business. When ECCI finally got around to replying to Münzenberg in late January 1922, the growing pile of aggressive film funding request letters from Berlin had set off alarm bells, especially in light of the escalating rumors that Münzenberg was starting to divert aid funds into buying industrial machinery. Wary of the "danger" that "our enemies [might] one day make use of revelations" about the misuse of aid monies, ECCI replied that it was already "self-evident" to Münzenberg that famine film proceeds "must entirely and exclusively be placed at the disposal of the famine aid campaign." Until this was understood, no seed money from Moscow would be forthcoming for Münzenberg's cinematic ambitions.[11]

Taking no for an answer was not, however, in Münzenberg's character. Figuring, as always, that the best way to loosen the Comintern's purse strings was to forge a fait accompli, he appropriated the necessary monies directly from the Berlin Hunger Committee's general collection fund in early January 1922. Over the next six weeks, more than four hundred thousand marks earmarked for the famine victims of the Volga were funneled into the purchase of film editing time in Berlin studios, labor, and censor fees. Much of this money had apparently been wasted, for by mid-February, when Münzenberg begged ECCI for the last time for famine film subsidies, no serviceable end product was ready for distribution.[12] In late March, the IAH-sponsored premieres of *Hunger in Soviet Russia* and *Starvation along the Banks of the Volga* were finally advertised in *Rote Fahne*, although by then it was far too late for the films to have much impact on the fund-raising efforts in Germany.[13] Perhaps sensing a lost cause, Münzenberg sent no more requests to ECCI that spring for reimbursement of his film outlays, concentrating instead on the IAH's industrial assistance campaign.

Had Münzenberg's short-lived efforts to turn his Berlin office into a do-it-yourself film processing operation been more successful, the developmental path of his entry into the motion picture industry might conceivably have resembled a viable alternative to the international "capitalist" model, as sympathetic film historians would have it. He might have served the communist cause through a blend of inexpensively produced Russian raw footage, German technical know-how, and a loyal audience base of foreign leftist sympathizers. Such a scenario might have seen Berlin imitating the continued successes of the FSR across the Atlantic, where William Kruse, an accomplished filmmaker, made his own famine movies on the cheap by editing Soviet newsreels. Kruse printed his films on twenty-eight-millimeter stock. This allowed him to use portable projection equipment for a successful series of one-time exhibitions in union halls and mining camps in the American Midwest, which ultimately drew in (according to Kruse's later recollection) almost forty thousand dollars.[14]

Münzenberg, however, unlike Kruse, had no experience making movies. Editing uncut famine footage was evidently no fun, and it was not long before Münzenberg realized that even completed propagandistic film shorts he acquired from the Soviet authorities offered little in the way of revenue, as not even his own IAH national committee chairmen wanted to put up money for them.[15] He saw more potential in the semiprivate Russian production companies that were beginning to thrive in the early NEP years, such as the so-called "North-West Cinema" or Sevzapkino, into which the Russian branch of IAH began to divert some of its cash flow in the winter of 1922–23.[16] On Münzenberg's instructions, negotiations had also begun between the Russian office of IAH and the state production companies Proletkino and Goskino in Moscow, although as yet to little effect.[17]

In the early days of the IAH, Münzenberg was mainly chasing down blind alleys in the Russian film business. This was perhaps inevitable as, aside from famine *agitki*, there was little serviceable Soviet product to be distributed abroad anyway. With the cities nearly emptied of people during the Civil War, Russia's fledgling film industry had all but ground to a halt in the first half-decade after the Revolution, due to a severe lack of capital, labor, and above all negative and positive film stock, which was not yet produced domestically. Only one studio had shown any promise: the so-called "Russ" collective, which had grown out of a tsarist-era private film studio of the same name, whose owner fled Russia with its cash after Lenin's coup —but not with its equipment or its employees. Moisei Aleinikov, a progressive Bolshevik admirer and longtime Russ employee, took over the studio's remaining assets and set up an artists' collective in early 1918, with shares distributed between himself and several like-minded political sympathizers with varying degrees of cinematic experience. Although the new Russ collective, like all the other old studios, remained all but idle at the height of the Civil War, when film stock and food to feed staff with were scarce, Aleinikov's grand ambitions and the idealistic atmosphere he cultivated helped attract the interest of some of Russia's leading actors. Among them was Ivan Moskvin, a popular veteran of the Moscow Art Theater, who had never before performed before the camera. Late in 1919, Moskvin happily accepted a title role for his film debut: the luckless, ignorant peasant of Lev Tolstoy's *Polikushka*, who fails in a futile mission he was charged with by a cruel landlord, and then hangs himself in despair.

The ultimate critical success of *Polikushka* in Germany made Russ's international reputation—and Münzenberg's, as he got credit for bringing the film to the West—but the legends surrounding this film have greatly obscured historical understanding. *Polikushka* was filmed under extremely trying conditions, during the harsh winter of 1919–20. It was bitterly cold in the unheated building in Petrovsky Park where the filming was done. Carefully controlled bonfires were lit underneath the sound stages merely to keep actors from freezing as they went about their business. The supply of negative film for *Polikushka* was limited to about twenty-five hundred meters, which meant that few second and third takes were allowed. This greatly frustrated Moskvin in particular, who as a lifetime stage actor was accustomed to lengthy rehearsal times and found himself barely able to prepare for his scenes at all.[18] Such conditions may have contributed to the film's nearly unanimous acclaim in Germany, where critics praised its stark visual "naturalism" and found Moskvin's performance unusually alive, if a bit histrionic. *Polikushka*, wrote the *Frankfurter Allgemeine Zeitung*'s reviewer in a tone of affectionately condescending approval in spring 1923, "was born in ice and cold, in hunger and deprivation."[19] Basking in the warm glow of *Polikushka*'s reception in Germany, film scholars have somehow misconstrued massive subsidies literally handed to Aleinikov and Kremlin distribution concessions gifted to Münzenberg as, respectively, profits and entrepreneurial talent.[20]

As an episode in Münzenberg's rise to prominence in the film business, the real *Polikushka* story is a classic illustration of the dictum that it is always better to be lucky than good. Aleinikov arrived in Berlin in summer 1922 with a copy of the film in hand, with specific instructions from Lenin to turn it over to Münzenberg.[21] This was not all. Gosbank had furnished Aleinikov with twelve million marks, in cash, with which he was to purchase positive and negative film stock in Berlin—purchases that were to benefit the Soviet film industry as a whole, and for which Aleinikov and Münzenberg would later take the credit (although neither of them had footed the bill). With his Kremlin slush fund, Aleinikov began purchasing reels of film from both Agfa and Kodak's Berlin office in November and December 1922, months before any revenues from *Polikushka* were reaped on the German market.[22]

All Münzenberg had to do in return for receiving the global distribution rights to *Polikushka* was—nothing. And in the second half of 1922, he did precisely that—nothing. Far from being the well-connected economic powerhouse Aleinikov had expected on Lenin's say-so, the IAH had no record at all distributing feature films in Germany, and Münzenberg was forced at last to enlist the services of the "bourgeois" German studio outfit Dafu to make copies of *Polikushka* and bring them to market. Not until March 1923 did the first ads for the film grace the pages of *Rote Fahne* and Münzenberg's own *Hammer and Sickle*—publicity, to be sure, was one thing Münzenberg could reliably deliver.[23] It is doubtful, though, that ads in either KPD or IAH organs made more than a minimal contribution to *Polikushka*'s success in Germany. Public curiosity about this first film export from the Soviet Union was high, and favorable advance notices were all over the "bourgeois" press. Once Dafu had done the grunt work of copying and distributing, Münzenberg was able to sit back and collect, not least from the resale of distribution rights for twenty thousand dollars in the United States —where interest in films coming out of the Soviet Union had been stimulated by Kruse's homemade *agitki* tours—and for two thousand dollars in Japan.[24]

In truth, Münzenberg had done little to distribute *Polikushka*—certainly nothing that more experienced film hands could not have done much better —but this did not stop him from taking the credit. With his usual boldness, Münzenberg declared a proprietary interest in the Russ studio based on his dubious *Polikushka* coup. During the opening session of the IAH World Congress convened in Berlin on 14 June 1923, Münzenberg referred to Russ as a "daughter organization," a boast he would try to make good on several weeks later while visiting Moscow.[25] According to a 26 June 1923 *udostvorenie*, or declaration of legal intent, signed by Münzenberg alone, the Russ collective, although retaining an "independent juridical identity," had "entered into the [organizational] structure of [Russian IAH]" and could thus be "termed a commercial organ of the IAH." Suspiciously, Münzenberg backdated a consent agreement here between the IAH and Russ to 6 March 1923—the exact date of *Polikushka*'s premiere in Berlin.[26] In this way, Münzenberg unilaterally laid claim to Russ's current and future output, much as he had earlier incorporated Aufbau to seize Russian commercial and real estate assets in 1922.

Unfortunately for Münzenberg, the Russ concession turned out to be no less strewn with economic and political landmines than the IAH's questionable industrial takeovers. In terms of its history, resident talent, and creative potential, Russ was a golden apple compared to the lumbering state giants Goskino and Proletkino, but in the communist world such apples were always poisoned by the possibility of political deviation. *Polikushka* was certainly a progressive film, populist in the classic tradition of Tolstoy in its moralistic condemnation of the idle Russian rich and selfish aristocracy, but it was hardly Marxist, let alone communist. As the first truly Soviet contribution to world cinema, *Polikushka* seems to have been granted an ideological pass by Lenin, who approved its export to Germany. But such political leeway could not possibly last forever.

Furthermore, when Münzenberg, buoyed by *Polikushka*'s success, brought several more prerevolutionary Russ films to Germany in 1923, even his own IAH employees complained. These films, especially *The Freemason* and Protozanov's *Satan Triumphant* (1917), scandalized delegates forced to sit through them at the IAH World Congress in June 1923. The first, complained one Swiss Communist, was "a frivolous monarchical feature through and through," while the second—heaven forbid!—was "religious." Catholics in Switzerland, the delegate exclaimed in horror, "would greedily hanker after this film" if the IAH sold it on the international market.[27]

Here was the same headache Münzenberg had faced with the decadent Moscow "workers' restaurant." Just as soon as the IAH got its hands on a product people might be willing to buy, sensitive Communists in the organization cried foul and demanded an ideological housecleaning. But Münzenberg was unperturbed. The dreary famine outtakes he had wasted months editing in Berlin in winter 1921–22 had drained precious cash and been total flops, whereas *Polikushka* all but publicized itself—and actually made money. Russ films may have been offensive to Communist doctrinaires, but people wanted to see them, unlike the straight agitprop productions being foisted on the world by the Soviet government, a painful fact confirmed by the constant refusal of IAH national branch offices to pay for them. Still, Münzenberg could not simply follow commercial imperatives in the film business—he was an avowed Communist, after all—especially in light of the ongoing IAH scandals in the Russian economy, where mixed motives and managerial incompetence had called the organization's very existence into question.

Münzenberg's position vis-à-vis the Soviet film industry was immeasurably complicated by the work of the IAH auditing commission, which after its inception in May 1923 was determined to turn Münzenberg's labyrinthine commercial empire into something resembling the international workers' collective it was supposed to be. One auditor in particular, Allan Vallenius, had it in for Münzenberg, and he was not impressed by the latter's Russ distribution coups. The IAH's greedy general secretary, Vallenius reported to ECCI in September 1923, "is more interested in breaking into the international bourgeois film market than in bringing proletarian films broadly to the workers."

This was a serious accusation in the communist world, and Münzenberg did not take it lightly. He admitted in a memo to ECCI while in Moscow in early October 1923 that the films he had put the most energy into distributing were the politically questionable *Polikushka* and *Satan Triumphant*, but he further claimed, somewhat disingenuously, to be on the brink of a breakthrough with the backlog of ideologically solid films in the IAH's possession that had not yet reached many viewers. Münzenberg further emphasized his willingness to collaborate with both the official Goskino studio and with Proletkino, the smaller production company set up by the Kremlin in early February 1923 to make propaganda films directly for Comintern use abroad, although he stopped short of agreeing to invest hard currency in the latter studio for the IAH, as Vallenius was demanding. Vallenius's accusation that the IAH was only interested in "bourgeois" films, Münzenberg concluded, was "outrageous and slaps the truth in the face."[28]

Strictly speaking, Münzenberg was right, but as always the more complex truth was hidden in the details. He was certainly willing to distribute Goskino and Proletkino products, if their films seemed saleable, but these studios were state-subsidized competitors of the more talented Russ collective, and there was no way Münzenberg was going to build them up at Russ expense with the IAH's dwindling capital resources if he did not have to. As it turned out, he did not have to put up any of his own cash to get what he wanted: a formal controlling stake in Russ confirming the rights he had already unilaterally claimed, which was handed to him on a silver platter by the Soviet government in December 1923.

The baroque terms of the Russ agreement typified Münzenberg's parasitic relationship with the Kremlin, which again decided to give him something for nothing in order to camouflage the IAH's real nature. The "Mezhrabpom-Russ" studio was formally capitalized with 1.5 million gold rubles ($750,000) in October 1923, with fifteen hundred shares written up at a value of 1,000 gold rubles (or $500) apiece. Half of these shares were sold, at face cost, to a consortium of American investors. The other 750 shares, all backed by government deposits at the Soviet Central Bank, were confusingly dispersed among the IAH and its affiliates. Two hundred and fifty shares were simply given to the IAH for free. Another 250 were "sold" to the IAH at cost (although the money was really to be put up by Goskino in exchange for films Münzenberg was expected to secure from German studios, which Goskino would then distribute in Russia). The remaining shares were distributed among the new corporation's board of directors and anyone else the Kremlin saw fit to give them to.[29]

This was a sweetheart deal for Münzenberg, but it did not come without some reciprocal obligation.[30] Aside from immediately buying rights on credit to five films owned by the German studio giant Dafu and turning them over to Goskino to distribute in Russia, Münzenberg was expected to devote the vast organizational machinery of the IAH to policing the international film market and ensuring that private Western distributors were locked out of the Russian market.[31] Münzenberg's IAH was named in 1923 as the key partner in an institutional troika that also included the Soviet trade Delegation in Berlin and the People's Commissariat of Enlightenment back in Russia. The duties of the troika were to protect Goskino's distribution monopoly inside Russian borders and cushion Soviet film producers against foreign competition. Although Münzenberg had his own designs on Goskino's Russian distribution monopoly, for the most part the policing initiative would serve to help both the IAH and Russ in the Russian market, so he readily assented to the policy. It would be disastrous, Münzenberg explained to his IAH colleagues, if Western films continued to sneak into the USSR through "Riga, Warsaw and especially Constantinople, of which a great many [would be] awful films worthy of a pigsty, which were perhaps shown in Italian villages twenty years ago [but] are brought to Russia as masterworks and sold for good money."[32] Better by far to restrict access to the Russian market to films bought by the IAH abroad or produced by Russ in Moscow.

In theory, Münzenberg's agreement with the Soviet government allowed him to do just this. But as in all the other realms of the Russian economy the IAH touched, Münzenberg's ability to capitalize on his concessions was curtailed by the limitations of the people who worked for him. The sale of German films purchased by the IAH to Goskino in Moscow continued to net serious revenue in 1924, but none of this cash made its way back to Berlin. By November, debts were piling up in Berlin, and there was little revenue to show for it. In theory, the forty-five thousand dollars Münzenberg owed to German filmmakers could easily have been covered by the eighty thousand dollars he estimated the Russian branch of IAH should have coughed up to date through the distribution agreement with Goskino. But Münzenberg's men in Moscow, including his old friend Francesco Misiano, were diverting these revenues right back into production, both at Russ and at the other semiprivate studio in which the IAH had an interest, Sevzapkino. Of the money properly accounted for by Misiano, at least ten thousand dollars had been earmarked for Russ's flagship production of 1924, a heavily publicized sci-fi picture, based on Alexei Tolstoy's cult novella *Aelita*, that had some commercial promise.[33] But most of Misiano's investments were squandered on more questionable projects, including a Russian-language film journal he had launched called *Cinema Week*. If the Russian IAH office did not start sending its share of Goskino revenues back to Berlin, Münzenberg feared, the entire IAH empire could go bust.[34]

In Misiano's defense, it must be said that he merely followed Jung's earlier example in throwing caution to the winds and throwing Russian IAH cash wherever he saw fit. This was certainly the way Münzenberg operated in Berlin, and there was no reason to think Münzenberg would have done anything differently if he had been the one with access to the Goskino cash in Moscow. Some of Misiano's investments—such as the thousands of dollars he poured into Russ productions, an investment backed to the hilt by the pool of foreign and government capital the Kremlin had put into the studio—stood to pay handsome artistic, if not necessarily economic, dividends. *Aelita* in particular impressed Communist critics with its optimistic futuristic plot and expensive sci-fi costumes.[35]

But if the IAH was able to penetrate the Soviet film market with German films made by others, and Russian films made by Russ, the organization proved singularly incapable of making a dent in the international film business outside Soviet borders. Münzenberg's financial desperation would not have been nearly so extreme if the IAH had been successfully distributing Soviet films abroad, as it tirelessly claimed to be doing. But the overly didactic schlock he received in Berlin from Proletkino (*The Red Devil*, 1924) and even Sevzapkino (*Castle and Fortress*, 1924) simply did not sell abroad, as Münzenberg complained to Piatnitskii in April 1924. In part, he diplomatically explained, this was because of anticommunist censorship. More fundamentally, the problem was that Soviet propaganda films were simply unwatchable. Contemporary Russian film production standards, Münzenberg concluded sadly in his letter to Piatnitskii, "can unfortunately not make the current global film industry obsolete, rather film production in Russia must temporarily adapt to the standards of the foreign film market."[36]

Rarely did Münzenberg reveal so directly as here the lie on which his whole business empire was premised. If the IAH could not, in fact, circumvent ordinary market imperatives based on its (theoretical) mandate to service the needs of the global proletariat, then what exactly was it doing that "capitalist" distributors could not?

Münzenberg's ambivalence about Proletkino, the only Soviet studio fully dedicated to producing straight propaganda films for Comintern use abroad, perfectly illustrated the conundrum. After he refused to invest IAH funds directly in Proletkino as Vallenius had recommended in autumn 1923, ECCI ordered all national Communist parties to begin negotiations with Proletkino about investing in the studio and distributing its films without Münzenberg's help. With his (theoretical) monopoly thus endangered, Münzenberg changed his mind and wrote to Moscow in March 1924, asking for another chance with Proletkino.[37] But he immediately hedged again on the question of putting up IAH cash, complaining to Piatnitskii in April that his film investments were already stretched too thinly on credit. There was no way, Münzenberg concluded after examining the current finances, that he could come up with the ninety to one hundred thousand dollars he estimated were needed to make Proletkino's production standards competitive on the world market. (He made no effort to explain where he got this figure.)[38] And if Münzenberg was unable to receive assurance that he would "have control over direction, can voice [approval] over which films get made, who acts [in them], how [they] are financed, and how they are marketed abroad," he refused to invest serious money in Proletkino.[39] He wanted, it seems, to protect his putative monopoly on Proletkino's overtly propagandistic films on the world market —so long as he did not actually have to distribute any of them.

By 1925, it was clear to anyone with even limited access to the IAH accounts that the global distribution capacity on which Münzenberg's film concession was premised was basically a phantom. Few of the IAH's national committees put up cash for Soviet films, and those that did, such as the English, did so only on credit—extended by Münzenberg. It is hard to say who lost more from the bizarre arrangement that saw the London office of Münzenberg's business subsidiary Aufbau "buy" films from Münzenberg with money provided by Aufbau's Berlin office—half of which was simply written off as a loss—and repay the remainder of the debt by taking out more loans from private English banks. Ideally, of course, these debts should have been repaid from the revenue generated by the distribution of the movies purchased on credit, but less than a tenth of the amount London paid Berlin for Soviet films in 1923–24 was ever recouped on the English market.[40]

The IAH's inability to make much of a splash in Western film markets can be explained in part by the unsaleable nature of Proletkino productions, for example, about whose amateurish and hopelessly didactic qualities Münzenberg never tired of complaining. But however bad some Proletkino films may have been, the IAH was hardly living up to its billing if it failed to bring them to Western viewers. Propaganda, after all, was what the organization was supposed to be all about. Münzenberg could blame whomever he wanted for his failures, but the fact remained that he simply was not very good at distributing or promoting films to broad audiences.

Francesco Misiano, Münzenberg's chief lieutenant on film questions in Moscow, all but pleaded guilty of incompetence in a rare moment of candor during a closed session of the IAH World Congress in Paris in mid-April 1925. Significantly, Münzenberg was in Moscow at the time. With the imposing German Gensek absent from the hall, Misiano, usually a reliable yes-man, uncharacteristically loosened his tongue while under attack from Comrade Humberdot, the French IAH spokesman. It was true, Misiano allowed after enduring Humberdot's complaints about Berlin's inability to deliver promised films on time, "that we have never had a perfect [distribution] network." But in Paris, Misiano objected, you "have never sold *any* films." This was, Humberdot in turn conceded, true—but only for the mundane reason that "we have never received any."

Misiano was now on the defensive, and without Münzenberg to cover for him, there was nowhere to hide. The transcript of his exchange with Humberdot provides a precious glimpse of the helplessness that plagued even the most able IAH functionaries when it came to the realities of the business world. "We have sent films," Misiano told Humberdot by way of explaining his failure to supply Paris, "to Australia, to Japan, to the United States and Canada . . . we never received any money for them, and these films cost us millions." The English, because they had actually paid (albeit on credit), had received more films than anyone else, but even there, Misiano was not entirely sure where Münzenberg stood. The English IAH secretary, Helen Crawfurd, Misiano tried to reassure Humberdot, "claims to have assured the sale of [distribution rights]." If the French could give similar assurances, then perhaps Misiano and Humberdot could work something out.

Unmoved by these protestations, Humberdot could not resist a little needling. "Not only have you not received money [for IAH films], you don't even know where you sent them." "Well," Misiano replied, groping for an answer, "films cost a lot and we usually obtain them on credit; we can't make gifts of them . . . we must be sure that in sending films off we will receive some money [for them]." And yet somehow it never worked out this way, in part because Misiano did not even know what to charge in the first place. "How much do films cost? I don't know how much films cost. That's a technical question that depends on [market] elasticity. Prices can't be the same in all countries." With this blithe admission of ignorance, Misiano concluded the discussion of film questions. And with no films worth distributing in Paris, Humberdot was summoned away to Berlin, where he would shortly be reassigned to the IAH's distant China office, in Peking.[41]

If the IAH's executives were incompetent in commercial enterprise generally, when it came to the film industry they were downright clueless. Similarly, if the organization's finances in most businesses were bad, when it came to movies they were simply "catastrophic," as Münzenberg confessed to ECCI in late April 1925—before asking for an immediate cash transfusion of fifteen thousand dollars. The IAH staff bloodletting in Berlin was well under way, and Münzenberg now promised to begin lopping off superfluous employees at Russ in Moscow as well—so long as his ownership stake in the studio was increased from the current 55 percent to 75 percent (presumably so the other shareholders wouldn't complain about the firings).[42] This was a typical Münzenberg move—masking incompetence with bravado—but it got him nowhere. By summer, the IAH's Berlin office, still waiting for Kremlin subsidies and for funds theoretically earmarked for Münzenberg through a profit-sharing agreement signed by Aleinikov and Misiano in August 1924, was nearly broke.[43]

Meanwhile, back in Moscow, due both to the IAH's financial difficulties and to the distraction of the turf war with International Red Aid, Misiano was beginning to lose control of M-Russ. Aleinikov's studio, far from being a profit-maker for Münzenberg (or any of its other shareholders), was turning into a giant money drain, in constant need of new capital. Aleinikov was nothing if not generous to members of his collective, putting all of his actors, directors, and sound and lighting engineers on permanent salary, whether or not they were currently filming. Top talents such as the director Protazanov (and Aleinikov himself) received upward of eight hundred gold rubles per month; actors such as Moskvin, along with indispensable technicians, pulled down around five hundred rubles; and even the interns were often paid nearly a hundred rubles. By decade's end the ever-expanding M-Russ had a permanent staff of nearly four hundred, and the studio was spending over fifty thousand gold rubles a month just on salaries. When spiraling production costs were figured in, the Russ collective was churning through serious money—far more than the IAH could possibly hope to provide in its crisis-ridden state of 1925.[44]

Small wonder, then, that Aleinikov sold foreign rights to no less than fourteen M-Russ films late that fall to a private Western distributor who, unlike Münzenberg, could afford his prices. Not even a letter of passionate protest from Münzenberg to ECCI, nor the personal lobbying of Clara Zetkin in Moscow, could prevent the deal from going through. Painfully, even *Aelita*, whose production costs had been largely covered by Misiano, was included in the package, which netted M-Russ over fifty thousand dollars of desperately needed hard currency.[45] So low had the IAH's Russian film operation sunk that Misiano wrote to Sovkino in late November 1925 asking for a concession, on the authority of the Central Committee of the Russian Communist Party (to which Misiano optimistically carbon-copied the same letter), to distribute all of the studio's upcoming films in the West—but only if these rights were turned over to the IAH "for free."[46] Here was a worthy Münzenberg man at his best, conjuring up phantom concessions by rhetorical alchemy, preserving the appearance of prosperity even in the face of bankruptcy.

And yet, in a sense both Münzenberg and Misiano were right in denying defeat. The IAH's film concessions, like its commercial properties, had always been capitalized by others, and there was no reason Aleinikov wouldn't come back in line if new investors could be found to provide the IAH's putative stake in the studio. In the meantime, there were more important matters afoot that winter, with Prombank moving to foreclose on the IAH's most valuable properties in the Russian economy due to the organization's inability to pay off its debts. The IAH's financial stake in M-Russ was much flimsier than it had been in its industrial ventures, and Münzenberg did not even dispute Prombank's claim to his shares in the studio. Significantly, in the same December 1925 letter to ECCI in which he protested Prombank's pending takeover of Ural-AG, the Astrakhan fishery, and the Moscow boot factory, Münzenberg disowned M-Russ as a secondary concern hopelessly "distant" from the IAH's "organizational ideology."[47]

But this was mere ideological bluster. In truth, Münzenberg cared little for the embarrassing commercial dinosaurs of the IAH's "industrial assistance" period, whose photogenic potential for Western agitprop had long since been exhausted. Only his interest in maintaining the propriety of the IAH workers' loan prevented him from disowning the troublesome properties of the *Wirtschaftshilfe* entirely. M-Russ, by contrast, was a far more glamorous, if revenue-draining, asset, and his acquiescence in Prombank's takeover of the IAH's shares in the studio was little more than a ploy. M-Russ's reputation at ECCI for making politically questionable films required that Münzenberg distance himself from the studio whenever possible, and agreeing so readily to forfeit his stake in M-Russ offered an easy opportunity to do this. Münzenberg's disingenuous objection to the foreclosures of the politically more saleable "industrial assistance" properties followed the same logic, from the opposite angle. The idea was to deny that IAH business interests served any purpose other than Communist propaganda.

Thus when Münzenberg protested the Prombank foreclosure agreements to his friends at ECCI, he made no effort to dispute the bank's financial claims. His objection, rather, was to the manner in which the parties had come to terms—despite the fact that Misiano had signed off on them, almost certainly with Münzenberg's prior approval. Such a "rearrangement" of organizational sovereignty, Münzenberg objected, "can only be possible after [formal] notification and [the] approval of the [IAH] Executive with the Comintern."[48] Translated into ordinary language, this meant that no matter who was really financing Münzenberg's business empire, the disputed properties belonged ultimately to ECCI and through it, to the Russian Communist Party. In the final analysis, Münzenberg knew, the financial details mattered much less than the relative political status of the players, and on this front he was not conceding anything.

While putting up a phantom fight for Ural-AG and the other old properties, Münzenberg settled on a policy of benign neglect of film questions during his winter of discontent, and it was not long before this policy paid off handsomely. Much as *Polikushka* had been dropped, unexpected, into Münzenberg's lap due to Lenin's personal intervention back in 1922, another promising Soviet film came into his grasp early in 1926, not from Aleinikov at M-Russ but from the Soviet Trade Delegation in Berlin, with a minor assist from the KPD. The film was Sergei Eisenstein's *Battleship Potemkin*, an enormously expensive Sovkino-produced agitprop extravaganza glorifying a sailors' mutiny during the Russian Revolution of 1905, filmed in summer 1925 on location in Odessa. Unlike *Polikushka*, whose relative lack of ideological content had ensured smooth sailing into German cinemas once Münzenberg contracted distribution duties out to Dafu, *Potemkin* was politically explosive, recognized by all who had seen even glimpses of it as a prime candidate for the censor's blade. The film's ideological potency owed much to outsize directorial talent. Whereas most early Soviet propaganda films killed audience interest with their ham-handed sloganeering, Eisenstein's carefully orchestrated crowd scenes build genuine suspense. *Potemkin* is hardly subtle. Only hard-core Soviet sympathizers would fail to notice that on-screen blood flows exclusively from the veins of the mutinous "revolutionaries," while their "class-enemy" victims are left to bleed, unmourned, away from the cameras. But it was still stunningly well-executed propaganda, and it is not surprising that Sovkino found no private distributors willing to brave the censors in a Europe still gripped by fears of Bolshevism.

This was where Münzenberg came in. Ironically, his increasingly low profile in the film business actually worked in his favor in the case of *Potemkin*. Sometime late in 1925, Emil Unfried, an old Communist chum from the Spartacist days in Stuttgart now working in the KPD's agitprop department, had contacted Münzenberg in Berlin, informing him that the party was looking to unload a small debt-ridden holding company, Prometheus, which had produced the KPD propaganda film *Nameless Heroes*. The only capital sunk into Prometheus came from the KPD; yet in exchange for assuming its debts, Münzenberg was immediately granted a majority stake of 55 percent.[49] Prometheus was obscure enough to offer a degree of political cover for *Potemkin*, and, more significantly, to swallow up the debts sure to accrue in what was expected to be a lengthy battle with the censors. In the event, slightly over three months elapsed between the day the Soviet Trade Delegation turned *Potemkin* over to Prometheus (21 January 1926) and the film's much-ballyhooed premiere in the Apollotheater on Friedrichstrasse on 29 April—more than enough time for the film to become a cause célèbre in the left-wing press and a bête noire in the right-wing press. Over twenty meters of film footage, despite the impassioned protests of Münzenberg and his lawyer, the former KPD chieftain Paul Levi (now the orthodox scourge of the SPD's left wing), fell to the German censor's blade. But this only served to heighten *Potemkin*'s dangerous appeal.[50]

Münzenberg had, in short, an inevitable smash-hit on his hands, and it came along just in the nick of time. With the already debt-ridden Prometheus firm drowning in censor's and lawyers' fees by spring 1926, Münzenberg finally liquidated the IAH's remaining shares in M-Russ, handing them over formally to Prombank on 6 April in exchange for a limited write-off of IAH debt to the bank.[51] Almost certainly the prospect of a successful *Potemkin* run gave Münzenberg the confidence to finalize this liquidation, not because he expected profits from Eisenstein's film to cover his debts, but rather because he believed his political capital in the film business was set to rise.

And rise it did. Just days after *Potemkin*'s successful premiere in Berlin on 29 April, the censor's office banned the film anew, which whipped up yet more publicity and gave Münzenberg the opportunity to hold a massive protest rally in the Charlottenburg Piccadilly-Palast. Still more objectionable footage was cut from the film, which was then legalized for good. Throughout spring and summer 1926, *Potemkin* packed in German audiences even larger than those which had greeted *Polikushka*. Ticket sales were brisk—more than RM 150,000 worth by the end of June—although they were not nearly lucrative enough to turn a profit, much less pull Prometheus out of debt, once the shares of the Soviet Trade Delegation (RM 75,000) and Sovkino (RM 120,000) were tabulated.[52]

Profits or no profits, the publicity surrounding *Potemkin* was enormous, and Münzenberg, as usual, knew how to take the credit. On the strength of the *Potemkin* coup alone, he reasserted his claim to M-Russ in September 1926, despite having no capital to invest. With incredible arrogance, Münzenberg in fact demanded 240,000 gold rubles from M-Russ on the dubious basis of past services rendered, which was to buy back the IAH's outstanding debts at Prombank and underwrite Münzenberg's new stake. Incredibly, precisely such a deal went through, due to the muscle of Prombank, without whose bottomless credit M-Russ would long ago have gone bust. In a settlement every bit as baroque as the earlier December 1923 M-Russ capitalization, Prombank gave Münzenberg a partial stake in the studio (though not, as previously, a majority interest), merely by manipulating the studio's cash holdings at the bank (about 350,000 gold rubles) to write off 180,000 *chervontsi* worth of IAH debt and underwrite over 60,000 gold rubles of studio stock for Münzenberg, in exchange for—nothing.[53] Tellingly, the studio's newly formulated capitalization was less than one-half what it had been three years earlier, although production expenses, and annual film output, had risen exponentially. The other half—significantly, the $375,000 contributed by the consortium of American investors, who were no longer listed as shareholders—had simply gone up in smoke.[54]

Although Münzenberg now held only a minority stake in M-Russ, in political terms he was back in the saddle, and it was not long before he tried to start bossing his backers around. When Comrade Axelrod, the director of Prombank, appointed a new chairman (B. M. Malkin) to run the M-Russ studio in accordance with the new capitalization agreement, Münzenberg cried foul, claiming that board members could be appointed only if approved mutually by both Prombank and himself.

Reversing his rhetorical tack of the year before, Münzenberg conceded that Prombank had been justified in taking over Aufbau's remaining industrial assets in Russia in view of the IAH's inability to pay off its debts, but argued that the Soviet government had demonstrated through the recent M-Russ recapitalization its belief that "the valuable work of the IAH in the Russian film industry should be preserved at any price."[55] Despite IAH's late recovery from bankruptcy due to Prombank's generosity, and regardless of the puny size of its recently gifted share of studio stock (less than 10 percent), Münzenberg wanted Axelrod to kneel down before him due to the size of his reputation.[56]

Here, then, was the Münzenberg model of movie moguldom. Let more talented individuals make the films. Get other, cash-richer institutions to pay for them, and, if necessary, distribute them. But make sure to take all the credit for any box-office successes. As it turned out, there were no more blockbusters coming out of the Soviet Union that would rival *Polikushka* or *Potemkin* in their impact on German screens, but M-Russ continued to churn out avant-garde pictures by the dozens in the late 1920s. Many of them, such as Pudovkin's *Mother* (1925) and *Storm Over Asia* (1928), along with Feodor Otsep's *The Living Corpse* (1929), are still known to cinema scholars (although not to the general public) today.[57] Nearly all of the money for these lavishly produced films was provided by Prombank, whose Kremlin-appointed directors did not seem to mind that M-Russ lost millions of rubles a year, due in part to its extremely generous salaries and pensions for its often idle employees. Factoring in redundant technical and administrative staff, the IAH auditing commission estimated in July 1929, the firing of superfluous or inactive personnel could have netted M-Russ over six hundred thousand gold rubles annually (although these savings would have only covered about one fiscal quarter's worth of the studio's enormous operating deficit).[58]

But that was not Münzenberg's problem. So long as someone else was footing the bill, and he was getting the credit, why split hairs over Aleinikov's indulgence of his artistes? Characteristically, Münzenberg himself made no effort to trim runaway expenses at M-Russ in the late 1920s, preferring to devote his own voluminous correspondence to lobbying for expanded Kremlin subsidies, write-offs of debts accrued to Sovkino for use of studio space and equipment, and import concessions that, he claimed, would finally allow the studio to break even.[59]

Profits? Those were for capitalists. In the Communist world, there was always another bureaucrat to pay the piper, so long as he played the right propaganda tune for the time. One propaganda blockbuster, like *Polikushka* or *Potemkin*, was enough to wipe out the memory of years of flops, even if you had neither invested in the film in question, nor made any particular effort to acquire it. Such were the forgiving economics of the film business, if your name was Münzenberg, and you had the confidence of the Kremlin.

CHAPTER 11 *Preempting the Peace*

Over the first half-decade of the IAH's existence, Münzenberg was able to carve out a seemingly viable, though always hotly contested, niche for the organization in the communist world. Whenever humanitarian crises arose, the IAH would lay formal claim to any revenues raised by Comintern member parties in the name of the disaster victims, whether or not the parties actually turned this money over to Münzenberg. This questionable model of fund-raising by wishful thinking was painfully exposed in the Volga funds embezzlement controversy and the turf war with MOPR. It reached ever more absurd apogees in the phantom "Japanese earthquake survivors" and "Chinese flood victims" and the "English miners' strike" campaigns of 1923, 1925, and 1926, respectively. It was perhaps fortunate that virtually no money was raised for the first two causes, as the IAH was unable to find any suitable "proletarians" willing to take it. As for the third campaign, it came to a halt when the English Communist Party forbade the IAH outright to raise money in England.[1]

Such putatively substantial "aid" causes were supplemented by smaller IAH agitprop campaigns on themes somehow related to Soviet Russia, from the ephemeral industrial assistance stratagem of 1922, to the premieres of Soviet-made films like *Polikushka* and *Potemkin*, to aggressive counterspin efforts meant to douse periodic flare-ups of anti-Soviet headlines in the Western press. Only Münzenberg's tireless self-promotion lent a semblance of coherence to these disparate activities, and only his ability to charm the purse masters in the Kremlin kept it all afloat.

The heart of the problem was a lack of vision. Münzenberg was, for the most part, reacting to events—the Volga famine, NEP, a new film, an English miners' strike—instead of shaping them or defining them. Even the most promising initiative—the antifascist campaign of 1923—had foundered as soon as Hitler faded from the political scene.

But Münzenberg had not forgotten the visceral appeal the antifascist campaign had had for celebrity intellectuals, and he longed to duplicate this success with a fashionable cause that had more traction. His retooling of the IAH from a charity into a media organization in the mid-1920s provided just such an opportunity. Significantly, the new monthly agitprop budget he sent to Moscow for approval early in 1926 included substantial subsidies for new IAH branch offices in China and Japan, through which he planned to launch a broad new "anti-imperialist" propaganda offensive in Asia to embarrass the European powers. That he conceived of this propaganda offensive independent of instructions from the Kremlin seems clear: he began diverting Kremlin gold into the anti-imperialist venture long before he had received authorization to do so.[2]

In summer 1926, Münzenberg moved the anti-imperialism campaign into high gear, christening a new Berlin IAH committee the "League Against Colonial Oppression." To secure a permanent new funding stream for the league, Münzenberg began lobbying Piatnitskii and the ascendant Ukrainian party boss Dmitri Manuil'skii at Comintern headquarters, before he finally hit pay dirt while Nikolai Bukharin was visiting Berlin in late August.[3] Buoyed by the endorsement of Bukharin, who was about to replace the disgraced "Trotskyist" Zinoviev at the reins of the Comintern, Münzenberg submitted a major article on the new agitprop theme to the official Comintern oracle, *Inprecorr*.[4] In early September he demanded fifteen thousand dollars to begin preparations for an international "conference against imperialism" scheduled for sometime early in 1927.[5]

Münzenberg's conference plans were nothing if not ambitious. Major Asian anticolonial radicals, such as China's Chiang Kai-shek and India's Mohandas Gandhi, along with selected rebel movement leaders from Africa and the Americas, were to be invited to western Europe, where they could preach independence in a specially chosen city that symbolized colonial oppression. To add spice to the ethnic mix, black American delegates would be recruited from the NAACP and the American Negro Labor Congress to come to Europe and denounce racial oppression in the United States.[6] To round out the assembly of notables, Münzenberg planned to add noncommunist "fellow travelers" with no particular connection to imperial regimes or opposition movements, who wanted to demonstrate their right-thinking opposition to colonialism, racism, and all the rest. Specifically, Münzenberg informed ECCI, he would invite about eighty "left-leaning intellectuals" and sixty "scientists and artists," with Albert Einstein—a longtime IAH supporter who had joined FSR-type front committees in 1921 and 1923—

leading the charge. Such a gathering was sure to raise the ire of the European ruling establishment, especially if Moscow's hand in organizing it were manifest, so Münzenberg (conveniently) offered to circumvent overt Comintern involvement by using the international apparatus of the IAH.[7]

Not incidental to Münzenberg's conference plans was the fact that ECCI planned to rule, yet again, in November 1926 on the necessity of funding the IAH.[8] To corral yet another Kremlin notable, Münzenberg supplemented his conference funding requests with a flattering letter to Stalin in which he outlined elaborate, month-by-month plans for celebrating the Soviet Union's tenth anniversary in 1927. From January to December in the anniversary year, Münzenberg promised Stalin, he would bring wave after wave of workers and journalists to tour the USSR, even as celebrated Russian artists, authors, and athletes would visit the West. The IAH would form "Friends of Soviet Russia" groups in all countries still lacking them, and their members would be invited to Moscow for a huge celebration in late summer. Fortified by their experience in the Soviet capital, the various IAH "friends" would return to their home countries to organize cascading pro-Soviet demonstrations that would peak in October and early November, as the actual tenth anniversary date drew near. Through it all, the IAH would trumpet the Revolution's achievements in its media organs and at Soviet film festivals. All this, Münzenberg assured Stalin, could be done—if the Kremlin came through with an early installment of ten thousand gold rubles by the end of 1926, just to get things moving.[9]

There was an inherent contradiction in Münzenberg's two propaganda schemes for 1927. By Münzenberg's own description, his anticolonial conference could only work if the Comintern's hand in organizing it was hidden; and yet he was simultaneously promising to crank up his entire media apparatus, for an entire year, for an ostentatious celebration of the USSR's tenth anniversary. While he was directing such an explicitly pro-Soviet campaign, how could anyone possibly be gulled into believing Moscow had nothing to do with the anticolonial conference? Moreover, why should the Kremlin support Münzenberg's expensive plans for an international gathering of "anti-imperialist" dignitaries, if it was not going to be able to take the credit?

In a sense this problem was endemic to communist propaganda generally—the Comintern's member parties, after all, were forever denying that their funding came from Moscow, contrary to what nearly all noncommunist politicians (correctly) suspected—but in the case of the anti-imperialist initiative it was particularly acute. Münzenberg's conference plan, as he sold it to the Kremlin, was premised on his ability to lure in famous noncommunist world leaders, so that their illustrious names would supplement the list of intellectual "fellow travelers" whose often gullible apologias for Soviet actions in Western media organs lent legitimacy to the Bolshevik regime internationally. Yet such political notables would hardly endorse Münzenberg's anti-imperialist program if, by doing so, they would appear to be Soviet stooges. Why should Chiang Kai-shek, for example, the most feared chieftain in China—and hardly a communist—want to toady so obviously to Moscow? But if he were unwilling to do that, why should the Kremlin invite him to Europe and pick up the not insubstantial travel costs for the man and his entourage?

To resolve this conundrum, Münzenberg was in effect forced to lie out of both sides of his mouth at once, assuring his paymasters that Moscow would bask in the prestigious glow of his gathering of notables, while denying to any conference participants who asked that the Kremlin was behind the affair. The former proposition required that Münzenberg downplay his own personal responsibility for the anticolonial conference by surrounding it with an interlocking web of more overtly pro-Soviet propaganda, which would reassure ECCI that Moscow was getting its money's worth. The latter meant, however, that Münzenberg could not allow Kremlin influence over the unfolding of the conference to trump his own, lest the lie of Moscow's noninvolvement be exposed. The whole game depended on Münzenberg's ability to promote the idea of his own indispensability as a buffer, as a presumably autonomous go-between between anticolonial fellow travelers and the men in Moscow who wanted to manipulate them.

The trouble was, it was a lie. Even as Münzenberg proactively dispatched his IAH lieutenants throughout Europe, Asia, and America in December 1926 with VIP invitations to his upcoming conference, he bombarded the Kremlin with a flurry of funding requests that revealed only too well where the real power behind the conference resided.[10] Despite Münzenberg's obsequious lobbying, though, the Kremlin continued to hedge, throwing his conference plans into turmoil. By the end of December 1926, Münzenberg had already selected a date (early February 1927) and location (Brussels) for the conference, where he wanted tribal chieftains from the Belgian Congo to play a starring role by denouncing the brutal practices of their colonial overlords.[11] The great distance that Africans and Asians needed to travel meant that they would need to set off for Brussels nearly two weeks in advance. Kremlin funds, then, were needed by mid-January at the latest. But on 8 January 1927, Münzenberg was informed that funding would not be forthcoming. With the IAH's organizational future still undecided, the Comintern Executive wanted Münzenberg to postpone his conference plans, to June or later.[12]

This was certainly bad news, but Münzenberg, ever the optimist, was inclined to see a silver lining. First of all, ECCI's new point man on the IAH, the Finnish Communist administrator Mauno Heimo, had picked up on nearly all of the agitprop talking points Münzenberg had been playing up, even if he was unable to deliver immediately on funding for the conference. Earlier in January, Münzenberg had sent in press clippings on a new anticommunist campaign heating up in the Western press, which (most disturbingly) was being led by the left-leaning *Manchester Guardian*, and these clippings had, according to Heimo, received due attention at ECCI. More encouragingly, a dubious new pet cause, which Münzenberg had recently mentioned only in passing—the anti-Soviet and therefore "fascist" government that had recently come to power in Lithuania—had struck a chord with the men in the Kremlin. They asked the official Soviet newspaper *Pravda* to reprint an IAH protest against the Lithuanian regime, endorsed by many of the organization's in-house intellectuals. And the Kremlin's demand that the IAH postpone its anticolonial conference until June entailed a tacit endorsement of the initiative, even if Moscow had not agreed on what Münzenberg believed to be the necessary timing.[13]

Reassured by Heimo's broad endorsement of his current propaganda thrust—and confident that Bukharin, whose stock in Moscow was now peaking, would intervene on his behalf if necessary because of the warm words the two had exchanged in Berlin—Münzenberg resolved to force the issue. The argument he made against postponement masterfully revealed the hidden premise of Münzenberg's manipulation of Communist sympathizers, which was that they were too stupid to realize they were being manipulated. The Brussels conference, he wrote Heimo on 11 January 1927, could on political grounds no longer be postponed, because many of the Asian delegates (including Chiang Kai-shek) had already left home, and if they were told to turn around and go back now it would be clear who was telling them to do so.[14] "These people have the belief," Münzenberg wrote in an arresting passage underlining his cynical attitude toward fellow travelers, "that they are actually doing this themselves. This belief must be preserved at any price."[15]

Münzenberg's argument was bold enough to excite Heimo's immediate attention. Heimo promptly excerpted the key passage on the need to deceive the fellow travelers, stamped it "secret," and distributed it to the members of the Comintern Secretariat who were still discussing the IAH's liquidation.[16] Bukharin, according to Heimo, was particularly impressed. By way of preliminary endorsement of Münzenberg's February conference date,

Heimo agreed to pay the travel costs for the Chinese delegation, although Münzenberg's further request that delegates from the Russian unions attend was tabled. To soothe Münzenberg's ego while Moscow was still deciding on his funding request for the conference, Heimo offered on 21 January to lean on MOPR to turn over money owed from the long-ago German hunger campaign.[17]

Heimo's letter clearly implied that a favorable ECCI ruling on the Brussels plans—and on the IAH's future more generally—was in the offing, but Münzenberg was not about to take chances. In a furious rush of last-minute activity (he was "working like a bear," he assured Heimo), Münzenberg covered all his bases with a mixture of cajolery, threats, and aggressive maneuvering that left his political rivals in MOPR and the KPD gasping for breath. Brandishing Bukharin's (reported verbal) endorsement of his plans like a sword—and claiming Stalin was behind him, too—Münzenberg stormed around Berlin in late January whipping up Communist support for a series of protest rallies to be held in Hamburg, Cologne, and Frankfurt on the theme of "the menacing danger of war against the Soviet Union." These rallies were also designed to recruit sympathizers for a new incarnation of the Friends of Soviet Russia clubs Münzenberg hoped to build as part of his "Ten Years of Soviet Russia" anniversary campaign.[18]

What a virtually nonexistent military threat against the USSR could possibly have to do with European colonialism in Asia—or either of them with resistance to Italian fascism, upon which theme Münzenberg was also building a new committee—were not questions Münzenberg expected ECCI's funding commissars to ask. What was important, rather, was that the Amsterdam Socialist International was working together with the Italian and Swiss Socialist parties to build an antifascist office, and that they would beat Moscow to the punch if Münzenberg was not immediately given the Kremlin's endorsement (over MOPR, that is, which was also maneuvering for the anti–Italian fascism portfolio).[19] Ingeniously, Münzenberg wrapped all these seemingly inchoate themes together with the USSR's tenth anniversary in a single catch phrase. His initially clunky double slogan "Ten Years of Soviet Russia/Against the Menacing War Danger" was now replaced by the concise yet open-ended "Against War, for the Soviet Union," which would be splashed on IAH posters and distributed at the Brussels conference.[20]

All this inspired agitprop legerdemain would have been for naught, however, if Münzenberg had not been able to play the unsuspecting new ECCI chieftain, Bukharin, like a fiddle. Bukharin, the most cerebral of the

Bolsheviks from Lenin's inner circle, was not fully initiated into how the Comintern actually worked. Münzenberg seems to have convinced him during their brief meeting in Berlin in August 1926 that the IAH was autonomous and self-financing. Bukharin had asked what Münzenberg needed from the Kremlin, by way of support—to which Münzenberg had slyly replied, "only that no one gets in our way." Such non-"interference" Bukharin had happily, and unconditionally, promised, so it is not surprising that Bukharin intervened repeatedly on Münzenberg's behalf in early 1927, endorsing by turns the "war scare" idea, the Russian Revolution anniversary plans, the new antifascist committees, the new Friends of Soviet Russia clubs, and most crucially, the Brussels conference dates for early February.[21]

Heimo and Otto Kuusinen, who actually had to figure out how to pay for the Brussels conference and the new German FSR clubs, were somewhat less sanguine than the excitable Bukharin. In light of unfavorable "bourgeois" press notices sniffing out Comintern involvement in the affair, they demanded that Münzenberg move the conference to Berlin, Basel, Geneva, or Copenhagen. Further, they ordered that Münzenberg work in tandem with the KPD Zentrale and MOPR in forming the new Friends of Soviet Russia clubs, so as not to ignite another unproductive turf war—and especially not to give more ammunition to the editors of *Rote Fahne*, who as usual were ready to pounce on any IAH improprieties.[22] Although ECCI had approved the February conference dates by the end of January (though not the Brussels location), the financing was still slow in coming. As of 7 February, three days before the conference was set to open, Münzenberg had received only half of the ten thousand dollars requested.[23]

Bureaucratic foot-dragging, though, was to be expected. The general thrust of the decisions of ECCI, due to Bukharin's interventions, was more favorable to the IAH than at nearly any time since 1921, and Münzenberg was never one to hesitate in claiming victory. A measure of the new balance of power in the ranks of German Communism could be taken in the dynamics of a bizarre meeting held between Münzenberg and a new "IAH committee" in the KPD Zentrale in late January 1927. Here, according to a witness present, the KPD heavyweights appointed to corral Münzenberg (Hugo Eberlein, Leo Flieg, Walter Ulbricht, and Ernst Thälmann) quickly backed down on every substantial issue of contention, such as the party's plan to take over publication of *AIZ*). This abject surrender made the leading figures in the KPD appear to be little more than "compliant managing directors of the firm W[illi] M[ünzenberg]."[24] Doubtless Ulbricht, Thälmann, and the others did not see things this way, but in politics appearances can often be more significant than reality, and to all appearances Münzenberg was the man of the hour on the eve of the massive pro-Soviet rallies to be held in Hamburg, Cologne, and Frankfurt in early February and the Brussels conference that would follow on their heels.

A lonely note of dissent registered in late January 1927 by a once-loyal Münzenberg man, grown wise to his master's ways, poignantly captures the absurdity of the IAH's newfound agitprop mission. "Soon," wrote Eduard Fuchs, secretary of the long-forgotten German Society of Friends of the New Russia whose mandate dated back to 1923, "W M will be able to report on relatively large successes.... there will be great demonstrations, he will recruit new members [for the new Friends of Soviet Russia clubs] and he will rashly increase the circulation of his newspapers. This will all allow him to expand his IAH apparatus and his influence... [and to claim that] only in Germany has resistance to the war threat against the Soviet Union been mobilized."

Such claims, Fuchs continued, "will all sound very imposing"—but only to "the unsuspecting and the stupid." For "only a fool or a malicious liar could summon the courage" to claim that, in the moderate political climate of 1927, he was able to "organize German intellectuals and petty bourgeois [sympathizers] into a movement for the defense of Soviet Russia." In fact, Fuchs explained, all the myriad IAH subcommittees Münzenberg had ever created were made up of the same tiny cadre of people—Fuchs himself was exhibit A, as he belonged to all of them—and the new clubs, along with the League Against Colonial Oppression to be set up at Brussels, would merely recycle the old (in most cases without even changing offices, merely their names). The next wave of Münzenberg clubs, about which ECCI would be hearing ad nauseam over the coming months, would, according to Fuchs, be little more than organizational "Potemkin villages."

Fuchs's warning went unheeded, in part because he made the mistake of sending it to two grand dames of the Kremlin, Clara Zetkin and Lev Kamenev's wife Olga, who had long ago fallen under Münzenberg's spell, but more significantly, because Münzenberg was too quick for him.[25] Hardly a fool, Münzenberg was in fact a consummate liar, who knew that every report he sent to Moscow about new committees being formed or increased newspaper circulation was registered as evidence in his favor, whether the committee members or newspaper subscribers were flesh and blood or phantoms. And every favorable ECCI decision, no matter how conditional or ambiguous, gave Münzenberg grounds to forge ahead with his plans back in Berlin, heedless of skeptical KPD rivals or cautious Kremlin overseers. Revealingly, once money finally came through for the anticolonial conference, Münzenberg's relentless correspondence with Moscow screeched to a halt, to the point where Heimo complained that he was receiving no reports from Brussels. Before the Brussels event kicked off, Münzenberg had already received approval for a follow-up conference he was planning for summer 1927 which would fuse the anticolonial theme with pacifism and antifascism (although Heimo insisted that the conference not officially be promoted as antifascist). So there was no need for further lobbying on the subject.[26]

Once Münzenberg's various "Potemkin" initiatives were conceived, then, it was nearly impossible for either rivals or skeptics to tear them down. The Brussels conference was the perfect example. One by one, Münzenberg blithely ignored every single objection laid down by Moscow, about the timing, financing, and location of the event, before he finally bulldozed right through the most substantial condition of all—that the Kremlin's involvement be carefully hidden. Due to Münzenberg's own conspicuous role in the event, along with his failure to relocate from Brussels, socialist delegates complained loudly about Muscovite manipulation of the proceedings. A furious debate ensued inside the Amsterdam secretariat after the conference about whether or not to collaborate with Münzenberg, which was closely followed by European intelligence observers.[27] So concerned about the Comintern's blown cover was Heimo, in fact, that he devised a comically overwrought new linguistic code for communicating with Berlin, requesting further that Münzenberg destroy the letter in which the code was established.[28]

But what was a blown cover to Willi Münzenberg? Due to Münzenberg's disregard for Comintern protocol, Western governments found it all too easy to blame Moscow for the Brussels Congress, which provided a megaphone for destabilizing rabble-rousers such as Jawaharlal Nehru (who attended in Gandhi's stead) and Chiang Kai-shek, not to mention famous political amateurs such as Einstein. All this notoriety made Münzenberg look good, even if it made a mockery of the premise of Comintern deniability on which the IAH's mandate was based. Merely that the Brussels conference had met at all was, as everyone in the Communist world knew—and many outside it as well—due to Münzenberg's personal initiative, and he was not about to let Moscow forget this.

With his mandate (and his subsidies) renewed on all the grounds Münzenberg had lobbied for—from Brussels to the "Ten Years of Soviet Russia" campaign to the "war scare" demonstrations to the new German FSR clubs —Münzenberg was now in a prime position to expand his media empire. The circulation of both *AIZ* and his new daily newspaper, *Welt am Abend*, grew geometrically in 1927, and these escalating figures translated into larger and larger subsidies from Moscow, just as Fuchs had predicted they would.[29]

Münzenberg clearly had an effective new propaganda formula, which might be summed up as one-third "the glorious reign of the proletariat in the Soviet Union is in danger"; a quarter anti-imperialism; another quarter pacifism aimed at women; and a dollop of vague "the fascists are coming" rhetoric thrown in for good measure. Subsumed in the deceptively simple slogan "Against War, for the Soviet Union," the new IAH religion could be bent at will in several directions at once, with the emphasis depending on the events of the day, as they were interpreted in Moscow. Thus the successor-to-Brussels conference, approved by ECCI in early February and held in Vienna in late summer 1927, played up the bogeymen war and fascism (with less emphasis on imperialism). Later gatherings, such as the most famous Münzenberg event, the Amsterdam conference of 1932, played mostly to the anti-imperialist pacifists—while (stunningly in light of Hitler's electoral triumphs that year) ignoring fascism entirely. Out of this ever-evolving smorgasbord of fashionable liberal causes, lovingly lavished with Moscow gold by Münzenberg, grew that strange political concoction later known as the Popular Front.

The new IAH mandate was sufficiently nebulous to encompass nearly any cause Münzenberg wanted to play up, and this was both its strength and its weakness. So wrapped up was Münzenberg for most of 1927 in glorifying the Soviet Union, building his FSR clubs, and hawking the anti-imperialist line in his rapidly expanding news organs, that he completely missed out on the greatest propaganda event of the year, the protests surrounding the execution of Sacco and Vanzetti in Massachusetts that August.[30] With the Sacco and Vanzetti campaign, MOPR finally reaped the reward of the FSR takeover in Chicago, netting, according to one estimate, almost five hundred thousand dollars in donations, most of which was filched by the American Communist Party.[31] Yet due to his dubious, but widely publicized, Brussels triumph (and the "Potemkin" coup of 1926), Münzenberg's reputation was already so inextricably intertwined with secret Comintern propaganda that his latest historian, on the basis of in-house IAH legends Münzenberg apparently delighted in cultivating, erroneously claimed he was behind the Sacco and Vanzetti campaign as well.[32]

Receiving credit for the victories of his most bitter rivals, convincing naysayers to step aside so that his plans might be realized due to their obvious inevitability, conjuring copycat committees out of phantom causes such as the "war threat" to the Soviet Union—Münzenberg increasingly seemed to have the touch of a magician whose ugly backstage maneuvering was witnessed only by powerless subordinates and the heedless paymasters who financed his deceptions. There would be no stopping him as he set out to put his few remaining Communist rivals in their place.

CHAPTER 12 *The Red Millionaire*

On the eve of his triumph at Brussels in February 1927, Münzenberg moved permanently into a luxurious new apartment in Berlin Tiergarten at Zeltenstrasse 9a, in a prestigious neighborhood populated mainly by retired military officers and government officials. Since leaving Switzerland eight years before, he had lived a more or less itinerant life in Berlin, spending long hours and frequently working all night at the IAH lair in the Soviet embassy, often switching apartments so as to frustrate police spies, and leaving the city for weeks at a time on official IAH business. Although the apartment Münzenberg most often stayed in before 1927 was in the relatively unfashionable working-class northeastern Berlin suburb of Pankow, he did not live badly. Münzenberg employed a full-time chauffeur in Berlin. When in Moscow, he and his bohemian wife and collaborator Babette Gross stayed, after 1923, in the elegant Hotel Metropole. Gross and Münzenberg usually flew back and forth between Berlin and Moscow at cut-market rates with Dereluft, a special Lufthansa subsidiary co-owned with the Soviet government, which was used by Comintern VIPs. While traveling on IAH business in Europe, Münzenberg and his entourage often stayed in the most expensive hotel in town—at the Comintern's expense.[1] But the lifestyle was exhausting, especially for a man whose health had never been good. It was clearly time to settle down.

Münzenberg's building was owned by Magnus Hirschfeld, an eccentric Communist sympathizer and wealthy self-described professor who ran an "Institute for Sexual Sciences" adjacent to Münzenberg's flat. The labyrinthine corridors of Zeltenstrasse 9a were "plastered with the sexual symbols of primitive peoples and other relevant photographic material." Hirschfeld's budding science of "sexology" was just then beginning to excite attention in left-wing circles and derision among conservatives—he would later become a favorite punching-bag of the Nazis.[2] After Münzenberg moved in,

Hirschfeld's building acquired, in Gross's recollection, "a considerable reputation in the Comintern." Aside from the visual curiosities in the corridors, Münzenberg's own quarters were stylish, even "bourgeois"—the furniture was Biedermeier—and visiting Moscow emissaries, such as the Bulgarian Communist Georgi Dimitrov, often used the building to meet contacts.[3]

Münzenberg's new dwelling seemed a perfect fit for his outsized and somewhat eccentric reputation. For years resentment had been building up inside the regular KPD apparat at Münzenberg's lavish lifestyle, his disregard for the both the written and unwritten protocols of proper party behavior. At one point in July 1926, Münzenberg's precarious position in the KPD had been seriously threatened when two earnest young functionaries from the Berlin party local produced a lengthy report recommending his expulsion from the party. Their grounds were his ideologically loose hiring practices, the "faithlessness" and "dishonesty" he consistently displayed toward loyal KPD foot soldiers—who were often fired from his enterprises even while Münzenberg continued to employ party outsiders—and above all his "corruption stinking to high heaven."[4]

Perhaps because this onetime provincial lumpen proletarian, unlike many KPD leaders, had actually known poverty, Münzenberg appreciated the pleasures that money could buy, and made no secret of it. He was chauffeured around Berlin in a Lincoln limousine, and shadowed by his own personal bodyguard. Unlike rich left "bohemians" who liked to dress down so as to condescend to the laborers they supposedly spoke for, Münzenberg dressed snappily and was shaved and manicured daily by a personal barber.[5] He frequented Berlin's fashionable restaurants and cafés, and considered himself a connoisseur of fine coffees, although he still avoided alcohol and cigarettes.[6]

The contrast between Münzenberg and his close friend Heinz Neumann, who also moved into Hirschfeld's building early in 1928, is instructive. On the surface, the two men had much in common. Both were handsome young Communist up-and-comers. In a pattern typical of fashionable Weimar society, they had attracted the notice of a pair of elegant young sisters, raised in the bourgeois luxury of prewar Potsdam, who had moved to Berlin after the war in search of bohemian adventure. Just as Babette Gross found Münzenberg's combination of coarse street toughness and entrée into the highest Bolshevik circles irresistible, so did her sister Greta fall for the precociously talented Neumann, whose rapid rise in the party ranks during the 1920s bespoke a fiery revolutionary determination. Both couples "married" in the unofficial bohemian style of radical Berlin, which forbade "bourgeois" niceties such as wedding ceremonies.

Münzenberg and Neumann, however, came from very different backgrounds. Already in the days of the Communist Youth International, Münzenberg was a warhorse of the European underground, respected by his Bolshevik comrades for having suffered long years in obscurity with them. He was also authentically "proletarian," in the sense that he had actually once worked in a factory and boasted no more than a grade school education. He also looked the part, with his squat frame and disproportionately long torso, which allowed him to give off an aura of physical authority that awed underlings.[7]

Neumann was not only Münzenberg's junior by thirteen years; he had nothing of the proletarian about him. Born in 1902 to a proper upper-middle class German family, he came of political age during the heady revolutionary struggles of postwar Berlin, where he studied philology at the Humboldt University from 1919 to 1921. He was, in short, a bourgeois intellectual, like Ruth Fischer and her allies in the so-called "Berlin Left" who had taken the reins of the KPD Zentrale in 1924. Neumann's uncompromising thirst for doctrinal purity owed much to Fischer's and Rosa Luxemburg's example.

Perhaps because he had never suffered like a true proletarian, Neumann affected a somewhat overwrought asceticism, disdaining "bourgeois" pleasures and toeing the party line in matters of dress and behavior. Ever the intellectual, he was both an urbanite and a homebody, preferring to spend his rare free time holed up alone in his rooms on Zeltenstrasse, reading or writing communist tracts. Gradually Münzenberg prevailed upon Neumann to leave the city on Sundays to go hiking in the forests near Berlin, but the young theoretician went on these excursions reluctantly. Away from the city, Neumann invariably complained that there was "nothing to see." Instead of enjoying nature, he would bombard Münzenberg with KPD gossip and questions on pressing agitprop issues.

Münzenberg liked to relax on weekends, and Neumann's persistent questions sometimes annoyed him, although he seldom lost patience with his young friend. Invariably Münzenberg would fault Neumann for "naïveté" or "foolish optimism" about the KPD's political prospects in Germany, whereupon the latter would chide his older rival for his "rotten opportunism" and satisfied complacency.[8]

For all their differences, there was clearly a deep respect between the men, who from different directions were both ascending high into the Comintern orbit in the late 1920s. While Münzenberg was famously bringing European anti-imperialists together in 1927, Neumann was out on the anticolonial front lines, implementing the Comintern's new "revolutionary" policy in China. In December 1927, Neumann personally directed a Communist uprising in Canton that was bloodily suppressed by none other than Münzenberg's honored guest from Brussels, Chiang Kai-shek.[9] Critics in the KPD called Neumann the "butcher of Canton" after the December disaster, but despite this sanguinary failure—or perhaps because of it?—he retained Stalin's confidence.[10] Clearly Neumann now had the kind of "revolutionary" credentials on his résumé with which he could chide even Münzenberg.[11] No wonder, then, that he refused to defer to Münzenberg. For all their disagreements, the men were now comrades-in-arms, related by (bohemian) marriage and united by common political experience.

With his idealistic, doctrinaire comrade Neumann as a foil, Münzenberg seemed to be settling down into a comfortable bourgeois existence in Berlin, with his own revolutionary struggles increasingly behind him. The favorable ECCI rulings of winter 1927 on his myriad new agitprop initiatives gave him the confidence to expand his propaganda empire, and he did so without a moment's hesitation. In April, Münzenberg launched a new venture, the Association of Workers' Photographers, with its own illustrated monthly, the *Worker-Photographer*. Whereas *AIZ* was filled with photographs of proletarians (or Communist leaders, anyway), these had mostly been taken by established "bourgeois" photographers; the new venture was meant to showcase up-and-coming photographers of working-class origin. A similar idea lay behind *Owlglass*, a satirical monthly Münzenberg created in May 1928 to showcase the drawings of "proletarian" artists. Financially speaking, the *Worker-Photographer* and *Owlglass* were small potatoes compared to *AIZ*. Neither publication ever developed even the sketchiest following—they failed to produce any advertising revenue—but they did provide employment for a few struggling artists in Berlin, in much the same way that Roosevelt's Works Progress Administration later would do during the New Deal in America.[12]

AIZ, despite its abysmal financial track record in Berlin, was also spawning imitators. German-language Austrian, Swiss, and Czech editions were an easy fix; they all simply parroted the Berlin *AIZ* and piggybacked on the party press, appearing as inserts in local Communist dailies, although the parties often balked when finances were tight.[13] It was tougher to mimic *AIZ* in Paris, where Communist leaders were implacably hostile to the IAH, but this did not stop Münzenberg from trying. An early effort called *La Russie nouvelle*, edited by the tiny Paris IAH committee, was printed only at the mercy of the PCF. It collapsed without a whimper in winter 1925–26. Münzenberg tried again in summer 1928 with a glossy called *Nos Regards*. This time, he invested money directly, dispatching Babette Gross to Paris with NDV funds in hand. Gross, on Münzenberg's instructions, used this cash to circumvent the hostile PCF apparat by enlisting the services of a private "bourgeois" publisher, Hachette. She also hired expensive editing talent. Only then did Münzenberg inform Moscow about the new venture.

Münzenberg's request for Kremlin subvention of *Nos Regards,* dispatched to ECCI in November 1928, splendidly illustrates the peculiar spirit of Communist "entrepreneurship" underwriting his media expansion drive. If the financial logic animating industrial assistance had been "throwing bad money after bad," the motto of the self-reproducing Münzenberg agitprop ventures of the late 1920s might well have been "spend first, ask questions later." By November, NDV had siphoned no less than RM sixty thousand from its Kremlin-subsidized accounts into *Nos Regards,* and most of this had disappeared into printers' fees at Hachette and bloated editors' paychecks. Monthly revenues were not even covering the salaries of the four senior editors. By November, *Nos Regards* was running monthly losses at a rate of over 400 percent. It was at this point that Münzenberg informed Moscow about the RM sixty thousand he had sunk into a Parisian black hole—and asked the Kremlin to share his losses by throwing in another forty thousand marks.[14]

Less ambitious than the expensive Münzenberg glossies in Paris and Berlin, but no less absurd, were the targeted special-interest publications that began sprouting, weed-like, from phantom IAH committees. Thus Münzenberg's anticolonial league published a French- and German-language *Anti-Imperialist Review,* although both it and the league would disappear in 1929. The phantom German FSR clubs founded in 1927 had their own monthly, *The Coming War,* which inexplicably went bi-weekly in 1928 despite the fact that no one was reading the monthly version.[15]

Not all of Münzenberg's media ventures were phantoms, of course. But as a general rule, the more "real" such enterprises were, the more red ink they bled. The anticolonial league was typical in this regard. The Brussels conference had been real enough, and so were the meetings that followed it—real enough to attract the attention of observers in the European intelligence community.[16] At one such gathering in Cologne in August 1927, Münzenberg's IAH lieutenant Louis Gibarti announced an Arab Freedom Congress to be held in Mecca the following spring. Yet the league's office overhead alone was already eating up so much revenue that the plans came to naught. By April 1928, Münzenberg was already dismantling his beloved anti-imperialist league. There would be no mass meeting in Mecca.[17]

A similar fate befell Münzenberg's much-ballyhooed Communist book of the month club, the Universum-Bücherei, run out of a Berlin warehouse just off the Unter den Linden. On paper, the idea was brilliant: Münzenberg would charge a monthly fee to left-wing intellectuals interested in Soviet affairs, which would help underwrite some of the IAH's publications overhead and provide a ready market for its books. In theory, Universum-Bücherei was modeled on the enormously successful "bourgeois" Deutsche Buchgemeinschaft, which in the late 1920s boasted more than three hundred thousand subscribers who paid one mark per month for membership, in addition to agreeing to buy at least one book every three months for five to six marks. Confident that he would win over a substantial number of subscribers, Münzenberg ordered large print runs of new novels by Soviet-friendly writers such as Maxim Gorky and the American muckraker Upton Sinclair. He further promised to acquire old titles of potential interest to communist sympathizers, by proletarian-friendly writers such as Mark Twain and Emile Zola.[18]

As it turned out, however, there just weren't enough Soviet sympathizers in Germany to underwrite a national book of the month club. Despite a barrage of free advertising in all of his newspapers, Münzenberg was able to win over only several thousand subscribers in 1927, roughly one-hundredth the membership of the Buchgemeinschaft, even though Universum, unlike its bourgeois rival, required no obligatory book purchases on top of the modest one-mark-per-month membership fee. Münzenberg's book club did cross the seven-thousand-member mark by April 1928—but these subscribers were still not buying very many books.[19] Astoundingly, the seemingly foolproof venture was actually losing Münzenberg money, since not enough books were being sold to cover the costs of the excessively optimistic print runs at Kosmos-Verlag, a new IAH publisher set up on Wilhelmstrasse to siphon debt away from NDV.[20]

Not that any of this stopped Münzenberg. When one venture went under (such as the anti-imperialism league), or proved enough of a money loser to warrant a Kremlin bailout (*Nos Regards*, Universum), he was always ready to divert cash into a new venture—waiting, as always, until it was up and running to inform Moscow about it. Thus with his Russian film debts being assumed by Prombank and his German obligations dumped into Prometheus, Münzenberg could throw money into ever more superfluous film projects. His Communist movie club, with monthly dues and its own illustrated magazine, proved nearly as unprofitable as his book club.[21] Another cash drain was the "proletarian film archive" Münzenberg established in a warehouse at Wilhelmstrasse 48.[22] Crowning them all was Weltfilm or "World Film," an audaciously titled sham company Münzenberg created to capitalize (i.e., siphon debts away from) all the other film ventures.[23]

With the Universum financial mess safely subsumed inside the new, dummy Kosmos publishing house, Münzenberg likewise opened up room in the NDV accounts for the mushrooming print ventures that accompanied the creation of each new IAH committee. By the early 1930s, these included *The Woman's Path*, to promote the IAH's outreach to female proletarians; *The Pioneer*, aimed at teenage communist sympathizers; and *Children in Battle*, which targeted youngsters. From the amateurish production quality of such ideological doggerel—and the total lack of paying advertisers in any of them—we may assume these publications were little read outside the Berlin committee offices which edited them.[24] But that was hardly the point. With sample issues sent to ECCI along with copies of more substantial print organs like *Welt am Abend* and *AIZ*, the groupthink bulletins of the women's, teen, and children's IAH divisions created the appearance of ubiquity and extensive penetration of the German print market for Kremlin overseers. They perfectly embodied, that is, the myth of Münzenberg's media genius.

With new IAH newspapers, book clubs, sympathizers' committees, and film societies multiplying every year in the late 1920s, it is no wonder the Münzenberg media "trust," as it was beginning to be called, attracted the attention of journalists seeking to penetrate its secrets. The most damaging revelations generally came from SPD and independent union rivals on the left, who had contacts inside the Münzenberg apparat. Such access had been crucial to the SPD exposé of Münzenberg's business concessions in the Soviet Union that led to the denunciation of the IAH as the "Third Column" of the Communist International in spring 1924, and the same would be true in 1929, when the SPD began running another investigative series on Münzenberg.[25]

"Where does the money come from? Where does it go?" asked SPD critic Eugen Prager about the mysterious "Münzenberg Trust," before sketching out a rough flow-chart, not entirely inaccurate, which guessed at a strange hybrid of worker donations, Soviet bank credits, Comintern subsidies, and membership dues. Like wealthy media magnates on the right such as Hugenberg and the late Hugo Stinnes, Münzenberg had seemingly escaped the economic constraints faced by mere mortals. He was able to accomplish "everything he desired," bound by no "scruples"; he seemed "to be answerable to no one." Even in the communist universe, Prager marveled, Münzenberg was somehow able to break the rules that kept others in their place. Earlier associated with discredited figures like Zinoviev, Münzenberg was now friendly with both Thälmann and Stalin. Others "come and go," wrote Prager, "but Münzenberg stays." The "Münzenberg Trust" seemed to exist in a kind of netherworld where the rules of "bourgeois" law and finance did not apply, but then neither was it subject to "any kind of proletarian influence." Did Münzenberg serve the Soviet Union? Or merely himself? The answer to this question, Prager lamented, was unknown to "anyone in Germany," and "perhaps not even [to] Stalin in Moscow." Thus when German workers donated money to IAH causes, Prager warned, they were unwittingly furthering the growth of an empire of "corruption of the most evil kind."[26]

Münzenberg set out to "refute" Prager's speculations later that spring in his new theoretical journal, *Rote Aufbau.* Yet by doing so, he ironically lent credence to Prager's concerns about the runaway Münzenberg media monolith—by using Prager's well-publicized attack to help advertise yet another superfluous press venture! To promote *Rote Aufbau,* born in 1922 as the theoretical organ of the short-lived industrial assistance campaign and now reincarnated in 1929 as the oracle of the first Soviet Five Year Plan, Münzenberg sold his response to Prager as a special supplement for ten pfennigs. *Rote Aufbau* needed something to live off, after all—not a single advertiser had braved its pages in 1922, and none had yet in 1929, either.[27]

Certainly there was no reason for Münzenberg to be seriously concerned by Prager's accusations. Even if Prager had made some errors in his guesswork (assuming, as most historians have as well, that MOPR's apparat was subordinate to the IAH, instead of being its most bitter rival), these only accentuated further the Münzenberg legend.[28] In the main Prager's account of the IAH empire was deeply flattering, making Münzenberg out to be a financial genius—the peer of Hugenberg, whose entrepreneurial talents were nefariously and secretly furthering the communist cause at the SPD's expense.

Instead of "refuting" Prager's imputation of omnipotence and brilliant financial chicanery, Münzenberg shrewdly took Prager's accusations and subtly amplified them. In one early draft of his reply, Münzenberg playfully denied that he really possessed the "phenomenal powers" Prager endowed him with.[29] In the final version, he toned down his backhanded "denials," but slyly played up the profitability issue. "Using our own resources and our own means," he lied, the IAH dutifully sank profits from its various "economic enterprises" into "revolutionary mass propaganda and agitation."[30] Prager and his SPD readers, like Bukharin in the Kremlin, erroneously believed the IAH media empire was self-financing. Why would Münzenberg want to disabuse them of this illusion? Press attacks on his seemingly unscrupulous finances played right into Münzenberg's hands, by promoting the myth of the IAH's financial "independence."

Although rivals and critics helped along the way, the true author of the

Münzenberg legend was none other than Münzenberg himself. Even the flattering "Red Millionaire" label, which Münzenberg's wife Babette Gross bandies about in her memoir of his career with a suspicious degree of indignation, as if it was some nasty right-wing epithet, seems to have been Münzenberg's own creation.[31] I have found no usage of this term by any of Münzenberg's rivals or enemies. The Nazis, for example, generally preferred to refer to him with their standard epithet (which was incidentally quite inaccurate), "Jewish."[32] One SPD critic called Münzenberg a "communist profiteer," and Prager described him as a "communist Hugenberg," but Hugenberg himself, for example, seems not to have been unduly flattered by the comparison.[33] Hugenberg's newspapers, unlike *Vorwärts*, wasted little ink on Münzenberg—and why should they have? Whereas SPD journalists worried that Münzenberg was trying to steal their left-leaning readers, Hugenberg's organs reached an entirely different audience of unapologetic national chauvinists. And Hugenberg's newspapers were in a different league than Münzenberg's in terms of market penetration. Although Berlin-area circulation figures for *Welt am Abend* were, on paper at least, comparable to those of Hugenberg's flagship *Berliner Lokal-Anzeiger* (about two hundred thousand in the early 1930s), the latter newspaper was actually read: it often ran as many as thirty-eight pages of paid advertisements on a weekday, whereas Münzenberg was rarely able to fill a single page even in a Sunday edition.[34] If Münzenberg was a media mogul at all, it was through audacious deficit spending and assiduous lobbying for Kremlin bailouts, as opposed to any sort of business acumen.[35]

The self-described "Red Millionaire" may not have been literally a millionaire.[36] But he certainly lived like one, with his chauffeur, his personal barber, his freshly tailored suits, his entourage, and his bottomless expense account. The secrecy of Münzenberg's personal finances only heightened his allure to jealous Communists and snooping Socialists. As a Reichstag deputy after 1924, his income was exempt from taxation, so that there was no public record of his investments. He did have a stock portfolio run through the investment bank Bett, Simon & Co., the value of which one Socialist critic guessed in 1930 at upward of seventy thousand marks, which may have included shares of I. G. Farben stock.[37] Archives in Moscow also indicate that Münzenberg was paid 150 gold rubles per page for *Solidarität*, an IAH vanity book ghosted in his name, which at a length of over five hundred pages netted him roughly forty thousand dollars according to official exchange rates—a fortune in early 1930s terms, and the equivalent of close to a million dollars today.[38] No wonder Münzenberg struck younger communists like Neumann as complacent and self-satisfied. No matter how devoted he was to the Revolution to come, in the present day he was already living like a high-powered postrevolutionary commissar, surrounded by devoted sycophants and all of the attributes of power and privilege.

If we look more closely at the content of the vaunted media organs of the "Red Millionaire," the sense of rhetorical drift in the late 1920s gives us some idea of what a Münzenberg-led propaganda regime might have been like if the KPD had actually seized power in Germany. On the surface, an extraordinary compartmentalization would have held sway, in which every last segment of the laboring classes, from preteen scouts to teenage apprentices to assembly line women and white-collar typists, was bombarded with specially targeted bromides about the proper proletarian life. The IAH's bulletin *Children in Battle* would have become the Bible of the "Thälmann Youth," Germany's answer to the Russian Komsomol. *The Pioneer* would have ushered enthusiastic teenage veterans of the Thälmann Youth into the arcana of party rule. And the IAH's feminist flagship, *The Woman's Path*, would have gradually evolved from its austere, capital-poor beginnings into a glossy guide to acceptable communist fashions. Feminist features might have mirrored *AIZ*'s *What to Do with Your Money?* segment from September 1927, which showed prospering proletarian wives how to accentuate their beauty with colorful clothes, instead of flaunting their wealth with conspicuous jewelry.[39]

The illustrated monthly *AIZ*, meanwhile, was already promoting the Stalinist personality cult. Flattering portraits of Lenin, Stalin, and Felix Dzerzhinsky, the founder of the Cheka, graced the covers of special issues of *AIZ* in 1925 and 1926.[40] Luxemburg and Zetkin were memorialized with similar cult-like reverence in 1927, and soon even lowly Russian Communist functionaries, such as uniformed Chekists on parade, were receiving the same glossy treatment.[41] If the KPD had come to power, one can imagine similar, cult-like photographic paeans to party martyrs (Luxemburg and Liebknecht); Politburo enforcers (Thälmann, Ulbricht); and the founder of the future German Cheka (or Stasi), who would probably have been Münzenberg's onetime roommate Leo Flieg.[42] From *AIZ*'s photographic flaunting of the glistening bodies of "proletarian athletes," we may further infer that anyone who won Olympic medals for Red Germany would have received the same treatment from Münzenberg's media machine.[43] Münzenberg himself might have preferred, like Goebbels, to shun the limelight, secure in his prestige as the propaganda mastermind, the power behind the throne.

Beneath this facade of party pieties, however, Münzenberg would have cultivated even under the most rigid KPD dictatorship a certain stylistic populism, with the Communist ideological cheese melted in a zesty gumbo of yellow journalism. After Münzenberg took over editorial control of *Welt am Abend* in spring 1926, the newspaper veered inexorably toward sensationalism, displaying a morbid lust for blood-and-guts mayhem of all varieties. Aside from the inevitable "war scare against the Soviet Union" blow-ups, Münzenberg's editors filled space with lurid features on the last days of the Romanovs and Hohenzollerns, romantic series on themes such as "spying during the war," gossip about Hitler and his adulterous entourage, and front-page disaster stories. It is not hard to imagine Münzenberg distracting Germans from the poverty sure to result from a Communist dictatorship, much as Goebbels would later divert them from the repression of Nazi rule, through a barrage of murder-and-mayhem headlines—though originating exclusively from outside Red Germany. Inside any future German Communist paradise, much like in the Soviet Union as it was already covered by the Münzenberg trust, there would have been no more disasters—none exposed by Münzenberg, anyway.[44]

Even short of a Communist takeover, the increasingly bland prosperity of Weimar Germany in the late 1920s offered Münzenberg broad license to experiment in his newspapers, unencumbered by the strict political mandates of the revolutionary postwar period. The protestations of young theorists like Neumann aside, Communists were not about to come to power in Germany; but this did not mean there was nothing for the party faithful to get excited about. Why not devote IAH Communist front organs to lurid Soviet hero worship, at a time when *Rote Fahne* was constrained to cover domestic affairs in a depressingly moderate political climate? Why not trade totalitarian party gossip and tell lurid stories of fallen royalty, if that was what readers of daily newspapers wanted? In the absence of strict ideological constraints, Münzenberg's daily newspaper flourished, with plenty of colorful graphics that soon rivaled those of the illustrated monthly *AIZ*.

But the days of comparative moderation inside the KPD were numbered, due not to anything happening in Germany but to a power struggle inside the Kremlin. Stalin was on the move again in 1928, turning violently against Bukharin, who from 1924 to 1927 had stood at his side as Trotsky, Zinoviev, and Kamenev were progressively stripped of their offices and their power. In a sense Bukharin's fate resembled that of Danton and the moderate "right" Jacobins during the French Revolutionary terror of 1794, who were guillotined after Robespierre had already crushed the "left" Jacobin faction of extremists. In the Soviet case, Trotsky, followed somewhat later by Zinoviev and Kamenev, had represented the "Left," in that they had all supported abandoning the concessions of NEP to the Russian peasantry, in order to begin a new "socialist offensive" of rigidly planned industrialization. Bukharin, by contrast, seemed to like NEP. While sharing the ultimate goal of all Leninists—abolition of the market and all private economic activity—Bukharin believed that the best way to "grow into socialism" was by allowing peasants to produce enough surplus wealth to finance industrialization—another catch phrase of Bukharin's was "socialism in one country," as opposed to Trotsky's "permanent revolution" in all. Stalin, like Robespierre before him—but more effectively—chose to adopt what he liked of both "deviations" once his rivals had been eliminated, deciding on a path of forced industrialization (à la Trotsky) in one country alone (as per Bukharin).[45]

The pretext for eliminating Bukharin was his ideological opposition to the first Soviet Five Year Plan. In western Europe, Bukharin's putative allies on the Communist "right" were eliminated as well, although both the timing and the ideological logic of the expulsions differed from country to country.

In Germany, the pretext for enforcing the new line, the so-called "Wittorf affair" of 1928, came about in wholly arbitrary fashion, and Münzenberg was lucky he was not blindsided by it. John Wittorf was Ernst Thälmann's brother-in-law, whom Thälmann had recently installed as KPD secretary in Hamburg. The Hamburg party local had long been the personal fiefdom of Thälmann, a Kremlin favorite who had run on the KPD ticket for president in the German elections of 1925, losing to the retired field marshal, Paul von Hindenburg. Thälmann, a bland-looking apparatchik who, with his shaved head, could easily have passed for one of the party's menacing street thugs, had grown up in Hamburg and was an active participant in the abortive insurrection there during the German October of 1923. When Wittorf brazenly embezzled party funds in August 1927, Thälmann's rivals in the KPD Zentrale moved gingerly at first but agreed on a course of expelling Wittorf after he confessed in June 1928. Thälmann, ostensibly in order to preserve the party's reputation in Hamburg, tried to hush up the affair that summer, going so far as to declare his solidarity with the confessed embezzler and to refuse to sanction his expulsion. This open tolerance for corruption was too much for the other members of the KPD Zentrale, who on 26 September 1928 unanimously resolved to suspend Thälmann from his functions (although Walter Ulbricht, significantly, quietly abstained by excusing himself to go to the lavatory before the vote).[46]

As would so often prove to be the case in subsequent scandals involving Communist Party leaders in the era of Stalin's burgeoning dictatorship, the deciding factor in the Wittorf affair was not politics so much as the pliancy (or lack thereof) of personalities. Thälmann was, to be sure, on the "left" inside the KPD, and the rivals who were most adamant about expelling him (including August Thalheimer, Hugo Eberlein, Paul Fröhlich, and Jakob Walcher) were on the "right," in the sense that they had all traditionally favored at least some political flexibility in dealing with German Socialists and independent unions. But when Stalin intervened on Thälmann's behalf, forcing through a resolution reinstating the fallen KPD leader at a rump session of the Comintern Presidium on 6 October 1928, the justification was a simple breach of party discipline: the Zentrale's members had suspended Thälmann without consulting Moscow. Worse, they had openly published their 26 September resolution, which expelled several Hamburg party leaders for corruption and chided Thälmann for his cover-up, in *Rote Fahne*. The "right" faction in the KPD had thus aired the party's dirty laundry in public, and this Stalin could not stomach. Eberlein, Thalheimer, and the others were now sacked from their positions in the party leadership.

Although he had played no role in it, the Wittorf affair proved a godsend for Münzenberg, allowing him to survive a new round of purges of the "right" that should, by all political logic, have targeted him as well. By its very definition, the Münzenberg trust was aimed at collaborating with non-Communist elements in European politics, at ensnaring sympathizers and independent union groups into unofficial Communist front activities. This stance of "conciliation" *(Versöhnheit)* was officially forbidden under Stalin's new "class against class" line, and if not for the accident of personality, it is likely Münzenberg's stock in the Kremlin would have now plummeted. Bukharin, after all, the scapegoat of the hour, had been Münzenberg's key patron during the "anti-imperialist" initiative of 1926–27 that had underwritten his media expansion. Of Münzenberg's earlier Bolshevik patrons, one (Lenin) was dead, and two more (Zinoviev and Radek) had long since fallen from favor. The fragility of Münzenberg's political position in Moscow was underscored by the attacks on political deviation in M-Russ films that were now lighting up otherwise dour Bolshevik arts journals.[47]

But the travails of Thälmann and Wittorf worked to Münzenberg's advantage, even though he had no personal connection to either of them. In the midst of the recriminations and backbiting following Stalin's October 1928 intervention in favor of Thälmann, Paul Fröhlich, an old Hamburg hand who was the best informed of Thälmann's critics in the party Zentrale about the corruption there, dropped Münzenberg's name at a KPD rally in Cologne in association with Wittorf and the financial scandals roiling the party. Informed by his friend Leo Flieg about Fröhlich's accusation of financial malfeasance inside the Münzenberg trust (which was actually vague and rather tame), Münzenberg lodged an indignant protest against Fröhlich at the KPD Zentrale on 5 December 1928, accusing him of spreading false rumors about the IAH. This was a shrewd move, for Fröhlich would soon be expelled from the KPD, and Münzenberg was now on record against him. Münzenberg also publicly defended his friend Neumann (a "left" ally of Thälmann) against personal attacks published in November 1928 by bitter "right" rivals in the Zentrale such as Thalheimer and Walcher—men who were also shortly expelled from the party.[48]

In this way Münzenberg threw in his lot unambiguously with the hard Communist Left, agreeing to enforce the new "class against class" line— never mind that the premise behind his entire media trust implied a moderate "right" position. Although no admirer of Thälmann, Münzenberg agreed to purge the KPD local in his electoral district of Hesse-Nassau, near Frankfurt-am-Main, of anti-Thälmann "conciliators." By publicly defending Stalin's purges, Münzenberg shored up his position in the new Thälmann-Neumann–dominated Zentrale and in the Kremlin. A measure of the effectiveness of Münzenberg's maneuvering inside the KPD may be taken in the vehemence with which *Gegen den Strom*, the organ of the anti-Thälmann opposition launched by ousted KPD renegades in November 1928, was soon attacking him.[49]

The next step was to whip the Münzenberg trust itself into line with the new "anticonciliatory" policy, an ostensibly daunting task made much easier by the fact that many of its most obviously "conciliatory" ventures were largely illusory. Thus the poorly capitalized anti-imperialism league was left to rot in 1929, as its *Anti-Imperialist Review* and its audacious conference plans, for Mecca and elsewhere, were simply abandoned. Münzenberg's vaunted book, film, and photo clubs were not killed off quite so quickly, but he scaled back on their expenses and ceased mentioning them entirely in his correspondence with Moscow after the new line was enforced in November 1928.[50] To distance himself from the politically questionable M-Russ film studio, meanwhile, Münzenberg merely danced the old Comintern two-step, informing his Russian IAH lieutenants at a November 1928 Executive meeting held shortly after Stalin's new "class against class" line was transmitted to Berlin that he was shocked at the poor ideological quality of the M-Russ films currently being produced in Moscow.[51]

Münzenberg faced a different ideological challenge in reforming the *Reichsabteilung*, or German branch, of the IAH, which was the only department in the Münzenberg trust still devoted primarily to fund-raising and charity. Under the competent, plodding direction of Paul Scholze, the *Reichsabteilung* had grown organically, if somewhat accidentally, out of the "German hunger" campaign of 1923–24 into the largest national branch of the IAH. It still ran soup kitchens in many German cities, although this network had contracted significantly due both to the alleviation of the economic situation and to the general indifference that had greeted the campaign.[52] The *Reichsabteilung* also ran a small network of "proletarian" summer camps and other charities aimed at worker children.

Even this paltry operation, though, posed a political problem. Of the five or ten thousand dues-paying members of the IAH *Reichsabteilung*, only about 30 percent were registered Communists. Although only about 3 percent of the rest belonged to the now taboo SPD, the other 67 percent or so were non–party-affiliated and thus also, in the crunch, ideologically unreliable.[53] Aside from the issue of consorting with potential political "enemies," the IAH's German branch was carrying out charitable activities that seemed passé in the new era of "class against class." No sooner had the new line been imposed in November 1928 than the *Reichsabteilung* found itself lambasted by KPD critics for the novel sin of "charity soup politics" *(Bettelsuppenpolitik)*, which failed to live up to the spirit of class warfare. If it did not abandon the old soup kitchen initiative, these critics warned, the IAH ran the risk of diluting workers' revolutionary tendencies, snuffing out their battle-readiness by filling their bellies.[54]

To clear the ideological air, Münzenberg, who had ignored his German division for years, personally attended the *Reichsabteilung* conference in Dresden in April 1929. The new line he laid down there was harsh. No longer could the IAH regard itself as an "aid organization." Instead of receiving free sojourns at summer camps merely because of their class origins, worker children must instead be recruited into disciplined IAH cells, where they would receive proper ideological instruction. Monthly dues would henceforth be smaller (only ten pfennigs, instead of fifty), but organizations and individuals failing to pay (which to date was most of them) would no longer be able to call themselves IAH members. And these dues would no longer finance anything so mundane as soup kitchens for the hungry, but rather must feed class warriors exclusively—that is, workers on strike who were thus engaged in "battle" with capitalist management. The IAH was to leave charity behind, and become an "organization of struggle." And there would be no debate regarding the new line: protests by IAH member committees against Berlin resolutions were now forbidden.[55]

To make sure the new line would be followed, Münzenberg established a new indoctrination seminar for IAH functionaries at Berlin headquarters in summer 1929, modeled on the International Leninist School in Moscow used to train foreign Communist party leaders. From now on, there would be no more excuses if national IAH committees deviated from the party line as laid down by Münzenberg. Propaganda commissars, trained in Berlin, would make regular visits to the IAH national branch offices to check up on the leadership and enforce any resolutions laid down by the Berlin Secretariat. The keywords everywhere were "strike support" and "class struggle."[56]

All this, however, was the easy part. Outside Germany, Münzenberg's aid committees were mostly phantoms anyway, and it was not a really difficult trick to make objectionably unwarlike charity operations vanish when they barely existed in the first place. Likewise, Münzenberg was able to extricate himself effortlessly from ideologically questionable fellow-traveling film, photo, and book clubs that had never really gotten off the ground. The FSR-type clubs, meanwhile, were by their very nature suited to the new hard left line—since all they did was promote hysteria about the "coming war against the Soviet Union." It was easy to transform them into outright apologists for Stalin's terror tactics, as Münzenberg did in fall 1930, when he formed a new subcommittee "For the Defense of the Soviet Union—against Imperialist Warmongers." The keynote act of this group was a public appeal (putatively) signed by "forty-two professors and intellectuals" who had all come to the inescapable conclusion that the show trials of "industrial wreckers" and saboteurs then taking place in Moscow proved "what had been clear to every politically conscious person, that influential imperialist trusts, groups, and general staffs are in league with the Russian counterrevolution preparing a well planned war of intervention against the Soviet Union." Among the signatories to this cynical whitewash of Stalinist tyranny were the art critic Alfred Kerr, the satirist Kurt Tucholsky, and the writer Kurt Hiller.[57]

Münzenberg's major print organs, though, were a different story. As ostensibly independent media ventures meant to appeal to uncommitted party outsiders, *AIZ* and *Welt am Abend* almost by definition fell afoul of the dictates of the KPD's "class against class" strategy. This line had hardened by fall 1929 to the point where KPD propagandists were expected to refer to everyone on the non-Communist left as "social fascists" who, by supporting the SPD-led government of Hermann Müller, had shown their true colors, their support for the capitalist ruling establishment, their hatred of the Soviet Union, and so on. Amazingly, the new doctrine of "social fascism" held the SPD to be even more guilty of "fascistic" tendencies than the real fascists, Hitler's Nazis. The latter, because still in opposition to the tottering Weimar regime, were seen as less dangerous than the Socialists, who by contrast provided its strongest support.[58] How could Münzenberg now justify his putatively independent newspapers, which for so long had sold themselves to Moscow on the grounds that they roped in sympathizers from the non-Communist left—that they appealed, that is, to that category of humanity now unmasked as the "social fascist" enemy?

The answer, of course, was to toe the harsh new Communist line in Münzenberg's ostensibly non-Communist newspapers, pretensions of independence be damned. Münzenberg would go ahead and smear Socialists and other wishy-washy left-wing sympathizers, even if those were exactly the people, he claimed, who were reading his newspapers. Or at least, he would insult them frequently enough to cover his flank in case anyone in Moscow was paying attention. In the main, *AIZ* and *Welt am Abend* continued running the same old yellow "Soviet Russia in danger" headlines in 1929 and 1930, but every so often Münzenberg would slip in a sucker punch against the German Socialists, accusing SPD ministers of financial corruption, or of cynical collusion with capitalist magnates, or of secretly conspiring to attack the Soviet Union.[59]

Perhaps in order to keep his beloved flagships relatively clear of frontal assaults on his putative audience of Socialist sympathizers, Münzenberg started publishing a morning edition of *Welt am Abend* in March 1929 that was soon renamed *Berlin am Morgen*. Although similar in both format and content to *Welt am Abend*, *Berlin am Morgen* was blunter in its attacks on the SPD, spelling out directly what its evening counterpart only hinted at. Thus Müller's SPD-led cabinet was not merely described as corrupt and pro-capitalist, but Müller himself was compared directly to Mussolini, the power-hungry former Socialist turned fascist dictator.[60] Remarkably, Münzenberg stuck to this line in *Berlin am Morgen* even after Müller quite voluntarily surrendered power to an SPD-less "bourgeois" coalition led by Heinrich Brüning of the Catholic Center Party in March 1930.[61]

Generally, though, Münzenberg preferred to keep the daily newspapers free of the truly swinish insults. These he confined to more theoretical organs like *Rote Aufbau*, the reborn oracle of Soviet industrialization, which, entirely devoid of advertisements, was obviously aimed exclusively at KPD apparatchiks and ECCI budget commissars. When Münzenberg was not singing of the heavenly glory of the Five Year Plan in its pages, he was descending into the gutter to savage Socialist enemies. In one typical broadside, he compared the SPD's Interior Minister Carl Severing to both Mussolini and Kerensky, with the blunt subtitle, "a dictator and his masses."[62] By toeing the "social fascism" line so blatantly in *Rote Aufbau*, Münzenberg effectively covered his political flank to the "left," allowing at least a measure of flexibility in the other, more popular IAH organs.

By the time the Müller Cabinet collapsed in March 1930, the Münzenberg trust was squarely in line with the "class against class" dogma, savaging Socialist treachery wherever it could be found, and in many places where it couldn't. Whether the SPD was in power or out, he discovered, the German Socialists offered a particularly congenial target for political abuse. Thus in Münzenberg's main agitprop labor of love of 1929, an autobiography of his prewar and wartime glory days that he finished writing in late October, he gleefully settled scores with his old adversaries, lacing the book with coded insults against the SPD leaders who had once humiliated him by taking over his beloved Erfurt Free Youth.[63]

The gloves were now off. There would be no compromise with Socialists who blocked the Communists' path to power. From his position atop a German media megalith, backed up by dozens of international agitprop divisions in the Münzenberg trust, the "Red Millionaire" would now intoxicate his followers with a heady brew of political warfare, pledging them to annihilate their class enemies and usher in a Communist dictatorship. The hour of social apocalypse was at hand.

CHAPTER 13 *Tango with the Devil*

On 29 October 1929, a date that would soon live in infamy as "Black Tuesday," a careening stock sell-off that had begun the week before on the New York Stock Exchange turned into a rout, and panic descended on most of the world's financial markets. An economic downturn had begun in Europe as early as 1928, drying up demand for U.S. exports and leaving few outlets for American goods when the Wall Street crash undermined domestic confidence the following autumn. The production crisis was exacerbated further by the doctrinal commitment of Western governments to the gold standard, which left central bank officials with little room to maneuver and kept credit tight. By winter 1929–30, a great deflationary spiral had ensued, in which contractionary fiscal policies pursued on both sides of the Atlantic reinforced one another, dampening demand still further.[1]

The political fallout from the Great Depression in central Europe was felt immediately. The German economy had slipped into recession even before the Wall Street crash, and the news from New York devastated the business climate even further. The Müller government, composed of an unwieldy coalition of Socialist, Catholic Center, and People's Party ministers, was already drowning under the political burden of a burgeoning employment crisis, which threatened to bankrupt the national unemployment insurance fund. Foreign Minister Gustav Stresemann of the People's Party, who had negotiated the far-reaching Young Plan of 1929 refinancing the German reparation payments over the long term and including a pledge from the Allies to evacuate their troops from the Rhineland, died just weeks before the Wall Street crash, depriving the Cabinet of its most talented statesman. Stresemann's death laid bare the impotence of the Müller Cabinet, which few expected to survive the difficult winter months.

If the Depression weakened the hand of political moderates in Germany, it inevitably did just the opposite for the extremists. The first beneficiaries were Hitler's Nazis, who, along with the Communists, were the most vociferous supporters of the campaign against ratification of the Young Plan.[2] Nominally, the campaign was led by Alfred Hugenberg, the wealthy media magnate who headed a national committee promoting an anti–Young Plan plebiscite. Yet by bringing the Nazis into his coalition, Hugenberg famously made Hitler *salonfähig,* or socially respectable, for the first time, thereby helping ensure his own political eclipse. The opportunistic Hugenberg plebiscite, which demanded the abrogation of the Versailles treaty and made any minister who acquiesced in reparations payments guilty of treason, was resoundingly defeated in December 1929, but this did not slow the extremist momentum Hugenberg had foolishly ignited. Buoyed by the entrée Hugenberg's embrace gave him into business circles, Hitler kicked Nazi fund-raising into high gear and succeeded in winning regional elections for the first time, including the mayorship of Coburg. This success with the voters also led to a ministerial position in the Thuringian state government, into which the Nazis ominously entered in January 1930.

As in the Ruhr crisis of 1923, the Communists fed on the economic chaos no less shamelessly than did Hitler. Yet once again, the Communists fell far behind the Nazis in their recruitment efforts. In much the same way that the KPD's confusing flirtation with fascism had alienated potential converts in 1923, Communist assaults on SPD and union leaders as "social fascists" now seriously damaged the party's capacity to win over workers in the early days of the Depression. "To be a Communist," *Rote Fahne* declared with typically savage bluster, one must be "a mortal enemy of social fascism."[3] Such shrill attacks on an avowedly worker-friendly, SPD-led Müller government, struggling for its life against the forces of political reaction, were simply too much for most German workers. Astonishingly, as the Depression cast a pall over Germany and unemployment rolls soared into the millions over the winter of 1929–30, the Communists actually lost fifteen thousand members, just as the Nazi membership rolls were exploding.[4]

Declining KPD membership rolls were hardly reassuring, however, to members of the Müller government, who saw the Nazis' inexorable expansion and the increasing stridency of Communist rhetoric as two sides of the same coin. Both parties, after all, drew on paramilitary forces for support, which at a moment's notice could be mobilized in support of an antirepublican coup. (The SPD had its own paramilitary arm, the Reichsbanner, but this group was pledged to defend the Republic.) In truth, the Communists' notorious M- and N-groups had declined significantly in strength since their heyday in the early 1920s; but if they were mobilized at the same time as

Hitler's storm troopers, the German army would have been stretched to the limit merely to reestablish public order, leaving the Polish border, among others, vulnerable to attack. Such was the reasoning behind the Defense of the Republic law that SPD Interior Minister Carl Severing introduced into the Reichstag on 13 March 1930 in one of the Müller government's last desperate efforts to keep the forces of political extremism at bay.[5] Since the last Defense of the Republic Act had expired on 22 July 1929, Severing noted, assassination attempts on government officials had dangerously accelerated. Paramilitary attacks on the Socialist government of Prussia alone in 1929 had yielded fourteen police deaths and more than three hundred injuries. Though Severing clearly considered Hitler's storm troopers public enemy number one, he took the Communists' paramilitary Roter Frontkämpferbund seriously as well, seeing in both forces a mortal threat not only to Germany's republican form of government, but to "our entire public life."[6]

In his (eminently plausible) depiction of both Communists and Nazis as mortal enemies of republican government, Severing provided rhetorical ammunition to the KPD's "social fascism" argument. So often in the 1920s, laws aimed at curtailing political extremism had been applied unevenly, with the courts applying a double standard that punished the Left more severely than the Right. Whereas convicted Communist agitators often languished for years in prison, renegade right-wing generals such as Ludendorff were sometimes acquitted completely. Hitler himself got away with only a short prison sentence after gleefully confessing to attempting to overthrow the Weimar government at his February 1924 trial. And charges of politically motivated murders by Nazi storm troopers were sometimes dismissed by judges who, understandably, feared reprisals.

Thus when Severing introduced this law designed to defend the Weimar Republic against its extremist foes, it merely "proved" to Communists that the SPD was their greatest enemy. "Social fascists" like Severing, armed with parliamentary resolutions and the backing of the government, seemed more dangerous to the workers' movement than the real fascists, even if the latter often murdered Communists in cold blood. After all, KPD foot soldiers could retaliate against such provocations by murdering Nazis—as they began to do when Nazi attacks grew more virulent later in 1930—whereas Communist violence against Weimar government officials would now be crushed by the regular army.

In this way the debate over the law allowed Communists to flesh out the "social fascism" argument, introducing a real and present danger into a doctrine that had previously relied on hysterical claims about phantom

SPD war plans against Soviet Russia. It is significant that the most vociferous parliamentary opposition to Severing's draft law came not from the Nazis—who still had only the insignificant twelve seats they had won in 1928, as their swelling membership rolls had not yet translated into parliamentary strength—but from the much larger Communist delegation, whose raucous members smelled blood.

No one exploited this rhetorical moment more effectively than Münzenberg. Although he had never really warmed up to parliamentary life, seldom appearing in the Reichstag in his first five years as a deputy, Münzenberg was known to comrades and political rivals alike as a talented orator who could hold audiences spellbound. Several surviving pictures of Münzenberg delivering speeches in this era, taken by Nazi photographers assigned to cover Communist rallies, give a sense of the man's demagogic firepower: Münzenberg all but glows with demonic energy, with the scorching intensity of his eyes giving sharp edge to his movie-star good looks. Far more handsome than Hitler, Münzenberg nevertheless shared his contemporary's bottomless capacity to feed off the energy of a crowd, to seem to lose himself in the passion of the moment, even while maintaining ruthless control over his ideological message (figures 4 and 5).

With an impeccable sense of timing, Münzenberg seized on Severing's appearance in the Reichstag to give one of his greatest speeches. After reminding his fellow deputies that the first Defense of the Republic Act had been applied mostly against Communists, Münzenberg dismissed Severing's claim that this law was aimed against the Nazis as "monstrous" cynicism. From Ebert and Noske to Müller and Severing, Münzenberg saw in Socialist ministers not representatives of the working class, but rather their "hangmen and prison wardens." You "speak against the fascists," he berated Severing, "and then [you] descend on the workers with tanks and machine guns and shoot them."

Münzenberg, like most Communists, simply did not believe that the SPD-led "bourgeois" government really feared the Nazis. The Hitler-Hugenberg accord during the anti–Young Plan plebiscitary campaign seemed proof that the Nazis, though claiming to be anticapitalist radicals, had in fact "long ago made their peace with the German bourgeoisie." How could the Republic possibly fear a capitalist magnate like Hugenberg? And—since Münzenberg (again, like most Communists) mistakenly believed that Hugenberg now controlled Hitler behind the scenes like a marionette—it stood to reason that no Defense of the Republic Act would ever be applied against the Nazis, as "no one in the ruling classes of the Republic" could possibly gain from

FIGURE 4. Münzenberg in the full flow of oratory addressing a Communist rally, circa winter 1931–32, photographed by a Nazi surveillance team. Source: Files of the Gesamtverband deutscher antikommunistischer Vereinigungen, Hoover Institution Archives, Stanford, California.

FIGURE 5. Another Nazi surveillance photo taken at a rally, showing Münzenberg in calmly authoritative mode. Source: Files of the Gesamtverband deutscher antikommunistischer Vereinigungen, Hoover Institution Archives, Stanford, California.

such repression. "For whom," Münzenberg demanded, would the law work, and "against whom" was it intended? The answer could only be that Severing's law defended the interests of "the Republic's financial backers" against "the workers" and "the Communist Party."

Having dismissed the Nazi threat as a red herring, Münzenberg proceeded to attack his true enemies—the "social fascists" who had designed the nefarious new law. Bringing back to life the ever-simmering old resentments of wartime, when Socialist leaders had transformed a party of Social Democrats into "Social Patriots" by supporting the war effort, Münzenberg traced the party's further evolution during the Weimar years into a complacent organ of prosperous "pensioners and rentiers of the bourgeois Republic." In its prewar glory days a militant workers' movement, the SPD by the late 1920s represented only "well-installed bureaucrats and police chiefs," whom the new law was obviously meant to protect against the true revolutionaries, the Communists.

Just as he had during his trial for treason after the Spartacist uprising in Stuttgart in 1919—and as Hitler had in his own treason trial in 1924—Münzenberg openly pled guilty to Severing's charges of antirepublican agitation, and dared him to do something about it—safe in the knowledge, of course, that he enjoyed parliamentary immunity. "*Jawohl*," he proclaimed, "we are a revolutionary party," the first in German history that "had paid for its program with the blood of its martyrs." "*Jawohl*," he continued, "we are proud that the German worker is finally awakening" to fight back against oppression. We will resist any effort to suppress the KPD, he promised Severing, "with tooth and claw." Citing a famous phrase uttered by one of the SPD's founding fathers, Wilhelm Liebknecht, in his trial for lèse-majesté in Leipzig, Münzenberg vowed that the Communist rank and file would "oppose violence with violence." When your laws defend a "capitalist dictatorship," Münzenberg taunted Severing, again turning Liebknecht's words against his own party, then "we consider it a positive duty . . . to break [them]."

Spurred on by the SPD's countertaunts that he was merely acting as Moscow's tool ("Kronstadt 1921!" was the one most frequently heard), Münzenberg built up to an apocalyptic climax that left no doubt as to who would bear the wrath of his vengeance when the KPD took power. "You laughed at us then," Münzenberg admonished the SPD's almost elderly Reichstag delegation, reminding them of the ridicule that once greeted Lenin and his tiny Zimmerwald Left fraction during the war. But your "moment . . . will come," he promised his SPD enemies, just as "it came for tsardom and for German kaiserdom." "Your 'Defense of the Republic' law," Münzenberg assured Severing, "is a sign of weakness," while for us, by contrast, it is "a spur to double our forces, to increase them tenfold." There was no doubt in Münzenberg's mind that the SPD was losing the war for the hearts of the working masses, who would soon all join the KPD's ranks in struggling toward "the destruction of bourgeois class society and the realization of communism."[7]

About one thing, at least, Münzenberg was right: the SPD-led government of Hermann Müller was too weak to defend the Weimar Republic. Over the Communists' increasingly shrill objections, Severing's Defense of the Republic Act did pass by a vote of 265 to 150 in the Reichstag the following week, but this symbolic triumph was not enough to save the government. Müller was, to be sure, handicapped by the stubbornness of his own party's Reichstag delegation, which on 27 March 1930 rejected compromise legislation devised by Heinrich Brüning of the Center Party on the crucial issue of bailing out the unemployment insurance fund from bankruptcy. But Müller could have weathered even this crisis had President Hindenburg had faith in his capacity, as a Social Democrat, to uphold social order in the face of extremist threats like those issued by Münzenberg. Knowing that Hindenburg had no intention of issuing a presidential decree on his behalf (which would have allowed him to circumvent Reichstag opposition on the unemployment insurance plan), Müller resigned. Brüning, the pragmatic Center Party moderate who had authored the compromise legislation, was now drafted by Hindenburg to replace him. Although Brüning himself had wanted to preserve the Müller coalition government, and now wished to establish his own parliamentary majority, in truth his claim to the chancellorship rested from the start with Hindenburg's advisers, most of them (like Hindenburg) military men, who were more interested in stamping out Socialist influence on German politics than in securing parliamentary support for economic initiatives. For better and for worse, with the advent of "presidential" Cabinets such as Brüning's, the army would now call the shots in Weimar politics.[8]

Under pressure from Hindenburg's cadre of reactionary advisers, Brüning reluctantly ousted from the government every one of the seven Socialists who had served under Müller. For reasons still debated to this day, he also pursued a deflationary policy which, by rejecting economic stimulus or work creation measures in favor of strict adherence to international financial obligations, exacerbated the unemployment crisis further and put his government on a collision course with the SPD and the unions.[9] All of this put the Communists in an odd position, rhetorically speaking. With the SPD stripped of its power (outside of the state government of Prussia), were Socialists still "social fascists"? And of course, Münzenberg and other Communists had been cruelly taunting Müller, Severing et al. for months. Should the attacks now cease and the gloating begin? Or did the advent of a Cabinet openly hostile to Socialism herald a time for contrition and reconciliation with the SPD? Where, in short, was the enemy?

A flicker of recognition of what the Communists' brutal assaults on Müller may have wrought can be found in the subtle shift in doctrine endorsed by the KPD Politburo the week following Müller's fall. In the opaque phraseology of party-speak, the new line, passed on 5 April 1930, was labeled "United Front from Below." This basically meant that SPD rank-and-file members would no longer be overtly attacked as "social fascists," and that their leaders, after being ousted from government, were now seen as mere "lackeys" of Germany's bourgeois ruling classes. "Fascism" was now understood as a kind of all-embracing phenomenon in the German governing bureaucracy, in which "SPD lackeys" were not necessarily worse than Brüning's coalition or the Nazis—who were no longer merely an opposition party, as they now held office in Thuringia. On the other hand, in the new doctrine Socialists were not seen as any better than the Nazis, either.[10]

One happy corollary of the new line was that Communist journalists were now free to criticize real fascists as well as imaginary ones. The threat posed by Hitler's Nazis was formally addressed for the first time in a Politburo resolution dated 4 June 1930, which expressed concern over storm trooper terror tactics and authorized attacks in the party press labeling the NSDAP as "fascist."[11] In his usual style, Münzenberg had already jumped out in front on this issue, launching his own press assaults on the Nazis as early as mid-May. Repeatedly during spring and summer 1930, Münzenberg ran inflammatory stories exposing Nazi brutality, leaving no epithet unused (one memorably alliterative headline compared SA storm troopers to the Ku Klux Klan).[12] The KPD's discovery of real fascism clearly helped the party's cause, reversing the membership declines of the preceding winter, although only about half of the losses were made up by August.[13]

The Communists' flirtation with moral principle, however, was short-lived. With new Reichstag elections called by Brüning for September, the Nazis' surging popularity alarmed Moscow enough that a new, more aggressive (and more cynical) doctrine was proclaimed for the KPD. On the positive side, the new line was less opaque than the last, summed up in the cardinal theme of "national liberation." The idea was to claim Nazi issues for the Communist camp, stepping up attacks on the Young Plan and on the Versailles settlement more generally, which was now officially labeled a "thieves' peace."[14] Through a perverse logic of backhanded flattery, the Communists hoped to beat Hitler at his own game, much as they had aped his anti-Semitic arguments in their attacks on Jewish industrialists in the Ruhr controversy of 1923. And the early returns were promising: after railing opportunistically against reparations in the campaign's final weeks, the KPD won 1.3 million more votes in the September 1930 elections than it had in 1928, increasing its Reichstag delegation to its greatest number yet, seventy-seven deputies.

And yet, just as in 1923, Nazi gains were much greater. Hitler's party increased its vote count by a factor of eight over the 1928 results, from 809,000 to 6.4 million, and its Reichstag delegation by a factor of ten, from twelve to 107. Nazis now outnumbered Communists in parliament for the first time, and by a substantial margin of thirty seats. The KPD "national liberation" campaign, pressed most enthusiastically in the Zentrale by Münzenberg's friend Neumann, may even have helped the Nazis. By encroaching on the Nazis' rhetorical turf, the Communists seemed to have played right into Hitler's hands.

Oddly, though, the Communists didn't see it that way. The Nazis, in spite of their electoral triumph, remained purely opposed to Brüning's government —unlike the SPD, which saw Brüning as a lesser evil than the Nazis and agreed not to support a no-confidence motion against him in the Reichstag. Thus the official Communist line labeled the Brüning cabinet a "fascist dictatorship" propped up by "social fascist henchmen."[15] In this sense, Hitler's gains in September were less important than the six hundred thousand votes lost by the moderate SPD to the uncompromising KPD. Such losses, in the blinkered "social fascist" worldview, left the putatively centrist but actually "fascist" Brüning regime weak and ripe for the plucking. The September elections, in this way, represented "Communism Advancing in Germany." Münzenberg's *AIZ* even put out a special issue celebrating "the electoral triumph of Red Berlin" in words and pictures.[16]

Münzenberg himself responded in much the same way in a postelection interview conducted by Hans Wesemann of the prestigious left-wing cultural review *Die Weltbühne*. On reading the transcript of this interview today, one is struck less by the predictable bombast about Communist gains in September than by the ideological confusion caused by the unexpected Nazi triumph. On the one hand, Münzenberg dismissed Hitler as a nonentity, calling him "little Adolf," and spent most of the interview gloating about the erosion of the Socialist voter base. When he was asked to defend the "class against class" strategy, which had clearly weakened the SPD and possibly strengthened the Nazis, Münzenberg was unapologetic, blaming the Socialists alone for disuniting the Left by opportunistically grasping at power. If the SPD were true to its "democratic and socialist" principles, Münzenberg unbelievably insisted, then it would form a government with Hitler (!) and make him "answerable" for his phony promises to the German workers. But the stodgy SPD bureaucrats would not do this, preferring instead to prop up the unpopular cabinet of Brüning, merely in order to protect the party's precious ruling posts in the Prussian state government. Holding ministerial office was, in Münzenberg's view, the Socialists' true pride and joy. The SPD, he declared, would "hold onto Prussia, its sole power base, at any price." Thus the SPD would continue to shy away from any decisive social struggle, leaving it to Communists alone to fight the true class war.

Somehow, though, Münzenberg seemed to recognize that the Nazis represented a serious threat on the political horizon, even if he was not sure quite how to meet it. In full obedience to the "class against class" line, he ruled out unequivocally any "tactical collaboration with the SPD bureaucracy" to counter the fascist threat. In part, this was because Münzenberg viewed the SPD as an enemy that the Nazis and Communists had in common. Both parties, after all, were trying to make inroads in independent German labor unions, which for the most part remained loyal to the SPD and hostile to both Red and "Brown" recruiters. Münzenberg was hardly going to "begrudge every lumpen proletarian who defected to [the Nazis] for Hitler's free beer." Then again, if Hitler's Brownshirts ever took power, Münzenberg was certain they would drop their quasi-socialist rhetoric in an instant and launch their "national liberation struggle" by "thrashing the weakest segment of the [German] working classes with their truncheons." Thus the Communists must carry out a "dual strategy," seeking to "avert the fascist danger" even while "winning over the working masses of the SPD" to the KPD strategy of escalating the class war.[17]

At root, the contempt Münzenberg and other Communists felt for the SPD's mostly elderly, comfortably well-paid leaders reflected a lack of respect for the Socialists' will to fight for their beliefs—a will the Nazis obviously possessed in abundance. For this reason, there was a grudging mutual respect between the two extremist parties, neither of which hesitated to copy and learn from the other. Hitler himself admitted that, although he despised the Communists' "boring social theory and materialist conception of history," he had learned a great deal from their "methods," from Lenin's ruthless militarization of politics and demonization of political enemies to the disciplined organizational techniques and elaborate propaganda apparat of the

Comintern.[18] Then there were the garishly red Nazi swastika banners and posters, which so shamelessly usurped the traditional color of the Left.

The Communists returned the compliment, both in 1923, when Radek and Ruth Fischer experimented with fascist themes and Hermann Remmele tried recruiting Communists at Nazi rallies, and in 1929–30, when the KPD jumped on the anti–Young Plan, anti-Versailles bandwagon to try to rope in nationalist malcontents. It is significant that the strongest Nazi and Communist gains in the early Depression years were registered among the unemployed, who proved especially susceptible to the no-holds-barred scapegoating practiced by demagogues like Hitler and Münzenberg. At the time of the September 1930 Reichstag elections, as many as 40 percent of registered KPD members were on the dole. The Nazis, too, drew much of their electoral support from voters who had lost their jobs (although the extent of Hitler's exploitation of the unemployment crisis has sometimes been exaggerated), and the unemployed made up a particularly large percentage of storm troopers, who were happy to join an organization that offered them work (of a sort—professional brawling, basically), and not infrequently, free food. Neither party, by contrast, made any kind of serious dent in the more numerous (though ever dwindling) ranks of organized and skilled labor, where electoral loyalty to the SPD was still fierce.[19]

It should not be surprising, then, that the Communists' new covert "antifascist combat alliance" created in December 1930 to replace their now illegal paramilitary arm, not only mirrored the Nazi SA's tactics but even recruited from its ranks. Among the Communist cadets Münzenberg addressed in a rousing speech at the combat alliance's founding congress was a former Freikorps lieutenant, Richard Scheringer, who had done time at Gollnow prison for illegal political solicitation in the army. At Gollnow, Scheringer was converted to communism along with a number of his fellow inmates. Following Münzenberg's speech, Scheringer rose up to declare his allegiance to the KPD and his readiness to take up arms against the Nazis. With Münzenberg's help, Scheringer began publishing a Nazi opposition rag styled "The Mouth-Piece of the Upright Soldiers of the German Revolution in the NSDAP." It was not long before Scheringer began receiving letters from SA men disillusioned by Hitler's apparent lack of revolutionary "sincerity." Many of these disgruntled storm troopers followed Scheringer in joining the KPD. Not all would stay, however—in fact "side-switching" between the two extremist parties' paramilitary wings occurred with great frequency in the early 1930s, with some turncoats moving back and forth between the Communists' combat alliance and the SA repeatedly.[20]

As such ideological defections by hardened street warriors suggest, the KPD's hostility to Nazism in no way reflected a pacifist aversion to Hitler's violent methods. The gulf between the two parties was not so much ethical in nature as eschatological. Certainly the two extremist parties reveled in publicizing atrocities committed by the other in the tactical struggle of the here and now, but for most of their leaders, it was the ends to which power would ultimately be put, not the means by which it was acquired, which really mattered. Münzenberg certainly believed this, which helps explain why, even as many of his Communist followers were being bludgeoned by Nazi thugs in the streets of Berlin, he agreed to tarry with the notorious Nazi renegade Otto Strasser in January 1931 at a friendly public debate on the theme of "National Unity or International Socialism?"[21]

Strasser's famous break with Hitler the previous spring had been occasioned by his contempt for the Nazi führer's indifference to the "socialist" and "worker" parts of his party's name. Unlike Hitler, Strasser actually believed in the ideal of a national *socialism*, in which the means of production —just as in Marxist socialism—would be turned over to the workers. In Strasser's scenario these would, of course, all be patriotic German workers, who would still look out for the national interest. Strasser's last illusions about the ultimate goals of Nazism were dispelled at an emotional meeting of the NSDAP leadership held in Berlin on 21 May 1930, when he learned that Hitler did not, in fact, intend to expropriate Germany's industrialists, whose support Hitler would need to carry out his goals for military expansionism. Unwilling to abandon his socialist ideals, Strasser was expelled from the Nazi party, whereupon he tried to recruit followers into a splinter party of "revolutionary national socialists."[22]

When Strasser and Münzenberg took the stage in Berlin's Pharussälen on 6 January 1931 for what was advertised as a "Frank Discussion between Communists and National Socialists," then, there was clearly common political ground to be exploited. The two men shared a passion for "socialist" ideology and for large-scale geopolitical theorizing, to the exclusion of the mundane tactical give and take of the everyday. Astonishingly, at a time when Nazi Brownshirts and Communist Redshirts were brawling in the streets and generally sowing terror wherever they went, neither man saw fit to bring up the issue of this political violence in the entire course of their exchange. Although both criticized Hitler severely, it was not out of distaste for his brutal anti-Semitism or for his goals—already published openly in *Mein Kampf*—of violent territorial conquest and extermination of his race enemies. Rather, their disagreements with Hitler—and with each other—

boiled down to the dialectical interpretation of current events. It was all a matter of historical eschatology, of the urgent need to predict the nature of the coming apocalypse and plan accordingly.

Significantly, Münzenberg opened his remarks by faulting Hitler for the cardinal sin of indifference to socialist doctrine. Citing Strasser's own recollection of the words spoken at his fateful meeting with the NSDAP leadership the previous spring, Münzenberg provoked loud indignation among the Communists present in the auditorium by declaring that for Hitler, "socialism [was] only a word, which we [the Nazis] use to mislead and defraud the masses." Since Hitler was not a serious socialist, he was not to be taken seriously. Münzenberg cruelly mocked the would-be Nazi dictator, to hearty laughs from the audience, as a clownish pretender to the Hohenzollern throne, who thought himself an "instrument of heaven," even though all he really spoke for was the vulgar "gramophone." "Hitler," Münzenberg assured his rough-and-ready followers, "we can ignore. He has no worldview, has never had one, and he never will have one."

Strasser, by contrast, actually did take socialism seriously—so Münzenberg saved his real rhetorical energy for him. By seeking to fuse nationalism with socialism, Strasser was in Münzenberg's view "unconsciously and unwittingly" acting as the stooge of the industrial profiteers who had sent millions of German workers to death in the war, and who were now preparing "an international war against . . . Soviet Russia to annihilate Bolshevism." Hitler, on the other hand—according to Münzenberg—acted "willingly" as a capitalist tool and was for that reason less dangerous to working-class unity. "Herr Otto Strasser," Münzenberg now counseled his adversary, to "stormy applause" from the Communist contingent in the hall, "your great political error" lies in the endorsement of "this nationalist heresy of the criminal capitalist classes" which "deceives" and "infatuates the German working masses."

Against this assault, Strasser mustered a surprisingly game defense. English and German workers, Strasser pointed out, even when employed in similar industries, neither thought nor behaved alike. Besides, millions of workers remained completely untouched by the economic world system. There was, then, no global "proletariat," whereas at least in Germany, one could point to a healthy population of workers with a similar cultural and political sensibility. Strasser further observed that in the world's preeminent capitalist country, the United States, there was not a single "Marxist deputy" in either House of Congress. If "there be any among you," Strasser challenged the Communists, "that dares [predict] that America will experience a socialist revolution at any time in the next thirty years, then I will bow down." Tell me then, he taunted Münzenberg, how many of "America's 120 million inhabitants belong to the Communist Party?"

In his reply to Strasser's challenge, Münzenberg showed his hand as seldom before, openly confessing that he never expected the German workers to rise spontaneously en masse, à la Rosa Luxemburg. Rather, he was a Leninist to the core, who, though faithful to the Marxist worldview, had no illusions that the great masses of humanity would ever fully share it. Yes, he agreed, there were 120 million Americans, and only about 80,000 of them, he estimated, were Communists. But then there had been only about 100,000 Bolsheviks in Russia at the time of Red October of 1917—and that was in "a country of 150 million." "Na ja, also!" Münzenberg's Communist supporters now shouted at Strasser: now that's an answer. You can't argue with success.

Or can you? In his retort to Münzenberg's apparent knockdown argument, Strasser offered a provocative interpretation of Bolshevism, in which Marxist ideology and political demographics were less important than personality and will. Lenin was in Strasser's view the first "national socialist," who, instead of "waiting until the international revolution had broken out," had simply decided "to make the revolution himself"—in Russia. If Lenin had not thus given birth to "national socialism," then "the tsar would still be sitting in the Kremlin." From an ideological standpoint, Strasser argued, Trotsky was the true "Marxist," with his focus on world revolution. But then Trotsky was a failure, whereas Lenin had achieved historical "greatness." Lenin had decided, in Strasser's formulation, that he "did not give a damn whether Marxist theory allows the model of socialism in one land or doesn't allow it." Strasser topped off this unorthodox tribute to the late Bolshevik leader with the crowd-pleasing send-off, "Long Live the Socialist Revolution!"[23]

Ultimately, no lasting cooperation grew out of Münzenberg's flirtation with Strasser, but the episode set a disturbing precedent whose echoes would not soon dissipate. It was not merely that Münzenberg echoed the Nazis in his merciless attacks on the SPD, but that the entire world of politics seemed upside down as viewed by the Münzenberg trust, with words denuded of any logical meaning. Thus in a typical installment of *Welt am Abend* in March 1931, readers learned of an IAH meeting held to promote "the struggle against fascism"—a meeting at which the only "fascists" criticized were Socialist and union leaders. And one of the critics invited to give a speech attacking the "social fascist leaders of the SPD and the unions" was—"a Nazi party spokesman"![24]

While dismissing the Nazis as cynical monarchist tools, Münzenberg spewed the bulk of his bile in the direction of the SPD. Münzenberg's flagship FSR club, the All-German Society of Friends of Soviet Russia, even held a benefit concert in Berlin in March 1931 to raise money for—noble cause!—yet more publicity smearing Socialists for their supposed complicity in "Menshevik" sabotage in Moscow.²⁵ As if this were not enough, Münzenberg next set out to discredit the last remaining "revolutionary" tradition to which the SPD adhered—May Day—by calling his own revolutionary counterdemonstration, an IAH-administered "Solidarity Day" march slated for 14 June 1931, at which no "open, brutal social fascist traitors" would be welcome.²⁶ The previous year, a similar IAH "Solidarity Day" march had attracted at least some interest among the non-Communist workers of Berlin, taking place as it did at the height of the short-lived spring 1930 thaw in KPD-SPD relations that had followed Müller's fall.²⁷ But no such brotherly love would be extended to SPD "class traitors" this year. Among the twenty-four political parties, union cells, paramilitary groups, cultural committees, and the like Münzenberg invited to participate on 14 June, not a single SPD affiliate was to be found.²⁸ As Münzenberg explained to his lieutenants at an IAH Executive meeting in Berlin on 19 May 1931, Germany's independent unions, just like the SPD, were no longer merely "reformist" but had transformed themselves into openly "social fascist organizations."²⁹ Or as he put the matter somewhat more colorfully in his formal Solidarity Day invitation to the workers of the world in *Inprecorr*, it was none other than Lenin himself who had taught the world during the war that "the international solidarity of the revolutionary proletariat is a fact *in spite of* the dirty scum of opportunism and social chauvinism."³⁰

Happily, none of the "dirty scum" from the Socialist parties dared show their faces at Münzenberg's Solidarity Day—but then neither did anybody else. So incendiary were the attacks on "social fascism" in Münzenberg's newspapers all through spring that the Prussian police—controlled as it was by the SPD—unsurprisingly laid down a comprehensive ban on street agitation of any kind on the planned Solidarity Day. Not even open-air concerts would be allowed in Berlin's working-class districts on either 13 or 14 June, lest they be used as a pretext for IAH demonstrations. Humbled by his SPD enemies yet again, Münzenberg backed down, vowing to fight another day.³¹

He did not have to wait long for another chance to smite the hated Socialist class traitors. Since Hitler's triumph at the polls in September 1930, the Nazis had been gearing up for a swipe at one of the last remaining props of Weimar democracy, the SPD-led government of Prussia. As in the anti–

Young Plan campaign that had brought Hitler to national prominence, the political vehicle chosen for the assault was a cynically demagogic no-confidence plebiscite. Once more, Hitler's key tactical ally was Hugenberg, and yet again his most vociferous rhetorical fellow travelers were Communists.

This was by no means an inevitable development. As late as 10 April, *Rote Fahne* was warning workers against joining forces with the "murderous strike-breaking bands of the Nazi [SA]."[32] But as the Communist assaults on the SPD grew fiercer over spring and early summer, the unthinkable became thinkable, and—after a nudge from Stalin—the KPD Zentrale chose on 22 July to throw in their lot with the Nazi plebiscite in order to weaken the Social Democrats. The SPD ministers of Prussia, Party Secretary Ernst Thälmann now declared, were to a man "deadly enemies of the working class," and it was now the duty of all truly revolutionary workers to strip them of their power, even if they would have to team up with Hitler and Hugenberg to do it.[33]

The KPD Zentrale's fateful decision came fairly late in the game, barely two weeks before the vote was scheduled for early August, but nevertheless the party press went all out to sell the "Red plebiscite," as it was now styled. No one embraced the campaign more vigorously than Münzenberg, who used the plebiscite as a springboard to publish one of his most scathing assaults ever on his "social fascist" enemies in a special supplement to the 6 August 1931 *Berlin am Morgen*. Astonishingly, Münzenberg saved his most passionate scorn for his own fellow-traveling clients, many of whom had come out against the plebiscite. The none too subtle sub-headline of his article was "an answer to all manner of critics and know-it-alls," whom he then dismissed in a boldface special section as "scribblers and intellectuals who fancy themselves radicals [but who] would support the social fascists Braun, Severing, Grzesinski and Co."[34]

Most readers of *Berlin am Morgen* understood these words to be directed most vehemently at one former "Münzenberg man" in particular, the self-described revolutionary pacifist writer Kurt Hiller, who had just published an open letter in several Berlin newspapers accusing Münzenberg of behaving as if he "had Nazi agents in [his] central committee." "If you personally, Willi Münzenberg," Hiller had written his former hero, soon after the Münzenberg trust began promoting the "Red plebiscite" in late July, "swallow this decision without damage to your health, then ... I admire your stomach."[35]

Certainly Münzenberg's stomach was stronger than Hiller's. In the voluminous records of Münzenberg's political correspondence in Moscow, I have found no expressions of soul-searching or undue concern for the precedent set by this stunning collaboration with Hitler. It may conceivably have helped Münzenberg's conscience, however, that the "Red plebiscite" was resoundingly defeated, due in part to a poor Communist turnout, as many of the party's rank and file refused, on principle, to vote for a Nazi-authored plebiscite.[36] Even Münzenberg's wife and collaborator Babette Gross, who in her memoir elsewhere takes great pains to protect her husband's reputation from any embarrassing stain of insufficiently antifascist tendencies (she avoids mentioning the Strasser meeting entirely, for example), is unable to muster up a shred of evidence to suggest that Münzenberg had second thoughts about pushing Hitler's plebiscite.[37]

At the time, there seemed no reason to mourn the defeat of the plebiscite, which, after all, had been a setback for the Nazis as well. Besides, Münzenberg had weightier matters on his mind that summer, such as the imminent release of his anniversary tome glorifying the IAH's first ten years, *Solidarität*. Münzenberg completed his introduction to this vanity volume in August, just days after the "Red plebiscite" was held. The book itself was ghosted by an NDV staffer who had been on the job since 1929, but Münzenberg was heavily involved in the editing of the proofs during spring and summer 1931. With his militant spirit unfazed by the plebiscite debacle, Münzenberg managed to slip in yet more attacks in *Solidarität* on the "social fascists of the Second International" who were, he claimed, struggling everywhere to exterminate revolutionary socialism and its most powerful exponent, the International Worker Relief.[38]

In addition to providing yet another venue for Münzenberg's inexhaustible vitriol against SPD traitors and saboteurs, *Solidarität* was also meant to set the stage for the tenth anniversary conference of the IAH, slated for October 1931. By downplaying his controversial media "trust" and other business interests in favor of a wildly overblown emphasis on his earlier, mostly imaginary charity campaigns, Münzenberg aimed yet again to cleanse the IAH's reputation. Not until page 493 of *Solidarität* was the once-ballyhooed *Wirtschaftshilfe* campaign of 1922–23 mentioned, and not until pages 509–21—the very last section of the book—did readers learn about Münzenberg's one true passion, the M-Russ film studio.[39] Rounding out the book's dishonesty was its heavy emphasis on the recent, post-1929 militant "strike aid" initiative—which in fact as yet had barely gotten off the ground.[40] The "strike aid" label was also opportunistically backdated to apply to earlier IAH failures, such as the English miners strike fiasco of 1926.[41] Taken as a whole, Münzenberg's *Solidarität* added up to an astonishingly dense farrago of lies.

It is unlikely, in any case, that Münzenberg expected his staffers and sympathizers to actually peruse this unreadable volume, beyond flipping through the pictures and the brief summary at the start of the book. Rather, *Solidarität*, like all of Münzenberg's productions, was above all aimed at one category of consumer: the ever-revolving cadre of Kremlin funding commissars. Certainly they were expected to notice Münzenberg's dramatic declaration that the IAH had independently "procured" the equivalent of 120 million gold marks during the organization's first decade.[42] How this money was "procured," of course, was not mentioned, beyond a vague flow chart, suspiciously buried on page 522, which mysteriously broke income down into "collections," "donations," and book and film "sales" without supporting documentation.[43] We may surmise that the book was especially intended for the eyes of Münzenberg's latest ECCI victim, Serafima Goptner, a Jewish Ukrainian apparatchik who had taken over Bukharin's role as senior Bolshevik-in-ignorance in charge of approving runaway Münzenberg trust expenses. Goptner, one of the last remaining party comrades of Lenin and Stalin from the days of tsarist exile, was the lucky recipient of all manner of IAH literary ephemera from Berlin after she ascended into the Comintern Secretariat in June 1931.[44]

Read by an IAH neophyte like Goptner, *Solidarität* might plausibly have made Münzenberg's media trust appear to be a lucrative financial asset of the Comintern, instead of its most corrupt spendthrift. Perpetuating this lie was more crucial than ever now, as requests for special expenses in 1931 —from elaborate preparations for the botched Solidarity Day in June (forty-one thousand dollars), to Münzenberg's book contract for *Solidarität* (forty thousand dollars), to the anniversary congress (another five thousand dollars, plus per diems)—were reaching unheard-of levels, just as the forced industrialization and agricultural collectivization of Stalin's Five Year Plan were beginning to bankrupt the Soviet economy.[45] And these elaborate expenses were on top of the nearly twenty thousand dollars a month the IAH's Berlin Secretariat was already receiving just for ordinary operating expenses.[46] Then there was Münzenberg's audacious request for fifty thousand dollars to conjure up an imaginary fund-raising windfall for a new "disaster" campaign taken from the headlines—an August 1931 flood in China—which he cynically hoped to showcase at the IAH's anniversary Congress.[47]

With his expensive vanity congress serenaded by the lies of his handsomely compensated vanity book, the "Red Millionaire" was in full stride when his admirers descended upon Berlin in early October 1931. Using Kremlin cash, as always, proactively, Münzenberg leased the Sportpalast, a cavernous indoor arena in Berlin's Alexanderplatz large enough to seat several thousand "friends of the IAH" who came from as far away as Australia. There were even two IAH reps from Iceland. Among those attending were famous fellow-traveling intellectuals like Henri Barbusse, along with hundreds of lowly Münzenberg staffers and hangers-on. No expense was spared to cover all the necessaries for the delegates, many of whom—reflecting the IAH's demographic base—were unemployed. And although nearly half of the attendees did not formally belong to any political party, there was little doubt where they stood.[48] The hall was bedecked with enormous banners with properly militant slogans—"Red Berlin Reads *Rote Fahne*," "Everyone for Red Unity," "Against Imperialist War"—along with poster ads for *Berlin am Morgen* and *Welt am Abend*. With a powerful megaphone mounted on the rostrum, the stage was set for a great demagogic harangue.

The crowd would not be disappointed. Münzenberg soared to great rhetorical heights in his keynote speech, infecting the delegates with his peculiarly demonic brand of apocalyptic optimism. "This capitalist system," he declared, "is on its last legs." "Our task," he instructed the IAH's international cadre of functionaries, "is to speed up its collapse and force it through completely everywhere in the world." Due to intensifying imperial rivalries, another world war was on the horizon, only this time—unlike in 1914—the workers did have a "fatherland": the Soviet Union. Whereas for most of the 1920s, the great strategic question in London and Paris had been, "When are we going to march to Moscow?" the economic collapse of capitalism in the early 1930s meant it was now, "When will Red Moscow be strong enough for the Red Army to march on the West?"

Bombarding his delegates with a rash of imposing armaments production statistics from Stalin's Five Year Plan, Münzenberg all but guaranteed victory over the capitalist West. "There is no longer any doubt," he promised the IAH rank and file, "who will be the victor"—the only question remaining was "when we will triumph." Thus whenever "fascism comes pounding on the door," whenever capitalism's most shameless tool, Adolf Hitler, chooses to "flaunt his power," whenever "Hitler threatens that heads will roll"—that will be the time, Münzenberg thundered, for us to say: "*Jawohl*, perhaps some heads will roll, but this only raises the question, which heads will do the rolling."

The great class war was coming. To prepare for it, Münzenberg instructed his legions, we must somehow "shake up the millions who are not yet aware." "We must awaken their hearts and their minds," Münzenberg explained, with "new, more cunning methods of agitation." "Our words," he counseled, "will grow cooler and more revolutionary, because the situation is sharper."

In short, amateur night was over. It was time for the IAH's employees to start acting like true Bolsheviks. "All of us," Münzenberg promised his IAH employees and committee members, "should no longer think of ourselves as functionaries in the workers' movement, but as the leaders of the coming German [or] French Soviet Union." We will, he assured them without betraying a whisker of doubt, take over the armies, the police, the newspapers, and the government. We will, he declared, "fulfill the legacy" of Marx, Engels, Bebel, and Lenin by "turning resolutions into active struggle towards the destruction of the bourgeoisie in all countries." When we have "convinced the last worker of the rightness of our cause," he promised the IAH commissars-in-waiting, whether this takes "two years or three," rest assured that "proletarian dictatorship [will] come."[49]

Intoxicated by Münzenberg's promises that they would soon share the fruits of an imminent global communist dictatorship, the IAH's national secretaries and functionaries returned home recharged and refreshed, ready to fight the class struggle all the harder. But most of them learned rapidly that revolutionary enthusiasm alone was not enough to ignite a class war, even in the midst of a Depression. Even the most rudimentary resolution for collective action passed at the World Congress in October 1931, which established plans for an internationally coordinated Solidarity Day on 12 June 1932, proved too much for many undersized, underfinanced national branch offices to handle.[50] In Canada, for example, despite the belated distribution of thousands of Solidarity posters in early June, not a single march took place anywhere on the twelfth, not even in front of the national IAH headquarters in Toronto, where staffers cowered together inside, in fear of the police.[51]

The Solidarity Day directive failed just as miserably south of the Canadian border, where the once-mighty American Münzenberg apparat was still reeling six years after the bitter MOPR takeover. Despite some inspired cultural agitprop—Upton Sinclair's musical *The Singing Jailbirds,* later performed in Vienna, was a particular highlight—the American office was now little more than an embarrassment.[52] Despite devoting months of redundant paperwork to the Solidarity Day initiative, the downsized American IAH office was unable even to advertise the 12 June 1932 festivities when the date drew near, because it had already squandered all of Berlin's subsidies on peripheral agitprop. Solidarity Day 1932, American IAH secretary Seyman Burns found himself obliged at last to report to Münzenberg, "was everywhere in the country a total fiasco."[53]

Tango with the Devil

The IAH was not faring much better in the countries of western Europe, which Münzenberg had somewhat overoptimistically singled out at the October 1931 congress as ripe for the plucking. The puny clout of the penny-ante English IAH section can best be assessed by the size of its currency transfer requests from Berlin, which were often for as little as ten or twenty pounds.[54] The IAH was not much stronger in Belgium, where the national secretary, honest to a fault, confessed to Münzenberg that nothing much was going to happen on Solidarity Day, as he had neither the funds nor the personnel to publicize it.[55] Nor was there much going on in Austria, where some one thousand IAH supporters marched in Vienna on 11 June 1932 to excite attention for Solidarity Day—attracting just enough notice to alert the police, who promptly forbade further demonstrations.[56]

In France, the IAH was hamstrung as always in the early 1930s, opposed not only by more the numerous "social fascists" of the French Socialist Party and the independent unions but also facing, as it always had, outright hostility from fellow Communists. *L'Humanité* still wouldn't promote any campaign with Münzenberg's name on it, and Communist union leaders would not even agree to meet with his representatives.[57] Nevertheless, there was a flicker of life during the Solidarity Day demonstrations in June 1932, when the French IAH office managed to lure nearly twelve thousand marchers onto the streets of Paris, although they did not stay there long, quickly fleeing the police cordons emplaced in the city center. This was no great feat in the heroic annals of Parisian revolutionary demonstrations, but in the history of the IAH in France, it was almost a miracle.[58]

Back in Berlin, the revolutionary situation was more promising. Münzenberg had reminded his German IAH lieutenants at the 1931 World Congress of the glory days of Spartacus—"we once nearly had power in our hands." In 1919, there had been no IAH and thus "there was no one to organize the power [of the workers]." Now things were different, and so Münzenberg offered a new slogan for the acceleration of the IAH strike aid campaign: "light in the mind, marrow in the bones, and fire in the belly!"[59]

Unlike the program force-fed to his *Reichsabteilung* during the sectarian "class against class" purges of spring 1929, Münzenberg's bold ideas for strike aid now had force—and hard cash—behind them. Enjoying the most generous Kremlin subsidies to date, Münzenberg was able to lubricate the IAH's domestic operations as never before. From the great metalworkers' strike at Hanau in November 1931, to a rash of walkouts staged in Berlin that winter, which touched industries as diverse as textiles and motorcar chauffeuring, to a twenty-four-day strike at the BMW motor works in

Bavaria in October 1932, the IAH flexed its newfound muscle as German class warriors.[60]

At Münzenberg's urging, the *Reichsabteilung* also threw new money at the old "Red soup kitchen" initiative, with special instructions to outspend and even infiltrate Nazi-supported kitchens so as to siphon followers away from Hitler. The main goal here was to invade "Brown Berlin," the districts where Communists had, as yet, made little headway among the unemployed. The IAH was already strong in the working-class and garment districts of the east, in Neukölln, Friedrichshain, Prenzlauer Berg, and Wedding, where it faced little opposition. The bulk of the new kitchens were organized in sections of the city that had proved most receptive to Nazism, such as Wilmersdorf, Mariendorf, Mitte (near Friedrichstrasse), Steglitz, and Friedenau. This was a bold undertaking and not without serious risk. As one of Münzenberg's Berlin staffers noted, Nazi attacks on IAH soup kitchens and their employees were all but inevitable, and they would almost certainly never be prosecuted in the "Brown" districts of Berlin.[61]

With its beefed-up strike support system and its bold new soup kitchen offensive, the Münzenberg's *Reichsabteilung* began to come into its own in 1932, scoring a number of political successes that would have been all but unthinkable in the past. Solidarity Day, for example, was for the most part a triumph, with significant marches taking place in many of Germany's major cities. Few of the demonstrations, to be sure, could have put much of a scare into Hitler's storm troopers. In most towns less than a thousand unarmed citizens took to the streets for Solidarity Day, many of them children. And in some cities either friendly to the Nazis (Munich) or where SPD and union strength translated into IAH weakness (Mannheim, Hanover), the turnout was negligible. Still, the results in Germany were not bad, especially in Berlin, where nearly fifty thousand marched, including some unionized workers and even a few members of the SPD's paramilitary Reichsbanner.[62]

Münzenberg's heightened impact on the German political scene can be measured by the fact that Hitler's spies now began taking serious notice of his apparat for the first time. Nazi agents snapped a number of pictures of Münzenberg giving speeches at IAH rallies, and began marshaling data on the Münzenberg trust. The Nazis' leading researchers of the Bolshevik "underworld," Adolf Ehrt and Dr. Julius Schweickert, took special note of the new "revolutionary strike support" line laid down in October 1931, citing in particular Münzenberg's exhortation that the IAH transform its "supply columns" into "assault battalions."[63] Hitler's propaganda chief, Joseph Goebbels, responded tit for tat to Münzenberg's creation of a new film club in Berlin in May 1932 by expanding his rival network of "Nazi cinemas" right into the IAH strongholds of East Berlin, paying kickbacks to "Red" theater owners who agreed to show films approved by the NSDAP.[64]

Another measure of the Communists' increasing belligerence came during the Reichstag election campaign of summer 1932, which took place amidst unprecedented bloodshed in the streets. Fatefully, Chancellor Brüning lifted the long-standing ban on Hitler's SA on 16 June, and the KPD's combat alliance came out of hiding as well. By July conditions in Prussia were approaching civil war, with hundreds of Redshirt-Brownshirt clashes and assaults by both extremist groups on the police taking a toll of nearly a hundred killed and over a thousand wounded. In July, Nazi casualties even outnumbered Communist ones, for the first time ever.[65] The violence built to a climax in Berlin during election weekend itself, 30–31 July, when in a span of barely more than a day twenty-two were killed and more than 150 wounded.[66]

One might have expected in such circumstances that the Communist combat alliance would have teamed up with the Socialist Reichsbanner in order to outgun Hitler's storm troopers. But party doctrine still squarely ruled out any collaboration with the "social fascists." If anything, the KPD's ideological flexibility was even more constrained in 1932 than in 1931, for Trotsky, in exile, had come out publicly against Stalin's "class against class" tactics over the winter, and Communists were now expected to denounce him. Münzenberg, for example, publicly attacked "Trotsky's fascist proposal to build a united SPD-KPD front."[67] In the presidential runoff vote held on 10 April 1932, the Münzenberg trust instructed Germans to spurn the Socialists' compromise strategy by refusing to vote for the musty old monarchist incumbent Hindenburg over Hitler as a "lesser evil." "A vote for Hindenburg," Münzenberg's circulars declared in an impressive feat of logical legerdemain, is "a vote for Hitler."[68]

For a few tantalizing moments in spring 1932 German Communist leaders, speaking as individuals, did flirt with the possibility of uniting the Left against fascism. Thälmann, possibly on his own initiative, issued a broad appeal to Socialist and Christian unions in a speech in Darmstadt on 12 June 1932 for strikes coordinated to weaken the unpopular new presidential cabinet of Franz von Papen. The same day, Münzenberg's Solidarity Day demonstrations saw a limited number of SPD supporters, including several members of the Reichsbanner, join a Communist march in southeastern Berlin, near Neukölln.[69] On 22 June, Thälmann's Politburo ally, Wilhelm Pieck, even hinted he might be willing to support the SPD and Catholic Center Party candidates in order to prevent the Nazis from taking over the presidency of the Prussian state parliament.[70]

But such moments were short-lived. The overtures by Thälmann and Pieck were dismissed as disingenuous by the Socialist editors of *Vorwärts*, and rightly so, as these "united front" gestures were later disowned by the KPD Zentrale after a reprimand for ideological heresy was issued by Moscow in late June.[71] When Chancellor Papen deposed the Prussian SPD government on 20 July 1932 on the grounds that it was incapable of maintaining public order, Communists did not raise a peep in protest. According to Babette Gross, Münzenberg did meet with the SPD's Reichsbanner chairman, Karl Höltermann, late in the morning of this fateful July day, to discuss the possibility of staging joint SPD-KPD paramilitary maneuvers to protest Papen's move. If this story is true, then it is not surprising that Höltermann sharply rebuffed Münzenberg, fearing betrayal by a man who, after all, had enthusiastically endorsed the Nazi plebiscite against the Prussian government the previous summer.[72]

In the Reichstag poll of 31 July 1932, the Communists reaped what they had sown. The KPD did win over eight hundred thousand new voters at the expense of the SPD, but just as in 1930, the Communists' refusal to unite the Left allowed Hitler to gain the most. KPD thugs may have killed more Nazi thugs than vice versa in July, but in a civil war–like atmosphere Hitler's messianic message that he would restore "order" to Germany won over millions of frightened Germans who blamed the Communists for the violence. The NSDAP more than doubled its vote count over the September 1930 results, surpassing the SPD for the first time as the strongest party in Germany, with nearly 14 million votes and 230 Reichstag seats, as against 8 million votes and 133 seats for the SPD and 5.4 million votes and 89 seats for Münzenberg's party. More ominously, the Nazi delegation had now outpolled and could outvote the SPD and KPD put together, even though the two "worker" parties were, of course, quite far from being united.[73]

Hitler's summer surge was alarming no matter how one looked at it, and it is hardly surprising that Stalin now moved to purge the KPD leadership. Stalin himself was, of course, ultimately responsible for the "class against class" line that was playing into Hitler's hands, but he was hardly going to blame this line, much less himself, for the electoral results of July. Instead, Münzenberg's friend Neumann was picked to shoulder the guilt, less for any particular policy innovation of his own than for the fact that he now had more enemies than anyone else in the KPD Zentrale. The "Neumann affair," much like the Wittorf affair of 1928, came down in the final analysis to personalities. Inevitably, the "Thälmann-Neumann" Politburo had split into rival factions since 1928, with the brilliant young theorist Neumann teaming up with the great orator Hermann Remmele, while the duller but more streetwise Thälmann gravitated toward thuggish enforcer types like union cell organizer Walter Ulbricht and Wilhelm Pieck, a militant onetime associate of Karl Liebknecht. Although Stalin had once been quite fond of Neumann, whom he had chosen to launch the bloody Canton uprising in 1927, it was perhaps inevitable that he would ultimately side with Thälmann, a loyal organization man who (apart from the brief "united front" mistake in June 1932, for which he properly repented) had never shown much of a capacity for political independence. Neumann was ejected from the Politburo in August for the old Comintern heresy of "antiparty group activity," and Remmele was stripped of his posts soon thereafter.[74]

In this way Stalin skinned his scapegoats for the distressing Reichstag election results, and yet again the true reasons for the KPD's failures were swept under the rug. As if to emphasize communism's dangerous aloofness from political reality, Münzenberg now moved to shore up his political flank by ignoring the depressing German situation almost completely. With a wary eye on Stalin's moves against his friend Neumann, Münzenberg mobilized his entire media trust behind a questionable campaign to free the "Rueggs," a Swiss "trade union" leader and his wife, arrested the previous year in Shanghai. In reality the Rueggs were Soviet spies from the Ukraine, traveling on borrowed passports, who had been caught red-handed ushering over fifty thousand dollars worth of Kremlin gold into China by way of eight different safety deposit boxes in Nanking. They also kept four separate apartments there and had been using no less than four different cable addresses at the Chinese Central Telegraph Office in Shanghai.[75] The overwhelming evidence pointing to the Rueggs' guilt did not prevent Münzenberg from trying to enlist the support of fellow travelers for their cause, including such American notables as Theodore Dreiser and John Dos Passos, who both, to their great credit, refused to bite. Among European writers, André Malraux, Bertolt Brecht, and the inevitable Henri Barbusse, unlike Dreiser and dos Passos, gullibly signed their names to Ruegg petitions and committees.[76]

The Ruegg case brilliantly illustrates Münzenberg's capacity for ideological dissembling, which would help him survive yet another round of purges in 1932. Almost certainly, Münzenberg knew the defendants were guilty. As financial guru of the defense he paid the lawyers' fees and received regular reports from the trial, which left no doubt how weak the Rueggs' case was.[77]

By cranking up every single one of his newspapers on their behalf, then, Münzenberg knowingly did violence to the truth, but in doing so he left an enormous paper trail of loyal service to the Soviet espionage apparat that he could point to if Stalin were ever to claim he had been disloyal.[78]

Nowhere did Münzenberg cover his tracks more audaciously than in *Inprecorr*. The Comintern's turgid official news bulletin, because read by few people outside the party bureaucracy, served Münzenberg as a kind of unambiguous public face that allowed him to camouflage any private doubts he might have had about the current political line. His ridiculously overblown article on the Rueggs was typical in this regard.[79] So was his official "Solidarity Day" invitation for 1932 attacking "social fascist war criminals" such as the Japanese Social Democrats, who were absurdly blamed for the recent "robber invasion" of Manchuria.[80] In this way Münzenberg watched his back, hewing to Comintern doctrine so cravenly in *Inprecorr* that no one in Moscow would be suspicious when in practice he allowed, and even encouraged, his followers to fraternize with Socialists in Berlin on Solidarity Day.

A similar tactic of dissembling was probably at work in the otherworldly Amsterdam "peace congress" of August 1932, where, despite the astonishing political advances made by Hitler in the last two years—a man who had already openly published many of his war aims, not least those involving a massive invasion of the Soviet Union—neither the civil war situation in Germany nor the Nazi threat were on the agenda. It is quite possible that Münzenberg, Barbusse, Heinrich Mann, and other notables who gathered in Amsterdam to discuss the "war danger" mentioned Hitler at some point, in informal conversation, if only in passing—but there is no evidence of this in the public record. Instead, Münzenberg, Barbusse et al. harangued legions of Communist fellow travelers about the imminent "imperialist war" to be fought against the Soviet Union, led by—of all countries—France. Because there were several hundred Socialist delegates present, Münzenberg toned down his usual nastiness about "social fascism" at Amsterdam. But in his rhetorical attacks on cowardly French imperialists, Münzenberg sounded like nothing so much as a Nazi party spokesman. Just as his commentaries on the Ruhr crisis of 1923 had eerily echoed Hitler's, so too could the venom he and others spewed at his "peace" congress against the Versailles Treaty—that "one-sided arrangement dictated by vengeance"— easily have issued directly from the pages of the *Völkische Beobachter*.[81]

Just what was Münzenberg thinking? Was he really more worried about the dangers to peace posed by "French imperialism" than about Hitler's unambiguous threats to annihilate Bolshevism?[82] Bizarre though it may seem to us today, the answer given by the historical record is an unequivocal yes. In the months following the Amsterdam Congress, Münzenberg stormed around Europe, rousing his fellow-traveling troops to enlist in yet another round of FSR and antiwar clubs. The catch phrases of the hour in the upside-down Münzenberg trust in fall 1932 were "Against French Imperialism," "Down with Warmongers and Saboteurs," and "Long Live the Soviet Union," slogans Münzenberg expounded no less proudly in Paris than in Leningrad.[83] And why not? After all, if there were another war—and Münzenberg was hardly alone in believing that this was imminent in the heated political atmosphere of the Depression, when one-upping tariffs and trade wars threatened to split the Western world apart at the seams—then it seemed best to throw in one's lot with Europe's largest military colossus, the Soviet Red Army.

Certainly the danger of a Russian invasion of Germany was taken seriously by security-minded officials in the German government, who throughout the political crisis of the early 1930s were keeping very close watch on Communist propagandists like Münzenberg. He was, after all, in the pay of the Soviet government—about this few serious observers had any doubt—and the more Münzenberg's propaganda directly serviced the needs of Soviet foreign policy, the more dangerous he seemed. Thus although the Nazis, by contrast, paid little attention to Münzenberg's pacifist congresses—possessed as they were of a truly bottomless contempt for pacifism—the Reich Interior Ministry stepped up its surveillance of Münzenberg to its highest levels after Amsterdam, seeing in every new district IAH cell a potential Trojan Horse for the Red Army.[84] On 1 September 1932, before Münzenberg had even returned from Holland, a phalanx of over sixty Prussian police officers raided the main Münzenberg trust offices in Berlin, confiscating papers related to the "pacifist" congresses and obtaining a list of eighty-nine key employees, who, though not arrested, were put under surveillance.[85] By the end of the year German intelligence had also marshaled evidence against Münzenberg's new round of FSR committees, producing another list of activists, including Heinrich Mann, believed to be Soviet agents.[86] In December 1932, IAH "women's" groups were placed under especially heavy surveillance, being seen as prime breeding grounds for dangerously pro-Soviet propaganda.[87]

The Reich Interior Ministry was, of course, keeping close tabs on the Nazi apparat as well.[88] Still, there is something disconcerting about the thought that idealistic pacifist girls had come to be seen as a prime security threat. Still more disconcerting is the thought that the Reich Interior Ministry may not have been far off the mark. For Münzenberg's hundreds of front organizations had, by late 1932, turned into unabashed servants of Stalin's foreign policy needs, whether or not all of the donors and committee joiners realized this. In a sense Neumann's recent ouster had brought Münzenberg back to where he had been during the era of Bukharin's fall from grace in 1927, when to preserve favor in the Kremlin he had first hit on the Stalin-pleasing formula of shamelessly prophesying the phantom war against the Soviet Union. The phony pacifist love-ins of Amsterdam and its aftermath were, in this sense, merely a blast from the past.

The difference in 1932, though, was that the IAH's growth in the preceding half-decade had given Münzenberg real power inside Germany, and yet, because he was forced to walk on eggshells to skirt the Moscow purges, he was wasting it. In late October, for example, on the eve of another round of historic Reichstag elections, the Münzenberg trust preoccupied itself with, of all things, the victims of a recent flood in Manchuria.[89] Münzenberg himself was too busy tending to his flock of Moscow loyalists—many of whom had recently been evicted from their luxurious apartments on Tverskaia-Iamskaia or were otherwise being harassed by Stalin's security services—to worry much about the Reichstag elections.[90] After all, his seat, as always, was secure. The beefed-up IAH "strike aid" apparatus did kick into gear in time to help Goebbels shut down the Berlin subways during the famous joint Communist-Nazi lockdown in November, but there is little evidence Münzenberg took much interest in this strike, much less expressed concern about yet another blatant display of collusion with fascism.[91]

If Münzenberg did have any pangs of conscience about the Communists' complicity in the descent of German politics into the gutter of brutal street violence, any second thoughts about toeing the Kremlin line even when it forced him to collaborate with Hitler—if he ever did wrestle with such demons, the only conclusion the historical record allows us to draw is that the demons won. The last great propaganda monuments Münzenberg left to the world in the final days of Weimar in January 1933, his last personal testaments to that contemptible façade of "bourgeois" democracy—freedom of speech—which would soon be snuffed out entirely in Germany, were several thoroughly mendacious attacks on the recently concluded Polish-French defense treaty, and a verbatim account of a speech by Stalin celebrating the work of the Soviet secret police in exterminating counterrevolutionary wreckers, saboteurs, conspirators, "truth-smearers," and other Menshevik enemies of Socialism.[92]

Of course Münzenberg could not have known that a series of maneuvers that were opaque to nearly all Germans at the time, involving former Chancellor Papen, President Hindenburg, and Papen's successor Kurt von Schleicher (who had himself put Papen into office) would bring Adolf Hitler to power, with all of the potential emergency power of the Reich Presidency behind him.[93] Hitler had actually lost two million votes in the November elections, whereas the Communists had continued their steady, if unexceptional, advance, gaining another seven hundred thousand or so votes from the Social Democrats and picking up eleven seats to reach triple digits for the first time, with one hundred seats altogether. More importantly for the Communists' ability to hold onto their illusions about winning over the masses of Germany, once again the combined vote totals of the SPD and KPD outnumbered that of the Nazis, unlike in July.[94]

Right up to the fateful events of 30 January 1933, most diehard Communists believed that the workers would rise up in the end, ushering in the great proletarian dictatorship that would consign that clownish capitalist tool, Hitler, to the dustbin of history. Münzenberg was no different. Had he not prophesied such a rising at the IAH's great "Red October" of 1931, when he had promised his foot soldiers that the great Marxist cataclysm would come to Europe, whether it took "two years or three"? The headlines from the IAH press in late January 1933 exude vigor and confidence, promising that proletarians will meet Nazi "provocations" with all the might of "Red Berlin."[95] Even rumors of Hitler's imminent accession to the Cabinet, which began to circulate openly around Berlin on the weekend of 28–29 January, prompted a militant vow from Münzenberg to fight the coming dictatorship of—Franz von Papen.[96]

But the workers did not rise to oppose Hitler, not on 30 January 1933 when he took office, nor on 4 February, when Münzenberg first began warning about "terror against the opposition press," nor on 8 February—a full week after the Nazis had taken over the government—when Münzenberg finally broached the idea of a "united front" to oppose Hitler's burgeoning dictatorship (but only if the Socialists first admitted past errors, of course).[97] Nor did the Red Army come riding into town to save the day. In the end, all Münzenberg and the Communists were left with were their Kremlin-financed newspapers, which had been crying wolf so often about phantom dangers to the German working-class that when a real wolf arrived on the scene, there was no one listening anymore. Heads would indeed be "rolling" in Germany, but it was not Münzenberg, but the man he had so cavalierly dismissed as "little Adolf," who would be choosing the heads to roll.

PART 3

Flight

"I am ready to do everything that will help normalize [our relations] and [allow me to] painstakingly fulfill the duties of a party member."

—Willi Münzenberg, 1938

CHAPTER 14 *The Fire This Time*

When Adolf Hitler was ushered into power on 30 January 1933, few in Germany really expected him to be an effective chancellor. Both Hugenberg and Papen, who took the (ostensibly) crucial positions of economics minister and vice chancellor in Hitler's government, believed the excitable would-be dictator was now under their control. The only other Nazis in the new Cabinet were Wilhelm Frick, the minister of the interior, and Hermann Göring, a minister without portfolio (although he was also Prussian minister of the interior). Hitler, outnumbered by non-Nazis eight to three in the Cabinet, appeared to be a weak "parliamentary" chancellor, backed by a Reichstag majority, but able to rule only at the mercy of the reluctant conservative allies who supplied him that majority. Ultimately Hitler's power rested on the support of President Hindenburg, who, so far as most informed observers knew, had no intentions of granting the new chancellor access to the almost limitless emergency presidential powers to which he held the key under the Weimar constitution. Hindenburg had accepted Hitler only with deep reluctance, on Papen's insistence, and he continued to express his contempt for the "Austrian corporal" with the big mouth. Hugenburg and Papen were no less dismissive. "We'll box Hitler in," Hugenberg famously promised his Stahlhelm chieftain, Theodor Düsterberg. Against the protestation of one anti-Hitler Junker aristocrat that he was unleashing a monster upon the world by bringing the Nazi führer to power, Papen vowed that "in two months we'll have Hitler pushed so far into a corner that he'll squeal."[1]

Papen's foolish disregard for Hitler has attained the status of legend, but in truth he was hardly alone in underestimating the ruthlessness and skill with which the Nazi leader would soon assemble dictatorial powers. Media reaction to Hitler's accession to power was initially very muted in Germany, and virtually nonexistent anywhere else. So often had chancellors come and gone over the past several years that millions of Germans had lost interest in the maneuverings of high politics. Henry Turner, in his acclaimed recent study, *Hitler's Thirty Days to Power*, noted that the installation of a new government was the last of six events depicted on a newsreel showing in film theaters around the country that week, "coming after . . . reports on a ski jump, a horse race, and a horse show."[2]

From his first days in office, though, Hitler gave signs of the storm to come. By brushing off overtures for cooperation from Catholic Center Party representatives just minutes after his swearing in as chancellor on 30 January, Hitler made new Reichstag elections necessary to secure a more decisive parliamentary majority. Hitler's immediate goal was to reverse the Nazi losses of November 1932 and put the Papen-Hugenberg conservatives in their place, by winning an outright Nazi parliamentary majority, or near enough to one, so that he could act independently. More fundamentally, Hitler wanted one last no-holds-barred election campaign to stamp the character of his regime on the country and establish the apocalyptic stakes of his rule: it was now all or nothing, a Nazified German renaissance or a descent into Bolshevism.

In his first radio address, delivered late in the evening on 1 February 1933, Hitler left no doubt where his wrath would first be directed. "Fourteen years of Marxism," he proclaimed, "have ruined Germany; one year of Bolshevism would destroy her." Were the KPD allowed to ride into power in Germany on the backs of the Red Army, Hitler prophesied, "the richest and fairest territories of the world would be turned into a smoking heap of ruins. Even the sufferings of the last decade and a half could not be compared to the misery of a Europe in the heart of which the Red Flag of destruction has been hoisted."[3]

Hitler's speech was not terribly subtle, and neither were his tactics in attacking the Marxist parties in the Reichstag election campaign that now ensued. On Frick's orders, copies of *Rote Fahne* were seized on newsstands in Berlin as early as 31 January 1933.[4] Using a presidential decree issued on 4 February, which authorized the prohibition of newspapers or public meetings in which "organs, institutions, authorities or leading state officials were insulted or brought into contempt," Hitler ordered police raids on opposition gatherings, including a Münzenberg-organized fellow-traveling extravaganza in Berlin on 19 February attended by Count Kessler and other notable Communist sympathizers.[5] Through both legal and illegal intimidation, made possible by Göring's aggressive purges of non-Nazis in the Prussian police and civil service, the Nazis were able to shut down *Vorwärts* and *Rote Fahne* entirely by the end of February. Because of its particularly inflammatory headlines about the Nazi "terror" against the opposition press, Münzenberg's *Berlin am Morgen* was banned even earlier, on 14 February (although *Welt am Abend* remained in business until the end of the month).[6]

Hitler didn't want to crush the Communists totally, however—at least not yet. He needed Communism as a foil, as a political lightning rod that he hoped would catch fire, just as Münzenberg and so many others had always promised it would. But there were few signs of revolutionary life in the KPD. Official Comintern doctrine still held the Socialists to be enemy number one even after Hitler had taken power, and for this reason the KPD attached impossible conditions to such calls for an armed uprising nor even for joint protest action with the SPD as it made.[7] True, the party had gone underground—its Berlin headquarters were empty when Göring's Nazi thugs, now dressed up in Prussian police uniforms, raided them on 24 February 1933—but this did not mean the Communists were actually preparing to take power. Göring's claim to have found "tons of treasonous materials" at KPD headquarters detailing plans for class warfare atrocities rang hollow when he failed either to produce the treasonous documents or to ban the Communist Party.[8] An outright ban might have thrown KPD voters into the arms of the SPD, and this was the last thing Hitler wanted to do. After all, the two parties combined had won more votes than the Nazis in November.

And so a strange endgame was now played out, in which Hitler prepared for the Communist revolution the Communists themselves refused to mount, and Stalin, too, waited, expecting the KPD to triumph in the end. In the Kremlin, the basic attitude toward the burgeoning Nazi dictatorship was summed up in the phrase "the worse the better," the idea being that every step Hitler took to consolidate his rule stripped away "bourgeois" illusions that had so long propped up capitalism. In this sense the Nazis were believed to be doing the Communists' work for them, preparing the inevitable Red revolution by sharpening the class struggle.[9]

In the event, both dictators were wrong in sizing up the other. Stalin had no intention of furnishing Hitler with a pretext for exterminating German Communism, but neither did Hitler wish to engage in class warfare that would play into the hands of the KPD. Their almost surreal waiting game was upended at last not because of any well-conceived strategy on either side, but instead by the action of one man, an estranged Dutch ex-Communist named Marinus van der Lubbe who was caught on the evening of 27 February 1933 setting fire to the Reichstag while still in the burning building, half-naked, completely disheveled, and dripping with sweat.[10]

The criminological controversy over the true guilty party behind Lubbe's arson began immediately and has not subsided to this day. It is by no means clear that the Nazis, as most of Hitler's contemporaries and historians presumed for decades, were behind the fire. All we can say with absolute certainty is that the mere fact of Lubbe's action—he was undeniably, whoever may have paid or manipulated or helped him, a longtime Communist, although he had left the party several years earlier—brought an abrupt halt to the Red-Brown tango that had bedeviled German politics for years. It furnished Hitler with exactly the pretext he needed to exterminate his Bolshevik enemies in Germany.[11]

The Nazi response to the Reichstag fire was swift and terrifying. Upon hearing the news on the fateful evening of 27 February of the fire and its presumed origins in a Communist conspiracy, Hitler, presumably stunned by his good fortune, famously remarked, "now I have them." Within the hour Göring, after "clambering over fire hoses" to reach the grand lobby of the Reichstag, spelled out in gruesome detail what Hitler meant. "Now there can be no mercy," the Prussian interior minister screamed in "an utterly uncontrolled manner," according to a witness present: "The German people will not put up with leniency. Every Communist functionary will be shot wherever we find him. The Communist deputies must be hanged this very night. Everyone in alliance with the Communists is to be arrested. We are not going to spare the Social Democrats and members of the Reichsbanner either!"[12]

These were not idle words. By the end of the night of 27–28 February nearly four thousand KPD functionaries had been arrested in Prussia alone. Next morning Hitler submitted a prepared decree outlining emergency powers to President Hindenburg, and Hindenburg signed, fatefully giving the Nazi leader carte blanche to arrest political enemies whomever, wherever, and whenever he liked. The right to habeas corpus, in fact every last right held by German citizens against the state, was now suspended indefinitely. In practice this meant open season on Communists, most of whom now rightfully feared for their lives.

It was Münzenberg's good fortune that he was nowhere near Berlin when the Reichstag was set ablaze, and was thus able to escape the first round of arrests that swept through Prussia. On the fateful evening of 27 February 1933, Münzenberg was giving a stump speech in his electoral district of Hesse-Nassau, in the tiny town of Langenselbold, just to the east of Frankfurt-am-Main. Taking the same precautions as all KPD functionaries now did, Münzenberg was whisked away from the rally by his chauffeur Emil immediately after finishing his speech. It was just in time: after receiving news of the Reichstag fire in Berlin by radio, a local SA detachment descended on the rally to arrest Münzenberg just minutes after he had left the scene.

Münzenberg himself did not learn of the fire until several hours later, after Emil had dropped him off at the home of an obscure local IAH functionary named Paul Schöfer. Around midnight, while Münzenberg and Schöfer were playing cards, Schöfer's wife rushed in, hysterical, with the news from Berlin, which had just gone out over short-wave radio. In shock, the men abandoned their game and tried, fitfully, to sleep. But there was much to worry about. Although Münzenberg did not know it yet, his Berlin Tiergarten apartment would be raided at dawn by Berlin police officers bearing a warrant for his arrest. There they would find only his assistant Hans Schulz and Schulz's wife, who fortunately was related to a former SPD Berlin police president, Karl Zörgiebel, known to one of the arresting officers. Politely warned that their lives were in danger, the Schulzes were allowed to flee, but it was now clear to them that Berlin was off limits to Münzenberg. They relayed this news shortly after dawn to Münzenberg's wife Babette when she called the Berlin apartment from a public phone in Frankfurt shortly after arriving by train from Switzerland that morning.[13]

The events that followed were worthy of a spy novel. When Emil had dropped him off at Schöfer's, Münzenberg had agreed to meet his chauffeur at a Frankfurt train station café the next day around noon. But the overnight news from Berlin meant that the station would almost certainly now be under heavy surveillance. Emil and Babette Gross (who had arrived at Emil's Frankfurt hotel shortly after dawn) therefore staked out the station square, positioning themselves as inconspicuously as possible at opposite ends of the main concourse to wait for Münzenberg's arrival. Emil, who spotted his boss first, "ran towards him and took him to the car." Together, the three sped off into the countryside, stopping at last in an obscure roadside diner where they planned their next move.

The trio resolved to make a run for Saarbrücken, where an acquaintance of Babette's sister Greta could take them in. The Saar was still a French protectorate under the Versailles settlement, so Hitler's agents had no legal authority there. Still, Münzenberg, certain Nazi border guards would have his photograph on file, needed false documents of some kind. This meant returning to Frankfurt, where a loyal staffer willing to part with his passport might be found in the IAH office. First, though, the trio drove to Mainz, where the spring carnival was under way. Münzenberg slipped into the carnival crowds, where he was to hide out until Gross and Emil returned. In Frankfurt,

Gross found a loyal IAH staffer who, though fourteen years younger than Münzenberg and bearing only a slight resemblance to him, courageously gave up his passport to save his boss. Back in Mainz, Gross and Emil found Münzenberg "wandering up and down the banks of the Rhine in a snow shower." So evidently exhausted was everyone that when they crossed the German border, the guards, assuming they were returning to the Saar after a long day's partying at the carnival, let them through with scarcely a glance at their documents.[14]

Münzenberg was not wrong in assuming he was high on the Nazis' hit list. On 2 March 1933, the *Völkische Beobachter* devoted an entire article to him, blaming him for being the "brain behind" Communist plans related to the "poisoning of food and water supplies" supposedly unearthed in the raid on party headquarters in Berlin. "So far," the Nazis lamented, "Münzenberg has evaded arrest." In the *Völkische Beobachter*'s special Sunday election edition, Münzenberg's picture was placed opposite Lubbe's next to the none too subtle cover headline, "Cankerous Core of Communist *Untermenschen*."[15]

Though he must surely have felt a rush of triumph in evading the Nazis' border guards, Münzenberg's swift flight risked doing serious damage to his reputation in the KPD. His preference for self-preservation over martyrdom had long been evident to anyone paying the slightest attention to his career, going back to his German draft evasion during the war, his strange voyage to Stockholm under German military escort in 1917, and not least, his refusal to be deported from Switzerland to certain imprisonment in Germany in 1918. In addition he had declined to go to Russia with Lenin to help overthrow the Provisional government in 1917, and he had backed down with suspicious ease during the Spartacist uprising in Stuttgart in 1919. After 1924 Münzenberg's parliamentary immunity had all but guaranteed his safety, even as his employees and committee joiners were often harassed or even arrested for their association with him.

Still, Münzenberg was hardly alone in fleeing during the unprecedented terror that followed the Reichstag fire. By the end of March 1933, nearly all of the senior figures in the KPD had left Germany. Münzenberg's closest friends in the party, Leo Flieg and Heinz Neumann, rapidly followed him into exile, the former to France and the latter to Switzerland. Even Thälmann's favorites, Walter Ulbricht and Wilhelm Pieck, who would both later try to make political hay out of Münzenberg's swift flight, were not able to wait out the year before fleeing. Thälmann himself was arrested even before the Reichstag elections, disappearing into the burgeoning Nazi prison network on 3 March 1933.

All in all, Münzenberg's extreme precautions proved justified by events. The Nazi raid on his Berlin apartment was only the beginning. Because of the heightened surveillance by the Reich Interior Ministry after the Amsterdam congress of August 1932, the Prussian police already had extensive information on the entire Münzenberg trust, from the locations of IAH affiliate branches, NDV editorial and printing offices, and affiliated businesses (such as several cigarette factories set up in 1932 to raise funds for the FSR clubs) to the names and addresses of no less than eighty-nine key Münzenberg loyalists.[16] Göring's thugs, on the strength of this intelligence, were able to suppress Münzenberg's publishing operations immediately, arresting most key editorial personnel and leaving Münzenberg without any media outlets in Germany during the final days of the Reichstag election campaign. By the end of March, the FSR clubs in Berlin were smashed, and the IAH's cigarette factories were closed down as well.[17] Only one IAH asset in Berlin escaped confiscation: a special hard currency reserve, probably worth tens of thousands of dollars, which Münzenberg held in the safe of the Russian consul at the Soviet embassy. Babette Gross, after dropping her husband off in Saarbrücken, was able to slip unnoticed into Berlin to collect this cash for Münzenberg's use abroad.[18]

Münzenberg's position vis-à-vis the German authorities had meanwhile become almost surreal. On 5 March 1933 he was elected, yet again, to the Reichstag from Hesse-Nassau—yet unless he could somehow make it physically to the Reichstag building in Berlin (which was anyway closed indefinitely due to the fire), the legal immunity his seat granted him was a mirage.[19] His picture was in all the papers, even in French-occupied Saarbrücken, where his reluctant host, upon learning the identity of his controversial guest, took the liberty of self-addressing a "warning" letter from his office to his home regarding Münzenberg's safety ("Depart immediately, Münz recognized"). Although the host's ruse was transparent and somewhat cowardly, he did, at least, agree to smuggle Münzenberg across the French border that night. Within days Münzenberg had established contact with members of the local French Communist apparat in the border town of Vorbach, who were able to furnish him with a temporary visa and send him on to Paris.

Once he was safe in the French capital, Münzenberg quickly recovered his political bearings. He had only visited Paris once before, the previous September, when he had attacked "French imperialism" in a speech to French Communist unionists. But he had been well received then, and he found an even more cordial reception in 1933. Through his writer friend Henri Barbusse and Alfred Kurella, an old Youth Socialist chum who now worked on Barbusse's journal *Le Monde*, Münzenberg was whisked into the heart of Paris' left-wing salon culture, where he was warmly embraced as a high-ranking refugee from Hitler's Germany. Lucien Vogel, a Communist sympathizer who published the illustrated glossy magazine *VU* and the fashion journal *Jardin des Modes*, put Münzenberg up in his country mansion in the forest of Maisons-Laffitte. Vogel had extensive connections in political and diplomatic circles, and he placed Münzenberg in touch with Gaston Bergéry, a prominent former Radical Socialist deputy who was friendly with the current premier, Camille Chautemps. By the end of March both Münzenberg and Gross, who had since returned from Germany with the secret IAH stash, were granted special residence visas as *réfugiés provenant de l'Allemagne* by authority of the French Cabinet, on the condition that neither would intervene in internal French politics.[20]

This condition Münzenberg gladly accepted, for his fevered political imagination had at last fastened upon a single rhetorical enemy: Hitler's Germany. Goebbels and Göring had smashed Münzenberg's operations in Berlin, but they fell well short of putting him out of business. So rapidly did Münzenberg begin to reconstitute his media trust that the Gestapo's overworked surveillance teams were unable to keep up with his movements. Confusingly, Münzenberg staffers had begun printing a version of *AIZ* in Prague (although it would appear only sporadically the rest of the year), and *Unsere Zeit* ("Our Time," formerly *Rote Aufbau*) was reborn in Basel, with a defiant cover story, penned by Münzenberg himself, entitled "Long Live Marxism!"[21] Was Münzenberg, then, in Switzerland? Or Czechoslovakia? Or still in Germany? Only in May, when Münzenberg's campaign to blame the Reichstag fire on the Nazis burst onto the international scene, were Hitler's agents able to confirm that he was in Paris.[22]

On 10 May 1933, the Nazis handed Münzenberg a perfect propaganda cause to rally Communist sympathizers around, when they began burning "objectionable" books in solemn ceremonies in Berlin and other German university towns, serenaded by the martial music of SA bands. News of this stunning suppression of intellectual freedom in Germany had an electric effect abroad, providing crucial political ammunition to the anti-Hitler émigré opposition. Within days Münzenberg had marshaled a wide array of international notables into a front called the "World Committee for the Relief of the Victims of German Fascism." Although Münzenberg initially chose Albert Einstein as honorary chairman (without Einstein having any say in the matter), a willing volunteer was soon found, the respected fellow-traveling English aristocrat and parliamentarian, Lord Marley. Count Michael Karolyi, the former head of the provisional Hungarian government overthrown by Bela Kun, enlisted as well.[23] Behind the scenes, Münzenberg had assembled a formidable team of the Kremlin's "confidence men," including Barbusse, the popular French Communist orators Jacques Doriot and Guy Jerram, and the trusted Czech Comintern jack of all trades, Bohumil Smeral.[24] "The isolation of the Hitler government in the international field," Münzenberg confidently proclaimed before the initial gathering of his new front of fellow-traveling notables, "is nearly complete."[25]

Among the Parisian expatriate community of German writers and intellectuals, Münzenberg's prospects looked even more promising. Heinrich Mann enthusiastically lent his name to Münzenberg's so-called "German Freedom Library," a kind of documentation center set up in a studio on the boulevard Arago for the collecting information about the Nazi dictatorship. Münzenberg's old Swiss friend Fritz Brupbacher, among many others, began sending in materials on request, such as an old radical polemic against capitalist justice relating to the Chicago of 1886 which Münzenberg hoped to use as a model for a publication that would pin guilt for the Reichstag fire on the Nazis.[26]

This project, the *Brown Book*, which Münzenberg spent most of 1933 organizing, was undoubtedly the propaganda highlight of his career. To throw snooping Nazi spies off the trail, he enveloped Paris in a multitiered network of fellow-traveling fronts that could be disassembled and reassembled at a moment's notice.

At the most public level there were the German Freedom Library, on the boulevard Arago; Marley's World Committee for the Relief of the Victims of German Fascism, provisionally headquartered on the rue Mondétour; and Henri Barbusse's vaguely pacifist-oriented "Amsterdam-Pleyel" committee on the rue Lafayette, which had grown out of the Amsterdam congress of 1932.

Slightly more submerged were Münzenberg's publishing fronts. These included the Imprimerie Française, on the place de Raben, where Bruno Frei, formerly chief editor of *Berlin am Morgen*, now churned out *Gegen-Angriff* (Counterattack), which aimed to counter Goebbels's *Angriff* (Attack); the Editions du Carrefour, a highbrow "bourgeois" publishing house on the boulevard St. Germain, previously devoted to poetry and art books, run by a Swiss Communist sympathizer named Pierre Lévi whom Münzenberg and Gross seemed to have bowled over merely with their charm; and the obscure and relatively secretive Editions Sociales Internationales on rue Racine, the only fellow-traveling publishing house Münzenberg founded entirely with IAH funds.[27]

At the most subterranean level was the web of private apartments and safe houses in which the *Brown Book* was assembled, nearly all of which were chosen to distance Münzenberg as far as possible from the project. One of the key locales was the hotel room on rue St. Roch of the talented, multilingual Jewish Czech writer Otto Katz (alias André Simon) a glib Comintern hack who had done time both at IAH headquarters in Berlin and at M-Russ in Moscow. Katz had a long history with Münzenberg, on whom he may have been spying for the NKVD, and his ability to intimidate subordinates was matched only by that of Münzenberg himself. Arthur Koestler, for example, remained under Katz's spell for years.[28] Another key *Brown Book* locale was the apartment of the exiled German writer Gustav Regler on the rue du Faubourg Saint-Honoré. Regler, though not previously acquainted with Münzenberg, was welcomed with open arms into the *Brown Book* project when he offered up photographs he had taken of the original blueprints for the Reichstag building while stopping over in his flight from Germany at the National Library in Strasbourg. Rounding out the team at the Faubourg Saint-Honoré were Max Schroeder, a Communist art historian, and several crusty old KPD bureaucrats from Berlin who, Regler recalled, always "smelt of tobacco."[29]

Because of the putatively significant photos of the Reichstag building he had produced (which in fact proved little), Regler was given a great degree of responsibility on the *Brown Book* project, and his memoir of the campaign gives a precious glimpse of Münzenberg in action at the height of his formidable powers.[30] Now forty-three, Münzenberg was unquestionably a senior figure in the underground world of German émigré Communism, one who commanded unquestioning obedience from his employees and collaborators.

> Always seeming to be busy with other projects elsewhere, Münzenberg was accustomed to pay brief daily visits to the scene of our labors and grin at the sight of our weary faces (he never seemed to realize how much he asked of us until someone collapsed). He read manuscripts, often tossing them aside after a perfunctory glance, and dictated telegrams, manifestos, and lengthy reports of political meetings. He was as foul-mouthed as a cab driver and as variable in his moods as only a genius can be, at one moment exultant and at the next filled with wrath and melancholy, exaggerating all things, seeing enemies everywhere, and no end to our defeat.[31]

For Münzenberg, Paris in 1933 must have seemed like heaven on earth, a mecca for political exiles all seeking, like him, to vindicate their radicalism by waging war against Goehbels's Nazi propaganda machine. "Paris," he wrote Brupbacher exultantly in May, "is becoming the city of émigrés. Hundreds are arriving every day . . . everything is coming together here. Life grows more cheerful."[32] Münzenberg's recruitment efforts were helped along, of course, by the fact that his fellow-traveling collaborators were paid. By fall 1933 nearly three hundred thousand francs (about twelve thousand dollars) worth of Moscow gold had churned through the World Committee, most of which went to the *Brown Book* project.[33] Any German who could provide information, or simply travel freely to and from Germany, was welcome. "Every new fugitive we could lay hands on," Regler recalled, "was invited to visit us and tell us his experiences . . . our offices were like an island where the shipwrecked struggled ashore, somebodies, nobodies and Quixotes, the broken and embittered victims of the new overlords—all were contributors to the *Brown Book*."[34]

For once, the political stakes for Münzenberg involved more than mere Soviet propaganda, and everyone involved drew inspiration from the gravity of the situation. This did not mean, however, that the *Brown Book* campaign was any more honest or truthful than the myriad fellow-traveling Münzenberg initiatives that preceded it. With a reckless disregard for evidentiary standards, Münzenberg's men mixed together a witch's brew of half-truths, forgeries, lies, and innuendo to convict the Nazis as the true authors of the Reichstag fire. The most important pseudo-evidence derived from Regler's misleading photos of early Reichstag blueprints, anachronistically captioned to point to a phantom "underground passage leading to Goering's house."[35] There was also a suspiciously detailed "insider account" of the fire, as planned and executed by Göring and Goebbels, ostensibly penned by an informed Hugenberg loyalist, Dr. Ernst Oberfohren. In a conveniently timed "suicide," Oberfohren had been shot in the head in early May and thus couldn't disown the forgery.[36] Finally, Münzenberg's team unearthed an entry in Lubbe's name in a Saxon parish register from June 1932, which supposedly pointed to incriminating contacts with local Nazis. The group also made none too subtle insinuations that Lubbe had served as a homosexual boy toy of SA chief Ernst Röhm.[37]

The *Brown Book* was, in short, a fraudulent hack job. To further its cause Münzenberg plastered the names of famous intellectuals unconnected to the project all over the ads hawking it.[38] Münzenberg even spread the rumor around Paris that Albert Einstein himself had sponsored the book, until Einstein himself stepped in to deny this.[39] But despite its glaring inaccuracies there was a certain intuitive logic to the *Brown Book*, which in the final analysis marshaled the case against the Nazis less on the basis of concrete evidence relating to the Reichstag fire than on the overall repressive character of Hitler's regime. Only about a third of the *Brown Book* was actually concerned with the fire, with the bulk of its pages devoted instead to such themes as Hitler's rise to power (which, of course, was blamed on the Social Democrats), the Nazis' destruction of the workers' organizations, their campaign against culture, their persecution of the Jews, and the concentration camps Hitler was already building for political enemies.

Much of the coverage of Nazi brutality since the Reichstag fire, though largely based on hearsay, rang true. Even so, anyone who read the *Brown Book* carefully might have been suspicious of the motives of the authors. Though professing a concern for human rights in Germany, they took pains to differentiate between the plight of proletarians and "capitalists." To "prove" that "in the last analysis the Jewish question . . . is not a question of race, but a class question," for example, the *Brown Book* cited no evidence of anything happening inside Germany, but a lengthy harangue Lenin had once devoted to the nefarious machinations of "rich Jews." Lenin's anti-Semitic tirade ostensibly helped explain why Hitler's regime was supported by rich "Zionists" and "Jewish capitalists" who had "not suffered the least inconvenience" under Nazi rule. Muddying the moral waters further, the *Brown Book* also declared that among sixty photographs supposed to be of Jews in a Nazi propaganda tract called *Jews are Watching You*, many were in fact of "Germans of pure race," who happened to be Marxists. Among those inaccurately represented was one Willi Münzenberg, in whom, the authors of the *Brown Book* indignantly proclaimed, "there is not a drop of 'Jewish blood'!"[40]

Aside from its fabrications and inaccuracies, then, the *Brown Book* was laced with bile against "class enemies" and even, astonishingly, against Jews. Somehow, though, Münzenberg's morally questionable tome found a real audience, both through sensational excerpts picked up by international wire services and through many separate national editions. A special German edition, printed in Basel, was even smuggled into Germany disguised as Goethe's *Hermann und Dorothea*, although several hundred copies of this version were seized by suspicious border police in Württemberg. Overall print runs were impressive, though not quite as immense as has sometimes been claimed. About twenty thousand copies, mostly in French and German, were published by Editions du Carrefour in Paris, and thousands more were published in English by Victor Gollancz in London.[41] The true measure of Münzenberg's—and the Communists'—success, though, is the fact that until the first serious historical examination of the evidence, Fritz Tobias's

Der Reichstagsbrand, was published in 1962, most historians adopted the *Brown Book*'s thesis about Goebbels planning and executing the Reichstag fire by sending a team of conspirators through Göring's "secret tunnel."

The *Brown Book*'s case against the Nazis was immeasurably strengthened by Münzenberg's greatest propaganda innovation to date, a so-called "countertrial" he modeled on the secret revolutionary courts of prewar Russia and pitched, successfully, to ECCI budget commissars while visiting Moscow in June 1933.[42] To establish a veneer of political independence for his countertrial, Münzenberg issued invitations to dozens of celebrity lawyers and famous intellectuals such as H. G. Wells and George Bernard Shaw. Inevitably, very few invitees agreed to participate, but those few who even bothered to respond to Münzenberg's summons had their names bandied about far and wide as members of an official "Commission of Inquiry into the Burning of the Reichstag." With their travel expenses picked up by Moscow, a grand total of six jurists eventually showed up in Paris, one each from France itself and the nearby countries of Belgium, Holland, Denmark, and Sweden, and one from the United States.[43] Those jurists who demanded to see actual evidence, such as the American legal expert, Arthur Garfield Hays (a former counsel for Sacco and Vanzetti), were rudely disappointed. Hays, who arrived in Paris on 13 September 1933, just one day before Münzenberg's "trial" was slated to open in London, was not even briefed before being whisked across the Channel, where he was expected to lend his name to the cause.

The London trial itself was largely a farce, presided over by obviously partial "judges" such as the French lawyer Maître de Moro-Giafferi, who had recently shouted at a public Münzenberg meeting in Paris that, "It is you, Göring, who are the real assassin and the real incendiary!" Moro-Giafferi was so unconcerned with sifting the "evidence" presented at the London proceedings that, overcome by boredom at one point, he scribbled a note to Bergéry, complaining that "there isn't a good-looking woman in the courtroom." At the conclusion of the "trial," Münzenberg's friend Bergéry penned a predictable "verdict" which regurgitated the *Brown Book*'s thesis and asserted, in a political aside, that Lubbe was "not a member but an opponent of the Communist Party."[44]

The London countertrial produced no new evidence of any kind, and the trial's financial backers in Moscow admitted this plainly in a sharply critical secret ECCI report on the proceedings handed down in October 1933.[45] On the eve of the London trial, in fact, the German Public Prosecutor had politely requested information from Münzenberg's commission that might be used to ensure a fair hearing for the Communist defendants in Germany, but he was flatly rebuffed. Münzenberg, of course, had no such information.[46]

Merely by announcing a verdict, though, Münzenberg's countertrial was able to grab headlines all over the world, which put the Nazis squarely on the defensive as the real trial opened in Leipzig. So widespread was the publicity accorded Münzenberg's countertrial that even Nazi papers felt obliged to report on its proceedings, in effect admitting that world opinion was lining up against the Nazis. This upside-down dynamic played out to dramatic effect in Leipzig, where the Communists acted more as prosecutors than defendants. Georgi Dimitrov, a brilliant Bulgarian Comintern agent fluent in German who had been arrested and blamed for organizing Lubbe's arson, berated his questioners for weeks with reverse accusations surrounding Nazi guilt for the fire and even the Beer Hall Putsch of 1923.

The Dimitrov show built to a climax when Hermann Göring himself entered the courtroom on 4 November 1933. Although theoretically only a witness called to testify to evidence relating to Lubbe's arrest and its aftermath on the night of the Reichstag fire, Göring chose foolishly to harangue the court with a stump speech, which played right into Dimitrov's hands. When the Nazi minister began exonerating himself against the slanders perpetrated by the *Brown Book* and at Münzenberg's countertrial, Dimitrov pounced on him with a slew of new accusations, in effect turning himself into the court prosecutor. Disconcerted by Dimitrov's questions, Göring retorted that "in my eyes you are nothing but a scoundrel, a crook who belongs to the gallows," before storming out of the courtroom.[47]

In the end the Nazis were able to prove the guilt only of Lubbe, which, of course, never been doubted in the first place. Dimitrov and the other Communists in the dock were acquitted. This limited verdict, handed down in Leipzig on 23 December 1933, resolved nothing about the true authors of the fire, as neither Nazis nor Communists were able to produce a shred of credible evidence linking Lubbe with conspirators from the other party. Fifty years later, another "International Commission of Inquiry" unearthed "new" evidence and concluded that a Nazi team led by Reinhard Heydrich was probably behind the blaze—but this evidence turned out to have been just as flimsily constructed as that provided in the *Brown Book*.[48] In December 1933, in any case, the mystery of Lubbe's true accomplices (if there were any) remained entirely impenetrable.

In the battle for public opinion, though, Münzenberg was the clear victor. Shrewdly remaining behind the scenes while the *Brown Book* and the London countertrial swayed public opinion in advance of the Leipzig proceedings, he was able to sit back and watch the Nazis incriminate themselves simply by failing to disprove his accusations. The Nazi terror following the Reichstag fire had all but destroyed the KPD, costing hundreds of party activists their lives and thousands more their freedom—but for Communists who escaped abroad, times had never been better. Helped along by Dimitrov's brilliant performance in Leipzig, Münzenberg was riding high as the fateful year of 1933 drew to a close, fresh from his greatest propaganda triumph and flush with the Moscow gold that had underwritten it. He could perhaps be forgiven for failing to realize that the political ground was already shaking beneath his feet.

CHAPTER 15 *Reckoning*

The stunning political developments in Germany in 1933 breathed new life into Münzenberg's propaganda network, but at the same time they uprooted the institutional framework that had so long sustained it. Reconstituting the once-mighty Münzenberg trust was not as simple as transferring headquarters from Berlin to Paris and winning new Kremlin subsidies for the London countertrial. Without a new, permanent mandate from Moscow, Münzenberg would need to beg continuously for ad hoc funding for his various Paris committees, which were eating up so much Kremlin cash already that there was little left over for the IAH. By November 1933, the tail of the Münzenberg trust was wagging the dog, with the IAH's rump apparat in central Europe relying on the World Committee for the Relief of the Victims of German Fascism for piecemeal handouts.[1]

The anti-Nazi crusade may seem, at first glance, to have been an ideal vehicle for a new Münzenberg mandate. Hitler, to all appearances, was firmly entrenched in power, his political standing in Germany unblemished by the general impression abroad that his agents were behind the Reichstag fire. The May book burnings, the suppression of the KPD and SPD and the unions, the mass imprisonments and general terror sown in opposition circles in Germany—all the evidence pointed to a dictatorial regime almost unprecedented in its brutality: a left-wing propagandist's dream.

But in totalitarian politics, appearances were often deceptive. Once the furor over the Reichstag fire countertrial and trial had died down, Stalin and Hitler made peace, of a sort, agreeing not to let the propaganda battle sully the productive diplomatic and economic contacts already linking their two authoritarian governments. Unbeknownst to much of the world, the Soviet Union had in fact been the first country to conclude a treaty of any kind with Hitler's Germany, agreeing in early May 1933 to a nonaggression pact and to the peaceful arbitration of trade disputes.[2] And Hitler backed down on some of Göring's threats after the Leipzig verdict was read, allowing Dimitrov and two other Bulgarian Comintern defendants from Leipzig to return triumphantly to Moscow in February 1934. Once Dimitrov and his men were released, there was little residue from the Reichstag fire left to raise an international hue and cry about. True, Ernst Torgler, the one German Communist in the dock, was packed off to a concentration camp, but he was a relatively obscure Reichstag deputy who had received little press coverage during the trial.

As a result, Münzenberg's seemingly formidable *Brown Book* team now disbanded into its constituent elements no less abruptly than it had been cobbled together. The World Committee, which had met on the rue Mondétour until the Leipzig trial, morphed briefly into the "Committee for the Liberation of Dimitrov, Popov, Torgler, and Tanev," which (presumably to establish a separate identity) held fund-raising meetings at no less than seven separate addresses in December 1933.[3] When the three Bulgarians were released, the committee moved to yet another address, at 10 rue Notre-Dame de Lorette, where it was restyled the "Committee for the Liberation of Thälmann and of All Imprisoned Antifascists"—presumably including Torgler.[4]

Thälmann, the KPD's secretary for almost a decade and twice a German presidential candidate, was the only one of Hitler's Communist victims prominent enough to attract a broad international audience, so it is not surprising that Münzenberg transferred his attention to him immediately after Dimitrov's release from prison.[5] Thälmann's picture was splashed across the new IAH bulletin, accompanied by possibly apocryphal remarks that he had made supporting Münzenberg's "Solidarity Days" in 1931 and 1932.[6] The American IAH branch in New York, renamed in 1933 the "National Committee to Aid the Victims of German Fascism," headquartered in the Flatiron Building on Broadway, followed Münzenberg's lead in changing the organization's letterhead in 1934 to "Rescue Ernst Thälmann!"[7] For reasons difficult to fathom today, the plight of the imprisoned Hamburg KPD party boss struck a powerful chord in Depression-era Greenwich Village. At the height of the craze, a pair of radical songstresses composed a lurid hymn exhorting the proletarians of the world to "Set Ernst Thälmann Free":

> Stone halls and stairways, sparks from boots fly,
> Brown-shirted henchmen drag him along;
> Ernst Thaelmann defies them. They wince at his glances,
> Fearing the strength of proletarian hate . . .[8]

So enthusiastically did American Communist sympathizers embrace Thälmann that Münzenberg made his first trip ever to the United States in June 1934, exploiting the cause to raise funds for his Paris committees at rallies held in Boston, Washington, Chicago, Cleveland, Milwaukee, and of course New York, where he addressed a large crowd in Madison Square Garden. As a refugee from Hitler's Germany, Münzenberg was given a hero's welcome by American left-wing admirers. Both Münzenberg and his wife Babette Gross, who accompanied him, were astonished by the generosity of American donors to the Thälmann campaign, and by the fact that they were allowed to travel freely by the U.S. government, which they had supposed to be the world's leading capitalist tyrant.[9]

Despite its apparent success in America, there was a certain air of political desperation about the Thälmann cause. Münzenberg himself had never been very fond of Thälmann, and most German Communists (if not their American counterparts) knew this. It was hardly a secret that Münzenberg had been close to Neumann and Remmele, two Thälmann rivals cut down to size by Stalin in 1932, and few were fooled by Münzenberg's sudden discovery of Thälmann's virtues in 1934. In this sense the Thälmann committee was a blatant defensive front allowing Münzenberg to shore up his fragile position in the KPD. He was also trying, of course, to shore up his position in Moscow, which had been tenuous ever since Remmele's fall. His new IAH mouthpiece *Our Time*, published jointly in Paris and Basel, blended opportunistic Thälmann mania with over-the-top Stalinist flattery throughout 1934. In one installment, a frontal portrait of Stalin's intimidating face accompanied the cover story on "Invincible International Marxism." In another issue, Stalin's face was displayed in profile with the imposing caption, "The Creator of the Five Year Plan, the Führer of the [Coming] Global October."[10]

Münzenberg's exuberant rendering of the Stalin personality cult was not the only sign of his weakening position in the Kremlin. Nearly all of his old Bolshevik friends and patrons were now powerless. Clara Zetkin, though not much more than a figurehead, had at least always been given access to the Kremlin; but she died in June 1933. During the same month, while visiting Russia, Münzenberg had seen his old allies Zinoviev and Kamenev for the first time since their fall from grace in 1926–27. Although both were still alive, they now lived in seclusion in small dachas outside Moscow, struggling to find enough to eat. Zinoviev in particular "broke down completely" when he saw Münzenberg, lamenting his cruel fate. The rump staff of Russian IAH employees, meanwhile, had seen many of their perks—most importantly their free apartments—revoked even before the Nazis' destruction of IAH headquarters in Berlin, and despite frantic lobbying, Münzenberg was unable to do anything to improve their lot during his 1933 visit.[11]

In one particularly ominous episode during his visit to Russia in 1933, Münzenberg nearly let slip a note of sharp criticism while his former colleague from the Volga aid campaign, Alexander Eiduk (now an NKVD slavedriver) was showing him around a forced labor camp for workers on the Moskva-Volga Canal near Shelkovo. "Münzenberg looked at the teeming mass of humanity," Gross later recalled of this awkward moment, "and commented beneath his breath that this reminded him of the building of the pyramids by the pharaohs." Luckily Eiduk did not hear him, and Münzenberg's tour through the glories of "socialist construction" continued without interruption. Certainly Münzenberg's conscience recovered in time for him to pepper the pages of *Our Time* with yet more praise for Stalin's industrialization campaign the following winter.

In the aftermath of the Reichstag fire campaign, Münzenberg seemed in many ways to be losing his political touch, remaining aloof from important political developments. He and Gross were vacationing on the French Riviera when violent street demonstrations rocked Paris on 6 and 9 February 1934.[12] The first involved clashes between French government troops and right-wing paramilitaries, the second a famously bloody Communist uprising in the working-class suburb of St. Denis that set off a crisis in the PCF leadership. In a manner even starker than the Wittorf and Neumann-Remmele affairs in Germany, the controversial 9 February Communist demonstration, following on the heels of a right-wing rising that some were already calling an attempted "fascist coup," exposed the party's hidden internecine squabbles to daylight. By April, allies of the popular St. Denis–based Communist orator Jacques Doriot, who had rallied against cowardly PCF Secretary Maurice Thorez on account of his refusal to take to the streets in February, were being disciplined for "antiparty" activity, just as the KPD leaders who had voted to expel Thälmann had been in 1928. As in Germany, the issue posed for Moscow by Doriot's rebellion concerned not ideology, but excessive independence—in fact ECCI began shifting over to Doriot's stated position in favor of greater "antifascist" cooperation with Socialists in May 1934, even as Doriot himself was being stripped of his posts.[13]

Münzenberg, of course, had explicitly promised the French government that he would not intervene in French politics, so he could hardly be blamed for missing out on the February events. But his distance from the PCF served him poorly as the Doriot-Thorez crisis built toward a climax in spring 1934. Because his World Committee had been launched the year before in cooperation with two now-discredited figures, Doriot and Jerram, Münzenberg should now have made a visible effort to distance himself from them. In spite of widespread gossip about Doriot's impending political demise, however, Münzenberg did no such thing. In fact he met with Jerram as late as 14 April 1934, and even dutifully sent a protocol of this meeting to Moscow.[14]

Worse, although the World Committee remained relatively open to party outsiders, Münzenberg himself remained stuck in "social fascism" mode well into April 1934, possibly misinterpreting Thorez's apparent victory over Doriot as a vote against greater cooperation with Socialists. Thus Münzenberg interpreted a series of ominous warnings about agitprop discipline problems at *Our Time* and *Counterattack*, sent to Paris by ECCI over the winter and early spring, as a signal to step up his attacks on Social Democracy.[15] In an almost surreally obsequious letter sent to Bela Kun in late March, Münzenberg promised to keep closer watch on his editors and to sack the "petty bourgeois journalist sympathizers" responsible for any recent political deviations.[16] Attached to this letter was a kind of executive summary outlining how *Our Time* had "driven home the campaign against Social Democracy and the Second International" over the past year.[17]

Although such obsequiousness was ordinarily welcome in the Kremlin, Münzenberg's promise to rid Paris of "social fascists" was especially ill timed in spring 1934. Already plans were under way at ECCI to merge the Amsterdam-Pleyel movement created out of the Amsterdam peace congress of 1932 and the Thälmann Committee into a single, entirely open antifascist organization uniting Socialists and Communist sympathizers in Moscow's orbit. When he got wind of this in mid-April, Münzenberg nearly choked on the news. He begged Kun that the committees be allowed to retain their separate identities, or that he be given at least another month to prepare for their union. Just recently, Münzenberg explained, he had launched plans for a new agitprop offensive against the Second International to purge the Thälmann Committee of undesirables before it was taken over by the Socialists. There was already a likelihood, then, that the Thälmann Committee would drift further "left," meaning become more exclusively Communist. This likelihood would only be increased by a merger with the Amsterdam-Pleyel group, which since 1932 had itself turned sharply "leftward," as many of its more moderate fellow travelers had left to join the Thälmann Committee. Throwing disparate sympathizers together so haphazardly, Münzenberg feared, could cost both front groups credibility among their intellectual patrons, especially the now-thriving Thälmann Committee, which was the only Münzenberg front that continued to expand internationally.

This argument was a weak one that did little to camouflage Münzenberg's true concern: that he was losing control of both committees, which had already replaced the nearly defunct IAH as the prime recipients of underground Comintern cash flow. The Amsterdam-Pleyel group, for example, was all but off limits to him by April 1934, due to especially heavy surveillance of its offices on the rue Lafayette by the Paris police prefecture, which had no illusions about the Communist nature of this front. The Paris police, more conservative than the left-leaning national Chautemps government that had granted Münzenberg his special refugee visa, harassed Münzenberg whenever they encountered him. Because of this, in the previous three months he had visited the Amsterdam-Pleyel headquarters only once. Meanwhile, the restyled Thälmann Committee offices were drifting "rightward," or becoming less exclusively Communist in orientation, which meant the police menaced them less often than Amsterdam-Pleyel. Yet for exactly the same reason, Thälmann Committee headquarters, too, remained off limits to Münzenberg, whose presence might blow its precarious cover. Being stripped of his power base in Germany had ironically raised Münzenberg's public profile enormously. Since he was the ranking KPD refugee in France, any organization he frequented was automatically tainted as Communist.[18]

The delicate situation surrounding Münzenberg's relationship to his own front groups was hardly his own fault, but in light of his heightened political visibility, it is not surprising that Moscow began looking to correct this liability by replacing him. The shift seems to have begun as early as March 1934, when longtime IAH loyalist Henri Barbusse was taken into confidences by ECCI about the political shakeout in French Communism before Münzenberg was.[19] Münzenberg's request that Moscow postpone the merging of his two main front groups even occasioned a sharp personal reprimand from Bela Kun that Münzenberg was trying to "take up the leadership of the whole [antifascist] movement, in order to receive a free hand" in Paris. Trying desperately to counter any imputation of independence, Münzenberg responded that he had "never had a 'free hand' with [the Paris front committees], but rather [had] run them from the beginning" in strict accordance with ECCI instructions. Besides, he was so exhausted from the strain of police surveillance that, in recent months, he had "been unable to take part in [the front committees' work]"—in fact he had "practically lost contact with them."[20]

Although he was assured by Kun that he was not going to be purged entirely from the new antifascist front, Münzenberg set off for America in late June, informing Kun shortly before departing that he needed some time away from the intrigues of Paris.[21] Although Münzenberg's inaugural visit to the United States was, to all appearances, a political triumph, it only underscored his slipping status. In fact much of the ground for his "free Thälmann" campaigning in America had already been paved by Barbusse, whose itinerary Münzenberg would follow closely. Where Barbusse had once blindly followed Münzenberg's directives, it was now the Frenchman who was breaking new ground.

Barbusse's simple, catchall Amsterdam-Pleyel cause—"Against War and Fascism"—was also better suited to the political atmosphere of 1934 than Münzenberg's increasingly complex agitprop maneuvers. Not only did Münzenberg fail to read the signs regarding Doriot's fall, he missed the boat entirely on the emergence of a French Popular Front between Socialist and Communists that followed in its wake. And much as he had been in the wrong place during the historic Paris street demonstrations in February, Münzenberg was physically absent during the crucial event that helped catalyze the official shift to a new policy: Hitler's so-called "Night of the Long Knives" of 30 June 1934, when the last element of radical "proletarian" energy in the Nazi movement—the SA storm troopers—were brutally purged in a veritable orgy of violence. Although various overtures between Socialist and PCF leaders had earlier hinted at a united front between the two main left parties, it was not until Hitler's stunning maneuver in Germany that the Comintern's proposal for joint "antifascist" action to oppose "the Hitler terror" was published in *L'Humanité*, leading to a Popular Front agreement in July.[22]

Münzenberg was at sea on his way to America when he heard the news about the SA purge.[23] He was already in the United States when the terms of Popular Front cooperation were being hammered out in Paris in July. During this seminal moment in the history of the European Left, then, Münzenberg found himself literally on the wrong continent. By the time Münzenberg returned to France in August, his newfound rival, Barbusse, was firmly in charge of the unified "World Committee against War and Fascism," whose journal *World Front* had now replaced the discredited *Our Time* and *Counterattack* as Moscow's favored propaganda mouthpiece.

Taking a cue from his former mentor, Barbusse had already spun off a mind-boggling array of affiliates from his new World Committee, including youth and women's leagues, which by September were already eating up more than a hundred thousand francs (about four thousand dollars) worth of Moscow gold a month. Roughly a fourth of this went into *World Front*, another quarter into the youth and women's leagues, and about a third into conference logistics, with the remainder devoted to office overhead and executive travel.[24]

With the advent of the Popular Front, then, the intellectual fellow travelers who had always been Münzenberg's most loyal foot soldiers finally took over the fort. Barbusse's transformation from craven IAH sycophant —he had once begged Münzenberg to make a movie out of his novel *Le Feu* (The Fire), even suggesting inventing new battle scenes to liven up the action—into full-fledged Comintern commissar was now complete.[25] Although Münzenberg was still listed as a member of the international secretariat, which served in an advisory role to the Thälmann Committee, he was now limited to once-a-month consultations, as any more frequent contacts, according to Barbusse, would jeopardize the new front group's reputation for political independence. "Speaking frankly," Barbusse wrote Moscow in September 1934, "Münzenberg's name, with its inveterate reputation for being the factotum of organizations affiliated with the Communist International, presents serious inconveniences."[26]

Though Barbusse's rather ungrateful coup dealt a serious blow to Münzenberg's standing in both Paris and Moscow, it was not necessarily a fatal one. Pierre Lévi's Editions du Carrefour imprint, though now a bastion of Communist propaganda, remained independent of party control.[27] Lévi and Münzenberg remained on exceptionally good terms, and together the two men cranked out an impressive run of books critical of the Nazi regime. The *Brown Book* on the Reichstag fire was followed by a *White Book* on the Night of the Long Knives. The exiled German Communist Walter Mehring penned a scathing series on Hitler's leading functionaries called "Nazi Leaders, Look at Yourselves." There followed political poems and novels, including a Bertolt Brecht poetry collection; an Egon Erwin Kisch novel called *No Entry*; and *In the Cross-Fire*, a dramatization of the upcoming plebiscite to determine if the Saar district would be returned to Germany, written by Münzenberg's new friend Gustav Regler.[28]

The campaign to sabotage the Nazis' expected victory in the Saar plebiscite, scheduled to be held under League of Nations auspices in January 1935, provided Münzenberg a welcome distraction from the painful Barbusse coup in Paris. Using all the tricks of the underground literature smuggling trade Münzenberg had mastered in wartime Switzerland, collaborators such as Gustav Regler stowed pamphlets in vegetable and flower seed packets, scented shampoo samples, and innocuous-looking weather balloons. Longer tracts such as the *Communist Manifesto* were often rebound into familiar-looking editions of German classics such as Schiller's *Maid of Orleans*.[29]

Without a new mandate from Moscow, though, Münzenberg was subsisting on leftover cash and borrowed time. By the time the Seventh Comintern Congress met in summer 1935, the ever malleable funding structures that had allowed Münzenberg's mania of reckless innovation to flourish for so long had dried up almost completely. There were still a few rump underground IAH locals in Germany, mainly in the Berlin area, but most of their reports sent in to Moscow dealt with such unpleasant matters as Gestapo harassment and mass arrests.[30] Despite a belated flurry of lobbying in Moscow, Münzenberg was unable to forestall the IAH's final liquidation. Some of his last-ditch cash-begging gambits were as impressively brazen as any he had conjured up in the past—he asked for no less than five hundred thousand rubles to renovate the Mezhrabpom-Film building—but the magic was gone.[31] In August, the IAH's debt-ridden film assets were at last taken over officially by the new Soviet state film monopoly, and MOPR absorbed the few remaining IAH branches in central Europe, in both Prague and Vienna.[32]

This was not necessarily the end for Münzenberg. The IAH's liquidation was little more than a sideshow in Moscow during the historic Seventh Comintern Congress, the first that had met since 1928, when the disastrous "class against class" line had been approved. The so-called "Congress of the New Tactical Reorientation," held in the grand setting of the Moscow Palace of Notables in summer 1935, dramatically announced the advent of a Europewide reconciliation with Socialists. In the German case, this meant repudiating the "social fascism" doctrine that, it was now tacitly admitted, had helped bring the Nazis to power. Officially, Neumann and Remmele were blamed for the flawed policy, which seemed to bode poorly for Münzenberg. But, just as in the Wittorf affair of 1928, Münzenberg slipped carefully through the personnel purges. This time he did so by throwing in his lot with Wilhelm Pieck, who in Thälmann's absence had emerged as a principal rival to Thälmann's favorite, Walter Ulbricht. Ulbricht was widely known to detest Münzenberg, and this is probably why Pieck now supported the latter's surprising election to the party Zentrale as a counterbalance to Ulbricht.[33] Although he had come only belatedly around to the Popular Front cause in France, Münzenberg was now officially enlisted in Moscow's efforts to reach out to the German Socialists' Prague-based party Executive (SOPADE). While Ulbricht and Pieck would handle the formal KPD-SOPADE negotiations in Prague, Münzenberg was expected to build bridges to party outsiders in Paris.

In addition to having his status in the KPD reconfirmed during the Seventh Comintern Congress, Münzenberg also received a substantial cash infusion of ten thousand gold rubles (about five thousand dollars) directly from the Kremlin, possibly to help cushion the blow of losing the IAH mandate. This money, officially earmarked for the vague purpose of promoting "antiwar literature," seems to have been intended to lubricate a new fellow-traveling committee in Paris that would complement Barbusse's World Committee against War and Fascism.[34] It may have been Georgi Dimitrov, Stalin's pick as new Comintern secretary, who authorized Münzenberg's new mandate. The two had teamed up impressively during the Reichstag fire controversy, with Dimitrov ingeniously deploying Münzenberg's *Brown Book* allegations against the Nazis at Leipzig. From the alacrity with which Münzenberg began reporting to Dimitrov from Paris in fall 1935, we may conclude that the two were on exceptionally good terms following the Seventh Congress.[35]

Münzenberg's position in Paris was also immeasurably strengthened by Barbusse's unexpected death in Moscow on 30 August 1935, which not only gave Münzenberg an excuse to reassert control over his own former front committees, but also gave occasion for a whole slew of fund-raising events held that fall in Barbusse's name. By December, Münzenberg had raised over 100,000 francs (about $4,000) in France and elsewhere for a "Barbusse memorial fund" (whose exact purposes, suspiciously, remained undefined), while Thälmann collections, especially in the U.S. and England, were bringing in a great deal more. Not that such campaigns were allowing the Thälmann Committee to turn profits—in fact these seemingly prolific collections were still running far behind the expenses of the agitprop that promoted them. While tactfully refusing to blame the Thälmann Committee's operating deficit on the late Barbusse's profligate stewardship, Münzenberg confessed to Dimitrov in December 1935 that he had run up debts of about 180,000 francs (about $7,200)—even before he had formed the new German Popular Front Paris committee envisaged at the Seventh Comintern Congress.[36]

The Red Millionaire, in short, was back in business. By early 1936 he had insinuated himself into a dizzying array of fashionable Popular Front causes, capitalizing on the openness of the new party line to rope in even more German émigré notables than during the *Brown Book* campaign. Along with his acquaintance Max Braun, a German journalist with contacts in SOPADE, Münzenberg laid the groundwork for a new round of antifascist periodicals to be fronted by Socialists, although secretly financed by Moscow. One weekly would supersede the now-outmoded *Counterattack* in exposing Nazi brutality; others would serve as mouthpieces for the new German united front and Popular Front committees; and if possible Münzenberg also hoped to found a true German-language daily newspaper in Paris along the lines of *Welt am Abend* and *Berlin am Morgen.*

There would be no shortage of sensational material to cover in such front organs. Among other agitprop gems, Münzenberg planned attacks on the new fascist anti-Comintern Axis of Germany, Italy, and Japan; campaigns against Nazi "cultural barbarism" and the upcoming "Hitler Olympics"; the promotion of new "Ethiopia" committees to protest Mussolini's recent aggression; more Barbusse memorial collections; the minting of Thälmann medallions and Dimitrov coins, along with stamps featuring both "antifascist" heroes; and the calling of a great new "peace congress" in Paris for sometime in spring 1936.[37] To lend political credibility to all the new ventures, Münzenberg planned to enlist exiled German Socialist heavyweights such as Rudolf Breitscheid and former Reichsbanner chairman Karl Hölterman; German émigré literary stars such as Heinrich and Thomas Mann, Ernst Toller, Lion Feuchtwanger, and Ludwig Marcuse; liberal German journalists and publishers like Georg Bernhard and Leopold Schwarzschild; French notables such as Moro-Giafferi, and English celebrities such as Lord Robert Cecil and Sir Norman Angell. The agitprop slogan unifying all these disparate themes and individuals, Münzenberg somewhat obsequiously promised Dimitrov, would be "Dimitrov Calls—and Millions Answer: Unity! Unity! Unity!"[38]

All of these themes received a hearing at the exploratory German Popular Front meetings Münzenberg held in the Hotel Lutetia in Paris over fall and winter 1935–36. Remarkably, nearly all of the German émigrés Münzenberg invited showed up at the inaugural gathering held in September 1935, even several notables from the publishing world previously hostile to Communism, such as Leopold Schwarzschild, editor-in-chief of the highly successful German émigré weekly *Das neue Tagebuch.* Schwarzschild was sufficiently concerned about Hitler's ever-strengthening dictatorship to respond warmly to Münzenberg's calls for antifascist cooperation, proposing that any new committee look seriously into forming a future German governing coalition (which he liked to call a "Fourth Reich") to take over if Hitler was ever ousted from power. Münzenberg, intrigued, placed Schwarzschild on the ten-man Lutetia executive committee, along with himself, Heinrich Mann (the chairman), Georg Bernhard, Max Braun, and Otto Klepper, the last Prussian minister of finance, who had been ejected by Papen's coup in 1932.[39]

Winning over such illustrious outsiders to the Lutetia initiative was a remarkable coup for Münzenberg, but their prominence inside the new front inevitably raised hackles among the KPD leadership in Prague. The core

Lutetia collaborators included a number of headstrong non-Communists whom Pieck and Ulbricht did not trust. At the third and largest Lutetia meeting in February 1936, among the 118 politicians and journalists in attendance Communists were outnumbered almost five to one by party outsiders, including even the notorious, hated former Prussian interior minister whom the Münzenberg trust had repeatedly pilloried as a "social fascist," Albert Grzesinski.[40] Not a single Communist was on the masthead of the official Lutetia organ, *Deutsche Informationen*. Even Münzenberg's Thälmann committees, once they opened their doors to party outsiders, dropped Thälmann's name from their registers. The Lutetia manifesto issued in February was similarly un-Communist in style. "All groups and all individuals who follow this appeal to unite," Münzenberg's new committee proclaimed to the German émigrés scattered around Europe and the Americas, "will help preserve Germans and the German nation and thereby other countries and other peoples from annihilation by a new world war."[41]

The biggest problem with Lutetia as far as Ulbricht and Pieck were concerned, though, may have been its very success. SOPADE-KPD negotiations were still bogged down in a swamp of mutual suspicion, stemming not only from the political resentments left over from the KPD's shameful "social fascism" doctrine in the early 1930s, but also from the risks inherent in sharing sensitive information about the parties' separate underground networks in Hitler's Reich. News of Münzenberg's euphoric Lutetia meetings therefore did not sit well in Prague. In February, Münzenberg received two aggressive demands for ideological "clarification" of the Lutetia initiative from the KPD Zentrale, both of which were copied and forwarded to Moscow.[42] Already rumors were swirling around Prague that clever SPD leaders such as Breitscheid and Greszinski were seeking to exploit differences "between the tactics of the [KPD Zentrale] and [those] of certain functionaries in Paris." To clear suspicions, Pieck and Ulbricht demanded that Münzenberg publish an article in the official KPD organ, *Rundschau*, which clearly laid out his adherence to the party line.[43]

Ulbricht and Pieck may have been justified in their suspicions. Münzenberg, cut loose from his IAH moorings and tossed into the backbiting maelstrom of the KPD-SOPADE negotiations, seems to have been hedging his bets in 1936, not yet sure himself where he was going with his new Lutetia initiative. Sometime late in February, he met secretly with senior SPD stalwarts Victor Schiff and Rudolf Breitscheid, along with two left-leaning independent German émigré journalists, Max Braun and Georg Bernhard. The latter was a brilliant but notoriously volatile editor who had famously been fired from the *Vossische Zeitung* in 1931 after accusing his boss Franz Ullstein's wife of being a French spy.[44] With no other Communists present, Münzenberg spoke quite frankly of his reservations about KPD Zentrale's united front tactics—perhaps a bit too frankly. Bernhard was so disturbed by Münzenberg's frankness that he dashed off a lengthy mea culpa letter to his friend Heinrich Mann describing the whole "tragicomedy." Finally he simply "had to explain to Münzenberg," Bernhard wrote, "that I under no circumstances would allow myself to be turned into a punching bag for Communist zigzag politics." Little did Bernhard know that Mann, probably on Münzenberg's own orders, was now forwarding copies of all essential Lutetia correspondence to Dimitrov in Moscow—who, in turn, was forwarding them back to Prague as well.[45]

Before word of Bernhard's unfortunate confession reached Moscow, however—in fact literally while his letter, forwarded by Mann, was still in the mails—Münzenberg, along with Ulbricht, was summoned to Moscow in March 1936 to give testimony on the ongoing tactical controversy to a special session of the Comintern Secretariat. Encouragingly, Münzenberg's Lutetia maneuvering received a strong endorsement as "a step forward." Ulbricht's negotiating strategy in Prague, by contrast, was deemed to have been "not elastic enough," as "not all opportunities for the promotion of a united front were utilized."

By the time Münzenberg returned to Paris, however, his apparent victory over Ulbricht on Popular Front doctrine had been transformed into a crushing defeat. In a sequence of events eerily similar to Thälmann's outmaneuvering of his KPD enemies in the "Wittorf affair" of 1928 and Thorez's defeat of Doriot in the battle for the soul of the PCF in 1934, Münzenberg's tactical triumph was undercut by evidence of a breach of discipline that overrode ideological considerations. Several days after Münzenberg left Moscow on 9 March 1936, certain of his strengthened standing, Bernhard's effusive letter, forwarded by Mann, reached Dimitrov. In a breathless sequence of resolutions on the German Popular Front mess, ECCI then officially endorsed Münzenberg's Lutetia initiative over Ulbricht's strategy as a model for future negotiations with party outsiders—but issued Münzenberg a sharp personal reprimand for washing the party's dirty laundry before a loose-tongued outsider such as Bernhard.[46]

This was a serious offense in the Kremlin, and Münzenberg knew he was in trouble. Stung by the pro-Münzenberg resolution issued by ECCI in March, Ulbricht began openly intriguing against his rival in Prague, although Pieck was still protecting Münzenberg against an outright expulsion.[47] Cut off almost entirely from Prague, Münzenberg was soon begging Dimitrov for some assurance of his standing in Moscow, declaring with more wishfulness than confidence that he had tried all year "to do good and serious work for the party and I am convinced that I have done that." But the stain of the "Bernhard letter," as it was called at ECCI, was difficult to wipe away. "I tried to talk Bernhard out of this nonsense," Münzenberg now pleaded, "I cited all of [your] resolutions, so that he could be certain that the line laid down at the Seventh Congress remained unchanged."[48]

But the damage was done. Although Münzenberg was not stripped of any of his functions, little further funding came through from Moscow for the Lutetia initiative. He did assure Moscow in April 1936 that the committee's SPD-edited front bulletin, *Deutsche Informationen*, was "developing well," but this was a lie.[49] The latest in a long line of Münzenberg agitprop productions was almost pitifully underproduced, often consisting of little more than a single typescript page with no graphics whatsoever.[50] So hard up was the venture for cash that Babette Gross asked Fritz Brupbacher to subscribe to *Deutsche Informationen* for twenty francs a month, which, she told him, would be "a real help."[51]

With the cash-strapped Lutetia venture floundering and his standing in Moscow undermined, it is little wonder that Münzenberg tried to branch out in 1936, setting his sights on the richest media organ in German émigré Paris. Sometime in early spring Bernhard, almost certainly with Münzenberg's cooperation, began intriguing to seize outright control over the *Pariser Tageblatt* from its owner and publisher, a rich, conservative White Russian Jewish émigré named Vladimir Poliakov. The *Tageblatt* was by far the most successful of several free German-language dailies that had sprung up in Paris after 1933, reaching a circulation of twelve thousand and an annual advertising turnover of over a million francs (about forty thousand dollars). Bernhard, a talented editor, clearly had contributed greatly to the paper's success after Poliakov hired him early in 1934, but due to Bernhard's Socialist leanings —not to mention his contacts with Communists like Münzenberg—there was political tension between the two men from the outset. After the Night of the Long Knives in 1934, Bernhard had even organized an editorial strike to mark the occasion, ostensibly to protest his boss's insufficiently anti-Nazi bent. This was nonsense—Poliakov, a Jew, was hardly pro-Nazi—but quite a few *Tageblatt* staffers had socialist leanings, and gradually Bernhard was able to organize them into a cabal hostile to Poliakov. When Poliakov refused to allow Münzenberg's Lutetia committee free publicity in his paper in 1936, Bernhard's cabal on the editorial staff resolved to launch a bold takeover bid.[52]

The evidence pointing to Münzenberg's role in planning Bernhard's editorial putsch is inconclusive, but the ingenious stunt bore all the hallmarks of Münzenberg's propaganda style.[53] On the occasion of a brief trip he made to the United States to attend an American Popular Front congress, Bernhard had several staffers declare (falsely) that Poliakov had fired him on the front page of the 11 June 1936 *Tageblatt*, claiming that Poliakov wanted a new editor who would "take a more loyal attitude towards Hitler and his aspirations." Because of Poliakov's "treachery"—he had supposedly been won over to the Nazi cause by one of Goebbels's henchmen while being observed visiting the German embassy in Paris—the renegade editors declared the 11 June paper "the last issue of the free anti-Nazi *Pariser Tageblatt*." They promised to retaliate by renaming Poliakov's paper the *Pariser Tageszeitung*, which would unite all anti-Nazi "writers, journalists and politicians of the German emigration."[54]

Suspiciously, the renegade editors still listed Georg Bernhard as chief editor on the same page as that on which Poliakov was said to have fired him—because in fact Bernhard had not been fired. On 12 June, the first issue of the *Pariser Tageszeitung* was printed in the *Tageblatt* offices, with a petition of "sympathy" for the fired Bernhard on the cover whose signatories, in effect, revealed themselves as the coup plotters. Bernhard's supporters turned out to be Rudolf Breitscheid, Max Braun, and Willi Münzenberg. Next day, a cablegram from New York graced the front page of the *Pariser Tageszeitung*, announcing Bernhard's solidarity with the editorial renegades. Poliakov was now accused, on the front page of the newspaper stolen from him, "of having made of the old *Pariser Tageblatt*, organ of the German emigration struggle, an object of bargaining and of treason with the Third Reich." "We challenge [Poliakov]," the plotters continued, "to meet us before any ordinary court or to face us before an arbitration tribunal composed of any impartial personalities of the emigration." Conveniently, Münzenberg had already formed a "commission of inquiry"—staffed entirely by obviously partial Lutetia luminaries such as Schwarzschild and Grzesinski. Not surprisingly, this commission was immediately endorsed by the editors of the new *Tageszeitung*—though not by Poliakov, who was shrewd enough to demand a "mixed commission" that was truly independent.[55]

Poliakov and his chief counsel, Richard Lewinsohn, though physically barred by the plotters from entering the *Tageblatt* offices on the night of 12–13 June, ultimately proved equal to the legal challenge. By the end of the year public opinion in the German émigré community had turned sharply against Bernhard, who, it was remembered, had once tried to smear Franz Ullstein at the *Vossische Zeitung* just as he now tried to ruin Poliakov.

Even Schwarzschild later switched sides, upholding Poliakov's honor as a Jew and a devoted opponent of Hitler in his *Neue Tagebuch*. Although it took almost two years to wind its way through the French courts, Poliakov's claim to the newspaper was ultimately upheld, and Bernhard was found guilty of defamation.[56]

Before this verdict was handed down in 1938, however, Bernhard and Münzenberg were able to retain control over the old *Tageblatt* offices by force, and this gave Münzenberg a crucial financial lifeline as his standing was sinking in Moscow. The *Pariser Tageszeitung* was not, at first, as lucrative as the *Tageblatt* had been, but Münzenberg did get his friend Hugo Simon to invest some capital that allowed the paper to keep going. Until July 1937, the Münzenberg-Bernhard-Simon trio continued publishing the *Tageszeitung*, ostensibly keeping it afloat through ad sales and the occasional capital contribution from Lutetia collaborators and admirers. Almost certainly, though, the three men exploited cash reserves produced during the *Tageblatt*'s years of prosperity. At one point during the ongoing legal struggle in early 1937, Bernhard offered to settle with Poliakov for 150,000 francs—implying that a significant amount had been embezzled from the old *Tageblatt* treasury. The offer was refused.[57]

Münzenberg was careful to cover his tracks during the *Tageszeitung* takeover battle. Unlike Bernhard, he emerged unscathed from the trials in 1938. But the affair did not much help his political standing in Moscow, where the "Bernhard letter" had already damaged his reputation. The next blow came in July 1936, when Münzenberg, summoned to Moscow to help prepare an upcoming pacifist front congress in Brussels, was asked to stay on to work in the Comintern's agitprop division. Although he wriggled out of this and was able to return to France, Münzenberg was now shadowed in Paris by his former Czech *Brown Book* collaborator Bohumil Smeral, who had been assigned to keep watch on his former boss. Furthermore, although he helped plan the Brussels conference, Münzenberg was not even allowed to make a public appearance there. Clearly, his stock in Moscow had slipped dramatically.[58]

General Franco's right-wing insurrection against the Spanish Popular Front government, launched on 17 July 1936, offered a potential new cause célèbre that might have served to renew Münzenberg's mandate. But when he and his wife Babette Gross asked all his Lutetia friends for support after returning to Paris in late July, they made little headway. "The most dreadful thing" about making such collections, Gross complained, "is the complete indifference and ignorance of all the people here."[59]

Desperation was setting in for Münzenberg. In late August 1936, news of the first in a series of lurid show trials of "old Bolsheviks" in Moscow sent shock waves through Europe. The two earliest victims were Kamenev and Zinoviev, both of them former Münzenberg patrons. Zinoviev was more than a patron, of course—he had been close to Münzenberg ever since the latter had joined Lenin's Zimmerwald Left circle in 1916. And now Zinoviev's execution, stunningly, was ordained by Lenin's own successor. While strolling around Brussels during the Peace Congress in early September—on direct orders from ECCI, he was not allowed into the conference hall—Münzenberg ran into an old Dutch ex-Communist acquaintance who blocked Münzenberg's path and shouted, "Cain, where is your brother Abel-Zinoviev?" Unable to muster a response, Münzenberg, "silently and profoundly depressed," turned and walked the other way.

With his standing in the Kremlin still uncertain, Münzenberg was summoned to Moscow again in October. Ominously, he and Gross, holed up in the new Hotel Moskva, were shunned by many Communist acquaintances. "No one dared to visit us," Gross later recalled: "after all we might be among the damned." Münzenberg tried to visit Radek, but learned that his last remaining friend from the Zimmerwald Left had just been arrested. Frantic, he tried to make an appointment with Dimitrov, with whom he still believed himself to be on good terms, but was told by ECCI that Dimitrov was "on holiday." Dimitrov's stand-in at ECCI, Palmiro Togliatti (Comintern alias "Ercoli"), repeated Dimitrov's July order that Münzenberg remain in Moscow to work in the Comintern's agitprop department, but this time informed the beleaguered organizer that Smeral, still in Paris, would now be taking over all of Münzenberg's functions there.

Even more ominously, Münzenberg was now ordered to appear before the International Control Commission recently created by Stalin to purge the Comintern apparat. The charge, "lack of revolutionary vigilance," related, on the surface, to one Liana Klein, a onetime Münzenberg employee who had fled to Spain in 1935 and was now believed to be a Franco spy. At first, Gross recalled, "Münzenberg treated this accusation as a joke, calling the whole affair 'flea killing.'" But he soon realized that the Klein connection was only one of hundreds the Control Commission could throw in his face if Stalin really wanted to destroy him. Münzenberg decided to toe the line, making a public declaration on 10 November 1936 of support for Zinoviev's death sentence. This act of political cowardice secured Münzenberg an exit visa, which allowed him to return, stripped of his functions and under strict surveillance, to France.[60]

In late November 1936, after arriving in Paris, Münzenberg dutifully began collecting the financial records and employee accounts of his various Lutetia-related committees and publications, in order to turn over his operations to Smeral. He omitted the *Pariser Tageszeitung*, in which his stake remained a closely guarded secret, and the Editions du Carrefour, which remained independent of Communist control.[61] Münzenberg did apparently slip Smeral's surveillance long enough to check into a sanatorium in the Parisian suburb of Chaténay-Malabry run by an old Russian Menshevik physician who now called himself Dr. Le Savouret. Safe for now, he wired Ulbricht and Pieck in Prague that he was taking sick leave. True to his word, Münzenberg, after conveniently being diagnosed with a "slight cardiac neurosis," went into political hibernation in Le Savouret's sanatorium for the rest of the winter, working on a polemic called *Propaganda als Waffe* (Propaganda as a Weapon) which aimed to deconstruct Nazi propaganda techniques.[62]

Propaganda as a Weapon, which Münzenberg wrote with the assistance of the German writer Kurt Kersten, was clearly intended as a magnum opus, an impassioned statement of all Münzenberg had learned about political manipulation during his years in the Communist party, which would serve the heroic cause of unmasking Hitler's treachery. The book does provide a fairly penetrating analysis of the propaganda methods used by Goebbels and Hitler to cow Germans into submission, from the exploitation of race prejudice, to the creation of the führer myth, to the appropriation of progressive words such as "socialism." Much as Münzenberg had condemned Hitler's contempt for "socialist" theory in his debate with Strasser in 1931, he now expressed shock that the Nazis had so blatantly appropriated the concept of "propaganda" itself, which had been a sacred term for Münzenberg ever since he joined the political club "Propaganda" as a teenager in Erfurt. For Münzenberg, "propaganda" had always signified the "intellectual transmission of scientific knowledge." For Goebbels, by contrast, propaganda was only a political "weapon" used to deceive. And of course, communists had conceived their "scientific" agitprop slogans on behalf of the working class, whereas the Nazis were the first party to exploit "mass propaganda for bourgeois interests."

Aside from such platitudes about the virtues of earnest socialist (as opposed to cynical "capitalist") propaganda, though, *Propaganda as a Weapon* disappointingly gives no real insight into Münzenberg's own secrets of political manipulation.[63] Münzenberg's would-be masterpiece was also politically opaque. Ulbricht soon used *Propaganda as a Weapon* as evidence of Münzenberg's ideological deviation, on the grounds that its principally "psychological" explanation of Hitler's appeal to the masses was "not Marxist." In fact, however, Münzenberg took pains to cite the proper ideological authorities throughout, citing Lenin for his expertise on propaganda theory, and Stalin (the "great leader of the Soviet Union and the architect of the world's first socialist state") on the inevitability of a capitalist war launched by Hitler. Dimitrov, though, was the real star, with Münzenberg quoting copiously from his celebrated "antifascist" speeches at the Leipzig trial of 1933 and the Seventh Comintern Congress of 1935 on no less than four separate occasions. There was something a bit tired about these citations, though; and Münzenberg also cited, as an expert on Hitler's plans for the conquest of Czechoslovakia, none other than Winston Churchill, about as un-Communist an authority as one could imagine.[64] *Propaganda as a Weapon,* in short, tried to offer a bit of something for everybody, and wound up pleasing almost no one.

At the least, writing the book provided Münzenberg a welcome distraction from the depressing news from Russia. It was a cold winter for those of Münzenberg's colleagues and collaborators who fell into Stalin's clutches in Moscow. In January 1937, one of Münzenberg's oldest and closest friends in the party, Radek, confessed to a list of crimes that included anti-Soviet terrorist activities and treasonous contacts with the German and Japanese governments.[65] Jacob Mirov-Abramov, the longtime Comintern finance liaison in Berlin who had been Münzenberg's neighbor in the Soviet embassy on Unter den Linden during the Russian and German relief campaigns, was arrested in the Soviet embassy in Paris just days after his wife visited Babette Gross. Not long thereafter Hans Schulz, Münzenberg's IAH assistant and roommate during the Tiergarten days of late Weimar, was interrogated by the NKVD. Schulz, fortunately, escaped arrest. Leo Flieg and Heinz Neumann, Münzenberg's two closest German Communist friends, were not so lucky. Both were summoned to Moscow and arrested in April 1937.[66] At about the same time, Münzenberg was approached for the first time by an NKVD agent named Beletskii, who would demand repeatedly over the coming months that he report to Moscow for further questioning. Somehow Münzenberg was able to avoid committing himself to such a trip, possibly by threatening to report Beletskii to the French government.[67]

Haunted by such clear omens of his impending doom, Münzenberg emerged from seclusion to make his first public appearance in months on 10 April 1937 at the first true German Popular Front conference, which met on the rue Cadet in Paris. Although he had been stripped of most of his Comintern posts and the funding that underlay them, Münzenberg was still technically a member of the KPD Zentrale, and in light of his still useful

Lutetia contacts, Pieck and Ulbricht had reluctantly agreed to allow him to represent the party at the April congress, though only after he had been briefed at length by Ulbricht on the ideological line he was expected to uphold. Münzenberg, though, refused to hold his tongue. Although the official Moscow-prescribed KPD position now pointed to the post-Hitler creation of a euphemistically named "Democratic People's Republic," Münzenberg played to the crowd by closing with the slogan, proscribed by Ulbricht in his briefing, "for a socialist Germany." To let his assault sink in, Münzenberg called in sick on the second day of the conference, on which date (11 April) a copy of his speech from the previous day was published in Bernhard's *Pariser Tageszeitung*, under the none too subtle headline, "Speech by the Leader of the German Communists."[68]

By the usually arcane standards of Communist party in-fighting, Münzenberg's presumptuous headline was fairly blunt, an unambiguous declaration of war on Ulbricht. Münzenberg's "socialist Germany" phrase was only a red herring. His differences with Ulbricht were in truth personal and tactical, not ideological. Münzenberg knew Ulbricht had both ECCI and the KPD Zentrale behind him—for now—but Münzenberg was the one with the contacts to party outsiders in Paris, and on the strength of this asset, he now sought to embarrass and discredit his rival.

In May, Ulbricht moved to Paris so as to keep closer watch over Münzenberg's activities as KPD liaison to the new Parisian Popular Front Committee that was headed, like Lutetia before, by Heinrich Mann. Münzenberg retaliated by making sure neither Mann, Breitscheid, nor his other friends on the committee would cooperate with Ulbricht. He further informed Mann that jealous KPD rivals were herding him out.[69] Mann responded by asking Dimitrov that Münzenberg be reinstated.[70] Breitscheid, meanwhile, ruined every German Popular Front committee meeting he attended in May and June 1937 by reviving old scores from the "social fascism" debacle of the early 1930s. He took particular pleasure in reminding Ulbricht of the Communists' support for the Nazi transport strike in Berlin in 1932—matters he had conspicuously neglected to discuss while Münzenberg had served as KPD liaison to the Lutetia committee. For his part, Münzenberg was content to observe from the sidelines as Ulbricht floundered. He offered his rival neither aid nor advice, and refused to attend further Popular Front committee meetings even after Ulbricht begged him to come back.[71]

Together, Münzenberg and Ulbricht, through their mutual hatred, helped to destroy the German Popular Front before it ever got off the ground. But Münzenberg didn't seem to mind. When rumors of the war inside the KPD

Zentrale began circulating openly in Parisian journalistic circles in July, Münzenberg published a coy statement in Bernhard's *Tageszeitung* that playfully attributed the rumors to the Gestapo and to White Russian gossips who, having given up on overthrowing the Bolsheviks, had nothing better to talk about.[72] Reports of any tension whatsoever between himself and the Comintern, Münzenberg wrote, were "so stupidly and clumsily ... fabricated and so nonsensically put together, that it really is not worth it, to waste a single word on them"—although he had in fact just "wasted" several hundred words refuting them![73]

In fact the political noose was tightening every day around Münzenberg's neck, although this stubborn political survivor still thought he could break its grip by the sheer force of his furious energy. Münzenberg's theatrical quarrel with Ulbricht may, in fact, have been a feint designed to distract his KPD rivals from what (he hoped) would be the real action: a popular movement to oust Hitler from power in Germany, in which Münzenberg himself would lead the charge. The impetus for this rebellion would not come from Ulbricht's floundering German Popular Front initiative, nor would its slogan be "for a socialist Germany," as Münzenberg had deceptively implied in his keynote speech to the German Popular Front congress. Rather, the nucleus of a "Fourth Reich" (the term was Schwarzschild's) would be formed by men with real political experience, ruthless and unprincipled enough to defeat Hitler; by men who, whether Communists or anti-Communists, would be willing to work with Moscow if that was what it would take.

The vehicle Münzenberg chose for his last stand with Stalin was the so-called "German Freedom Party," an intentionally amorphous group of like-minded émigré notables who began sending "German freedom letters" to selected groups inside Hitler's Reich in early 1937. The second letter, penned by Münzenberg's Lutetia colleague, the former Prussian minister of finance, Otto Klepper, and distributed to Berlin correspondents of foreign newspapers in April, alarmed the Nazis enough that Gestapo surveillance teams were assigned to track down Klepper's collaborators in Paris. Klepper's appeal defined the German Freedom Party as a "fraternal league of determined men and women, who share one goal ... to serve Germany ... to fight for freedom."[74]

Klepper didn't name these men and women—it took the Gestapo until late autumn 1937 to determine who most of them were—but Münzenberg knew them all.[75] They included Dr. Karl Spiecker, onetime press chief in Brüning's Cabinet, and Spiecker's Center Party allies Father Muckermann and Monsignor Poels, who were publishing a Catholic opposition journal called *Deutsche Weg* in Holland. Rounding out the Freedom Party team were Münzenberg's close friends Heinrich Mann and Georg Bernhard, whose *Tageszeitung* was its main publicity organ in Paris; Karl Emont, a union organizer with contacts with the underground SOPADE and KPD, and whose house in Eupen, near the Belgian-German frontier, was used for smuggling the letters into the Reich; and Emont's nephew Georg Walter, a Nazi Party member who served as the group's principal informant on conditions inside Germany.[76]

All in all, the Freedom Party collaborators were a motley lot, and it is hard to imagine them holding together if they had ever been given a chance to form a post-Hitler government. Still, the "freedom letters," of which some twenty had made their way into the Reich by fall 1937—smuggled by way of Emont's house, or sent directly to Berlin inside the French embassy's diplomatic bag—were, to all appearances, inspiring a lot of discussion inside Germany. The intensity of the Gestapo surveillance efforts certainly attests to this. The letters had an impressive moral authority, claiming to represent the anti-Hitler consensus of a broad range of German public opinion, spanning "all classes, occupations, religions, and groups," from Catholics and nationalists to Protestants and Social Democrats, and even certain renegade Nazis. All of these groups, the letters proclaimed, desired freedom from Hitler's tyranny, his political persecutions and terror tactics against opposition groups, and wanted to save Germany from the abyss of war, death, and destruction Hitler seemed so bent on opening up.[77]

Although hardly Communist in its message, the Freedom Party was broad enough in its potential appeal to represent, to Münzenberg at least, a much more promising nucleus for seizing power in Germany than the floundering German Popular Front. This belief was what prompted Münzenberg to make an extraordinary appeal in July 1937, over the heads of Ulbricht and Pieck in Prague and Dimitrov at ECCI, to the general secretary of the Communist Party of the Soviet Union himself, Comrade Joseph Stalin. Openly confessing to his fratricidal enmity with Ulbricht, Münzenberg seems to have thought Stalin would take his side in the struggle once he saw how bankrupt the Popular Front had become since Münzenberg had been ousted in April. "Ties . . . which were created over a period of years with German opposition groups and their leaders," he wrote Stalin, "were criminally destroyed [by Ulbricht] and may now be buried forever." Among these leaders, Münzenberg singled out Spiecker, Brüning's former right-hand man who had powerful contacts in the chancellery in Berlin, in the German army, and in the opposition underground in the Reich through the union organizer

Otto Wels. Like an imbecile, Ulbricht had recently denounced Spiecker in the pages of the *Deutsche Volkszeitung* as a "man who works with the Reichswehr"—thus faulting a powerful contact, who had shown himself willing to work with the Communists, on account of the very contacts that made him powerful. Ulbricht had further attacked the German Freedom Party more generally as a "bourgeois" venture worthy only of Communists' contempt.

On the assumption that Stalin, like him, now dreamed of nothing greater than ousting Hitler from power in Germany, Münzenberg repudiated Ulbricht's current policies as inimical to this purpose. He was loath to reveal the names of all of the men he was working with, such as Bernhard, whose loose tongue was still thought ill of at ECCI, and Karl Emont, a former Communist who had broken with Moscow in 1923. Still, Münzenberg was surprisingly effusive in laying out his plans before Stalin. He envisioned a broad, politically eclectic émigré coalition that would work toward seizing power in Germany, open to representatives of all parties and persuasions—excepting, of course, Trotskyists. Somewhat counterintuitively, Münzenberg promised Stalin that if he were put in charge of the KPD, he would step up the war against Trotskyists even while working more openly with party outsiders. He thought, that is, that a truly "Stalinist" political line would focus its venom more intensely on deviant Communists like Ulbricht, while remaining friendly to powerful German émigrés who did not bother even to pretend they were Communists, like Spiecker. If given a chance to make his case personally before Stalin, Münzenberg was sure the Soviet dictator would resolve the dispute with Ulbricht in his own favor. Signing off his letter with a "Bolshevik salute" and a "vigorous handshake," Münzenberg placed his trust in Stalin, and waited for a verdict on his political fate.[78]

The verdict, though slow in coming from Moscow, was not good. Stalin had no intention of ousting Ulbricht, who was nothing if not a loyal Bolshevik—virtually everything the KPD secretary did in Prague and Paris was in response to direct orders from ECCI. Münzenberg, by contrast, even when flattering Stalin's pretensions to political omniscience, had always done so proactively and on his own initiative. Stalin had not asked him for his opinion of Moscow's Popular Front policy in spring 1937, and there is no evidence that he responded to Münzenberg's appeal. Beletskii's harassment in Paris did not cease: Münzenberg was still expected to report to Moscow for questioning.

In both his extraordinary appeal to Stalin and his refusal of the summons to report to Moscow, Münzenberg displayed the same independent streak that had for so long allowed him to flourish, while less imaginative Communists had simply shifted with the ideological wind. Still, there were limits to this independence. It was the time of the Great Terror in Moscow, which was beginning to spread through Europe, as key Comintern "confidence men" and spies were beginning to be hunted down by the NKVD and murdered for what they knew. That summer Ignace Reiss, a Soviet military intelligence officer based in Switzerland, became the highest-ranking defector from Moscow when he published a letter calling Stalin a "traitor" to the Revolution. His corpse was found riddled with bullets in Lausanne in September. Walter Krivitsky, the Soviet military attaché in Switzerland who was initially ordered to liquidate Reiss, sought asylum in Paris in November after declining the assignment, and sailed for New York in December.[79] Because of his contacts with the French government, Münzenberg could easily have broken with the party like Krivitsky, and told his story to the world. In summer 1937 a number of "bourgeois" journalists, mostly French, approached Münzenberg, dying to hear the inside scoop on the shakeout in the KPD. But he remained silent.[80]

Though he refused to meet with Ulbricht and other KPD representatives in Paris, Münzenberg held out the hope that Dimitrov, at least, would still lobby Stalin on his behalf. When he received another summons from Dimitrov himself in late September, Münzenberg responded with a telegram in which, for the first time in years, he began waving the "bloody shirt," reminding Dimitrov that he had served with Lenin since 1915 and remained "loyal" to the Bolsheviks for two decades.[81] When Dimitrov refused to back down, Münzenberg played the Lenin card more and more brazenly, dispatching a flood of letters over fall and winter, each one longer than the last, in which he endlessly repeated homilies about his "collaboration with Lenin during the war." No one in Moscow should forget that Münzenberg was "of all German Communists and earlier Socialists the first who hooked up with Lenin in winter 1914–1915."[82] Münzenberg even brought out a new edition of his memoir *Dritte Front* through Editions du Carrefour, the ads for which promised exciting insider details of Lenin and the Zimmerwald Left in Switzerland.[83]

When this did not work, Münzenberg smeared Ulbricht with a rash of trumped-up accusations involving his "sectarian" policies dating all the way back to the Heinrich Brandler and Ruth Fischer eras of the early and mid-1920s and the "social fascism" electoral disasters of 1930–32. He even accused Ulbricht of illegal "mail theft" (of several of Münzenberg's letters to Moscow), and filed formal "party complaint" *(Parteiverfahren)* against Ulbricht with the KPD Zentrale for slander.[84]

With all his usual bravado, Münzenberg continued insisting he was the sole leader of the KPD, answerable only to the Kremlin. In one breathless dispatch, he demanded Dimitrov grant him a long paid vacation from his party duties (which he had neglected to fulfill for months!) so he could have time to write two more agitprop masterpieces on Hitler.[85] He categorically declined to see any KPD or ECCI leaders—unless they would come to Paris and meet him on his terms.[86] Although Münzenberg's final expulsion from the Zentrale was a foregone conclusion, his defiant attitude was only galvanized further by the molasses-like pace of the party proceedings against him. So timid were Ulbricht and Pieck that even after the Zentrale finally, officially, and belatedly resolved to expel Münzenberg on 14 May 1938, it took them another week to muster up the courage to announce this in public —and they left even this apparently final expulsion conditional on a future resolution by ECCI![87]

Thus Münzenberg, contrary to popular legend, never did "break" with Moscow.[88] Months after his expulsion, he was still arguing with Pieck, Ulbricht, Dimitrov, et al. in favor of his reinstatement as the true leader of the KPD, as if nothing had happened.[89] Münzenberg had evidently been in the party too long to imagine any other political orientation. Since 1917, he had faithfully served his friend Lenin's Russian Revolution with every last fiber in his body; but Lenin's heir, Stalin, had decided that the Revolution no longer required Münzenberg's service. It was a bitter blow, and if Münzenberg had to take the fall, he was going to go down swinging.

CHAPTER 16 *A Paris Exile*

As war clouds gathered over Europe in 1938, Münzenberg entered a strange political twilight, where the boundaries between loyalty and disloyalty, truth and falsehood, friends and enemies, were nebulous and ill defined. Although the KPD renegade had no illusions about Hitler's plans for a war of conquest—made increasingly plain over the course of the year through the Austrian Anschluss in March and the abject Munich agreement of September—Münzenberg no longer knew on whom he could rely politically to oppose Hitler's advance. Although he had given up on Ulbricht, Münzenberg still thought Dimitrov and Stalin would come around to his point of view and build a true anti-Hitler coalition for seizing power in Germany. And he still wanted this coalition to be led by Communists. After receiving what he considered to be a surprisingly friendly letter from Dimitrov in early June, Münzenberg eagerly wrote the ECCI secretary a long declaration of his continued loyalty, in which he claimed to have asserted himself "against Trotsky and for Stalin" at every critical historical juncture, not simply in *Our Time* but in "all my political activities."[1] "I am ready," he further wrote Pieck in late August, "to do everything that will help normalize relations and painstakingly fulfill the duties of a party member."[2]

Although he knew his life was in mortal danger due to NKVD surveillance of his movements, Münzenberg steadfastly refused to break his ties to Moscow in 1938. At one point in July he even sent a telegram to ECCI, indicating that he was ready to travel to Russia "at once," so long as he would be allowed to return to Paris by the end of the month.[3] This was clearly a bluff. As always, Münzenberg had a series of ready-made excuses to explain his continued refusal to report to Moscow. He outlined a number of these in a letter sent directly to Dimitrov on 30 August, objecting to the manner in which he had been excluded from the KPD Zentrale, which stood "in flagrant violation with the statutory rules of the KPD and the Communist

International." If Münzenberg were reinstated, then this would be the first step in the restoration of the KPD as a truly "Communist and Leninist" party. This time he appealed over the head of even Lenin and Stalin, citing as an authority to justify his restoration to good standing no less than Karl Marx. A real proletarian revolution, he argued, could only be led by "living men animated by faith in the justice of their ideas"—by men like himself, that is, instead of by bland automatons like Ulbricht. The goal must be not merely to oppose Hitler in doctrine, but to pursue "a real and concrete political program [aiming at] the seizure of power."[4]

Such hopes for a change in Moscow's policy were optimistic, to say the least, in autumn 1938. For Stalin, the Munich conference, from which the Soviet Union had been excluded, was proof of Western impotence against Hitler. Both the French and German Popular Fronts were in shambles, and even Stalin's relatively successful promotion of the Spanish Republican cause, which had inspired legions of political volunteers and idealistic adventure-seekers from America, England, France, and elsewhere to join the battle against Franco, was now marred by brutal sectarian violence that was disillusioning almost everyone. George Orwell's *Homage to Catalonia*, published earlier in 1938, exposed to the world for the first time the harrowing infighting on the Republican side, which by the end of 1937 had seen the Communists, aided by NKVD thugs, bloodily suppress the various anarchist and "Trotskyist" factions and unions on the left who threatened Stalin's control over the Republican government.[5] The signs were loud and clear for anyone who wanted to read them. Moscow no longer had any intention of backing a serious, popular "antifascist" coalition, in Germany or anywhere else.

Fitfully, reluctantly, and with bitter disappointment, Münzenberg seems to have gotten the message at last by early fall. While still hesitating to break with the Comintern openly, he began calling on non-Communist friends and colleagues for editorial and financial support for a new publishing venture, a weekly political broadsheet that he optimistically styled *Die Zukunft* (The Future). According to Babette Gross, the funds required to launch *The Future* came principally from Olof Aschberg, a wealthy Swedish banker and Communist sympathizer whom Münzenberg had first met at the Stockholm Youth Socialist Congress of 1917. Aschberg, born in Stockholm of Russian Jewish parents, had been one of the main conduits in the early years after 1917 in circumventing the international boycott on looted Bolshevik gold, which he sold on the Stockholm market after having the ingots melted down and given new markings. Münzenberg and Aschberg furthered their acquaintance in the 1920s, when Aschberg's Berlin-based Guarantee and Credit

A Paris Exile 297

Bank for the East handled repayment of the IAH workers' loan, although as we have seen, the cash came from Soviet government banks. Aschberg had moved to Paris even before the Nazis had taken power in Germany, and throughout the 1930s Münzenberg and Gross were regularly invited to his townhouse on the place Casimir-Périer. With Aschberg's help, Münzenberg hired an obscure printing house, Editions Sebastien Brant, located on boulevard Haussmann, with which neither he nor any other Communists had prior ties. Münzenberg's old *Brown Book* collaborator Arthur Koestler agreed to edit *The Future*, and on 12 October, the first issue rolled off the presses.[6]

Münzenberg's editorial reunion with Koestler uncannily illustrated his continued ambivalence about communism. Koestler himself had only recently arrived back in Paris, by way of London, after a dramatic ordeal in Spain, where he had been arrested by Franco while serving the Comintern apparat under cover as a reporter for the English *News Chronicle*. Although Moscow had almost certainly orchestrated the publicity campaign in England that ultimately convinced Franco to release him, Koestler was not in a grateful mood. He had witnessed, at first hand, the same Communist treachery in Catalonia that had so disturbed Orwell. Disillusioned by the purges in which Communists were required to publicly denounce former comrades "in the most violent way possible," Koestler had resigned his KPD membership. He did so in a private letter, however, and eerily echoed Münzenberg's own attempt to have it both ways by ending with a declaration of loyalty to the USSR. "Whoever goes against the Soviet Union," Koestler wrote in an intriguing formulation that hinted at the conflicted sentiments that might guide his editorship of the new publication, "goes against the future."[7]

The Future was one of Münzenberg's most ambitious publishing ventures ever—the periodical equivalent of *Propaganda as a Weapon*, which aimed to reach beyond the fellow-traveling audience to the broadest possible cross section of the German émigré Left. And yet, as with *Propaganda as a Weapon*, its coherence suffered from Münzenberg's political confusion, his inability to extricate himself fully from Communist ideology. For one thing, he was reluctant to sign on to the venture openly, whether through fear of police harassment (or detection by the Gestapo or the NKVD) or because he didn't want to taint *The Future* as Communist by associating himself with it.[8] All kinds of illustrious names were optimistically plastered on the cover of the inaugural issue as future contributors, including even Thomas Mann, who had shown no prior interest in Münzenberg's committees, but there was no masthead. Münzenberg did contribute a long article to the first issue, in which he vaguely argued for Socialist-Communist cooperation in the struggle against Hitler, but he mentioned none of his KPD rivals by name. There wasn't any kind of discernible mission statement, other than the injunction that "there should be no German group in exile, no German colony, no union of German-speaking individuals in any country, that does not read *The Future* and help to promote it."

Nor was there much of a financial plan. Advertising placements in *The Future* scarcely filled a third of a page in most twelve-page issues, of which tiny space fully half was usually taken up by in-house ads for other periodicals and books put out by Editions Sebastien Brant. Judging by this poor advertising volume, Münzenberg did not win over many loyal readers. He had trouble finding copy too, as illustrated by his devoting much of the first several issues to excerpts of novels by friends such as Kurt Kersten and Lion Feuchtwanger. The most substantial stories were generally concerned with Hitler's war plans, but even these sometimes missed the mark badly, such as a 28 October 1938 cover feature predicting that the Wehrmacht would use Czechoslovakia as a springboard for a spring push through Rumania into the Soviet Union.[9]

Still, *The Future* attracted some notice as an alternative German émigré voice in Paris to the Communist *Deutsche Volkszeitung* and Schwarzschild's "bourgeois" *Tagebuch;* the *Tageszeitung,* for its part, was still reeling from the court battle between Bernhard and Poliakov. Thomas Mann did contribute a short article, as promised, in late November, and his piece was flanked by another impressive celebrity coup, an essay by Sigmund Freud on anti-Semitism. Neither published further pieces in Münzenberg's weekly, but before long some of Koestler's progressive English writer friends, such as H. G. Wells, contributed their literary prestige to the venture. An offer of free delivery to willing subscribers paid some dividends as well, as a number of German émigrés from as far away as Los Angeles and even Colombia, signed up for this service. (Remarkably, one subscriber from Orlando, Florida, even offered to pay for his subscription.) And *The Future* sometimes delivered impressive reportage on developments inside Germany, as in a January 1939 cover graphic that outlined the growing nexus of concentration camps inside Hitler's Reich.[10]

There was something awfully half-hearted, however, about a political newsweekly without a real masthead. In every sense, Münzenberg was still in hiding politically over the winter of 1938–39, afraid to come out against Stalin, afraid even to criticize Ulbricht and Pieck in print. Although *The Future* was clearly under Münzenberg's control, he seems to have covered his tracks very well. The Gestapo, for example, which erroneously believed

The Future to be the official organ of the German Freedom Party and did not doubt that Münzenberg was behind it, was unable to obtain any documentary confirmation of this.[11] In a special January 1939 appeal for funds to the "friends and readers" of *The Future* which listed the journal's illustrious contributors, Münzenberg's name was buried among about seventy others.[12] Münzenberg wasn't involved in the day-to-day editing of *The Future*, which the Catholic journalist Werner Thormann took over as soon as Koestler left to write *Darkness at Noon*. It is unlikely that Münzenberg visited the Editions Sebastien Brant offices regularly. But informed observers suspected Münzenberg's control of this publisher no less surely than his control of *The Future*. ECCI even cited the Brant house's publication of a book by a known "Trotskyist" in its resolution, which officially expelled Münzenberg from the KPD.[13]

Something had to give in this treacherous game of political cat and mouse between Münzenberg and his enemies in Moscow. ECCI's official expulsion of Münzenberg from the KPD, handed down on 16 February 1939 and communicated to Paris soon thereafter, did the trick.[14] Münzenberg, to be sure, had almost certainly been preparing for months a statement outlining his differences with Moscow. Significantly, though, he did not publish this declaration until after he was expelled from the party—until, that is, there was no longer any hope for a reconciliation. There was an air of sadness about Münzenberg's KPD demission statement, which he sent personally to Pieck shortly before publishing it in *The Future* of 10 March 1939. Citing the principle of working-class unity laid down at the Seventh Comintern Congress in 1935, Münzenberg expressed his dismay that the KPD leadership seemed to have abandoned this goal. Far from disowning Communism or the necessity of a "proletarian revolution," Münzenberg claimed the mantle of Lenin in calling for enhanced revolutionary discipline among the workers—which was only possible if they were "convinced of the righteousness of the political, strategic, and tactical course of their leadership." Since 1906, Münzenberg's ideological conception of the "revolutionary movement" had remained unaltered. It was only the current (unnamed) KPD leadership that had altered its course. Thus Münzenberg now "parted with these leaders and their apparat," but not from the "thousands with whom I have struggled since 1906, first in the Socialist and then in the Communist movement." And, like Koestler, he did not come out against either Stalin or the Soviet Union, which he still viewed as "the first country where Socialism has been constructed." "I hold to the place," Münzenberg concluded defiantly, "that I have taken since 1906 at the side of Karl Liebknecht, . . .

Rosa Luxemburg, Clara Zetkin, and ... Lenin ... in the ranks of struggle of revolutionary Socialism."[15]

Although he had stopped short of attacking his enemies by name, Münzenberg's ideological war cry finally let loose the floodgates in the KPD Zentrale. That spring, the *Deutsche Volkszeitung* assaulted Münzenberg with relish, surrounding his name with all kinds of foul allegations, of which the most sinister was the imputation that his *Future* had turned into an organ of the Russian emigration. That Münzenberg took these accusations personally is abundantly clear; at one point in June he distributed a three-page letter to dozens of his friends and colleagues in which he denied them at length. The breathless tone of indignation in this letter is revealing: although no longer a Communist, Münzenberg still believed himself to be a revolutionary, and could not stomach the allegation that he had turned into a "White" reactionary. "I believe that everything must be done," he wrote, "to restore the old ideals of proletarian morality and honor in the international revolutionary workers' movement." And no "insolent provocations," slanders, or lies were going to prevent Münzenberg from using all of his powers to form a truly "independent German revolutionary workers' party."[16]

Münzenberg had taken the first steps in this direction in April, when he organized an exploratory meeting in an office building on the rue Sarpente aiming at the foundation of a new "German Socialist Unity" party. The initial turnout—about twenty-five or thirty Münzenberg loyalists, mainly consisting of *The Future* staffers, plus Koestler, a few ex-Communists, and one delegate from the splinter "German Workers' Party"—was not terribly impressive. The gathering did attract the notice of the Gestapo, but then it was not hard for German émigrés to do this in 1939 Paris.[17] By June, another sixty or seventy shipwrecked German leftists from such ephemeral groupings as Dr. Karl Frank's "Neues Beginnen" had climbed on board Münzenberg's new committee, now styled, in the old IAH mode, the "Friends of Socialist Unity." Possibly they were attracted by the catering provided in Olof Aschberg's elegant Left Bank townhouse, where the second meeting was held. The tentative nature of this organization was underlined by Münzenberg himself at the gathering, when he explained to the hundred or so curious guests that his goal was to create a "revolutionary socialist workers' party" that would be strong enough to inspire the Communists to negotiate terms of an alliance, ostensibly so Münzenberg could win Moscow over to his views.[18]

Since neither the KPD nor SOPADE had, as yet, made any effort to approach Münzenberg's new group, let alone send delegates to his meetings, such a scenario was more than a bit fanciful.[19] In the absence of serious political prospects for the Friends of Socialist Unity, Aschberg's townhouse was gradually transformed into a kind of all-purpose Münzenberg salon, with an ever-revolving guest list whose composition depended on the cause being hawked that night. At one celebrity function, attended mainly by exiled German aristocrats and French parliamentary deputies, guests celebrated the life and work of the Weimar poets Walter Mehring and Kurt von Tucholsky.[20] A more explicitly political, yet still nonpartisan gathering saw Otto Klepper invited to speak on behalf of the German Freedom Party on the theme "the future Germany and the European question."[21] At the most reliably left-leaning salon, Münzenberg distributed a pamphlet promoting his idea for an "independent revolutionary workers' party" which closed with a somewhat timid attack on SOPADE and the KPD (the parties, and their leaders, remained curiously unnamed): "Enough of the sabotage of unity! Enough of the Popular Front maneuvers, which only delay true and honest unity! Long live the great, strong, active German Unity Party!" Münzenberg's party did not, optimistic sloganeering withstanding, live long. By August 1939 it had already died a quiet death, unmourned except, perhaps, by the Gestapo agents who were no longer able to spy on its meetings.[22]

The very ease with which Münzenberg made new friends of all political stripes prevented him from organizing any kind of coherent new political movement. The Left Bank townhouse Münzenberg was using for his salons, under surveillance by the Gestapo as the presumed headquarters of the German Freedom Party and the Friends of Socialist Unity, was also watched by the right-leaning Paris police department, which suspected it of harboring a defeatist front Münzenberg had organized, known as the "French-German Union." The Paris police were not off the mark, either: on 30 June 1939, *The Future* openly announced itself as the organ of this pacifist union, which if we are to believe Münzenberg's "adherents list" counted as members over a hundred French notables, mostly professors and parliamentary deputies, along with German émigré heavyweights such as Otto Klepper.[23] On the other hand, the French police spies went a bit overboard in their speculation about the nature of this front, suspecting Münzenberg might have been turned into a Nazi agent by Else Kantrowitsch, the mistress of the German ambassador in Paris, with whom Münzenberg was known to be having an affair.[24]

Most of this political confusion was cleared up by the Molotov-Ribbentrop pact of 23 August 1939, which, by giving Hitler permission to invade Poland without Russian interference, plunged Europe into war and forced just about everybody to take sides, even though the secret protocols allowing Stalin a free hand in eastern Europe were not yet revealed to the world. For the first time, Münzenberg may have been glad to have been ejected from the KPD: for while Communists all over Europe were tripping over themselves to come up with plausible ideological justifications for Stalin's cynical deal with Hitler, Münzenberg was able to denounce the treaty freely and openly as a betrayal of Socialism. After the Red Army crossed into Poland on 17 September to claim the Soviet Union's share of the spoils, Münzenberg at last summoned the courage to call Stalin himself a "traitor" to the Revolution. "Socialist Russia is no more," he proclaimed with disgust. Rather there was now only "a Russia, which has announced its imperialist ambitions with fire and sword."[25]

This declaration of political independence must have been far more exhilarating—and terrifying—than the one Münzenberg had made in March. For the first time, he had come out openly against Stalin. No longer would Münzenberg hide behind a mask of anonymity. After the Russian invasion of Poland, he plastered his own name all over *The Future*, writing his own copy and putting it on the cover. His headlines now sang the glory of "German Freedom in the Struggle against Hitler and Stalin," and invited Germans all over the world to join him in staging a "People's Revolution against Hitler."[26]

If the advent of war allowed Münzenberg to speak at last with moral authority and consistency, however, he lost the last remnants of his ever-dwindling audience in the process. It is one of the saddest of ironies in the career of this inveterate propagandist that when he finally stood on his own two feet, publishing his own principled views under his own name, he lost at once his collaborators, his paying advertisers, and most of his readers. After September 1939, *The Future* was barely able to fill eight pages worth of copy a week, and not a single ad graced the paper for months. This sorry situation was not exactly Münzenberg's fault, of course. His readers, like his editorial co-workers and his advertisers, were almost all German nationals, who, after France had declared war on Hitler in early September, were progressively rounded up by the French government and sent to internment camps. Whatever Münzenberg wrote in the pages of *The Future* would not bring back the audience he had lost due to the exigencies of war.

Still, there was a kind of poetic justice to Münzenberg's predicament. Once again he was able to escape the personal risks faced by many of his colleagues and co-workers, although this time by a mere accident of fate. On 14 August 1939, less than three weeks before the war began, Münzenberg had turned fifty—the exact age of exemption set by the French government for the first round of internments. To his credit, Münzenberg did send a dossier outlining the antifascist, anti-Stalinist mission of *The Future* to the

French Interior Ministry in October 1939, accompanied by a letter arguing for the release of some of his editorial collaborators. One suspects, however, that Münzenberg may have been more keen to preserve his own freedom. "I would be elated," he concluded this plea, "to be allowed to continue my political activities which serve the liberation of the German people, the cause of France, and humanity in its entirety."[27]

Whether or not the French government believed that *The Future* served "the cause of France," Münzenberg was allowed to continue publishing it through the winter, through the whole interminable *drôle de guerre* which saw the Western Allies dither while Hitler prepared his further conquests.[28] This privilege to publish his views was surely a great emotional salve in a difficult time for Münzenberg, who had never before spoken with such consistent moral courage. He minced no words, for example, in holding Stalin to account for his invasion of Finland and the Baltics, and even published the names of forty German Communists murdered in the Great Terror.[29] But the only readers paying the slightest attention anymore were the NKVD, the Gestapo, and the French police.[30]

With the Soviet Union actively collaborating with Hitler in dismembering Europe, the time for a clean break with Münzenberg's Communist past had arrived. He was in a position to furnish France and Britain with information about the Comintern apparat in Europe, from names of agents to addresses of safe houses, weapons depots, and the like. In fact, Münzenberg was approached repeatedly during the first winter of the war by figures such as Paul Willert, an elegant young English diplomat, fluent in both French and German, who debriefed prominent German refugees from Hitler's Reich in Paris for British counterintelligence. According to Willert's later recollection, Münzenberg was so sought after by young Allied spies that he began holding an informal salon for them in the back room of a Left Bank restaurant, a location meant to frustrate the Gestapo agents who had staked out Aschberg's townhouse.[31] Was Münzenberg feeling out the Western intelligence apparatus, possibly to locate NKVD plants inside it who might be trying to entrap him? Was he seeking to protect himself from Stalin's assassins by making powerful new friends? Was he planning a true defection to the democratic camp, a renunciation of his lifelong revolutionary principles to serve the greater cause of the Western anti-Hitler coalition? Or was he simply playing for time?

With an NKVD death sentence almost certainly hanging over his head, and the Western intelligence services riddled with Soviet informers, we can hardly blame Münzenberg for stalling in revealing what he knew about the most sensitive secrets of the Communist International (if he indeed wanted to). But with a war on, time was not on his side. When the Wehrmacht invaded France on 10 May 1940, and the remaining German nationals at large were ordered to report to internment camps immediately, there was no one left to save Münzenberg. After parting with Gross at the Stade de Colombes in Paris (where men and women were separated before being interned elsewhere in France), Münzenberg was packed off to a camp at Chambaran, near Lyons, on the grounds of a former French artillery training center.[32]

Characteristically, Münzenberg was able to ingratiate himself with his superiors at Chambaran, obtaining a pleasant job tending the garden of the camp commandant while most of the detainees were sent to work in the forests. Just as in Switzerland during the last war, this German political exile whiled away his prison time in relative comfort, with his fate depending ultimately on the success or failure of the German army. This time, unfortunately for Münzenberg, the Germans won. At 3 A.M. on 20 June 1940, the Chambaran camp was evacuated. Münzenberg fled southward in the direction of the Swiss border in a small group that included his *Brown Book* collaborator Hans Siemsen, and a former SPD trade union official, Valentin Hartig. They were joined shortly by a mysterious comrade unknown to the others, probably an obscure German Communist named Heinz Hirth. Hirth may have been acting as an informant for the NKVD.[33] Münzenberg disappeared several days later, somewhere between Lyons and Grenoble.

On 22 October 1940, in the hush of late autumn, after the furious battle of France had given way to a strangely quiescent peace of German occupation, two hunters and their dogs were making their way through the woods just to the north of the French town of Montaigne, in the Vichy or unoccupied zone of southern France, not far from Grenoble. It was the dogs that first noticed the stench of human remains near the foot of an old oak. Although the corpse was propped upright on its knees, its limbs and torso were so buried by leaves and other debris that the hunters noticed it only after nearly stumbling over it. The sight was gruesome. So far gone was the body that the head, left exposed to buzzards along with the rain and wind, had been stripped to the bone. Around the skull was a knotted cord, which had apparently snapped quite soon after the body had been suspended from an overhanging branch.

When the hunters returned to the death scene with the mayor and the town coroner, they found papers on the body that provided clues to its identity. Among them were Münzenberg's special refugee visa, granted by the Chautemps government back in 1933; membership cards from several German cultural organizations with offices in Paris; a postcard from Babette Gross, sent to Münzenberg at the Chambaran camp; and several stamped certificates that appeared to repudiate Münzenberg's German citizenship. None of the men had any idea who this man was or why he had been hanged, and they were not terribly keen on finding out. If these Vichy officials even entertained the possibility of a homicide involving a prominent German political refugee who seemed intent on denying his nationality, it might invite interference from the dreaded Gestapo. A suicide ruling was clearly the path of least resistance, even though no suicide note had been found. The pathologist reported Münzenberg's death to have been self-inflicted by hanging, sometime in late June 1940, the rather circular explanation being that the corpse had been found with a noose around its neck. Suspiciously, no technical details were provided on the strength of the rope, or even about the rupture of cervical vertebrae one would expect from a hanging.[34]

The frustratingly uninformative coroner's report on the death of Willi Münzenberg gave birth to one of the great mysteries of twentieth-century politics. The suicide explanation is unsatisfying, first of all, because of what nearly everyone who knew him noted—Münzenberg's incredible will to live. Although his physical health was often poor, there is simply no evidence of a depressive strain in the character of this energetic, indefatigable man anywhere in the fifty full years of his life. Hartig, Siemsen, and all the other eyewitnesses who saw Münzenberg in his last days at Chambaran and in the first days of his flight spoke unanimously of his high spirits.

If not by suicide, then surely the life of this inveterate political conspirator might have been itself taken by some sort of political conspiracy? Münzenberg had, of course, been shadowed for years by the NKVD and Gestapo alike, not to mention the French government, which had imprisoned him only weeks before his death. But the French secret services had much more important things to worry about in June 1940, when the Wehrmacht was dismembering their country. Hitler? He would have wanted Münzenberg alive, to extract information from him on the European Communist underground. Stalin, by contrast, clearly had cause, and probably the means, to eliminate Münzenberg.[35] If Stalin's tentacles reached as far as Mexico—where Trotsky was assassinated amidst the fog of world war in summer 1940—then surely the NKVD could get to Münzenberg in southern France. And Stalin, suspicious of any Communist whose position in the movement, like Trotsky's, traced to Lenin instead of himself, had already eliminated all of Münzenberg's oldest friends from the Zimmerwald days—Radek, Zinoviev, and Fritz Platten.[36]

At the least, we may conclude that whether or not Stalin's agents succeeded in murdering Münzenberg on the exodus road in France in 1940, they undoubtedly wanted to, and they would have gotten to him sooner or later. Even if Münzenberg had defected to serve the Western democracies during the war, there is no guarantee he would have found true safe haven. Walter Krivitsky, for example, the highest-ranking defector of the Great Terror period, who sought the protection of the U.S. government and even testified before Congress, outlived Münzenberg by only eight months. His violent death by gunshot wound, like Münzenberg's by hanging, was ruled a suicide, though few close to either man believed this explanation.[37] Having latched so passionately onto the Bolshevik cause, Münzenberg was unable to sever the many cords that now linked his own fate with Bolshevism. Though no longer in the KPD, Willi Münzenberg died as he lived, a Communist to the core. He was, in the end, a victim of the same ruthless revolutionary energy that had given meaning to his life.

Willi Münzenberg was more than a victim, of course—he was also a perpetrator of some of the most colossal lies of the modern age. In our postcommunist era it is no longer shocking news that the greatest political ideals often give birth to the most heinous political crimes, but we must never let our increasing familiarity with manmade horrors dull our capacity for judging them. Viewed on its own terms, Münzenberg's use of Bolshevik blood money to whitewash Communist tyranny in Western public opinion is probably only in the second tier of crimes against humanity and common decency. Münzenberg was not the only Social Democrat to make a pact with the Bolshevik devil between the two world wars, nor the only Communist responsible for dividing the German Left so fatally before Hitler's onslaught. Still, his singular position as the senior Bolshevik "confidence man" in the West from Lenin's inner circle at Zimmerwald; his exceptionally easy access to Moscow gold; and his uniquely reckless unaccountability to either his own party colleagues or the working-class patrons he supposedly spoke for— such factors gave Münzenberg a special responsibility for the tragedy of socialism between the world wars. By shilling so shamelessly for Moscow, Münzenberg gave endless ammunition to his propaganda counterparts on the right, who matched him lie for lie, smear for smear, fatally poisoning the well of European politics. The historical halo the Communists wore for so long as "Hitler's first victims" must be torn off at last. Had Münzenberg himself come to power in Germany, there is no telling how much blood of "bourgeois class enemies" would have been on his hands.

It is hardly an accident that the kinds of fronts Münzenberg invented

—redundant, self-replicating cultural committees, innocuous-sounding political newspapers financed by distant paymasters, and above all, phony charities—are now exploited by the world's most formidable terrorist organizations. Nor is it a coincidence that today's masterminds of suicide bombings cloak their operations in the two most successful "progressive" propaganda themes Münzenberg pioneered in the 1920s, anti-imperialism and antifascism. In the same way the Communist International, arguably the greatest terrorist conspiracy of the last century, sought to destroy Western "bourgeois" society by infiltrating its institutions from within and playing brilliantly on its own tendency to self-criticism, so now twenty-first century Islamic terrorists exploit the very openness of our society to move money, men, and munitions across borders, and use our own technology to kill us.

We must be careful not to lose our ability to be shocked by conspiracies to commit mass murder, no matter how commonplace their increasing frequency seems to make them. Hitler made explicitly racial genocide, at least, taboo. If terrorists cloak their crimes in some sort of left-leaning political doctrine, however—whether "antifascist" or "antiracist" or "anti–colonialist occupation"—even the most proudly maniacal tyrants will still find liberal journalists to apologize for them. As Münzenberg so brilliantly grasped, fellow travelers will always be found to endorse the most violent means employed for political ends, so long as those ends are seen as furthering the dialectic of human "progress."

Like so many other Communists in their contempt for individual human beings and stubbornly modest human aspirations, Willi Münzenberg helped unleash a plague of moral blindness upon the world from which we have still not recovered. His example should remind us that the great lies no less than the great crimes of history are conceived by flesh-and-blood men, who, in their bottomless contempt for the truth, enable evil to flourish in front of our eyes. In Münzenberg's ghastly death there is a kind of justice, although for the millions of victims of communism, there will never be justice enough.

NOTES

The following source abbreviations are used in the notes.

AIZ	*Arbeiter Illustrierte Zeitung*
AN	Archives Nationales, Paris
BB	Schweizerisches Bundesarchiv, Bern
DBB	Deutsches Bundesarchiv, Berlin Lichterfelde
IISH	International Institute for Social History, Amsterdam
NA	National Archives, Washington, D.C.
RGALI	Russian Government Archive of Literature and Art, Moscow. Cited as RGALI.fond-opis-del', list
RGASPI	Russian Government Archive of Social-Political History, Moscow. Cited as RGASPI.fond-opis-del', list
SS	Schweizerisches Sozialarchiv, Zurich
TsKhIDK	Center for Preservation of Historico-Documentary Collections, Moscow. Also known as the "Osoby" archive of documents captured from the Germans in World War II. Cited as TsKhIDK.fond.opis.del', list

INTRODUCTION

1. The most important files on Münzenberg's activities are in Moscow at the Russian Government Archive of Social-Political History (RGASPI, formerly RTsKhiIDNI) on ulitsa Bolshaia Dimitrovka. Some of the relevant material in the general Comintern archive (fond 495) remains closed, but the voluminous files of Münzenberg's organizational clearinghouse, the International Worker Relief (fond 538) have been open since the early 1990s. Gestapo files on Münzenberg can also be found in Moscow, in the so-called *Osoby* or "special" archive of materials taken back to Russia by the Red Army after World War II. A limited number of captured Gestapo files are also available at the Hoover Institution in Stanford, California. Some of the captured records of the German Communist Party, long housed in the "Osoby," have been repatriated to Germany, where they accompany scattered Communist files from the former East German Institut für Marxismus-Leninismus, now located at the Bundesarchiv at the former American army base in Lichterfelde. There are also archival materials on Münzenberg from army and police intelligence in Bern, Paris, and Washington.

But many crucial documents have disappeared. After Münzenberg's arrest in Zurich in November 1917, many of his early letters, to Karl Radek, Lenin, Zinoviev, and others, were lost (although some materials were preserved by Münzenberg's Young Socialist colleague Edi Meyer, who deposited them in the Schweizerisches Sozialarchiv in Zurich). Similarly, most of Münzenberg's correspondence from his Berlin years was seized by the Nazis after the Reichstag fire in 1933, and most of the material from his Paris years, 1933–40, was taken by the Gestapo in 1940.

2. Alfred Hugenberg was a wealthy right-wing media mogul who controlled a chain of successful newspapers in Weimar Germany, of which the most successful was the *Berliner Lokalanzeiger.*

3. The most popular source text remains Babette Gross's informative, yet often inaccurate, memoir of her husband's career, *Willi Münzenberg: Eine politische Biographie* (Stuttgart: Deutsche Verlags-Anstalt, 1967). Recent literature on Münzenberg usually follows Gross in emphasizing Münzenberg's vaunted "antifascism," trying to rehabilitate him as a Third Way *(Dritte Weg)* socialist who has something to teach modern liberals and social democrats. See, for example, Harald Wessel's *Münzenbergs Ende* (Berlin: Dietz, 1991), or the 1992 Aix-en-Provence conference volume *Willi Münzenberg (1889–1940): Ein deutscher Kommunist im Spannungsfeld zwischen Stalinismus und Antifaschismus,* ed. Tania Schlie and Simon Roche (Frankfurt-am-Main: Peter Lang, 1995).

The most significant critical appraisal of Münzenberg to date is Stephan Koch's *Double Lives: Spies and Writers in the Secret Soviet War of Ideas against the West* (New York: Free Press, 1994). Koch's book, though sharply written and quite readable, is ultimately a careless polemic. None of Koch's often dramatic claims, unfortunately, are backed up with solid evidence. Amazingly, the research assistant Koch hired to do his work for him in Moscow missed the Münzenberg files in fond 538 entirely. The impression of Münzenberg in Koch's book is of a cold-hearted, cynical communist "tycoon"—he is "Stalin's willing tool." In fact, I will demonstrate, Münzenberg believed quite sincerely in the snake oil he was selling, and would not have been successful in keeping the money flowing if he hadn't—his grasp on Moscow's purse strings was in fact always precarious, and demanded constant flattery on his part to retain the Kremlin's favor over many rival Communist propagandists who resented and despised him.

4. The myth of Münzenberg's "financial genius," which originates both from self-serving propaganda and from the testimonials of co-workers such as Babette Gross and Arthur Koestler, seems to be unshakable. Relying largely on Koestler's vague say-so, David Caute once famously wrote that Münzenberg "demonstrated that if communism could not smash capitalism in an afternoon, it could at least make money while it was trying." Caute, *The Fellow Travellers: A Postscript to the Enlightenment* (New York: Macmillan, 1973), 57.

5. In this vein, see especially Koch, *Double Lives.*

6. See Edward J. Epstein's recent biography *Dossier: The Secret History of Armand Hammer* (New York: Random House, 1996).

CHAPTER 1. *Erfurt*

1. "Abschrift des Lebenslaufs von Wilhelm Münzenberg," unpublished autobiographical ms in BB, E 21 11326, 1–11.

2. Münzenberg, "Lebenslauf," 13. In his wife Babette Gross's often unreliable biography, this episode has been altered somewhat, so that his father's rage stems from Willi's failure, one day, to clean the oil lamps in the inn his father ran. It is certainly possible that the lashing incident occurred in the context of Willi's household chores, instead of while

he was practicing the piano. It seems more likely, however, that Willi made up the bit about cleaning the lamps when he related the story to fellow communists (like his wife) because it sounded more "proletarian" than a bourgeois melodrama about piano practice. In his wife's biography, there is no mention of piano lessons. Gross, *Willi Münzenberg: A Political Biography,* trans. Marian Jackson (East Lansing: Michigan State University Press, 1974), 10. Unless otherwise indicated, further references to Gross, *Willi Münzenberg,* are to this translation.

3. Münzenberg, "Lebenslauf," 6–18.

4. Willi left this embarrassingly romantic episode out of his autobiography. We know of it thanks only to his wife, who gave it a typically ideological treatment: it illustrated Münzenberg's lifelong "urge to translate theory into practice." Gross, *Willi Münzenberg,* 11.

5. Münzenberg, "Lebenslauf," 18–23, 26.

6. On the SPD's dominant role in upholding Marxist orthodoxy in European socialism see James Joll, *The Second International 1889–1914* (London: Weidenfeld & Nicolson, 1955).

7. The best introduction to the dilemmas faced by SPD leaders before World War I is still Carl Schorske's classic study, *German Social Democracy 1905–1917: The Development of the Great Schism* (Cambridge, Mass.: Harvard University Press, 1955). For a more recent discussion of the reform-versus-revolution tension inside the party, see the essays of Karl Rohe and Peter Witt-Christian in the useful anthology *Der Aufstieg der deutschen Arbeiterbewegung: Sozialdemokratie und Freie Gewerkschaften im Parteisystem und Sozialmilieu des Kaiserreiches,* ed. Elisabeth Müller-Luckner and Gerhard A. Ritter (Munich: Oldenbourg, 1990).

8. On party demographics generally, see Guenther Roth, *The Social Democrats in Imperial Germany* (Totowa, N.J.: Bedminster Press, 1963).

9. Münzenberg, *Die Dritte Front* (Berlin: Neue Deutsche Verlag, 1930), 15–19; Gross, *Willi Münzenberg,* 13–15.

10. Münzenberg recalled in his memoirs stumbling upon a rape perpetrated by "four or five older girls" upon a fourteen-year-old boy. Münzenberg, "Lebenslauf," 25.

11. Münzenberg, "Lebenslauf," 29.

12. There is an enormous literature on the growth of the Socialist youth movement in Germany after the turn of the century. Unfortunately, most of it was cooked up by East German intellectuals to provide a radical lineage for their Communist Party rulers. See, for example, Gerhard Roger, *Die pädagogische Bedeutung der proletarischen Jugendbewegung Deutschlands* (Berlin: Volk und Wissen, 1956).

13. Bernstein's once rock-solid belief in orthodox Marxism had eroded considerably by the late 1890s, when he observed that the dramatic growth in Europe's, and especially Germany's, economy had made nonsense of Marx's claim that progressive "immiseration" of the working classes would lead to a violent proletarian takeover of the means of production. In fact, general prosperity seemed to be benefiting workers too. He published this argument in *The Evolution of Socialism* in 1899, and was immediately denounced by the leading Marxists of Europe for the heresy of "Revisionism." A thorough, if often tendentious, analysis of Bernstein's political evolution is provided in Peter Gay, *The Dilemma of Democratic Socialism: Bernstein's Challenge to Marx* (New York: Collier, 1962). For a more recent account emphasizing the pacifist and youth issues in Bernstein's thinking, see Francis Ludwig Carsten, *Eduard Bernstein 1850–1932: Eine politische Biographie* (Munich: Beck, 1993).

14. The theoretical idea for a general strike (or *Massenstreik,* as the Germans called

it) had been bandied about in Socialist circles for at least a decade before 1905, but the basically spontaneous—and effective—Russian work stoppage in that year gave the idea currency it had never had before, and it was thereafter always an urgent topic of Socialist debate at the conferences of the Second International.

15. Münzenberg, "Lebenslauf," 27–29.

16. Münzenberg, *Dritte Front*, 31.

17. Ibid., 26, 28, 33, 36–37. With about thirty members, Erfurt Free Youth's monthly revenues would have been only ninety pfennigs. At this rate, it would have taken twenty-three months' worth of revenue to pay off even one fine for political agitation.

18. Münzenberg, *Dritte Front*, 43–47. Although Prussia enjoyed universal male suffrage, the electoral system was tipped significantly in favor of the rich. The suffrage was indirect, with the richest third by tax bracket choosing the same proportional representation as each of the bottom two-thirds, although their numbers were much smaller; the delegates chosen by the great mass of voters in the lowest tax bracket could thus be outvoted by the minority delegates who occupied the middle and upper brackets.

19. Münzenberg, *Dritte Front*, 35.

CHAPTER 2. *Zurich*

1. Münzenberg, *Dritte Front*, 50–55, 56–59.

2. This is all according to Münzenberg's recollections, so we may just have to take his word on faith that Socialist-sympathizing pharmacists in Zurich sometimes offered generous terms of employment for unqualified young political activists. He does not name his boss, nor have I found independent confirmation of this employment contract.

3. Most of what we know of the Aussersihl *Jungburschenverein* comes from Münzenberg's later recollections, and he almost certainly exaggerated the group's wild anarchistic qualities for dramatic effect, to make his own later efforts to discipline them seem more effective. Still, a glance at the records of Max Bock's national Socialist Youth Bureau, deposited in the Schweizerisches Sozialarchiv in Zurich by his assistant Eduard Meyer, seems to confirm the group's renegade qualities: there is virtually no regular correspondence from Aussersihl, and the group in fact is not listed as a contributing branch member in the financial records for 1911. SS, Ar.5.10.3, folder "Jungburschenvereine 1911," document headed "Jahresrechnung des Verbandes Schweiz, Jungburschenvereine 1911." By contrast, there are at least some weekly reports from July and August 1912 on group activities sent in from Aussersihl to national headquarters that Willi signed off on, found in the Nachlass Meyer from 1912, in SS, Ar.5.10.4.

4. Cited by Münzenberg, *Dritte Front*, 68.

5. Ibid., 69–70; and group circular preserved in SS, Ar.5.10.3, Nachlass Meyer, folder "1910," 24 June 1910 document headed "Jungburschen Verein Aussersihl."

6. Most, whose controversial writings included *Vive la Commune* (1888) and *Der kommunistische Anarchismus* (1889), was a Bavarian socialist who embraced anarchism in the late 1870s and was expelled from the SPD. He was later expelled from Germany, Austria, and even the tolerant exile's haven, England. He ended up in New York, where he edited a radical paper called *Freiheit* and promoted violent labor agitation, playing a small part in inciting the bloody Chicago Haymarket riot of 1886. Perhaps his single legacy was his terrorist how-to pamphlet, *The Science of Revolutionary Warfare*, published in 1885.

7. This was the argument Kropotkin advanced in *Mutual Aid*, published in Ger-

man as *Gegenseitige Hilfe in der Tier- und Menschenwelt* (Leipzig: Verlag von Theod. Thomas, 1910).

8. *Dritte Front*, 74–77.

9. Ibid., 92–95. Brupbacher's extensive ms notes from these salons, remarkably, have been preserved in SS, Ar. 5.30.1. See, for the discussion of *A Doll's House*, the ms notes headlined "Nora," 16 July 1912. Unfortunately, the records for 1911, when Willi reported on *Crime and Punishment*, are missing, so we simply have to wonder what this budding Marxist propagandist had to say about the moral absolutes endorsed in Dostoevsky's Orthodox Christian, extremely un-Marxist novel.

10. A representative sample of the poems penned by Aussersihl Youth Socialists has been preserved, some handwritten, some typed, in SS, Ar.5.20.2, folder marked "Jungburschen-Gedichte." The most that may kindly be said of them is—they rhyme. The final, didactic installment in the *Weihnachtsglocken* series, "Zum frohen Feste. Eine Sammlung ernster und heiterer Gedichte zum Rezitieren an Arbeiterfesten," omits these amateurish efforts in favor of classic poems, for which Münzenberg probably paid no royalties. A copy of this collection survives in SS, Ar.5.40.1, Band 2. On Barthel's enviable lifestyle as a wandering proletarian poet, see his memoirs, *Kein Bedarf an Weltgeschichte* (Wiesbaden: Limes, 1950), 11–26. His patron was the German writer Alfons Paquet, who had met Barthel while the latter was working in a furniture factory near Dresden, early in 1912.

11. *Dritte Front*, 121. At the time, the poem Münzenberg was most proud of was doubtless "Der Arbeit junges Volk," which he published in "Zum frohen Feste," 42: "Tremble there, you priests! / Wake up from your slumber, you servant! / We are fighting for the truth, for freedom and justice. / We will break the power of the masters, / that made us into servants, / we are the heirs of the future, / of the work of the young masses." His favorite play was probably *Jungvolk*, a protest against the corporal punishment of children, which he had performed several times before captive audiences of Youth Socialist groups.

12. Münzenberg, *Dritte Front*, 100–105.

13. Ibid., 89. For a taste of Münzenberg's ideas on gender issues, see the programs for the Sozialdemokratische Jugendorganisation Zürich for January to July 1914, in SS Ar.5.10.6. While the male members hear speeches on such subjects as the French and German Revolutions (both by Münzenberg), on SPD's "Erfurt Program," and the "International Socialist Youth Movement," the women are addressed on the importance of educating themselves, housework, and child care.

14. Münzenberg, *Dritte Front*, 105–10.

15. *Free Youth*, like most Socialist papers in prewar Europe, may very well have been read by more workers than would be directly reflected in its circulation figures, as individual copies were often passed around in factories or read aloud in coffee houses.

16. Münzenberg, *Dritte Front*, 114. For Brupbacher's own explanation of his expulsion from the SPS (which conveniently neglects to mention the objectionable article), see Brupbacher, *60 Jahre Ketzer. Selbstbiographie. 'Ich log so wenig als möglich'* (Zurich: Verlag B. Ruppli, 1935), 179–82.

17. *Dritte Front*, 113–17. In the event, Willi secured a substitute speaker at the last minute, when his aides stopped the Bulgarian Socialist Sakasov as he was attempting to change trains on his way to Basel. They besieged him with requests until he consented to offer Youth Socialists some personal observations of the recent war in the Balkans. The night had a respectable take of 230 Swiss francs.

18. *Dritte Front*, 126–28. For the personal details on Willi's assistants, see the Zurich

cantonal police report in BB, E 21 9778 ("Untersuchung betr. die Tätigkeit der sozialdemokratischen Jugendorganisationen der Schweiz in Zürich").

19. For the fiscal year 1914, Willi was paid a total of 1,289.98 francs, with a personal expense budget on top of that of 184.25 francs; in all, the expenses on Münzenberg made up almost one-fifth of the total operating budget of 7,842.88 francs. See *Die Zukunft. Jahrbuch der Sozialdemokratischen Jugendorganisation der Schweiz* for 1914, 16–17.

20. Ibid., 11.

21. *Dritte Front*, 136.

22. Enthusiasm for the war in Germany was not universal, however, as Jeffrey Verhey shows in his recent study *The Spirit of 1914: Militarism, Myth, and Mobilization in Germany* (Cambridge: Cambridge University Press, 2000). On the reaction of socialists more generally to the dilemma presented by the war, see also Arno J. Mayer, *Political Origins of the New Diplomacy, 1917–1918* (New Haven, Conn.: Yale University Press, 1959), 22–34.

23. *Dritte Front*, 141–43.

24. The issue's cover and several articles are reproduced ibid., 144–47.

25. Ibid., 153.

26. The French, Austrian, and German replies to Münzenberg's invitation are reproduced in Münzenberg, *Die Sozialistische Jugend-Internationale* (Berlin: Verlag Junge Garde, 1919?), 39.

27. *Dritte Front*, 154.

28. The women's Bern Conference of March 1915 has not inspired much historical comment, but a workable account of the proceedings is provided in R. Craig Nation's recent study *War on War: Lenin, the Zimmerwald Left, and the Origins of Communist Internationalism* (Durham, N.C.: Duke University Press, 1989), 67–71. On Armand, see Michael Pearson's recent *Lenin's Mistress. The Life of Inessa Armand* (New York: Random House, 2001).

29. The text of the resolution is reproduced in Münzenberg, *Die Jugend-Internationale*, 40–41.

30. *Dritte Front*, 160–63.

31. Willi estimated the total number of Youth Socialists from neutral countries represented at Bern at 33,800, of which 16,000 were in Norway, 8,000 in Sweden, and 7,000 in Denmark. *Dritte Front*, 158–60. Italy's stance of neutrality, incidentally, was short-lived after Bern. Tempted by the prospect of acquiring territory from Austria-Hungary, whose army's capacity was already stretched near the breaking point by the Russians, Italy entered the war against the Central Powers on 24 May 1915.

32. *Dritte Front*, 164; see also Nation, *War on War*, 70.

33. See the "Reglement für das international Jugendsekretariat," passed at the Bern Conference. Those countries without active members who could be easily counted, such as Russia, were to use the circulation numbers of any Youth Socialist publications to determine their level of contribution to Münzenberg's Secretariat. "Bericht über die internationale Konferenz der sozialistischen Jugendorganisation abgehalten zu Bern am 4., 5., und 6. April 1915," 36–37. In SS Ar.5.40.1, Band 2. Karl Liebknecht, the only German Reichstag deputy to vote against war credits during the second such balloting, in December 1914, was jailed early in 1915 for wartime lèse-majesté, so his name had become synonymous with antiwar political martyrdom. Luxemburg, too, was jailed for the same reason, but as a Polish Jew and a woman, she was a somewhat less popular symbol for German Socialists to rally around.

34. *Die Sozialistische Jugend-Internationale*, 44–45; Gross, *Willi Münzenberg*, 47.

35. Quoted by Nation, *War on War*, 85.

36. The Lenin-Zinoviev list was confined to the radical Dutch Tribunists, the opposition "International Socialists" in the SPD, the Polish-Lithuanian "Regional Presidium," the Lettish Social Democratic Party, and the Scandinavian Youth Leagues. See Nation, *War on War*, 79. Although Grimm had his way with the invitations list, not everyone he invited was able to attend. Significantly, both Liebknecht and Luxemburg were absent from Zimmerwald, as both were in prison. The British socialist delegation, meanwhile, failed to obtain the necessary exit visas and didn't show up at all. The somewhat ungenerous description of Lenin was made by the Belgian Socialist Emile Vandervelde. Quoted by Barbara Tuchman in *The Proud Tower: A Portrait of the World before the War, 1890–1914* (New York: Macmillan, 1966), 435.

37. See Nation, *War on War*, 85–92.

38. Quoted ibid., 81.

39. Quoted by Richard Pipes in *The Russian Revolution 1899–1919* (London: Harvill, 1990), 380.

40. Karl Marx, *Der Bürgerkrieg in Frankreich* (many separate editions).

41. Lyrics by Eugène Poitiers.

42. The Zimmerwald Left group initially comprised the core three of Lenin, Zinoviev, and Radek, along with Fritz Platten, Jan Berzin, Julian Borchardt, Carl Zeth Höglund, and Ture Nerman. Trotsky's remark denouncing them is quoted by Nation, *War on War*, 95. The Russian Social Democratic Party had split into two irreconcilable factions at their London Congress of 1903. On one side were those, led by the orthodox Marxist Georgi Plekhanov, who believed Russia must pass through a "bourgeois" revolution before achieving socialism. On the other side, Lenin and his supporters insisted in a direct revolutionary leap into a "dictatorship of the proletariat." Only sixty delegates were in attendance, but the doctrinal split stuck for the long haul: Lenin won a majority and thus deemed his followers *Bolsheviks*, while the Plekhanovites became the "minority" or "Menshevik" faction. On *Vorbote*, see Nation, *War on War*, 112–14.

43. Quoted by Gross, *Willi Münzenberg*, 51. Lenin's remark is quoted by Pipes, *Russian Revolution*, 383.

44. *Dritte Front*, 233.

45. Münzenberg circular "An die jugendlichen Redner," 24 September 1915, in SS, Ar.5.10.6.

46. Münzenberg circular headed "Zürich/ 5. Juli 1916," procedural orders for Swiss Young Socialist conference on 16 July 1916, in SS, Ar.5.10.6.

47. See *Dritte Front*, 173–74.

48. The central discussion topic of this meeting, "propaganda in the army," was clearly meant to be provocative. See undated Münzenberg circular for 30 July 1916 Volkshaus meeting, in SS, Ar.5.10.6.

49. Münzenberg circular "An unsere Sektionen!" 4 December 1916, in SS, Ar.5.10.6; and Münzenberg, *Dritte Front*, 178, 185.

50. Münzenberg circular "An unsere Sektionen!" 1 September 1916, in SS, Ar.5.10.6.

51. "Regierungsratsbeschluss betreffend Verbot von Versammlungen u. Umzügen auf öffentlichen Strassen und Plätzen," 2 September 1916, in BB, E 21 9783.

52. See "Platzkommando (Zürich) für die Tage vom 2. bis 4. September," in BB, E 21 9783.

53. See "Regierungsratsbeschluss betreffend Verbot von Versammlungen u. Umzügen auf öffentlichen Strassen und Plätzen," 2 September 1916, and "Platzkommando (Zürich)

für die Tage vom 2. bis 4. September," both in BB, E 21 9783. It is curious that Münzenberg was allowed to remain in Switzerland for so long, despite the fact that, unlike other political exiles, his political agitation was largely domestic and directed at Swiss men of draft age. He does not appear to have had any special residence visa. Nor did he ever apply, to my knowledge, for Swiss citizenship. Although the Swiss Public Prosecutor's Office began preparing a dossier on Münzenberg as early as 1915, it was not until a series of bloody riots overwhelmed Zurich in fall 1917 that Münzenberg was finally arrested.

54. See Münzenberg circular, 1 September 1916.

55. Report from Chur to the Public Prosecutor's Office in Bern, 21 September 1916, in BB, E 21 9791.

56. Polizeikommando des Kantons Zürich. "Es erscheint Wilhelm Münzenberg...," 13 September 1916, in BB, E 21 9778.

57. "Brief des Generalanwalts der Schweizerischen Bundesanwalt an den Chef des schweiz. Justiz- und Polizeidepartements Bern," 7 September 1916, in BB, E 21 11326.

58. Münzenberg circular, 29 December 1916, in SS, Ar.5.20.2.

59. Not everyone of the Left wanted to use the war as a springboard to seizing power, of course. On the antiwar activities and plans of more pacifistic socialists and liberals, see Mayer, *New Diplomacy*, 36–44.

60. French soldiers' defiance did fall short of the classic definition of "mutiny," as John Keegan recently pointed out: they did not direct their rage against their officers and many made it clear that they wished them "no harm." See Keegan, *The First World War* (London: Pimlico, 1998), 356.

61. The "February Revolution" is so called because Russia then worked according to the Julian calendar, which was calculated thirteen days behind the Gregorian one used in the West; the principal events occurred on 25 February–2 March/10–15 March. On Vienna's support for Lenin, see the accounting statement from December 1914 which reveals that the Ukraine Liberation Union, financed by the Austrian Ministry of Foreign Affairs, "has given support to the Majority faction of the Russian Social-Democracy in the form of money and help in the establishment of communications with Russia. The leader of that faction, Lenin, is not hostile to Ukrainian demands. . . ." Cited by Pipes, *Russian Revolution*, 377. On the machinations of the German Foreign Office, including support for Trotsky, see Z. A. B. Zeman and W. B. Scharlau, *The Merchant of Revolution: The Life of Alexander Israel Helphand (Parvus) 1867–1924* (London: Oxford University Press, 1965), 132–33, 155, 187–88. Trotsky, to be fair, almost certainly did not know the money was coming from the Germans—he received it through backdoor channels, notably from his friend Christo Rakovsky, a Rumanian socialist who had received one million gold marks from the German Foreign Office in Bucharest.

62. Edmund Wilson, *To the Finland Station* (London: Collins, 1940), 466–69. For Münzenberg's recollection of Lenin's words, see *Dritte Front*, 236; and his short memoir piece, "Mit Lenin in der Schweiz," *Internationale Presse Korrespondenz*, 6 (27 August 1926): 1838.

63. It was not, as was once thought, General Ludendorff, then ruling Germany's war economy as virtual dictator, who was behind the Lenin operation, but rather Parvus and the Foreign Office. For details and citations, see Zeman and Scharlau, *Parvus*, 136, 208–18. Parvus's remark about Lenin being "raving mad" was made to Philipp Scheidemann of the German SPD; it is quoted by Pipes, *Russian Revolution*, 390.

64. The Russians sold mainly foodstuffs and other raw materials processed by the German war machine, while the Germans provided surgical equipment, medicines, and

processed chemicals. For details of German financial support for the Bolsheviks, see Zeman and Scharlau, *Parvus*, 164–65, 216–19; and Pipes, *Russian Revolution*, 410. There is still a considerable amount of controversy as to the nature of Lenin's relationship with the German authorities who financed his trip to Russia. Although the appropriations for Bolshevik propaganda are clearly documented in the archives of the German Foreign Office, there has as yet been no documentary evidence to prove exactly how this money reached Lenin in Russia. Richard Pipes, in *The Unknown Lenin: From the Secret Archive* (New Haven, Conn.: Yale University Press, 1996) implies there is serious reason to believe that Lenin was acting on behalf of German interests or even as a "German agent." As Martin Malia argues in a critical review of *The Unknown Lenin* (in *Times Literary Supplement*, 31 January 1997: 6–7), however, this issue is in a political sense a bit of a red herring: Lenin's propaganda efforts and more importantly, his actions upon taking power, were determined by his own rigid ideological beliefs, and would not have been any different if his coup had or hadn't been financed by the Germans.

65. Zeman and Scharlau, *Parvus*, 220–26.

66. See the Swiss Public Prosecutor's 25 February 1918 report on Münzenberg to the Swiss Justice Department, in BB, E 21 11328, 22.

67. Romberg's request is reproduced in Werner Hahlweg, ed., *Lenins Rückkehr nach Russland 1917: Die deutschen Akten* (Leiden: Brill, 1957), 58.

68. See the document reproduced ibid., 109.

69. Letter in BB, E 21 11326. The author of this letter, Jakob Feldner, instructed its recipients to destroy it after reading it. Feldner, a socialist journalist with anarchist leanings, was an associate of Jules Humbert-Droz, Romain Rolland, and left intellectual notables in wartime Geneva. He claims to have negotiated British support for the instigation of a "German Revolution" while in London early in 1917.

70. Münzenberg, *Die Sitzung des internationalen sozialistischen Jugendbureaus am 19. bis 20. Mai in Stockholm und meine Teilnahme, Separat-Abdruck aus Jugend-Internationale* 9 (Zurich, 1917). Little was resolved at this meeting, apart from an increase in the contribution requirements for Socialist Youth organizations in neutral nations (from twenty-five francs a year per thousand members to fifty francs). The date of his reentry into Switzerland is revealed in "Berichtsbogen für den Deserteur oder Refraktär: Münzenberg Wilhelm," 21 November 1917, in BB, E 21 11326.

71. Münzenberg, *Dritte Front*, 210–11.

72. See various flyers and leaflet advertisements in SS, Ar.5.20.2, "Flugblätter, Zirkulare 1916"; and Münzenberg et al., circulars "Durchführung der Beschlüsse von Aarau," circa June 1917, and "Jakob Herzog und die Wahrheit," circa September 1917, in folder "1917 Jungburschenverein," in SS, Ar.5.10.6.

73. See Münzenberg circular, "Durchführung der Beschlüsse von Aarau" and untitled Münzenberg circular, 6 August 191[6], both in SS, Ar.5.10.6; and "Es erscheint Wilhelm Münzenberg . . . ," 13 September 1916, in BB, E 21 9778.

74. The result was the 12 July 1917 "Abkommen zwischen Partei, Gewerkschaftsbund und Jugendorganisation," in SS, Ar.5.20.2, "Flugblätter, Zirkulare 1917." For an example of Münzenberg's specialized instructions for giving speeches to rural audiences, see Münzenberg circular, circa 1916, for a recruiting drive in Bettlach, in SS, Ar.5.10.6.

75. Letter from the Public Prosecutor in Bern to Polizeidepartement des Kantons Solothurn, 7 April 1917; "Bericht des Tit. Polizeikommando des Kantons Solothurn," stamped recd. by Schweizerische Bundesanwaltschaft, 12 April 1917, in BB, E 21 9780. Yet again, this

episode demonstrates the liberal nature of the Swiss law of associations. In Germany, by contrast, a police observer would not possibly have left a political gathering merely because an organizer asked him to leave.

76. See Münzenberg's comments on Waibel in "Abschrift. Es erscheint auf Vorladung ... Wilhelm Münzenberg ...," 27 March 1918, in BB, E 21 11326. The "Waibel affair," as it came to be known, is described in some detail in several undated executive circulars, circa June 1917, in SS, Ar.5.10.6; see also "Jakob Herzog und die Wahrheit," and Herzog's undated reply, "Münzenberg und die Wahrheit," in SS, Ar.5.20.2., "Flugblätter, Zirkulare 1917."

77. Herzog, "Münzenberg und die Wahrheit," undated circular in SS, Ar.5.20.2, "Flugblätter, Zirkulare 1917."

78. The novel in question was *Looking Backward*, translated as *Ein sozialistischer Roman: Ein Ruckblick, 2000–1887* (Berlin: Verlag der "Berliner Volks-Tribune," 1889).

79. Münzenberg letter to Heinzmann, 5 July 1917, in SS, Ar.5.10.6.

80. There are literally hundreds of accounts of the October Revolution. I have mainly followed Pipes, *Russian Revolution*, 439–96. For a more sympathetic account of the Bolsheviks' Red October, see Sheila Fitzpatrick, *The Russian Revolution* (New York: Oxford University Press, 1982), 54–60.

81. There were few eyewitnesses on this first day, but it is unlikely that there were more than fifty or so demonstrators present at first (although more may have joined in once the group began its march on the weapons factories), as only about two hundred showed up in the Helvetiaplatz on the sixteenth, after the *Volksrecht* had publicized the previous day's events and flyers promoted a follow-up demonstration. See "Bericht über die Unruhen in Zürich umfassend den Zeitraum vom 15. bis 21. November 1917," 21 November 1917, in BB, E 21 9849; and Münzenberg, *Dritte Front*, 243–44.

82. Münzenberg, *Dritte Front*, 243–44. Under police questioning, Münzenberg later admitted financing the flyers. See the Swiss Public Prosecutor's 25 February 1918 report to the Swiss Justice Department, 18; and "Abschrift. Es erscheint auf Vorladung ... Wilhelm Münzenberg ..."

83. I have followed here mainly the eyewitness report volunteered by a number of local student pacifists in the pamphlet "Zu den Ereignissen in Zürich nach Berichten von Augenzeugen," 20 November 1917, in SS, Ar.5.20.2. Their account is factually consistent with the report of the local military command, "Bericht über die Unruhen in Zürich umfassend den Zeitraum vom 15. bis 21. November 1917."

84. "Bericht über die Unruhen in Zürich ... vom 15. bis 21. November 1917"; "Aus dem Protokoll des Regierungsrates 1917," Sitzung vom 23. November 1917, in BB, E 21 9855; "Zu den Ereignissen in Zürich nach Berichten von Augenzeugen"; Münzenberg, *Dritte Front*, 246–48.

85. Aus dem Protokoll des Regierungsrates 1917, Sitzung vom 23. November 1917.

86. Münzenberg's draft notice was issued on 7 September 1917, and he received it on the eighth. The Swiss Public Prosecutor's 19 November 1917 report is preserved in BB, E 21 11326.

87. For examples of these protests, see those listed in the Swiss Public Prosecutor's letter to Keller, 25 March 1918, in BB, E 21 11328; in the anonymous executive circular "An die Sektionen der sozialdemokratischen Jugendorganisation," 19 November 1917, in SS, Ar.5.20.2; and Fritz Platten's circular "An die Sektionen der Soziald. Jugendorganisation der Schweiz," 23 November 1917, in SS, Ar.5.10.6. Only one Münzenberg piece out of the twenty-odd reprinted in Willi Trostel, ed., *Was wollte Münzenberg?* (Zurich: Buchhandlung Freie Jugend, 1918) was on the military question.

Notes to Pages 62–67 319

88. *Berner Tagwacht*, 7 January 1918. For examples of international protests, see the telegrams and letters headed "Sozialistische Litteratur (Neues aus der Schweiz): W.MUENZENBERG: 'JUNG-VOLK' Schauspiel in 3 Akten 1915 Zürich 1915," in SS, Ar.5.10.9.

89. Polizeikommando des Kantons Zürich. "Es erscheint vorgeführt Münzenberg Wilhelm von Erfurt . . . ," 1 December 1917, in BB, E 21 11326.

90. Keller letter to the Swiss Bundesrat, 13 December 1917, in BB, E 21 11328, 6.

91. Ibid., 3.

92. Münzenberg letter to the Bundesrat, 27 December 1917, in BB, E 21 11328, 1. What Münzenberg vaguely hints here—that Switzerland, as an "advanced" country with an established "capitalist" legal system, is not yet ripe for socialism—of course contradicts the views of most orthodox socialists of the Second International, who envisioned the advanced industrial democracies of the West as the vanguard of the ultimate proletarian revolution. Münzenberg had obviously adopted Lenin's view that socialist revolution would come first to weakened, battered societies where the bourgeois order was weak, especially in the chaos of wartime—as Lenin himself "proved" with his October coup in Petrograd.

93. Münzenberg letter to the Bundesrat, 27 December 1917, in BB, E 21 11328, 1–3.

94. Swiss Public Prosecutor's 25 February 1918 report on Münzenberg to the Swiss Justice Department, 7, 9, 12, 13.

95. Ibid., 17, 21.

96. Münzenberg was suffering from a mild pulmonary infection, leading to a shortage of breath. See Keller letter to Herr Bundesrat Müller, 27 January 1918, in BB, E 21 11328. Münzenberg's bail release form, Bezirksanwaltschaft Zürich, signed by Münzenberg, 28 January 1918, in BB, E 21 11328. His declaration of intent was recorded in a letter to Keller, 24 January 1918, in BB, E 21 11328.

97. Münzenberg was not permitted to return to his old apartment-headquarters. His book, *Der Kampf und Sieg der Bolschewiki* (Stuttgart: Spartakus, 1919), was first published under the pseudonym "E. Arnold," although he later released the book under his own name in 1919.

98. Telegram from Kommando 6. Division to the Public Prosecutor's Office in Bern, 7 March 1918, in BB, E 21 11328.

99. Platten's motion was defeated 98 to 17; the counterresolution, sponsored by Musy, passed 77 to 19. For an example of media outrage at Münzenberg's continued presence in Switzerland, see the French-language *Gazette de Lausanne*, which claimed on 7 February 1918 to have from "serious sources" that Münzenberg was "inexplicably . . . enjoying a quasi-official protection in Zurich and Bern as well." For an example of leading industrialists' lobbying against Münzenberg, see the letter from F. Meyer of the Meyer & Stüdeli S.A. watchmaker "An den h. Bundesrat, Bern," 1 June 1918, in BB, E 21 11328.

100. See letter from Brunner, First State Prosecutor of the Canton of Zurich, to the Justice Department, 11 May 1918; letter from Wettstein, director of the Zurich Cantonal Justice Department, to the Public Prosecutor's Office in Bern, 17 May 1918; letter from the Swiss Public Prosecutor to the Swiss Justice Department, 25 May 1918; and protocol of the Sitzung des Schweizerischen Bundesrats, 31 May 1918, all preserved in BB, E 21 11328.

101. Münzenberg letter to Herr Bundesrat, 7 June 1918, in BB, E 21 11328. For further details see also Münzenberg, *Dritte Front*, 254.

102. See Münzenberg to Keller, 10 June 1918; Münzenberg letter to Herr Müller, Bundesrat Bern, 7 July 1918; and letter from Strafanstalt Witzwil to the Swiss Justice Department, 10 July 1918, all in BB, E 21 11329. On Münzenberg's queries at the U.S. consulate

in Zurich, see M. Churchill telegram to military attaché, Bern, 10 June 1918, in the U.S. Military Intelligence Division (MID) files at the National Archives in Washington, D.C., PF 13709.

103. Münzenberg letter to Platten, 4 August 1918, in BB, E 21 11329.

104. On this episode, see Pipes, *Russian Revolution*, 624–670.

105. Münzenberg letter to Platten, 4 August 1918.

106. See letter from Wettstein, Director of the Justice Department of the Canton of Zurich, to the national Justice Department in Bern, 31 August 1918, in BB, E 21 11329.

107. Münzenberg made this boast to Rosa Meyer-Leviné, who recorded it in her memoirs, *Im inneren Kreis: Erinnerungen einer Kommunistin in Deutschland 1920–1933*, ed. Hermann Weber (Cologne: Kiepenhauer & Witsch, 1979), 322–24.

108. There is no date attached to Münzenberg's typescript "Lebenslauf," which has been preserved in the Swiss police archives. But it can almost certainly be traced to the Meilen period, when he was cut off at last from his usually furious correspondence with colleagues. The abrupt tailing off of the manuscript (which ends just before Münzenberg takes over the Erfurt Free Youth in 1906–7) suggests strongly that he was suddenly interrupted before he could finish, almost certainly when the kaiser's fall on 9 November 1918 finally allowed the Swiss government to expel him to Germany, without fear of provoking protests.

109. Münzenberg, "Lebenslauf," 3–4.

110. Ibid., 4–5.

111. Ibid., 27.

112. Münzenberg telegram to Bundesrat, 9 November 1918, in BB, E 21 11330. Münzenberg later made the audacious claim that the end of the war made his deportation possible because it would no longer excite "the protest of the Entente [powers]." Münzenberg, *Dritte Front*, 262. This self-important scenario makes no sense. The only objection the Western Allies might have had to Münzenberg's expulsion from Switzerland during the war was if he proselytized for peace inside one of the Entente powers—this was the grounds for refusing him entry into France and the United States, for example. Certainly there was no threat, and possibly a benefit, to the Entente, if Münzenberg worked for peace in Germany (as the British in fact nearly hired him to do in spring 1917).

113. The final deportation saga is recounted in the Polizeikommando's report, 14 November 1918, in BB, E 21 11330.

114. See Urs Rauber's recollection in *Willi Münzenberg: Eine Dokumentation zur Muenzenberg-Tagung im September 1918 in Zuerich*, ed. Theo Pinkus (Zurich: Studienbibliothek zur Geschichte der Arbeiterbewegung, 1990) 5, 24.

CHAPTER 3. *Stuttgart*

1. Münzenberg, *Dritte Front*, 267–69. Münzenberg took the officer's name and number, but tore up the slip he had written them on soon after boarding the train for Stuttgart.

2. See Barthel's comments under Swiss police questioning in "Es erscheint vorgeführt: Barthel, Max . . . ," Polizeikommando Zürich, 5 December 1918, in BB, E 21 10682, 3; Münzenberg, *Dritte Front*, 270–71; and Gross, *Willi Münzenberg*, 73.

3. Barthel, *Kein Bedarf*, 45.

4. Münzenberg telegrams to Platten, 14 November 1918, and to Schweide and Platten, 15 November 1918, were intercepted by Swiss army intelligence and passed on to the Public

Prosecutor's Office in Bern, 18 November 1918, in BB, E 21 11414. See also Swiss Public Prosecutor's report on Schweide to the Swiss Justice Department, 4 December 1918, in E 21 10681.

5. "Es erscheint vorgeführt: Barthel, Max ... ," 3–4; and "Vor dem a.o. eidg. Untersuchungsrichter Dr. Bickel und seinem Schriftführer O. Gloor erscheint auf Vorführung aus dem Verhaft und erklärt als Beschuldigter: Marti Ernst ... ," Zürich 10 December 1918, in E 21 10677.

6. Undated Meyer letter dispatched "freiwillig" to the Public Prosecutor in Bern, circa mid-December 1918, in BB, E 21 10677; Kascher letter to Münzenberg, intercepted by Polizeikommando Zürich, 27 November 1918; and "Vor dem a.o. eidg. Untersuchungsrichter Dr. Bickel und seinem Schriftführer O. Gloor erscheint auf Vorführung aus dem Verhaft und erklärt als Beschuldigter: Marti Ernst ..."; intercepted Arnold letter to Münzenberg, 3 March 1919, in BB, E 21 10677.

7. See "Beilage zum Bericht über die Untersuchung betreffend die bolshewistischen Umtriebe," in BB, E 21 10527, which catalogues the extent of the bank transfers from Moscow.

8. Vor dem a.o. eidg. Untersuchungsrichter Dr. Bickel erscheint auf Vorführung und erklärt in Anwesenheit des Schriftführers O. Gloor als Beschuldigte: Kluser Adele ... ," in BB, E 21 10677.

9. Münzenberg telegram to Kluser, intercepted by Swiss army intelligence and passed on to the Public Prosecutor's Office in Bern, 8 December 1918, in BB, E 21 10677.

10. *Dritte Front*, 272–74. The workers' councils did take a fairly radical stand on military questions, voting for the immediate dismissal of Field Marshal Paul von Hindenburg and the dissolution of the elite schools which turned out most of Germany's officer corps; the councils wished to replace the old Prussian system with a popular militia. These demands were rejected by acting Chancellor Ebert, who knew that if he granted them he would lose the support of the regular army. Ebert's refusal to acquiesce to the radicals on the military issue cost him the support of the USPD, whose representatives in his Cabinet resigned in late December. Still, the councils' support for the upcoming elections was a blow to Spartacus, which interpreted this decision, correctly, as a rejection of Spartacists' demands for a comprehensive social revolution that would sweep all the old power structures away.

11. Keller letter to examining magistrate Dr. S. Bickel, 9 January 1919, in BB, E 21 10677. One of Keller's chief priorities was to recover love letters between Münzenberg and Kluser, a task at which he seems ultimately to have succeeded, for none of them survive in the police files.

12. On the KPD's founding congress, see Richard Lowenthal, "The Bolshevisation of the Spartacus League," in *St. Antony's Papers*, no. 9: *International Communism*, ed. David Footman (London: Chatto & Windus, 1960), 27–28; David W. Morgan, *The Socialist Left and the German Revolution: A History of the German Independent Social Democratic Party, 1917–1922* (Ithaca, N.Y.: Cornell University Press, 1975), 206–8; and Eric Waldman, *The Spartacist Uprising of 1919 and the Crisis of the German Socialist Movement* (Milwaukee: Marquette University Press, 1958), 149–58.

13. In response to Lenin's *What Is to be Done?* (1902), Luxemburg published a lengthy commentary in both the Russian-language *Iskra* and the German-language *Neue Zeit* on "Organizational Questions of the Russian Social Democracy." Her famous denunciation of Jaurès was lodged at the Amsterdam Congress of 1904, when Bebel tried to enforce the SPD's Dresden Resolution of 1903, which forbade political actions which might be construed as "accommodation to the existing order."

14. Rosa Luxemburg, "Was will der Spartakusbund?" *Rote Fahne*, 14 December 1918, 1–2.

15. On the Revolutionary Shop Stewards, see Peter von Oertzen, *Betriebsräte in der Novemberrevolution* (Düsseldorf: Droste, 1963); and also Eberhard Kolb and Klaus Schönhausen, *Regionale und lokale Räteorganisationen in Württemberg 1918/19* (Düsseldorf: Droste, 1976), 1, 26, 358.

16. On the so-called "Spartacist" uprising of January 1919, I have followed principally Waldman, *Spartacist Uprising*, 161–97.

17. This according to Münzenberg's own account published the next day in the short-lived *Rote Flut* of 10 January 1919. Article reproduced in Münzenberg, *Dritte Front*, 274–78.

18. Münzenberg, *Dritte Front*, 278–81.

19. See Münzenberg's account in *Der Spartakistenprozess in Stuttgart* (Stuttgart: Spartakus, 1919), and Münzenberg, *Dritte Front*, 284–85.

20. Although Liebknecht was more popular in his day, Luxemburg has turned into the darling of historians, in large part because she was a much more prolific propagandist than Liebknecht and thus left many more texts for sympathetic exegesis. The most colossal monument to her career is J. P. Nettl's *Rosa Luxemburg*, 2 vols. (London: Oxford University Press, 1966). Among more recent productions, Luxemburg plays the hero's role in Eric Weitz's *Creating German Communism, 1890–1990* (Princeton, N.J.: Princeton University Press, 1997), 78–99.

21. Münzenberg, *Nieder mit Spartakus!* (Chemnitz: Buchhandlung d. Kommunistischen Partei, 1919), 9, 11, 15, 19, 20.

22. Levi, *Generalstreik und Noske-Blut-Bad in Berlin* (Berlin: Verl. "Rote Fahne," 1919); "Die Lehren der ungarischen Revolution," in the Hanau *Freiheit*, 24 March 1919; "Die Kehrleite," *Die Internationale*, 4 August 1919.

23. Münzenberg, *Der Spartakistenprozess in Stuttgart*, 60–61; Münzenberg, *Dritte Front*, 286.

24. Trostel letter to Münzenberg, 3 March 1919, in BB, E 21 10677.

CHAPTER 4. *Berlin*

1. Quoted by Anton Gill in *A Dance Between Flames: Berlin Between the Wars* (London: John Murray, 1993), 28.

2. That Münzenberg received money regularly from Moor while in Berlin is suggested by a passage in Barthel's memoirs in which Barthel accompanies his friend to visit Moor and the two are provided casually with cash infusions, no questions asked. Barthel, *Kein Bedarf*, 53–55. Thomas, who also went under the alias of Rubinstein, was a multilingual Polish exile who had been implicated in an unsuccessful assassination attempt on the Russian governor general of Warsaw during the Revolution of 1905. Münzenberg's early contacts with Thomas are mentioned in Karl Retzlaw's memoirs, *Spartakus: Aufstieg und Niedergang: Erinnerungen eines Parteiarbeiters* (Frankfurt-am-Main, 1971), 218–22. See also Gross, *Willi Münzenberg*, 69, 93. On the role of WEB emissaries in financing the Western Communist parties in the early 1920s, see Branko Lazitch, "Two Instruments of Control by the Comintern: The Emissaries of the ECCI and the Party Representatives in Moscow," in *The Comintern: Historical Highlights*, ed. Milorad M. Drachkovitch and Branko Lazitch (Stanford, Calif.: Hoover Institution Press, 1966), 45–65.

3. Münzenberg, *Dritte Front*, 293, 298, 301.

4. Citations from Münzenberg, *Dritte Front*, 295–97; and from Alfred Kurella, *Gründung und Aufbau der Kommunistischen Jugend-Internationale* (Berlin: Verlag der Jugendinternationale, 1929), 31.

5. Münzenberg, *Dritte Front*, 305–9.

6. Babette Gross, in her biography of her husband, claims Münzenberg's youth staff passed out guns to each other at a secret meeting held during the putsch and that Münzenberg, who had never held a gun before, "was given a quick instruction course," as he was "convinced that it would come to a clash between the workers and the army." This whole scenario smells of later embellishment, especially since Gross stops here in mid-thought, telling us nothing of what the Youth Socialists tried to do once they were armed. Gross, *Willi Münzenberg*, 91. Münzenberg himself makes no mention at all of the Kapp putsch in his memoirs, possibly because to have been in Berlin and done nothing to stop the right-wing coup in March 1920 was not much of an advertisement for the Communist Youth International. On the Kapp Putsch more generally, see Gerald D. Feldman, *The Great Disorder: Politics, Economics, and Society in the German Inflation, 1914–1924* (New York: Oxford University Press, 1993), 207–8.

7. According to Barthel, Münzenberg would receive eight hundred gold marks on a typical visit to Moor (because he was a "politician/organizer"), although Barthel himself received merely four hundred (the amount "for tramps and writers"). Barthel, *Kein Bedarf*, 55. See also Gross, *Willi Münzenberg*, 92–93.

8. Münzenberg, *Dritte Front*, 314–15.

CHAPTER 5. *Moscow*

1. The legitimately "foreign" delegates came, one apiece, from the Netherlands, Austria, Sweden, Norway, and Germany. Only the German, Hugo Eberlein-Albrecht, carried a mandate (though the distinctive honor of being the first accredited foreign Communist delegate to the Third International did not prevent Eberlein-Albrecht from later being executed during Stalin's purges). See Angelica Balabanoff, *Impressions of Lenin* (Ann Arbor: University of Michigan Press, 1964), 69–70; and Julius Braunthal, *Geschichte der Internationale*, vol. 2 (Berlin: Dietz, 1974), 181.

2. Cited in Pipes, *Russia under the Bolshevik Regime 1919–1924*, 177.

3. Lenin, *'Left Wing' Communism, an Infantile Disorder* (1920).

4. Münzenberg, *Dritte Front*, 317.

5. Münzenberg, "Ein Tag in Dietskoje-Selo," *Jugend-Internationale* 2 (November 1920): 34–36.

6. Orlando Figes, *A People's Tragedy: A History of the Russian Revolution* (London: Viking, 1996), 739.

7. Münzenberg, *Dritte Front*, 321.

8. Such was the reason Balabanoff herself gave for her dismissal, and although self-flattering, her explanation is plausible. Balabanoff, *Impressions of Lenin*, 15–16.

9. Münzenberg, *Dritte Front*, 319. Münzenberg, incidentally, knew no Russian; but nearly all of the leading Bolsheviks, who had spent years in exile, were fluent in German, and even wrote theoretical articles in the language—Lenin included.

10. See Braunthal, *Internationale*, 2:189.

11. On the splitting of the German Independent Socialist delegates during the Second World Congress and the subsequent splitting of the USPD membership at the party congress

in Halle in October 1920, see Werner T. Angress, *Stillborn Revolution: The Communist Bid for Power in Germany, 1921–1923* (Princeton, N.J.: Princeton University Press, 1963), 64–73; and David Morgan, *The Socialist Left and the German Revolution. A History of the German Independent Social Democratic Party, 1917–1922* (Ithaca, N.Y.: Cornell University Press, 1975), 355–80.

12. Münzenberg, *Dritte Front*, 323.

13. The first time, Makhno blew up a bridge the delegates' train car was to pass over; the second time, he tore up the tracks in front of the oncoming train; the third time, he occupied an entire town with troops loyal to him, thinking the foreigners were about to arrive (they had in fact just passed through). Barthel, *Kein Bedarf*, 112; Figes, *People's Tragedy*, 662.

14. Barthel, *Kein Bedarf*, 103, 105.

15. Ibid., 114.

16. Gross, *Willi Münzenberg*, 99.

17. Münzenberg, *Dritte Front*, 329–31.

18. Cited by Kurella, *Gründung und Aufbau der Kommunistischen Jugend-Internationale*, 155. Münzenberg did support the Twenty-One Conditions in print. See, for example, "Anerkennung der Moskauer Thesen und 21 Bedingungen," in Münzenberg, "Ein Tag in Dietskoje-Selo," 36.

19. Münzenberg, "Ein Präzendenzfall?" in *Jugend-Internationale* 2 (10) (June 1921): 280–83.

CHAPTER 6. *Selling the Famine*

1. Cited by H. H. Fisher, *The Famine in Soviet Russia 1919–1923: The Operations of the American Relief Administration* (New York: Macmillan, 1927), 51.

2. This according to the data of the Soviet Central Statistic Bureau as furnished to the Nansen Relief Mission in 1922, as reproduced in Fisher, *Famine*, 483. The 1913 level was 4.08 million poods; that in 1920, 1.74 million poods. A pood is about 33 pounds, or one-sixtieth of a ton.

3. Quoted from the memoir of a Volga German pastor in Fisher, *Famine*, 500–501.

4. Figes, *A People's Tragedy*, 753.

5. See Fisher, *Famine*, 496–503.

6. Telegram from Lenin and Molotov to all Provincial and Regional Party Committees of the RKP(b), 30 July 1921, translated by Catherine A. Fitzpatrick and reproduced in Pipes, *Unknown Lenin*, 130–31.

7. Pipes, *Russia und the Bolshevik Regime*, 416–17.

8. Citations from Pipes, *Unknown Lenin*, 416; and Fisher, *Famine*, 55–56.

9. For a critical view of Hoover's political motivation in taking on the Volga aid project, see Benjamin M. Weissman, *Herbert Hoover and Famine Relief to Soviet Russia: 1921–1923* (Stanford, Calif.: Hoover Institution Press, 1974).

10. Lenin, note to Molotov, secret, 23 August 1921, reproduced in Pipes, *Unknown Lenin*, 133–34.

11. Quoted by Pipes, *Bolshevik Regime*, 416.

12. Quoted by Münzenberg in *Solidarität. Zehn Jahre Internationale Arbeiterhilfe* (Berlin: Neue Deutsche Verlag, 1931), 188.

13. A Russian original draft of this charter can be found in the RGASPI.538-3-1, 20–22. The second, explicitly political aspect of the committee's mandate was spelled out

Notes to Pages 106–12

only in very oblique language in the founding charter, which hinted that "in view of the possibility of difficulties arising in connection with the famine and the organization of aid on the part of bourgeois states and their organs," Münzenberg's committee should "work systematically with the working masses and their organizations to strengthen the position of Soviet Russia in its relations with capitalist countries." Translated from the German-language version of the charter, in RGASPI.538-3-1, 28. In practice this meant the famine's continued severity was to be blamed on the governments of the West, who would presumably benefit from Soviet Russia's weakness.

14. This according to Babette Gross's recollection in *Willi Münzenberg*, 113.

15. The transcript of the "Verhandlung der Mitglieder des internationalen Büros" held on Sunday 14 August 1921 in the Hotel Baltie, is reproduced in RGASPI.538-2-1, 1–25.

16. RGASPI.538-2-1, 11, 18, 22.

17. RGASPI.538-2-1, 20–21.

18. RGASPI.538-2-1, 24; Gross, *Willi Münzenberg*, 115.

19. RGASPI.538-2-1, 23.

20. Münzenberg circular "An die Zentralleitungen aller kommunistischen Parteien und Organisationen," 18 August 1921, in RGASPI.538-2-1, 26–28; Münzenberg letter to Zinoviev and Radek at the Comintern's "Kleinbüro" (henceforth "ECCI Little Committee"), 2 September 1921, in RGASPI.538-2-3, 7–7c.

21. Münzenberg letter to Zinoviev, Radek, and Kamenev at ECCI Little Committee, 6 September 1921, in RGASPI.538-2-3, 1–6.

22. Münzenberg letter to Zinoviev at ECCI Little Committee, 21 September 1921, in RGASPI.538-2-3, 20–21.

23. Münzenberg letter to Zinoviev, 4 October 1921, in RGASPI.538-2-3, 32 and back.

24. Münzenberg circular "An die Zentralleitungen der Kommunistischen Parteien!" 9 September 1921, in RGASPI.538-2-1, 31–32.

25. Münzenberg circular "An die Zentralen der kommunistischen Parteien und Organisationen und Arbeiter-Hilfskomitees!" 21 September 1921. In DBB, RY 1 / I 6/7/1, 8–15.

26. "Bericht über den Stand der Hilfsaktion in der Tschechoslowakei," in RGASPI.538-2-2, 1–5.

27. See the 20 October 1921 document headed "Die Arbeit des Berliner Komitees der Arbeiterhilfe für Sowjet-Russland" in RGASPI.538-2-2, 59–70; and a Boris Souvarine letter to Zinoviev at the Presidium of ECCI, from Berlin, 16 October 1921, in RGASPI.538-2-3, 54–55.

28. The protocol of this meeting is reproduced in RGASPI.538-2-2, 59–61.

29. The KPD had not mobilized its "party apparatus for even one day" for the famine relief week of October 9–16, Münzenberg complained to ECCI on 22 November 1921. In DBB, RY 1 / I 6/7/1, 109–10.

30. "Die Arbeit des Berliner Komitees der Arbeiterhilfe für Sowjet-Russland," RGASPI.538-2-2, 70.

31. Münzenberg telegram to ECCI Little Committee, stamped received 20 October 1921, in RGASPI.538-2-3, 68.

32. Fisher, *Famine*, 80–82.

33. Souvarine letter to Zinoviev, 16 October 1921, RGASPI.538-2-3, 54–55. On the events leading to Souvarine's eventual sacking in 1924, see Branko Lazitch, "Two Instruments of Control by the Comintern: The Emissaries of the ECCI and the Party Representatives in Moscow," in Drachkovitch and Lazitch, *The Comintern*, 54–56.

34. Münzenberg letter to Radek and Zinoviev, 5 October 1921, in RGASPI.538-2-3, 33–37.

35. Undated document headed "Die Arbeit des Berliner Komitees der Arbeiterhilfe für Sowjet-Russland," stamped received at Comintern 20 October 1921, in RGASPI.538-2-2, 16–17; Münzenberg letter to Kun, 16 October 1921, RGASPI.538-2-3, 59–61.

36. See Münzenberg letter to Fimmen, 24 October 1921, in RGASPI.538-2-1, 41–44.; Münzenberg circular "An alle Arbeiter-Hilfskomitees, kommunistische Parteien und Organisationen," 14 October 1921, in RGASPI.538-2-1, 37–40; unsigned Münzenberg letter to the KPD Zentrale, ms dated 29 October 1921, stamped received at Comintern headquarters 10 November 1921, in RGASPI.538-2-1, 50; letter from "Friesland" (Ernst Reuter) at KPD Zentrale to Münzenberg, 2 November 1921, in RGASPI.538-2-3, 74.

37. Copy of unsigned Münzenberg letter to the KPD Zentrale, ms dated 29 October 1921, stamped received at Comintern headquarters 10 November 1921, in RGASPI.538-2-1, 49; Münzenberg letter to Bela Kun, 10 November 1921 (although not stamped received at Comintern headquarters until 10 December 1921), in RGASPI.538-2-3, 91–92; and Münzenberg letter to ECCI, 22 November 1921, in RGASPI.538-2-3, 100–101.

38. See FSR's "Financial Summary" for August 9 to October 15, 1921, in RGASPI.538-2-5, 1.

39. Donor numbers 1197 through 1208, for example, as listed in the FSR's November 1921 Financial Report, were all individuals from the state of Oregon who gave between fifty cents and five dollars. In RGASPI.538-2-15, 4. On the ineffectual early history of the American Communist Party, see Guenter Lewy, *The Cause That Failed: Communism in American Political Life* (New York: Oxford University Press, 1990), 3–12; and Harvey Klehr et al., *The Soviet World of American Communism* (New Haven, Conn.: Yale University Press, 1998), 14–18.

40. This letterhead from the FSR's financial summary, August 9 to October 15, 1921.

41. See the roster of contributors from the FSR's November 1921 financial report.

42. An undated FSR letterhead, circa November 1921, dropped "Counter-Revolutionary" from its headline slogan, "Famine Relief without Conditions," and dropped Hoover's name as well. In RGASPI.538-2-5, 11.

43. Letter from A. B. Martin addressed "Dear comrade," stamped received by Comintern Secretariat, 11 February 1922, in RGASPI.538-2-9, 7.

44. From an undated Hartmann circular entitled "Instruction Bulletin—No. 1," in RGASPI.538-2-5, 46–50.

45. Münzenberg letter to Bela Kun, 1 November 1921, in RGASPI.538-2-3, 86.

46. From the protocol of this 5 December 1921 conference, RGASPI.538-1-1, 15, 17.

47. Protocol of the 5 December 1921 Berlin conference, in RGASPI.538-1-1, 26–28; Münzenberg request letter to Zinoviev, 5 December 1921, in RGASPI.538-2-3, 115–16. The first issue of *Sowjet-Russland im Bild* appeared on 7 November 1921, featuring a number of widely available pictures of Bolshevik leaders, Soviet public buildings, etc.

48. Münzenberg letter to ECCI Little Committee, 16 December 1921, in RGASPI.538-2-3, 117–19. See also below, chapter 10.

49. Münzenberg letter to Radek, 22 December 1921, in RGASPI.538-2-3, 142–43.

50. See Münzenberg letter to the Comintern Secretariat, 2 January 1922, in RGASPI.538-2-9, 14–16. At least eighty photos simply disappeared in the mails. The 20 January 1922 issue of *Sowjet-Russland im Bild* was dominated by stock shots of Lenin, Radek, et al., the Red Army on parade, etc.

51. Münzenberg letter to Radek, 23 December 1921, in RGASPI.538-2-3, 144; and Münzenberg letter to the Comintern Secretariat, 30 March 1922, in RGASPI.538-2-9, 33.

52. *Bulletin des Auslandskomitees zur Organisierung der Arbeiterhilfe für die Hungernden in Russland,* 12 July 1922, in RGASPI.538-2-12, 50a. The Dutch had raised 302,000 guilders, or about $116,000. The French turned over about 145,000 francs out of 1,850,000 collected, or just under 8 percent; the Italians, 187,500 lire of 1,850,000 collected, or about 10 percent.

53. See *Bulletin des Auslandskomitees,* 26 April 1922, which adds together all the funds collected by national Communist parties and their affiliates (less than 10 percent of which was sent to his committee in Berlin) along with that collected by Fimmen's unions (none of which was sent to Berlin) to come up with the impressive-sounding figure of five hundred million marks putatively sent "through" Münzenberg's "Foreign Committee to Aid the Hungry in Russia." In RGASPI.538-2-12, 23.

54. "Hoover Reports Communists Work Under Relief Guise," *New York Times,* 11 February 1922. This article, and the dozens of follow-up pieces on the scandal, were clipped and sent to Moscow by Münzenberg's men in New York.

55. The first photos did not appear until the ninth issue of *Sowjet-Russland im Bild,* dated 20 June 1922. Another two issues later, the first ads appeared, on 20 August 1922.

56. See unsigned Münzenberg letter to Jung, 21 December 1921, in RGASPI.538-2-3, 139–41, which mentions a cash transfer from Berlin to Moscow of forty thousand marks; Münzenberg letter to Comintern Secretariat, 2 January 1922, in RGASPI.538-2-9, 14–16, in which Jung is described as Münzenberg's "confidence man" in Russia; and Münzenberg letter to Comintern Secretariat, 12 January 1922, RGASPI.538-2-9, 23–25, in which he asks that ECCI support Jung with "all of [its] authority."

57. "Auslandskomitee zur Organisierung der Arbeiterhilfe für die Hungernden (Bericht der russischen Vertretung)," type signed at end Franz Jung, dated Moscow, 8 January 1922, in RGASPI.538-3-4, 1–4.

58. Münzenberg letter to Jung, 16 January 1922, in RGASPI.538-2-10, 9–11; protocol of the IAH Russia meeting, 30 August 1922, in RGASPI.538-3-3, 10.

59. The care package program was launched sometime in spring 1922; it was discussed, for example, at the international conference Münzenberg held in Berlin from 5–9 July 1922, the protocol of which can be found in RGASPI.538-1-2, 1–5. Otto Roth, an employee of Münzenberg's Russian office of the Foreign Committee, later baldly confessed that his people were having problems with "the nonarrival of the packages, the nonreturn of receipts, the seizure of entire package shipments, etc.," before suggesting the program be terminated outright. In RGASPI.538-1-3, 68. The French editors of the flagship Communist newspaper, *L'Humanité,* refused to publicize a German hunger campaign Münzenberg later tried to launch in October 1923 on the grounds that Münzenberg had never accounted for the aid packets from the Russian aid program. See Münzenberg letter to ECCI, 8 November 1923, with attached report, in RGASPI.538-2-19, 144–48.

60. From the protocol of the 5–9 July Foreign Committee conference, in RGASPI.538-1-2, 1.

61. See, for example, the "children of Tsaritsyn" pictured on the cover of the ninth issue of *Sowjet-Russland im Bild* (20 June 1922).

62. In an expense account statement for the Berlin office written up sometime in late June 1922, these expenses show up under such obvious labels as "machines," "tools and spare parts," and "agricultural equipment," along with less obvious ones such as "travel"

and "support of workers sent to Russia." Münzenberg hinted very obliquely at what he was doing as early as a 12 January 1922 letter to Radek, in which he asked that his old Zimmerwald Left comrade support Jung's various actions in the famine region "with all your authority." In the unsigned ECCI reply to this letter, dated 24 January 1922, the writer (possibly Radek) openly complains that Münzenberg has begun diverting money from the "collection funds" for tools, machines, etc. for the factories and workshops of the famine region," and worries that disclosure of such fund diversion could later be used by "our enemies" to discredit Communism. In RGASPI.538-2-9, 30.

63. This all according to Jung's "Report on the Workers' Relief in Russia," an English translation of his German-language dispatch from Moscow dated 28 June 1922, in RGASPI.538-3-4, 56–65. See also Jung's secret 9 April 1922 "Bericht der Hunger- und Produktionshilfe," in RGASPI.538-3-4, 24.

64. See Münzenberg letter to "Lieber Genosse," probably Zinoviev, 15 July 1922, in RGASPI.538-2-9, 39; and Münzenberg letter to Comintern Secretariat, 15 July 1922, in RGASPI.538-2-9, 45–47.

CHAPTER 7. *Building Socialism*

1. Figes, *A People's Tragedy*, 727, 730; Alan M. Ball, *Russia's Last Capitalists: The Nepmen, 1921–1929* (Berkeley: University of California Press, 1987), 8–9.

2. On the peasant uprisings that began in 1920, see Taisia Osipova, "Peasant Rebellions: Origin, Scope, Dynamics, and Consequences," in *The Bolsheviks in Russian Society. The Revolution and Civil Wars*, ed. Vladimir N. Brovkin (New Haven, Conn.: Yale University Press, 1997), 154–76; and Pipes, *Bolshevik Regime*, 373. On the Tambov rebellion, see Oliver Henry Radkey, *The Unknown Civil War in Soviet Russia* (Stanford, Calif.: Hoover Institution Press, 1976); and the more recent article by Sergei Pavliechenkov on "Peasant Wars in Tambov Province," in Brovkin, *Bolsheviks*, 177–98. The best overview of all the peasant revolts is Figes, *Peasant Russia, Civil War: The Volga Countryside in Revolution, 1917–1921* (New York: Oxford University Press, 1989). The best short account of the Kronstadt uprising is Paul Avrich's *Kronstadt 1921* (Princeton, N.J.: Princeton University Press, 1970). On the use of Chekist terror in Russia in 1921–22, see S. P. Mel'gunov, *Krasnyi terror v Rossii* (Moscow: Puico, 1990), 69–85.

3. Quoted by Pipes, *Bolshevik Regime*, 391.

4. Ball, *Nepmen*, 20–21.

5. Pipes, *Bolshevik Regime*, 393–94.

6. See Epstein, *Dossier*, 59–69.

7. Letter from Lenin to Molotov for Politburo members, 19 March 1922, reproduced in Pipes, *The Unknown Lenin*, 152–53. The best brief account of the assault on the Church is Figes', in *A People's Tragedy*, 748–49. For analysis of the campaign in the context of Bolshevik cultural policy, see Jonathan W. Daly, "The Bolshevik Assault on the Church," in Brovkin, *Bolsheviks*, 235–68.

8. For the diplomatic nuts and bolts of Rapallo, see Xenia Joukoff Eudin and Harold H. Fisher, in collaboration with Rosemary Brown Jones, *Soviet Russia and the West 1920–1927: A Documentary Survey* (Stanford, Calif.: Stanford University Press, 1957), 167–70. For economic and political details, see Gerald Freund, *Unholy Alliance: Russian-German Relations from the Treaty of Brest-Litovsk to the Treaty of Berlin* (London: Chatto and Windus, 1957), 118–21.

9. Some of these tractors may have been supplied by Ford, which exported some

238 Fordsons through a nominally private company in Petrograd, Ivan Stacheef & Co., according to Epstein, *Dossier*, 75. FSR expenses relating to these tractors are difficult to trace. Only $283.95 was collected by FSR affiliates specifically for the tractor campaign. The real expense for these tractors was probably diverted from miscellaneous FSR accounts relating to "tools and spare parts" for the famine aid campaign, which totaled nearly $30,000 from 1921 to 1923. See the FSR's own German-language budget report for its first three fiscal years, dated 31 July 1924, in RGASPI.538-2-24, 38–40. For the ethnic composition of the managers employed by Jung's operation, see his secret 9 April 1922 "Bericht der Hunger- und Produktionshilfe," in RGASPI.538-3-4, 30.

10. "The leasehold agreements," Jung himself wrote in the English-language version of his 28 June 1922 "Report on the Workers' Relief in Russia," "are in conformity with local conditions, and they all of them contain a clause to the effect that on the dissolution of the Workers' Relief the leasehold property must go back to the State organs." RGASPI.538-3-4, 57.

11. From Jung's secret "Bericht der Hunger- und Produktionshilfe," RGASPI.538-3-4, 29–30.

12. Reliable exchange rates during the inflationary period of 1921–24 for the Soviet paper ruble, or *sovznak*, are extremely hard to come by, as the currency was not traded on the global market. Newly printed *sovznaki* were converted in October 1922 at a rate of one million to one against the pre-1921 ruble, which would imply that the IAH start-up capital of April 1922 was equal to slightly more than ten million old, gold-backed rubles, or about one-half what the Soviet government spent on famine relief (twenty million gold-backed rubles, or $10 million, disbursed directly into the ARA food assistance fund. Although the value of the paper ruble in which this credit was granted was steadily declining, the size of the IAH's start-up capital grant was clearly substantial. See Alexander Baykov, *The Development of the Soviet Economic System* (New York: Macmillan, 1947), 88–90; and L. E. Hubbard, *Soviet Money and Finance* (London: Macmillan, 1936), 41–43.

13. See Münzenberg letters to Jung, 12 January 1922, RGASPI.538-2-10, 6–8; and 16 January 1922, RGASPI.538-2-10, 9–11. According to Münzenberg's letter to Jung, 27 April 1922, RGASPI.538-2-10, 21, the request would not be fulfilled until early May.

14. Münzenberg letter to Jung, 4 February 1922, in RGASPI.538-2-10, 16–19; Münzenberg letter to Jung, 27 April 1922, RGASPI.538-2-10, 20; and protocol of the IAH Russia meeting, 30 August 1922, in RGASPI.538-3-3, 19.

15. In a three-page letter sent to Eberlein at Comintern Secretariat, dated 30 June 1922, Jung confessed to giving Januschek the money used to buy the toys, but disavowed knowledge of what was apparently done with it. In RGASPI.538-3-4, 86 (back).

16. According to an English-language translation of the "Protokol [*sic*] of the General Meeting of the citizens of the village of Toikino numbering 210 men . . . ," 24 July 1922, more than half of the town's 250 residents were without any access to horses, and the rest were awkwardly sharing 60, which were already exhausted, underfed, and overworked. RGASPI.538-3-4, 68.

17. Undated English-language letter "Dear Comrades," ms signed Audrey Faline? from a member of the American Communist Party who worked with the Ware party at Toikino in summer 1922, letter circa August or September 1922. In RGASPI.538-3-4, 70. The amount of groceries purchased was 2,950 poods or about fifty tons.

18. From Comrade Baum's report for "Uralbuero," as recorded in the protocol of the IAH Russia meeting, 30 August 1922, RGASPI.538-3-3, 20–21.

19. Ware letter to Jung at Hotel Lux Moscow, 1 August 1922, RGASPI.538-3-4, 66.

20. Undated English-language letter "Dear Comrades," RGASPI.538-3-4, 70–71.

21. Winninger's scheme was to buy "third-rate" used clothes, instead of new ones, with the money. He used the difference to buy horses, which he then resold on the black market.

22. See Edwin Hörnle's "Bericht über den Stand der Kinderheime der IAH im Ural," circa April 1923, in RGASPI.538-3-9, 49–52. Although this report is unsigned, it is virtually identical to the less informative one Hörnle gave at the June 1923 IAH Congress in Berlin. It is clear this is Hörnle's work.

23. Protocol of the Russian IAH meeting, 30 August 1922, in RGASPI.538-3-3, 12. The addresses are listed, and the exact nature of the various properties in Moscow best described, in a Russian-language report of the first IAH auditing commission, circa October 1922, in RGASPI.538-3-6, 25–28.

24. From the German-language version of Jung's "Report on the Workers' Relief in Russia," 28 June 1922, in RGASPI.538-3-4, 41.

25. On the cocoa and clothing dumping schemes, see letter from the German Communist Günther Tonn to Münzenberg, 4 January 1923, RGASPI.538-3-11, 2; Münzenberg's same-day response to Tonn, in which he makes no effort to dispute Tonn's allegations but indicates that he will be very unhappy if Tonn mentions any of this to either the KPD or Comintern headquarters, RGASPI.538-3-11, 3–4; a letter from Schacht to Münzenberg, 18 January 1923, RGASPI.538-3-11, 5-6, which again confirms Tonn's allegations; and a lengthy Schäfer-Eiduk report dated 29 January 1923, RGASPI.538-3-11, 17–35, which owns up to everything that went on and provides details lacking in the other sources, such as the escalating price of cocoa in the black markets of Petrograd and Moscow, and the salary and administrative costs which prevailed in August 1922, before (they claim) the mess began to be cleaned up.

26. Münzenberg letter to Zinoviev, 1 August 1922, RGASPI.538-2-9, 52–54.

27. Münzenberg letter to Comintern Secretariat, 12 June 1922, RGASPI.538-2-9, 37.

28. See the English-language contract signed on 20 July 1922 by Münzenberg for IAH, Juliet Stuart Poyntz for FSR, and Frank P. Walsh as legal counsel. "A corporation is to be organized in America," the contract reads, "in the state having laws most favorable to the successful promotion of the undertaking." IAH headquarters in Berlin receives a controlling stake of 51 percent of the American branch, on the basis of compensation it will itself determine. Copy of contract signed by Münzenberg, Poyntz, and Walsh, 20 July 1922, RGASPI.538-2-8, 92–93.

29. Münzenberg had been playing around with the "workers' loan" idea since October 1921, when he formed the first IAH commission of experts, headed by Professor Alfons Goldschmidt, to look into the possibility. (Protocol of the emergency IAH meeting, 11 October 1921, RGASPI.538-2-1, 59–61.) Although the loan is not mentioned in the founding statutes of the Industrie- und Handels-Aktiengesellschaft, it was clearly part of the plan; the new corporation gave Münzenberg the first plausible organizational cover for the loan, which was launched by the Berlin office on 22 August 1922 and approved by the Council of People's Commissars on 13 September 1922. Gross, *Willi Münzenberg*, 126.

30. Münzenberg had, in fact, already established an IAH subcommittee with the express purpose of "the liquidation of the relief [campaign]." See protocol of IAH meeting in Berlin, 9 September 1922, RGASPI.538-2-8, 7–10.

31. Copy of contract signed by Münzenberg, Poyntz, and Walsh, 20 July 1922, RGASPI.538-2-8, 92. See also "Statuten der Industrie- und Handels-Aktiengesellschaft.

Internationale Arbeiterhilfe für Sowjet-Rußland. Gründer: Wilhelm Münzenberg, Francesco Misiano, Juliet Stuart Poyntz, Johannes Brommert, John William Kruyt. Berlin, den 28. Juli 1922." RGASPI.538-2-8, 94–97 (back).

32. Schäfer-Eiduk report dated 29 January 1923, RGASPI.538-3-11, 25.

33. Protocol of the executive meeting at IAH headquarters in Berlin, 23 September 1922, RGASPI.538-2-8, 7–10.

34. Schäfer-Eiduk report dated 29 January 1923, RGASPI.538-3-11, 18–19.

35. Gross, *Willi Münzenberg*, 129.

36. *Sowjet-Russland im Bild*, 10 (July 1922) and 12 (September 1922); Münzenberg, *Das neue Russland* (Berlin, Verlag der I.A.H. 1922).

37. Oehring/Hofer Russian IAH circulars, 10 and 27 August 1923, RGASPI.538-3-14, 23, 25.

38. Several of the Toikino tractors were resold for eighteen thousand dollars in 1923, according to the "Bericht über den Stand der Moskauer Geschäftsstelle zum 20.XII.23," RGASPI.538-3-9, 29.

39. Letter cited by Gross, *Willi Münzenberg*, 124.

40. Hal Ware plays a starring role in Sam Tanenhaus's recent biography, *Whittaker Chambers* (New York: Random House, 1997).

41. See the German-language translation of a Russian-language report by E. Lindwart from Astrakhan to Russian IAH headquarters, 27 September 1923, RGASPI.538-3-12, 92–93.

42. According to the protocol of the IAH Congress in Berlin, June 1923, in RGASPI.538-1-3, 64.

43. See 15 February 1923 Russian IAH report, RGASPI.538-2-17, 22.

44. From Kruyt's report for the auditing commission, as transcribed in the protocol of a Russian IAH Executive meeting, 16 June 1923, RGASPI.538-2-17, 62–63.

45. See the protocol of the auditing commission meeting with Moscow IAH leaders, 5 to 9 July 1923, RGASPI.538-3-9, 1–2.

46. Protocol of the 29 June 1923 meeting of the Russian IAH with Udov, Oehring, Kruyt, Kress, Blanchet, Eggebrecht, and Hofer present, RGASPI.538-3-9, 7.

47. The loss on the felt boots was $4,016.35 on revenues of $3263.71, according to Münzenberg's own report at the June 1923 IAH Congress, in RGASPI.538-1-3, 39.

48. "Kassen-Umsatz der I.A.H. vom 15/XII 1922–15/XII 1923, account for "Schuhfabrik." RGASPI.538-3-16, 38.

49. Protocol of the Berlin Executive IAH "Arbeitssitzung," 30 October 1923, RGASPI.538-2-17, 89. For this period, the hair salon's losses were 900 gold rubles on revenues of 136 rubles.

50. From Münzenberg's report at the June 1923 IAH Congress, 538-1-3, 31. For details on the American aid bounty, see FSR's "Jahresbericht 'B.' Vergleichende Aufstellung der Ueberweisungen von Hilfsgeldern für drei Finanzjahre—vom 9. August 1921 bis 31. Juli 1924." Over $124,000 collected for famine relief was sent directly to Berlin between 1921 and 1924.

51. "Bericht über die Moskauerabteilung der int. Arbeiterhilfe z.H. des Zentralkomité in Berlin und dem Schweizerbureau," 16 April 1923, RGASPI.538-3-9, 13; protocol of the June 1923 Berlin IAH Congress, 538-1-3, 57; and "Bericht der Revisionskommission der I.A.H. Die Arbeit in Russland," 5 June 1923, 538-2-18, 134. Significantly, the restaurant was the one property on which Münzenberg refused to discuss liquidation in the second half of 1923, when the scrutiny of the auditing commission called all of his concessions into question

before the governing bodies of ECCI. He pointedly refused to hand the restaurant back to the Soviet authorities, for example, at the Executive IAH "Arbeitssitzung" in Berlin which was attended by leading Russian IAH employees on October 30, 1923. RGASPI.538-2-17, 90.

52. From the protocol of the June 1923 Berlin IAH Congress, 538-1-3, 36.

53. "Bericht ueber die Besichtigung des Gutes Pinajewo durch die Kontrollkommission der I.-A.H. vom 23–26-ten Mai 1923. Delegierter: Jakob Fausch," RGASPI.538-2-18, 63–65.

54. "Bericht ueber die Revision der Unterstelle Saratow . . . ," RGASPI.538-2-18, 110–11.

55. Jung mentioned this loan—floated in 1922 for one million dollars by Hillman of the American tailors union—in connection with his plans for Ural-AG in his "Bericht über die Arbeiterhilfe in Russland," 28 June 1922, RGASPI.538-3-4, 43.

56. "Bericht über die Tätigkeit der A.G. Traktor-Meschrabpom im Ural," 6 December 1923, RGASPI.538-3-9, 25 and back.

57. See the German translation of a Russian-language field report by Bartaschewitsch addressed "An die Leitung der I.A.H.," circa May 1923, RGASPI.538-2-18, 55–56; and Otto Roth's report at the June 1923 Berlin IAH Congress, 538-1-3, 55. The legend about Jung sticking a gun under Münzenberg's nose is recounted by Gross, *Willi Münzenberg*, 123.

58. This entirely typical comment was Kress's in his "Bericht ueber die Fischerei der I.A.H. in Astrachan," RGASPI.538-2-18, 112–14.

59. Auditing commission letter, from Kress, Fausch, et al., to IAH Berlin, 16 May 1923, RGASPI.538-2-18, 116–18.

60. Münzenberg letter to Comintern Secretariat, 27 June 1923, 538-2-19, 94.

61. *Die Dritte Saüle der kommunistischen Politik. I.A.H.* (Berlin: Verlagsgesellschaft des Allgemeinen Deutschen Gewerkschaftsbundes, 1924).

CHAPTER 8. *Germany Red or Black*

1. The best account of the March action and its aftermath is that of Angress, "The 'Unauthorized' Bid for Power (1921)," in *Stillborn Revolution*, 105–219.

2. Angress, *Stillborn Revolution*, 293–94.

3. Quoted by Joachim Fest, *Hitler*, trans. Richard and Clara Winston (New York: Penguin, 1974; original German edition 1973), 163–64. For analysis of the ideological context of this position, see also Ian Kershaw, *Hitler 1889–1936: Hubris* (New York: Norton, 1998), 191–93.

4. Münzenberg, "Eine neue Ruhrbesetzung," in *Hammer and Sickle* (February 1923): 7.

5. Quoted by Fest, *Hitler*, 164.

6. Angress, *Stillborn Revolution*, 298.

7. Radek, "Russisches Brot für deutsche Klassenkämpfer!" *Rote Fahne*, 8 March 1923: 5.

8. The Russian grain shipment to the Ruhr is not mentioned in the protocols of any of the IAH Executive's Berlin meetings held on 1, 5, 6, and 8 March, in RGASPI.538-2-17, 17–38. Münzenberg mentions the upcoming Russian grain shipment only after Radek announced it in *Rote Fahne*, in two letters to Moscow dispatched on 13 March 1923, in RGASPI.538-2-19, 32–33.

9. Gross, *Willi Münzenberg*, 136.

10. Radek, "Russisches Brot für deutsche Klassenkämpfer!"

11. Angress, *Stillborn Revolution*, 323.

12. On the Radek affair with the German Foreign Office in late May 1923, see Angress, *Stillborn Revolution*, 320–25. That Russian military advisors and intelligence operatives were in the Ruhr as early as 7 February 1923 is confirmed in Walter Krivitsky's memoirs, *In Stalin's Secret Service* (New York: Harper, 1939), 38–41. See also David J. Dallin's critical study of *Soviet Espionage* (New Haven, Conn.: Yale University Press, 1955), 72–75.

13. See, for example, Pipes, *Russia under the Bolshevik Regime 1919–1924*, 431–32. Among diplomatic historians, the case is made most strongly by Freund, *Unholy Alliance*, 157–63.

14. Cited in Angress, *Stillborn Revolution*, 333–34.

15. Krivitsky, *Stalin's Secret Service*, 42. Krivitsky's claim is buttressed by the amount of hand-wringing ink spilled on this subject in Moscow. Münzenberg himself wrote a report on the theme "Radek, Reventlow und die Folgen" in early August, a report he forwarded to Brandler at the KPD Zentrale on 8 August 1923, according to his same-day letter to Brandler, DBB, RY 1/I 6/7/1, 179. On Ludendorff's forays into politics, see Gerald D. Feldman, *Army, Industry, and Labor in Germany, 1914–1918* (Princeton, N.J.: Princeton University Press, 1966), 141–45; 158–62; 180–88; 407–8; 455–56; and 499–500; and Feldman, *Great Disorder*, 207–8, 741–45.

16. See, for example, Radek, "Kommunismus und deutsche nationalistische Bewegung," in *Rote Fahne*, 17 August 1923: 5.

17. "Nieder mit der Regierung der nationalen Schmach und des Volksverrat!" ibid., 29 May 1923: 1.

18. Onetime KPD activist Franz Borkenau recalls taking the "Schlageter campaign" to university students in spring and summer 1923, with very limited success. Borkenau, *World Communism: A History of the Communist International* (Ann Arbor: University of Michigan Press, 1962), 248.

19. Fischer's tirade was transcribed by an SPD eyewitness and reproduced in *Vorwärts*, 22 August 1923. Cited by Angress, *Stillborn Revolution*, 340.

20. "Die jüdischen Kommerzienräte Stresemanns," *Rote Fahne*, 7 August 1923: 2.

21. "Rede des Genossen Remmele in der Faschistenversammlung in Stuttgart," ibid., 10 August 1923: 9.

22. Aktionsausschuss der Kommunistischen Internationale und der Roten Gewerkschafts-Internationale, Moscow, 3 March 1923, as reprinted ibid., 9 March 1923): 1.

23. "Auf zum Kampf gegen den Faschismus!" ibid., 10 March 1923, 1.

24. Angress, *Stillborn Revolution*, 333.

25. See the protocol of the June 1923 IAH Congress, in RGASPI.538-1-3, 284; and Zinoviev letter to Münzenberg, 18 May 1923, in RGASPI.538-2-17, 55.

26. Misiano et al. letter to ECCI, 14 May 1923, in RGASPI.538-2-19, 49–50.

27. Münzenberg letter to ECCI, 4 June 1923, in RGASPI.538-2-19, 69.

28. See ECCI resolution no. 55, 7 June 1923, in RGASPI.538-3-19; and ECCI letter to Münzenberg, 7 June 1923, in RGASPI.538-2-19, 66.

29. Münzenberg letter to ECCI, 21 June 1923, in RGASPI.538-2-19, 80.

30. See, for example, Münzenberg's rambling memorandum to Zinoviev from his Moscow hotel room, 12 July 1923, in which neither the Ruhr crisis nor the nascent German hunger campaign is mentioned once. RGASPI.538-2-19, 100–101.

31. "Hände weg von Sowjetrussland!" *Rote Fahne*, 13 May 1923: 5.

32. This really was the convoluted political logic of the new IAH campaign, although

I left out the part about the conspiratorial assassination of a Soviet diplomat by pro-British, Turkish oil interests. Actually the Bolshevik was murdered by a White Russian who despised the Bolshevik regime.

33. According to Barthel, Sinclair complained about the misuse of his name for many of the IAH's campaigns in the early 1920s, of which "Hands off Soviet Russia" was undoubtedly one. Barthel, *Kein Bedarf,* 159.

34. See the somewhat amateurish-looking document headed "Gesellschaft der Freunde des Neuen Russlands," preserved in DBB, RY 1 / I 4/7/4, 113. There are, however, no actual signatures to prove that any of these figures were really actually involved.

35. At least as an ideological flavor of the month. The Society of Friends of the New Russia lasted hardly a year, although it would later reappear in various similar versions.

36. See Münzenberg letters to Piatnitskii, 8 August 1923; to ECCI, 10 August 1923; to Piatnitskii, 13 August 1923; and to Kuusinen, 13 August 1923, in RGASPI.538-2-19, 106–10. Although Münzenberg's name appears nowhere on the masthead, *Swastika* was clearly his brainchild, a propagandistic labor of love he put considerable time into. He mentioned it for the first time in a letter to the Comintern Presidium on 2 August 1923 (RGASPI.538-2-19, 103–5) and proudly sent the inaugural issue to Piatnitskii on 28 August 1923 (enclosure with letter, RGASPI.538-2-19, 116) before it was first distributed in Germany.

37. *Das Hakenkreuz,* September 1923.

38. See graphics "Gedenkblatt an den Verfassungstag in Weimar" and "Der Budenzauber," in *Das Hakenkreuz,* 15 September 1923; and "Das 'Hakenkreuz' verboten! Politische Karikaturen als Verbotsgründe," *Rote Fahne,* 20 September 1923: 3.

39. See Feldman, *Hugo Stinnes: Biographie eines Industriellen 1870–1924,* trans. Karl Heinz Siber (Munich: Verlag C. H. Beck, 1998), 886–87; English edition forthcoming from Cambridge University Press. See also Feldman, *Great Disorder,* 741–45.

40. See Fest, *Hitler,* 168–70.

41. Membership in the largest national union organization, the ADGB, dropped from about seven million at the beginning of the Ruhr crisis to merely four million early in 1924.

42. See Angress, *Stillborn Revolution,* 380–87.

43. The date of the Politburo decision is suggested by Boris Bajanov in his memoirs, *Avec Staline dans le Kremline* (Paris: Les éditions de France, 1930), 190–98. For the Communist plans more generally, see Wolfgang Leonhard, *Völker hört die Signale: Die Anfänge des Weltkommunismus 1919–1924* (Munich: Bertelsmann, 1981), 337–40; and Angress, *Stillborn Revolution,* 398–404.

44. On the questionable figures chosen by the French to lead the separatist uprising, see Robert G. L. Waite, *Vanguard of Nazism: The Free Corps Movement in Postwar Germany 1918–1923* (New York: Norton, 1952), 234.

45. Krivitsky, *Stalin's Secret Service,* 43. For a lurid and somewhat unreliable memoir of a veteran of the KPD T-groups, see Walter Zeutschel, *Im Dienst der kommunistischen Terror-Organisation (Tscheka-Arbeit in Deutschland)* (Berlin: Dietz, 1931).

46. The best account of the inflation, and all its social repercussions, is Feldman's *Great Disorder.* See also Feldman, "Bayern und Sachsen in der Hyperinflation 1922/23," *Historische Zeitschrift* 238 (3) (June 1984): 569–609.

47. Alexander Barmine, *One Who Survived: The Life Story of a Russian under the Soviets* (New York: Putnam, 1945), 139.

48. Ruth Fischer, *Stalin und der deutsche Kommunismus* (Frankfurt-am-Main: Verlag der Frankfurter Hefte, 1948), 379–80.

49. Citations in Angress, *Stillborn Revolution*, 427–28.

50. See Grégoire Bessedovsky, *Oui, j'accuse! Au service des Soviets* (Paris: Librairie de la Revue Française, 1930), 62.

51. See Ruth Fischer, *Stalin*, 445.

52. Dallin, *Soviet Espionage*, 73–74; Angress, *Stillborn Revolution*, 417–23.

53. According to Zeutschel (*Terror*, 13), Brandler bragged in Moscow that nearly five hundred thousand had been armed, but Zeutschel puts the real figure at one-tenth that amount.

54. Angress, *Stillborn Revolution*, 431.

55. I have been unable to establish exactly when or how this shipment reached Germany, but from later references to its size (3,000 tons), it appears highly likely that the grain Münzenberg gave as gifts to the governments of Thuringia (788 tons) and Saxony (2,000 tons) came from the strategic reserve in Petrograd. See, for example, Russian IAH memo to Piatnitskii, 6 February 1924, in RGASPI.538-3-19, 30. See also "Russisch-Sächsischer Getreidelieferungsvertrag," *Rote Fahne*, 20 October 1923: 1; and Heinz Habedank, *Zur Geschichte des Hamburger Aufstandes 1923* (Berlin: Dietz Verlag, 1958), 80.

56. The most extensive (if rather biased) account of the Hamburg uprising is DDR historian Heinz Habedank's *Zur Geschichte des Hamburger Aufstandes 1923*.

57. Angress, *Stillborn Revolution*, 460–61.

58. Ibid., 463–74.

59. Münzenberg letter to Zinoviev, "persönlich," 9 November 1923, in RGASPI.538-2-19, 142.

60. Orgburo resolution no. 97, 25 October 1923, in RGASPI.538-3-19, 143. This resolution followed up on a 22 October 1923 Comintern resolution, co-signed by Barthel for IAH and Piatnitskii for ECCI, which had created an "All Soviet Unified Committee to Aid the Hungry Workers of Germany and Their Children." RGASPI.495-60-12, 2.

61. Barthel circular "An alle Unterstellen der Internationalen Arbeiterhilfe in Russland," 1 November 1923, in RGASPI.538-3-12, 75.

62. Barthel memo to Zinoviev, 1 November 1923, in RGASPI.538-3-10, 52.

63. "There is in the current moment," Zinoviev earnestly intoned, "no greater duty for internationally minded workers than to send aid to the hungry, struggling workers of Germany and their children." *Hunger in Deutschland* 1 (5) (13 November 1923): 1.

64. ECCI resolution no. 31, 10 November 1923, reproduced in RGASPI.-538-3-19, 140.

65. The short-lived bulletins have been preserved in RGASPI.538-2-21, 39–60.

66. According to a memo from Barthel to Zinoviev, 20 October 1923, in RGASPI.538-3-10, 48.

67. Münzenberg letter to Piatnitskii at Comintern Secretariat, 28 October 1923, in RGASPI.495-60-12, 19. He also sent a deliberately vaguer report on the new campaign to Zinoviev on the same day, which gave the misleading impression that the IAH was already being swamped with donations for the German hunger campaign, and thus needed no help from anyone. Münzenberg letter to Zinoviev, 28 October 1923, DBB, RY 1/I 6/7/1, 189–90.

68. The liaison man was Comrade Dogadov, who was to oversee the IAH fund-raising campaign in the USSR on behalf of the ECCI. ECCI letter to Münzenberg, 6 November 1923, in RGASPI.538-2-19, 143. See also Münzenberg letter to ECCI, 9 November 1923, RGASPI.538-2-19, 140.

69. See the "Secret Müller Report, 9 November 1923," RGASPI.538-2-19, 144–48.

70. Angress, *Stillborn Revolution*, 390.

71. Barthel letter to Zinoviev, 20 October 1923, in RGASPI.538-3-10, 48.

72. Notarized document on Russian IAH stationery, addressed to the Comintern on 13 November 1923, RGASPI.538-3-10, 55. "Prombank" was the state-owned Bank of Industry and Trade of the USSR, the "prom" being short for the Russian word for "industry," *promyshlennost'*.

73. From the Protokoll of the IAH World Congress in Berlin, 11 December 1923, exclusive Communist-only session. In RGASPI.538-1-4, 20.

74. See "Richtlinien für die Organisation der Komitees der IAH in Deutschland," enclosure with Münzenberg letter to Piatnitskii, 5 February 1924, in RGASPI.538-3-19, 20.

75. According to a member of Berlin's city council who reported at the open session of the IAH World Congress in December, in September 1923 there had been 106 suicides in Berlin and 11 deaths directly attributable to hunger. RGASPI.538-1-4, 26.

76. See the protocol of the December 1923 IAH Congress, RGASPI.538-1-4, 3, 144.

77. "Richtlinien für die Organisation der Komitees der IAH in Deutschland," RGASPI.538-3-19, 21, 28.

78. "Liste der Speisestellen der I.A.H. in Deutschland," circa February 1924, RGASPI.538-3-18, 10.

79. Although the IAH still purported itself to be "nonpartisan," its new organizational base in Germany was inevitably superimposed on the preexisting KPD structures, as a 24 January 1924 Münzenberg request to the KPD secretariat for district party addresses in Kiel, Essen, Stettin, Bremen-Bremerhaven, Lübeck, and other German cities, suggests. Letter preserved in DBB, RY 1/I, 2/3/225, 23.

80. Police report sent in from Gelsenkirchen to Berlin, 10 July 1924, in RGASPI.538-2-23, 145.

CHAPTER 9. *Follow the Money*

1. By way of apologizing to his Berlin boss, the self-confessed embezzler, Comrade Martin, promised to send fifteen thousand dollars of this stash to support Münzenberg's German hunger campaign, so long as ten thousand dollars could be used directly by the Communist Party, which at the time was "completely broke." See Münzenberg letter to ECCI, 28 December 1923, RGASPI.538-2-19, 193 (and back), 194 (and back).

2. "Streng vertraulich" ECCI reply to Münzenberg, circa late December 1923, RGASPI.538-2-19, 199.

3. See letter from Gosbank to Russian IAH headquarters, asking for written proof of authorization for the debt write-off from the Kremlin, 22 March 1923, RGASPI.538-3-14, 12. The ECCI resolution that officially turned the IAH worker loan obligations over to the Soviet government passed on 25 April 1923 (RGASPI.538-3-19, 138). The earliest written evidence of IAH debt to Prombank I have found is a receipt of payment, dated 14 April 1923, which lists a credit of £4,237 10s. or slightly over $20,000, extended "through Prombank." RGASPI.538-3-14, 17. Ultimately Prombank would become the principal financial guarantor of the IAH's solvency in Russia, and would in fact legally foreclose on many of its operations in 1925–26.

4. Münzenberg authorized the initial capital expense, according to the protocol of the IAH executive meeting held in Berlin on 19 January 1923, RGASPI.538-2-17, 13. That the rent went unpaid is established in a complaint filed with Russian IAH headquarters by comrades Kosakov and Parakhkin of the Tsentral'noe Upravlenie Rybolovstvo, Arendno-Khoe. otdel., 28 December 1923, RGASPI.538-3-14, 45.

5. Kassen-Umsatz der I.A.H. vom 15/XII–15/XII 1923, RGASPI.538-3-16, 38.

6. With the exception of members of the hated auditing commission, who to their chagrin were charged full price while staying at Lux in late May 1923, a slight which may have contributed to their foul mood when they wrote up their scathing audit. See IAH auditing commission memo sent to ECCI, ms signed Kress, Jak. Fausch, E. Kruse, 2 June 1923, RGASPI.538-2-17, 119. I have been unable to determine the provenance of the IAH stake in the Hotel Lux, mentioned by Münzenberg at an IAH executive meeting held in Berlin with representatives of the Russian IAH Moscow office on 2 March 1923, RGASPI.538-2-17, 25. It may have been given to Jung during the fire sale of summer 1922. The only commercial account showing revenues exceeding expenses is the workers' restaurant, which showed a profit of 190 *chervontsi* on income of 1,200 gold rubles.

7. See Kassen-Umsatz der I.A.H. vom 15/XII–15/XII 1923, RGASPI.538-3-16, 38. By far the most substantial credit listed in this financial statement, a net income of roughly 40,000 gold rubles on revenues of 46,251 rubles, is labeled merely "pro diverse." This is clearly a euphemism for loans taken out from Gosbank and Prombank, with the debit being interest payments to date on the loans. The only other sizeable credit listed in this Russian IAH financial statement, 4,000 gold rubles income against zero outlays, is unambiguously labeled "Laufende Rechnung i.d. Stadtbank," i.e., a running credit account opened up at one of the several banks controlled by the Moscow city government.

8. Financial statement for "Kinderhilfe," ms signed by Bailly, director of the Finance Department at Russian IAH, 8 December 1923, RGASPI.538-3-16, 31. Expenses (debits) for the children's homes were 92,497 gold rubles, revenues (credits) 9,023 rubles. Income from the "Paketabteilung" was 2,192 gold rubles. Expenses were fifteen *chervontsi* (on what exactly, I can't venture to imagine).

9. "Auszug aus dem Konto der Ural Aktien—Gesellschaft," ms signed Bailly for Russian IAH, 12 December 1923, RGASPI.538-3-16, 33.

10. This cynical arrangement was later described by Karl Müller, an IAH executive staffer in Berlin, in a 30 October 1924 letter to Piatnitskii, RGASPI.538-3-19, 209.

11. See the protocol of the closed IAH executive meeting held in Berlin on 30 October 1923, with Münzenberg, Misiano, Kruyt, and Oehring present, RGASPI.538-2-17, 89–92.

12. Münzenberg letter to Comintern Secretariat, 17 January 1924, RGASPI.538-2-23, 12.

13. See, for example, the 10 January 1924 letter to Münzenberg written by Käthe Dunker, chair of MOPR's Thuringia office, which Münzenberg proudly forwarded to Moscow. RGASPI.538-2-23, 6–7.

14. See ECCI resolutions on the German hunger campaign dated 19 February and 24 March 1924 both mentioned in Misiano's written complaint lodged with ECCI on 2 April 1924, in RGASPI.538-3-19, 82. See also Münzenberg letter to Comintern Secretariat, 2 April 1925, RGASPI.538-2-19, 86–87.

15. According to Münzenberg's letter to ECCI, 5 April 1924, RGASPI.538-2-23, 95; and Misiano letter to the Comintern Secretariat, 12 April 1924, RGASPI.538-3-19, 86–87, which repeats the allegations.

16. Münzenberg letter to Zinoviev, 27 April 1924, RGASPI.538-2-23, 110.

17. It is possible, of course, that this shift was engineered simply in order to protect FSR accounts from prying Communist Party hands in New York.

18. See 31 July 1924 FSR finance report labeled "Jahresbericht 'A.' Vergleichende Aufstellung. Für das dritte Finanzjahr, das am 31. Juli 1924 endete. (Mit jährlichen

Totalsummen für drei Finanzjahre vom 9. August 1921 bis 31. Juli 1924." The general donation funds for Russian relief had dropped from over $700,000 (fiscal year August 1921–July 1922) to under $40,000 in the third fiscal year (August 1923–July 1924). Donations for German relief totaled over $73,000 for the third fiscal year, of which about $49,000 had been collected by 30 April 1924.

19. See the 31 July 1924 FSR finance report labeled "Jahresbericht 'A' (Fortsetzung)" and "Jahresbericht 'B,'" RGASPI.538-2-24, 39–40. Of $133,000 raised by the FSR in the third fiscal year, from August 1923 to July 1924, some $102,000 were devoted directly to Russian and German food and clothing "aid." Of this, just under $28,000 went through Münzenberg's office in Berlin.

20. These and other names are listed on the letterhead of a letter from Chicago FSR secretary Rose Karsner to Münzenberg, 15 May 1924, RGASPI.538-2-24, 26.

21. See, for example, a letter from a Chicago man requesting help for his deaf-mute nephew who had been turned away from an IAH home upon his return from a Moscow hospital where he had been sent after taking ill, forwarded by Karsner to Münzenberg in late January 1924, RGASPI.538-2-24, 4; and the letter from "a foster mother to her adopted child [in the Soviet Union]," forwarded by Karsner to Münzenberg on 14 May 1924, RGASPI.538-2-24, 25.

22. See ECCI resolution no. 141, 5 May 1924, reproduced in RGASPI.538-3-19, 146.

23. The exact date of the MOPR takeover in Chicago is unclear. Münzenberg confessed, at a private IAH executive session held with his three principal lieutenants on 4 November 1924, that he was no longer receiving revenue from the United States (RGASPI.538-2-22, 41–42). See also Münzenberg's letter to the Comintern Secretariat on 22 December 1924, RGASPI.538-2-23, 201–3, and the 1 August 1924 report on the FSR's finances prepared by a New York–based accountant, J. B. Collings Woods, who may have been hired to audit the organization before its accounts were to be taken over by MOPR. In any case, this audit, preserved in RGASPI.538-2-24, 28–37, is the last FSR finance report preserved in the IAH files, and I have found no evidence FSR sent money to Berlin after 1 August 1924.

24. This, at least, was how Lovestone represented the "majority" view in the Chicago office when he met with Münzenberg in Berlin in late January 1925, according to Münzenberg's recollection in the protocol of an IAH executive meeting held in Berlin on 27 January 1925, RGASPI.538-2-26, 22a.

25. See, for example, the first page of Münzenberg's long letter to Zinoviev, 5 February 1924, in which he impugns the KPD generally for its rudderless inactivity over the preceding winter but contends that he sympathizes more and more with the left figures, who represent the most "rapidly forward-looking fraction in the KPD." RGASPI.538-2-23, 21.

26. Misiano confessed to the fund-raising diversion in a 2 April 1924 report to ECCI, RGASPI.538-3-19, 82. Two members of the Russian Communist Party's branch office in the Krasnopresnenskaya District were, soon thereafter, "invited" to join the Russian IAH Executive (RGASPI.538-2-20, 92), and a leading member of the party's Moscow apparat, B. M. Malkin, joined Russian IAH's film department in June (RGASPI.538-2-20, 97).

27. Undated Münzenberg letter "An das Nationalkomitee der I.A.H. Moskau," circa late December 1924, RGASPI.538-2-24, 123–24.

28. See Münzenberg letter to Kun, 15 December 1924, RGASPI.538-2-23, 194.

29. See protocols of the IAH executive meetings in Berlin on 27 January, 5 and 7 February, 4 and 8 March, and 27 April 1925, RGASPI.538-2-26, 23, 25, 26–27, 34–35, 38, 42.

30. This was the budget Münzenberg outlined to his staff at a meeting held in Berlin

on 28 April 1925, RGASPI.538-2-26, 45–48, before dispatching a request to Moscow for an immediate infusion of $16,000.

31. Münzenberg letter to Kornblum at ECCI, 29 April 1925, RGASPI.538-2-27, 49.
32. Münzenberg letter to Zinoviev, 7 May 1925, RGASPI.538-2-27, 51–52.
33. Münzenberg letter to Stalin, transcribed in Russian, 2 May 1925, RGASPI.538-2-28, 34. Münzenberg's request was fulfilled, although not until months later. He finally put Stalin on the cover of the 25 March 1926 *AIZ*.
34. See Münzenberg letter to Piatnitskii, 21 July 1925, RGASPI.538-2-27, 101.
35. I have been unable to locate copies of the preliminary foreclosure agreement with Prombank, but it is described in great detail by Münzenberg in his letter to Kornblum at ECCI, 18 December 1925, RGASPI.538-2-27, 240–43. The amount of total debt accrued by the IAH to Prombank by the end of 1925 was approximately 715,000 gold rubles, according to a four-page report Misiano sent to Kornblum at ECCI on 27 May 1926, reproduced in RGASPI.538-2-37, 77–80.
36. See Münzenberg's letter to ECCI, 10 December 1925, RGASPI.538-2-27, 222–25. He provides no evidence to support the contention that five thousand dollars a month (in profits?) was the amount of income that would be forfeited after foreclosure by Prombank. Expenses at Berlin headquarters, incidentally, were to be fifteen hundred dollars a month, not including outlays for conferences and executive travel.
37. The new subsidies did not arrive in time to prevent another round of staff bloodletting in January 1926, as three of the four remaining staff secretaries were fired. See Münzenberg letter to Kornblum and Zetkin, 20 January 1926, RGASPI.538-2-37, 3. Münzenberg's budgetary demands of December 1925 were not exactly met, but the five thousand dollars he demanded corresponds fairly closely to the total of the monthly ECCI subsidy for the Russian IAH office (five thousand gold rubles, or twenty-five hundred dollars, according to a report Misiano sent to Kornblum on 26 May 1926 [RGASPI.538-2-37, 79]), plus the RM 12,500 (about three thousand dollars) Berlin would receive monthly from Moscow, as reported in the IAH budget from September 1926 in RGASPI.538-2-34, 22–25.

Overall, in the first eight and a half months of 1926, some RM 110,000 worth of hard currency were transferred from Moscow to the Berlin IAH office, or about twenty-five thousand dollars. The budget for the Berlin office, incidentally, was in practice even larger as a percentage of overall revenue by September 1926 (roughly 60 percent) than Münzenberg had projected in his December 1925 projections. No less than RM 7,950, or around nineteen hundred dollars, was spent monthly by late summer 1926 on Münzenberg's executive office.

38. Misiano report to Kornblum, 27 May 1926, RGASPI.538-2-37, 77.

CHAPTER 10. *Hollywood East*

1. "Mezhrabpom" was a contraction of the Russian name of International Worker Relief, "Mezhdunarodnaia rabochaia pomoshch'."
2. Vance Kepley, Jr., "The Origins of Soviet Cinema: A Study in Industry Development," in *Inside the Film Factory*, ed. Richard Taylor and Ian Christie (London: Routledge, 1991), 70.
3. Ian Christie, "Introduction," in *The Film Factory: Russian and Soviet Cinema in Documents 1896–1939*, ed. and trans. Richard Taylor (London: Routledge & Kegan Paul, 1988), 5.
4. Kepley, "The Workers' International Relief and the Cinema of the Left 1921–1935," in *Cinema Journal* 23 (1) (fall 1983): 7–23.

5. Kepley's 1983 article on the "Workers' International Relief," which has served as the standard reference for all subsequent literature on the subject, primarily relies on Münzenberg, *Solidarität,* Münzenberg's self-glorifying whitewash of the IAH's finances (for which he was handsomely paid by the Kremlin).

6. The IAH charter is in RGASPI.538-3-1, 20–22.

7. See Münzenberg's (unsigned) letter to Zinoviev, 12 December 1921 (RGASPI.538-2-3, 115); and ECCI letter to Münzenberg, 24 January 1922, in RGASPI.538-2-9, 30.

8. Münzenberg letter from Moscow to the Comintern Secretariat, 7 March 1922, in RGASPI.538-2-9, 32.

9. Münzenberg letter to Zinoviev, 12 December 1921, RGASPI.538-2-3, 115.

10. Münzenberg's 16 December 1921 letter to ECCI's Little Bureau (RGASPI.538-2-3, 117–19), for example, was stamped received only on 29 December, by which time Münzenberg had gone ahead and appropriated the requested sum out of the IAH's general collections fund.

11. ECCI letter to Münzenberg, 24 January 1922, RGASPI.538-2-9, 30.

12. See Münzenberg letters to the Comintern Secretariat, 2 January and 7 March 1922, RGASPI.538-2-9, 14–16, 32.

13. *Rote Fahne,* 30 March 1922.

14. Kruse's most successful homemade *agitki* were *Russia Through the Shadows* and *Fifth Year.* See Kepley, "The Workers' International Relief and the Cinema of the Left 1921–1935," 10–11. Kepley's source for the figure of forty thousand dollars is an interview he himself conducted with Kruse in 1975.

15. Münzenberg tried to sell delegates to the IAH World Congress in June 1923 on a number of Soviet propaganda films, including *Das neue Russland, Völkermai, Die Rote Armee,* and a lurid cinematic eulogy to murdered Soviet diplomat Vaslav Vorovsky. Protocol of the June 1923 World Congress, in RGASPI.538-1-3, 268–69. No one, however, was buying, according to a later Münzenberg letter to the Comintern Secretariat, 4 December 1923, RGASPI.538-2-19, 185–86.

16. According to the minutes of an IAH Executive meeting held on 8 March 1923, the IAH had a "credit" of twenty-three thousand dollars at Sevzapkino. RGASPI.538-2-17, 40.

17. "Bericht über den Stand der Moskauer Geschäftstelle zum 20.XII.23," in RGASPI.538-3-9, 29.

18. See M. N. Aleinikov, "Zapiski kinematografista," chap. 5, typescript and ms memoirs, RGALI.2734-1-21, 38–40.

19. This review, circa spring 1923, was clipped and placed in an album in the Aleinikov fond, RGALI.2734-1-94, 34. The reviewer's initials are E. von P.

20. See, for example, Jay Leda's *Kino: A History of the Russian and Soviet Film* (London: George Allen & Unwin, 1960), 145–47. Leda, though he examined Aleinikov's memoirs, missed a crucial passage, where we learn that the money used to purchase film stock for Russ in Berlin in 1922—twelve million marks—came not from the sale of distribution rights to *Polikushka* but directly from Gosbank. See Aleinikov, "Zapiski kinematografista," RGALI.2734-1-22, 7–11 and 19–20.

21. According to Aleinikov, "Zapiski kinematografista," Maria Fedorovna Andreeva, a leading Bolshevik consultant on arts policy, passed along Lenin's instructions personally. Andreeva told Aleinikov soon before his departure for Berlin in 1922 that he must "get to know Willi Münzenberg . . . he will help you with advice and business [connections]."

22. In all the literature on the IAH and its involvement in the film business, Münzenberg is credited with providing necessary capital and film stock, etc., which allowed the Russ collective to thrive in the 1920s. But extant documents prove that Aleinikov received official permission from the Commissariat of Foreign Trade and Commerce, the Soviet Import Board, and the Board of Chemical Acquisitions to bring *Polikushka* to Germany on the express condition that he would return with positive and negative film stock, bought with money from Gosbank. See, for example, the contracts between Russ and Agfa for negative and positive film signed on 9 February, 22 November, 30 November, and 9 December 1922, in the Aleinikov fond, RGALI.2734-1-39, 3, 6, 8, 10.

23. Ads for showings of the movie first appear in *Rote Fahne*, for example, on 4 March 1923, where the IAH is declared to have a world monopoly on the film. *Rote Fahne*, 4 March 1923: 9. Max Barthel also reviewed Polikushka in Münzenberg's *Hammer and Sickle* (March 1923): 5.

24. According to Münzenberg's report to the June 1923 World IAH Congress in Berlin, in RGASPI.538-1-3, 270. I have been unable to determine the IAH's share from *Polikushka*'s gate revenues in German theaters, but it is likely the sum was insignificant in dollar terms, due both to the weakness of the mark and to the share claimed by Dafu, a studio to which Münzenberg soon fell deeply into debt.

25. From the protocol of the June 1923 World Congress, in RGASPI.538-1-3, 32.

26. The 26 June 1923 declaration of legal intent has been preserved in the Aleinikov fond, RGALI.2734-1-43, 1. Because Aleinikov kept copies of virtually all the important documentation of the evolving relationship between the IAH and the Russ collective over the years, he would almost certainly have preserved the 6 March 1923 agreement Münzenberg hinted at if it had existed elsewhere than in Münzenberg's own mind. It is more likely that any agreement reached between the parties in March was a verbal one, or that Münzenberg was merely referring to the successful premiere of *Polikushka* on that date, which in his mind justified the IAH's claim to special rights to the output of the Russ studio.

27. This was the verdict of Comrade Siegrist, in RGASPI.538-1-3, 273.

28. Most of the passages quoted were cited in Münzenberg's 6 October 1923 memo to ECCI, in RGASPI.538-2-19, 127–28. Among the reliably "communist" films Münzenberg named were *Hunger in Soviet Russia* and *Starvation on the Banks of the Volga*, which had long since come and gone, and were hardly topical in October 1923 now that the Soviet famine was over and the German "revolution" was on the immediate horizon. For Vallenius's perspective, see his report on Proletkino, circa autumn 1923, RGASPI.538-3-10, 35–37. Vallenius wanted to corral Münzenberg's film activities by forcing him to invest twenty thousand gold rubles in Proletkino, thus effectively tying the IAH's fortunes to those of Proletkino, then still woefully undercapitalized. On Proletkino generally, see A. Gak, "K istorii sozdaniia Sovkino," *Iz istorii Kino* 5 (1962): 132–33.

29. See the capitalization agreement preserved in RGASPI.538-3-12, 2–3.

30. Although Münzenberg's stake was, in theory, a controlling one, it fell short of what he was demanding in the way of revenue sharing, an 80-20 split between the IAH and Russ in the former's favor. See the protocol of the Executive IAH meeting in Berlin, 19 September 1923, RGASPI.538-2-17, 77–78.

31. The German films were: *Wilhelm Tell, Zirkus Jimmi, Caroline, Schreckensnacht*, and *Stadt in Sicht*. The IAH was to receive 25 percent of ticket sales for these films at Goskino theaters (regardless of administrative costs) and 60 percent of Goskino's take at non–

Goskino-owned cinemas. Distribution costs were to be picked up by the IAH until the films crossed the Russian border. See the German translation of Russian contract, headed "Vertrag No. 101," dated Moscow 12 December 1923, RGASPI.538-3-15, 8.

32. From the protocol of the June 1923 Berlin IAH Congress, RGASPI.538-1-3, 266.

33. Protocol of the Russian IAH meeting held on 27–28 June 1924 in Moscow with Münzenberg present, RGASPI.538-3-17, 12–15.

34. Protocol of the Berlin IAH Executive meeting, 4 November 1924, RGASPI.538-2-22, 41–42.

35. *Aelita*, directed by celebrated auteur Iakov Protazanov, is one of those curiosities of the silent film era that has been madly overpraised by film critics and historians for reasons that escape me. Certainly its bizarre costumes had the appeal of novelty to contemporary audiences, but its flimsy plot and inconsistent production values have hardly allowed it to stand the test of time against silent classics like *Birth of a Nation, Potemkin, Dr. Caligari*, or the films of Charlie Chaplin and Buster Keaton, for example.

36. Münzenberg letter to Piatnitskii, 29 April 1924, RGASPI.538-2-23, 114.

37. Münzenberg letter to Kolaroff, 31 March 1924, RGASPI.538-2-23, 82–83.

38. Münzenberg letter to Piatnitskii, 29 April 1924, RGASPI.538-2-23, 115–16.

39. "Fortsetzung des Protokolls der Verhandlungen zwischen Genosse Misiano und Münzenberg," circa December 1924, RGASPI.538-2-22, 57 and back.

40. Aufbau A.G. (London Office), balance sheet for the year ending 31 December 1924, RGASPI.538-2-25, 47–48. Previous to fiscal year 1924, £462 worth of film stock had already been purchased but remained unused; another £650 was spent on films in 1924. Total revenue for fiscal year 1924 from the sale of distribution rights and from ticket sales at IAH fund-raisers, etc., was £102. Roughly half of the £3,300 provided to London by Aufbau Berlin, approximately £1,600, was written off as a loss, and by the end of the fiscal year 1924 Aufbau London's total outstanding debts to private creditors, some of which had been incurred in order to pay back Berlin, stood at £2,615.

41. From the French-language protocol of the IAH Congress held in Paris from 14–17 April 1925, RGASPI.538-1-6, 28–30. This exchange took place in the Hotel Bellevilloise on 15 April.

42. Münzenberg letter to Kornblum at Comintern Secretariat, 29 April 1925, RGASPI.538-2-27, 49.

43. See the 1 August 1924 agreement in the Aleinikov fond, RGALI.2734-1-44, 1. The loophole in this contract revolved around the terms "profit" *(pribyl')* and "losses" *(ubytki)* which were rather malleable concepts in the IAH universe. Russ films were anyhow, as a general rule, so absurdly expensive by the standards of the time, that profit on even the most popular films simply never materialized.

44. I am basing these figures on a 1929 budget report that lists individual salaries, many of which remained constant throughout the 1920s. Aleinikov, for example, who was both studio chief and a producer of many of its films, was paid 800 gold rubles a month beginning in 1917; Protazanov received 750 gold rubles a month beginning in 1924. Moskvin's salary was 500 gold rubles in 1928, but this was almost certainly after a contract renegotiation; he may have made more before, when he was younger and more active. In all, 380 individual salaries are listed, which collectively add up to 56,639.09 gold rubles a month. See document titled "Spisok shtatnykh sotrudnikov 'Mezhrabpom-Fil'm' po sostoiano na 1.7.29," in the Aleinikov fond, RGALI.2734-1-49, 1–9.

45. See Münzenberg letter from Berlin to the Comintern Secretariat, 9 December 1925, RGASPI.538-2-27, 218–21. Fourteen M-Russ films were sold to the Lloyd film company for fifty-two thousand dollars. Münzenberg claims to have made a rival bid of sixty-two thousand dollars for the same package, but this is unlikely to have been taken seriously. The IAH had all but gone into receivership in December 1925, with its Russian assets being held in escrow by Prombank.

46. Misiano letter to Sovkino, copied to Malt'sev at ZK RKP, 18 November 1925, RGASPI.538-2-27, 189.

47. Münzenberg letter to Kornblum at ECCI, 18 December 1925, RGASPI.538-2-27, 241–42.

48. Ibid., RGASPI.538-2-27, 240.

49. According to a Münzenberg report to ECCI, 4 October 1926, RGASPI.538-2-34, 148. On the origins of the Prometheus deal with the KPD, see also Gross, *Willi Münzenberg*, 168. I have been unable to find the original documentation of the IAH's takeover of Prometheus, but Gross's story of a backroom deal between old friends seems plausible. There is no mention of Prometheus in Münzenberg's correspondence before 1926, which suggests that he acquired the company somewhat haphazardly—certainly it was not a carefully planned and executed takeover.

50. See letter from "Prometheus Filmverleih- und Vertriebs GmbH" to Sergei Eisenstein, reproduced in *Eisenstein und Deutschland: Texte, Dokumente, Briefe*, ed. Oksana Bulgakova (Berlin: Akademie der Künste/Henschel Verlag, 1998), 74–75.

51. See document labeled "Eingabe der Gründer der Aktien-Gesellschaft 'MESCHRABPOM-RUSS' der Industrie- und Handelsbank der USSR (PROMBANK), des Zentralkomitees der Internationalen Arbeiterhilfe (MESCHRABPOM) und der vollen kinematographischen Genossenschaft 'Künstler-Kollektiv RUSS,'" 4 September 1926, RGASPI.538-2-38, 73.

52. See "Bericht über eine Revision in der 'Prometheus' Filmverleih und Vertriebs GmbH am Mittwoch, den 30. Juni 1926," RGASPI.538-2-35, 72–73. Despite its success, *Potemkin* clearly did not pull Prometheus into the black. According to an IAH financial report from 1928, the founding capital of Prometheus, which had been fronted by the KPD, was RM 10,000. By September 1927, the outstanding obligations at Prometheus had reached RM 400,000 (about $100,000), according to the "Sept. 1927 Revisionsbericht." And the firm's (optimistic) projected operating deficit for 1928, which incorporated interest payments on debts incurred to date, was RM 300,000, or thirty times the firm's founding capital. From a sixty-page report titled "Bericht über die Tätigkeit der IAH in den letzten Jahren," ms signed "Heimo" for the Comintern Executive, circa late May–early June 1928, RGASPI.538-2-44, 292–93.

53. See M-"Russ Eingabe," 4 September 1926, RGASPI.538-2-38, 73 (back).

54. In the periodic recapitalizations of M-Russ that occurred almost annually from 1924 to 1930, the original private American investors in the studio who had put up $375,000 (750,000 gold rubles) in 1923 were never again listed as shareholders. I have been unable to determine their names, or what became of them. Based on the exponentially expanding studio budget, though, I think it is safe to conclude that Aleinikov spent their money without qualms—and that they never saw a penny of it again.

55. Münzenberg letter to Axelrod at Prombank, 28 September 1926, RGASPI.538-2-38, 82–83. In a letter dispatched to the other members of Prombank's governing body on 29 September 1926, the day after he wrote Axelrod, Münzenberg admitted that all of

the IAH's Russian ventures had stayed afloat due to the bank's endless extension of credit. In RGASPI.538-2-38, 85.

56. This according to the 4 September 1926 "Eingabe," which assigned the IAH 61,000 gold rubles worth of shares out of 700,000. Inevitably, Münzenberg and his Moscow staffers disputed the size of their shares repeatedly over the coming months. Misiano was creative enough at one point to subtract the 180,000-ruble debt write-off from Prombank's own share (actually a clear majority stake, 450,000 rubles) and add it to the IAH's minority stake. See Misiano letter to Prombank, 15 October 1926, RGASPI.538-2-38, 109. But that was merely wishful thinking. In a sharply worded 3 November 1926 communiqué dispatched from Moscow to Berlin, Axelrod tried to put an end to such claims, reminding Münzenberg that the 3 September 1926 recapitalization agreement had been signed under the full authority of the Soviet government. Unsigned Axelrod letter to Münzenberg, 3 November 1926, RGASPI.538-2-38, 112.

57. This last Otsep film was actually a co-production of Russ and Prometheus, filmed in Berlin with a joint Russian-German crew.

58. From the twenty-page "Bericht der Revisionskkomission [sic] der Internationalen Arbeiter Hilfe über die bei Meschrabpom-Film durchgeführte Revision," 3 July 1929, RGASPI.538-2-52, 53–57.

59. For a brief summary of these claims, see the five-page letter from Münzenberg and Misiano "An das Rat der Volkskommissare der UdSSR," 11 December 1928, RGASPI.538-2-47, 58–62.

CHAPTER 11. *Preempting the Peace*

1. In the Japanese campaign, Münzenberg's envoy, Comrade Rothkegel, remained stuck in Shanghai, unable to obtain permission to see the Japanese consul about arranging aid shipments to Japan until he had first obtained papers from the German ambassador to China who, in turn, refused to see him. See Rothkegel letters from Shanghai to IAH Russian in Moscow, 20 and 26 December 1923, RGASPI.538-3-11, 47–50.

The Chinese campaign, though unsuccessful, was not quite so embarrassing. At least five thousand marks earmarked for the flood victims had made it to the IAH's Peking office by 1926. But this all came from direct Moscow subsidies, as the IAH was unable to secure any donations in Europe. Further, nearly 70 percent of this sum was funneled into supplementing IAH salaries in the Peking office. See the IAH finance report dated 17 September 1926, RGASPI.538-2-34, 23.

On the abortive English miners' strike campaign, see Münzenberg's own complaint lodged in a letter sent to Geschke or Kornblum at ECCI on 27 September 1926, RGASPI.538-2-37, 149–51.

2. Approximately a thousand marks per month were thrown at the *Kolonial-Abteilung* in 1926, according to the September 1926 IAH budget in RGASPI.538-2-34, 22–25.

3. For examples of Münzenberg's vigorous lobbying, see his letters to Kornblum, 6 July 1926, RGASPI.538-2-37, 101; to Piatnitskii, 17 August 1926, RGASPI.538-2-37, 115; and to Manuil'skii, 17 August 1926, RGASPI.538-2-37, 110. Manuil'skii, already a member of the ECCI Präsidium, joined Piatnitskii in the new Comintern Secretariat, which took over effective control from departing ECCI President Zinoviev in November–December 1926. Münzenberg reported on his meeting with Bukharin in a letter to Kuusinen at ECCI, 24 August 1926, RGASPI.538-2-37, 118. As part of the judgment against Zinoviev at ECCI,

his office of president was abolished at the seventh enlarged plenum of the Comintern Executive in November 1926. Bukharin, his successor, became primus inter pares in the new Comintern political secretariat.

4. Münzenberg, "For a Colonial Conference," *International Press Correspondence* (London edition), 26 August 1926.

5. Münzenberg first made this demand in a letter to Kuusinen at ECCI, 9 September 1926, RGASPI.538-2-37, 124–25. The anti-imperialism conference was already in the planning stages at ECCI the previous spring, although Münzenberg was then considered only one possible candidate for handling the affair. See the "Resolution der Kommission zur Prüfung der Angelegenheit eines Kolonialkongresses in Brüssel," dated 30 March 1926, in RGASPI.495-60-76, 2–3.

6. This plan was outlined in an attachment to Bukharin's letter to Kuusinen at ECCI, RGASPI.538-2-37, 126–35.

7. See the "Bericht des Gen. Münzenberg über die vorbereitende Kommission anlässlich des 10. Jahrestages der Oktoberrevolution," 25 May 1927, RGASPI.495-60-117, 36–41.

8. The monthly subsidies were to be reviewed in November 1926, according to a report Misiano sent to Kornblum on 26 May 1926, RGASPI.538-2-37, 79.

9. Münzenberg letter to Stalin, 26 November 1926, RGASPI.538-2-37, 170–71, with accompanying six-page attachment outlining plans for the Russian Revolution tenth anniversary celebrations, RGASPI.538-2-37, 172–77. In typically indirect style, Münzenberg waited until the final page of this dispatch to broach the subject of cash.

10. See, for example, the top-secret Russian-language Münzenberg memo to the Soviet Finance Ministry's Special Currency Committee, 4 December 1926, RGASPI.538-2-38, 121.

11. See letter from Paris addressed "Lieber Willi," possibly from Misiano, 24 December 1926, RGASPI.538-2-38, 123.

12. Letter from Comintern Secretariat, probably from Heimo, to Münzenberg, copied to Kuusinen, 8 January 1927, RGASPI.538-2-40, 12–15.

13. See letter from Comintern Secretariat, probably from Heimo, to Münzenberg, copied to Kuusinen, 8 January 1927, RGASPI.538-2-40, 12–15. Heimo, a Finnish associate of Otto Kuusinen, worked for nearly fifteen years on organizational matters at ECCI, from 1920 to 1935. He and his wife were executed in 1937 during Stalin's purges.

14. Whether or not it was true the Asian delegates had left by January 11, it seems clear that Münzenberg had already diverted IAH funds to pay for Chiang Kai-shek's trip: RM 8,260 show up under the label "Kuomintang" in an IAH budget report covering income and expenses for 1 January 1926 to 30 September 1927. RGASPI.538-2-41, 9. Since the income for "Kuomintang" matched the expenses exactly, we may conclude that the money Münzenberg put up for Chiang Kai-shek's trip was reimbursed by Moscow, as Heimo promised in his 21 January 1927 letter to Münzenberg, RGASPI.538-2-40, 33–35.

15. Münzenberg letter to Heimo, 11 January 1927, RGASPI.538-2-40, 20–23.

16. A copy of this excerpt, stamped 18 January 1927, is preserved in RGASPI.538-2-40, 24.

17. See Heimo's letter to Münzenberg, 21 January 1927, RGASPI.538-2-40, 33–35.

18. On Münzenberg's maneuvering on the eve of the Brussels conference, see Eduard Fuchs letter to Kameneva, 27 January 1927, in DBB, Nachlass Clara Zetkin, NL 5/73, 36. Münzenberg's remark to Heimo was made in a 24 January 1927 letter, RGASPI.538-2-40, 36.

19. For examples of Münzenberg's maneuvering for the new Italian fascism portfolio, see his 25 January 1927 letters to Heimo (RGASPI.538-2-40, 43) and to Bohumil Smeral (RGASPI.538-2-40, 52).

20. Münzenberg's final slogan was reported in a letter to Heimo dispatched from Berlin on 5 February 1927, just days before the Brussels congress was to begin. RGASPI.538-2-40, 82.

21. Münzenberg later reminded Bukharin of their prior conversation in Berlin, in a 1 February 1927 letter, RGASPI.538-2-40, 72. Bukharin's various endorsements were reported by Heimo in letters to Münzenberg dispatched on 26 January and 9 February 1927, RGASPI.538-2-40, 55–58, 108.

22. Most of the press speculation was centered in Amsterdam and New York, according to Heimo's letter to Münzenberg, 26 January 1927, RGASPI.538-2-40, 55, 57. Kuusinen, who helped direct the campaign that ousted Zinoviev from the Comintern presidency in 1926, was a Stalinist to the core. He would outlast both Heimo and Bukharin, and would later be installed as president of Stalin's puppet Finno-Karelian Republic from 1940 to 1956.

23. Münzenberg letter to Heimo, 7 February 1927, RGASPI.538-2-40, 83.

24. Eduard Fuchs's description, invited to the meeting as a representative of the old IAH-affiliated Society of the Friends of the New Russia, in a letter to Olga Kameneva, 27 January 1927, in DBB, NL 5/73, 33.

25. Fuchs's 27 January 1927 letter to Kameneva, DBB, NL 5/73, 37–38. Fuchs asked in a postscript that Kameneva forward the letter to Zetkin, who dutifully preserved it in her papers.

26. Although Münzenberg did still need to be reimbursed for Brussels, as he had borrowed substantially from private German banks to foot the bill. See Münzenberg's letter to the Comintern Secretariat, 19 March 1927, RGASPI.538-2-40, 159. Heimo's complaints were registered in letters to Münzenberg of 5 and 19 February 1927, RGASPI.538-2-40, 81, 117.

27. The German Reichssicherheitshauptamt, for example, took note of the hand-wringing in the Amsterdam secretariat in its 15 October report on Münzenberg's "Liga gegen koloniale Unterdrückung," DBB, RY 1/R/134/35, 107–9.

28. Heimo letter to Münzenberg, "Zu vernichten!" 23 February 1927, RGASPI.538-2-40, 121–22.

29. The official renewal of the IAH's general mandate was registered in ECCI's "Resolution zur Frage der Internationalen Arbeiter-Hilfe," 7 February 1927, RGASPI.495-60-114, 3–6. On the eve of the Brussels conference, *AIZ*'s circulation, according to Münzenberg's 7 February 1927 letter to Heimo, crossed 200,000 for the first time. He predicted at this time that it would reach 500,000 by the end of the year (RGASPI.538-2-40, 83–85). But although the Kremlin's subsidies gradually increased, he was still unable to sell more than about 350,000 copies by early 1928, according to a 20 April 1928 Münzenberg report to Heimo, RGASPI.538-2-44, 66. *Welt am Abend* also had a banner year, on paper anyway, expanding its circulation from around 125,000 in winter 1927 to 200,000 by the following October, according to Münzenberg's boast in a 10 October 1927 letter to Piatnitskii, RGASPI.538-2-40, 326.

30. Münzenberg did dispatch a telegram to the U.S. government protesting the upcoming execution in April 1927, but he paid little heed to the protests as they heated up over the summer. A resolution outlining the agitprop priorities of the IAH's reconstructed American branch office, which Münzenberg forwarded to ECCI on 1 August 1927, makes no mention of Sacco and Vanzetti. RGASPI.538-2-40, 300.

31. The money was collected through International Labor Defense, the new moniker of the Chicago FSR office after it was taken over by MOPR in 1925. The office, run by an able organizer named James Cannon, collected nearly five hundred thousand dollars, of which only about six thousand dollars was turned over to the Sacco and Vanzetti Defense Committee, according to Johannes Zelt, *Proletarischer Internationalismus im Kampf um Sacco und Vanzetti* (Berlin: Dietz, 1958), 127–28. Zelt, an East German Communist, was given access to selected Comintern archives in Moscow, but still, his five-hundred-thousand-dollar total sounds suspiciously round. I have found no independent corroboration of Zelt's claims in my own research.

32. Stephen Koch gives Münzenberg credit for International Labor Defense's fundraising windfall, citing little evidence other than Babette Gross's recollection. Münzenberg, Koch writes, was the "guiding spirit of Red Aid," whereas in fact, Red Aid was one of Münzenberg's most bitter enemies, whom he never forgave for the devastating FSR takeover in Chicago. Koch, *Double Lives,* 31–37, 346–47.

CHAPTER 12. *The Red Millionaire*

1. Gross, *Willi Münzenberg,* 123, 173, 175, 186. Gross claims that Münzenberg frequently had to "escape" from the police, but so far as I have been able to determine, no warrant for his arrest was issued after the Stuttgart warrant from 1919 was dropped in summer 1921. As a Reichstag deputy from April 1924, Münzenberg enjoyed immunity from prosecution—which did not prevent the Prussian police from tailing him and keeping voluminous files on him, although these related mostly to public events and open IAH publications.

2. After his death in 1934, Hirschfeld would achieve international fame when Münzenberg's Communist collaborator Arthur Koestler edited an improbable bestseller promoting his theories, *Sexual Anomalies and Perversions (etc.) (1938).*

3. Gross, *Willi Münzenberg,* 186–87.

4. See the 12 July 1926 "Antrag auf Einsetzung gegen den Genossen Willi Münzenberg, M.d.R.," DBB RY 1/I 2/6/2, 99–106. The proposal for Münzenberg's expulsion was warmly received at the Berlin-Brandenburg district party headquarters, but was then quietly hushed up at the KPD Zentrale. Clearly mere local functionaries had no jurisdiction over a high-ranking apparatchik like Münzenberg, who after all served directly under ECCI. See letter from KPD Zentrale Sekretariat to Bezirksleitung Berlin-Brandenburg, 15 July 1926, DBB, RY 1/I 2/6/2, 118.

5. These details were apparently reported by Babette Gross when she was interviewed by Koch in 1989, for (typically) he gives no attribution or reference for them. Koch, *Double Lives,* 8, 12. While not all of Gross's recollections are reliable, these at least seem to fit the picture of Münzenberg painted by others who knew him well, such as Margarete Buber-Neumann, Gustav Regler, Manès Sperber, and Arthur Koestler.

6. Margarete Buber-Neumann, *Kriegsschauplätze der Weltrevolution: Ein Bericht aus der Praxis der Komintern 1919–1943* (Stuttgart: Seewald Verlag, 1967), 262.

7. See, for example, the recollection of Münzenberg by his onetime staffer Manès Sperber in his autobiography *All Our Yesterdays,* vol. 2: *The Unheeded Warning, 1918–1933,* trans. Harry Zohn (New York: Holmes & Meier, 1991), 168–70.

8. See Buber-Neumann, *Von Potsdam nach Moskau: Stationen eines Irrweges* (Stuttgart: Deutsche Verlags-Anstalt, 1957), 200.

9. After receiving IAH funds to attend Münzenberg's anti-imperial conference,

Chiang had returned to China, turned against his Communist benefactors, and seized power by crushing their first major putsch in the famous Shanghai "bloodbath" of 12 April 1927. On the Chinese uprisings of 1927, see S. A. Smith, "The Comintern, the Chinese Communist Party and the Three Armed Uprisings in Shanghai, 1926–1927," in *International Communism and the Communist International 1919–1943*, ed. Tim Rees and Andrew Thorpe (New York: Manchester University Press, 1998), 254–70. On Neumann's role in Canton, see Richard C. Thornton, "New Comintern Strategy for China," in Drachkovitch and Lazitch, *Comintern*, 66–110.

10. See Gross, *Willi Münzenberg*, 205. Neumann's standing with Stalin was greatly reinforced at the August 1927 Comintern Congress, where he was one of the most vocal denouncers of Trotsky and Zinoviev.

11. And Münzenberg paid Neumann respect for taking charge of the bloody uprising in Canton, serenading the martyrs of Neumann's foolhardiness in *AIZ* 9 (49) (December 1930), in a graphic captioned, "Den Helden der Kantoner Kommune vom Dezember 1927 gewidmet."

12. See the Münzenberg request for direct subsidies for all of his German illustrated publications, lodged with the Special Foreign Currency Commission at the Soviet Finance Ministry circa summer 1930, RGASPI.538-2-58, 85 (and back). Whereas *AIZ* was churning through $2,250 a month, its poor agitprop stepsisters had to make do with a mere $200 between them to cover monthly expenses.

13. See Münzenberg's finance report on the IAH press, sent to Kornblum at the Comintern Orgburo, 2 January 1926, RGASPI.538-2-35, 66–67.

14. The projected November 1928 revenues for *Nos Regards* added up optimistically to 11,200 francs, of which 1,500 came merely from Berlin subsidies and 5,000 from suspicious-sounding "collective subscriptions." Total projected expenses were 53,381 francs, of which no less than 13,100 francs were earmarked for the salaries of the four senior editors. See the budget reproduced in Münzenberg's letter to the ECCI publishing department, 14 November 1928, RGASPI.538-2-44, 198–200, 202. See also Gross, *Willi Münzenberg*, 151.

15. For fiscal year 1928, advertising and other revenues for *The Coming War* totaled the miserly sum of RM 201.22, according to the IAH "Bericht über die finanzielle Entwicklung der einzelnen Betriebe und Organisationen im Jahre 1928" forwarded to Heimo by Misiano on 4 January 1929, RGASPI.538-2-44, 122–27. On the anti-imperialist league, see also Gross, *Willi Münzenberg*, 194.

16. In its 15 October 1927 report, the German Reichssicherheitshauptsamt took note of Münzenberg's plans for conferences in Paris, Mecca, and elsewhere. DBB, RY 1/R 134/35.

17. Nor could there have been, as non-Muslims are not allowed in Mecca (though Münzenberg seems to have been unaware of this). On the runaway expenses of the anti-imperialist league, see Münzenberg's letter to Heimo, 20 April 1928, RGASPI.538-2-44, 65.

18. See the ad for the Universum-Bücherei in *Welt am Abend*, 22 November 1926. The financial plan for the book club was described in "Bericht über die Tätigkeit der IAH in den letzten Jahren" (circa late May–early June 1928), in RGASPI.538-2-43, 281.

19. Universum's income for April 1928, for example, totaled RM 10,628, of which most came simply from the dues paid by the club's seventy-two hundred members. Revenues from book sales were only about RM 2,500. At typical prices for NDV fare (usually around RM 5), the number of books sold, then, was about five hundred, or about one for every fifteen members. This, in the sixteenth month of the book club's existence.

20. In its first year, Universum ran up a deficit of RM 58,452, or about $15,000, according to a secret financial report distributed at the September 1927 IAH World Congress labeled "Revisionsbericht an die Executive der IAH." The red ink at Universum prompted Münzenberg to ask ECCI for money to cover the venture, which could no longer be financed by diverting monies from other accounts. See Münzenberg letter to Heimo, 20 April 1928, RGASPI.538-2-44, 67.

21. *Film und Volk* was published by Prometheus from February 1928 to March 1930. Monthly dues for the film club were fifty pfennigs, according to "Bericht über die Tätigkeit der IAH in den letzten Jahren" (circa late May–early June 1928), RGASPI.538-2-43, 280. The venture was not a total failure, drawing in about four thousand marks in monthly dues in the second half of 1928, which would imply it had about eight thousand loyal members. But this was still not enough to cover monthly expenses of fifty-five hundred marks on equipment, staff salaries, and *Film und Volk* (which alone cost a thousand marks monthly). See "Bericht über die finanzielle Entwicklung der einzelnen Betriebe und Organisationen im Jahre 1928," RGASPI.538-2-44, 123.

22. The address of this warehouse is provided in a 13 October 1927 Reichssicherhauptsamt report on the German Left, DBB, RY 1/R 134/35, 56, which mentions the proletarian film archive.

23. Weltfilm was created to facilitate the "coordination of proletarian film organizations in European countries," and to further the "creation and distribution of films made by affiliated organizations." See the 17 August 1928 IAH Executive circular, signed by Münzenberg, 538-2-44, 19. In its first four months, Weltfilm spent about sixteen thousand marks on various IAH film-related ventures, and earned nothing, according to the "Bericht über die finanzielle Entwicklung der einzelnen Betriebe und Organisationen im Jahre 1928," RGASPI.538-2-44, 122. Clearly the venture was a dummy corporation, designed as a financial scapegoat for revenue-draining IAH film projects. In September 1929, for example, Münzenberg blamed Weltfilm for a rash of cash-flow problems, and ordered its directors to be fired. See the protocol of the 2 September 1929 IAH Executive meeting, RGASPI.538-2-52, 4–5.

24. The IAH files in Moscow are filled with "sample" and "special" issues of these bulletins, the production qualities of which are unimpressive, to say the least. The layout and editing seem to have been done by total novices, who were not even given access to the printers ordinarily used by NDV and Kosmos.

25. *Die Dritte Saüle der kommunistischen Politik. I.A.H.* (Berlin: Verlagsgesellschaft des Allgemeinen Deutschen Gewerkschaftsbundes, 1924).

26. Eugen Prager, "Der Münzenberg-Konzern. Die Geschäfte des kommunistischen Hugenberg," *Volksrecht*, 28 March 1929. Prager's article was published the next day in the Berlin *Vorwärts* and was soon reprinted by most provincial SPD organs as well.

27. Throughout 1929 and 1930, the "Münzenberg-Konzern?" offprint was advertised in other IAH media organs at a price of ten pfennigs a copy.

28. Prager's flow-chart erroneously depicts Rote Hilfe as one of the cash sources of the "Münzenberg-Konzern."

29. Draft typescript "Willi Münzenberg/Unser Konzern," circa spring 1929, RGASPI.538-2-75, 55.

30. Cited in Gross, *Willi Münzenberg*, 197.

31. Clearly the term enjoyed popular currency in the IAH and NDV offices where

Gross worked. Gross titles an entire section of her book "The 'Red Millionaire,'" and uses the term repeatedly. But she gives no attribution for the phrase, aside from her own memory of working with Münzenberg.

32. At least after they took power, when the *Völkische Beobachter* described Münzenberg as, for example, "a cunning individual endowed with a truly Jewish business sense." Cited by Gross, *Willi Münzenberg*, 252. Until 1931, the Nazis paid little attention to Münzenberg, although the *Völkische Beobachter* did gleefully cite the SPD's labeling of him as a "Communist Hugenberg" in April 1929. See "Hinter den Kulissen der K.P.D. und S.P.D. Die kapitalistische Durchsetzung des Marxismus. Der Münzenberg-Konzern—Ullstein als Manager," *Völkische Beobachter*, 13 April 1929: 2.

33. "Ein kommunistischer Raffke. Willi Münzenbergs Bankkonto," *Arbeiterzeitung*, 16 September 1930.

34. John A. Leopold, *Alfred Hugenberg: The Radical Nationalist Campaign against the Weimar Republic* (New Haven, Conn.: Yale University Press, 1977), 96.

35. Paid advertisements in *Welt am Abend* typically took up less than one-third of a page in an eight-page daily spread. *AIZ*, which relied mostly on the same advertisers, did not do much better, filling up between half a page and one full page of a sixteen-page spread with ads—even though it was a monthly (until 1927, when it went bi-weekly, and 1928, when it went weekly). The costs of these newspapers, then, were obviously picked up by the IAH, which in turn received most of this money from Moscow—and from private bank loans, also later to be paid back by Moscow. From 1 January 1926 to 30 September 1927, for example, NDV ran up nearly two hundred thousand marks (about fifty thousand dollars) of debt, of which about a quarter came from *Welt am Abend*, according to the "Revisionsbericht an die Executive der IAH," RGASPI.538-1-7, 56a, 58.

By the early 1930s, when circulation figures for all of Münzenberg's flagship publications peaked, direct Kremlin subsidies earmarked for the IAH press reached upward of 60 and 70 percent of operating costs, making indirect subsidies from the IAH (not to mention advertising revenues) all but unnecessary. No less than seventy-five hundred dollars of the eleven thousand dollars NDV spent each month on the IAH's newspapers was provided directly by Moscow subsidies, according to a lengthy financial report drawn up by Misiano and sent to the Special Currency Commission at the Soviet Finance Ministry on 27 October 1931, RGASPI.538-3-145, 23 (and back), 24 (and back). Thus it is highly unlikely the circulation figures—i.e., the number of copies Münzenberg ordered to be printed—corresponded even remotely to the number of loyal readers such figures implied.

36. Officially, Münzenberg's monthly salary was only RM 450, about the same as that of most senior Communist functionaries. See the 1927 "Monatsbudget für Büro Berlin," RGASPI.538-2-41, 12.

37. This claim from "Ein kommunistischer Raffke. Willi Münzenbergs Bankkonto."

38. Münzenberg, *Solidarität*. The original Russian-language version of this contract is in RGASPI.538-3-144, 46.

39. "Wohin mit dem Geld?" *AIZ*, 14 September 1927: 6.

40. Ibid., January 1925, March 1926, December 1926.

41. "Frauen der Revolution," ibid., 29 June 1927; "G.P.U.," ibid., 23 January 1928.

42. Flieg was the main liaison from the KPD Zentrale to the party's military and "terror" units during the preparation for the October uprising of 1923. If the KPD had taken power in Germany by force in the late 1920s or early 1930s, he would almost certainly

have become the security chieftain. As it turned out, because of his ties to Münzenberg and Neumann, he would fall victim to Stalin's purges. Flieg died in a Soviet prison in 1939.

43. See, for example, the rather revealing view from behind as two male "proletarian divers" take flight on the cover of *AIZ*, 30 May 1928.

44. "Die letzten Tage der Romanows" ran in installments in late March and early April 1926; "Die Kurtisanen der Hohenzollern. Diskrete Geheimnisse eines deutschen Fürstenhofes" ran in May 1928. The "Spionage im Weltkrieg" serial ran in September 1927. The *Welt am Abend* cover story for 27 April 1928 was "Adolf Hitler und seine Kanaille. Politik und Ehebruch bei den Nationalsozialisten." For the murder-and-mayhem aesthetic, see, for example, the 16 April 1928 *Welt am Abend* headline, "Die mörderische Strassenbahn. Furchtbare Katastrophe an der Heerstrasse," accompanied by graphic photographs of the carnage caused by the streetcar accident.

45. The best analysis I have found of the ideological struggles between Bolshevik rivals in the 1920s is Martin Malia's chapter on "The Road Not Taken: NEP, 1921–1928," in *The Soviet Tragedy: A History of Socialism in Russia, 1917–1991* (New York: Free Press, 1994), 139–75. For a more sympathetic view of the "Bukharin alternative," see Stephen Cohen, *Bukharin and the Bolshevik Revolution: A Political Biography 1888–1938* (New York: Oxford University Press, 1971).

46. This detail is reported by Gross, *Willi Münzenberg*, 203. The corruption in the Hamburg apparat is discussed at length in the rump Zentrale's 18 October 1926 protest sent "An das Exekutivkomitee der Kommunistischen Internationale in Moskau" after Stalin had come down on Thälmann's side, signed by Thalheimer, Walcher, Schreiner, Köhler, Fröhlich, and Enberle, preserved in DBB, RY 1/I 2/3/70, 160–62. The amount embezzled from party coffers by Wittorf was RM 1550. The KPD Zentrale resolution dismissing Thälmann from his posts is preserved in DBB, RY 1/I 2/3/70, 153.

47. Due to both financial and political problems, production at Mezhrabpom-Film, as the M-Russ studio was now called, was severely scaled back after 1928, to the point where Soviet critics of the studio were speaking of the "disbanding" of the "Mezhrabpomfilm cell and its leadership." See, for example, "Za rekonstruktsiyu sovetskoi kinematografii," *Na literaturnom postu*, February 1930: 2–4.

48. According to Fröhlich, all he said was that "if we [the so-called "conciliators" punished by ECCI for voting against Thälmann] really wanted to clean up the party, then we should long ago have tried to uncover corruption in the Münzenberg Trust." From Fröhlich's letter to Münzenberg, 4 December 1928, in DBB, RY 1/I 2/3/70, 109. Münzenberg's cover letter to the KPD Zentrale, dated 5 December 1928 (DBB, RY 1/I 2/3/70, 107), was accompanied by a copy of the protest letter he sent to Fröhlich the previous day (DBB, RY 1/I 2/3/70, 108). See also Gross, *Willi Münzenberg*, 204.

49. See, for example, "Münzenberg spaltet die IAH," *Gegen den Strom* 1 (1) (17 November 1928); "Der neue Kurs in der IAH," ibid., 1 (13) (30 March 1929); and "Diktator Münzenberg," ibid., 1 (22) (1 June 1929).

50. In the voluminous correspondence between IAH headquarters in Berlin and ECCI in Moscow preserved in opis' 2 of fond 538 at the Comintern archives in Moscow, Münzenberg mentions the Arbeiter-Fotografen-Bewegung, Universum-Bücherei, and the Volks-Film-Verband venture dozens of times in letters dating 1928 and earlier, but not once between 1929 and 1931. The first time, after 1928, when the book club is mentioned is in an IAH "Abschrift" sent to Moscow, dated 28 January 1932, RGASPI.538-2-80, 4. The film

and photo clubs seem to have died quiet and slow deaths. I have found no reference to either of them in the IAH files after 1928.

51. See the protocol of the 13 November 1928 IAH Executive meeting, RGASPI.538-2-44, 24–25.

52. As Münzenberg later complained, in the German hunger drive the IAH had fed "a hundred thousand workers" but won over barely four thousand of them as loyal IAH members. See Münzenberg et al. circular to all national IAH committees, 6 September 1929, in RGASPI.538-2-52, 84.

53. This percentage breakdown is based on the 1,430 members of the IAH in Saxony, in the IAH report titled "Die politische Zusammensetzung der IAH-Mitglieder," from the "Bericht über die Tätigkeit der IAH in den letzten Jahren" (circa late May–early June 1928), in RGASPI.538-2-44, 270.

54. This accusation against the IAH was leveled in *Gegen den Strom*, the organ of the KPD renegades ousted after the Wittorf affair. Münzenberg cited it in a speech he gave at the IAH *Reichsabteilung* conference at Dresden in April 1929. In DBB, RY 1/I 6/7/3, 16.

55. These were the key points in the "Dresden resolutions," as disseminated in the 6 September 1929 Münzenberg et al. circular to all national IAH committees, RGASPI.538-2-52, 83–86. See also undated report, circa late April 1928, entitled "Das Verhältnis des Zentralkomitees zu den einzelnen Unternehmungen," RGASPI.538-2-44, 70, and the critical article "Diktator Münzenberg," *Gegen den Strom* 1 (22) (1 June 1929).

56. See Münzenberg/Scholze circular to all national IAH central committees, copied to and ms signed off on by Heimo at ECCI, 4 June 1929, RGASPI.538-2-52, 33–39. A program for a typical seminar week, headed "Tagesordnung für den internationalen Schulungskursus des ZK der IAH, Herbst 1929," is preserved in RGASPI.538-2-52, 101.

57. Gross, *Willi Münzenberg*, 208. See also "Münzenberg gegen die Heuchler. Oeffentliche Diskussion mit dem Märchen vom russischen Blutterror auf," *Welt am Abend*, 6 November 1930. On the grounds for the trials themselves, see "Incendiaries. On the Trial of the Counter-Revolutionary 'Industrial Party' in the Soviet Union" and the "Text of Indictment: Indictment in the Matter of the Counter-Revolutionary Organisation," *Inprecorr*, 20 November 1930: 1061–62, 1077–1103.

58. The best explanation of the origins and implementation of the doctrine of "social fascism" in Germany is Hermann Weber's *Hauptfeind Sozialdemokratie: Strategie und Taktik der KPD 1929–1933* (Düsseldorf: Droste, 1982).

59. See, for example, "Hilferdings Zehnmilliarden-Etat. Neue Millionensteuern. Was die vier sozialdemokratischen Minister dem Volke bescheren," *Welt am Abend*, 19 January 1929; "Geheimer Korruptionsvertrag. Sozialdemokratische Minister als Ullstein-Angestellte," ibid., 2 April 1929; and "SPD-Geheimplan gegen Sowjetunion," ibid., 14 February 1930.

60. "Von Müller zu Mussolini," *Berlin am Morgen*, 28 May 1929.

61. "Geheimverhandlungen enthüllt! Sozialdemokraten bieten Zustimmung zum Diktaturkurs," ibid., 10 September 1930.

62. See, for example, Münzenberg, "Zum 12. Jahrestag der Sowjetunion," *Rote Aufbau* 2 (7) (November 1929); and "Argus," "Mussolini, Kerenski und Severing. Oder: Diktator und Masse," ibid., 3 (7) (July 1930).

63. Aside from his attacks on then Youth Socialist chairman Friedrich Ebert, Münzenberg depicted the "Erfurt party bureaucrats" as embodying a "mixture of shamelessness, stupidity, and commonness." Inevitably, such craven careerists were now perched high atop Weimar institutions, fat, old, lazy, and self-satisfied. Münzenberg, *Dritte front*, 29–34.

CHAPTER 13. *Tango with the Devil*

1. For a provocative recent argument that attributes the Great Depression to the blind faith of Western leaders in an antiquated gold standard, see Barry Eichengreen, *Golden Fetters: The Gold Standard and the Great Depression, 1919–1939* (New York: Oxford University Press, 1995).

2. Although the KPD was not directly involved in Hugenberg's plebiscite campaign, the party Zentrale put through a strong resolution condemning the Young Plan, with rhetoric every bit as extremist as that coming from the Nazis, on 24–25 October 1929. Weber, *Hauptfeind*, 122.

3. "Kommunist sein heisst Todfeind des Sozialfaschismus sein." *Rote Fahne*, 9 February 1930.

4. At the end of 1929, the party counted 135,000 dues-paying members. This number had dropped to 120,000 by April 1930. Weber, *Hauptfeind*, 26.

5. The original law, enacted for a duration of five years under Chancellor Josef Wirth of the Catholic Center Party in 1922, had been extended for another two years in 1927. See Heinrich August Winkler, *Der Schein der Normalität: Arbeiter und Arbeiterbewegung in der Weimarer Republik 1924 bis 1930* (Berlin: Dietz Verlag, 1985), 308, 678, 796–97.

6. From Severing's speech in the 141st session of the Reichstag elected in 1928, held on 13 March 1930, as transcribed in the *Verhandlungen des Reichstags. IV. Wahlperiode 1928* (Berlin: Druck und Verlag der Reichsdruckerei, 1930), 4420.

7. From Münzenberg's speech, ibid., 4431–40.

8. For a sympathetic portrayal of Brüning's futile efforts to form a true parliamentary coalition, see William Patch, Jr., *Heinrich Brüning and the Dissolution of the Weimar Republic* (New York: Cambridge University Press, 1998), 72–117. On the army's role behind the scenes in Brüning's accession to the chancellorship, see Gordon Craig, *The Politics of the Prussian Army, 1640–1945* (New York: Oxford University Press, 1955), 433–37.

9. The issue of whether Brüning's essentially deflationary economic policies can be blamed for the depth to which the German Depression sank between 1930 and 1932—with all the attendant political consequences—has sparked passionate historiographical debate. For a summary of the controversy, see Jürgen Baron von Kruedener, ed., *Economic Crisis and Political Collapse: The Weimar Republic 1924–1933* (New York: St. Martin's Press, 1990).

10. On the "Einheitsfront von unten" line, see Weber, *Hauptfeind*, 26–30.

11. Resolution cited by Weber, *Hauptfeind*, 27.

12. "Ku-Klux-Klan stürmt Kinderlager. 2000 Faschisten brennen IAH-Lager nieder," *Welt am Abend*, 16 August 1930. See also, for example, "Drei Arbeiter heute Nacht von Nationalsozialisten ermordet," ibid., 17 May 1930; and "Blütige Wahlschlacht. Nazitrupps überfallen kommunistische Versammlung. 70 Verletzte," ibid., 18 July 1930.

13. The KPD membership rolls, which dropped from 135,000 to 120,000 between December 1929 and March 1930, were back up to 127,000 by August. Weber, *Hauptfeind*, 26–31.

14. Cited by ibid., 31. See also Thälmann's "Programmatic Declaration of the C.P. of Germany on the National and Social Emancipation of the German People," *Inprecorr*, 28 August 1930: 825–27.

15. Th. Neubaner, "Fascist Dictatorship with the Help of the Social Democratic Party of Germany," ibid., 9 December 1930: 1178.

16. Werner Hirsch, "Communism Advancing in Germany. The Result of the German Reichstag Elections," ibid., 18 September 1930: 901–2; and "Der Wahlsieg des roten Berlin," *AIZ* 9 (39) (September 1930): 762.

17. As transcribed in Hans Wesemann, "Interview mit Willi Münzenberg," *Die Weltbühne* 26 (37) (9 September 1930): 474–76.

18. Cited by Fest, *Hitler*, 126.

19. On KPD demographics in the Depression years, see Heinrich Winkler, *Der Weg in die Katastrophe: Arbeiter und Arbeiterbewegung in der Weimarer Republik 1930 bis 1933* (Berlin: Dietz Verlag, 1987), 595–600. The most thorough study of the demographics of Nazi voters, by Jürgen Falter, shows at once that the Nazis did very well among the unemployed, but that their substantial overall electoral gains between 1928 and 1932 in fact lagged behind the norm in districts in which unemployment was rising the fastest. Jürgen W. Falter, *Hitlers Wähler* (Munich: Beck, 1991), 296–303. See also Kershaw, *Hitler*, 404–5.

20. On the radical milieu in which such "side-switching" flourished, see Tim Brown's recent University of California, Berkeley, dissertation "Constructing the Revolution: Nazis, Communists and the Struggle for the 'Hearts and Minds' of the SA, 1930–1935" (2000), 80–81, 175–86. On Scheringer personally, see ibid., 80–101. See also Gross, *Willi Münzenberg*, 311.

21. "Nationale Einheit oder internationaler Sozialismus?" This was Strasser's formulation. Münzenberg himself re-phrased it before the debate as "Nationale Einheitsfront mit der Bourgeoisie oder internationale proletarische Solidarität und Klassenkampf?" For Münzenberg's own public gloss on the theme of the debate, see "Münzenberg gegen Otto Strasser," *Berlin am Morgen*, 7 January 1931: 2.

22. On the genesis of Strasser's splinter party, see Brown, "Constructing the Revolution," viii.

23. From the transcript labeled "Aussprache zwischen Kommunisten und Nationalsozialisten in den Pharussälen zu Berlin. Dienstag, den 6. Januar 1931, abends 8 Uhr," RGASPI.538-2-65, 1–2, 8, 10–13, 42–44, 45, 54.

24. "Der Kampfkongress gegen den Faschismus," *Welt am Abend*, 9 March 1931: 2.

25. See the ad for "Grosse internationale Kundgebung," ibid.

26. Münzenberg, "International Solidarity—Workers International Relief," *Inprecorr*, 13 May 1931: 467.

27. According to a Berlin police report, "Verbot der oeffentlichen Demonstrationen und Aufmaersche zum Solidaritaetstage der IAH durch das Berliner Polizeipraesidium," circa June 1931, RGASPI.538-2-66, 169.

28. See the groups listed in an IAH press release dated 15 May 1931 (RGASPI.538-2-71, 51–52).

29. From Münzenberg's speech as transcribed in the "Protokollauszüge der Exekutivsitzung der I.A.H. vom 19. und 20. Mai 1931 in Berlin," RGASPI.538-2-65, 60.

30. Münzenberg, "International Solidarity—Workers International Relief." Emphasis added.

31. Münzenberg forwarded the draconian terms of the SPD police ban to Moscow, presumably to justify having backed down from holding the Solidarity Day demonstrations. RGASPI.538-2-66, 169.

32. Citations in Weber, *Hauptfeind*, 40.

33. According to Weber, who has seen the transcripts of the relevant Zentrale meetings, the decision was made on 22 July after significant pressure in favor of joining the plebiscite campaign from Stalin, who was backed strongly by Molotov. Weber, *Hauptfeind*, 40–42.

34. Münzenberg, "Warum für den roten Volksentscheid? Eine Antwort an allerhand Kritiker und Besserwisser," *Berlin am Morgen*, 6 August 1931, suppl.: 5.

35. The letter is reproduced in Hiller's memoirs, *Köpfe und Tröpfe: Profile aus einem Vierteljahrhundert* (Hamburg: Rowohlt, 1950), 39–40.

36. The plebiscite received only about 37 percent support in all, and did especially poorly in Communist districts, where most voters simply stayed home. Weber, *Hauptfeind*, 41.

37. Gross, *Willi Münzenberg*, 215–16. Her account of the plebiscite campaign is more accurate than her treatment of most questionable episodes in Münzenberg's career, but as always she tries to absolve him of responsibility with all means at her disposal. She does it in this instance by blaming the "plebiscite" idea exclusively on "the Russians."

38. The ghostwriter, hand-picked by Münzenberg, was a certain Comrade Parwig, according to the protocol of an Executive IAH meeting held in Berlin on 2 September 1929, RGASPI.538-2-52, 4–5. Münzenberg's drafts of his introduction, along with assorted editorial comments and suggestions, take up an entire file folder in the Comintern archives in Moscow, RGASPI.538-2-69. The final attacks on "social fascists" wound up in Münzenberg, *Solidarität*, 12–13.

39. "Die erste Phase der wirtschaftlichen Tätigkeit," *Solidarität*, 493–509; "Die Tätigkeit der Meschrabpom-Film-A.G., Moskau," ibid., 509–21.

40. See Düninghaus's self-criticism delivered at the IAH German Congress that accompanied the October 1931 World Congress, RGASPI.538-2-67, 27–29.

41. See, for example, the introductory section, "Die Internationale Arbeiterhilfe und die Unterstützung von Massenstreiks und Wirtschaftskämpfen," ibid., 25–30; and extensive sections in the body of the book, such as "Von der Katastrophenhilfe zur Streikhilfe," ibid., 256–302.

42. Ibid., 8.

43. "Gesamtleistungen der IAH in zehnjähriger Tätigkeit 118,5 Millionen Mk.," ibid., 522.

44. Goptner had joined the Russian Social Democratic Party in 1903, and the Bolshevik faction while exiled in Paris in 1910. After the Revolution in 1917, she assumed high office in her native Ukraine, where she served as education commissar for most of the 1920s. In 1928, after Bukharin and his followers were removed from their functions in the Comintern leadership, she was called in to Moscow to serve in ECCI. By spring 1931 she was the senior Bolshevik inside the ECCI Secretariat. It was in June of that year that Münzenberg began sending his prized advertorial items—special issues of *AIZ*, *Solidarität*, and the like—to Goptner. See, for example, Münzenberg letters to Goptner, 2 June 1931, RGASPI.538-2-66, 19; 22 June 1931, RGASPI.538-2-66, 30; 29 June 1931, RGASPI.538-2-66, 37, etc.

45. Misiano originally requested forty-one thousand dollars (eighty-two thousand gold rubles) for Solidarity Day in March 1931, although it is likely that much of this never made it to Berlin, once the police ban was announced. See Misiano's letter to the Currency Department of Narkomfin, 16 March 1931, RGASPI.538-3-145, 14. On the anniversary congress, see the Russian translation of Münzenberg's note to Rudsutak, 9 September 1931, RGASPI.538-2-66, 62 (in which the formal request for the ten thousand gold rubles [five thousand dollars] was made); and Münzenberg's complaint that only half the money was received, lodged in a letter to Kaganovitch on 23 October 1931, RGASPI.538-2-66, 65. Ultimately this money was nowhere near enough, and Münzenberg had to dip deeply into IAH reserves, accruing debts that were, of course, ultimately paid back by Moscow.

46. See Misiano's 12 December 1930 budget for 1931 addressed *Zamestitelu Predsedatelya Soveta Narodnikh Komissarov SSSR*, RGASPI.538-2-144, 88, which requests 450,000 gold rubles for the year ($225,000); and his 27 November 1931 budget for 1932, addressed to the Special Currency Commission of Narkomfin, which demands $220,000, all of it devoted to ordinary operating expenses. RGASPI.538-2-145, 23–24 (and back). Most of the $18,000 or so in monthly subsidies was to be spent in Berlin, with $3,000 going to Münzenberg's office overhead and another $11,000 for NDV publications.

47. See Münzenberg's note on the "Ueberschwemmungskatastrophe in China," dispatched to Moscow from Berlin on 27 August 1931, and Misiano's follow-up Russian language note, dated 30 August 1931 and marked "top secret," forwarded to the All-Russian Central Council of Professional Unions, RGASPI.538-2-66, 52, 54 (and back). To all appearances this money never came through, as little attention was paid to the recent Chinese flood at the October Congress.

48. Münzenberg paid the travel expenses of most of the delegates with the first $2,500 installment from ECCI, waiting to buy their return tickets until he had received the second, according to an executive IAH memo headed "'I. Auswertung des Kongresses,' Vertretung in M.," dispatched to Moscow sometime between 9 and 16 October 1931, RGASPI.538-2-66, 130–31. The $2,500 was clearly not enough to cover delegates' total travel expenses, which ultimately totaled RM 24,494 (about $6,000). Individual IAH delegates did come up with nearly RM 21,000 (about $5,000) out of pocket for travel and other costs, but this would have offset less than a third of Münzenberg's expenses for the week, which included hotel bills, paper and printing costs, the hiring of stenographers, translators, and so on. The room and board expenses for the delegates, listed in the "Gesamt-Budget" as "sonstige Ausgaben—Aufenthalts-Spesen etc.," came to RM 34,924, or nearly $9,000. In all the conference cost over RM 66,000 (about $18,000). "Gesamt-Budget" for the October 1931 World IAH Congress, 538-1-10, 172–81. For details on attendees and their origins, see the "Bericht vom 8. Weltkongress der IAH. Berlin 1931," RGASPI.538-2-66, 94–97, and the attendance list at the top of the October 1931 conference protocol, RGASPI.538-1-8, 5.

49. From the protocol of the October 1931 IAH Congress, RGASPI.538-1-8, 40, 49–52, 54, 64–67.

50. A copy of this resolution is preserved in RGASPI.538-1-10, 25.

51. Letter from William Clarke to IAH headquarters in Berlin, 15 June 1932, RGASPI.538-2-81, 70.

52. See the program for the IAH's "revolutionäre Kulturwoche" of October 1930, RGASPI.538-2-59, 130–31; and undated Austrian IAH report, circa summer 1931, RGASPI.538-2-68, 56.

53. Burns letter to Münzenberg, 30 June 1932, RGASPI.538-2-81, 92–94.

54. See Isabel Brown's telegram to IAH headquarters in Berlin, 14 June 1932, RGASPI.538-2-81, 57; and her letter to Münzenberg, 23 June 1932, RGASPI.538-2-81, 84–86.

55. Karel Van Dooren letter to IAH headquarters in Berlin, 13 May 1932, RGASPI.538-2-81, 21.

56. Unsigned report from IAH Vienna, sent to Berlin on 13 June 1932, RGASPI.538-2-81, 47–48.

57. See Misiano's lengthy letter of complaints sent to PCF secretary Maurice Thorez from Berlin on 31 March 1932, RGASPI.538-2-80, 16–18.

58. See Onof letter to Münzenberg, 13 June 1932, RGASPI.538-2-81, 50–51.

59. From the transcript of Münzenberg's speech to the IAH Reichsabteilung, 8 October 1931? RGASPI.538-2-67, 134–35.

60. "Bericht über die Hilfsaktionen der Internationalen Arbeiterhilfe bei Streiks und wirtschaftlichen Massenkämpfen seit dem 8. Weltkongress der IAH (Oktober 1931)," circa November 1932, RGASPI.538-2-66, 181–202.

61. See Berlin IAH report on "Die Solidaritätskuchen des 'proletarischen Selbsthilfekomitees' gegen Erwerbslosennot. Bericht vom Oktober 1931 bis April 1932," circa May 1932, RGASPI.538-2-78, 10, 12.

62. "Bericht vom internationalen Solidaritätstag 1932," circa June 1932, RGASPI.538-2-81, 140–43.

63. Ehrt and Schweickert, *Entfesselung der Unterwelt: Ein Querschnitt durch die Bolschewisierung Deutschlands* (Berlin: Eckart-Verlag, 1932), 239–42. They cited Münzenberg's words from the IAH World Congress as they were published openly in the 11 October 1931 *Berlin am Morgen*.

64. See Reich Interior Ministry report dated 1 July 1932, DBB, R 1501/alt St 10/57, Bd. 1, 316; and the *Welt am Abend* articles of July 1932, "Die Nazikinos von Berlin" and "Um die Berliner Nazikinos" (both clipped and stored in the Reich Interior Ministry files, DBB, R 1501/alt St 10/57, Bd. 1, 152 and 154).

65. Fest, *Hitler*, 338–39; Winkler, *Der Weg in die Katastrophe*, 650–51.

66. Winkler, *Der Weg in die Katastrophe*, 683–84.

67. Münzenberg, "Trotskis faschistischer Vorschlag einer Blockbildung der KPD mit der SPD," *Rote Aufbau* 5 (4) (15 February 1932). On Thälmann's attacks on Trotsky in 1932, see Weber, *Hauptfeind*, 50–51.

68. See IAH Reichsabteilung circulars Nr. 8/32 (19 March 1932) and Nr. 18/32 (4 June 1932) RGASPI.538-2-79, 27, 61.

69. "Bericht vom internationalen Solidaritätstag 1932," RGASPI.538-2-81, 140.

70. Weber, *Hauptfeind*, 54.

71. Winkler, *Der Weg in die Katastrophe*, 623; Weber, *Hauptfeind*, 54.

72. Gross, *Willi Münzenberg*, 229.

73. Electoral results from Winkler, *Der Weg in die Katastrophe*, 684.

74. For a thorough, although rather biased explanation of the reasons for Neumann's ouster in August 1932, the best source is his wife Greta's memoir, *Von Potsdam nach Moskau*, 258–60.

75. From an English-language translation of the prosecution dossier prepared in Shanghai against the Rueggs, RGASPI.538-2-83, 49–55.

76. According to IAH Ruegg committee lists preserved in RGASPI.538-2-82, 35–63.

77. IAH records relating to the dubious "save the Rueggs" campaign fill no less than three entire folders, nos. 82 to 84 in RGASPI.538.2.

78. Aside from the correspondence, the three folders in the Comintern archives also contain literally hundreds of news clippings from *Welt am Abend*, *AIZ*, *Berlin am Morgen*, etc., relating to the Ruegg case.

79. Münzenberg, "The World Protest against the Intended Murder of the Trade Union Secretary in Shanghai," *Inprecorr*, 27 August 1931: 852.

80. Münzenberg, "Proletarian Solidarity against Imperialist War Criminals," ibid., 19 May 1932: 432.

81. "Manifesto of the Amsterdam World Congress Against Imperialist War," ibid., 15 September 1932: 866. For accounts of the congress, including speech excerpts by

Münzenberg, Barbusse, Cachin et al, see also "Einheitsfront gegen den Krieg," *Welt am Abend*, 29 August 1932; "Gorki, Schwernik und Münzenberg," ibid., 31 August 1932; "Kampfbündnis der Massen gegen imperialistischen Krieg," ibid., 1 September 1932. For the most informative (although hardly unbiased) short secondary account of the Amsterdam Congress, see Gross, "The Parade of the Freedom Fighters," in *Willi Münzenberg*, 221–27.

82. For some of Hitler's more colorful saber-rattling threats against his Communist enemies, see, for example, Kershaw, *Hitler*, 339.

83. See "Willi Münzenbergs Rede vor den Pariser Arbeitern. Kampfruf gegen den kommenden Weltkrieg," and "Willi Münzenberg vor Leningrader Arbeitern," *Welt am Abend*, 21 and 27 September 1932.

84. Ehrt and Schweickert, *Entfesselung der Unterwelt*, for example, doesn't even mention the Amsterdam congress.

85. Wessel, *Münzenbergs Ende*, 15.

86. See Reich Interior Ministry report dated 8 October 1932, "Betrifft: KPD.—Antigkriegsarbeit—Deutsches Kampfkomitee gegen den Krieg," DBB, R 1501/alt St 10/57, Bd. 1, 253–54.

87. See, for example, Interior Ministry circular "Betrifft: Weltkongress gegen den imperialistischen Krieg (Frauenkonferenz)," dispatched from Berlin "an die Nachrichtenstellen der Länder" on 14 December 1932, DBB, R 1501/alt St 10/57, Bd. 1, 313–14.

88. Reich Interior Ministry surveillance on the Nazi movement, for example, has been used to excellent effect by Henry Ashby Turner in *Hitler's Thirty Days to Power: January 1933* (1996; London: Bloomsbury, 1997).

89. See IAH circular from headquarters to all member sections, 27 October 1932, RGASPI.538-2-80, 21–29.

90. See Münzenberg's letter of complaint, sent to the Central Committee of the Communist Party of the Soviet Union, 27 October 1932, RGASPI.538-2-80, 20 (and back).

91. On the IAH's involvement in the Nazi-Communist transport strike, see the section labeled "BVG Berlin" for November 1932 in the "Bericht über die Hilfsaktionen der Internationalen Arbeiterhilfe bei Streiks und wirtschaftlichen Massenkämpfen seit dem 8. Weltkongress der IAH (Oktober 1931)," RGASPI.538-2-66, 200–202.

92. Münzenberg, "Keine Illusionen! Die Nichtangriffspakte und die Kriegsgefahr," published in both *Unsere Zeit* (the renamed *Rote Aufbau*), 5 January 1933: 6–8, and *Berlin am Morgen*, 8 January 1933: 4; Münzenberg, "Einige Fragen unseres Kampfes gegen den imperialistischen Krieg," *Unsere Zeit*, 20 January 1933: 67; "Stalin/Ueber die GPU," ibid., 5 January 1933: 4–5.

93. See Turner, *Hitler's Thirty Days to Power*.

94. Election results from Winkler, *Der Weg in die Katastrophe*, 774.

95. "Mittwoch: Bülowplatz! Nach der Sonntags-Provokation der Nazis die grosse Kampfkundgebung des roten Berlin," *Berlin am Morgen*, 24 January 1933.

96. "Hindenburg will Hitler zum Reichskanzler ernennen. Soll es zu einem neuen 20. Juli kommen?" ibid., 29 January 1933.

97. "Terror gegen die oppositionelle Presse," ibid., 4 February 1933; "Einheitsfront! Der Massenwille auf der Lustgarten-Demonstration. Abg. Torgler will eine Erklärung der KPD. verlesen," ibid., 8 February 1933.

CHAPTER 14. *The Fire This Time*

1. Quotations in Turner, *Hitler's Thirty Days to Power*, 147.
2. Ibid., 159.
3. Quoted by Fest, *Hitler*, 388–89.
4. "'Rote Fahne' beschlagnahmt," *Welt am Abend*, 31 January 1933.
5. The presidential decree is cited by Martin Broszat, *The Hitler State*, trans. John W. Hiden (1969; London: Longmans, 1981), 62. On the raid on the Kroll halls gathering, see Gross, *Willi Münzenberg*, 232.
6. See the cover of the 14 February 1933 *Welt am Abend*.
7. The conditions KPD leaders set down before they would stage joint maneuvers with the SPD basically involved Socialists repenting for past political sins and renouncing their own leadership. See "Einheitsfront! Der Massenwille auf der Lustgarten-Demonstration Abg. Torgler will eine Erklärung der KPD. verlesen," *Berlin am Morgen*, 8 February 1933.
8. Fest, *Hitler*, 392.
9. Nikolai Tolstoy, *Stalin's Secret War* (New York: Holt, Rinehart and Winston, 1981), 84.
10. Fritz Tobias, *The Reichstag Fire*, trans. Arnold J. Pomerans (New York: Putnam, 1964), 28.
11. The Nazis immediately claimed publicly to have found Lubbe with a party membership card on him, but later backed down from this claim once it was proved false. Under police questioning, Lubbe himself claimed to have left the Dutch Communist Party in 1929, although he appears to have belonged to a Dutch Communist splinter group, Rade, after that. Tobias, *Reichstag Fire*, 35. According to the *Brown Book of the Hitler Terror and the Burning of the Reichstag* by Münzenberg et al. (London: Victor Gollancz, 1933), Lubbe also belonged to the Young Communist League of Leyden until April 1931. Since he did not, to anyone's knowledge, join the Dutch Social Democrats or any non-Communist parties after 1931, it seems best to describe him as an estranged former Communist.
12. Cited by Fest, *Hitler*, 396.
13. Gross, *Willi Münzenberg*, 234–35.
14. Ibid., 236.
15. Citations in Gross, 237, 246.
16. The cigarette business was a sort of fund-raising craze in Communist circles in the early 1930s, possibly because smoking tended to increase with unemployment levels. The KPD and Red Aid had their own cigarette labels, which they used for fund-raising, and in 1932 the IAH followed them into the business by spinning off two labels of its own, "Solidarität" and "Liga" (profits from which were earmarked for the FSR clubs). See Reichssicherheitshauptamt reports dated 3 and 10 November 1932, DBB, R 58/516, 143–44. See also Harald Wessel, *Münzenbergs Ende: Ein deutscher Kommunist im Widerstand gegen Hitler und Stalin. Die Jahre 1933 bis 1940* (Berlin: Dietz Verlag, 1991), 15.
17. See Berlin police reports dated 14 and 22 March 1933, in the Gestapo file labeled "Bund der Freunde der Sowjetunion 1933–1935," DBB, R 58/791, 37–40; Reichssicherhauptamt report dated 28 March 1933, DBB, R 58/516, 168. The factory where the "Solidarität" and "Liga" labels were produced, located at Köpenickstrasse 118, was closed on 28 March 1933.
18. Gross, *Willi Münzenberg*, 237–38. Gross does not mention the sum involved, but implies that it came from the rich NDV accounts, from which Münzenberg had been diverting sizable sums monthly into the reserve stash for almost two years. From what we know

of the NDV's generous Moscow subsidies, more than ten thousand dollars a month by 1932, it seems reasonable to guess that several years' worth of monthly cash diversions may have yielded as much as thirty or forty thousand dollars. At the least we may conclude that the sum was significant enough for Gross to risk her life to obtain it, at the height of the Nazi terror against leading Communists.

19. This immunity would later be lifted for good, based on a legal technicality, in a sweeping decree issued by Göring on 23 August 1933. See *Reichssteuerblatt*, 1 September 1933.

20. Gross, *Willi Münzenberg*, 238–41.

21. See the 8 April 1933 IAH circular on the upcoming Prague *AIZ* edition, RGASPI.538-2-90, 27–28; and Münzenberg, "Es lebe der Marxismus!" *Unsere Zeit* (Basel edition), 1 April 1933.

22. There is no reliable record of Münzenberg's whereabouts during the months of March and April 1933, when he deliberately left as few tracks as possible. For surveillance speculations, see Berlin Gestapo report dated 15 March 1935, in the Institut für Zeitgeschichte, MA 699, (2) 799461–62; and the Zürich cantonal Polizeikommando file on "Münzenberg Wilhelm" in BB, E 21 9246, entry for 13 March 1933.

23. See protocol of the initial exploratory meeting for the World Committee for the Relief of the Victims of German Fascism, held in Paris on 21 April 1933 with Münzenberg, Doriot, Smeral, Barbusse, and Jerram present, in RGASPI.495-60-242, 8–16.

24. Smeral, one of the most popular leaders of the Czech Social Democratic Party before the war, was converted to Bolshevism by Lenin during a visit to Moscow in 1919. For the next five years he was a leading member of the Czechoslovak Communist Party, before emigrating to Moscow permanently in 1925. He was sent as a direct emissary of ECCI to various hot spots in the 1920s and 1930s, including Paris in 1933, where he teamed up with Münzenberg and helped reconstitute the IAH publishing apparat.

25. From the English-language protocol in RGASPI.495-60-242, 22–24.

26. This was *Der Justizmord in Chicago*, by Pierre Ramus, a copy of which Münzenberg urgently demanded from Brupbacher in a letter dispatched from Paris to Zürich on 25 May 1933, preserved in IISH, Brupbacher archive.

27. See the French Interior Ministry file labeled "Comité mondial contre la guerre impérialiste et le fascisme," in AN F7 13148; and Gross, *Willi Münzenberg*, 243–44. Münzenberg's new living quarters with Gross, in the Hotel Jacob, were only several blocks away from the offices of Editions du Carrefour. For the ESI address, see the Gestapo surveillance report on Münzenberg captured by the Red Army and returned to Moscow, in the "Osoby" archive, TsKHIDK.500-3-182, 177.

28. See Koestler, *The Invisible Writing*, 255–56; and Michael Scammell's forthcoming biography *Cosmic Reporter, The Life of Arthur Koestler* (Yale University Press), esp. chapters 11, 13, and 14.

29. Regler, *The Owl of Minerva*, trans. Norman Denny (New York: Farrar, Straus and Cudahy, 1959), 160–62.

30. Regler's out-of-date photos came from the original blueprints drawn by architect Paul Wallot in *Das Reichstagsgebäude in Berlin* (1899).

31. Regler, *Owl of Minerva*, 162–63.

32. Münzenberg letter to Brupbacher, 15 May 1933, in IISH, Brupbacher archive.

33. Total expenses for the World Committee, up to 31 October 1933, were 294,147.23 francs, according to an attachment to the "Bericht der Revisionskommission ueber das

Finanzgebahren des Welthilfskomitees," circa early November 1933, RGASPI.495-60-244, 133–34.

34. Regler, *Owl of Minerva*, 163.

35. Münzenberg et al., *Brown Book*, 133. The *Brown Book* took pains to "prove" with Regler's photos of Wallot's 1889 plans that there was a secret underground passage leading from the Reichstag to the official residence of Hermann Göring as Reichstag president. In fact the "underground passage" was a narrow 450-foot-long tunnel filled with steam pipes from the boiler room, which had been constructed at a distance from the Reichstag "in order that there should be no source of fire within Parliament itself." The Speaker's residence, built after Wallot drew his plans, was then also connected to the boiler room, through its own steam-pipe tunnel. The entrance to this underground pipe network from the Reichstag was further protected by an almost impenetrable "maze of corridors and [locked] doors," in which a court investigator, sent to test the thesis of a team of incendiaries entering through the speaker's house, got lost and had to be rescued by a search team. See Tobias, *Reichstag Fire*, 74–76.

36. Oberfohren was almost certainly murdered by Nazi thugs. His break with Hitler's brutal policies had long been evident at the time his corpse was discovered, and the official "suicide" explanation was suspicious, in light of the fact that the pistol he had been shot with was found laid neatly beside Oberfohren's blown-off head (and not in or near his hand, as one would suspect would follow a suicide attempt). See, among other sources, Erich Matthias and Rudolf Morsey, *Das Ende der Parteien 1933* (Düsseldorf: Droste Verlag, 1960), 596, 598, 606. For the most thorough examination of the Oberfohren Memorandum controversy, see Tobias, *Reichstag Fire*, 104–16.

37. Münzenberg et al., *Brown Book*, 56–57; 60–62; Tobias, *Reichstag Fire*, 54–56.

38. Among others, Münzenberg listed Sherwood Anderson, Martin Alexander-Nexö, Egon Erwin Kisch, Romain Rolland, Lincoln Steffens, John Strachey, Ernst Toller, André Gide, and Henri Barbusse as having made "original contributions" to the *Brown Book*, in an ad published in *Unsere Zeit* (Basel edition), 15 July 1933: 24. Since these names do not appear anywhere in the *Brown Book* itself, it is likely that Münzenberg exaggerated, or simply lied about, their involvement in the project. It is also possible that some of these celebrities may have contacted Münzenberg to disown involvement in the project, although I have uncovered no evidence of this.

39. See the letter to Bela Kun, ms marked "Misiano," dispatched to Moscow from Paris on 4 September 1933, with accompanying "Text der Erklärung" on Einstein's denial of involvement in the *Brown Book* campaign, in RGASPI.538-3-154, 50–51.

40. Münzenberg et al., *Brown Book*, 235–36, 284–85.

41. In Paris, the books were actually printed at Imprimerie R. Bussiere à Saint-Amand (Cher), according to a 9 October 1933 French Interior Ministry report on the Reichstag fire campaign in France, preserved in AN, F7 13432. This report gives the figure of eight thousand for the French edition's print run, and no figures for the German edition printed in Paris. Since Gross estimates the breakdown at Editions du Carrefour as about half French and half German, twenty thousand seems a reliable estimate for the total published in Paris (although Gross guesses fifty thousand, without citing any sources).

42. Gross, *Willi Münzenberg*, 263. The earliest documentary confirmation I have of this ECCI budgetary approval is the 6 September 1933 resolution in RGASPI.495-60-242, 61–63. The funding figures, which ultimately came to about 270,000 francs, can be found in the 28 November 1933 ECCI auditing commission report, RGASPI.495-60-242, 160–62.

43. Travel expenses still amounted to thirty-five thousand francs, or about fourteen

hundred dollars, according to the 28 November 1933 ECCI auditing commission report, RGASPI.495-60-242, 160–62.

44. Tobias, *Reichstag Fire*, 120–27. See also Gross, *Willi Münzenberg*, 250–52. The Paris meeting where Moro-Giafferi shouted his already formed opinion was well attended, with the speeches by Moro-Giafferi and Gaston Bergéry taken note of by the French Interior Ministry, among others. See report dated 4 October 1933 on the meeting in the Salle Wagram, AN, F7 13432.

45. See report headed "Politische Bemerkungen zum Londoner Prozess," marked "Vertraulich," type signed "Koppel" on 4 October 1933 and stamped "ECCI" on 7 October 1933, RGASPI.495-60-244a, 35.

46. This letter, and the rebuff returned by Münzenberg's commission, penned by the Swedish lawyer Georg Branting, are reproduced in Tobias, *Reichstag Fire*, 122.

47. Tobias, *Reichstag Fire*, 125, 227.

48. See Walter Hofer and Christoph Graf, "Neue Quellen zum Reichstagsbrand," *Geschichte in Wissenschaft und Unterricht* 27 (2) (1976): 65–88. A number of historians, most recently Alexander Bahar (*Wilfried Kugel: Der Reichstagsbrand. Wie Geschichte gemacht wird* (Berlin: Edition q, 2000), have drawn on this account to indict the Nazis as the guilty party behind the fire, but none has succeeded in refuting charges that Hofer's evidence was fabricated. For a useful survey of the controversy, see Henning Köhler, "Bis sich die Balken biegen. Ein gescheiterter Versuch, die Schuld der Nationalsozialisten am Reichstagsbrand nachzuweisen," *Frankfurter Allgemeine Zeitung*, 22 February 2001: 8.

CHAPTER 15. *Reckoning*

1. About thirty-eight thousand francs, or roughly fifteen hundred dollars, were transferred from the World Committee to IAH projects such as "Emigrantenhilfe" in 1933, according to the document headed "Zu dem vorliegenden Kassenbericht ist folgendes zu erklären," circa early November 1933, RGASPI.495-60-244, 133–34.

2. This was the so-called Berlin Treaty of 6 May 1933. For background on its negotiation, see Julius Braunthal, *A History of the International*, vol. 2: *(1914–1943)*, 396–98.

3. See French Interior Ministry reports dated 2, 6, and 16 December 1933, in AN, FY 13432.

4. This address according to, among other sources, a captured Gestapo surveillance report preserved in the "Osoby" Archive, TsKhIDK.500.3.182, 175.

5. According to a January 1934 letter to ECCI, Münzenberg had organized demonstrations for Thälmann in Paris as early as spring 1933—although it is curious that he waited until 1934 to inform Moscow of this. See Münzenberg letter "Werte Genossen," 7 January 1934, in DBB, RY 1/I 6/10/68, 6.

6. *Arbeiter-und Bauern-Solidarität* (Amsterdam edition), 20 February 1934, 1–3.

7. This address from a document headed "Für sofortige Freilassung. New-Yorker Hilfskomitee für die Opfer des deutschen Faschismus, 870 Broadway, New-York-City," RGASPI.495-60-242, 148.

8. Etc. "Set Ernst Thälmann Free," music by F. Szabo, lyrics by Anne Bromberger and Frances May, Copyright, 1934. A copy of the sheet music is preserved in RGASPI.538-2-98, 114. (and back).

9. Gross, *Willi Münzenberg*, 270.

10. *Unsere Zeit* (Paris/Basel), February 1934: 1–3; ibid., July 1934: 1–7.

11. See Münzenberg's letter to the Central Committee of the Communist Party of the Soviet Union, 27 October 1932, RGASPI.538-2-80, 20 (and back); and Gross, *Willi Münzenberg*, 262, 265–66.

12. Gross, *Willi Münzenberg*, 265–66, 269.

13. On the Thorez-Doriot affair, see Stéphane Courtois and Annie Kriegel, *Eugen Fried: Le grand secret du PCF* (Paris: Editions du Seuil, 1997), 223–31; and McMeekin, "From Moscow to Vichy," *Contemporary European History* 9 (1) (2000), 29.

14. See "'Protokoll der Sitzung der Fraktionsleitung vom 14:4:34.' Anwesend: Romer, Schultz, Ullrich, Jerram, Muenzenberg," stamped received at ECCI, 28 April 1934, RGASPI.495-60-245, 18–19.

15. Basically, ECCI's complaints revolved around the excessive bragging in both journals about the London countertrial, connection to which Moscow still wished to deny. See, for example, letter from "Ulrich" "An den Kameraden Willi persönlich," 23 February 1934, RGASPI.495-60-246, 53.

16. Münzenberg letter to Kun, 27 March 1934, RGASPI.495-60-246, 107–9.

17. Undated document headed "Wie die Zeitschrift 'Unsere Zeit' den Kampf gegen die Sozialdemokratie und die II. Internationale führte," RGASPI.495-60-246, 110–13.

18. Münzenberg letter to Kun, 17 April 1934, RGASPI.495-60-246, 143–45.

19. See letter from "Ulrich" to Barbusse, 9 March 1934, RGASPI.495-60-246, 54–58. In this dispatch from Moscow, Barbusse was specifically warned to distance himself from Guy Jerram. Münzenberg, so far as I have been able to determine, received no such warning—at least not in time to forestall his April meeting with Jerram, on which he foolishly reported to Moscow.

20. Münzenberg letter to Kun, 1 May 1934, RGASPI.495-60-246, 165–68.

21. See unsigned letter "Lieber Freund," circa early May 1934, almost certainly from Kun to Münzenberg, RGASPI.495-60-246, 169–70; and letter to Kun from "Ihr W.," ms marked "Münzenberg," circa June 1934, RGASPI.495-60-246, 228.

22. On the Night of the Long Knives, see Fest, *Hitler*, 449–75.

23. Gross, *Willi Münzenberg*, 270.

24. In yet another nod to Münzenberg's preferred modus operandi, Barbusse listed no less than three thousand francs a month for his personal expenses. See the French-language original of a forty-page Barbusse report later translated into Russian and dated 20 September 1934 (the French version is undated), RGASPI.495-60-246a, 142–44, 150.

25. See Barbusse letter's to Münzenberg, 14 November 1927, in RGASPI.538-3-97, 48; and his follow-up plea to Misiano, RGASPI.538-2-97, 54.

26. Barbusse report, 20 September 1934, RGASPI.495-60-246a, 135.

27. Gross claims the imprint was taken over by the Comintern, but she provides no evidence of this. Gross, *Willi Münzenberg*, 243. From the later history of Editions du Carrefour in 1936–38, when Münzenberg was accused by Communist colleagues of publishing "un-Marxist" books there, it seems likely that the Comintern never did achieve this takeover. Münzenberg himself, so far as I have been able to determine, had no formal stake in the publishing house, although he clearly had significant influence there due to his friendship with Lévi.

28. See Editions du Carrefour brochure titled "Deutsche Bücher 1933–1934," RGASPI.538-2-102, 27–32; and Gross, 266–67.

29. See Misiano report sent to Kun at ECCI, 16 November 1933, RGASPI.538-2-242, 128; and Regler, *Owl of Minerva*, 172–75.

30. See "Bericht über die deutsche IAH," dated February 1935, RGASPI.538-2-103, 26–28.

31. The most expensive item was the new saunas Münzenberg wanted for his employees. See undated Russian-language translation of Münzenberg letter to "Zamestiteliu Predsedatelia Soveta Narodnikh Krmissarov [sic] Tovarishchu Chubar," circa mid-August 1935, RGASPI.538-2-103, 4.

32. See letter from Münzenberg "An das ZK der WKP / b/ z. Hdn. des Genossen Angarow," 31 August 1935, RGASPI.538-2-103, 10–11, 11a. See also Gross, *Willi Münzenberg*, 277.

33. This is my own interpretation of Münzenberg's surprising election to the Zentrale in 1935, based on the insider recollection of Herbert Wehner, "Erinnerungen" (unpublished ms), in the Wehner archive at the Institut für Zeitgeschichte in Munich, F 81/1, 110–14. Wehner remarks somewhat blandly that Pieck supported Münzenberg's election "in order to . . . tie [him] down to the [KPD]," but it seems obvious that Pieck must have been looking out for his own interests as well.

34. See top-secret Russian-language document marked "Postanovlenie soveta narodnikh kommissarov soiuza SSR. Moskva Kreml'. 19 June 1935. sov. sekretno," RGASPI.538-2-103, 2.

35. Münzenberg's prolific correspondence with Dimitrov from August to December 1935 is preserved in a folder at DBB, RY 1/I 6/10/68.

36. Münzenberg letter to Dimitrov, 17 December 1936, DBB, RY 1/I 6/10/68, 253–55.

37. See unsigned worksheet dated 17 September 1935, headed "Zwischen W.M. und M.B. wurde grundsaetzlich ueber die gemeinsame Herausgabe einer Zeitung verhandelt, d.h. eine Zeitung, an der die durch W.M. vertretene Organisation und M.B. interessiert sind," DBB, RY 1/I 2/3/418, 217–18.

38. Münzenberg letter to Dimitrov, 17 December 1936, DBB, RY 1/I 6/10/68, 249–58. See also Victor Schiff letter to Münzenberg, 22 September 1935, DBB, RY 1/I 6/10/69, 30–33; and undated documented headed "1935–1937. Uebersicht über die Arbeit der KPD seit dem VII. Weltkongress im Zusammenhang mit der Arbeit des Ausschusses zur Vorbereitung der Deutschen Volksfront in Paris," in the Nachlass Wilhelm Pieck, DBB, NL 36/558, 102.

39. "1935–1937 Uebersicht," 101–2. On Schwarzschild's "Fourth Reich" idea, see Gross, "The German Communists' United-Front and Popular-Front Ventures," in Drachkovitch and Lazitch, *Comintern*, 128–29.

40. "1935–1937 Uebersicht," 108.

41. Cited by Gross, *Willi Münzenberg*, 284 (although she gets the date of the February Lutetia conference wrong, claiming it took place on the sixth). On the formation of the Lutetia committee see also "1935–1937 Uebersicht," 102–8; Wehner, "Erinnerungen," 114; and for the exact roll call of attendance, see document marked "Sitzung am 2. Februar 1936," DBB, RY 1/I 6/10/68, 273–75.

42. See, in this vein, letters from "Deine Freunde" and "Eure Freunde," both addressed "An Willi M.," 13 February 1936, DBB, RY 1/I 2/3/419, 22, 24. Both of these letters, marked "top secret," were forwarded to ECCI by "Walter [Ulbricht]," 14 February 1936, DBB, RY 1/I 2/3/419, 21.

43. Letter from "Deine Freunde" "An Willi M.," 13 February 1936, DBB, RY 1/I 2/3/419, 22.

44. See the typescript titled "The 'Pariser Tageblatt' Affair," authored by a "Committee of Patronage" headed by Paul Miliukov and Jules Brutzkus in Paris in 1939, excerpted in DBB, RY 1/I 2/3/358, 216.

45. See the copies of Bernhard's letter lodged in the files of the ECCI Secretariat, one of which was forwarded from "Eure Freunde" to Wilhelm Pieck, DBB, RY 1/I 6/10/68, 20–25.

46. "1935–1937 Uebersicht," DBB, NL 36/558, 112–15.

47. I am inferring this based on the contents of a Pieck letter to KPD colleagues in both Prague and Paris, dispatched on 14 June 1936, in which Pieck reveals himself to have served as a friendly go-between for Münzenberg and Ulbricht during the spring. DBB, NL 36/558, 99–101.

48. Münzenberg letter to Dimitrov (unaddressed), marked "Streng vertraulich," 17 May 1936, DBB, RY 1/I 6/10/68, 42–45.

49. Münzenberg letter to Ercoli, 14 April 1936, DBB, RY 1/I 6/10/68, 33.

50. See, for example, *Deutsche Informationen* 69 (15 August 1936), which includes nothing more than a half-page appeal "Für den Sieg der spanischen Demokratie."

51. Gross letter to Brupbacher, 17 April 1936, in IISH, Brupbacher archive.

52. "The 'Pariser Tageblatt' Affair," DBB, RY 1/I 2/3/358, 240.

53. The best documentary evidence I have found on Münzenberg's inside knowledge of the coup is a 12 July 1936 letter from Heinrich Mann to Münzenberg that alludes repeatedly to the "the Poliakov case." But this letter was dispatched after the coup took place, by which time Mann, Münzenberg, and most of the Lutetia committee members had rallied around Bernhard. It does not confirm that Münzenberg was involved in planning the putsch.

54. From a photostat reproduction of the "Erklärung" on the cover of the 11 June 1936 *Tageblatt* in "The 'Pariser Tageblatt' Affair," 217–19.

55. From "The 'Pariser Tageblatt' Affair," 222–23.

56. The final judgment, made in the XIIth Correctional Chamber and upheld by the French Court of Appeal in October 1938, found Bernhard liable for court expenses and defamation damages. He was arrested on 20 October 1938. "The 'Pariser Tageblatt' Affair," 225.

57. "The 'Pariser Tageblatt' Affair," 224. This text, though biased in favor of Poliakov, is based on the legal affidavits produced during the trials of 1937 and 1938. No exact information is given on the size of Münzenberg's, Bernhard's, or Simon's investment, nor on their compensation, but it seems clear the three did subsist on the paper's existing capital and income until 24 June 1937, when they declared bankruptcy.

58. Gross, *Willi Münzenberg*, 287–89.

59. Letter from Gross to "Liebe Madame Paulette," 23 July 1936, in IISH, Brupbacher archive.

60. Gross, *Willi Münzenberg*, 287–88, 290; see also Stéphane Courtois, "La seconde mort de Willi Münzenberg," *Communisme* 38–39 (1994): 30. Although under the terms of his agreement with Togliatti, he was still expected to return to Moscow to take up work in the Comintern's agitprop department. In order to play up her husband's "antifascist" track record, Gross fancifully claims Münzenberg's exit visa was granted expressly by Togliatti so that Münzenberg could "return to Paris and see through the campaigns for Spain which he had started and which included the procuring of arms." Stephen Koch makes mountains out of this claim, constructing an elaborate scenario whereby the Spanish Civil War becomes Münzenberg's "sheet anchor," allowing him to survive the purges, and giving him the opportunity to manipulate Communist fellow travelers who went to Spain, such as Ernest Hemingway and John Dos Passos. See Koch, "The Spanish Stratagem," in *Double Lives*, 265–97.

While this all makes exciting reading, I have found no documentary evidence in Moscow, Paris, or Berlin to support either Gross's or Koch's claims that Münzenberg was very deeply involved in organizing the Spanish brigades.

61. According to Gross, Münzenberg copied these records, unbeknownst to Smeral, and had friends stash the copies "in the safe of a Catholic press service," where they remained until the Catholic fathers guarding the safe burned them in 1940 to keep them from falling into the hands of the Gestapo. Those records from the 1930s which survived, scattered in archives in Moscow, Berlin, and Stanford, California, were Smeral's originals, which later turned up in the Paris hotel room of the writer and Communist sympathizer Friedrich Wolf and were seized by the Gestapo. Gross, *Willi Münzenberg*, 292.

62. See secret KPD Politburo report headed "Abschrift . . . zum fall Münzenberg. Vertraulich!" 25 March 1938, DBB, RY 1/I 6/10/67, 1; and Gross, *Willi Münzenberg*, 292–93.

63. Münzenberg, *Propaganda als Waffe* (Paris: Éditions du Carrefour, 1937), 9–12, 19. Münzenberg was clearly unaware that this word had also been used before by the Vatican's Office of Propaganda, the department charged with "propagating" the Catholic faith.

64. Münzenberg, *Propaganda als Waffe*, 11, 26–27, 126, 160–61, 274, 277, 280. For Ulbricht's use of *Propaganda als Waffe* against Münzenberg, see undated document headed "Willi Münzenberg: 'Propaganda als Waffe,'" ms marked "Pieck," circa spring 1937, in the Nachlass Pieck, DBB, NL 36/515, 48–49. See also the official later denunciation "Zu Willi Münzenbergs Buch 'Propaganda als Waffe'" in the new KPD official organ, *Deutsche Volkszeitung*, 7 November 1937: 4.

65. Radek escaped with a ten-year sentence, but was killed in his concentration camp in 1939. Walter Laqueur, *Stalin: The Glasnost Revelations* (New York: Scribner's, 1990), 81.

66. Gross, *Willi Münzenberg*, 293.

67. In a personal statement turned over to the French minister of the interior in October 1939, Münzenberg obliquely thanked "the French authorities" for having helped him evade Beletskii's clutches. See document reproduced by Courtois, "La seconde mort de Willi Münzenberg," 136.

68. "Rede des Führers der deutschen Kommunisten." For the details of this account of the Communist maneuvering surrounding the 10–11 April 1937 German Popular Front congress, I am relying on the admittedly biased account provided in the secret KPD Politburo report headed "Abschrift . . . zum fall Münzenberg. Vertraulich!" 25 March 1938, DBB, RY 1/I 6/10/67, 1–3. But Münzenberg, in his many later complaints against Ulbricht lodged with both Dimitrov and Stalin, makes no effort to dispute the facts as presented by his rivals in this episode.

69. See unsigned 13 June 1937 KPD Politburo report marked "Streng vertraulich," in the Nachlass Pieck, DBB, NL 36/515, 42.

70. This letter is cited by Tania Schlie in her article "Der 'Fall Münzenberg' in den Akten von KPD und Komintern," in Schlie and Roche, *Willi Münzenberg*.

71. See "Abschrift . . . zum Fall Münzenberg. Vertraulich!" 3–6.

72. Specifically, this accusation related to an article in the White Russian newspaper *Poslednie Novesti*, which began running a series of speculative articles on Münzenberg in July 1937.

73. "Erklärung Münzenbergs," *Pariser Tageszeitung*, 24 July 1937.

74. From excerpts of the second "freedom letter" reproduced in a 22 September 1937 Gestapo report on the Freiheitspartei, DBB, RY 1/R 58/645, 2.

75. The first Gestapo report I have found listing a significant number of *Freiheitspartei* collaborators, including Münzenberg, Bernhard, and the union organizer Karl Emont, was dated 25 October 1937. DBB, RY 1/R 58/645, 154–58. Not until 1938, apparently, was the

Gestapo informed about the participation of Catholic Center Party notables such as Spiecker, Father Muckermann, and Monsignor Poels. Gestapo report dated 18 August 1938, DBB, RY 1/R 58/645, 170–75.

76. From the 18 August 1938 Gestapo report, DBB, RY 1/R 58/645, 172–74.

77. For an example of the political flavor of the "freedom letters," see the 22 September 1937 Gestapo report on the Freiheitspartei, DBB, RY 1/R 58/645, 2.

78. From a French translation of a Münzenberg letter to Stalin dated 14 July 1937, a copy of which was seized by French intelligence in 1939 and later obtained by Stéphane Courtois, who published it in "La seconde mort de Willi Münzenberg," 50–51, 54–55. The German original, probably housed in the Stalin files in the so-called "Presidential archive" in the Kremlin, is unavailable.

79. Tanenhaus, *Whittaker Chambers*, 123.

80. On these contacts, see the German-language translation of the article "Willi Münzenberg und die Komintern," *Poslednie Novosti*, 25 July 1937, preserved in the Nachlass Pieck, DBB, NL 36/515, 70.

81. French-language translation of Münzenberg telegram to Dimitrov, 8 October 1937, reproduced in Courtois, "La seconde mort de Willi Münzenberg," 57.

82. From Münzenberg's letter to Dimitrov, circa February 1938, DBB, RY 1/I 6/10/67, 26.

83. The new edition of *Dritte Front* was advertised in *Propaganda als Waffe*.

84. Münzenberg letter to Dimitrov, 15 December 1937, DBB, RY 1/I 6/10/67, 5–12; "Schreiben Münzenbergs an das Sekretariat des ZK," 1 November 1937, in the Nachlass Pieck, DBB, NL 36/515, 116.

85. Münzenberg letter to Dimitrov, circa February 1938, DBB, RY 1/I 6/10/67, 27. The two proposed book titles were "Hitlerpropaganda" and "Kann Hitler den Krieg ohne Gefahr einer Revolution führen?"

86. See Pieck letter (for Secretariat) to Münzenberg, 11 November 1937, in the Nachlass Pieck, DBB, NL 36/515, 129.

87. "Parteiverfahren gegen Genossen Münzenberg," 14 May 1938, in the Nachlass Pieck, DBB, NL 36/515, 175; "Beschluss des ZK der KPD über W. Münzenberg," *Deutsche Volkszeitung*, 22 May 1938.

88. The legend of Münzenberg's voluntary "break" with Moscow, first propagated by his collaborators such as Gross, Regler, Koestler, and Kurt Kersten, has received approbation in virtually all the historical literature on Münzenberg, with the notable exception of Stephen Koch's *Double Lives*.

89. See, for example, Münzenberg's letter to the KPD Zentrale, with attached letter to ECCI, 29 August 1938, in the Nachlass Pieck, DBB, NL 36/515, 182–86.

CHAPTER 16. *A Paris Exile*

1. From the French-language translation of Münzenberg's letter to Dimitrov, 14 June 1938, reproduced in Courtois, "La seconde mort de Willi Münzenberg," 95.

2. Münzenberg letter to Pieck at the KPD Zentrale, with attached letter to ECCI, 29 August 1938, in the Nachlass Pieck, DBB, NL 36/515, 186.

3. Telegram cited by Gross, *Willi Münzenberg*, 306. She kept a copy in her possession.

4. Citations from the French-language translation of Münzenberg's letter to Dimitrov, 30 August 1938, reproduced in Courtois, "La seconde mort de Willi Münzenberg," 99, 105.

5. Orwell, *Homage to Catalonia* (London: Secker and Warburg, 1938).

6. On Münzenberg's relationship with Aschberg, see Gross, *Willi Münzenberg*, 127–28, 268–69, 315.

7. Koestler, *The Invisible Writing*, 473. For the best explanation of Koestler's reasons for resigning from the party, see Scammell, *Cosmic Reporter*, chap. 14.

8. Apparently Münzenberg's Communist reputation still preceded him, as the KPD organ *Deutsche Volkszeitung* felt compelled to carry a clarification on 30 October 1938 that denied Communist involvement in *Die Zukunft*. Cited in Courtois, "La seconde mort de Willi Münzenberg," 37.

9. "Aufruf an die Leser und Freunde der Zeitschrift 'Die Zukunft,'" *Die Zukunft*, 12 October 1938: 12; ibid., 25 November 1938: 16; Feuchtwanger, "Ein deutscher Junge in Paris" and Kersten, "Ade Rudolf Thomas," ibid., 21 October 1938: 8; "Der Nächste Vorstoss," ibid., 28 October 1938: 1.

10. Thomas Mann, "Zu diesem Frieden"; Freud, "Ein Wort zum Antisemitismus," ibid., 25 November 1938: 2; Wells, "Wie soll die Welt beschaffen sein?" ibid., 9 December 1938: 3; ibid., 20 January 1939: 12; "Konzentrationslager Deutschland," ibid., 27 January 1939: 1.

11. See 15 May 1939 Gestapo report on the Deutsche Freiheitspartei, DBB, RY 1/R 58/645, 189–92; and accompanying flow-chart graphic, dated 22 March 1939, which links Münzenberg and Spiecker to a kind of anti-Nazi conspiracy box labeled "'Zukunft' Paris."

12. "An die Leser und Freunde der 'Zukunft'!" *Die Zukunft*, 13 January 1939: 12.

13. See Courtois, "La seconde mort de Willi Münzenberg," 38.

14. "Beschluss der IKK im Fall Münzenberg," in the Nachlass Pieck, DBB, NL 36/515, 236–37. See also Reinhard Müller, ed., *Die Akte Wehner: Moskau 1937–1941* (Berlin: Rowohlt, 1993), 327–30.

15. From the original text of Münzenberg's "Ertrittserklärung" (*sic*) from the KPD, preserved in the Nachlass Pieck, DBB, NL 36/515, 240–45. Published in slightly altered form as "Alles für die Einheit," *Die Zukunft*, 10 March 1939: 11.

16. Münzenberg, 26 June 1939 letter "An einige Freunde," to be found, among many other locations, at IISH, Brupbacher archive, 1–3.

17. Gestapo report on "Die Zukunft Gruppe," 28 April 1939, DBB, RY 1/R 58/627, 10–11.

18. Gestapo report on the "Münzenberg Gruppe," 13 June 1939, DBB, RY 1/R 58/627, 20–24 (and back).

19. There is no mention of negotiations with SOPADE or the KPD, or even attention paid by them to Münzenberg's group, in any of the well-informed Gestapo reports I have come across for 1939. Münzenberg himself left no documentary trace of such contacts, at least none that survives. He didn't even mention the "Friends of Socialist Unity" party in *Die Zukunft*, unlike other groupings the paper habitually promoted, such as the "German-French Union" and the "Friends of *The Future*."

20. Gestapo report on the "Münzenberg Gruppe," 3 July 1939, DBB, RY 1/R 58/627, 32.

21. Gestapo report on the "Münzenberg Gruppe," 21 July 1939, DBB, RY 1/R 58/627, 50.

22. Gestapo report on the "Münzenberg Gruppe," 26 July 1939, DBB, RY 1/R 58/627, 55.

23. "Union Franco-Allemande—Deutsch-Französische Union," *Die Zukunft*, 30 June 1939: 11.

24. Paris, Préfecture de Police archives, Box M 12: Dossier "Munzenberg Wilhelm."

25. Münzenberg, "Der russische Dolchstoss," *Die Zukunft*, 22 September 1939: 1.

26. Münzenberg, "Die deutsche Freiheit im Kampf gegen Hitler und Stalin," ibid.,

29 September 1939: 1; Münzenberg, "Her zu uns! Offener Brief an Freunde in Deutschland und im Ausland," ibid., 6 October 1939; "Der Weg zur Rettung: Volksrevolution gegen Hitler!" ibid., 13 October 1939.

27. Reproduced in Courtois, "La seconde mort de Willi Münzenberg," 136–39.

28. Münzenberg's Interior Ministry dossier and letter may simply have been ignored. I have found his name in neither special French Interior Ministry files from 1937 to 1940 relating to German nationals regarded as suspect due to nationalistic views (AN, F/7/14715: "Dossiers personnels et notes de renseignements sur des ressortissants allemands suspects; 1937–1940."); nor in those relating to German émigrés held to be reliable (AN, F/7 14823: "Refugiés politiques notoirement connus pour leur loyalisme a l'égard de la France et présentant toutes garanties au point de vue moral," Stamped 22 September 1938). On the other hand, Münzenberg was a prominent enough figure that it is entirely possible his case was handled at a higher level.

29. Münzenberg's March 1940 *Zukunft* article, "Il y a des victoires qui sont des défaites!" reproduced in Courtois, "La seconde mort de Willi Münzenberg," 147–49. Münzenberg published the names of the murdered German Communists in the Belgian newspaper *Le Peuple* (30 January 1940); cited by Koch, *Double Lives*, 310.

30. The Gestapo files on *Die Zukunft* are located in the "Deutsche Freiheitspartei" files, DBB, RY 1/R 58/645. See also the Paris Préfecture de Police archives, Box M 12: Dossier "Munzenberg Wilhelm."

31. Willert spoke of his contacts with Münzenberg in an interview with Koch. See Koch, *Double Lives*, 308–9, 387. For more on Willert, see also Scammell, *Cosmic Reporter*, chap. 15.

32. Gross, *Willi Münzenberg*, 322.

33. Hirth's account of Münzenberg's death, written five years after the fact in summer 1945, was later found in the files of the "KPD in exile" organization which operated in loose association with the French resistance during the Nazi occupation. It was housed in PCF archives for most of the Cold War, and later transferred to the Institut für Marxismus-Leninismus in East Germany in 1988. It has been reproduced in Karlheinz Pech, "Un nouveau témoin dans l'affaire du décès de Willi Münzenberg," in *Willi Münzenberg: Un homme contre* (Aix-en-Provence: La Bibliothèque Méjanes, 1992), 178–79.

Hirth's entire testimony is an obvious effort to discredit Münzenberg posthumously. There is no explanation, first of all, why he wrote about the circumstances of Münzenberg's death at all, five years after the fact. Suspiciously, this document is not part of a coherent memoir, but rather appears to have been written independently, in order to counter the impression that Münzenberg had been murdered by the NKVD. Even in 1945, Hirth was carrying on the old KPD polemic against Münzenberg, labeling him a "Trotskyist" and describing his "anti-Russian politics."

Even more suspiciously, Hirth claims to have specifically joined Münzenberg's group "in order to keep watch on him." He claims Münzenberg was suffering from "an extraordinary nervous tension" and declares that "he had committed very great errors that he could never make good." Upon confessing his "errors," Münzenberg, according to Hirth, began crying uncontrollably. The next morning, Hirth discovered the corpse of Münzenberg, who had supposedly hanged himself from a tree.

This whole story strains credulity almost comically. Hartig, Siemsen, and all the other eyewitnesses who saw Münzenberg in his last days at Chambaran and in the first days of his flight spoke unanimously of his high spirits. Hirth's suicide scenario was obviously concocted to dispel rumors, already widely circulating in Communist circles during the war, that Münzenberg had been liquidated by the NKVD. Either he invented the entire story about accompanying Münzenberg and finding his corpse, or he was in fact the mysterious, unnamed companion Hartig remembered seeing with Münzenberg shortly before his departure. The second possibility strikes me as most plausible, which would make Hirth the guilty party who informed the NKVD hit squad about Münzenberg's movements.

34. The pathologist's report and other materials relating to the discovery and disposal of Münzenberg's corpse have been reproduced as "Rapport de gendarmerie sur la mort de Willi Münzenberg," in Courtois, "La seconde mort de Willi Münzenberg," 157–67.

35. As yet, no "smoking gun" has appeared in Moscow archives that really connects Stalin with Münzenberg's death. In the early 1990s, Arkadi Vaksberg did unearth a high-level NKVD order, dated December 1943, from Colonel Zhukov to former Comintern Secretary Dimitrov for documents regarding Münzenberg, who "is said to have been killed in 1941 in attempting to cross the French-Swiss border." Since it seems unlikely that a ranking NKVD officer such as Zhukov would not have known Münzenberg had in fact died in summer 1940, this coy demand for information from Dimitrov may have been intended to dispel further rumors of NKVD involvement in Münzenberg's murder, which had apparently begun circulating in Moscow as well. See Vaksberg, *Hôtel Lux: Les partis frères au service de l'Internationale communiste*, trans. Olivier Simon (Paris: Fayard, 1993), 185–93. Of course, it is possible, too, that Zhukov really did know nothing of Münzenberg's death.

36. Although not informed by the latest archival research, the best introduction to the liquidation of the Zimmerwald Left is still Branko Lazitch's article "Stalin's Massacre of the Foreign Communist Leaders," in Lazitch and Drachkovitch, *Comintern*, 139–74. For more recent accounts of individual cases, see Laqueur, *Stalin: The Glasnost Revelations;* Christopher M. Andrew and Oleg Gordievsky, *KGB: The Inside Story of Its Foreign Operations from Lenin to Gorbachev* (London: Hodder & Stoughton, 1990); Pavel Sudoplatov, *Special Tasks: The Memoirs of an Unwanted Witness, a Soviet Spymaster* (Boston: Little, Brown, 1994); and Christopher M. Andrew et al., *The Sword and the Shield: The Mitrokhin Archive and the Secret History of the KGB* (New York: Basic Books, 1999).

37. Krivitsky was found in his hotel room in Washington, D.C. on 10 February 1941, with a "bullet in his temple and a .38 caliber pistol in his hand." Suicide notes, which may have been forgeries, were also found at the scene. Tanenhaus, *Whittaker Chambers*, 168–69.

SELECT BIBLIOGRAPHY

Archival Sources

Archives Nationales, Paris
    F7 13148. "Comité mondial contre la guerre impérialiste et le fascisme."
    F7 14715. "Notes diverses et affaires concernants des allemands internés; 1939–1940."
    F7 14823. "Refugiés politiques notoirement connus pour leur loyalisme a l'égard de la France et présentant toutes garanties au point de vue moral."

Center for Preservation of Historico-Documentary Collections, Moscow ("Osoby" archive of documents captured from the Germans in World War II)
    Fond 500, opis 3, del' 182.

Deutsches Bundesarchiv, Berlin Lichterfelde
    NL 36/515 and NL 36/558. Nachlass "Pieck, Wilhelm."
    NL 5/73. Nachlass "Zetkin, Klara."
    RY 1/I 2. KPD Politburo files, 1920–39.
    RY 1/R 58/645. Gestapo files on the "Deutsche Freiheitspartei."
    RY 1/R 58/627. Gestapo files on the "Münzenberg Gruppe."
    RY 1/R 134. Reichssicherheitshauptamt files, 1918–33.
    RY 1/R 1501. Reichsministerium des Innern files, 1918–33.

Hoover Institution Archives, Stanford, California
    "Gesamtverband deutscher antikommunistischer Vereinigungen" collection, box 32, folder 2.

Institut für Zeitgeschichte, Munich
    MA 644, 699. Gestapo files on Münzenberg.

National Archives, Washington, D.C.
    Military Intelligence Division file PF 13709

Paris Prefecture Archives, Paris
    Box M 12. "Münzenberg, Wilhelm."

Russian Government Archive of Literature and Art, Moscow
    Fond 2734, opis 1, del' 21, 22, 39, 43, 94. "Aleinikov, Moises."

Russian Government Archive of Social-Political History, Moscow
    Fond 538, opisi 1–3. Internationale Arbeiterhilfe (1921–35).
    Fond 495, opis 60. Comintern Orgburo and Special Commissions.

Russian State Film Archive, Moscow.
   Fond 1–17909 I, "MXAT/Mezhrabpom-Russ."
Schweizerisches Bundesarchiv, Bern
   E 21, 9849–9855. Platzkommando Zürich, files relating to the public disturbance of 15–21 November 1917.
   E 21, 9778–9783. Zurich cantonal police files on public disturbances, 1916–18.
   E 21, 11326–11330. Bern Public Prosecutor's Office file on Münzenberg, 1915–18.
Schweizerisches Sozialarchiv, Zurich
   5.10, Nachlass Edi Meyer. Socialist Youth Bureau files, 1909–18.

NEWSPAPERS AND PERIODICALS

Arbeiter Illustrierte Zeitung aller Länder (1924–34).
Arbeiter- und Bauern-Solidaritaet (1934).
Arbeiterfotograf (1928–29).
Berlin am Morgen (1929–33).
Berliner Lokalanzeiger (1929–33).
Chronik des Faschismus (1923–24).
Deutsche Informationen (1936–37).
Der drohende Krieg (1928–30).
Eulenspiegel. Zeitschrift für Scherz—Satire—Ironie und Tiefere Bedeutung (1928–29).
Film und Volk. Organ des Volksfilmverbandes (1928–30).
Gegen den Strom (1928–29).
Das Hakenkreuz (September 1923).
Hunger in Deutschland (1923–24).
International Press Correspondence (Inprecorr) (1929–33).
Nos Regards (1928–32).
Pariser Tageblatt (1934–38).
Rote Aufbau (1922, 1929–32).
Rote Fahne (1918–33).
Ruhr Echo (1923).
Sichel und Hammer (1922–23).
Sowjet-Russland im Bild (1921–22).
Unsere Zeit (1933–34).
Völkische Beobachter.
Vorwärts (1919–33).
Völkische Beobachter (1919–33). *Vössische Zeitung* (1919–33).
Die Welt am Abend (1925–33).
Die Weltbühne (1929–33).
Die Zukunft (1938–39).

Bibliography

CONTEMPORARY ARTICLES, POLEMICS, AND TREATISES

Die Dritte Saüle der kommunistischen Politik. I.A.H. Berlin: Verlagsgesellschaft des Allgemeinen Deutschen Gewerkschaftsbundes, 1924.

Ehrt, Adolf, and Dr. Julius Schweickert. *Entfesselung der Unterwelt: Ein Querschnitt durch die Bolschewisierung Deutschlands.* Berlin and Leipzig: Eckart-Verlag, 1932.

"Hoover Reports Communists Work Under Relief Guise." *New York Times*, 11 February 1922.

Illustrierte Geschichte der russischen Revolution. Berlin: NDV, 1927.

Kropotkin, Peter. *Gegenseitige Hilfe in der Tier- und Menschenwelt.* Leipzig: Verlag von Theod. Thomas, 1910.

Lenin, Vladimir Ilich. *What Is to Be Done?: Burning Questions of Our Movement.* Moscow: Foreign Languages Publishing House, 1947.

Levi, Paul. *Generalstreik und Noske-Blut-Bad in Berlin.* Berlin: Verlag "Rote Fahne," 1919.

———. "Die Lehren der ungarischen Revolution." *Freiheit* (Hanau), 24 March 1919.

———. "Die Kehrleite." *Die Internationale* 1 (9/10) (4 August 1919).

———. *Unser Weg: Wider den Putschismus.* Berlin: A. Seehof & Co., 1921.

Luxemburg, Rosa. *Reform or Revolution?* New York: Three Arrows Press, 1937.

Maslow, Arkady. "Bolshewismus und Menschewismus. Die Spaltung der U.S.P. in Deutschland." *Jugend-Internationale* 2 (3) (November 1920): 40.

Münzenberg, Wilhelm. "Brennende Tagesfragen der Kommunistischen Internationale." *Jugend-Internationale* 2 (8) (April 1921): 199–201.

———. *Der Kampf und Sieg der Bolschewiki.* Stuttgart: Spartakus, 1919.

———. "Der 2. Kongreß der Kommun. Internationale und die Kommunistische Jugendinternationale." *Jugend-Internationale* 2 (4) (December 1920): 86–89.

———. *Das neue Russland.* Berlin, 1922.

———. *Nieder mit Spartakus!* Chemnitz: Buchhandlung d. Kommunistischen Partei, 1919.

———. "Ein Präzendenzfall?" *Jugend-Internationale* 2 (10) (June 1921): 280–83.

———. *Propaganda als Waffe.* Paris: Editions du Carrefour, 1937.

Münzenberg, Wilhelm, et al. *The Brown Book of the Hitler Terror and the Burning of the Reichstag.* London: Victor Gollanzcz, 1933.

Prager, Eugen. "Der Münzenberg-Konzern. Die Geschäfte des kommunistischen Hugenberg." *Volksrecht,* 28 March 1929.

DOCUMENT COLLECTIONS AND PARLIAMENTARY PROCEEDINGS

Die Akte Wehner: Moskau 1937–1941. Berlin: Rowohlt, 1993.

Bulgakova, Oksana. *Eisenstein und Deutschland: Texte, Dokumente, Briefe.* Berlin: Akademie der Künste/Henschel Verlag, 1998.

Degras, Jane, ed. *The Communist International, 1919–1943. Documents.* Vol. 1. New York and Oxford: Oxford University Press, 1956.

Drachkovitch, Milorad M., and Branko Lazitch, eds. *The Comintern: Historical Highlights*. Stanford, Calif.: Hoover Institution Press, 1966.

Eudin, Xenia Joukoff, and Harold H. Fisher, in collaboration with Rosemary Brown Jones, eds. *Soviet Russia and the West 1920–1927: A Documentary Survey*. Stanford, Calif.: Stanford University Press, 1957.

Hahlweg, Walter, ed. *Lenins Rückkehr nach Russland 1917: Die deutschen Akten*. Leiden: E. J. Brill, 1957.

Kerbs, Diethart, ed. *Willi Münzenberg*. Berlin: Edition Echolot, 1988.

Pipes, Richard. *The Unknown Lenin: From the Secret Archive*. New Haven, Conn.: Yale University Press, 1996.

Verhandlungen des Reichstags. IV. Wahlperiode 1928. Stenographische Berichte der 135. Sitzung am 6. März 1930 bis zur 168. Sitzung am 20 Mai 1930. Berlin: Druck und Verlag der Reichsdruckerei, 1930.

Memoirs

Abschrift des Lebenslaufs von Wilhelm Münzenberg. Glashütten im Taunus: Verlag Detlev Auvermann KG, 1972.

Bajanov, Boris. *Avec Staline dans le Kremline*. Paris: Les Editions de France, 1930.

Balabanoff, Angelica. *Impressions of Lenin*. Ann Arbor: University of Michigan Press, 1964.

Barbé, Henri. "Souvenirs de militant et de dirigeant Communiste," typescript memoirs (circa 1949–1950?). Hoover Institution Archives, Hoover Institution on War, Revolution and Peace, Stanford University.

Barmine, Alexander. *One Who Survived: The Life Story of a Russian under the Soviets*. New York: Putnam's, 1945.

Barthel, Max. *Kein Bedarf an Weltgeschichte*. Wiesbaden: Limes Verlag, 1950.

Bessedovsky, Grégoire. *Oui, j'accuse! Au service des Soviets*. Paris: Librairie de la Revue Française, 1930.

Brupbacher, Fritz. *60 Jahre Ketzer. Selbstbiographie. 'Ich log so wenig als möglich.'* Zürich: Verlag B. Ruppli, 1935.

Buber-Neumann, Margarete. *Kriegsschauplätze der Weltrevolution: Ein Bericht aus der Praxis der Komintern 1919–1943*. Stuttgart: Seewald Verlag, 1967.

———. *Von Potsdam nach Moskau: Stationen eines Irrweges*. Stuttgart: Deutsche Verlags-Anstalt, 1957.

Fischer, Ruth. *Stalin und der deutsche Kommunismus*. Frankfurt-am-Main: Verlag der Frankfurter Hefte, 1948.

Globig, Fritz. *. . . aber verbunden sind wir mächtig*. Berlin: Verlag Neues Leben, 1958.

Gross, Babette. *Willi Münzenberg: Eine politische Biographie*. Stuttgart: Deutsche Verlags-Anstalt, 1967.

Habedank, Heinz. *Zur Geschichte des Hamburger Aufstandes 1923*. Berlin: Dietz Verlag, 1958.

Hiller, Kurt. *Köpfe und Tröpfe: Profile aus einem Vierteljahrhundert.* Hamburg: Rowohlt, 1950.

Koestler, Arthur. *The Invisible Writing.* New York: Macmillan, 1969.

Krivitsky, Walter. *In Stalin's Secret Service.* New York: Harper, 1939.

Kurella, Alfred. *Gründung und Aufbau der Kommunistischen Jugend–Internationale.* Berlin: Verlag der Jugendinternationale, 1929.

Meyer-Leviné, Rosa. *Im inneren Kreis: Erinnerungen einer Kommunistin in Deutschland 1920–1933*, ed. Hermann Weber. Cologne: Verlag Kiepenhauer & Witsch, 1979.

Münzenberg, Wilhelm. *Die dritte Front.* Berlin: NDV, 1930.

———. "Ein Tag in Dietskoje-Selo." *Jugend-Internationale* 2 (3) (November 1920): 34–36.

———. "Mit Lenin in der Schweiz." *Internationale Presse Korrespondenz* 6 (27 August 1926): 1838.

———. *Die Sitzung des internationalen sozialistischen Jugendbureaus am 19. bis 20. Mai in Stockholm und meine Teilnahme.* Reprinted from *Jugend-Internationale* 9. Zurich, 1917.

———. *Solidarität: Zehn Jahre Internationale Arbeiterhilfe.* Berlin: NDV, 1931.

———. *Die Sozialistische Jugend-Internationale.* Berlin: Verlag Junge Garde, 1919?

———. *Der Spartakistenprozess in Stuttgart.* Stuttgart: Spartakus, 1919.

Orwell, George. *Homage to Catalonia.* London: Secker and Warburg, 1938.

Regler, Gustav. *The Owl of Minerva*, trans. Norman Denny. New York: Farrar, Strauss and Cudahy, 1959.

Retzlaw, Karl. *Spartakus: Aufstieg und Niedergang. Erinnerungen eines Parteiarbeiters.* Frankfurt-am-Main: Verlag Neue Kritik, 1971.

Sieger, Walter. *Die junge Front.* Berlin: Verlag Neues Leben, 1958.

Sperber, Manès. *All Our Yesterdays*, vol. 2: *The Unheeded Warning, 1918–1933*, trans. Harry Zohn. New York: Holmes & Meier, 1991.

Zeutschel, Walter. *Im Dienst der kommunistischen Terror-Organisation (Tscheka-Arbeit in Deutschland).* Berlin: J. H. W. Dietz Nachf., 1931.

SECONDARY LITERATURE

Andrew, Christopher M., and Oleg Gordievsky. *KGB: The Inside Story of Its Foreign Operations from Lenin to Gorbachev.* London: Hodder & Stoughton, 1990.

Andrew, Christopher, et al. *The Sword and the Shield: The Mitrokhin Archive and the Secret History of the KGB.* New York: Basic Books, 1999.

Angress, Werner T. *Stillborn Revolution: The Communist Bid for Power in Germany, 1921–1923.* Princeton, N.J.: Princeton University Press, 1963.

Avrich, Paul. *Kronstadt 1921.* Princeton, N.J.: Princeton University Press, 1970.

Ball, Alan M. *Russia's Last Capitalists: The Nepmen, 1921–1929.* Berkeley: University of California Press, 1987.

Baykov, Alexander. *The Development of the Soviet Economic System: An Essay on the Experience of Planning in the U.S.S.R.* New York: Macmillan, 1947.

Beradt, Charlotte. *Paul Levi: Ein demokratischer Sozialist in der Weimarer Republik.* Frankfurt-am-Main: Europäische Verlag, 1969.

Berlin, Isaiah. *Karl Marx: His Life and Environment.* London: Oxford University Press, 1939.

Borkenau, Franz. *World Communism: A History of the Communist International.* Ann Arbor: University of Michigan Press, 1962.

Bracher, Karl Dietrich. *Die Auflösung der Weimarer Republik: Eine Studie zum Problem des Machtverfalls in der Demokratie.* Stuttgart and Dusseldorf: Ring-Verlag, 1957.

Braunthal, Julius. *Geschichte der Internationale.* Vol. 2. Berlin: Dietz, 1974.

Brown, Timothy. "Constructing the Revolution: Nazis, Communists and the Struggle for the 'Hearts and Minds' of the SA, 1930–1935." Ph.D. diss., University of California, Berkeley, 2000.

Carsten, Ludwig. *Eduard Bernstein 1850–1932: Eine politische Biographie.* Munich: Beck, 1993.

Caute, David. *The Fellow Travellers: A Postscript to the Enlightenment.* New York: Macmillan, 1973.

Christie, Ian. "Introduction. Soviet Cinema: A Heritage and Its History." In *The Film Factory: Russian and Soviet Cinema in Documents 1896–1939*, ed. and trans. Richard Taylor. London: Routledge & Kegan Paul, 1988.

Cohen, Stephen. *Bukharin and the Bolshevik Revolution: A Political Biography 1888–1938.* New York: Oxford University Press, 1971.

Courtois, Stephane, and Annie Kriegel. *Eugen Fried: Le grand secret du PCF.* Paris: Editions du Seuil, 1997.

———. "La seconde Mort de Willi Muenzenberg," *Communisme* 38–39 (1994): 25–44.

Craig, Gordon. *The Politics of the Prussian Army, 1640–1945.* Oxford: Clarendon Press, 1955.

Dallin, David J. *Soviet Espionage.* New Haven, Conn.: Yale University Press, 1955.

Daly, Jonathan. "The Bolshevik Assault on the Church." In *The Bolsheviks in Russian Society: The Revolution and Civil War*, ed. Vladimir N. Brovkin. New Haven, Conn.: Yale University Press, 1997.

Drachkovitch, Milorad M., and Branko Lazitch. *Biographical Dictionary of the Comintern.* Rev. ed. Stanford, Calif.: Hoover Institution Press, 1986.

Eichengreen, Barry. *Golden Fetters: The Gold Standard and the Great Depression, 1919–1939.* New York: Oxford University Press, 1995.

Falter, Juergen W. *Hitlers Wähler.* Munich: Beck, 1991.

Feldman, Gerald D. *Army, Industry, and Labor in Germany, 1914–1918.* Princeton, N.J.: Princeton University Press, 1966.

———. "Bayern und Sachsen in der Hyperinflation 1922/23." *Historische Zeitschrift* 238 (3) (June 1984): 569–609.

———. *The Great Disorder: Politics, Economics, and Society in the German Inflation, 1914–1924.* New York: Oxford University Press, 1993.

———. *Hugo Stinnes: Biographie eines Industriellen 1870–1924,* trans. Karl Heinz Silber. Munich: Verlag C. H. Beck, 1998.

Felix, David. *Protest: Sacco–Vanzetti and the Intellectuals.* Bloomington: Indiana University Press, 1965.

Fest, Joachim. *Hitler,* trans. Richard and Clara Winston. New York: Penguin, 1974.

Figes, Orlando. *Peasant Russia, Civil War: the Volga Countryside in Revolution, 1917–1921.* New York: Oxford University Press, 1989.

———. *A People's Tragedy: A History of the Russian Revolution.* London: Viking, 1996.

Fisher, H. H. *The Famine in Soviet Russia 1919–1923: The Operations of the American Relief Administration.* New York: Macmillan, 1927.

Freund, Gerald. *Unholy Alliance: Russian-German Relations from the Treaty of Brest-Litovsk to the Treaty of Berlin.* London: Chatto and Windus, 1957.

Gak, A. "K istorii sozdaniia Sovkino." *Iz istorii Kino* 5 (1962): 132–33.

Gay, Peter. *The Dilemma of Democratic Socialism: Bernstein's Challenge to Marx.* New York: Collier, 1962.

Gill, Anton. *A Dance Between Flames: Berlin between the Wars.* London: John Murray, 1993.

Goldbach, Marie-Louise. *Karl Radek und die deutsch-sowjetischen Beziehungen 1918–1923.* Bonn: Verlag Neue Gesellschaft, 1973.

Graf, Christoph, and Walter Hofer. "Neue Quellen zum Reichstagsbrand." *Geschichte in Wissenschaft und Unterricht* 27 (2) (1976): 65–88.

Habedank, Heinz. *Zur Geschichte des Hamburger Aufstandes 1923.* Berlin: Dietz Verlag, 1958.

Hubbard, L. E. *Soviet Money and Finance.* London: Macmillan, 1936.

Huebsch, B. W. Introduction to *Militarism by Karl Liebknecht,* trans. B. W. Huebsch. New York: B. W. Huebsch, 1917.

Illustrierte Geschichte Deutsche Arbeiterjugendbewegung 1904–1945. Berlin: Verlag Neues Leben, 1987.

Koehler, Henning. "Bis sich die Balken biegen. Ein gescheiterter Versuch, die Schuld der Nationalsozialisten am Reichstagsbrand nachzuweisen." *Frankfurter Allgemeine Zeitung,* 22 February 2001: 8.

Joll, James. *The Second International 1889–1914.* London: Weidenfeld & Nicolson, 1955.

Keegan, John. *The First World War.* London: Pimlico, 1998.

Kennedy, David. *Freedom from Fear: The American People in Depression and War, 1929–1945.* New York: Oxford University Press, 1999.

Kepley, Vance, Jr. "The Origins of Soviet Cinema: A Study in Industry Development." In *Inside the Film Factory: New Approaches to Russian and Soviet Cinema,* ed. Richard Taylor and Ian Christie. London: Routledge, 1991.

———. "The Workers' International Relief and the Cinema of the Left 1921–1935." In *Cinema Journal* 23 (1) (Fall 1983): 7–23.

Kershaw, Ian. *Hitler 1889–1936. Hubris.* New York: Norton, 1998.

Klehr, Harvey, et al. *The Soviet World of American Communism.* New Haven, Conn.: Yale University Press, 1998.

Koch, Stephan. *Double Lives: Spies and Writers in the Secret Soviet War of Ideas against the West.* New York: Free Press, 1994.

Kolb, Eberhard, and Klaus Schoenhausen. *Regionale und lokale Räteorganisationen in Württemberg 1918/1919.* Düsseldorf: Droste Verlag, 1976.

Kruedener, Jürgen Baron von, ed. *Economic Crisis and Political Collapse: The Weimar Republic 1924–1933.* New York: St. Martin's Press, 1990.

Laqueur, Walter. *Stalin: The Glasnost Revelations.* New York: Scribner's, 1990.

Lazitch, Branko. "Two Instruments of Control by the Comintern: The Emissaries of the ECCI and the Party Representatives in Moscow." In *The Comintern: Historical Highlights,* ed. Milorad M. Drachkovitch and Branko Lazitch. Stanford, Calif.: Hoover Institution Press, 1966.

Leda, Jay. *Kino: A History of the Russian and Soviet Film.* London: George Allen & Unwin, 1960.

Leonhard, Wolfgang. *Völker hört die Signale: Die Anfänge des Weltkommunismus 1919–1924.* Munich: C. Bertelsman Verlag, 1981.

Leopold, John A. *Alfred Hugenberg: The Radical Nationalist Campaign against the Weimar Republic, 1919–1925.* New Haven, Conn.: Yale University Press, 1977.

Lewy, Guenter. *The Cause That Failed: Communism in American Political Life.* New York: Oxford University Press, 1990.

Lowenthal, Richard. "The Bolshevisation of the Spartacus League." In *St. Antony's Papers,* no. 9: *International Communism,* ed. David Footman. London, 1960.

Malia, Martin. *The Soviet Tragedy: A History of Socialism in Russia, 1917–1991.* New York: Free Press, 1994.

———. Review of Pipes, *The Unknown Lenin. Times Literary Supplement* 4896 (31 January 1997): 6–7.

Mayer, Arno J. *Political Origins of the New Diplomacy, 1917–1918.* New Haven, Conn.: Yale University Press, 1959.

McMeekin, Sean. "From Moscow to Vichy: Three Working-Class Militants and the French Communist Party, 1920–1940." *Contemporary European History* 9 (1) (2000): 1–35.

Morgan, David W. *The Socialist Left and the German Revolution: A History of the German Independent Social Democratic Party, 1917–1922.* Ithaca, N.Y.: Cornell University Press, 1975.

Müller-Lückner, Elisabeth, and Gerhard A. Ritter. *Der Aufstieg der deutschen Arbeiterbewegung. Sozialdemokratie und Freie Gewerkschaften im Parteisystem und Sozialmilieu des Kaiserreiches.* Munich: Oldenbourg, 1990.

Nation, R. Craig. *War on War: Lenin, the Zimmerwald Left, and the Origins of Communist Internationalism.* Durham, N.C.: Duke University Press, 1989.

Nettl, J. P. *Rosa Luxemburg.* 2 vols. London: Oxford University Press, 1966.

Oertzen, Peter von. *Betriebsräte in der Novemberrevolution; eine politikwissenschaftliche Untersuchung uber Ideengehalt und Struktur der betrieblichen und wirtschaftlichen Arbeiterräte in der deutschen Revolution 1918/19.* Hrsg. von der Kommission fur Geschichte des Parlamentarismus und der Politischen Parteien. Düsseldorf: Droste Verlag, 1963.

Osipova, Taisia. "Peasant Rebellions: Origin, Scope, Dynamics, and Consequences." In *The Bolsheviks in Russian Society: The Revolution and Civil Wars*, ed. Vladimir N. Brovkin. New Haven, Conn.: Yale University Press, 1997.

Patch, William, Jr. *Heinrich Bruning and the Dissolution of the Weimar Republic.* New York: Cambridge University Press, 1998.

Pipes, Richard. *The Russian Revolution 1899–1919.* London: Harvill Press, 1990.

———. *Russia under the Bolshevik Regime 1919–1924.* London: Harvill Press, 1997.

Radkey, Oliver Henry. *The Unknown Civil War in Soviet Russia: A Study of the Green Movement in the Tambov Region, 1920–1921.* Stanford, Calif.: Hoover Institution Press, 1976.

Rauber, Urs. "Willi Münzenberg in Zürich 1910–1918. Einige Anmerkungen zu bisher nicht ausgewerteten Quellenmaterialien." In *Willi Münzenberg: Eine Dokumentation zur Münzenberg-Tagung im September 1918 in Zürich*, comp. Peter Vonderhagen und Brigitte Walz-Richter, ed. Theo Pinkus. Zurich: Studienbibliothen zur Geschichte der Arbeiterbewegung, 1990.

Roger, Gerhard. *Die pädagogische Bedeutung der proletarischen Jugendbewegung Deutschlands.* Berlin: Volk und Wissen, 1956.

Roth, Guenther. *The Social Democrats in Imperial Germany.* Totowa, N.J.: Bedminster Press, 1963.

Russell, Francis. "Sacco-Vanzetti: The End of the Chapter." *National Review* 22 (17) (5 May 1970): 454.

Rütz, Günter, and Wolfgang Uellenberg. *75 Jahre Arbeiterjugendbewegung in Deutschland.* N.p.: Stiftung Deutsche Jugendmarke, n.d.

Scharlau, W. B., and Z. A. B. Zeman. *The Merchant of Revolution: The Life of Alexander Israel Helphand (Parvus) 1867–1924.* London: Oxford University Press, 1965.

Schlie, Tania, and Simon Roche. *Willi Münzenberg (1889–1940). Ein deutscher Kommunist im Spannungsfeld zwischen Stalinismus und Antifaschismus.* Frankfurt-am-Main: Peter Lang, 1995.

Schorske, Carl. *German Social Democracy 1905–1917: The Development of the Great Schism.* Cambridge, Mass.: Harvard University Press, 1955.

Schüddekopf, Otto Ernst. *Linke Leute von rechts: Die national-revolutionäre Minderheiten und der Kommunismus in der Weimarer Republik.* Stuttgart: Kohlhammer, 1960.

Smith, S. A. "The Comintern, the Chinese Communist Party and the Three Armed Uprisings in Shanghai, 1926–1927." In *International Communism and the Communist International 1919–1943*, ed. Tim Rees and Andrew Thorpe. New York: Manchester University Press, 1998.

Sudoplatov, Pavel. *Special Tasks: The Memoirs of an Unwanted Witness, a Soviet Spymaster.* Boston, Mass.: Little, Brown, 1994.

Tanenhaus, Sam. *Whittaker Chambers.* New York: Random House, 1997.

Tobias, Fritz. *The Reichstag Fire,* trans. Arnold J. Pomerans. New York: Putnam's, 1964.

Tolstoy, Nikolai. *Stalin's Secret War.* New York: Holt, Rinehart and Winston, 1981.

Tuchman, Barbara. *The Proud Tower: A Portrait of the World Before the War 1890–1914.* New York: Macmillan, 1966.

Turner, Henry Ashby. *Hitler's Thirty Days to Power: January 1933.* London: Bloomsbury, 1997.

Vaksberg, Arkadi. *Hotel Lux: Les partis freres au service de l'Internationale communiste,* trans. Olivier Simon. Paris: Fayard, 1993.

Verhey, Jeffrey. *The Spirit of 1914: Militarism, Myth, and Mobilization in Germany.* Cambridge: Cambridge University Press, 2000.

Waite, Robert G. L. *Vanguard of Nazism: The Free Corps Movement in Postwar Germany 1918–1923.* New York: Norton, 1952.

Waldman, Eric. *The Spartacist Uprising of 1919 and the Crisis of the German Socialist Movement.* Milwaukee: Marquette University Press, 1958.

Weber, Hermann. *Hauptfeind Sozialdemokratie: Strategie und Taktik der KPD 1929–1933.* Düsseldorf: Droste, 1982.

Weissman, Benjamin M. *Herbert Hoover and Famine Relief to Soviet Russia: 1921–1923.* Stanford, Calif.: Hoover Institution Press, 1974.

Weitz, Eric. *Creating German Communism, 1890–1990.* Princeton, N.J.: Princeton University Press, 1997.

Wessel, Harald. *Münzenbergs Ende: Ein deutscher Kommunist im Widerstand gegen Hitler und Stalin.* Berlin: Dietz, 1991.

Wilson, Edmund. *To the Finland Station.* London: Collins, 1940.

Winkler, Heinrich August. *Der Schein der Normalität: Arbeiter und Arbeiterbewegung in der Weimarer Republik 1924 bis 1930.* Berlin: Dietz, 1985.

———. *Von der Revolution zur Stabilisierung: Arbeiter und Arbeiterbewegung in der Weimarer Republik 1918 bis 1924.* Berlin: Verlag Dietz, 1984.

———. *Der Weg in die Katastrophe: Arbeiter und Arbeiterbewegung in der Weimarer Republik 1930 bis 1933.* Berlin: Dietz, 1987.

"Za rekonstruktsiyu sovetskoi kinematografii." *Na literaturnom postu,* February 1930: 2–4.

Zelt, Johannes. *Proletarischer Internationalismus im Kampf um Sacco und Vanzetti.* Berlin: Dietz, 1958.

ACKNOWLEDGMENTS

During the years I have worked on this book, which began as a dissertation at the University of California, Berkeley, I have incurred a number of debts. What follows is a sincere attempt to make good on the most important of these.

Although sometimes underestimated, financial support is possibly the most important precondition for doing research, especially when traveling abroad, where there is enough to worry about without having to figure out how to pay for one's next meal. I have been especially lucky in this regard, receiving support from the UC Regents on numerous occasions, through UC Berkeley's Graduate Fellowships Office; from the U.S. Department of Education, through the FLAS program, which allowed me to master Russian; from the American Council of Teachers of Russian and the State Department, which financed an especially fruitful trip to Moscow; and not least from the German Chancellor's Office, which not only underwrote a fantastic year in Germany but even footed the bill for (yet another) crucial research visit to Moscow.

I would like to make special mention of Professors Keith Baker and James Sheehan of Stanford University, my undergraduate mentors, who first pointed me toward the intellectual satisfaction possible in serious historical scholarship. At UC Berkeley, thanks go to Professor Carla Hesse, who is more responsible than anyone else for the wonderful opportunities I enjoyed there (although she may be disappointed that I abandoned her field, the French Revolution); to Susanna Barrows, who directed the seminar paper from which this project drew inspiration; to Anthony Adamthwaite, for his encouragement and perennial good cheer; and especially to Martin Malia, whose work on communism has been endlessly stimulating and thought-provoking. Although Malia (because now retired) did not serve on my dissertation committee, he was kind enough to read the entire manuscript. His comments, contacts, and support were invaluable.

The research itself could not have been accomplished without the help of dozens of knowledgeable archivists, at the Russian Government Archive of Social-Political History (RGASPI, formerly RTsIiKhDNI), the Osoby Archive, the State Film Archive, and the Russian Government Archive of Literature and Art (RGALI) in Moscow; at the Bundesarchiv in Berlin-Lichterfelde; the Institut für Zeitgeschichte in Munich; the Friedrich-Ebert Archiv in Bonn; the Schweizerisches Sozialarchiv in Zurich; the Schweizerisches Bundesarchiv in Bern; the Archives Nationales in Paris; and the National Archives in Washington. I owe the same debt to the entire staff at the Hoover Institution in Stanford, California. At the Hoover, special mention goes to Natasha and Olga (for allowing me to practice my Russian); Linda Bernard and Carol Leadenham, for handling touchy technical requests; and above all Elena Danielson, who discovered the photograph of Münzenberg, taken by a Nazi surveillance team, that appears here as figure 4. And Mabel Lee, the tireless graduate assistant in Berkeley's History Department whose mastery of the arcane details of academic bureaucracy never ceases to amaze me, provided institutional expertise of a different, yet no less valuable, kind. Thank you, Mabel! You are the best.

Neither the research nor the agonizing process of writing this work would have been possible without the constant guidance and mentoring of my committee members. Professor Ken Jowitt of the political science department took time out of his busy schedule to read an entire draft and iron out the ideological details. Professor Gerald Feldman has given me not only the example of his own indispensable work on the Weimar period but also recommendations and contacts that helped open many doors in Germany. His meticulous reading of my dissertation draft greatly improved the final copy. Yuri Slezkine has been an incomparable guide to all things Russian, however mysterious (such as transliteration), and his critical comments on the draft yielded great dividends.

Professor Peggy Anderson has been the most honorable, reliable, and conscientious chair a dissertation writer could possibly hope for. Her energy and devotion never cease to amaze me, nor does the care with which she reads every line of every single page of my work (even—especially—the endnotes). It is not always easy to make good on all of her invariably astute comments and criticisms, but it is an inspiration merely to try. Thank you, Peggy, for all of your hard work and support for this project. I will never forget your dedication, which will serve as a model for me as I begin my own academic career.

In the progress of this project from academic dissertation to publishable manuscript, I received invaluable assistance from Ron Radosh, who first put me in contact with Jonathan Brent of Yale University Press. Tony Judt invited me to NYU for an extremely fruitful postdoctoral year of research, revision, and most enjoyable teaching, and Jair Kessler helped make my stay on Washington Square extremely pleasant and comfortable. Michael Scammell was not only kind enough to show me relevant chapters of his forthcoming biography of Arthur Koestler but also to provide a healthy critique of several chapters of my own work. Norman Stone's wisdom and incomparable sense of humor helped me keep things in perspective as I wound through the final stages of editorial agony.

At Yale, Gretchen Rings and Mary Pasti have been tireless in guiding me through the details of manuscript preparation. But Jonathan Brent is the person to whom I owe the most. Jonathan's belief in this manuscript, along with his historical and political vision, have both surprised and challenged me. Thank you, Jonathan, for giving me this chance, and for demanding so much from me. I hope that the final product has not greatly disappointed your expectations.

Among friends and family, special mention goes above all to my mother, Susan, who rarely complained about handling practical details (such as mail forwarding) during my sometimes interminable trips abroad. My father, Thomas, too, has never ceased to believe in me, no matter how many times I complain about the various financial miseries of the graduate student life. And my good friends Ethan Rundell and Andrew MacDowell have come through in the crunch for me, the former by handling difficult tasks in Berkeley when I was abroad, the latter with a careful reading of the text from the perspective of a budding novelist. Andrew has also done double duty as my computer consultant.

In every city in which I have stayed, I have found good friends willing to help me out with the kind of essential knowledge only a local can provide. In Paris, Olivia and Sylvain Boulouque have been invaluable as guides and contacts; in Moscow, Katia Prokopova was a veritable doyenne of my well-being; and in Berlin, Anna Kossatz never once tired of my endless queries about the mysteries of German bureaucracy. Responsibility for any mistakes of fact or interpretation remains solely my own.

INDEX

Aelita, 174, 183–84, 187, 342. *See also* Misiano, Francesco; M-Russ
AIZ (Arbeiter Illustrierte Zeitung), 136–37, 145, 151, 171, 180, 199, 201, 207, 210, 213–14, 219, 231, 262. *See also* IAH
Aleinikov, Moisei, 178–79, 187, 189, 192, 340–42. *See also* M-Russ
Alexander-Nexö, Martin, 361
American Communist Party, 163. *See also* FSR
Amsterdam "Peace" Congress (1932), 202, 248–50, 274. *See also* Amsterdam-Pleyel movement; Barbusse, Henri
Amsterdam-Pleyel movement, 202, 263, 274–76. *See also* Amsterdam "Peace" Congress (1932); Barbusse, Henri
Amter, Israel, 166–67. *See also* MOPR
Anderson, Sherwood, 361
Andreeva, Maria Fedorovna, 340
Andrew, Christopher M., 370
Angell, Norman, 280
Angress, Werner T., 324, 332, 333–35
Anti-Imperialist Review, 208
ARA (American Relief Administration), 105–6, 111, 114, 118, 121, 133, 146. *See also* Hoover, Herbert; Volga famine (1921)
Armand, Inessa, 30–31, 37, 314. *See also* Lenin, Vladimir Ilyich
Arnold, Emil, 72, 76, 85
Aschberg, Olof, 296, 301, 303, 367
Aufbau (Industrie- und Handels-Aktiengesellschaft: Internationale Arbeiterhilfe für Sowjet-Russland), 135–36, 171, 180, 185, 330. *See also* IAH
Avrich, Paul, 328
Awensparger, Fanny, 69, 71

Bahar, Alexander, 362
Bahnhofstrasse incident (1916), 39–43
Bajanov, Boris, 334
Bakunin, F. N., 21, 51, 53
Balabanoff, Angelica, 30–31, 67, 95–97, 323
Ball, Alan M., 328
Barbusse, Henri, 1, 150, 241, 247–48, 261, 263, 361; and takeover of Münzenberg's Paris Popular Front committees (1934–35), 274–77, 279, 363. *See also* Amsterdam "Peace" Conference (1932); Amsterdam-Pleyel movement
Barmine, Alexander, 334
Barthel, Max, 23, 74–77, 82, 96–98, 313, 320–24, 334–35, 341; and "German hunger" campaign (1923), 159, 161
Battle of France (1940), 304
Battleship Potemkin, 174–75, 189–92, 342–43. *See also* Eisenstein, Sergei
Baykov, Alexander, 329
Bebel, August, 11, 242
Beletskii, 288, 292, 366. *See also* NKVD
Bellamy, Edward, 54
Bergéry, Gaston, 262, 267, 362
Berlin am Morgen, 220, 238, 257, 263, 280
Berliner Lokal-Anzeiger, 212. *See also* Hugenberg, Alfred
Berlin transport strike (1932), 250, 289
Bernhard, Georg, 280–85, 290–91, 298, 366. *See also* Pariser Tageblatt Affair; Poliakov, Vladimir
Bern women's antiwar conference (1915), 30–31. *See also* Zetkin, Clara
Bern youth antiwar conference (1915), 31, 39
Bernstein, Eduard, 13, 311

385

Berzin, Jan, 315
Bessedovsky, Grégoire, 335
Birth of a Nation, 342
Black Tuesday stock market crash (1929), 222–23
BMW, 243
Bock, Max, 19, 23–25, 40, 312. *See also* SPS
Böhny, Ferdinand, 38, 72
Bolshevik Party (Russian Social Democrats, "Majority" faction), 3, 46, 61, 67–68, 103. *See also* Bukharin, Nikolai; Kamenev, Lev; Lenin, Vladimir Ilyich; Radek, Karl; Soviet Union, history of; Stalin, Joseph; Zinoviev, Grigori
Borchardt, Julian, 315
Borkenau, Franz, 333
Brandler, Heinrich, 153, 158–59, 293
Branting, Georg, 362
Braun, Max, 279–80, 284. *See also* Lutetia committee
Braunthal, Julius, 323, 362
Brecht, Bertolt, 1, 247, 277
Breitscheid, Rudolf, 280–81, 284, 289
Brest-Litovsk Treaty (1918), 91, 328
Brommert, Johannes, 135, 331
Broszat, Martin, 359
Brovkin, Vladimir N., 328
Brown, Isabel, 356
Brown, Tim, 354
Brown Book, 263–68, 277, 279, 297, 359–61. *See also* Leipzig trial (1933); London Counter-Trial (1933); Reichstag fire
Brüning, Heinrich, 220, 229, 231, 291, 353
Brupbacher, Fritz, 22–25, 263, 283, 313, 359, 365, 368
Brussels Anti-Imperialism Congress (1927), 196–201
Brutzkus, Jules, 364
Buber-Neumann, Greta, 205, 259, 347
Bucher, Alfred, 51, 58, 72–73
Bukharin, Nikolai, 92, 211, 214–15, 240, 351; and patronage of Münzenberg (1926–28), 194, 197–99, 250, 344–46
Bulgakova, Oksana, 343
Bülow, Prince Bernhard von, 15
Burns, Seyman, 242

Cabinet of Dr. Caligari, 174, 342
Cachin, Marcel, 92
Catholic Center Party, 245

Carsten, Francis Ludwig, 311
Caute, David, 310
Cecil, Lord Robert, 280
Chambers, Whittaker, 138, 331, 367, 370
Chaplin, Charlie, 342
Chautemps, Camille, 262, 305
Cheka (All-Russian Extraordinary Commission for Combating Counter-Revolution and Sabotage), 105, 124, 128, 213. *See also* NKVD
Chemin des Dames offensive (1917), 43
Chiang Kai-shek, 194, 196, 197, 201, 207, 345, 347–48
Chicherin, Georgii, 92, 95, 108
Children in Battle, 210
Christie, Ian, 175, 339
Churchill, Winston, 288
Clarke, William, 356
Cohen, Stephen, 351
Comintern (Communist International, 1919–43), 277, 307; and Department for International Liaison, 156; Executive Committee (ECCI), correspondence and decisions of, 95, 98–99, 109, 111–13, 148–49, 151, 160–61, 163, 165–69, 171–72, 176–77, 181, 184, 187–88, 195, 197–200, 202, 210, 220, 274–75, 282–83, 286, 289, 291–92, 294–95, 299–300; First Congress of (1919), 91–92; Second Congress of (1920), 90, 92–96; Seventh Congress of (1935), 278–79; Third Congress of (1921), 99, 106. *See also* Bukharin, Nikolai; Piatnitskii, Iosif; Zinoviev, Grigori
Communist Manifesto, 277
Courtois, Stéphane, 363, 365, 366–70
Counterattack, 263, 274, 276, 279
Craig, Gordon, 353
Crawfurd, Helen, 186
Crispien, Arthur, 96
Cuno, Wilhelm, 144, 148, 154

Dallin, Alexander, 334–35
Daly, Jonathan W., 328
Danneberg, Robert, 29–32
Danton, Georges Jacques, 214
Darkness at Noon, 299
Dättwyler, Max, 56–58, 60, 63
Däumig, Ernst, 96
Deutsche Informationen, 281, 283. *See also* Lutetia committee

Deutsche Volkszeitung, 298, 300, 368. *See also* KPD
Dickens, Charles, 50
Dimitrov, Georgi, 205, 268–69, 271, 364–65, 367, 370; and Popular Front, 278–80, 282, 286, 288, 293–95. *See also* Comintern; Leipzig trial (1933)
Dittman, Wilhelm, 96
Dooren, Karel von, 356
Doriot, Jacques, 263, 273, 363
Dos Passos, John, 1, 247, 365
Dostoevsky, Fyodor, 23, 313
Drachkovitch, Milorad M., 322, 325, 348, 364, 370
Dreiser, Theodore, 247
Dritte Front, 45, 293, 311–15, 319–20, 322–24, 352
Dunker, Käthe, 337
Dzherzhinsky, Felix, 213

Eberlein, Hugo, 169, 199, 216, 323, 329
Ebert, Friedrich, 225, 321, 352; as Central Youth chairman of SPD, 19; as leader of Majority SPD (1917–19), 48, 70; as president and chancellor of Weimar Germany (1919–25), 151, 153, 155. *See also* Spartacus and Spartacist uprising; SPD
ECCI. *See* Comintern
Editions du Carrefour, 263, 266, 277, 287, 293
Editions Sebastien Brant, 297–98
Ehrt, Adolf, 244, 357–58
Eichengreen, Barry, 353
Eichhorn, Emil, 80–81
Eiduk, Alexander, 119, 128, 273, 330–31
Einstein, Albert, 1, 150, 194, 201, 262
Eisenstein, Sergei, 174, 189–90, 343. *See also Battleship Potemkin*
Eisner, Kurt, 70
Emont, Karl, 291–92, 366. *See also* German Freedom Party (1937–39)
Engels, Friedrich, 11, 242
Epstein, Edward, 310, 328–29
Eudin, Xenia Joukoff, 328

Falter, Jürgen, 354
Fausch, Jakob, 141
Feldman, Gerald D., 323, 333–34
Feldner, Jakob, 317
Fest, Joachim, 332, 357–59, 363
Feu, 277

Feuchtwanger, Lion, 280, 298, 368
Figes, Orlando, 97, 323–24, 328
Fimmen, Edo, 107–9, 112–13, 326. *See also* International Federation of Trade Unions
Fischer, Ruth, 147, 158, 168, 206, 293, 334–35. *See also* KPD
Fisher, H. H., 324, 328
Fitzpatrick, Catherine A., 324
Fitzpatrick, Sheila, 318
Flieg, Leo, 199, 213, 217, 260, 288, 350–51
Foreign Relief Committee for the Organization of Worker Relief for the Hungry in Soviet Russia. *See* IAH
"Fourth Reich" project, 284, 290. *See also* German Freedom Party (1937–39); Schwarzschild, Leopold
Franco, Francisco, 285–86
Franco-Prussian War (1870–71), 7, 18, 36
Frank, Dr. Karl, 300
Frankfurter Allgemeine Zeitung, 179, 362
Franz Josef, Emperor, 43
Freiligrath, Ferdinand, 11, 22, 50
French Communist Party. *See* PCF
French-German union (1939), 301
French internments of German nationals (1939–40), 302–4
French Popular Front, 274, 276–77, 296. *See also* Comintern; PCF
Freud, Sigmund, 298, 368
Freund, Gerald, 328
Frick, Wilhelm, 255–56
Friedländer, Paul, 116
Frisch, Heinrich, 22
Friends of Socialist Unity (1939), 300
Fröhlich, Paul, 216–17, 351
FSR (Friends of Soviet Russia), 114–18, 128, 135, 163, 166–68, 171. *See also* IAH
Fuchs, Eduard, 200, 202, 345–46
Fürstenberg, Jakob ("Kuba"), 46
Future, 296–303

Gak, A., 340
Gandhi, Mohandas, 194, 201
Gay, Peter, 311
"general strike," socialist theory of, 13
German Communist Party. *See* KPD
German Foreign Office, 45–46
German Freedom Party (1937–39), 290–92, 299, 366. *See also* "Fourth Reich" project; Schwarzschild, Leopold

German Popular Front, 278–83, 288–90, 296. *See also* Comintern; KPD; SPD
German Revolution of 1918, 70–71, 74
German Socialist Unity Party (1939), 300–301
German Workers' Party (1939), 300
Gessler, Otto, 155
Gestapo: surveillance of Münzenberg, 1, 258–62, 290–92, 297–306, 366, 368–70. *See also* NSDAP
Gibarti, Louis, 208
Gide, André, 361
Gill, Anton, 322
Goebbels, Joseph, 1, 244–45, 262–64, 284, 287. *See also* NSDAP
Goethe, Johann Wolfgang von, 50, 266
Gogol, Nikolai, 23
Gollancz, Victor, 266
Golos Pravdy, 46
Goptner, Serafima, 240, 355
Gordievsky, Oleg, 370
Göring, Hermann, 255–58, 261–62, 268, 359. *See also* NSDAP
Gorky, Maxim, 94, 105, 150, 209
Goskino, 178, 180, 182–84. *See also* M-Russ
Graf, Christoph, 362
Greulich, Hermann, 29
Grimm, Robert, 30–31, 35, 37
Gross, Babette, 136, 170, 204–5, 207–8, 239, 258–60, 273, 283, 285, 296, 303–5, 310–11, 314–15, 322–23, 325, 332, 343, 347–51, 352, 354–55, 357–67, 369. *See also* Münzenberg, Willi; NDV
GRU (Red Army intelligence), 119. *See also* Cheka; NKVD
Grzesinski, Albert, 281, 284

Habedank, Heinz, 335
Hahlweg, Werner, 317
Hammer, Armand, 2, 126–27
Hammer and Sickle. See *AIZ*
Hartig, Valentin, 304–5, 369
Hartmann, Dr. Jacob W., 116
Hays, Arthur Garfield, 267
Heimo, Mauno, 197–99, 201, 343, 345–46, 349
Heine, Heinrich, 11, 22, 50
Helphand, Alexander Israel ("Parvus"), 45–48, 316
Helvetiaplatz incident (1917), 58–65

Hemingway, Ernest, 365
Herzen, Alexander, 23
Herzog, Jakob, 51–54, 58, 60, 63, 96, 317–18
Heydrich, Reinhard, 268
Hiden, John W., 359
Hilferding, Rudolf, 151, 352
Hiller, Kurt, 219, 238, 355
Hindenburg, Paul von, 229, 245, 251, 255, 258
Hirsch, Werner, 354
Hirschfeld, Magnus, 204, 347
Hirth, Heinz, 304, 369–70. *See also* Münzenberg, Willi: death of
Hiss, Alger, 138
Hitler, Adolf, 1, 71, 220, 263, 266, 281, 284–85, 287, 290, 296, 298, 301, 303, 306, 332, 351, 358–59, 367; and Beer Hall Putsch (1923), 158; and book-burning, 262, 270; and cooperation with Stalin, 270–71; and genocide, 307; and Night of the Long Knives (1934), 276; and 1936 Olympics, 280; in power, 255–59; and rise to power, 223–25, 228, 231–33, 237–39, 241, 244–45, 248, 250, 255–56; Ruhr crisis (1923), 144–45, 147–48, 152–53, 158. *See also* NSDAP
Hofer, Walter, 362
Höglund, Carl Zeth, 315
Höltermann, Karl, 246, 280
Homage to Catalonia, 296, 367
Hoover, Herbert, 105–6, 114, 118–19, 121, 125, 127, 133, 146. *See also* ARA; Volga famine (1921)
Hörnle, Edwin, 74, 82, 132–33, 330
Hubbard, L. E., 329
Hugenberg, Alfred, 1, 210–12, 223, 225, 310, 350. See also *Berliner Lokal-Anzeiger*
Humanité, 160, 243, 327. *See also* PCF
Humbert-Droz, Jules, 92, 317

I. G. Farben, 212
IAH (Internationale Arbeiterhilfe/International Worker Relief): and Auditing Commission, 139–43, 181, 192; and Berlin transport strike (1932), 250; and children's homes in Ural region, 132–33, 138, 164–65; and corruption scandals (1922–23), 129–36, 138–43, 164–65, 188, 239; and dumping of aid supplies on Russian black market, 135–36; and "German hunger" campaign (1923–24), 159–62, 165, 169;

and "German October" (1923), 156–58; and June 1923 World Congress, 143, 149; liquidation of (1935), 278; and miscellaneous fundraising campaigns, 193; and M-Russ film company, 174–75, 178, 180, 182, 187–92; and national branch offices, 242–44; and persecution by Nazis, 261–62, 272–73; and Prombank debts, 161, 164, 171–72, 188, 190–91, 336, 343–44; and real estate concessions in Moscow and Petrograd, 133–34; and *Reichsabteilung* (German branch), 217–19, 243–44; and Ruhr crisis (1923), 150–51; and Solidarity Days (1931–32), 237, 242, 244, 248, 271; and surveillance by Reich Interior Ministry, 249–50; and Ural-AG scandal, 141–42, 164–65, 188; and Ten-Year Anniversary Congress (1931), 240–42; and Volga famine campaign, 106–22, 193; and *Wirtschaftshilfe* campaign (1922–23), 122, 127–43, 164–65, 171–72, 188, 239. See also *AIZ;* Comintern; FSR; Jung, Franz; Münzenberg, Willi

Ibsen, Henrik, 23, 313
Inprecorr (International Press Correspondence), 194, 248, 352
International Federation of Trade Unions, 107–9, 113, 148. See also Fimmen, Edo
International Socialist Youth Secretariat (1915–19), 31–32, 40, 47–49, 60–61
International Worker Relief. See IAH
In the Cross-Fire, 277

Jardin des Modes, 262
Jaurès, Jean, 321
Jerram, Guy, 263, 274
Jews are Watching You, 266
Jogisches, Leo, 78
Joll, James, 311
Jones, Rosemary Brown, 328
Jung, Franz, 327–29, 330, 332; and Volga famine campaign, 118–21; and Ural-AG scandal, 141–42, 164–65; and *Wirtschaftshilfe* campaign, 122, 126–28, 130, 133–36, 141–42, 164–65. See also IAH

Kahr, Gustav von, 152
Kamenev, Lev, 124, 169, 200, 214–15, 272, 286, 325
Kameneva, Olga, 200, 345–46

Kapp putsch (1920), 89, 144, 322
Karolyi, Count Michael, 262
Karsner, Rose, 168, 338
Kascher, Leonie, 76, 321
Katz, Otto ("André Simon"), 264. See also NKVD, surveillance of Münzenberg
Kautsky, Karl, 11
Keaton, Buster, 342
Keegan, John, 316
Keller, Albert, 62–63, 64, 67, 78, 318–19, 321
Keller, Helen, 168
Kepley, Vance, 174–75, 339–40
Kerensky, Alexander, 47, 55–56, 352
Kerr, Alfred, 219
Kershaw, Ian, 332, 354, 358
Kersten, Kurt, 287, 367–68
Kessler, Count Harry von, 86, 256
Kiel mutiny (1918), 70
Kisch, Egon Erwin, 277, 361
Klehr, Harvey, 326
Klein, Liana, 286
Klepper, Otto, 290, 301
Kluser, Adele, 24, 69, 71, 73, 75, 77–78, 85, 321
Koch, Stephen, 310, 347, 365, 367–68
Kodak, 179
Koenen, Wilhelm, 108
Koestler, Arthur, 264, 296–300, 347, 359, 367
Köhler, Henning, 362
Kolb, Eberhard, 322
Kollwitz, Käthe, 116, 150
Kornilov, Lavr Georgievich, 55
KPD (Kommunistische Partei Deutschlands/German Communist Party), 85, 270, 306; and Berlin transport strike (1932), 250, 289; executive (Zentrale) correspondence and decisions of, 109–11, 147–48, 158–59, 278–83, 288–90, 293–96; and film propaganda, 180, 189; formation of, 78–79; and "German hunger" campaign (1923–24), 162; and German Popular Front, 278–83, 288–90, 293–94; and "German October" (1923), 153–59; and Kapp putsch (1920), 89; March action of (1921), 112, 144; and Münzenberg's expulsion from, 293–96, 299–300; and paramilitary branches, 147, 153–58, 223, 233–34, 245–46; and persecution by Nazis, 256–58, 270–71; and Ruhr crisis (1923), 144–48, 153–58; and "social fascism" doctrine, 4, 220–21, 223–25, 228–32, 236–39;

KPD *(continued)*
　Spartacist uprising (1919), 80–83; and tensions with Münzenberg, 199–200, 205–6; and Volga famine campaign, 109–12, 117; and 1932 elections, 245–46, 251. *See also* Comintern; German Popular Front; Pieck, Wilhelm; SPD; Thälmann, Ernst; Ulbricht, Walter
Kress, Wilhelm, 139, 141, 331
Kriegel, Annie, 363
Krivitsky, Walter, 147, 293, 306, 333–34, 370
Kropotkin, Prince Peter, 21, 312
Kruedener, Jürgen, Baron von, 353
Kruse, William, 177–78, 180, 340
Kruyt, John William, 135, 170, 331, 337
Ku Klux Klan, 230
Kun, Bela, 84, 105, 116, 169, 263, 274–75, 326, 361, 363
Kurella, Alfred, 261, 323–24
Kuskova, Ekaterina, 105
Kuusinen, Otto, 199, 334, 345–46
"Kuzbus" concession (1922), 129–32, 137–38. *See also* IAH; Smith, Jessica; Ware, Harold

Lang, Fritz, 174
Laqueur, Walter, 366, 370
Lazitch, Branko, 322, 325, 348, 364, 370
League of Nations, 277
Leda, Jay, 340
Leipzig trial (1933), 268–69, 271, 279, 288
Lenin, Vladimir Ilyich, 77, 88, 99, 132, 148, 199, 213, 216, 232, 236, 240, 242, 286, 288, 294, 296, 300, 305–6, 309, 314, 321, 323–24, 326, 340; and anti-Church campaign (1921–22), 126–28, 138; and IAH *Wirtschaftshilfe* mandate, 128; and Krupskaya, 38; and Münzenberg, 2–4, 36–39, 62, 71, 73, 179, 181; political ideas and writings of, 32–39, 93; quoted, 101; and Russian Revolution of 1917 (October), 55–57; and "sealed train car" journey to Finland Station (1917), 45–48; and Second Comintern Congress (1920), 92–95; and Volga famine (1921), 104–6; and Zimmerwald Left, 36–37, 228, 293, 305–6. *See also* Armand, Inessa; Russian Revolution of 1917 (October); Zimmerwald Left
Leonhard, Wolfgang, 334
Leopold, John A., 350
Levassor, F., 170

Levi, Paul, 48, 79, 84, 190, 322
Lévi, Pierre, 263, 277
Lewinsohn, Richard, 284
Lewy, Guenter, 326
Liebknecht, Karl, 13, 25, 32, 36, 78, 122, 132, 213, 247, 299, 314–15, 322; and military draft issue, 15, 39–40; and Spartacist uprising (1919), 80–83. *See also* KPD; Luxemburg, Rosa
Liebknecht, Wilhelm, 228
London Counter-Trial (1933), 267–68. See also *Brown Book;* Leipzig trial (1933)
Lovestone, Jay, 168
Lowenthal, Richard, 321
Lubbe, Marinus van der, 257–58, 268. *See also* Reichstag fire
Ludendorff, Erich, 89, 151, 224, 333
Lunacharskii, Anatolii, 95
Lutetia committee, 280–83, 285, 289
Lüttwitz, Walther Freiherr von, 89
Luxemburg, Rosa, 13, 25, 36, 45, 120, 132, 206, 213, 236, 300, 315, 321–22; and general strike question, 13; political beliefs of, 78–81; and Spartacist uprising (1919), 80–81, 83. *See also* KPD; Liebknecht, Karl

MacDonald, Ramsey, 108
McMeekin, Sean, 363
Maid of Orleans, 277
Makhno, Nestor, 97, 324
Malia, Martin, 351
Malkin, B. M., 191
Malraux, André, 247
Manchester Guardian, 197
Mann, Heinrich, 248, 249, 280, 282, 289, 291, 365. *See also* German Popular Front; Lutetia committee
Mann, Thomas, 280, 297, 368
Manuil'skii, Dmitri, 194
Marcuse, Ludwig, 280
Marley, Lord, 263. *See also* World Committee for the Relief of the Victims of German Fascism
Marti, Ernst, 51, 58, 60–61, 72, 76, 321
Martin, A. B., 326, 336
Marx, Karl, 51, 132, 140, 242, 296, 315
Marxism, theory of, 11
Maslov, Arkadi, 158
Matthias, Erich, 361
Mayer, Arno J., 314, 316

Index

Mehring, Franz, 13
Mehring, Walter, 277, 301
Mein Kampf, 234. *See also* Hitler, Adolf
Mel'gunov, S. P., 328
Menshevik Party (Russian Social Democrats, "Minority" faction), 56, 315. *See also* Bolshevik Party (Russian Social Democrats, "Majority" faction)
Meyer, Edi, 26, 76, 312, 321
Meyer-Leviné, Rosa, 320
Mezhrabpom-Film. *See* M-Russ
Miliukov, Paul, 364
Mimiola, Guilio, 26
Mirov-Abramov, Jacob, 156, 288
Misiano, Francesco, 78, 135, 172, 331, 344–45, 355–56; and M-Russ film company, 183–84, 186–88, 337, 339. *See also* IAH; M-Russ
Molotov, Vyacheslav, 301–2, 354
Molotov-Ribbentrop Pact, 301–2
Monde, 262
Moor, Karl, 323
MOPR (Mezhdunarodnaia Organizatsia Pomoshchi Revolutsioneram/International Red Aid), 165–69, 187, 193, 198–99, 211, 242, 278. *See also* Amter, Israel; IAH
Morf, Anni, 72
Morgan, David W., 321, 324
Moro-Giafferi, Maître de, 267, 280, 362. *See also* London Counter-Trial (1933)
Morsey, Rudolf, 361
Moskvin, Ivan, 174, 178–79, 187
Most, Johann, 21, 312
M-Russ (Mezhrabpom-Russ/Mezhrabpom-Film), 174–75, 178, 180, 182, 187–92, 217, 278. *See also* Aleinikov, Moisei; IAH; Misiano, Francesco
Muckermann, Father, 366
Müller, Alfred, 157
Müller, Hermann, 219–22, 225, 229–30, 237. *See also* SPD
Müller, Karl, 335, 337
Müller, Reinhard, 368
Münzenberg, Karl, 7–9; death of, 9
Münzenberg, Mina, 7–9, 69–70
Münzenberg, Willi: and Allied intelligence contacts (1939–40), 303; and Amsterdam "Peace" Congress (1932), 248–50; and anarchism, 21–22, 51, 53; and antifascist committee (1923–24), 148–52, 193; and anti-imperialism campaign (1926–27), 171, 194–203, 208; and anti–Young Plan plebiscite (1929–30), 223; and apologies for Stalin's tyranny, 219, 272–73; and archival sources, 309–10; autobiographical writings of, 8, 69–71; and Bahnhofstrasse incident (1916), 39–43; barbershop apprenticeship of, 9; and Berlin apartment, 205–6; and Berlin transport strike (1932), 250; and Bern youth antiwar conference (1915), 31, 39; and British Foreign Office, 48–49; and *Brown Book*, 263–68; and Brussels Anti-Imperialism Congress (1927), 195–201; childhood of, 7–10; and Communist Youth International, 87–90, 98–99, 106, 169; death of, 1, 305–6, 369–70; and dumping of IAH aid supplies on Russian black market, 135–36; early political education of, 11–12; and ECCI reprimand (1936), 282–83; and Erfurt Free Youth, 12–13, 15–17, 19, 99; and expulsion from KPD, 293–96, 299–300; and fellow travelers, 194, 196–97, 238; and film holdings, 174–92, 209, 217, 343; financial holdings of, 212, 350; and flight from Nazi Germany (1933), 256–62; and French internments of German nationals (1939–40), 302–4; and *Future*, 296–303; and general strike issue, 50–51; and German Freedom Party (1937–39), 290–92; and "German hunger" campaign (1923–24), 159–62, 165, 169; and German Popular Front, 278–83, 288–90; and "German October" (1923), 156–58; and German Socialist Youth movement, 12–17; and Gestapo surveillance, 1, 258–62, 290–92, 297–306, 366, 368–70; and Goebbels, 244–45; health problems of, 8; and Helvetiaplatz incident (1917), 58–65; and historical responsibility, 306–7; and historical sources, 1; and Hitler, 1, 71, 144–45, 225, 228, 237–39, 241, 244, 251; and Hugenberg, 1, 211–12; and IAH Solidarity Days (1931–32), 237, 242, 244, 248, 271; and IAH Ten-Year Anniversary Congress (1931), 240–42; and incorporation of Aufbau, 135, 330; and International Youth Secretariat, 31–32, 40, 47–49, 60–61, 67, 75–78; and Kapp putsch (1920), 89, 144; and KPD March action (1921), 144; and

Münzenberg, Willi *(continued)*
last stand with Stalin, 290–92; lavish lifestyle of, 205–6, 212–13; and Leipzig trial (1933), 268–69; and Lenin, 2–4, 36–39, 45–48, 62, 71, 73; and liquidation of IAH (1935), 278; and London Counter-Trial (1933), 268–69; and loss of Paris Popular Front committees (1934–35), 274–77, 279; and Lutetia committee, 280–83; and media "trust," 200–202, 207–14, 217–20; and Meilen prison period, 68–71; and military draft issue, 38–39, 47, 61, 63–64; and Molotov-Ribbentrop Pact, 301–2; and Moscow show trials, 286–88; and myth of "break" from Moscow, 293–94; NKVD surveillance of, 1–2, 286, 288, 292–93, 295, 368–70; and oratorical skills, 225–27; and Pariser Tageblatt Affair, 283–85; pictured, 14, 52, 72, 226–27; and poetic inclinations of, 22–23; political beliefs of, 2–4, 54–55; and political group "Propaganda," 10–12; political instincts of, 82–84; and *Propaganda as a Weapon*, 287–88; and pseudonym "E. Arnold," 319; quoted, 253; recruitment abilities of, 12; and recruitment of renegade Nazis, 233–37; and "Red Millionaire" label, 211–13, 240, 279; and "Red Plebiscite" on Prussian SPD government (1931), 238–39; and Red Sunday incident (1916), 41–43, 49; in Reichstag, 168, 225, 228–29; and Reichstag fire campaign, 263–68; and relationship with mother, Mina, 69–70; and "Rescue Ernst Thälmann" campaign (1934), 271–72, 274–75, 277; and rivalry with Ulbricht, 199, 278, 281–82, 287, 289–90, 293–94; and "Ruegg" case, 247–48; and Ruhr crisis (1923), 144–46, 148–52, 156–58; and run-ins with police (Erfurt), 9, 15–16; and run-ins with police (Switzerland), 39–43, 49, 53, 55–65; and run-ins with police (Weimar Germany), 84–85, 88–90, 249–50; and Saar plebiscite campaign (1934–35), 277; and Second Comintern Congress (1920), 93–98; and Seventh Comintern Congress (1935), 278–79; and "social fascism" doctrine, 4, 220–21, 223–25, 228–32, 236–39, 248–49; and *Solidarität*, 212, 239–40; and SOPADE, 278–82; and Spanish Civil War, 365; and Spartacist uprising in Stuttgart (1919), 82–85, 144; and Stalin, 195, 198; and Stuttgart Youth Conference (1914), 27, 29; and Swiss Socialist Youth movement, 18–27, 39–43, 49–55, 60–61; teetotalism of, 12, 50; and tensions with KPD, 199–200, 205–6; and tensions with SPD leadership, 15–17, 19, 143, 210–12; and tensions with SPS leadership, 22, 24, 28, 40–43, 74–75; and Third Comintern Congress (1921), 99, 106; and U.S. military intelligence, 67; and visit to America (1934), 272, 275–76; and Volga famine relief campaign, 106–22, 324–25; and *Wirtschaftshilfe* campaign, 122, 127–43, 164–65, 171–72; and Wittorf affair, 216–17; and Witzwil prison period, 65–68; and work experience in Erfurt shoe factory, 10–13, 17. *See also* German Freedom Party (1937–39); Gross, Babette; IAH; KPD; Lutetia committee; M-Russ; Zimmerwald Left

Mussolini, Benito, 151–52, 352

Nabokov, Vladimir, 86
Nashe Slovo, 44
Nation, 105, 114
Nation, R. Craig, 314–15
Nazis. *See* NSDAP
NDV (Neue Deutsche Verlag), 170, 208, 250. *See also* Gross, Babette
Nehru, Jawaharlal, 201
Nerman, Ture, 315
Nettl, J. P., 322
Neubaner, Th., 353
"Neues Beginnen," 300
Neue Tagebuch, 285, 298
Neumann, Heinz, 205–7, 213–14, 216–17, 246–47, 260, 288, 348. *See also* KPD; Stalin, Joseph
New Deal, 207
New Republic, 105, 114
News Chronicle, 297
New York Times, 118
Night of the Long Knives, 276–77, 283. *See also* Hitler, Adolf; SA (Sturmabteilung/Storm Troop Section)
NKVD, surveillance of Münzenberg, 1–2, 286, 288, 292–93, 295, 297–306, 368–70. *See also* Beletskii; Cheka

Index 393

No Entry, 277
Noske, Gustav, 225
Nos regards, 207–9
Nötri, Ernst, 72
NSDAP (Nationalsozialistische Deutsche Arbeiterpartei/National Socialist German Workers' Party), 222–28, 230–39, 244–45, 248–49, 251; and anti-Young Plan plebiscite, 222–23; and Beer Hall Putsch (1923), 158–59, 268; and Berlin transport strike (1932), 250, 289; and book-burning, 262; and Leipzig trial (1933), 268–69; and Night of the Long Knives, 276–77, 283; and 1932 elections, 245–46, 251; and 1936 Olympics, 280; in power, 255–60, 262, 270–71, 277; and Ruhr crisis (1923), 144–45, 147–48, 152, 155, 158–59. *See also* Gestapo; Goebbels, Joseph; Göring, Hermann; Hitler, Adolf; Night of the Long Knives
Nüssli, Gustav, 64

Oberfohren, Ernst, 265, 361
"Oberfohren memorandum," 265, 361. *See also Brown Book;* London Counter-Trial (1933); Reichstag fire
Oehring, Walter, 331, 337
Oertzen, Peter von, 322
Okopnaia Pravda, 46
Orwell, George, 296–97, 367
Osipova, Taisia, 328
Otsep, Feodor, 192, 344
Our Time, 262, 272–74, 276
Owlglass, 207

Papen, Franz von, 245–46, 251, 255
Pariser Tageblatt, 283–85
Pariser Tageblatt Affair, 283–85. *See also* Bernhard, Georg; Poliakov, Vladimir
Pariser Tageszeitung, 284–85, 287, 289–90, 298
Patch, William, Jr., 353
Pavliechenkov, Sergei, 328
PCF (French Communist Party), 111–12, 160, 208, 243, 273–75. *See also Humanité;* Souvarine, Boris
Pearson, Michael, 314
Pech, Karlheinz, 369
Pflüger, Paul, 20–21
Piatnitskii, Iosif, 160, 163, 166, 169, 184–85, 334–37, 339, 342, 344
Pieck, Wilhelm, 245–47, 260, 298, 364, 366, 367–68; and German Popular Front, 278, 281–82, 287, 289, 294; and Spartacist uprising (1919), 80–82. *See also* German Popular Front; KPD
Pinkus, Theo, 320
Pioneer, 210
Pipes, Richard, 92, 315–16, 318, 323–24, 328, 333
Platten, Fritz, 37, 47, 61–62, 66–68, 71–72, 75, 305, 315, 320. *See also* Zimmerwald Left
Plekhanov, Georgi, 315
Poels, Monsignor, 290, 366
Poincaré, François, 144
Poitiers, Eugène, 315
Poliakov, Vladimir, 283–85, 298, 365. *See also* Bernhard, Georg; Pariser Tageblatt Affair
Polikushka, 178–80, 189–90, 192–93, 341. *See also* Aleinikov, Moisei; M-Russ
Pomgol (All-Russian Committee to Aid the Hungry), 105–6. *See also* Volga famine (1921)
Popov, Simon, 271
Popular Front. *See* French Popular Front; German Popular Front; Spanish Popular Front
Poslednie Novosti, 366–67
Poyntz, Juliet, 135, 330–31
Prager, Eugen, 210–12, 349
Pravda, 46, 103, 137, 197
Profintern (Red Labor International), 165–66
Prokopovich, S. N., 105
Proletkino, 178, 180, 182, 184–85. *See also* IAH; M-Russ
Prometheus, 190, 209, 343
Propaganda as a Weapon, 287–88, 297
Protazanov, Yakov, 174, 179, 181, 187, 342
Pudovkin, 192

Radek, Karl, 34–35, 71, 73, 99, 132, 134, 216, 305, 309, 315, 332–33; and Lenin's "sealed train car" journey to Finland Station (1917), 45–46; and Ruhr crisis (1923), 146–48, 155, 158; and Second Comintern Congress (1920), 94–95; and show trials (1930s), 286; and Volga famine campaign, 110, 326–28; and Zimmerwald Left,

Radek, Karl *(continued)*
 36–37, 106, 305. *See also* Lenin, Vladimir Ilyich; Zimmerwald Left
Radkey, Oliver Henry, 328
Rakovsky, Christo, 316
Ramus, Pierre, 359
Rapallo Treaty (1922), 126–27, 145–46, 148, 328
Rauber, Urs, 320
"Red Sunday" incident (1916), 41–43, 49
Rees, Tim, 348
Regler, Gustav, 264, 277, 347, 359, 363, 367
Reich, James ("Thomas"), 87, 89–90
Reich Interior Ministry, 249, 261
Reichstag fire, 257–58, 277, 362
Reiss, Ignace, 293
Remmele, Hermann, 148, 155, 247, 333
Retzlaw, Karl, 322
Reuter, Ernst, 326
Reventlow, Count Ernst zu, 147, 333
Ribbentrop, Joachim von, 301–2
Ritter, Gerhard A., 311
Robespierre, Maximilien, 214
Roche, Simon, 310
Roger, Gerhard, 311
Rohe, Karl, 311
Rolland, Romain, 317, 361
Romanov family, dynasty and looted wealth of, 98–99, 351
Roosevelt, Franklin Delano, 207
Rote Aufbau, 141, 211, 220–21, 262
Rote Fahne, 75–76, 109, 113, 117, 147, 155, 177, 180, 199, 214, 223, 256, 333, 341. *See also* KPD
Roth, Guenther, 311
Roth, Otto, 140, 142
Rotter, Max, 56
"Ruegg" case (1932), 247–48, 357
Ruhr crisis (1923), 143–58, 160
Rundschau, 281
Russian Civil War (1918–21), 91–92, 96–97, 103–4, 123, 178; and Kronstadt uprising (1921), 124; and peasant rebellions (1921), 124; and War Communism (1918–21), 3, 123, 125, 149. *See also* Volga famine (1921)
Russian Revolution of 1905, 13
Russian Revolution of 1917 (February), 44, 70
Russian Revolution of 1917 (October), 55–57, 65. *See also* Lenin, Vladimir Ilyich
Russie Nouvelle, 207

SA (Sturmabteilung/Storm Troop Section), 152, 155, 224, 233–34, 237–39, 244, 262, 276. *See also* Hitler, Adolf; Night of the Long Knives; NSDAP
Saar plebiscite campaign (1934–35), 277
Sacco, Nicola, 202, 346–47
Säufen, Fritz, 72
Scammell, Michael, 359, 367
Schäfer, Franz, 134–36, 330–31
Scharlau, W. B., 316–17
Scheidemann, Philipp, 48, 316
Schiff, Victor, 281, 364
Schiller, Friedrich, 50, 277
Schlageter, Albert Leo, 147–48
Schleicher, Kurt von, 251
Schlie, Tania, 310, 366
Schmidt, Robert, 15
Schöfer, Paul, 259
Scholze, Paul, 170, 218, 352
Schönhausen, Klaus, 322
Schorske, Carl, 311
Schroeder, Max, 264
Schulz, Hans, 259, 288
Schumann, Georg, 11–13, 15
Schwarzschild, Leopold, 280, 284, 290, 298. *See also* "Fourth Reich" project
Schweickert, Julius, Dr., 244, 357–58
Schweide, Isaak, 75, 320
Second Workingman's International (1890–1914), 11, 29, 31–32, 88. *See also* Lenin, Vladimir Ilyich; Luxemburg, Rosa
Seeckt, Hans von, General, 89, 151–52, 155, 158
Serrati, Giacinto Menotti, 92
Severing, Carl, 224–25, 229, 352–53. *See also* SPD
Sevzapkino, 178, 183
Shaw, George Bernard, 267
Siber, Karl Heinz, 334
Siemsen, Hans, 304, 369
Sigg, Johann, 28
Simon, Hugo, 150, 285, 365
Simon, Olivier, 370
Sinclair, Upton, 1, 150, 168, 209, 242, 334
Singing Jailbirds, 242
Skoblevsky, Pëtr Aleksandrovich, General, 156
Smeral, Bohumil, 263, 285, 287, 346, 365–66
Smith, Jessica, 131–32. *See also* "Kuzbus" concession (1922); Ware, Harold

Smith, S. A., 348
"social fascism," Communist doctrine of, 4, 220–21, 223–25, 228–32, 236–39, 248–49, 281, 289. *See also* Comintern; KPD; Stalin, Joseph
Soldatskaia Pravda, 46
Solidarität, 212, 239–40, 340, 355
SOPADE (SPD in exile after 1933), 278–82, 291, 300–301. *See also* German Popular Front; KPD; SPD
Souvarine, Boris, 111, 325. *See also* PCF
Soviet Russia in Pictures. See *AIZ*
Soviet Union, history of: First Five Year Plan and collectivization (1929–34), 3, 240–41, 272–73; New Economic Policy (1921–29), 124–28, 133, 136, 142–43, 150, 193; show trials (1930s), 219, 286, 288. *See also* Lenin, Vladimir Ilyich; Russian Civil War (1918–21); Stalin, Joseph
Sovkino, 188–90, 192. *See also* M-Russ
Spanish Popular Front, 285, 296
Spartacus and Spartacist uprising (1919), 80–85, 144. *See also* KPD; Liebknecht, Karl; Luxemburg, Rosa; USPD
SPD (German Social Democratic Party), 99, 223, 229–30, 245, 257, 270; leadership of, 11, 15–17; and persecution by Nazis, 256–58, 270; and Ruhr crisis (1923), 144, 152–53, 157; and Spartacist uprising (1919), 80–83; and surveillance of Münzenberg, 143, 210–12, 350; and 1932 elections, 245–46, 251. *See also* Ebert, Friedrich; KPD; Müller, Hermann; Severing, Carl; SOPADE
Sperber, Manès, 347
Spiecker, Karl, Dr., 290, 292, 366
SPS (Swiss Social Democratic Party), 19, 22, 24, 37, 59. *See also* Bock, Max; Platten, Fritz
Stalin, Joseph, 169, 171, 195, 198, 210, 291–94, 295–96, 299, 302, 339, 346, 348, 359, 366; and "class against class" line (1928–34), 213–15, 217, 245–47, 250; First Five Year Plan and collectivization of (1929–34), 240–41, 272–73; and Ruhr crisis (1923), 155, 157–59; and show trials (1930s), 219, 286, 288; and Trotsky's murder, 305. *See also* Soviet Union, history of; "social fascism," Communist doctrine of
Stasi, 213

Steffens, Lincoln, 261
Stinnes, Hugo, 152, 210
Stirner, Max, 21
Stoecker, Walter, 96
Strachey, John, 361
Strasser, Otto, 234–37
Stresemann, Gustav, 147, 154–55, 222
Sudoplatov, Pavel, 370
Swiss Socialist Party. *See* SPS

Tagliatti, Palmiro ("Ercoli"), 286
Tanenhaus, Sam, 331, 369–70
Tanev, Vassili, 271
Taylor, Richard, 339
Thalheimer, August, 351
Thälmann, Ernst, 158, 199, 210, 213, 260, 271, 274–75, 277, 281, 353, 362; and "class against class" line (1928–34), 215–17, 245–47; and Wittorf affair (1928), 215–17, 351. *See also* KPD
Third International. *See* Comintern
Thorez, Maurice, 273, 282, 356, 363
Thormann, Werner, 299
Thornton, Richard C., 348
Thorpe, Andrew, 348
Tobias, Fritz, 359, 361–62
Toller, Ernst, 280, 361
Tolstoy, Alexei, 183
Tolstoy, Lev, 178, 180
Tolstoy, Nikolai, 359
Tonn, Günther, 330
Torgler, Ernst, 271, 359
Trade Union Council of Germany, 15
Trostel, Willi, 26, 39, 58, 60–62, 73, 75, 85, 318, 322
Trotsky, Lev, 34, 36, 44, 62, 91–92, 214–15, 245, 292, 295, 299, 316; and Kronstadt uprising (1921), 124; murder of, 305; and Ruhr crisis (1923), 153, 158. *See also* Lenin, Vladimir Ilyich; Stalin, Joseph
Tucholsky, Kurt, 219, 301
Turner, Henry Ashby, 256, 358
Twain, Mark, 209
Twenty-One Conditions, 95–96, 98
"Two and a Half" Socialist International. *See* Vienna Socialist International

Ulbricht, Walter, 213, 260, 296, 298, 365–66; and "class against class" line (1928–34), 215, 247; and German Popular Front, 278,

Ulbricht, Walter *(continued)* 281–82, 287, 289–90, 293–94; and rivalry with Münzenberg, 199, 278, 281–82, 287, 289–90, 293–94; and Wittorf affair (1928), 215. *See also* German Popular Front; KPD; SOPADE
Ullstein, Franz, 282, 284
Unfried, Emil, 189
Universum-Bücherei, 208–9, 351
USPD (Unabhängige Sozialdemokratische Partei Deutschlands/Independent German Social Democratic Party), 75; and Second Comintern Congress, 96; and Spartacist uprising (1919), 80–83. *See also* Spartacus and Spartacist uprising

Vaksberg, Arkadi, 370
Vallenius, Allan, 181–82, 184
Vanzetti, Bartolomeo, 202, 346–47
Verhey, Jeffrey, 314
Vienna Socialist International, 108, 201
Vogel, Lucien, 262
Volga famine (1921), 103–7, 123, 149, 163
Völkische Beobachter, 147, 248, 260, 350. *See also* Goebbels, Joseph; NSDAP
Vossische Zeitung, 282
Vorovski, V. V. ("Orlovsky"), 47
Vorse, Mary Heaton, 168
Vorwärts, 81, 212, 256. *See also* SPD

Wagner, Max, 146
Waibel, Toni, 51, 96
Waite, Robert G. L., 334
Walcher, Jakob, 216
Waldman, Eric, 321–22
Wallot, Paul, 359
Walsh, Frank P., 330
Walter, Georg, 291
Ware, Harold, 129–32, 138, 141, 329–31. *See also* "Kuzbus" concession (1922); Smith, Jessica
WEB (Comintern's Western European Bureau), 87, 90. *See also* Comintern
Weber, Hermann, 320, 352–55, 357
Wehner, Herbert, 364, 368
Weismann, Adolf, 150
Weissman, Benjamin M., 324
Weitz, Eric, 322

Wells, H. G., 267, 298, 368
Wels, Otto, 291–92
Welt am Abend, 201, 210, 214, 219–20, 236, 257, 280
Weltbühne, 231
Wesemann, Hans, 231, 354
Wessel, Harald, 359
White Book, 277
Wilhelm II, Emperor, 25, 70
Willert, Paul, 303, 369
Wilson, Edmund, 45, 316
Winkler, Heinrich August, 353–54, 357
Wirth, Josef, 353
Witt-Christian, Peter, 311
Wittorf, John, 215–17, 246, 351. *See also* Thälmann, Ernst
Wittorf affair (1928), 215–17, 246, 351. *See also* Thälmann, Ernst
Wolf, Friedrich, 366
Woman's Path, 210
Woods, J. B. Collings, 338
Worker-Photographer, 207
World Committee Against War and Fascism, 276. *See also* Barbusse, Henri
World Committee for the Relief of the Victims of German Fascism, 262–63, 265, 267–68, 270, 271, 273–76
World Front, 276
World War I, 28, 29, 32–33, 43–45, 67–71, 113; and French army mutinies (1917), 43; and *Revolutionierungspolitik*, 43–49

Young Plan, plebiscite against (1929–30), 223, 230. *See also* Hugenberg, Alfred; Hitler, Adolf

Zeigner, Erich, 157
Zelt, Johannes, 347
Zeman, Z. A. B., 316–17
Zetkin, Clara, 30–31, 187, 200, 213, 273, 300, 339, 345–46; and Ruhr crisis (1923), 148; and Spartacist uprising (1919), 82; and Volga famine campaign, 106, 108, 116
Zeutschel, Walter, 334–35
Zhukov, Georgy Konstantinovich, 370
Zimmerwald antiwar conference (1915), 34–35
Zimmerwald Left, 36–37, 53, 106, 149, 228,

Index

286, 293, 305–6, 315

Zinoviev, Grigori, 71, 88, 99, 108, 163, 166–67, 169, 171, 194, 210, 273, 309, 315, 325, 328, 333, 335, 339–40, 344–45; purged (1928), 214–16; and Ruhr crisis (1923), 148–49, 153, 155, 158–59; and Second Comintern Congress (1920), 92–93; and show trials (1930s), 286, 305; and Volga famine campaign, 110; and Zimmerwald conference, 34–35. *See also* Comintern; Soviet Union, history of; Zimmerwald Left

Zohn, Harry, 347

Zola, Emile, 209

Zörgiebel, Karl, 259